EDUCATION 91/92

Eighteenth Edition

Annual Editions
A Library of Information from the Public Press

Editor

Fred Schultz
The University of Akron

Fred Schultz, professor of education at the University of Akron, attended Indiana University to earn a B.S. in social science education in 1962, an M.S. in the history and philosophy of education in 1966, and a Ph.D. in the history and philosophy of education and American studies in 1969. His B.A. in Spanish was conferred from the University of Akron in May 1985. He is actively involved in researching the development and history of American education with a primary focus on the history of ideas and social philosophy of education. He also likes to study languages.

Cover illustration by Mike Eagle

The Dushkin Publishing Group, Inc.
Sluice Dock, Guilford, Connecticut 06437

The Annual Editions Series

Annual Editions is a series of over fifty volumes designed to provide the reader with convenient, low-cost access to a wide range of current, carefully selected articles from some of the most important magazines, newspapers, and journals published today. Annual Editions are updated on an annual basis through a continuous monitoring of over 200 periodical sources. All Annual Editions have a number of features designed to make them particularly useful, including topic guides, annotated tables of contents, unit overviews, and indexes. For the teacher using Annual Editions in the classroom, an Instructor's Resource Guide with test questions is available for each volume.

VOLUMES AVAILABLE

Africa
Aging
American Government
American History, Pre-Civil War
American History, Post-Civil War
Anthropology
Biology
Business and Management
Business Ethics
Canadian Politics
China
Comparative Politics
Computers in Education
Computers in Business
Computers in Society
Criminal Justice
Drugs, Society, and Behavior
Early Childhood Education
Economics
Educating Exceptional Children
Education
Educational Psychology
Environment
Geography
Global Issues
Health
Human Development
Human Resources
Human Sexuality

Latin America
Macroeconomics
Management
Marketing
Marriage and Family
Microeconomics
Middle East and the Islamic World
Money and Banking
Nutrition
Personal Growth and Behavior
Psychology
Public Administration
Race and Ethnic Relations
Social Problems
Sociology
Soviet Union and Eastern Europe
State and Local Government
Third World
Urban Society
Violence and Terrorism
Western Civilization,
  Pre-Reformation
Western Civilization,
  Post-Reformation
Western Europe
World History, Pre-Modern
World History, Modern
World Politics

Library of Congress Cataloging in Publication Data
Main entry under title: Annual editions: Education. 1991–92.
      1. Education—Addresses, essays, lectures. I. Schultz, Fred, *comp*. II. Title: Education.
370'.5   73–78580   ISBN: 1-56134-008-1
LB41.A673

Eighteenth Edition

Manufactured by The Banta Company, Harrisonburg, Virginia 22801

Editors/ Advisory Board

To the Reader

In publishing ANNUAL EDITIONS we recognize the enormous role played by the magazines, newspapers, and journals of the *public press* in providing current, first-rate educational information in a broad spectrum of interest areas. Within the articles, the best scientists, practitioners, researchers, and commentators draw issues into new perspective as accepted theories and viewpoints are called into account by new events, recent discoveries change old facts, and fresh debate breaks out over important controversies.

Many of the articles resulting from this enormous editorial effort are appropriate for students, researchers, and professionals seeking accurate, current material to help bridge the gap between principles and theories and the real world. These articles, however, become more useful for study when those of lasting value are carefully *collected, organized, indexed,* and *reproduced* in a *low-cost format,* which provides easy and permanent access when the material is needed. That is the role played by *Annual Editions.*

Under the direction of each volume's *Editor,* who is an expert in the subject area, and with the guidance of an *Advisory Board,* we seek each year to provide in each *ANNUAL EDITION* a current, well-balanced, carefully selected collection of the best of the public press for your study and enjoyment. We think you'll find this volume useful, and we hope you'll take a moment to let us know what you think.

This year's rhetoric on the purposes and possible restructuring of North American educational goals sets a vibrant tone for the 1990s as another decade of serious reassessment. Possible choices open to us range from "cultural literacy," to present-day child-centered and existentialist approaches to schooling as a therapeutic and informative endeavor, all the way to vigorous debate over "deconstructing" and "reconceptualizing" how people are to be educated. It is quite a liberating discourse that is opening up before us. Amidst this vigorous debate on the means and ends of education is the continuation and expansion of "knowledge-based" inquiry on the conduct of instruction and the organization of curriculum. Undergraduate curricula in teaching education programs continue to change as the recently-developed revisions in teacher licensure and certification standards fall in place. The competition for the "minds and hearts" of those who teach in and those who govern educational systems, is as intense as ever. This is a healthy situation, and it is adding significantly to the quality as well as the variety of research in the field.

There is a momentum behind the drive to "reform" educational systems, but a national consensus on the broad general goals, specific attainable purposes, or the means for their achievement is still needed. The value assumptions of those who debate these issues are fundamentally different. Dialogue and compromise continue to be the order of the day. The various interest groups within the educational field reflect a broad spectrum of perspectives from various behaviorist and cognitive development perspectives to various humanistic ones. Practice-based approaches to field inquiry on teaching and learning in classrooms continue to produce fascinating alternatives to discovering the "knowledge base" of teaching. Case study approaches to teaching teachers are opening up new directions for teacher education programs. The interests of students, parents, state or provincial governments, and the corporate world continue to challenge traditional views on how people should learn.

Economic, military, and political pressures continue to affect the programs and planning agendas of those who wish to see educational systems respond to the social problems of North America. A cultural malaise created by continuing economic realignments, large numbers of rural and urban poor, and instability in financial networks still inhibits the improvement of conditions in many school systems. President Bush is determined to support the calls of state governors and corporate leaders for more emphasis upon improving the quality of learning in schools as well as alternative means for licensing teachers. However, his educational policies have been affected by the demands of diplomatic and military concerns. He continues to receive pressure from those who say there is a need for a more specific set of national educational policy priorities. He remains committed to supporting the national reform effort to improve the quality of education, but more specific federal policy initiatives to support such change is needed. As this year's *Annual Editions* goes to press, state governors are expected to report on the condition of education at their annual summer conference in 1991.

Some states are continuing to develop "alternative" certification programs for new teachers that bypass the respective states' programs (generally very behaviorist ones) for teacher certification. The state and provincial legislatures and the leaders of educational reform do not have a working consensus yet.

In assembling this volume, we make every effort to stay in touch with movements in educational studies and with the social forces at work in the schools. Members of the advisory board contribute valuable insights, and the production and editorial staff at the Dushkin Publishing Group coordinates our efforts. Through this process we collect a wide range of articles on a variety of topics relevant to education in the United States and Canada.

The following readings explore the social and academic goals of education, the current condition of North American educational systems, the teaching profession, and the future of American education. In addition, these selections address the issues of change, the moral and ethical foundations of schooling, and the many varieties of educational experiences available to people in North America.

As always, we want you to help us improve this volume. Please rate the material in this edition on the form at the back of the book and send it to us. We care about what you think. Give us the public feedback we need.

Fred Schultz

Fred Schultz
Editor

Contents

Unit 1

Perceptions of Education in North America

Five articles examine the present state of education in America. Topics include school reform, school quality, the future of teaching, and current public opinion on public schools.

Unit 2

The Reconceptualization of the Educative Effort

Six selections discuss the effects of equal opportunity, the reorganization of school programs, educating homeless children, and the challenges facing education today.

The concepts in bold italics are developed in the article. For further expansion please refer to the Topic Guide and the Index.

Unit 3

Striving for Excellence: The Drive for Quality

Five articles discuss the current aims for excellence in American education. Topics include teacher quality and curriculum development.

The concepts in bold italics are developed in the article. For further expansion please refer to the Topic Guide and the Index.

**Unit
4**

Morality and Values in Education

Four articles examine the role of American schools in teaching morality and social values.

The concepts in bold italics are developed in the article. For further expansion please refer to the Topic Guide and the Index.

Unit 5

Discipline and Schooling

Four articles consider the necessity of judicious and effective discipline in the American classroom today.

Unit 6

Equal Opportunity and American Education

Five articles discuss the current state of equality and opportunity in the American educational system. Racism, welfare reform, and the history of school desegregation are some of the topics considered.

The concepts in bold italics are developed in the article. For further expansion please refer to the Topic Guide and the Index.

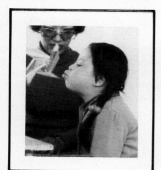

Unit 7

Serving Special Needs and Humanizing Instruction

Eight selections examine some of the important aspects of special educational needs—mainstreaming, teen pregnancy, and education at home.

The concepts in bold italics are developed in the article. For further expansion please refer to the Topic Guide and the Index.

Unit 8

The Profession of Teaching Today

Seven articles assess the current state of teaching in American schools. Topics include the historical background of major teaching issues, teacher education, and what makes an effective teacher.

The concepts in bold italics are developed in the article. For further expansion please refer to the Topic Guide and the Index.

Unit 9

A Look to the Future

Three articles look at the future of education in American schools. Curricula for the future, demographic changes, and educational reform are considered.

The concepts in bold italics are developed in the article. For further expansion please refer to the Topic Guide and the Index.

Topic Guide

This topic guide suggests how the selections in this book relate to topics of traditional concern to students and professionals involved with the study of education. It is useful for locating articles that relate to each other for reading and research. The guide is arranged alphabetically according to topic. Articles may, of course, treat topics that do not appear in the topic guide. In turn, entries in the topic guide do not necessarily constitute a comprehensive listing of all the contents of each selection.

TOPIC AREA	TREATED IN:	TOPIC AREA	TREATED IN:
Academic Freedom	43. Who Decides What Schools Teach? 44. Developing and Sustaining Critical Reflection	**Curriculum and Instruction (cont'd)**	8. Inside the Classroom 11. A Brief Historical Perspective 12. Fixing the System From the Top Down 15. Teacher Preparation 30. The ABC's of Caring 37. Rethinking Retention 38. What Makes a Good Teacher? 39. Fixing the Teaching, Not the Kids 42. 'It Was a Testing Ground' 43. Who Decides What Schools Teach? 44. Developing and Sustaining Critical Reflection
Accountability and Teaching	12. Fixing the System From the Top Down 13. Forging a Profession 14. Rift Over Teacher Certification Rules 15. Teacher Preparation 39. Fixing the Teaching, Not the Kids 40. Now You See Them, Now You Don't 41. Research on Teaching and Teacher Research 43. Who Decides What Schools Teach? 44. Developing and Sustaining Critical Reflection		
		Discipline	21. Design a Classroom That Works 22. Order in the Classroom 23. 'I Cried in Front of Fifth Period' 24. Charm School for Bullies
AIDS	36. Is Your School Ready for AIDS?	**Economics of Education**	1. Now Comes the Hard Part 3. Rethinking Education Reform 4. Public Schools and Public Mood 25. Children of Poverty 26. Welfare Reform
Alternatives in Education	6. A Reconceptualization of Teacher Education 7. A Reconceptualization of Educational Foundations 8. Inside the Classroom 9. Navigating the Four C's 10. 'Those' Children Are Ours 11. A Brief Historical Perspective 12. Fixing the System From the Top Down 30. The ABC's of Caring 31. *Honig v. Doe* 32. Teen-age Pregnancy 33. Home Remedy 35. When School Is a Haven 36. Is Your School Ready for AIDS? 37. Rethinking Retention	**Educational Policy**	1. Now Comes the Hard Part 2. A National Priority 3. Rethinking Education Reform 4. Public Schools and Public Mood 5. The 22nd Annual Gallup Poll 9. Navigating the Four C's 10. 'Those' Children Are Ours 11. A Brief Historical Perspective 12. Fixing the System From the Top Down 15. Teacher Preparation 26. Welfare Reform 27. Gender Issues in Teacher Education 34. Adolescence 35. When School Is a Haven 36. Is Your School Ready for AIDS? 37. Rethinking Retention 39. Fixing the Teaching, Not the Kids 43. Who Decides What Schools Teach? 44. Developing and Sustaining Critical Reflection
Carnegie Reports	13. Forging a Profession 14. Rift Over Teacher Certification Rules 15. Teacher Preparation		
Competency and Teaching	4. Public Schools and Public Mood 10. 'Those' Children Are Ours 12. Fixing the System From the Top Down 13. Forging a Profession 14. Rift Over Teacher Certification Rules 15. Teacher Preparation 16. How Do You Spell Distinguished? 38. What Makes a Good Teacher? 39. Fixing the Teaching, Not the Kids 40. Now You See Them, Now You Don't 41. Research on Teaching and Teacher Research 42. 'It Was a Testing Ground' 43. Who Decides What Schools Teach? 44. Developing and Sustaining Critical Reflection	**Equality of Educational Opportunity**	8. Inside the Classroom 10. 'Those' Children Are Ours 25. Children of Poverty 26. Welfare Reform 27. Gender Issues in Teacher Education 28. Race and Ethnicity 29. Social Class, Race, and School Achievement 30. The ABC's of Caring 31. *Honig v. Doe* 34. Adolescence 35. When School Is a Haven
Curriculum and Instruction	6. A Reconceptualization of Teacher Education 7. A Reconceptualization of Educational Foundations	**Future of Education**	45. Educational Renaissance 46. Proper Behavior for the 21st Century 47. Will the Social Context Allow a Tomorrow

Perceptions of Education in North America

The social demographics of North America are continuing to change rapidly. People are interested in how the schools will respond to dramatic changes in the population and the economy. Powerful forces for creating more open and extensive opportunity structures in state or provincial educational systems are evident. Yet the debate continues on state or federal government funding for the anticipated high costs of public educational needs. Perceptions of the effectiveness and adequacy of educational systems affect the public's willingness to support them. With one-quarter of all children or adolescents of school age in the United States living at or below the poverty level and more than 30 percent of them living in nontraditional family settings, the needs of the student population have seldom been more evident to those in the educational systems.

The importance of public confidence in the capacity of school systems to educate effectively is self-evident. There are serious concerns on how well schools meet the needs of youth to survive and develop their full potential in multi-problem educational environments. President Bush and the governors of the states are aware that education is a topic of great public interest. In the midst of this national interest, many innovative programs are being developed in both the public and the private sectors. The cultural malaise caused by dramatic economic changes in recent years have tended to aggravate, rather than to allay, the public's concerns about the efficacy of public schooling as it is currently conducted.

Varying political, corporate, and philanthropic forces continue to articulate alternative educational agendas for national educational development. At the same time, the "incumbents" of the educational system (teachers, administrators, and others) respond with their own educational agendas reflecting their views of the system from the inside. The well-being and academic progress of students is the motivating force behind the recommendations of all well-meaning interest groups in this dialogue. New national strategic goals for future educational development will come from this dialogue. The American public is ever more sensitive to the relevance of educational policy at the local, state, and national levels.

The public is concerned that several severe educational problems need to be addressed. They perceive the importance of teaching young children learning-readiness skills, and there is widespread concern to eliminate the severe drug usage problems among children and adolescents. The problem of illiteracy is important as a significant minority percentage of the American population are unable to read or write effectively. They are concerned about the increasing school dropout rate (around 24 percent) nationally—particularly in the large cities and rural poverty areas. Issues as to "parent choice" plans, extending the school day or year, and proposals for year-round school in areas experiencing rapid population growth are now being given serious public discussion. Recent declines in nationally standardized school achievement test scores have also created citizen concern for the quality of the teaching-learning process in American schools. Whether these public concerns for improvement in the conditions and outcomes of learning can be successfully resolved with effective new curricula (some of which involve the restoration of older, traditional educational ideals) remains to be seen. The decade is running apace, as all the others have, and "we have miles to go before we sleep" with any concrete assurance that these great educational issues can be resolved in the short-term future.

There have been massive shifts in American public opinion regarding the quality of the nation's schools throughout the history of the United States. Never have North American schools confronted a more pluralistic world-wide ideological and economic environment than the one they face today. The history of school reform efforts in nineteenth and twentieth century Canadian and American education reflects a continuing public concern for the quality of teachers and the quality of learning. Improving the qualitative outcomes of schooling has never been easy; today the American public sees the connections between effective schooling and national development in the light of dramatically changing national demographic and economic circumstances. (These circumstances are discussed further in the essays in Unit 6.) If there is any optimism in public perceptions of the "state" of schooling in North America, it is a guarded optimism.

North Americans sense the present intense competition for world markets and the demands for a more literate, learning-oriented workforce. There are public calls for curricular changes in schools that will better prepare American youth for the complex demands of becoming more literate and more able to work and to learn independently. The public seems to believe that American education problems are not additive or quantitative, but qualitative.

It must also be noted that fewer American young adults entering college or university studies today wish to consider seriously the possibility of becoming teachers. Teacher education enrollments are up significantly in some universities, but still not enough to meet anticipated

national demands for teachers projected for the early and mid 1990s. At least 45 states in the United States have developed new teacher education programs, but the "alternative" certification programs are defeating (in large part) the intentions of these efforts, for reasons that will be discussed in the overview essay to Unit 3.

American business leaders perceive their ability to compete effectively with Asian and European competitors as dependent on their intervention into the efforts to improve the quality of learning in North American schools. They have established working partnerships with many public school systems to improve the academic performance of students and to assist high school students in being more ready for entrance level positions in industry. The business community and the defense establishment both perceive some level of "computer literacy" as a "new essential" for today's high school graduates.

The public's perception of the costs and effectiveness of new school programs is vague at best, because we are uncertain as to the long-term success of certain models for innovation that are being placed in schools. For instance, some state departments of education are imposing 9th and 12th grade exit standards that are academically demanding, as well as "tiered diplomas" (qualitatively different exit credentials) for high school graduates. We are not sure what the overall public reactions to such innovations will be even though the competency testing has been going on in some states and provinces for some time.

There is great public uncertainty, as well, as to whether state and provincial legislators will accept a greater state government role in funding needed changes in the schools. People are generally convinced that it is unreasonable to expect local communities to finance local educational systems to a much greater extent than they are at present. There is a general public consensus that the challenges confronting North American educational systems in the 1990s are different from earlier educational problems that were confronted in the 1960s and earlier.

Looking Ahead: Challenge Questions

What educational issues are of greatest concern to citizens today?

What ought to be the policy directions of national and state governments regarding educational reform?

What are the most important problems blocking efforts to improve educational standards?

What technological changes in the world economy influence the directions of educational change?

What economic factors affect educational development?

How can we best build a national public consensus regarding the structure and purposes of schooling?

What social factors encourage at-risk students to leave school early?

What are the differences between the myth and the reality of North American schooling? Have the schools done anything right?

What are the best ways to accurately assess public perceptions of the educational system?

What is the functional effect of public opinion on national public policy regarding educational development?

What generalizations can one draw concerning public schools in the United States from the Gallup Poll data?

How can existing public concerns regarding schooling be addressed more effectively by state or provincial legislatures?

Now Comes The Hard Part

Many observers argue that the President's education goals are unrealistic, if not meaningless, without a strategy to reach them

When President Bush laid out six national goals for education in his January State of the Union Message, an eerie sense of déjà vu accompanied his speech.

More than five years earlier, in September 1984, then-President Reagan also presented a set of national education goals—four targets to be reached by 1990. One of those goals—to raise the high school graduation rate to more than 90 percent—was among the challenges Bush has embraced for the year 2000.

Reagan adapted his objectives from those first issued by former Secretary of Education Terrel Bell in December 1983, at the conclusion of the nation's first "education forum" in Indianapolis. At the meeting, attended by 2,500 of the nation's key education policymakers, Bell called on each state to meet four education goals by the end of the decade.

In addition to increasing the graduation rate, they included raising scores on college-admissions tests above the 1965 average, making teachers' salaries competitive with those for entry-level college graduates in business and engineering, and stiffening high school graduation requirements.

The list of people attending the forum was impressive, including 8 governors, 10 members of Congress, 150 state legislators, about 30 chief state school officers, and some 60 college and university presidents.

But the goals pronounced there faded from public memory well before the date set for reaching them. Now, many people are asking what will make the current goals-setting endeavor any different.

"The real danger here is, if you repeatedly set goals that are not met, and there is no accountability for failing to meet them, you make the announcement of future goals a dead letter," says Gary Bauer, who held several top Education Department posts during the Reagan Administration. "You raise false expectations, and you also may divert attention from asking the hard questions about why we are in this fix."

There are some differences between the current goals-setting effort and those that preceded it. Bell's goals were created in response to *A Nation at Risk*, the report by the National Commission on Excellence in Education that is widely credited with quickening the pace of school reform. That report was the work of a relatively small number of individuals. Outside the group, "No one accepted the goals, as such, or very few did," Bell says.

In contrast, the current set of national goals represents the combined efforts of the President, the Secretary of Education, and all 50 of the nation's governors. That could be a powerful coalition for change, particularly given Bush's campaign pledge to be the "education" President.

Even so, there may be more similarities than differences between the two occasions. Many problems that way-laid the last goals-setting initiative still exist and could sandbag the current one. Observers question the White House's commitment to move beyond rhetoric, and they point to a dearth of financial resources needed to make lofty national goals attainable. Nor does the nation have appropriate measurements and data to let the public know if goals have been met.

Without some careful planning, Bell cautions, the "results" could be much the same this time around.

"The country has always set national goals," notes John Chubb, senior fellow with the Brookings Institution. "We set national goals for education after Sputnik, and we set them during the War on Poverty, and we set

---

'Ambitious Aims'

The goals announced by President Bush promise that, by the year 2000:

• All students "will start school ready to learn."

• The percentage of students graduating from high school will increase to at least 90 percent.

• Students will "demonstrate competency over challenging subject matter, including English, mathematics, science, history, and geography" in assessments in grades 4, 8, and 12.

• American students "will be first in the world" in achievement in science and mathematics.

• Every adult American will be literate and possess the skills "necessary to compete in a global economy and exercise the rights and responsibilities of citizenship."

• All schools will be free of drugs and violence and "offer a disciplined environment conducive to learning."

"Ambitious aims? Of course. Easy to do? Far from it," the President said. "But the future's at stake. The nation will not accept anything less than excellence in education."

them in 1983, and we're going to set them again.

"There's nothing wrong with keeping the country focused on what we're trying to achieve, but the question is always, 'What's the follow-up?' Nearly 90 percent of the issue should not be the goals, but what people have in mind for achieving them."

Many educators describe the goals that President Bush unveiled in January as disappointing and unrealistic. For example, few people think that U.S. students can rank first, worldwide, in math and science by the year 2000 when they currently come in last or near last on international comparisons.

"The goals I've read about thus far strike me as pablum," says Dorothy Rich, president of the Home and School Institute Inc. "They are too big to be doable. It's like saying, 'No one will be killing each other in automobile accidents by the year 2000.' It's almost like the Wizard of Oz."

Indeed, the national targets remain nearly as vague as those President Bush first described in September, when he and the governors agreed to work on national goals. The governors had promised to develop, by their midwinter meeting in late February, a more explicit set of national goals than those listed in the President's speech. But they also needed a plan to reach them. So far, many educators observe, there has been little talk about means.

"I don't think one has to be cynical to say that the President didn't say very much" in his State of the Union Message, says Theodore Sizer, chairman of the department of education at Brown University.

"He ordered the cars to drive faster; that's about what it was," Sizer adds. "He didn't say how the engine was going to be souped up, or whether the tires had to be fixed, or whether the road should be any different."

Indeed, some worry that, in the race to come up with a list of goals by this winter, the President and the governors chose rapidity over content.

"Our view here was that they were pushing these goals out much too fast without giving enough thought to the strategies for attaining them," says Sandra Kessler Hamburg, director of education studies for the Committee for Economic Development. Without more detailed performance targets and a believable implementation plan, another observer suggests, the current effort "just doesn't look serious."

Bush's federal budget proposals, for example, are hardly a windfall for education. He calls for an additional $500 million for Project Head Start in 1991. But college student aid comes in for cuts. And the Education Department's $500 million increase does not even keep pace with inflation.

For now, many educators are withholding judgment. They say they will give more credence to the goals-setting initiative if Bush and the governors enact some visible new mechanisms for helping to reach their targets.

"When President Kennedy said we had to beat the Russians to the moon and get a person there," notes F. James Rutherford, chief education officer for the American Association for the Advancement of Science, "we didn't just strap some rockets on the side of an airplane."

Rutherford would like the federal government to create an independent national council that could translate the goals into a workable action plan, monitor progress, and report on results. Marian Wright Edelman, president of the Children's Defense Fund, has suggested devising a National Assessment of Educational Practice to measure who is taught what, by whom, when, for how long, and with what support.

Sizer wants the government to underwrite a research-and-development fund that is generous enough to help redesign the schools.

The governors themselves suggested a number of policies that could help achieve national goals in 1986, when they released *Time for Results: The Governors' 1991 Report on Education.* That document described an array of initiatives for improving the schools that the governors promised to work on over the next five years. Michael Cohen, director of education programs at the National Governors' Association, says the governors will devise more specific plans for reaching national goals before their annual meeting this summer.

But for now, many people note, there is little relationship between the goals-setting process going on in Washington and the realities of most schools. How to combine the current thrust toward national goals with the myriad innovations being tried in individual schools around the country is unclear. Some people worry that the move toward standardization which national goals imply could discourage much-needed creativity at the school level.

What the governors and the President choose to do in the next six months could determine whether the nation's goals for the year 2000 become more than a mere wish list. "Everyone's fear—or some people's hope, I suppose—is that this will be the end of it," notes one observer. "There aren't that many people out there reminding the decisionmakers that they have an obligation here."

—Lynn Olson, *Education Week*

A National Priority: The Search for Common Goals

This month, President Bush and the nation's governors will unveil a specific plan that could transform America's public schools

The nation's governors—possibly alongside President Bush—will unveil an unprecedented intergovernmental compact this month at the National Governors' Association conference in Washington: an agreement spelling out performance goals for the nation's schools.

This goal-setting initiative, begun last September at a ballyhooed "education summit" amid the photo-opportunity-perfect historical grandeur of the University of Virginia in Charlottesville, may ultimately be judged a mere public relations exercise, signifying nothing.

But it could also prove to be a key catalyst for the transformation of American education.

Participants in the September summit forged a pact calling for a system of education that is at once more centralized and less bureaucratic, which gives educators more authority, but also demands greater accountability for results.

The plan would be nothing short of revolutionary if it were actually carried out. The question is, to what extent will it be carried out?

"For the first time in our history, we are seriously considering the question of a national agenda, and it has the potential to alter our entire system," says Ernest Boyer, president of the Carnegie Foundation for the Advancement of Teaching. "More important is what follows the goals. We may not have the structure or leadership to carry it forward; I'm not at all clear in my own mind where it should come from."

The goals to be announced this month were drafted by Administration officials and the National Governors' Association's education task force, after consultation with such "stakeholders" as educators, parents, and business leaders.

That "consultation" essentially amounted to a Dec. 7 meeting in Washington, D.C., with representatives from education, civil rights, and business; a request for written comments; and state-level conferences and hearings in which governors sought advice and suggestions from constituents.

In effect, every summit-related agreement, from the agenda for the Charlottesville meeting to the final joint statement, was negotiated by White House officials and a group of key governors—NGA Chairman Terry Branstad of Iowa, and task force co-chairmen Bill Clinton of Arkansas and Carroll Campbell of South Carolina. It is likely that the goals will be drafted similarly.

At press time, White House sources said that the President would preview the goals in his January State of the Union Message and that they would parallel those outlined in the summit agreement, which specifically listed as priorities:

• Ensuring that children are ready to start school.
• Raising student performance on international achievement tests, particularly in math and science.
• Reducing the drop-out rate and improving performance of at-risk students.
• Decreasing the number of illiterate adults.
• Ensuring a "competitive workforce" through adequate training.

• Improving the supply of qualified teachers and "up-to-date technology."
• Ensuring "safe, disciplined, and drug-free schools."

But even those who support such goals believe they are meaningless without a strategy to achieve them.

Summit participants promised in their September agreement to announce "detailed strategies" for meeting the goals. But it is unclear when or how that announcement will be made.

A majority of governors have begun work at the state level by holding conferences and forming task forces. And several have promised to include education-reform proposals in their 1990 budget messages.

Governors and Administration officials say the goals they announce will be quantifiable, such as increasing the national graduation rate from 71 percent to 95 percent. Educators and officials at the state and local levels, they say, will then be left to determine the best way to reach the goals.

This dovetails with the summit agreement's call for greater flexibility and decentralization of authority.

The governors and Federal officials have said they will seek to loosen state and Federal rules and regulations in exchange for demonstrated improvements in student achievement—to "trade red tape for results."

They also declared their commitment to "restructuring education" and outlined a number of initiatives that could be implemented to further that effort, such as site-based decisionmaking, parental choice, alternative teacher certification, and program s that provide both rewards for excellence and "real consequences" for failure.

How and the extent to which this agenda is carried out will vary from state to state. But the summit agreement is likely to have one universal effect: It will apply pressure on states and local districts to meet national goals and measure up favorably on the comparative assessments.

"A lot of this is persuasion," Clinton noted at the summit. "You have to be willing to give them flexibility and hold them accountable for results."

Gov. Garrey Carruthers of New Mexico, chairman of the Education Commission of the States, was more specific, suggesting that, in some situations, states may have to take over school districts.

Will the goal-setting and monitoring process spur more states to consider such drastic moves? "If governors have any influence in states, absolutely," Carruthers said.

Although the education system evoked by the summit agreement would give educators more flexibility and more responsibility, innovations such as school-based management cannot be implemented nationally or even by governors; they must be instituted at the local level, often through collective bargaining.

What is a national issue, however, is whether to reduce the amount of Federal red tape that accompanies many of the national compensatory education programs. Such a reduction would require legislation, which is opposed by many advocates for the disadvantaged, who are the recipients of most categorical education aid. Advocates fear that regulations are the only reason some schools endeavor to serve those students.

But cutting the red tape is understandably popular among educators tired of tangling with bureaucratic rules like the ones preventing the after-school use of computers bought for Chapter 1 classes. And an idea so popular with constituents can be difficult for a lawmaker to stand against.

Many educators are encouraged by the summit-agreement's proposal to give them more autonomy and authority on the job. They note, however, that in exchange, they would be held directly accountable for their students' performance.

The trade could be a bad one for educators if performance standards are adopted without other reforms and without increases in resources, particularly for less affluent schools.

"We need a commitment to equity, and until there is equity, I don't want to be compared to the districts in the richer suburbs," says Constance Clayton, superintendent of the Philadelphia Public Schools.

The call for greater accountability also focused "summiteers' " attention on the issue of student assessment. In a brief statement that belies its potential for controversy, the agreement calls for establishing "clear measures of performance" and issuing "annual report cards on the progress of students, schools, the states, and the Federal government."

Says Ramsay Selden, director of the education-assessment center of the Council of Chief State School Officers: "If we declare those kinds of learning goals, we'd better develop an assessment to measure them or the goals will go by the wayside.

"The message to local schools is: What's important is what is tested. Goals are ineffective if they don't follow what is measured."

Some educators, like Clayton, are concerned that achievement will be assessed almost exclusively with standardized tests. That would be unfair to poor states and poor school districts, she and other opponents say, and could result in a single-minded focus on raising test scores.

Despite concerns about the adequacy of existing assessments, there is little sentiment for delaying goal-setting until it improves.

"We should not be held hostage by the fact that we don't have the right measures at this time," Frank Newman, executive director of the Education Commission of the States, said at the Dec. 7 meeting. "We should set the goals in such a way to force the system to change."

Whatever the ultimate result, the summit, and its aftermath, is virtually certain to increase public awareness of the need for change in American education. Perhaps the most revolutionary outcome of all is that a nation traditionally antipathetic toward Federal encroachment on the local control of education is on the verge of establishing national benchmarks.

Says former U.S. Secretary of Education Terrel Bell, "We've reached a point in our national life when we need more unity of purpose in education."

The findings of a recent Gallup Poll seem to indicate that the American public is coming around to this line of thinking. The poll found that 70 percent of respondents favor requiring that public schools conform to national achievement goals.

Bell and others believe that the focus on national goals portends an enhanced role for the Federal government in education. Says Bell: "I think we're going to spend more money on education at the Federal level. I think we're going to set nationwide standards, not federally imposed but nationwide standards, and that's going to demand a much more meaningful role for the U.S. Department of Education."

But finally, most agree, the success of national goals depends on the people who must meet them: educators. Some question whether the goal-setting process included sufficient involvement of those who would actually carry out the strategies being mapped.

In fact, some Congressional leaders are pushing for another summit, a conference of school officials, teachers, and parents. A law enacted in 1984 authorized $500,000 in Federal funds for such a conference, but the Reagan Administration never held it.

"I don't care what you do from the top if you don't get the people in trenches willing to make the change," says Rep. Bill Goodling of Pennsylvania, a former teacher and ranking Republican on the House Education and Labor Committee.

"You can't mandate excellence," he adds. "It won't just happen because someone waved a magic wand and said that's the way it will be."

—Julie A. Miller, *Education Week*
The plan would be nothing short of revolutionary, if carried out. The question is, will it be?

Rethinking Education Reform In the Age of George Bush

HENRY A. GIROUX

HENRY A. GIROUX is a professor in the Department of Educational Leadership and director of the Center for Education and Cultural Studies at Miami University, Oxford, Ohio. He is the author of Schooling and the Struggle for Public Life *(University of Minnesota Press, 1988).*

THE ELECTION of George Bush as the 41st President sets the stage for a new round in the national debate about the future of higher education and public schooling in this country. The growing interest in such a debate can be seen in Bush's promise to become the nation's first Education President, in the attempts by various interest groups to influence Bush's education platform, and in the concern expressed by growing segments of the general public over the declining quality of American schools.

There is little doubt that the ferment that has characterized the debate on education in the 1980s will continue. One can only hope that the next stage of this debate will address a more significant set of questions, provide a stronger and deeper language of analysis, and embrace an emancipatory set of interests for defining the purpose and meaning of public education.

For most of the 1980s, the views of Reaganite conservatives dominated the debate on education. The pursuit of "excellence" became a way of granting privileges to the children of the rich and of the middle classes, while simultaneously justifying the poor quality of education meted out to students from subordinate groups. In this view, high dropout rates, low reading scores, absenteeism, drugs, boredom, and student resistance served as cultural markers to let us know that students who were poor, black, "ethnic," or simply "devalued" for other reasons didn't count for much. School

The nation needs a new philosophy of education and policy making that makes hope practical for those generations of children for whom schooling will be their most important introduction to public life, Mr. Giroux avers. At risk is the very fate of democracy itself.

failure was viewed as a matter of poor character. Equity was denounced as a liberal trick to cheat the offspring of the rich out of an opportunity to get into Ivy League schools. *Authority* and *basics* became thinly veiled code words for invoking a military model of discipline when Reagan Administration officials talked about reforming schools in troubled urban areas.

In the current education reform movement, schools have become the new scapegoat for the increasing failure of the American economy to compete in the world market. At the same time, the notion of schooling as a vehicle for social justice and public responsibility has been replaced by the imperatives of the marketplace and the logic of the test score. "Making it" in schools is now defined in terms fashioned out of the language of Wall Street; it has become competitive, individualistic, and heartless. Important school problems stemming from inadequate resources, overworked teachers,

understaffed schools, visionless administrators, and powerless students are no longer taken seriously as part of the language of education reform. The result is often a notion of schooling that has a great deal to do with oppression and too little to do with educating those who are not rich, white, or native speakers of English to locate themselves in their own histories as part of the task of learning the knowledge and skills they will need to shape the world in which they live.

At the same time, community and democracy have become subversive categories as the language of schooling has been stripped of its ethical and public functions. For a number of spokespersons in the Reagan Administration the meaning of public schooling had nothing to do with the celebration of cultural differences or the creation of a democratic public culture. Rather, it was about respect, order, and submission. Such a view of schooling was more appropriate to British-run India of the 19th century than to 20th-century America.

THE BUSH Administration and the school reformers need to construct a new frame of reference for the debate over education reform by reclaiming schools in the interest of extending democratic possibilities, combating domestic tyranny, and preventing assaults on human freedom and dignity. These are not the kinds of concerns that Bush voiced as part of his campaign rhetoric, which was little

From *Phi Delta Kappan*, May 1989, pp. 728, 730. Reprinted by permission of the author and *Phi Delta Kappan*.

more than a recycling of the tired Reagan philosophy in which schools are defined in terms of building a more competitive America, raising test scores, developing accountability schemes for testing teachers, and pushing money into "merit schools" that teach down-home values.

As President, however, George Bush need not be a slave to ideological consistency. Given the educational problems that his Administration will have to face, it is reasonable to hope that he will rediscover his own voice and rethink his attitude toward public education.

The innovations and insights that have been developed during the last decade by a variety of critical school reformers and practitioners must be integrated into the language of the education reform movement. The reform of public schooling must come to be seen as part of a wider revitalization of public life; teachers must be viewed as empowered intellectuals who reflect upon the principles that inform their work, connect what they do to wider social issues, and work under conditions that allow them to share ideas and exercise power over the conditions of their labor.

Similarly, within the critical tradition, *empowerment* of students means providing them with a curriculum and an instructional agenda that enable them to draw on their own histories, voices, and cultural resources in developing new skills and knowledge. It also means teaching students to take risks, to struggle with power relationships, and to critically appropriate knowledge that exists both within and outside their immediate experiences.

This position is at odds with forms of schooling that treat knowledge as a received truth, that view student learning as a matter of adapting to existing social forms, and that regard student achievement as a way of describing success without acknowledging the messy social problems of the larger society. Clearly, this position is at odds with traditional forms of schooling in which students are asked to slug down great gulps of information that has little to do with their lives or their world.

Education reform needs to address the most basic questions of purpose and meaning. What kind of society do we want? How do we educate students for a truly democratic society? What conditions must we provide for both teachers and students for such an education to be meaningful and workable? These questions link schooling to the issues of critical citizenship, democratic community,

and social justice. A serious debate on education reform would make them central rather than marginal.

PRESIDENT Bush needs to articulate a vision of schooling that bears a closer affinity to some of the most important insights provided by this critical tradition. Let me offer a few suggestions.

First, the Bush Administration needs to reclaim the legacy of defending public schools as democratic spheres responsible for providing an indispensable public service to the nation: that of awakening the moral, political, and civic consciences of its youth. Education reformers need to put forth a clear vision of what education is supposed to do over and above meeting the needs of industry, and they must explain why education is important as a public, rather than merely private, endeavor. By linking public education to the imperatives of democracy rather than to the narrow demands of the marketplace, reformers can situate the debate on the meaning and nature of public education within the broader context of issues of citizenship, politics, and the dignity of human life.

In this view it becomes possible to provide a rationale and purpose for public education that aims at developing critical citizens and reconstructing community life by extending the principles of social justice to all spheres of economic, political, and cultural life. By viewing public schooling as essential to the formation of a critical and engaged citizenry, we can come to see the school as a social site from which to organize our national moral energies. This means challenging the sterile instrumentalism, selfishness, and contempt for democratic community that has become such a marked feature of American life. It also means ennobling the meaning of education by giving the schools a central place in the social life of the nation, as public forums for addressing the needs of the poor, the dispossessed, and the disenfranchised.

Second, the Bush Administration and other education reformers need to redefine what it means to be a teacher. The reforms of the last decade have seriously undermined the possibilities for teachers to expand the role that schools might play as public incubators of democracy. In fact, the conservative agenda for schooling — with its emphasis on standardized testing, massive accountability schemes for teacher evaluation, standardized curricula, and top-down, get-

tough approaches to school discipline — has further contributed to the de-skilling and disempowerment of teachers.

There is a growing need to generate policies that improve working conditions for teachers as well as dignify their role as public servants. Instead of defining teachers as clerks or technicians, we should see them as engaged and transformative intellectuals — professionals who reflect on the ideological principles that inform their practice, connect pedagogical theory and practice to wider social issues, and work together to share ideas, exercise power over the conditions of their labor, and embody in their teaching a vision of a better and more humane life.

Central to this position is the need for reforms that enable teachers to work under conditions in which they have time to reflect critically, conduct collaborative research, engage in dialogue with their students, and learn about the communities in which their schools are located. At the very least such changes will entail raising teacher salaries, extending opportunities for sabbaticals, redistributing power in schools, providing increased funding for inservice training, creating national public information networks that provide resources and funds for teachers to engage in individual or collective research projects related to their teaching, and forming parent/teacher resource centers that offer opportunities for teachers, parents, and community members to work together in shaping school policy. In addition, schools must be given the resources to help meet the social, cultural, economic, and political problems they encounter: drugs, teenage pregnancy, illiteracy, improper nutrition, and inadequate or unaffordable health care.

Third, the Bush Administration must address the issue of learning for empowerment. Central to a critical theory of education reform is the assumption that power and knowledge are inseparable. The real battle should be over what counts as knowledge, who decides if the knowledge that students already possess is valuable, and what else they must learn and for what purpose. The education reform movement inspired by Reagan conservatives has consistently defined learning in ways that ignore the diversity of experiences, traditions, voices, histories, and community traditions that students bring to school. Cultural differences have often been treated as deficits.

A curriculum policy must be put forth that argues for the importance of drawing on the cultural resources that students bring to school as a way to begin developing new skills and engaging existing knowledge. For example, a traditional approach to teaching contemporary American history would focus on history as the transmission of knowledge, facts, and information far removed from the everyday experiences of students. An alternative approach would begin with an investigation of the cultural resources that are at work in the community in which the school is located and would capitalize on those resources by building them into history lessons.

For example, a school with a large number of minority students could develop a series of lessons on the civil rights movement. The students could interview people in their neighborhoods who have stories to tell about the civil rights movement, how it affected them, what it meant to them, and how they evaluate that period of their lives. The students could then work together to organize the stories and develop a script dramatizing that period in the history of their community. Their production could be videotaped and could serve as a point of critical dialogue about a particular part of American history as it affected the nation and the neighborhood. Stories generated by the community on the civil rights movement could be compared with standard and alternative texts. In this example, teaching history becomes organic to, rather than removed from, the voices of the students who attend the class, both confirming and critically engaging the knowledge and experience through which they give meaning to their lives.

While this approach is meant to conform to the language forms, modes of reasoning, dispositions, and histories that students use in defining the world, it is also meant to make student experience the object of critical analysis and debate. This entails teaching students how to identify, unravel, and critically appropriate the codes, vocabularies, and deep grammar of different cultural traditions. Such a pedagogy provides the foundation for developing curricula and pedagogical models that replace the authoritative language of standard lectures and textbooks with an approach that allows students to speak from their own histories and traditions while simultaneously challenging the very foundations of knowledge and power.

A curriculum that respects the diversity of student voices also provides a referent for the principle of democratic tolerance as an essential condition of social life in a democracy. Schools need to incorporate the diverse and contradictory stories that emerge from the interplay of experience, identity, and possibility that students bring to the classroom. For too many students, schools are places of dead time — "holding centers" that have little or nothing to do with their lives or dreams. Reversing that experience for students is a central pedagogical and political issue.

Finally, the Bush Administration needs to address the federal government's role

F*or too many students, schools are "holding centers" that have little or nothing to do with their lives or dreams.*

in financing the school reform movement. Enduring and high-quality improvement cannot take place without adequate and equitable funding. Three issues need to be dealt with in innovative ways.

First, new sources of revenue need to be found as alternatives to the inequitable property-tax system that favors the children of the wealthy. Such sources might include: taxing large corporations through a corporate profit tax, developing a graduated income tax, instituting a corporate property tax, or placing a tax on real estate speculation. In addition, federal spending for defense could be reduced so that spending for education could be substantially increased. Instead of financing cruise missiles and Star

Wars, the federal government could invest in the future of this country's children.

Second, the financing of school reform must be tied to the wider issue of developing an alternative economic program committed to full employment or — at the very least — to extensive youth employment through the creation of public programs.

Third, while the issue of federal financing of education reform does not exhaust the debate about improving the quality of education in this country, money does make a difference in providing suitable conditions for teaching and learning. Schools with broken toilets, inadequate school supplies, low teacher salaries, lead-based paint, and limited resources for substitute teachers fail to educate well at least partly because they lack financial resources.

Nor can the federal government get away with ignoring problems of education that are not directly related to the school reform movement. The federal government needs to finance programs for at-risk children, e.g., Head Start, day-care centers, and health and human services programs. In addition, the federal government should provide funding for minorities who want to become teachers. President Bush could start by establishing 1,500 scholarships for minority students as an affirmative pledge of his own and the nation's commitment. Moreover, the federal government should restore grants, loans, and scholarship funds, so that prospective and practicing teachers can once again afford to become full-time students in schools of education.

In summary, George Bush has a historic opportunity to reestablish the importance of public schooling as a basis for critical citizenship, civic responsibility, and democratic public life. Creating a new context for the current debate by rethinking the meaning and purpose of public schooling in the U.S. is a challenge that must not go unmet. The nation needs a new philosophy of education and policy making that makes hope practical for those generations of children for whom schooling will be their most important introduction to public life. Not only is the future of our children at risk, but the very fate of democracy itself.

THE PUBLIC SCHOOLS AND THE PUBLIC MOOD

Since the birth of the nation, the public's
perception of the quality of public schools has
swung from approval to dismay and back again.
Here an eminent historian traces the course of
school reform and finds that neither conservative
nor liberal movements ever fully achieve their
aims—which may be just as well.

Carl F. Kaestle

Carl F. Kaestle is Vilas Professor of Educational Policy Studies and History at
the University of Wisconsin at Madison.

In a historic meeting at Charlottesville, Virginia, last September, President George Bush and the nation's
governors promised to revitalize
America's public schools by establishing "clear national performance goals,
goals that will make us internationally
competitive." Their language recalled
the document that had inspired school
reforms earlier in the 1980s, *A Nation
at Risk*. President Reagan's first Secretary of Education, Terrel Bell, a quiet
educator from Utah, had been appointed in 1981 under the cloud of a Reagan

promise to abolish the department.
Insecure in his cabinet position and
never the public figure his successor,
William J. Bennett, proved to be, Bell
was nonetheless determined to do
something about the mounting evidence of poor performance in the nation's public schools. He appointed
a National Commission on Excellence
in Education, whose 1983 report reso-
nated deeply with the public mood.

"Our nation is at risk," the commission warned. "If an unfriendly foreign
power had attempted to impose on
America the mediocre educational performance that exists today, we might
well have viewed it as an act of war.
. . . We have, in effect, been commit-
ting an act of unthinking, unilateral

educational disarmament." This message reverberated through the rest of
the Reagan years. It was cited again
and again as the nation entered a period of major educational stocktaking,
hand wringing, and reform. Within a
year several new commissions had
echoed its theme. A Twentieth Century
Fund task force worried that "by almost
every measure—the commitment and
competency of teachers, student test
scores, truancy and dropout rates,
crimes of violence—the performance
of our schools falls far short of expectations." The Education Commission
of the States said the schools were
"adrift," and a report by the Carnegie
Foundation said that a "deep erosion
of confidence in our schools" was cou-

From *American Heritage*, Vol. 41, No. 1, February 1990, pp. 66-68, 70, 72, 74, 76, 78, 81. Copyright © 1990, American
Heritage, a division of Forbes, Inc.

pled with "disturbing evidence that at least some of the skepticism is justified." Reformers called for higher graduation standards, tougher course content, more homework, better teacher training, and merit pay for teachers. The mass media took up the cry, and television networks ran prime-time documentaries on the school crisis.

This crisis did not come out of the blue. Publicity about declining standardized test scores in the late 1970s strengthened a backlash against open education, open campuses, and easy elective courses—things that people associated with the permissive sixties. Problems like racial segregation and illiteracy had proved difficult to solve, and people were disillusioned with the liberal reforms of a previous generation. Complex and coercive federal and state programs designed to correct discrimination had multiplied in the 1970s, and they taxed the bureaucratic capacity of local schools. Principals' and teachers' decisions about where a given child should be at a given moment were beset by contradictory rules about compensatory education, bilingual education, mainstreaming of the handicapped, and desegregation. Many critics and parents became convinced that traditional academic programs were suffering from neglect.

Respect for American public schools declined. In 1974 Gallup pollsters began asking people to grade the public schools. By 1981 the percentage of people who gave the schools an A or a B had declined from 48 percent to 36 percent while the percentage of people who gave the schools an F or a D nearly doubled, from 11 percent to 20 percent. The combination of a disillusioned public and a powerful group of critics had a dramatic effect. Legislatures in many states passed major education-reform bills: graduation requirements were beefed up, teacher salaries were increased, and a flurry of experimental programs were implemented. Although Secretary Bennett left office in 1988 warning that the schools were "still at risk," and reformers are now busy advocating newer programs for teacher training and for inner-city children, there is no doubt that many

As some School Houses look.

As the School House should look.

Reform-minded illustrations from *The Common School Almanac,* 1839.

states took the first wave of criticism seriously and implemented several of the suggested reforms of the mid-1980s.

This was not the first time in American history that critics aroused an anxious public about the quality and content of public schooling. The schools always have had plenty of critics, but widespread reform has succeeded only when there has been a general crisis of confidence in the schools and reformers have solidified public consensus about what changes are needed. Some efforts to mobilize public opinion have worked; others have not.

The nation was barely born when critics first warned of the terrible condition of schoolhouses and the ignorance of schoolmasters. Schools were "completely despicable, wretched, and

contemptible," said Robert Coram of Delaware in 1791, and the teachers were "shamefully deficient." Thomas Jefferson and Benjamin Rush suggested school-improvement schemes at the state level, arguing that the fragile Republic could be preserved only by creating an intelligent citizenry. The public was not impressed, and state legislatures refused to pass school-reform bills. People did not think that government intervention in local education was necessary, and they didn't see an urgent need for improvement. "There is a snail-paced gait for the advance of new ideas on the general mind," complained Jefferson in 1806. "People generally have more feeling for canals and roads than education." Thirty years went by before a successful school-reform movement blossomed.

Horace Mann, whose name became synonymous with that movement, grew up when Massachusetts was beginning to industrialize. Born in 1796 to a struggling farm family in Franklin, Massachusetts, he recalled bitterly the endless hours of work and the hellfire-and-brimstone religion of the local Congregationalist minister. When Mann's brother drowned in a local swimming hole on a Sunday, the minister preached about the eternal damnation of sabbath breakers.

Mann was determined to escape this heartless Puritan religion and the marginal economic position of his family. Under the direction of an eccentric but brilliant itinerant teacher named Barrett, Mann put together a course of study that propelled him into the sophomore class of Brown University. A splendid record there led him to a teaching post at Brown and then to the law school at Litchfield, Connecticut. In 1827 he began his political career as a member of the Massachusetts legislature. By the 1830s Mann was a leading figure in the state senate, supporting economic development through the expansion of railroads, as well as new state institutions like insane asylums and prisons.

Both Mann's distaste for orthodox religion and his desire to shape the developing capitalist economy played a role

Students ranged in age from three to eighteen—all in one room—and teachers struggled to keep order, some by love, most by applying the birch.

in his educational views. Appointed secretary of the commonwealth's board of education in 1837, he made public schooling his main focus and led the first successful school-reform movement in American history. When he considered Massachusetts's tiny rural school districts and its burgeoning mill towns, Mann was alarmed by low enrollment and poor attendance, as well as by the shoddy facilities, the short sessions, and the poor quality of teachers. Like the *Nation at Risk* panel of the 1980s, Mann argued that failure to educate all children would sabotage American society: "Is it not a fearful thing to contemplate that a portion of our children passed through the last year without the advantages of any school, public or private? What would be said, if we saw a large portion of our fellow citizens treasonably engaged in subverting the foundations of the republic, and bringing in anarchy or despotism?"

Mann had many fellow reformers. In New York a legislative committee complained that public funds for education were "utterly wasted" because "one-third to a half of the pupils were daily absent." A report on Albany's schools complained of "low, vulgar, obscene, intemperate, ignorant, profane and utterly incompetent" teachers. In Vermont the new state superintendent of schools said in 1846 that schoolhouses were in "miserable condition" and that tiny rural districts were "the paradise of ignorant teachers." All over the country the call for reform was the same. Schoolhouses were poorly built, poorly equipped, and poorly located; teachers were incompetent and lacked supervision; sessions were too short and attendance too irregular.

Memoirs that describe early-nineteenth-century district schools tell about a year divided into two terms: a few months in the winter for all the children and another in summer for those

too young to be working. The students ranged in age from three to eighteen, and all studied in the same room, so teachers relied on endless recitations by small groups and struggled to keep order, some by love or persuasion, most by boxing ears and applying birch switches.

The picture of untrained, overburdened teachers struggling to maintain control and teach the three Rs by rote is confirmed in many memoirs of students as well as teachers. As a little boy in winter school in the Catskills, Warren Burton said his ABCs four times a day for his teacher. "This exercise he went through like a great machine, and I like a little one." Otherwise Burton watched the older children, napped, and fidgeted on the hard bench. In Woonsocket, Rhode Island, Elizabeth Chace remembered that "at twelve years of age I had recited *Murray's Grammar* through perhaps over a dozen times without a word of explanation or application from the book or the teacher."

These old district schools had their supporters and produced some fond memories. They sufficed to teach rudimentary literacy to a large part of the population in a basically rural nation, they accommodated the seasonal need for child labor, they were inexpensive, and local religious preferences were often observed in prayer and Bible-reading lessons. Although attendance was voluntary, the sketchy figures we have suggest that more than 60 percent of school-age children went to school for some part of a term during the early nineteenth century.

This wasn't enough for Mann and his fellow school reformers. By the 1840s the district schools seemed clearly inadequate to answer the troublesome problems that industrialization and immigration posed for the nation. Samuel Galloway called schooling in the state of Ohio "the prostrate cause."

Caleb Mills revealed the "humiliating fact" that one-seventh of Indiana's adults were "not able to read the charter of her liberties." In the South a report to the Virginia House of Delegates warned, "It would be a fatal delusion to suppose that under the neglect or decay of education, free institutions could preserve a healthful existence." In North Carolina, the state with the most advanced public school law in the South, reformers complained in the 1850s that some local school committees neglected their duties and others misappropriated school funds.

Everywhere there was resistance to reform from those who opposed increased state involvement, standardization, and higher taxes. In upstate New York an opponent of reform complained that school tax laws authorized some people "to put their hands in their neighbors' pockets." A delegate to the Michigan constitutional convention of 1850 warned that if districts were given the power to tax residents for schools, it would endanger passage of the whole revised constitution. In Massachusetts a legislative committee complained that Horace Mann and his board of education were "the commencement of a system of centralization and of monopoly of power in a few hands, contrary, in every respect, to the true spirit of our democratical institutions."

Among Mann's opponents were Congregationalists who saw state regulation of education as a threat to religion in the schools. They joined in an effort to have Mann's position abolished. Mann referred to this opposition as "an extensive conspiracy" and wrote to a friend that "the orthodox have hunted me this winter as though they were bloodhounds and I a poor rabbit." In his journal Mann wrote, "I enter another year not without some gloom and apprehension, for *political madmen* are raising voice and arm against the Board." To Henry Barnard, his Connecticut counterpart, Mann wrote, "Let us go on and buffet these waves of opposition with a stout arm."

School reformers promised not only improved intellectual education but improved morals. They emphasized that moral training was crucial to the republican form of government and to work habits and day-to-day behavior as well. They offered to reduce ethnic and class tensions by providing a common meeting ground and a common culture. And despite a long, hard fight, determined opposition, and some setbacks, they won. Devotion to local control of schools gave way by the mid-nineteenth century to anxieties about immigration and economic change and to conflict between Protestants and Catholics. People realized that a higher level of education was needed for the market-oriented economy that industrialization brought with it. A majority of the public in the North had become disillusioned with untrained teachers, short sessions, and makeshift schoolhouses, so they voted for bigger budgets and more state involvement in supervising education.

By 1860 most Northern states had established school funds, state superintendents of instruction, county supervisors, and summer institutes for teachers. Enrollments continued to rise even though schooling did not become mandatory until the late nineteenth century. Small neighborhood school districts were consolidated under townwide school committees, and these committees gradually established longer school sessions and better schoolhouses. The public mood had shifted. The appeal to cultural cohesion and economic progress had succeeded.

There were still dissenters, of course. In the 1870s critics charged that the public schools had not made good on their promises of moral education. Bribery, divorce, crime, disrespect for parents—"this is the condition in which we are after more than half a century of experience of our public-school system," said Richard Grant White in the

North American Review in 1880. He urged the abolition of all public education above the elementary level. A few years later a U.S. Assistant Attorney General named Zachariah Montgomery wrote a book urging the same policy. Public education was a "monstrous usurpation of parental authority" and should be ended, he declared. Montgomery included testimonials from various Protestant clergy to prove that he wasn't just a champion of Catholic schools, and he argued against the "deep-seated and constantly fomented prejudice in favor of the public-school system, which makes politicians afraid to attack the monster."

These were conservative voices crying in the wilderness, though. Not until the 1890s did the public mood shift enough to foster another major reform movement. The problems of labor strife, immigration, and economic depression had escalated by then, intensifying concerns about whether the public schools were doing an adequate job of moral education and cultural assimilation. In the judgment of many observers, the schools had become stagnant —lifeless bureaucracies for the educators and stultifying memorization factories for the children.

The person most responsible for spreading this view was Joseph Mayer Rice, a New York pediatrician interested in education. In 1892 Rice received an invitation from Walter Hines Page, editor of the monthly opinion magazine *The Forum*, to tour thirty-six cities throughout the United States and to inspect their schools. The resulting series of nine articles, beginning in October 1892, caused a sensation. Starting with New York's schools, Rice lambasted the boredom and passivity of rote learning. "In no single exercise is a child permitted to think. He is told just what to say, and he is drilled not

only in what to say, but also in the manner in which he must say it." One of Rice's main complaints was the unscientific nature of teaching, a cry that would echo throughout the subsequent reform movement. "The typical New York city primary school," he said, is a "hard, unsympathetic, mechanical-drudgery school, a school into which the light of science has not yet entered." In Baltimore, Rice noted, "the schools . . . *are almost entirely in the hands of untrained teachers*," and "political influence appears to play a much greater part in their appointment than merit."

There were a few bright spots. Teachers in Indianapolis showed great sympathy for children's interests (another watchword of the developing reform movement), and in Minneapolis Rice found a system free from politics, staffed by well-trained teachers who engaged children in active, creative work. But mostly Rice's series exposed corruption, mindlessness, and failure. "In nearly every class that I visited," he wrote of Philadelphia's schools, though he could have been speaking about the nation's, "the busywork meant little more than idleness and mischief. It was the most aimless work that I have ever found."

School officials, of course, reacted defensively to Rice's findings. One professional journal sneered about the "cheap criticisms and the charlatanism of an alleged expert." But Rice caught the public mood. A new reform movement developed in the 1890s, and its name—progressive education—linked it with the larger political reform movement of the day. Actions were taken to distance the schools from ward politics in large cities. Smaller school boards hired "captains of education" to run urban school systems according to efficient, scientific principles. New schools of education churned out research on motivation, individual differences, and specialized curricula for different children.

Two goals were at the heart of progressive education: efficiency and individual growth. The tension between these goals went unrecognized by many reform enthusiasts, who patched together new ideas and new programs in a general effort to make schools more relevant to the world of work and more responsive to children's individual needs. Others recognized the problem but made the kinds of practical compromises necessary in large school systems. In Seattle, for instance, the superintendent Frank Cooper resisted much of the enthusiasm for factory-like efficiency in the schools, but he still believed that testing and grouping were necessary: "The teacher's greatest problem is to diagnose the individual needs of her pupils and then so to adjust her work that she may be able to give each child the thing that he especially needs."

Many educators embraced scientific efficiency and the industrial metaphor without qualms. Franklin Bobbitt, an influential education professor at the University of Chicago, argued that education was like industry: "Whether the organization be for commerce or for manufacture, philanthropy or education . . . the fundamental tasks of management, direction, and supervision are always about the same." He hoped that the business world "would state in specific terms the kind of educational product that it desires," just as railroad companies specify what kinds of rails they need from steel plants.

Meanwhile, John Dewey was advocating a very different version of progressive education. A Vermont farm boy trained in philosophy at Johns Hopkins University, Dewey had already proved himself a brilliant philosopher and a powerful teacher at the University of Michigan when he became head of both philosophy and education at the new University of Chicago in 1894. In the university's Laboratory School, Dewey and his associates tried to provide education that balanced the children's interests with the knowledge of adults, that engaged the children in cooperative, active work, and that integrated social and intellectual learning. The concepts of growth and active learning imbued the curriculum. Children learned about earlier societies through studying people's productive activities. In 1906, for example, the eight-year-olds of the Laboratory School were studying Phoenician civilization. "The occupational work centered around

---

T**wo very different goals were at the heart of Dewey's program for progressive education: school efficiency and individual growth.**

---

the trading and maritime activities of the Phoenicians," wrote one of the teachers, "and then moved on to the larger topic of world exploration and discovery." Teachers tried to relate all the work the class did to the Phoenician unit. "As each group passed from home room to shop, to laboratory, to studio, to music room, the things they did or expressed, related to or illustrated as far as possible the activities that went on in the historical study they were dramatizing." This is what Dewey meant by education's involvement with "occupations."

Outright occupational training was something altogether different. When David Snedden, a curriculum expert at Columbia's Teachers College, advocated separate vocational high schools for future factory workers, Dewey debated him in the pages of *The New Republic*. Dewey objected to the "acquisition of specialized skill in the management of machines at the expense of an industrial intelligence based on science and a knowledge of social problems and conditions." He wanted the kind of knowledge that would "make workers, as far as may be, the masters of their own industrial fate." Chicago labor unions joined the battle, complaining that dual school systems were designed to put the education of working-class children "under the complete control of corporations," with the aim of turning out "meek little manikins." Separate schools for vocational education were defeated in Illinois, as in most other places. Despite the vogue of efficient education for industrial productivity, the most extreme schemes failed because they sounded too undemocratic.

The "child-centered" school also encountered opposition, not only from Dewey himself, who considered it too permissive, but also from many parents and teachers. When the public schools in Greenwich Village, New York City, began a progressive elementary school in the 1920s, an Italian mother in the parent-teacher association complained: "The program of that school is suited to the children of well-to-do homes, not to our children. We send our children to school for what we cannot give them ourselves, grammar and drill. . . . We do not send our children to school for group activity; they get plenty of that in the street." Not surprisingly, the New York experiment was soon canceled. Indeed, in the decades that followed, educators adopted efficiency-minded reforms more enthusiastically than child-centered reforms. By the 1950s attempts to combine efficiency and individual development had resulted in an intellectually weak program called Life Adjustment Education. The time was again ripe for school reform, and two conservative strains of criticism—the right-wing anti-Communists of the McCarthy years and the academic traditionalists—emerged to provide it.

The anti-Communists knew more about what they didn't like (any liberal textbook or leftist teachers' union) than about what they wanted. In Tenafly, New Jersey, parents identified 131 library books that "follow the Communist line and . . . are written by Communist sympathizers," one of a rash of

With Sputnik as a catalyst in 1957, American educators launched the schools into a period of frenetic—and ultimately successful—reform.

such attacks in the early 1950s. A number of right-wing organizations sprang up to promote and distribute such publications as *Progressive Education is REDucation*. In Council Bluffs, Iowa, the former congressman Charles Swanson was upset by textbooks that listed Thomas Jefferson, Andrew Jackson, and Franklin Roosevelt as great Presidents but not William Howard Taft. These books, he said, "should be thrown on a bonfire—or sent to Russia."

The time in the limelight of the obsessed anti-Communists was brief. The champions of traditional academic learning, however, became a considerable voice. They assaulted everything they thought progressive education stood for: a low priority for intellectual training, time wasted on trivial social topics, and an endless string of worthless education courses for teachers. (They often confused John Dewey's original and demanding philosophy with that of his much more permissive and fuzzier disciples.)

A spate of books in the first half of the decade voiced these complaints. The titles tell the story: *Quackery in the Public Schools*, *The Diminished Mind*, *The Miseducation of American Teachers*, *Let's Talk Sense about Our Schools*, and *The Public School Scandal*. The most widely debated book was Arthur Bestor's *Educational Wastelands: The Retreat from Learning in Our Schools*. Bestor, a respected historian of nineteenth-century utopian communities, taught at the University of Illinois. So did Harold Hand, a professor of education and one of the leading defenders of Life Adjustment Education. The two could hardly have been more different. Bestor was the epitome of the college professor; he was reserved, dressed conservatively, and spent his free time in the library. Hand was an outdoorsman and amateur pilot who wore work boots and open shirts, a self-conscious man of the people, yet highly regarded by his colleagues for his intelligence and judgment. His willingness to depart from traditional subject matter stemmed from his experience as a young boy in school in the Dust Bowl in the 1930s, listening to a teacher reading Tennyson's *The Lady of the Lake* while outside, through the window, he could see the topsoil blowing away.

It was a classic confrontation. The two advocates were personally gracious toward each other, but their views were irreconcilable. Hand was convinced that Life Adjustment Education was a necessary and democratic response to the ever-increasing number of young people who were going to high school. Bestor would have none of it. He gave himself over wholly to the debate, dropping his scholarly work and mounting a campaign to convince the public that education professors had expelled traditional learning from the schools. Unlike some of the other antiprogressive traditionalists, Bestor did not blame the abandonment of traditional learning on Dewey. In fact, he said that progressive education had been "on the right track" up through the 1920s, when he himself had gone to the Lincoln School, a showcase of progressive education at Columbia's Teachers College. But then too many educators forgot about Dewey's efforts to balance the child's interests with a concern to impart traditional knowledge. Life Adjustment Education emphasized social rather than intellectual learning, especially for students with average or low academic ability. This, fumed Bestor, "declares invalid most of the assumptions that have underlain American democracy." Like conservatives in the 1980s, Bestor took the high ground on the issue of democracy: All students should have the same highly academic curriculum, in order to make opportunity equal, convey high expectations, and prepare students for intelligent citizenship.

No doubt Bestor exaggerated the loss of traditional academic subjects in most schools, and he overestimated the power of education professors. Hand argued vociferously that *Educational Wastelands* was full of "falsehoods and misleading statements" as well as "sleight-of-hand" and "bloopers." But Bestor found a receptive audience for his complaints, and he got widespread publicity. In the Life Adjustment curriculum, Bestor complained, "trivia are elaborated beyond all reason," and to prove it, he cited details about helping students develop hobbies and choose a dentist.

Bestor's biting criticisms, however, got more publicity than his program for reform. He called for the abolition of the undergraduate education major so that all teachers would get a liberal education. He also argued that experts should have more say in curriculum decisions, hoping that this would lead to a restoration of the traditional disciplines in the schools. And of course he wanted higher standards and tougher exams for students.

Whether this conservative program would have resulted in a successful reform movement simply on the strength of its critique of Life Adjustment Education is doubtful. In any case, it had not done so by October 1957, when the launching of the Russian space satellite *Sputnik* dramatically raised Americans' anxieties about the Cold War. Many Americans erroneously viewed the satellite as evidence that the Russians had a generally superior school system. Adm. Hyman Rickover wrote that *Sputnik* proved that the Russian schools caused "all children to stretch their intellectual capacities to the utmost." President Eisenhower called upon the schools to give up the path "they have been following as a result of John Dewey's teachings." And *Life* ran a series on the hardworking Alexei Kutzkov, who studied difficult math and science in a Moscow high school and did homework most of the time when he wasn't in a museum. Kutzkov was contrasted with two American children: goofy Steve Lapekas from Chicago, who had fun in school and spent most of his after-school hours fooling around, and Barry Wichmann of Rockwell City, Iowa, the neglected genius with an IQ of 162, whose school had no time, no concern, and no competence to deal with his talents.

With *Sputnik* as the catalyst, Americans launched into a period of frenetic educational reform, led by James Conant and Jerome Bruner. Conant, a former Harvard president and a prestigious spokesman for public education, had an answer to the dual demands of democracy and the Cold War: large comprehensive high schools that grouped students primarily according to ability. Bruner, the premier psychologist of education in the country, gathered some university experts and a smattering of school people at Woods Hole on Cape Cod to talk about the structure of the disciplines and then wrote a landmark book, *The Process of Education*, which inspired new curricula in mathematics and science. The federal government joined the reform movement with a major new initiative, the National Defense Education Act of 1958, which bolstered math, science, and foreign-language training at every level. Again, a successful educational-reform movement had resulted when political and social anxieties coincided with a public perception that the schools were not in tune with the needs of the society.

The curriculum reforms of the late 1950s and early 1960s had a special focus on math, science, and talented children. By the mid-1960s these concerns had been overtaken by another shift in the public mood. The civil rights movement, dramatized by the grassroots efforts of blacks and encouraged by the Johnson administration, resulted in a major effort to address poverty and racial prejudice through government action. Education was assigned a key

role in this effort, just as it had been assigned a key role in solving the national problems brought about by industrialization in the 1840s, immigration and urbanization in the early 1900s, and the Cold War in the 1950s.

The momentum lasted until the early 1970s. Gaps between the basic skills of minority and majority students narrowed among younger students; a revolution in school integration occurred, particularly in the South; schools recognized and institutionalized the rights

---

Reforms have limited effects compared with their goals, but they do force teachers to think about the enterprise they are engaged in.

---

of women, the disabled, and non-English-speaking students. But by the mid-1970s the public's tolerance for the disruptions of new programs and regulations was exhausted. Even before Reagan's electoral victory, education officials in the Carter administration were winding down massive student-aid programs, going more slowly on rights enforcement, and reducing the tangle of regulations and reporting required of local districts. A grassroots back-to-basics movement, declining college-entrance-exam scores, economic recession, and foreign competition set the stage for Terrel Bell and his Commission on Excellence in Education. The pendulum had swung again.

Major reforms of public education seem to come in cycles. Some people characterize the swings as conservative or liberal. The progressive decades of 1895 to 1915 and the 1965–75 reform movement are "liberal," meaning that they emphasized equal access to education and recognition of student diversity; the 1950s and the 1980s

are "conservative" because they place an emphasis on the nurturing of standards, talent, and traditional academic knowledge. Swings of reform might also be seen as alternating between periods of centralization and professionalization (as in the 1840s, the progressive era, and the 1960s), and periods of reasserted localism, private initiative, and challenges to the education establishment (as in the 1950s and the 1980s).

The cycles of public-school reform in our history have had limited effects compared with their goals. They did not achieve full equality of opportunity, harmonious social relations, effective character education, universal literacy, and satisfactory levels of academic excellence. The links between policy makers and teachers in the classroom have always been weak, and schools are rather inert institutions. They have limited resources of time and money to devote to change. Perhaps it is a good thing that schools don't swing radically from one reform agenda to another, but it is frustrating to reformers—both "conservative" and "liberal"—when they try to assess the impact of their heartfelt efforts.

Nonetheless, even if school reforms have limited effects and run in somewhat predictable pendulum swings, they serve two very useful purposes. They force educators to think about what they are doing, to defend it, to fine-tune it, and to think about the whole enterprise they are engaged in, not just their specific daily roles. More important, school reforms encourage the public to think about public education—not just about its failings but about its purpose and its importance. To the extent that schools respond successfully to widespread reform sentiment, they give people a sense of having a stake and a voice in the conduct of public schools.

The metaphor of the pendulum is probably too tame for the intense difficulties our public schools will face in the 1990s as reformers try to fashion a movement that addresses the unfinished agenda: dropouts, the problems of low-income and single-parent families, the restructuring of teacher training and teachers' working conditions, the debate over common learning for a highly diverse population, the consolidation of equal rights that have been promised but imperfectly granted, drugs, and, most important, more effective instruction, both in basic skills and in problem solving.

At Charlottesville, President Bush said that "the American people are ready for radical reforms." The next few years will tell how long that mood can be sustained. Meanwhile, school reformers have their work cut out for them.

TO FIND OUT MORE

The best history of American education is Lawrence Cremin's prizewinning three-volume work, culminating in his recent *American Education: The Metropolitan Experience* (New York: Harper and Row, 1988). Three books on school reform in different periods, written from very different points of view, are: Carl F. Kaestle, *Pillars of the Republic* (New York: Hill and Wang, 1983), on the pre–Civil War period; David B. Tyack, *The One Best System* (Cambridge: Harvard University Press, 1974), on the progressive period; and Diane Ravitch, *The Troubled Crusade* (New York: Basic Books, 1983), on the period after World War II.   **—C.F.K.**

The 22nd Annual GALLUP POLL Of the Public's Attitudes Toward the Public Schools

Stanley M. Elam

STANLEY M. ELAM (Indiana University Chapter) is contributing editor of the Phi Delta Kappan. *He was Kappan editor from 1956 through 1980 and has been coordinating Phi Delta Kappa's polling program since his retirement.*

National Goals for Education

People strongly believe in the six education goals for the Nineties announced last February, with appropriate fanfare, by President George Bush and the 50 state governors. They believe in them so strongly that they would like to vote for political candidates who support these goals. But people are also profoundly skeptical about the possibility that the goals can be reached within this decade, which was part of the plan put forth by the President and the governors.

These conclusions are drawn from answers to three key questions asked in the 22nd Annual Poll of the Public's Attitudes Toward the Public Schools, sponsored by Phi Delta Kappa and conducted by the Gallup Organization in April and May 1990.

More than three-quarters of the 1,594 adults interviewed for the poll attach very high or high priority to all six of the national goals for education. They give highest priority to the last goal: to free every school in America from drugs and violence and offer a disciplined environment conducive to learning. But only 5% of the respondents think it very likely that we will achieve this goal by the year 2000, and 36% think it very *unlikely* that we will. The only goal among the six that even 50% of the people think we might reach in this decade is that of readying children to learn by the time they start school.

This pessimism echoes the judgment of many experts, some of whom, like Dorothy Rich, president of the Home and School Institute and a member of the governing board for the National Assessment of Educational Progress, regard the goals as political pabulum. "They are too big to be doable," she asserts. "It's like saying, 'No one will be killing each other in automobile accidents by the year 2000.' "*

The nation's education goals for the Nineties, as stated by President Bush at the conclusion of his February conference with the 50 state governors, are:

A. By the year 2000, all children in America will start school ready to learn [i.e., in good health, having been read to and otherwise prepared by parents, etc.].
B. By the year 2000, the high school graduation rate will increase to at least 90% [from the current rate of 74%].
C. By the year 2000, American students will leave grades 4, 8, and 12 having demonstrated competency in challenging subject matter, including English, mathematics, science, history, and geography. In addition, every school in America will insure that all students learn to use their minds, in order to prepare them for responsible citizenship, further learning, and productive employment in a modern economy.
D. By the year 2000, American students will be first in the world in mathematics and science achievement.
E. By the year 2000, every adult American will be literate and will possess the skills necessary to compete in a global economy and to exercise the rights and responsibilities of citizenship.
F. By the year 2000, every school in America will be free of drugs and violence and will offer a disciplined environment conducive to learning.

The first question:

This card describes several national education goals that have been recommended for attainment by the year 2000. First, would you read over the description of the different goals on the card. Now, as I read off each goal by letter, would you tell me how high a priority you feel that goal should be given during the coming decade — very high, high, low, or very low?

Goal	Very High %	High %	Low %	Very Low %	Don't Know %
		Priority Assigned Each Goal			
A	44	44	6	2	4
B	45	42	8	1	4
C	46	42	7	2	3
D	34	42	16	3	5
E	45	37	11	3	4
F	55	26	9	6	4

*For a roundup of expert opinion on the goals, see Lynn Olson, "Lessons Learned? Old Goal-Setting Stirs New Doubts," *Education Week*, 14 February 1990, pp. 1, 23. The same article appears in the April 1990 issue of *Teacher*, under the title "Now Comes the Hard Part" (pp. 12-15).

From *Phi Delta Kappan*, September 1990, pp. 41-55. Reprinted by permission.

The second question:

As I read off each goal by letter again, would you tell me whether you think reaching that goal by the year 2000 is very likely, likely, unlikely, or very unlikely?

Likelihood of Attainment

Goal	Very Likely %	Likely %	Unlikely %	Very Unlikely %	Don't Know %
A	12	38	33	12	5
B	10	35	37	12	6
C	9	38	36	12	5
D	6	23	41	24	6
E	7	25	42	21	5
F	5	14	40	36	5

The third question:

As I read off each goal by letter again, please tell me how much influence a political candidate's support for that goal would have on your decision to vote for him or her — a great deal, a fair amount, not very much, or almost none.

Influence of Candidate's Support on My Vote

Goal	A Great Deal %	A Fair Amount %	Not Very Much %	Almost None %	Don't Know %
A	29	37	18	11	5
B	30	36	19	10	5
C	32	36	17	10	5
D	26	35	21	13	5
E	33	36	16	10	5
F	43	30	12	10	5

Trends in Support for Parental Choice

Beginning in 1979, these annual polls have probed the sensitive issue of parental choice of schools. In that year parents were asked if they would like to send their eldest child to a public school different from the school that child currently attended. The great majority of parents (78%) whose eldest child was 12 or younger said no; only 12% said yes. An even larger majority (85%) of parents whose eldest child was older than 12 said no, while 11% said yes. This was hardly a resounding endorsement of school choice.

In 1986, however, two related questions were asked, with considerably different results. In that year 68% of public school parents said they wished they had the right to choose the public schools their children would attend, while 25% said they did not. Mothers were particularly intrigued with the idea; 73% of mothers (but only 62% of fathers) said they wished they could choose their children's schools. The percentage of public school parents who said they would choose the same schools their children currently attended dropped from the higher 1979 level down to 65%, again with women particularly favoring change.

In 1987 all respondents were asked whether they thought parents in their community should have the right to choose which local schools their children would attend. Seventy-one percent of the total sample (and 81% of all nonpublic school parents) said yes; only 20% of the total sample said no.

A question intended to reveal attitudes toward vouchers was asked several times in these surveys. The question was worded as follows: "In some nations, the government allots a certain amount of money for each child's education. The parents can then send the child to any public, parochial, or private school they choose. This is called the 'voucher system.' Would you like to see such an idea adopted in this country?" The national totals were:

	1987 %	1986 %	1985 %	1983 %	1981 %	1971 %	1970 %
Favor	44	46	45	51	43	38	43
Oppose	41	41	40	38	41	44	46
Don't know	15	13	15	11	16	18	11

The 1987 poll followed this voucher question with another, asking people whether they thought the voucher system would help or hurt the local public schools. Forty-two percent said they thought vouchers would hurt the public schools, and 36% said they thought vouchers would help. Of those who *favored* vouchers, 73% thought that vouchers would help the local public schools; of those *opposed* to vouchers, 81% thought that vouchers would damage the local public schools.

Now that several states have begun experimenting with parental choice plans and the idea of school choice has the backing of President Bush and the U.S. Department of Education, the question on choice has been asked in a new form. As framed in 1989, it avoided the issue of public versus nonpublic schools that arises when vouchers are discussed. People were simply asked whether they favor or oppose allowing students and their parents to choose the public schools that students attend, regardless of where they live. (Respondents were not asked to consider the many ramifications of public school choice.) A sizable majority supported the idea in 1989 (60% in favor to 31% opposed), and the results were virtually identical when the same question was asked again this year.

In the 1989 poll, the question on school choice was followed by three other questions intended to reveal opinions regarding whether choice would improve all or only some schools, whether choice would improve student achievement, and whether choice would increase student satisfaction with the local schools. A majority (51%) thought choice would improve some schools and hurt others. Forty-two percent thought that choice would not make much difference in student achievement, but another 40% thought that achievement would increase. Half of the respondents (49%) thought that student satisfaction with the schools would improve; 37% said that choice would make little difference; and 7% said that student satisfaction would be lower.

It seems clear from the above record that the idea of public school choice is attractive, much as motherhood, freedom, and apple pie are attractive. It remains to be seen whether choice plans can be carried out in ways that preserve other values that may be equally important to people. The current experiments in Minnesota, Arkansas, and Iowa should give us clues.

The question:

Do you favor or oppose allowing students and their parents to choose which public schools in this community the students attend, regardless of where they live?

	National Totals %	No Children In School %	Public School Parents %	Nonpublic School Parents %
Favor	62	60	65	81
Oppose	31	33	30	14
Don't know	7	7	5	5

Further breakdowns for the 1990 question:

	Favor %	Oppose %	Don't Know %
NATIONAL TOTALS	62	31	7
Sex			
Men	61	34	5
Women	63	29	8
Race			
White	60	34	6
Nonwhite	72	18	10
Age			
18 - 29 years	72	23	5
30 - 49 years	63	31	6
50 and over	54	38	8
Community Size			
1 million and over	64	27	9
500,000 - 999,999	61	36	3
50,000 - 499,999	60	33	7
2,500 - 49,999	61	36	3
Under 2,500	60	33	7
Education			
College	62	33	5
Graduate	62	30	8
Incomplete	63	34	3
High school	65	28	7
Graduate	66	28	6
Incomplete	62	29	9
Grade school	44	43	13
Income			
$40,000 and over	59	37	4
$30,000 - $39,999	62	32	6
$20,000 - $29,999	67	27	6
$10,000 - $19,999	60	30	10
Under $10,000	60	31	9
Region			
East	62	27	11
Midwest	57	38	5
South	66	28	6
West	62	34	4

Reasons for Choosing a School

In 1990 a new dimension was added to the survey's treatment of parental choice. Respondents were asked what aspects of a public school would be most influential in decision making should parental choice be adopted in their community. Teacher quality, student discipline, and the curriculum were judged very important by three-fourths or more of all respondents, but class size, the track record of graduates in college or on the job, school size, and proximity to the student's home were also rated either very or fairly important by large majorities.

These are all legitimate considerations. But one set of responses calls attention to the same concern about parental choice in public education that critics of voucher systems raise: Would not parental choice encourage and/or permit segregation on the basis of race, ethnicity, and perhaps socioeconomic status? Civil libertarians insist that a democracy cannot tolerate this kind of elitism and discrimination in the public schools.

Forty-eight percent of the respondents admitted that the racial or ethnic composition of the student body would be either a very or a fairly important consideration in decision making. This response puts racial and ethnic considerations near the bottom of the list. In interpreting such data, however, it is well to remember a distinction between public opinion and private sentiment drawn by historian John Lukacs: public opinion is the formal remarks that folks make to pollsters; private sentiment is the set of beliefs and biases that people are often too embarrassed to disclose. It is pos-

sible that racial and ethnic considerations are much more important factors in school choice than people admit to pollsters.

The question:

This card lists different factors that might be considered in choosing a public school for a child, assuming that a free choice of public schools was allowed in this community. As I read off each of these factors one at a time, would you tell me whether you would consider it very important, fairly important, not too important, or not important at all in choosing a local school?

	National Totals				
	Very Important %	Fairly Important %	Not Too Important %	Not Important at All %	Don't Know %
Quality of the teaching staff	87	8	2	*	3
Maintenance of student discipline	78	17	1	1	3
Curriculum (i.e., the courses offered)	73	22	2	*	3
Size of classes	56	32	8	1	3
Grades or test scores of the student body	48	41	7	1	3
Track record of graduates in high school, in college, or on a job	43	38	12	3	4
Size of the school	35	37	21	4	3
Proximity to home	31	43	19	4	3
Extracurricular activities, such as band/orchestra, theater, clubs	24	50	20	3	3

	Very Important %	Fairly Important %	Not Too Important %	Not Important at All %	Don't Know %
Social and economic background of the student body	22	37	31	7	3
Racial or ethnic composition of the student body	21	27	34	15	3
Athletic program	20	38	32	7	3

*Less than one-half of 1%.

Parental Control of Public Schools

Since 1987 the public schools of Rochester, New York, have been run by a team of parents, teachers, and administrators. In Chicago locally elected councils composed predominantly of parents have been in charge of all the city's 541 public schools since last fall.

Responses to a question asked in last year's poll suggest that similar experiments would be warmly received elsewhere. The 1989 poll showed that more than 40% of the general public believed that parents should have a greater say regarding the allocation of school funds, the content of the curriculum, the hiring of teachers and administrators, and the choice of textbooks and instructional materials.

The 1989 question:

Do you feel that parents of public school students should have more say, less say, or do they

have about the right amount of say regarding the following areas in public schools?

	More Say 1989 %	Less Say 1989 %	Right Amount 1989 %	Don't Know 1989 %
Allocation of school funds	59	10	27	4
Curriculum (i.e., the courses offered	53	9	36	2
Selection and hiring of administrators	46	14	37	3
Books and instructional materials	43	13	41	3
Selection and hiring of teachers	41	17	38	4
Teacher and administrator salaries	39	17	39	5
Books placed in the school libraries	38	15	44	3

In the current poll, people were asked for their opinion on how much influence public school parents actually do exercise in most of these same areas. The responses show that the public perceives parental influence to be minimal. In areas such as salaries and hiring, half of the respondents said that parents have almost no say.

The question:

In your opinion, how much say do the parents of public school students have about the following areas in the public schools in this community — a great deal, a fair amount, very little, or almost none?

	A Great Deal %	A Fair Amount %	Very Little %	Almost None %	Don't Know %
Books placed in the school libraries	5	17	29	37	12
Curriculum (i.e., the courses offered)	4	21	37	28	10
Books and instructional materials	3	14	31	41	11
Teacher and administrator salaries	3	12	25	50	10
Selection and hiring of administrators	3	11	26	50	10
Selection and hiring of teachers	2	8	29	52	9

Examinations for Promotion

Because many policy-making bodies have recently declared war on what they view as soft or shoddy academic standards, a question about promotion policy was included in this poll.

Public opinion continues to oppose promotion from one grade to the next unless the student can pass examinations — presumably grade- and curriculum-appropriate examinations. Opinion seems not to have changed on the issue since the question was first asked in 1978. But it is probably accurate to say that a majority of educators hold a different opinion. Although few teachers approve of strictly "social" promotion, most believe that considerations other than passing an exam must be taken into account when decisions about promotion are made. There is much research evidence to support their belief. Certainly, making a child repeat a grade without taking other steps to help him or her

learn is often counterproductive. This is an area in which the profession needs to educate the general public.

The question:

In your opinion, should children be promoted from grade to grade only if they can pass examinations?

	National Totals %	No Children In School %	Public School Parents %	Nonpublic School Parents %
Yes	67	67	66	71
No	29	28	31	27
Don't know	4	5	3	2

	National Totals			
	1990 %	1984 %	1983 %	1978 %
Yes	67	71	75	68
No	29	25	20	27
Don't know	4	4	5	5

Retention in Grade and Dropout Rates

Get tough! This is the advice commonly offered to educators by critics who regard student achievement in public schools as unsatisfactory. To them, getting tough often means retention in grade for the student who can't or won't master the curriculum. At the same time, many of the same critics deplore today's public school dropout rate. Is there a connection between retention in grade and the dropout rate? This year's poll explored current opinion on the issue.

The question:

Just your impression — which children are more likely to drop out of school: those who fail achievement tests and have to repeat a grade, or those who fail achievement tests and are promoted anyway?

	National Totals %	No Children In School %	Public School Parents %	Nonpublic School Parents %
More of those who repeat a grade will drop out	32	34	28	31
More of those promoted anyway will drop out	54	52	60	56
Don't know	14	14	12	13

As well-informed educators will recognize, the majority view on this question is at odds with the findings of research. In *Flunking Grades: Research and Policies on Retention* (Falmer Press, 1989), Lorrie Shepard and Mary Lee Smith report the findings of a meta-analysis of 63 studies, which shows that students who are retained in grade are far more likely to drop out than students of similar ability and achievement who are promoted. It is easy to oversimplify the Shepard/Smith findings, but there is little doubt that their chief conclusion is correct. Thus the majority view on this question is merely opinion, and it is erroneous.

It is interesting to note that opinion expressed by nonwhites on this question is closer to the findings of research than is the opinion of whites. Forty-four percent of nonwhites (but only 30% of whites) believe that repeaters are more likely to drop out. By contrast, 57% of whites (but only 41% of nonwhites) believe that students who are promoted despite unsatisfactory performance are more likely to drop out.

Access to Personal Information About Students

Research recently conducted by members of Phi Delta Kappa under the direction of Jack Frymier, senior fellow at Phi Delta Kappa International Headquarters, shows that teachers have only limited access to the kinds of personal background information about students that would help them adapt their methods to individual needs.* Because of privacy considerations, schools have been hesitant to collect this kind of information and make it available to teachers, even under rules designed to guarantee strict confidentiality.

Answers to a question asked in the current poll show that a majority (60%) of the respondents favor giving educators more latitude to collect and use personal information. However, the size of this majority is by no means overwhelming, as it should probably be before policies are changed. This is a case in which local polls would be useful to policy makers.**

The question:

Some educators say that the public schools could do a better job of educating students if they had more personal information about the home situations of students, for example, whether the parents are divorced, whether there is a family history of alcoholism, or whether there are other factors that put the student at risk. Assuming that the information is kept confidential, do you think that the public schools in this community should or should not have access to more personal information about students than they now have?

	National Totals %	No Children In School %	Public School Parents %	Nonpublic School Parents %
Should	60	61	56	61
Should not	32	30	37	32
Don't know	8	9	7	7

Equal Educational Opportunity

Whites in America seem convinced that, on the whole, blacks and other minority children have the same educational opportunities as whites. This conviction has not changed since 1975, when the question was first asked in these surveys.

But nonwhites (who make up 14% of the sample in the current poll) have a considerably different view. A disturbing 38% see inequality of opportunity in education. Much of the

*Jack Frymier and Bruce Gansneder, "The Phi Delta Kappa Study of Students at Risk," *Phi Delta Kappan*, October 1989, pp. 142-46.

**Phi Delta Kappa distributes a manual titled *PACE* (Polling Attitudes of the Community on Education), which explains in detail how to conduct accurate local polls. For information, contact Neville Robertson, Director, Center for Dissemination of Innovative Programs, Phi Delta Kappa, P.O. Box 789, Bloomington, IN 47402. Ph. 812/339-1156.

dissatisfaction appears in larger cities, where minority populations are concentrated.

The question:

In your opinion, do black children and other minorities in this community have the same educational opportunities as white children?

	National Totals %	No Children In School %	Public School Parents %	Nonpublic School Parents %
Yes	79	78	81	77
No	15	16	14	19
Don't know	6	6	5	4

Further breakdowns:

	Yes %	No %	Don't Know %
NATIONAL TOTALS	79	15	6
Sex			
Men	80	15	5
Women	79	15	6
Race			
White	83	11	6
Nonwhite	56	38	6
Age			
18 - 29 years	73	22	5
30 - 49 years	81	13	6
50 and over	82	12	6
Community Size			
1 million and over	71	23	6
500,000 - 999,999	82	17	1
50,000 - 499,999	81	13	6
2,500 - 49,999	90	8	2
Under 2,500	86	6	8
Education			
College	79	15	6
Graduate	78	15	7
Incomplete	80	15	5
High school	80	15	5
Graduate	79	15	6
Incomplete	82	14	4
Grade school	78	15	7
Income			
$40,000 and over	80	13	7
$30,000 - $39,999	83	12	5
$20,000 - $29,999	80	16	4
$10,000 - $19,999	82	15	3
Under $10,000	75	19	6
Region			
East	80	13	7
Midwest	80	11	9
South	81	17	2
West	76	20	4

Desirability of Teaching as a Career

Perceptions of the desirability of public school teaching as a career have been measured seven times since this series of polls began in 1969. The attractiveness of the occupation has fluctuated considerably, related no doubt to changing popular attitudes toward the schools and to impressions about teacher income. Unfortunately, only about half of today's parents (compared with 75% in 1969) would like to see one of their children become a public school teacher. Interestingly, college-educated and high-income respondents are as likely as poorly educated and low-income respondents to perceive teaching as a desirable career for their children today.

The question:

Would you like to have a child of yours take up teaching in the public schools as a career?

	National Totals %	No Children In School %	Public School Parents %	Nonpublic School Parents %
Yes	51	49	56	51
No	38	39	37	40
Don't know	11	12	7	9

	National Totals						
	1990 %	1988 %	1983 %	1981 %	1980 %	1972 %	1969 %
Yes	51	58	45	46	48	67	75
No	38	31	33	43	40	22	15
Don't know	11	11	22	11	12	11	10

Teacher Salaries, Working Conditions, And School Quality

In 1969 more people thought teacher salaries in their communities were about right (43%) than thought them too low (35%). Today 50% of poll respondents think salaries are too low, and 31% think them about right. Only a small minority has ever thought that teachers are paid too much for their services.

Respondents to the current poll were asked whether they think raising teacher salaries would improve school quality. A substantial majority (79%) do think that higher salaries would have this effect, but 17% said that there would be almost no improvement. (Respondents were not given the option of saying that higher salaries would damage school quality.)

A similarly worded question asked about the possible effect on public school quality of better working conditions for teachers. Responses differ little from those obtained for the salary question. However, there is a hint that people think better working conditions would yield more school improvement than higher salaries. Teachers themselves often espouse the same belief.*

The first question:

Do you think salaries for teachers in this community are too high, too low, or just about right?

	National Totals %	No Children In School %	Public School Parents %	Nonpublic School Parents %
Too high	5	5	3	1
Too low	50	49	54	54
Just about right	31	31	32	34
No opinion	14	15	11	11

*Stanley Elam, *The Second Gallup/Phi Delta Kappa Survey of Public School Teacher Opinion: Portrait of a Beleaguered Profession* (Bloomington, Ind.: Phi Delta Kappa, 1989).

	National Totals					
	1990 %	1985 %	1984 %	1983 %	1981 %	1969 %
Too high	5	6	7	8	10	2
Too low	50	33	37	35	29	33
Just about right	31	43	41	31	41	43
No opinion	14	18	15	26	20	22

The second question:

Do you think that raising teacher salaries would improve the quality of education in the schools in this community a great deal, a fair amount, not very much, or almost not at all?

	National Totals %	No Children In School %	Public School Parents %	Nonpublic School Parents %
A great deal	16	14	18	21
A fair amount	35	36	35	33
Not very much	28	28	28	23
Almost not at all	17	17	17	18
Don't know	4	5	2	5

The third question:

Do you think that providing better working conditions for teachers would improve the quality of education in the public schools in this community a great deal, a fair amount, not very much, or almost not at all?

	National Totals %	No Children In School %	Public School Parents %	Nonpublic School Parents %
A great deal	25	24	29	31
A fair amount	37	38	34	36
Not very much	21	21	20	19
Almost not at all	12	11	14	12
Don't know	5	6	3	2

Appropriate Salaries for Teaching And Other Occupations

In the 1984 Gallup/Phi Delta Kappa poll, people assigned numerical values to their impressions of the prestige and value to society of each of 12 different occupations. Public school teachers were ranked third, after the clergy and physicians, in value to society, but they were ranked seventh in prestige or status.

A related question in the current poll suggests that the public does not believe that the value of a profession to society should necessarily determine the income of those who practice that profession. Respondents were asked to indicate what annual salary should be paid to people in each of seven different occupations. As the table below shows, people think teachers should be paid less than medical doctors, lawyers, engineers, pharmacists, and even nurses. Interestingly, the clergy, whose societal contribution the public considers so valuable, are dead last in terms of the salary the public would assign them.

The question:

As I mention the name of an occupation or profession, would you please tell me the annual

salary you feel people in that occupation should be paid in this community?

	$50,000 And Over %	$40,000-$49,999 %	$30,000-$39,999 %	$29,999-Or Less %	Don't Know %
Medical doctors	73	6	3	10	8
Lawyers	66	10	6	8	10
Engineers	53	20	11	6	10
Pharmacists	38	23	18	14	7
Nurses	26	22	26	18	8
Public school teachers	21	21	28	22	8
Plumbers	18	19	30	25	8
Clergy	12	14	26	37	11

Required Core Courses

For the sixth time, this poll gathered data on the public's perception of which subjects should be required of high school students who are bound for college and of high school students who are not college-bound. Public opinion on these issues has changed little over the past decade. For students who plan to attend college, more than 70% of the respondents would require at least five basic subjects: math, English, history, science, and computer training. More than half would require geography, career education, business education, foreign language, and health education. People would place less emphasis on several of these subjects for non-college-bound students, particularly foreign language and science, but they would require vocational education instead.

The question:

Please look over this card, which lists high school subjects. If you were the one to decide, what subjects would you require every public high school student who plans to go on to college to take? What about those *not* planning to go on to college?

For Those Planning to Go to College

	1990 %	1987 %	1985 %	1984 %	1983 %	1981 %
Mathematics	96	94	91	96	92	94
English	92	91	88	94	88	91
History/U.S. government	84	84	76	84	78	83
Science	81	83	76	84	76	76
Computer training	75	72	71	–	–	–
Geography	63	–	–	–	–	–
Career education	62	63	57	–	–	–
Business education	59	59	59	68	55	60
Foreign language	56	56	53	57	50	54
Health education	53	54	48	52	43	47
Physical education	40	45	40	43	41	44
Vocational training	29	31	27	37	32	34
Art	24	23	23	24	19	28
Music	22	23	24	22	18	26

(Figures add to more than 100% because of multiple answers.)

For Those *Not* Planning to Go to College

	1990 %	1987 %	1985 %	1984 %	1983 %	1981 %
Mathematics	90	88	85	92	87	91
English	86	85	81	90	83	89
Vocational training	74	78	75	83	74	64
History/U.S. government	67	69	61	71	63	71

	1990 %	1987 %	1985 %	1984 %	1983 %	1981 %
Computer training	63	61	57	–	–	–
Business education	63	65	60	76	65	75
Career education	60	61	57	–	–	–
Science	58	57	51	61	53	58
Health education	50	49	43	50	42	46
Geography	48	–	–	–	–	–
Physical education	38	41	40	44	40	43
Foreign language	25	20	17	19	19	21
Art	17	17	15	18	16	20
Music	16	15	15	18	16	20

(Figures add to more than 100% because of multiple answers.)

Subjects High Schools Should Emphasize

Respondents to this poll were asked which subjects should receive more — and which subjects should receive less — emphasis in high school. People tend to want more emphasis on the same subjects that top their required lists. For example, 80% would increase emphasis on mathematics. But it is something of an anomaly that foreign language is given short shrift, since so many people would require it for college-bound students. Not surprisingly — although most educators will deplore this finding — many respondents would deemphasize music and art.

The question:

As I read off each high school subject, would you tell me if you think that subject should be given more emphasis, less emphasis, or the same emphasis it now receives in high school — regardless of whether or not you think it should be required?

	National Totals			
	More Emphasis %	Less Emphasis %	Same Emphasis %	Don't Know %
Mathematics	80	3	14	3
English	79	3	15	3
Computer training	79	5	12	4
Career education	73	6	16	5
Science	68	11	18	3
History/U.S. government	65	9	23	3
Vocational education	65	9	22	4
Health education	62	10	25	3
Business	60	11	25	4
Geography	53	18	25	4
Foreign language	37	34	25	4
Physical education	32	27	37	4
Music	13	39	43	5
Art	12	42	40	6

Beyond the Basics

People would like their public high schools to do much more than teach the so-called basics. In fact, more people would require drug abuse education in high schools than would require any subjects other than math and English. Alcohol abuse education, AIDS education, sex education, and information about environmental issues and about teen pregnancy are also high on the public's list of subjects to be required. Character education, which is uncommon as a formal subject in public high schools, has as much support as a required subject as does driver education.

The question:

Please look over this card, which lists areas in which some public high schools offer instruction

beyond the standard academic courses. If you were the one to decide, which subject areas would you *require* every public high school student to study?

	National Totals %	Public School Parents %	No Children In School %
Would Require			
Drug abuse education	90	92	89
Alcohol abuse education	84	86	82
AIDS education	77	77	77
Sex education	72	74	71
Environmental issues and problems	66	65	66
Teen pregnancy	64	64	65
Driver education	59	62	59
Character education	57	56	57
Parenting/parent training	46	48	45
Dangers of nuclear waste	30	29	31
Dangers of nuclear war	28	28	28
Communism/socialism	24	23	25

(Figures add to more than 100% because of multiple answers.)

	National Totals		
	1990 %	1984 %	1983 %
Would Require			
Drug abuse education	90	82	81
Alcohol abuse education	84	79	76
AIDS education	77	–	–
Sex education	72	–	–
Environmental issues and problems	66	–	–
Teen pregnancy	64	–	–
Driver education	59	73	72
Character education	57	–	–
Parenting/parent training	46	55	58
Dangers of nuclear waste	30	61	56
Dangers of nuclear war	28	51	46
Communism/socialism	24	57	51

(Figures add to more than 100% because of multiple answers.)

Success in High School And in Later Life

Educators are well aware that there is a close correlation between academic success in high school and academic success in college. This relationship has been extensively explored and documented. The current poll shows that the general public is also aware of this correlation: 76% of poll respondents said that the relationship between success in high school and success in college is either very close or fairly close.

The relationship between academic success in high school and success in one's occupation is less extensively researched and documented, partly because of the difficulty of measuring "success" in an occupation. But as the answers to the second question below demonstrate, nearly as many laypeople believe that high school grades correlate with occupational success as believe in the connection between high school grades and college success. These findings are congruent with earlier poll findings that show how important people believe a good education to be for success in one's life work.

The first question:

Just your impression — how close a relationship do you feel there is between how high a student's grades are in high school and how academically successful he or she will be in college? Do you feel the relationship is very close, fairly close, not very close, or not close at all?

	National Totals %	No Children In School %	Public School Parents %	Nonpublic School Parents %
Very close	25	25	26	21
Fairly close	51	51	51	63
Not very close	13	13	13	11
Not close at all	4	3	4	1
Don't know	7	8	6	4

The second question:

Just your impression — how close a relationship do you feel there is between how good a student's grades are in high school and how successful he or she will be after completing school, that is, in an occupation or profession? Do you feel the relationship is very close, fairly close, not very close, or not close at all?

	National Totals %	No Children In School %	Public School Parents %	Nonpublic School Parents %
Very close	21	19	23	12
Fairly close	49	49	48	68
Not very close	19	20	18	11
Not close at all	5	5	7	1
Don't know	6	7	4	8

Grading the Public Schools

Over the past seven years there have been no statistically significant changes in the ratings people give their local public schools. During this period, between 40% and 43% of poll respondents have graded their local schools A or B. The highest ratings were given in 1974, when this question was first asked. In that year nearly half (48%) of all respondents gave their schools an A or a B. The low point came in 1983, just after *A Nation at Risk* was released by the National Commission on Excellence in Education and was widely publicized by the media. Only 31% of poll respondents gave local schools an A or a B in that year. Even allowing for some sampling error, the drop of 17 percentage points in approval ratings between 1974 and 1983 represented a negative shift in opinion for perhaps 25 million of the 170 million or more voting-age adults in the U.S. Now we seem to have gained back about 10 points. These trends are presented in the tables below.

One interesting but unexplained feature of the 1990 findings is the fact that, for the first time in several years, whites and nonwhites award very similar ratings to their local public schools. In past polls nonwhites tended to give their schools measurably lower ratings. For example, in 1987 only 35% of nonwhites gave their schools A or B ratings; 43% of whites did so. This year the figures are virtually identical for the two groups.

As past polls have amply demonstrated, people tend to give higher grades to their local public schools than they give to public schools nationally. There is a suggestion in the tables below of a slow deterioration in the national ratings in recent years. It is tempting to attribute this change to increasingly negative media coverage, but I know of no hard evidence to support such a conclusion.

The contrast between ratings given the nation's schools and ratings given local schools by the people who should know them best — parents of children currently attending the schools — is striking and instructive. Note that 72% of parents believe the public school their eldest child attends is worthy of a rating of A or B. Compare this with the 21% A or B rating given to the nation's public schools by all respondents, parents included. The most reasonable explanation for this phenomenon is that the more firsthand knowledge one has about the public schools (i.e., knowledge that doesn't come from the media), the better one likes and respects them.

Other tables presented below reveal the public's opinion on how well elementary teachers, high school teachers, and parents are doing their jobs for America's children.

The first question:

Students are often given the grades A, B, C, D, and FAIL to denote the quality of their work. Suppose the *public* schools themselves, in this community, were graded in the same way. What grade would you give the public schools here — A, B, C, D, or FAIL?

	National Totals %	No Children In School %	Public School Parents %	Nonpublic School Parents %
A & B	41	39	48	32
A	8	7	12	6
B	33	32	36	26
C	34	34	36	37
D	12	12	9	18
FAIL	5	5	4	6
Don't know	8	10	3	7

Ratings Given the Local Public Schools

	1990 %	1989 %	1988 %	1987 %	1986 %	1985 %	1984 %	1983 %	1982 %	1981 %	1980 %
A & B	41	43	40	43	41	43	42	31	37	36	35
A	8	8	9	12	11	9	10	6	8	9	10
B	33	35	31	31	30	34	32	25	29	27	25
C	34	33	34	30	28	30	35	32	33	34	29
D	12	11	10	9	11	10	11	13	14	13	12
FAIL	5	4	4	4	5	4	4	7	5	7	6
Don't know	8	9	12	14	15	13	8	17	11	10	18

The second question:

How about the public schools in the nation as a whole? What grade would you give the public schools nationally — A, B, C, D, or FAIL?

	National Totals %	No Children In School %	Public School Parents %	Nonpublic School Parents %
A & B	21	20	23	18
A	2	2	2	1
B	19	18	21	17
C	49	49	51	50
D	16	16	14	24
FAIL	4	4	4	5
Don't know	10	11	8	3

The third question:

Using the A, B, C, D, and FAIL scale again, what grade would you give the school your oldest child attends?

	Public School Parents %
A & B	72
A	27
B	45
C	19
D	5
FAIL	2
Don't know	2

Ratings Given the School Oldest Child Attends

	1990 %	1989 %	1988 %	1987 %	1986 %	1985 %
A & B	72	71	70	69	65	71
A	27	25	22	28	28	23
B	45	46	48	41	37	48
C	19	19	22	20	26	19
D	5	5	3	5	4	5
FAIL	2	1	2	2	2	2
Don't know	2	4	3	4	3	3

The fourth question:

What grade would you give the public *elementary* school teachers in this community?

	National Totals %	No Children In School %	Public School Parents %	Nonpublic School Parents %
A & B	58	55	67	49
A	18	15	26	10
B	40	40	41	39
C	21	22	21	31
D	6	5	6	12
FAIL	3	2	3	2
Don't know	12	16	3	6

	National Totals	
	1990 %	1987 %
A & B	58	53
A	18	18
B	40	35
C	21	21
D	6	4
FAIL	3	2
Don't know	12	20

The fifth question:

What grade would you give the public *high school* teachers in this community?

	National Totals %	No Children In School %	Public School Parents %	Nonpublic School Parents %
A & B	43	42	44	37
A	8	8	8	7
B	35	34	36	30
C	28	29	28	32
D	10	10	9	12
FAIL	4	4	4	5
Don't know	15	15	15	14

	National Totals	
	1990 %	1987 %
A & B	43	43
A	8	12
B	35	31
C	28	24
D	10	8
FAIL	4	3
Don't know	15	22

The sixth question:

What grade would you give the parents of students in the local public schools for bringing up their children?

	National Totals %	No Children In School %	Public School Parents %	Nonpublic School Parents %
A & B	26	25	28	27
A	3	3	3	1
B	23	22	25	26
C	40	36	47	44
D	20	22	17	19
FAIL	7	9	4	2
Don't know	7	8	4	8

	National Totals	
	1990 %	1984 %
A & B	26	33
A	3	7
B	23	26
C	40	36
D	20	16
FAIL	7	6
Don't know	7	9

Have the Schools Been Improving?

On two occasions — first in 1988 and now in 1990 — Gallup interviewers have asked people whether they think the public schools in their communities have improved, gotten worse, or stayed about the same over the preceding five years. This question is intended to determine whether people believe the current wave of school reform has been successful. Evidently, not many people do. Whereas 29% of those surveyed in 1988 saw improvement over the preceding five years, only 22% did so this year. This finding seems congruent with the opinions people offered about the education goals announced by President Bush and the 50 governors last fall, which were discussed earlier in this report. Not only does a sizable group of respondents think

that the schools haven't gotten better recently, but they also think that no great improvement is likely to occur within the current decade.

This preponderantly negative opinion is fairly evenly distributed among the major demographic groups that the Gallup Organization defines. However, the pessimism seems stronger in large cities, in the South and the West, and (ominously) among 18- to 29-year-olds. In cities of a million or more people, only 17% think their public schools have improved, while 35% think they have gotten worse. However, in communities of 50,000 and under, more people believe that their schools have improved than believe that they have deteriorated.

The question:

Would you say that the public schools in this community have improved from, say, five years ago, gotten worse, or stayed about the same?

	National Totals %	No Children In School %	Public School Parents %	Nonpublic School Parents %
Improved	22	20	29	18
Gotten worse	30	30	27	37
Stayed about the same	36	36	36	39
Don't know	12	14	8	6

	National Totals	
	1990 %	1988 %
Improved	22	29
Gotten worse	30	19
Stayed about the same	36	37
Don't know	12	15

Further breakdowns:

	Improved %	Gotten Worse %	Stayed About The Same %	Don't Know %
NATIONAL TOTALS	22	30	36	12
Sex				
Men	24	27	38	11
Women	20	32	35	13
Race				
White	22	29	37	12
Nonwhite	21	34	34	11
Age				
18 - 29 years	24	37	25	14
30 - 49 years	24	26	39	11
50 and over	18	29	41	12
Community Size				
1 million and over	16	36	35	13
500,000 - 999,999	22	32	39	7
50,000 - 499,999	26	28	33	13
2,500 - 49,999	27	23	39	11
Under 2,500	25	24	39	12
Education				
College	21	27	38	14
Graduate	19	22	44	15

	Improved %	Gotten Worse %	Stayed About The Same %	Don't Know %
Incomplete	23	31	33	13
High school	22	33	35	10
Graduate	22	32	35	11
Incomplete	22	35	35	8
Grade school	25	23	36	16
Income				
$40,000 and over	21	21	44	14
$30,000 - $39,999	23	33	34	10
$20,000 - $29,999	22	32	35	11
$10,000 - $19,999	24	34	32	10
Under $10,000	24	30	32	14
Region				
East	21	27	37	15
Midwest	21	22	45	12
South	25	37	30	8
West	20	31	33	16

Biggest Problems Facing Local Public Schools in 1990

In 1986, for the first time, the use of drugs edged out lack of discipline as the most frequently mentioned problem that people see besetting the local public schools. Every year since then more people have mentioned the drug problem. In 1989, 34% of the public cited drug use as the most important problem facing the schools; the comparable figure in 1990 is 38%, exactly double the percentage of people who mention lack of discipline. In other respects, the 1990 responses are similar to those given in other recent Gallup/Phi Delta Kappa surveys. However, one problem appears for the first time on this year's list: how to deal with the increasing number of students whose first language is not English. This problem was mentioned by 1% of the respondents and so moved out of the miscellaneous category.

The question:

What do you think are the biggest problems with which the public schools in this community must deal?

	National Totals %	No Children In School %	Public School Parents %	Nonpublic School Parents %
Use of drugs	38	40	34	39
Lack of discipline	19	19	17	25
Lack of proper financial support	13	18	17	21
Poor curriculum/poor standards	8	9	7	6
Large schools/ overcrowding	7	6	10	16
Difficulty getting good teachers	7	6	10	10
Pupils' lack of interest/ truancy	6	7	3	3
Low teacher pay	6	5	6	8
Crime/vandalism	5	7	4	1
Integration/busing	5	5	4	6
Parents' lack of interest	4	5	3	3
Drinking/alcoholism	4	4	4	3
Teachers' lack of interest	4	3	5	5
Moral standards	3	4	2	1
Lack of respect for teachers/other students	3	3	3	4
Lack of needed teachers	3	3	3	1
Lack of family structure	3	3	3	2
Lack of proper facilities	2	1	2	4
Parents' involvement in school activities	2	2	2	2

	National Totals %	No Children In School %	Public School Parents %	Nonpublic School Parents %
Mismanagement of funds/ programs	2	1	2	1
Problems with administration	2	2	3	3
Communication problems	2	2	2	2
Fighting	2	2	2	*

	National Totals %	No Children In School %	Public School Parents %	Nonpublic School Parents %
Lack of after-school programs	1	1	2	2
Transportation	1	1	1	2
Taxes are too high	1	1	1	1
Too much emphasis on sports	1	1	1	*
School board politics	1	1	2	*
Non-English-speaking students	1	1	*	*
Peer pressure	1	1	*	*
There are no problems	1	1	2	3
Miscellaneous	5	4	6	6
Don't know	6	7	2	5

*Less than one-half of 1%.
(Figures add to more than 100% because of multiple answers.)

Assigning Blame: Schools or Society?

Educators can take some comfort, perhaps, from responses to a question asking where the blame for the problems confronting public education should be placed—on the schools themselves or on society in general. People evidently blame society, not the schools. Note that parents of children who do not attend public schools—those who have already opted out of the public school system—tend to put more blame on the public schools.

The question:

In your opinion, which is more at fault for the problems currently facing public education in this community — the performance of the local public schools or the effect of societal problems?

	National Totals %	No Children In School %	Public School Parents %	Nonpublic School Parents %
Performance of schools	16	14	18	26
Effect of societal problems	73	73	75	63
Don't know	11	13	7	11

Research Procedure

The Sample. The sample used in this survey embraced a total of 1,594 adults (18 years of age and older). It is described as a modified probability sample of the nation. Personal, in-home interviewing was conducted in all areas of the nation and in all types of communities. A description of the sample can be found below.

Time of Interviewing. The fieldwork for this study was carried out during the periods of 6-18 April and 4-22 May 1990.

The Report. In the tables used in this report, "Nonpublic School Parents" includes parents of students who attend parochial schools and parents of students who attend private or independent schools.

1. PERCEPTIONS OF EDUCATION IN NORTH AMERICA

Due allowance must be made for statistical variation, especially in the case of findings for groups consisting of relatively few respondents, e.g., nonpublic school parents.

The findings of this report apply only to the U.S. as a whole and not to individual communities. Local surveys, using the same questions, can be conducted to determine how local areas compare with the national norm.

Composition of the Sample

Adults	%
No children in school	67
Public school parents	30*
Nonpublic school parents	6*

*Total exceeds 33% because some parents have children attending more than one kind of school.

Sex	%
Men	48
Women	52

Race	%
White	86
Nonwhite	14

Age	%
18-29 years	23
30-49 years	41
50 and over	36

Occupation (Chief Wage Earner)	%
Business and professional	29
Clerical and sales	7
Manual labor	37
Nonlabor force	16

Occupation (Chief Wage Earner)	%
Farm	3
Undesignated	8

Income	%
$40,000 and over	28
$30,000-$39,999	17
$20,000-$29,999	16
$10,000-$19,999	20
Under $10,000	13
Undesignated	6

Region	%
East	25
Midwest	25
South	31
West	19

Community Size	%
1 million and over	37
500,000-999,999	8
50,000-499,999	19
2,500-49,999	11
Under 2,500	25

Education	%
College	43
High school	49
Grade school	8

Design of the Sample

The sampling procedure is designed to produce an approximation of the adult civilian population, age 18 and older, living in the U.S., except for persons in institutions such as prisons or hospitals.

A replicated probability sample is used, down to the block level in urban areas and down to segments of townships in rural areas. More than 300 sampling locations are used in each survey.

The sample design included stratification by these seven size-of-community strata, using 1980 census data: 1) incorporated cities of population 1,000,000 and over, 2) incorporated cities of population 250,000 to 999,999, 3) incorporated cities of population 50,000 to 249,999, 4) urbanized places not included in 1 and 2, 5) cities over 2,500 population outside of urbanized areas, 6) towns and villages with populations less than 2,500, and 7) rural places not included within town boundaries. Each of these strata was further stratified into four geographic regions: East, Midwest, South, and West. Within each city-size/regional stratum, the population was arrayed in geographic order and zoned into equal-sized groups of sampling units. Pairs of localities were selected in each zone, with probability of selection of each locality proportional to its population size in the 1980 census, producing two replicated samples of localities.

For each survey, within each subdivision for which block statistics are available, a sample of blocks or block clusters is drawn with probability of selection proportional to the number of dwelling units. In all other subdivisions or areas, blocks or segments are drawn at random or with equal probability.

In each cluster of blocks and each segment, a randomly selected starting point is designated on the interviewer's map of the area. Starting at this point, interviewers are required to follow a given direction in the selection of households until their assignment is completed.

Interviewing is conducted at times when adults, in general, are most likely to be at home, which means on weekends, or, if on weekdays, after 4 p.m. for women and after 6 p.m. for men.

Allowance for persons not at home is made by a "times-at-home" weighting* procedure rather than by "callbacks." This procedure is a method for reducing the sample bias that would otherwise result from under-representation in the sample of persons who are difficult to find at home.

The prestratification by regions is routinely supplemented by fitting each obtained sample to the latest available Census Bureau estimates of the regional distribution of the population. Also, minor adjustments of the sample are made by educational attainment by men and women separately, based on the annual estimates of the Census Bureau (derived from its Current Population Survey) and by age.

*A. Politz and W. Simmons, "An Attempt to Get the 'Not at Homes' into the Sample Without Callbacks," *Journal of the American Statistical Association*, March 1949, pp. 9-31.

Sampling Tolerances

In interpreting survey results, it should be borne in mind that all sample surveys are subject to sampling error, i.e., the extent to which the results may differ from what would be obtained if the whole population surveyed had been interviewed. The size of such sampling errors depends largely on the number of interviews.

The following tables may be used in estimating the sampling error of any percentage in this report. The computed allowances have taken into account the effect of the sample design upon sampling error. They may be interpreted as indicating the range (plus or minus the figure shown) within which the results of repeated samplings in the same time period could be expected to vary 95% of the time, assuming the same sampling procedure, the same interviewers, and the same questionnaire.

The first table shows how much allowance should be made for the sampling error of a percentage:

Recommended Allowance for Sampling Error of a Percentage

In Percentage Points
(at 95 in 100 confidence level)*
Sample Size

	1,500	1,000	750	600	400	200	100
Percentages near 10	2	2	3	3	4	5	8
Percentages near 20	3	3	4	4	5	7	10
Percentages near 30	3	4	4	5	6	8	12
Percentages near 40	3	4	5	5	6	9	12
Percentages near 50	3	4	5	5	6	9	13
Percentages near 60	3	4	5	5	6	9	12
Percentages near 70	3	4	4	5	6	8	12
Percentages near 80	3	3	4	4	5	7	10
Percentages near 90	2	2	3	3	4	5	8

*The chances are 95 in 100 that the sampling error is not larger than the figures shown.

The table would be used in the following manner: Let us say that a reported percentage is 33 for a group that includes 1,000 respondents. We go to the row for "percentages near 30" in the table and across to the column headed "1,000."

The number at this point is 4, which means that the 33% obtained in the sample is subject to a sampling error of plus or minus four points. In other words, it is very probable (95 chances out of 100) that the true figure would be somewhere between 29% and 37%, with the most likely figure the 33% obtained.

In comparing survey results in two samples, such as, for example, men and women, the question arises as to how large a difference between them must be before one can be reasonably sure that it reflects a real difference. In the tables below, the number of points that must be allowed for in such comparisons is indicated.

Two tables are provided. One is for percentages near 20 or 80; the other, for percentages near 50. For percentages in between, the error to be allowed for lies between those shown in the two tables.

Recommended Allowance for Sampling Error of the Difference

In Percentage Points
(at 95 in 100 confidence level)*

TABLE A	Percentages near 20 or percentages near 80					
Size of Sample	1,500	1,000	750	600	400	200
1,500	4					
1,000	4	5				
750	5	5	5			
600	5	5	6	6		
400	6	6	6	7	7	
200	8	8	8	8	9	10

TABLE B

Size of Sample	Percentages near 50					
	1,500	1,000	750	600	400	200
1,500	5					
1,000	5	6				
750	6	6	7			
600	6	7	7	7		
400	7	8	8	8	9	
200	10	10	10	10	11	13

*The chances are 95 in 100 that the sampling error is not larger than the figures shown.

Here is an example of how the tables would be used: Let us say that 50% of men respond a certain way and 40% of women respond that way also, for a difference of 10 percentage points between them. Can we say with any assurance that the 10-point difference reflects a real difference between men and women on the question? Let us consider a sample that contains approximately 750 men and 750 women.

Since the percentages are near 50, we consult Table B, and, since the two samples are about 750 persons each, we look for the number in the column headed "750," which is also in the row designated "750." We find the number 7 here. This means that the allowance for error should be seven points and that, in concluding that the percentage among men is somewhere between three and 17 points higher than the percentage among women, we should be wrong only about 5% of the time. In other words, we can conclude with considerable confidence that a difference exists in the direction observed and that it amounts to at least three percentage points.

If, in another case, men's responses amount to 22%, say, and women's to 24%, we consult Table A, because these percentages are near 20. We look in the column headed "750" and see that the number is 5. Obviously, then, the two-point difference is inconclusive.

Acknowledgments

About 100 delegates and officers attending Phi Delta Kappa's Biennial Council last October responded to a call for help in framing this 22nd Gallup/Phi Delta Kappa opinion poll. Their suggestions were carefully considered by a panel of advisers composed of six members of the Phi Delta Kappa professional staff, and a number of topics and questions suggested have been used in this poll in some form. The form of these questions was largely determined by Alec Gallup of the Gallup Organization.

We wish to thank all Kappans who submitted suggestions — and especially the following persons, whose ideas were used:

James Brazee, Northeast Nebraska Chapter; Joseph Naples, Westminster College Chapter; J. C. Hainsworth, Murray State University Chapter; Jane-Ellen Brereton, Suffolk County Chapter; Laverne Warner, Sam Houston State University Chapter; Judy Parsons, University of Missouri Chapter; Donald E. Wilson, Greater Kansas City Missouri Chapter; Mary Kilgallen, Big Rapids Michigan Chapter; Larry McNeal, Southern Arkansas Chapter; Shelbie Johnson, Northeast Georgia Chapter; Ralph E. Helser, Northwest Georgia Chapter; Christian H. Cherau, Southwest Florida Chapter; Fred C. Hansen, La Canada California Chapter; Linda G. Huggins, Florence South Carolina Chapter; Joyce L. Chapman, Eastern Panhandle West Virginia Chapter; Margaret Schoelles, St. Leo Florida Chapter; and C. R. Wall, Southwest Kansas Chapter. — SME

The Reconceptualization of the Educative Effort

There is a great deal of dialogue today in the teaching profession regarding how best to reconceive the structure of schooling at the elementary, secondary, and university levels. "Reconceptualist" ideas concerning alternative ways of conceiving teacher education programs reflect fundamental debate over the best way to improve the intellectual quality and curiosity of prospective teachers. The debate over the restructuring, or reconceptualization, of teacher education is addressed in Unit 3.

In this unit, the efforts to reconceive, redefine, and "deconstruct" existing patterns of curriculum and instruction at the elementary and secondary levels of schooling are considered and related to the efforts to reconceive existing conflicting patterns of teacher education. In "A Reconceptualization of Educational Foundations," Jonas Soltis calls for the clarification of what is meant by "professional literacy" in efforts to redirect commonly shared concepts and concerns about curricular reconstruction. There is a broad spectrum of dialogue developing in North America, the British Commonwealth, the Soviet Union, and other areas of the world regarding the redirecting of the learning opportunities of citizens.

Prospective teachers are encouraged to question their own educational experiences as a part of the process of becoming more reflective professional persons. Cultural institutions and values affect our ideas about curriculum content and the purpose of educating others. This is perceived as vitally important in the developing dialogue over liberating students' capacities to function as independent inquirers. The interrelationships among cultural factors, processes of economic change, the social contexts of students' lives as learners in classrooms, and the content of school curricula are basic components in the debate over restructuring the social and intellectual purposes of schools. The dramatic economic and demographic changes in North American society encourage a fundamental reconceptualization of how schools ought to respond to the social contexts in which they are located.

Fundamental rethinking is underway regarding the process of curriculum development in elementary and secondary schools and in teacher education. This has developed as an intellectual movement with participants in the dialogue coming from the entire range of ideological, political, and cultural perspectives reflected in public debate regarding the social purposes of educational systems and the quality of teaching and learning. The current efforts to restructure and to redefine professional purposes are closely related to the efforts to achieve meaningful qualitative improvement in what and how students learn in schools. The varied and pluralistic perspectives that shape the lives of students in their formal educational experiences in schools has been under critical review. This process is leading to fascinating reconception of what is possible in our efforts to educate others.

This movement in our thought about education is reflected in the views of school board members, school administrators, teachers, students, as well as the views of scholars in teacher education and the arts and sciences. The effort to reassess and reconceive the education of others is a part of broader reform efforts in society, as well as a dynamic dialectic in its own right. How can schools, for instance, better reflect the varied communities of interest that they serve? How can they be better perceived as more just, fairer places in which young people seek to achieve learning and self-fulfillment?

This is not the first period in which North Americans have searched their minds and souls to redirect, construct, and, if necessary, "deconstruct" their understandings regarding formal educational systems. The debate over what ought to be the conceptual and structural underpinnings of national educational opportunity structures has continued since the first mass educational system was formed in the nineteenth century. The vital work in the development of critical perspectives of learning that has developed in the past thirty years is represented in the language of empowerment and personal liberation that helps students think critically and commandingly about self and others.

Alternative approaches to improving the quality of educational experiences for young people develop in most decades. In any given year, many interesting, innovative programs are initiated in some schools to facilitate and enrich student learning. When we think of continuity and change, we think of the conceptual balance between cherished traditions, and innovations that may facilitate learning without compromising cherished core values or standards. On the other hand, some innovations do challenge traditional ideas. This is a sensitive balance. When one thinks of change in education, one can be reminded of such great educational experiments of earlier times as (1) the late John Dewey's Laboratory School at the University of Chicago, (2) the late Maria Montessori's Casi di Bambini (children's houses), and (3) the late A. S. Neil's controversial Summerhill School in England, as well as many other earlier and later innovative experiments in learning theories. Our own time has seen similarly dramatic experimentation.

Questions regarding educational change have to be considered in terms of their feasibility, anticipated effectiveness, and the values premises that underlie them. One

Unit 2

person's desired change is often another person's "poison." What constitutes desirable change is directly related to one's own core values regarding what the purposes and content of educational experiences ought to be. When considering a proposed change in an educational system or a particular classroom, some questions to ask include: What is the purpose of the proposed change? What are the human and social benefits and costs of the proposed change (in teachers' work, in students' learning tasks, etc.)? What defensible alternatives are possible? What are our best ideas? How does the proposed change affect traditional practice? These are but a few of the questions we must ask. They suggest others. The past thirty or more years of research on teaching and learning have led us to be more concerned over the need to improve the quality of learning while also broadening educational opportunity structures for young people. Broadening opportunities structures provides a high degree of equity in access to educational services, as well as developing alternative educational experiences. We must strive to be fair with our colleagues and our students in the spirited debates now going on regarding changes needed to make school systems and teachers more effective.

It is still of some value to remind ourselves of that ideal expressed so well by Matthew Arnold in the late nineteenth century that "education" ought to be "the best that has been thought and said." It is necessary to confront the issue regarding what subjects should be retained in school curricula, as well as what new bodies of knowledge ought to be added. Part of this task involves consideration as to how knowledge from related areas can be developed in interdisciplinary curricular efforts. We must prepare young persons to be humane, caring individuals, and this needs to be done while also teaching them the technical skills that they need to persevere and to succeed in a highly competitive "high-tech" international marketplace. This dispute over the content of school and university curricula, as a part of the debate regarding general studies for all students, has been going on ever since Thomas Huxley and Matthew Arnold debated, in the late nineteenth century, the places of the sciences and the humanities in school curricula.

Each of the essays in this unit relates directly, in some relevant ways, to the conceptual tension involved in reconceiving how educational development should proceed.

Looking Ahead: Challenge Questions

What are the most important problems to be considered when we talk about restructuring schools?

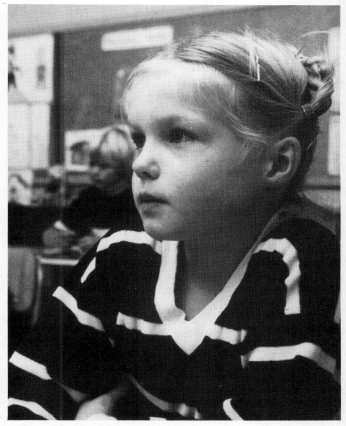

What concepts in our thoughts about "education" need "reconceptualization"?

What are the social forces that affect human responses to change?

What can teachers do to improve critical reasoning skills in themselves and their students?

To what extent can schooling be reconstructed to most effectively emphasize academic achievement as well as intangible but important factors such as character or initiative or freedom of thought?

Are there more political and economic pressures on educators than they can reasonably be expected to manage? Is this sort of pressure avoidable? Why or why not?

What knowledge bases (disciplines or interdisciplines) ought senior high school students study?

If it is true that there should be a common curriculum at the primary and middle grade levels, should there also be a common curriculum at the secondary level?

What values ought to be at the basis of any effort to reconceptualize the social purposes of schools?

A Reconceptualization of Teacher Education

William F. Pinar

Pinar is Professor and Chair, Department of Curriculum and Instruction, College of Education, Louisiana State University.

Pinar focuses on the political and curricular aspects of reconceptualization. Addressing the issue of "academic bankruptcy" in schools, he examines selected Holmes proposals that serve as a response to the public's disillusionment. Pinar defends the Holmes proposals, but suggests that they be modified to meet reconceptualist goals. Otherwise, it remains to be seen whether the Holmes reforms will fall victim to the current zeal for standardized tests and quantifiable data, or whether the new programs will reflect the ideals of reconceptualization.

The theoretical apparatus is now in place for a curricular reconceptualization of teacher education. If schools are to be the "second site" of reconceptualization, teacher education will be an important instrument. Consideration of political and curricular issues accompanying such a reconceptualization is the subject of this paper.

The reconceptualization of curriculum studies began in a critique of the traditional field (see Pinar, 1975), a field largely identified with the Tyler Rationale (Tyler, 1949). After a decade of declining enrollments and a national curriculum reform movement led not by curriculum specialists but by disci-plinary specialists, the field was vulnerable to critique (Pinar and Grumet, 1988). In 1969 Joseph Schwab delivered the first of a decade-long series of critiques, one consequence of which was to accelerate the "breakdown" of the Tylerian "paradigm" (Brown, 1988). In its place surfaced an effort to understand the curriculum as well as to develop it. That effort was to be informed by history, political theory, aesthetic theory, phenomenology, gender research, and feminist theory. During the 1970s curriculum as a field became absorbed with the complex of ways that culture and individuals reproduce and transform themselves via public institutions, particularly the school and specifically school knowledge or curriculum. Reconceptualization had twin emphases: the school as microcosm of society and the school as experienced by the individual (Pinar, 1975). Reconceptualization has ended as a social and intellectual movement within curriculum studies. Indeed, within curriculum theory, the reconceptualization has occurred (Pinar, 1988).

The forms this multifaceted, complex, and evolving understanding of curriculum would take in teacher education programs vary according to external influences (such as the political climate of the local schools) and internal influences, including the perspectives of those involved most closely, even if these individuals were all "reconceptualists." This paper sketches qualities of one possible version of a "reconceptualist" teacher preparation program. This version makes use of the controversial Holmes Group proposals, proposals which, in modified form, can advance teacher education significantly. The three most interesting Holmes proposals are (a) eliminating the undergraduate major in education, (b) reconceptualizing teacher education coursework, and (c) linking teacher education programs to the schools.

In Our Interest

Politically, the Holmes proposals are in the political best interests of education faculties. They represent a way of claiming defeat as victory, that is if we act decisively and take reconceptualization seriously. Now education faculties are given the blame for the perceived failure in the schools. We know that is only partly true, but that public perception is not going to be corrected soon or easily, and certainly not by the accused. Shifting the responsibility for undergraduate learning to our colleagues in arts and sciences also shifts the political responsibility for the quality of those students who graduate from their disciplines and enter ours. Creating clinical faculty from colleagues in the schools to teach methods courses and supervise student teachers or interns helps shift political responsibility to existing teachers. Reducing the number of coursework hours we have teacher education students reduces the responsibility of teacher educators.

Despite its dangers, the differentiated staffing idea is smart politically and economically. The major problem will involve keeping internal bureaucratic politics minimal so that the most intelligent and professional of teachers are those who are promoted to the highest category and thus earn the highest salaries. If intelligent, well-trained and dedicated people are appointed to the promotion boards which make these decisions, there is a chance. If behavioristic schemes are used, mostly by existing administrators, especially principals, one can be less sanguine. Even the instructor class, those with a bachelors degree in an arts and science discipline but no or little education coursework, is a risk worth taking in the short term. If significant amounts of new money are not forthcoming, a conservative if not reasonable assumption for most school districts, then keeping entry-level salaries low will help free monies to create higher-paying, "career professional" positions. The Rochester, N.Y., top salary of $70,000 is one with which all districts ought to compete. Most districts will not have the absolute increases in their budgets Governor Cuomo has provided New York State districts, and so starting salaries must be considerably below the Rochester ones of nearly $30,000. If, for example, a history major were paid $14,000 to begin a teaching career, then experienced, educated, intelligent and dedicated teachers could be paid considerably more. Unless this monetary incentive is built in the system soon, all reform efforts will be undermined. And the public will be unwilling to provide additional monies unless discernible (if not dramatic) reform is underway.

From a political point of view, then, the Holmes proposals provide a diversification of responsibility for the quality of teachers, thus reducing the risk of liability for education faculties. They ensure fundamental educational experience in the basic arts and sciences disciplines anterior to the study of teaching and curriculum. Finally, a reduction in the number of coursework hours available to teacher education faculties requires those faculties to reconceptualize those courses along more academically rigorous and complex lines. The curricular sketch which follows points toward one such reconceptualization.

Liberal Arts Education

Undergraduate education majors do not sufficiently study the arts and sciences. No matter how sophisticated it may be, and at many institutions it is hardly sophisticated, the study of teaching, learning, and the curriculum always derives from the arts and sciences disciplines. The arts and sciences disciplines constitute orders of information and experience that are epistemologically anterior to the rigorous study of teaching. Curriculum is always, in a fundamental sense, an extrapolation from arts and sciences disciplines. To reduce prospective teachers' arts and science work is to reduce the knowledge a teacher can bring to elementary and secondary school students.

Exemplary teaching is not universal in arts and sciences disciplines. Vocationalism, an orientation which views undergraduate work as primarily preparatory to graduate work, is present in those disciplines. A bachelor's degree in one of the arts, humanities, and sciences in no way guarantees expertise in working with children. And the differentiated staffing proposal does pose the possibility of creating a permanent "underclass" of teachers in the "instructor" category. However, students whose undergraduate experience has been limited to methods and foundations courses (often courses not academically rigorous or as information-rich as arts and sciences courses) sometimes cannot pass minimal competency tests imposed by some states, nor are they perceived by the public as having succeeded with the nation's schoolchildren. Indeed, the Holmes, Carnegie, and NCATE reports are responses to a widespread judgment of academic bankruptcy for our schools. While the reasons for this bankruptcy are complex, and responsibility belongs to no one group, such as education faculties, the point is that a fundamental reorganization of the teacher preparation process is politically required. Even if this judgment of bankruptcy were false, as many mainstream teacher educators seem to believe, the public believes it by and large, the politicians believe it, and most others in the higher education community believe it.

Coursework for Preservice Teachers

Tom (1987) expresses a well-grounded skepticism regarding "the knowledge base of teaching" mentioned in the Holmes proposals. Efforts to develop a science of teaching have indeed failed. One would hope that reconceptualist scholarship has laid to rest this false ambition. It rests on a mechanical view of humankind which, if accurate, would not require a technology of teaching, given that human behavior would then be manipulable and predictable (Pinar, 1988). Pseudo-scientific, "practice-oriented" teacher preparation emphasizes a narrow vocationalism over the cultivation of professional judgment.

The cultivation of judgment and professional wisdom, provided they are grounded in serious study in the arts, humanities, sciences and in curriculum theory, is an appropriate aspiration. This general and important distinction between academic vs. vocational or technical curriculum is well expressed in the following catalogue statement, which was taken from the University of Michigan Law School Announcement.

> [T]he Law School is very much a professional school. But it is distinctly not a vocational school. Students are not trained to perform many, or even most, of the tasks that its graduates may be called upon to perform as lawyers, and should not expect to be fully prepared to deliver a wide range of legal services on the day of graduation. [S]tudents may acquire or begin to develop some practical or technical skills and may gain confidence in their ability to perform as lawyers. Our practice-oriented courses and clinics provide, however, only an introduction to skills and a framework for practice which can only be defined through years of experience. The majority of our graduates join law firms where numerous opportunities exist for skill development under supervision of experienced practitioners who share with the novitiate responsibility for the quality of service rendered. Michigan, more than many other law schools, *seeks to provide students with the intellectual and theoretical background with which an attorney can undertake a more reflective and rewarding practice.* It is felt that too much haste or emphasis on vocational skills, without a broader and more critical view of the framework in which lawyering occurs, runs the risks of training technicians instead of professionals. (p. 15) (emphasis added)

The production of technicians is ill-advised also because it polarizes the undergraduate experience and professional training. Graduate study in education must not be severed from the undergraduate liberal arts curriculum; rather it must enhance and surpass the experiences and understandings that students have accumulated during these pre-education years. A "reconceptualist" M.A. preservice year would intersect but not coincide with undergraduate experience. It would critically grasp and extend that experience. What a reconceptualist fifth year can offer students is an analysis of arts and science knowledge grounded in curriculum theory and suggested by specializations such as the history of science (mathematics, etc.), the sociology of knowledge (including science), gender analyses of the disciplines, phenomenology of educational experience, aesthetic ways of knowing, and the politics of school knowledge. The graduate of such a curriculum is more likely to become a "transformative intellectual" than a technician-functionary (Giroux, 1988).

These affiliated areas of curriculum theory can be taught in several courses with interdisciplinary content. For instance, rather than the conventional child development psychology course, an "Experience of Childhood" course drawing upon undergraduate knowledge in arts and sciences disciplines could be developed. It would include readings in developmental psychology, but also in the history of childhood, in fictional accounts (both novels and poems) of growing up, as well as political and economic analyses of the family, children, and schooling. Other interdisciplinary courses might include the "Nature of Knowledge," including characteristic ways of knowing from arts, sciences, and the humanities, with particular attention to teaching exemplifications of each epistemological mode. Non-European knowledge as well as material from marginalized classes and groups must be included.

While thematic organizations of knowledge are hardly novel (Barnes, 1987), "reconceptualist" teacher preparation curricula would explicitly occupy the intersections between undergraduate study of the liberal arts and institutional demands of practitioner performance. These courses could be taught, if economy required, in large lecture sections. Intense small group workshop experiences could accompany them. These courses must be rigorous academic experiences constructed to integrate undergraduate knowledge in the various disciplines with knowledge of curriculum and instruction. Considerations of practice are best left to the methods courses that would be taught later in the program by Ph.D. students in interdisciplinary curriculum theory programs or

by clinical faculty, who, under ideal circumstances, would be graduates of such programs. Clinical faculty trained in such programs would be more likely to give the program continuity.

The early courses would be intensely academic experiences; later experiences would be intensely practical. That is, methods courses could be taught in the schools by working teachers who have already undergone a thoroughly theoretical preparation. Supervision of student teaching ought to include sponsor teachers and at least one university person. Testimonial material from students, parents, and administrators ought to be included in a candidate's portfolio. This material ought to be used in a reflective supervisory practice, as this permits the student critically to analyze his or her performance (Garman, 1986). Standardized instruments are best avoided, as they force a mechanization of teaching. Versions of Eisnerian "aesthetic" evaluation are preferable. Student teaching sites ought to be multiple, and include public and non-public schools, as well as demographically diverse experiences.

During a student's M.A. year, he or she should maintain a journal in order to address both phenomenological and gender-related experience (Grumet, 1988). Each M.A. student might be assigned to a faculty member or to an advanced Ph.D. student who would meet weekly with the student throughout the program. This person, trained in autobiography and journal work, would help the student reflect upon and analyze the experiences. This person would also serve as an advocate for the student, but not necessarily be in a grade-conferring position. After student teaching, this "advisor" would be included in the Committee judgment regarding conferral of the Master of Arts degree.

Schools

The Holmes Group calls for more closely linking education faculties with schools and for reorganizing schools. Clinical faculty who would have offices in education faculty buildings and who would interact with education faculty will help link education faculties to schools. Further, so-called "professional development schools," sites where collaborative training and research projects might be formulated and pursued, will permit closer ties between schoolteachers and university profes-

sors. Preferably, not only education faculties will be involved, but education schools will facilitate arts and science faculties involvement on part-time bases.

Closer links to the schools ought not be viewed uncritically. The powerful press of daily life in the school can function as a kind of "black hole" into which theory disappears. Survival can come to mean coinciding uncritically with situations as they are (Baldwin, 1987). While we are friends with our colleagues in the schools — they are our former students — we must maintain a respectful distance from them. We cannot advise or educate those with whom we have thoroughly identified. For teacher educators, the school must remain an object of study as well as a site for success (Pinar and Grumet, 1988).

A Caution

There is a fear that Holmes Group reforms will make more difficult the recruitment of minority teacher candidates (see Martinez, 1988). This fear must be taken seriously but must also be situated in a larger economic context. Minority students will return to teaching if and when it becomes lucrative and respected. This is, in large measure, a market-driven matter. Making the field more prestigious and more appropriately compensated should make it easier to recruit minority students. Accommodations in admission criteria will have been made on occasion, especially when GRE scores or other culturally narrow and standardized instruments are an essential factor in admissions decisions (Barone, 1987). Retention of minority teacher candidates can be made more likely by incorporating appropriate cognitive "styles" (Anderson, 1988). Acknowledgement of and support for cultural, class, and specifically ethnic variabilities in modes of cognition are important aspects of a reconceptualist agenda.

The diversity of teacher education institutions would probably be reduced (Tom, 1987), and that is not necessarily unfortunate. Most nonresearch universities, including many small colleges, have very limited resources for teacher education. Common to many small colleges is an education department of two to five overworked faculty with one hundred or more students among them. With little time or institutional support to keep abreast of current scholarship or to attend annual professional meetings, these faculty, despite their intelligence, good training, and commitment cannot offer what research universities can offer prospective teachers.

Conclusion

The Holmes proposals represent concession portrayed as victory, and reconceptualists must claim the victory as partially their own, as we have been critical of the vacuous pseudo-science that has sometimes characterized mainstream teacher education in the past. Behavioral objectives, instruction interaction analysis, and standardized forms of evaluation have contributed to the "deskilling" and "dis-empowerment" of educators and to the deterioration of American public education. The Holmes proposals, by promising increased teacher autonomy and higher salaries, intersect with the reconceptualist agenda. Vigorous intervention on behalf of women and minorities — in recruitment and in curriculum content — are an essential item of a reconceptualist-Holmes agenda.

The real battle is not over whether a reconceptualization of teacher education will occur. That battle is over, lost in the perceptions of politicians and the public. The battle concerns the content of fifth-year or extended programs and whether that content will remain or become even more standardized, behavioristic, and technological or whether it will reflect the critical and reflective content and goals of the recent reconceptualization of curriculum studies. Reconceptualists can enter the battle in the professional journals, in their own faculty meetings, and in legislative sessions, arguing for a reconceptualization that will authorize truly interdisciplinary and critically rigorous teacher preparation programs.

Acknowledgement

Special thanks to Tony Whitson for bringing the University of Michigan Law School announcement to my attention.

—————— References ——————

Anderson, J. A. (1988). Cognitive styles and multicultural populations. *Journal of Teacher Education, 39* (1), 2-9.

Baldwin, E. E. (1987). Theory vs. ideology in the practice of teacher education. *Journal of Teacher Education, 38* (1), 16-19.

Barnes, H. L. (1987). *Journal of Teacher Education, 38* (4), 13-18.

Barone, T. E. (1987). *Journal of Teacher Education, 38* (2), 12-17.

Brown, T. (1988). How fields change: A critique of the "Kuhnian" view. In W. F. Pinar (Ed.), *Contemporary curriculum discourses*. Scottsdale, AZ: Gorsuch Scarisbrick.

Bass de Martinez, B. (1988). Political and reform agendas' impact on the supply of black teachers. *Journal of Teacher Education, 39* (1), 10-13.

Garman, N. (1986). Reflection, the heart of supervision. *Journal of Curriculum and Supervision, 2* (1), 1-24.

Giroux, H. A. (1988). Liberal arts, teaching, and critical literacy: Toward a definition of school as a form of cultural politics. In W. F. Pinar (Ed.), *Contemporary Curriculum Discourse* (pp. 243-263). Scottsdale, AZ: Gorsuch Scarisbrick.

Pinar, W. F. (Ed.) (1975). *Curriculum theorizing: The reconceptualists.* Berkeley, CA: McCutchan.

Pinar, W. F. (1988). "Whole, bright, deep with understanding": Issues in qualitative research and autobiographical method. In W. F. Pinar (Ed.), *Contemporary curriculum discourse* (pp. 134-154). Scottsdale, AZ: Gorsuch Scarisbrick.

Pinar, W. F., & Grumet, M. R. (1988). Socratic *caesura* and the theory-practice relationship. In W. F. Pinar (Ed), *Contemporary curriculum discourse* (pp. 92-100). Scottsdale, AZ: Gorsuch Scarisbrick.

Tom, A. (1987). *How should teachers be educated? An assessment of three reform reports.* Bloomington, IN: Phi Delta Kappa Education Foundation.

Tyler, R. W. (1949). *Basic principles of curriculum and instruction.* Chicago: University of Chicago Press.

University of Michigan Law School Announcement, 1986-87.

A Reconceptualization of Educational Foundations

Jonas F. Soltis

Teachers College, Columbia University

Soltis claims that the members of any profession need a "professional literacy" of concepts and concerns held in common if they are to communicate effectively in debate and cooperative problem-solving. Properly conceived, he argues, social and psychological foundations instruction can provide teachers with a common background of theoretical frameworks, major concepts, alternative models, and historical precedents necessary for shared understanding and communication. Toward this end, Soltis suggests several fundamental educational questions that each prospective teacher should be equipped to reflect upon in informed ways.

The reconceptualization of foundations of education that I will offer here rests on a basic set of philosophical and normative assumptions. In spirit, they are Deweyan. Dewey's idea of community as a form of associative living, as a sharing of common language, concepts, and interests, as the free interaction among different groups and the using of collective intelligence in the solution of common problems, is very basic to my view of what a community of professional educators should be. So too is Dewey's pragmatic view of knowledge.

Many think in shorthand terms of pragmatism as a view of knowledge as that which is useful and of truth as that which works. This way of characterizing Dewey's view of knowledge may contain an ounce of accuracy, but it also conveys a pound of distortion. The key to understanding Dewey's view of knowledge-in-use is his conception of educative experience and education as growth. Previous experience that enters into present experience to inform it, organize it, transform it, and reconstruct it is not just useful knowledge in the technical sense of knowing how to do something. It is useful in the richer and broader sense of being able to use one's past experience to orient oneself in a new situation, to interpret its manifold dimensions, to analyze its components, to guess at or antici-

pate its future, and to bring one's purposes to bear on the ongoing interaction of self and situation. This richer view of knowledge-in-use is basic to the view of foundational knowledge that I want to put before you, but I am getting ahead of myself. Let me start at the beginning.

THE FOUNDATIONS METAPHOR

We are here today at a very crucial time in the history of the education of teachers to reconsider the idea of the foundations of education. Although only a half century old, foundations is a venerable idea in teacher education. Even those who doubt its potency for practice still tend to treat it with respect. There is something magic and majestic in the root metaphor of foundations. It suggests something solid, sound, basic, fundamental, and supportive of the whole superstructure of educational practice. Nevertheless, in the teacher education community today, there are serious doubts about the efficacy and essentiality of foundations.

The foundations metaphor is problematic. It suggests a false logical necessity. We all know that people can teach and even teach well without ever having studied foundations; yet we act as if that were not so. When foundations is claimed to be the essential theoretical knowledge base for educational practice, the lie is cast in indefensible form. Just as knowledge of oceanography is not a prerequisite for skillful fishing and there are superb mountain climbers who have not studied geology, so too there is a lack of necessary connection between foundations and teaching. No matter how natural and appealing this interpretation of the root metaphor is, it is just plain wrongheaded and our belief in the importance of foundations suffers from this misinterpretation, however understandable it may be.

Of course we could remedy this situation by replacing the metaphor of foundations with a new metaphor. That would not be an easy bill to fill, however. A new metaphor would have to be as elegantly suggestive of the power and value of foundational studies as the old. It would have to fit comfortably into the space left in college catalogs when all the references to foundations are removed. Or failing to find a new metaphor, we could change the name of foundations departments or submerge foundations people in other less metaphorically suggestive departments called policy studies, administration, or curriculum and theory as some institutions already have done. But what would happen to the powerfully suggestive idea of the basic importance of educational foundations if we all did so? Would the sense of something being fundamental to teacher education disappear? Would we lose something important to the proper normative conception of the educating profession? If a "foundation" for teaching is not logically necessary, might having one be professionally or morally desirable? Is there any way to conceive of foundations that remains true to the force of the powerful original root metaphor and yet avoids a mistaken view of the relationship between theory and practice, knowledge and use?

I think so and that is what I am here to offer you today. I would like to recast the argument for foundations-as-basic from one that is directly practical and technical to one more philosophical, cultural, and normative in form. I would like to expand the concept of knowledge-in-use beyond the technical sense of application to include the interpretive, perspectival, creative, imaginative, sensitive, normative, critical, and formative uses of knowledge. I would like to offer a reconceptualization of foundations for educators that befits the profession of teaching; a profession not in the sociological sense of having or seeking elevated status, but in the human service sense of intelligent and sensitive practitioners talking, thinking, and debating about good practice as they engage in it; a profession that cares about what it does and constantly strives to do it better.

THE ARGUMENTS FOR FOUNDATIONS RECONSIDERED

There are two very popular recent scholarly books about education that have surprised their publishers, drawn much scorn as well as support from the academic community, and received a great deal of attention from the media and the public. They are so strident in their recommendations for education that nearly everyone has strong feelings pro and con about them. I cite them today not to join the controversy, but because they seem to speak to fundamental issues regarding education that the American public is concerned about. They are Bloom's *Closing of the American Mind: How Higher Education Has Failed American Democracy and Corrupted the Souls of Today's Students* and Hirsch's *Cultural Literacy: What Every American Needs to Know.*[1]

Forget for the moment your personal reactions to these controversial works. Consider instead what each tries to do. Think with me for a moment about the central arguments in Bloom and Hirsch that the public finds so appealing. Let us see if we can use the themes of these arguments to sketch a parallel direction for a more philosophical and cultural argument for the role foundations of education in teacher education can take.

Bloom claims that our conception of the educated person has become too relativistic, too narrow, and too technical. We need, he says, to reinstitute the idea that the educated person is one who has been asked in his or her college education to seriously consider the fundamental questions of life. He takes these to be: What is the nature of man (sic)? What is truth? What is beauty? He sees the college experience as the only time when these fundamental questions of human existence can be raised in a supportive environment and their gnawing persistence injected into the consciousness of the students being educated so that, forevermore, they will wrestle with being human no matter what else they do with their lives.

With a little extrapolation, I think we can argue (and many have) that there also are persistent and perennial educational questions that are equally fundamental to the education of educators and that well-educated educators need to meet and wrestle with them and incorporate them into their consciousness throughout their whole careers if they are to be truly educated professionals. Some of these questions are: What are the aims of education? How do human beings learn? What is the relation of school to society? What knowledge is of most worth? For those charged with the education of our young, these are no less fundamental questions than are questions about the meaning of life, truth, and beauty.

We have here an old, yet seemingly timeless philosophical argument for raising the fundamental questions of education in the minds of all teachers. In today's climate of reform, the serious raising of these questions takes on a new urgency. If reform is to be more bottom-up than in the past, teachers themselves must raise and answer these fundamental questions in their own situations. It is time for us to reaffirm this kind of philosophical argument for the importance of foundational studies, which urges question-asking rather than misleadingly promising technical knowledge essential for practice. We need to raise the consciousness of each new generation of teachers to what is eternally problematic in their profession and in need of their persistent critical and creative attention.

When we turn to Hirsch, we find the cultural strand for our reconsidered argument. Hirsch bemoans the fact that in our society we lack cultural literacy. By cultural literacy he means a set of concepts, ideas, and common knowledge that gives us as members of a common culture the requisite background to engage in public dialogue, to understand each other, and to engage in meaningful debate. Just as people who know no quantum physics or microeconomic theory cannot engage in dialogue about such subjects, he argues, so too those of us whose educations did not produce a common core of our culture's shared concepts cannot fully understand each other or communicate effectively as members of our society.

I do not think the answer to this problem lies in Hirsch's lists-of-words approach or in his dictionary, but that is beside the point. He is correct about the need for a community to share a set of common concepts and knowledge as a background against which they can speak to each other meaningfully and without which not only is understanding of the everyday written and spoken word very difficult, but meaningful and responsible debate is impossible. The same is true in education.

Professionals in any field need to communicate effectively if responsible debate and problem solving are to be achieved. As a community of professionals, educators, too, need to achieve a high level of intragroup literacy. They need to acquire the language and concepts of education, the background history, basic theoretical frameworks, central ideas, and common knowledge and traditions that give them the associative conceptual background that permits serious communication, dialogue, and debate as professionals. Much of this will come from various education courses, of course, but without foundations, the broad historical, social, psychological, and philosophical dimensions of professional literacy will be haphazardly treated if at all and our teachers will be merely literate technicians rather than broadly educated and morally sensitive literate professionals.

A SPECIFICATION OF EDUCATIONAL FOUNDATIONS

Superficially, it would seem that we already have the wherewithal for providing professional cultural literacy in our current foundations courses and requirements. Yet we all know that across and even within institutions, very few if any basic foundations courses contain the same common elements and students often are allowed to choose among a variety of courses. To say that students can take any courses they wish to meet the foundations requirements and to openly admit that we all do very different things in teaching foundations is to reveal an appalling truth about our lack of agreement about what we believe we should be doing in common, and what we believe is culturally and normatively essential to teacher education. Our contentless agreement that foundations should provide interpretive, normative, and critical perspectives[2] notwithstanding, I do not think that we have been

specific enough about the core of common content essential to the education of the literate professional. Nevertheless, I also believe that a highly specific list of such things would be as bad a solution to this problem as is our current, overly broad description of foundations requirements and purposes.

What I think is needed is a middle-range specification of what should be core and common. It should specify the key fundamental questions in education and include a set of theoretical frameworks, major concepts, alternative models, competing arguments, and historical precedents sufficient to provide an appropriate cultural and professional literacy. Such a literacy could serve all educators throughout their careers as background with which they can communicate and understand each other as they puzzle over the major perennial, persistent, and profound educational questions that arise in each new generation in different guises and in unanticipated forms.

Let me illustrate the kind of specificity I have in mind by way of a concrete example. A few years ago I designed and coauthored a set of five textbooks called the Thinking about Education series.[3] Utilizing a case-studies approach, the series offers a version of this mid-range specification of core concepts, of shared background knowledge, and the questions fundamental to education. I cite it here only as an illustration of what I am arguing for. It is one version, only a first effort, but it points in the direction I believe we need to go if we are to provide a common core of foundational cultural literacy for educators. The fundamental questions that are raised and the current conceptual frameworks for dealing with them that I and my coauthors have explored in our five short textbooks are sketched below.

I will start with *Approaches to Teaching* because I think that the question of how to approach teaching is one of the most fundamental questions a teacher can ask. It is akin to asking how to lead one's life. In order to provide the professional background literacy needed to be able to think about and discuss this question, Gary Fenstermacher and I offered three possibilities drawn from the current forms that teaching practice actually takes. We called them the executive approach, the therapist approach, and the liberationist approach. The executive teacher is one who is committed to using the best knowledge available from educational research to effectively manage the classroom and achieve the goal of maximizing learning. A teacher using the therapist approach views each student as unique and in need of nurturing to achieve innate potential. Self-concept and personal growth are the goals so that an autonomous, capable person emerges at the end of the process. The liberationist teacher works toward the goal of freeing the mind. In the liberal arts tradition, this teacher models the moral and intellectual virtues while initiating students into the disciplinary forms of knowledge of liberal learning. These conceptions give teachers a way to think and talk about approaches to teaching that stress very different yet legitimate goals and values, a way to think about what kind of teacher one should be and how to lead their lives as teachers.

Related to the question of what approach to teaching one should take is a second question: How do human beings learn? The shared literacy needed to begin to struggle with this question is rooted in the different theories of learning that have been produced from Plato and Locke to the present array of competing theories including behaviorism, Gestalt, discovery learning, information processing, and artificial intelligence. Denis Phillips and I argued that each of these theories lacks universal adequacy. We illustrated this using clear cases in which at least one theoretical explanation failed. We showed how different theories explained the same phenomenon. We also tried to show that each of them, even the classical ones, offers helpful insights into the multiple and complex situations that define a teacher's struggle to help people learn. In this way teachers see that learning theories provide perspectives on teaching—and ways to think about how to nurture it in different settings—rather than providing single-minded directives for practice.

The third question our series proposes is: What should be the aims of education? Two corollary questions are: What constitutes being an educated person? What should the curriculum be? The history of human thought includes a great tradition of answers to these questions from Plato, Rousseau, and Dewey to the progressive and traditionalist debates early in this century to the current discussions of educational reform. Decker Walker and I sketched these and also dealt with the dominant Tylerian form of curriculum rationalization, different ways to conceive of subject matter, and the politics of determining aims in a pluralistic society. We argued that after thinking and weighing different views on teaching and learning, curriculum questions become personally more meaningful to teachers and are not just exercises in grand theory. Constructing curriculum can then become a personally engaging activity, sometimes in debate with others, and not just something done *by* others and given *to* the teacher to execute with skill but without much deliberative thought.

The fourth question we propose is: In what ways does the school as a social institution serve our ideals of nurturing and developing educated persons and in what ways does our social structure constrain us? Walter Feinberg and I saw the needed literacy to deal with this question along three dimensions. We saw the dominant form of interpretation of the role of school and society to be the functionalist view represented by positivist researchers and we contrasted that with the conflict theorist's and neo-Marxist's critical views of social reproduction. The third perspective was an interpretativist view of the newer ethnographic and qualitative researcher bent on studying how people negotiate their socially constructed world. We argued that these three broad conceptualizations provide the perspective needed for professionals—including teachers—to begin to analyze schooling and make sense of the school as a social institution.

Finally, the fifth question: What moral obligations do teachers share with their colleagues as educators, and its corollary, how can one be an ethical professional? Ken Strike and I tried to lay out the options along consequentialist and nonconsequentialist views of ethics using realistic case studies in which the ethical issues of education arise on a day-to-day basis. Our emphasis, recognizing the pervasiveness of relativism today, was on the principles of benefit maximization and respect for persons and on a rational, objective approach to ethical thinking for educators. We argued that education is a moral enterprise and that foundations has the obligation to help professionals see *their* obligations—in part by learning to share a language and a mind set for identifying and dealing with ethical issues in an objective and rational way.

These may not be the best ways to specify the basic philosophical questions of education and to supply the alternative concepts and theoretical frameworks we currently have available to us to think about and debate our answers to them, but I do believe that this is the kind of middle-range specification we need to have and the format it should take. As for the fundamental aspects of education that the series treats, that is, curriculum and aims, teaching, learning, the school as a social institution, and the ethical obligations of educators, I can think of no others that we need to add that are equally or more essential to understanding the nature of education as a human enterprise. These, in my judgment, constitute the basic core of foundational topic areas.

Even if you were to grant that I have the philosophical questions and cultural literacy topics and arguments right, the reconceptualization of foundations that I promised you when I started has only just begun. We need to explore and understand more fully the normative nature of a community of practitioners and make more explicit the range of uses to which fundamental professional knowledge can be put. I have talked so far only about what might be the core *content* of foundations. It is time to reconceptualize the role of foundational knowledge as it is used in a professional community.

A COMMUNITY OF PRACTICE

A genuine community of practice is not just an aggregate group of practitioners. It is a community with a past, a present, and a future. It exists by virtue of the older practitioners' transmitting the skills and guiding traditions of the practice to the initiates and instilling in them a commitment to the overarching purpose of the practice and a normative desire to practice well.

Dewey displays these ideas of community, transmission, and solidarity quite nicely in *Democracy and Education* when he talks about the nature of social groups in general. I quote him at length because he gives depth to the idea of foundations that I am trying to develop here. His normative view of social living gives us not only a way to think about a kind of foundation that provides a common base of knowledge to be used in practice, but a foundation of philosophical questions and theoretical frameworks to be infused and diffused in the dialogues of practitioners.

> [A social group] not only continues to exist *by* transmission, *by* communication, but it may fairly be said to exist *in* transmission, *in* communication. There is more than a verbal tie between the words common, community, and communication. Men live in a community **in** virtue of the things which they have **in** common; and communication is the way in which they come to possess things in common. What they must have in common in order to form a community or society are aims, beliefs, aspirations, knowledge—a common understanding—a like-mindedness as the sociologists say. . . . The communication which insures participation **in** a common understanding is one which secures similar emotional and intellectual dispositions—like ways of responding to expectations and requirements. . . . Individuals do not even compose a social group because they all work for a common end. The parts of a machine work with a maximum of cooperativeness for a common result, but they do not form a community. If, however, they were all cognizant of the common end and all interested in it so that they regulated their specific activity in view of it, then they would form a community. But this would involve communication. Each would have to know what the other was about and would have to have some way of keeping the other informed as to his own purposes and progress. Consensus demands communication. . . . Not only is social life identical with communication, but all communication (and hence all genuine social life) is educative.[4]

The facilitation of professional communication and consensus on the deepest level possible is what the study of foundations must be about. Of course, consensus and communication can also be secured by indoctrination into a single, pervasive point of view. That is why foundations must create a genuine quest for answers to perennial questions with the recognition that our answers may not converge and may have to change over time in response to new problems, new insights, and new social contexts. It is why foundations needs to help people see the alternatives available for making sense of curriculum and aims, teaching and learning, schooling and society, and professional ethics.

Competing conceptions open up the minds and conversations of practitioners. Their conversations should be aimed at securing what is of mutual interest and benefit. Without common basic questions (shared interests) and shared understandings of the best available answers (alternative conceptualizations), the educational community would have little to think with or about. They might be good, effective, hard-working parts of the educational machine, but they would not be professionals who were able to be thoughtfully responsible for the well-being of the learners in our society.

A professional community's normative dimension is even more complex than I have suggested thus far. It is normatively both conservative and progressive; it looks to the past as well as to the future. It is conservative in that it is based on a tradition of practice with time-tested standards of excellence built into it. It is conservative because it is based on historically shared values and interests and on favored ways to organize and communicate knowledge. its members share a traditional canon of literature in which high ideals, goals, aspirations, and images of good practice both collective and individual are enshrined.

While a community with a tradition is thus conservative, it can also be progressive. Built into the tradition of educational theory and practice are fundamental questions that motivate a seeking of the good, the right, the better, and the best. By continually seeking better answers to questions about curriculum and aims, teaching and learning, and the school and society, we display our progressive and melioristic tendency. Through our own practice and through our ongoing dialogue and debate in the community of practitioners, we seek the improvement of practice and of education. Foundational knowledge serves this progressive normative cause not in a how-to fashion, but by raising the basic philosophical questions of practice, by supplying the needed basic conceptual and theoretical literacy, by instilling the desire to improve practice, and by sensitizing educators to the ethical and normative dimensions of their practice.

PROFESSIONAL KNOWLEDGE-IN-USE

In this sketch of education as a community of practice, I have suggested that knowledge, especially that of the sort we teach about in foundations, can be variously used. Some, like knowledge of learning theories, for example, may be directly applied in practice. Thus far, however, I have argued for two basic, yet not so direct, uses of foundational knowledge among professionals. The philosophical questions of education are to be used, in this view, to create a hunger for understanding and improving education as a human enterprise. The cultural literacy core is used as the medium for professional dialogue, discussion, and debate, and the location and resolution of common issues and problems. Both of these "uses" provide perspective and interpretive power. Such knowledge is useful in "seeing," in making sense of what is going on and critically seeking its improvement rather than as knowledge of how to do something in particular.

Our dominant technical sense of knowledge-in-use as how-to knowledge is much too narrow a view for a profession to take, however necessary it may be to the transmission of sophisticated skills and well-meaning directives for establishing good practice. Knowledge-in-use is a much richer concept when viewed from a broader context outside of being told what to do and how to do it.

One of the most dynamic and richest conceptions of knowledge-in-use that I know of is also to be found in Dewey.[5] His model of experience leading to growth fits very well with what I am trying to convey here. One component of his model is funded experience, and that means knowledge that is meaningful for the individual because of its connection with past experience. What we know enters into a present situation both because it was meaningful to us in the past and because it is meaningfully useful to us in the present. The possible uses of knowledge in any particular situation, however, are multiple. It might be used to express our interests or our purposes. It might suggest possible actions or desirable ends. It might be used to assess the means at our disposal to act in the situation. It might be used in the form of executive to secure our ends-in-view. It might be used as a standard of judgment applied to the results of our actions. It might generate alternative hypotheses for action. I could go on. If not endless, the uses of knowledge, on Dewey's view, are many and expansive. Still, this is only the start for understanding his view of knowledge-in-use.

The activity that one is engaged in when using knowledge should also be an occasion for the reconstruction, reorganization, and transformation of one's fund of knowledge. We build on what we know. In the process of using our knowledge we often find that it needs modification or is added to by present experience. Such transformation and reorganization of our knowledge gives us added power to project into and anticipate the future forms that experience might take. There is a dynamic, creative, transactive, and continuous quality to the growth of personal knowledge and our ability to act effectively in the world in the pursuit of our purposes. This kind of knowledge-in-use is cumulative not in some simple additive way, but organically and transformationally.

Moreover, this Deweyan view of educative experience and education as growth is applicable not only to the individual psyche, but also to a social group as a whole. Foundational knowledge not only provides the individual with empowering perspectives, but also makes possible a community of practitioners who share a fundamental set of interests in improving teaching, learning, schooling, curriculum, aims, and the ethics of their craft. By using their collective experience in making sense of education and developing new meanings and new ways to address future education problems and situations, as a professional community they also grow and progress. This broader view of foundational knowledge-in-use coupled with the concept of a core of literacy provides the glue that holds the community of educators together and moves them forward. The foundations metaphor works if only we reconceptualize it this way. In fact, I would argue that the conception of foundations that I have sketched here is what education in general is and should be about. It provides a model for the effective teaching and learning of any subject. We should teach our teachers as we would have them teach.

NOTES

1. Allan B. Bloom, *Closing of the American Mind: How Higher Education Has Failed American Democracy and Corrupted the Souls of Today's Students* (New York: Simon & Schuster, 1987); and E. D. Hirsch, *Cultural Literacy: What Every American Needs to Know* (Boston: Houghton Mifflin, 1987).

2. Council of Learned Sciences in Education, *Standards for Academic and Professional Instruction in Foundations of Education, Educational Studies, and Educational Policy Studies* (Ann Arbor, Mich.: Prakken Publications, 1986).

3. Gary D. Fenstermacher and Jonas F. Soltis, *Approaches to Teaching* (New York: Teachers College Press, 1986); D. C. Phillips and Jonas F. Soltis, *Perspectives on Learning* (New York: Teachers College Press, 1985); Decker F. Walker and Jonas F. Soltis, *Curriculum and Aims* (New York: Teachers College Press, 1986); Walter Feinberg and Jonas F. Soltis, *School and Society* (New York: Teachers College Press, 1985); and Kenneth A. Strike and Jonas F. Soltis, *The Ethics of Teaching* (New York: Teachers College Press, 1985).

4. John Dewey, *Democracy and Education* (New York: Macmillan, 1961), pp. 4–5. Emphasis in original.

5. Ibid.

Inside the Classroom: Social Vision and Critical Pedagogy

William Bigelow

Jefferson High School, Portland, Oregon

Bigelow, a secondary school teacher in Portland, Oregon, believes that public schooling in the United States serves social and economic class interests very unequally, and that one justifiable response for the educator is to help equip students to understand and critique the society in which they live. This article portrays students and teachers engaging in the kind of structured dialogue that Bigelow says is essential to the critical pedagogy he employs.

There is a quotation from Paulo Freire that I like; he writes that teachers should attempt to "live part of their dreams within their educational space."[1] The implication is that teaching should be partisan. I agree. As a teacher I want to be an agent of transformation, with my classroom as a center of equality and democracy—an ongoing, if small, critique of the repressive social relations of the larger society. That does not mean holding a plebiscite on every homework assignment, or pretending I do not have any expertise, but I hope my classroom can become part of a protracted argument for the viability of a critical and participatory democracy.

I think this vision of teaching flies in the face of what has been and continues to be the primary function of public schooling in the United States: to reproduce a class society, where the benefits and sufferings are shared incredibly unequally. As much as possible I refuse to play my part in that process. This is easier said than done. How *can* classroom teachers move decisively away from a model of teaching that merely reproduces and legitimizes inequality? I think Freire is on the right track when he calls for a "dialogical education."[2] To me, this is not just a plea for more classroom conversation. In my construction, a dialogical classroom means inviting students to critique the larger society through sharing their lives. As a teacher I help students locate their experiences socially; I involve students in probing the social factors that make and limit who they are and I try to help them reflect on who they *could* be.

STUDENTS' LIVES AS CLASSROOM TEXT

In my Literature in U.S. History course, which I co-teach in Portland, Oregon, with Linda Christensen, we use historical concepts as points of departure to explore themes in students' lives and then, in turn, use students' lives to explore history and our society today. Earlier this year, for instance, we studied the Cherokee Indian Removal through role play. Students portrayed the Indians, plantation owners, bankers, and the Andrew Jackson administration and saw the forces that combined to push the Cherokees west of the Mississippi against their will. Following a discussion of how and why this happened, Linda and I asked students to write about a time when they had their rights violated. We asked students to write from inside these experiences and to recapture how they felt and what, if anything, they did about the injustice.

Seated in a circle, students shared their stories with one another in a "read-around" format. (To fracture the student/teacher dichotomy a bit, Linda and I also complete each assignment and take our turns reading.) Before we began, we suggested they listen for what we call the "collective text"—the group portrait that emerges from the read-around.[3] Specifically, we asked them to take notes on the kinds of rights people felt they possessed; what action they took after having their rights violated; and whatever other generalizations they could draw from the collective text. Here are a few examples: Rachel wrote on wetting her pants because a teacher would not let her go to the bathroom; Christie, on a lecherous teacher at a middle school; Rebecca, on a teacher who enclosed her in a solitary confinement cell; Gina, who is black, on a theater worker not believing that her mother, who is white, actually was her mother; Maryanne, on being sexually harassed while walking to school and her subsequent mistreatment by the school administration when she reported the incident; Clayton, on the dean's treatment when Clayton wore an anarchy symbol on

From *Teachers College Record*, Vol. 91, No. 3, Spring 1990, pp. 437-448. Reprinted by permission of the publisher from William Bigelow, "Inside the Classroom: Social Visions & Critical Pedagogy" in Tozer, Steven, Anderson, Thomas H. and Armbruster, Bonnie B., eds. FOUNDATIONAL STUDIES IN TEACHER EDUCATION: A RE-EXAMINATION, pp. 139-150. (New York: Teachers College Press, © 1990 by Teachers College, Columbia University. All rights reserved.)

his jacket; Bobby, on convenience store clerks who watched him more closely because he is black. Those are fewer than a quarter of the stories we heard.

To help students study this social text more carefully, we asked them to review their notes from the read-around and write about their discoveries. We then spent a class period interpreting our experiences. Almost half the instances of rights violations took place in school. Christie said, "I thought about the school thing. The real point [of school] is to learn one concept: to be trained and obedient. That's what high school is. A diploma says this person came every day, sat in their seat. It's like going to dog school." A number of people, myself included, expressed surprise that so many of the stories involved sexual harassment. To most of the students with experiences of harassment, it had always seemed a very private oppression, but hearing how common this kind of abuse is allowed the young women to feel a new connection among themselves—and they said so. A number of white students were surprised at the varieties of subtle racism black students experienced.

We talked about the character of students' resistance to rights violations. From the collective text we saw that most people did not resist at all. What little resistance occurred was individual; there was not a single instance of collective resistance. Christie complained to a counselor, Rebecca told her mother, many complained to friends. This provoked a discussion about what in their lives and, in particular, in the school system encouraged looking for individual solutions to problems that are shared collectively. They identified competition for grades and for positions in sought-after classes as factors. They also criticized the fake democracy of student government for discouraging activism. No one shared a single experience of schools' encouraging groups of students to confront injustice. Moreover, students also listed ways—from advertising messages to television sitcoms—through which people are conditioned by the larger society to think in terms of individual problems requiring individual solutions.

The stories students wrote were moving, sometimes poetic, and later opportunities to rewrite allowed us to help sharpen their writing skills, but we wanted to do more than just encourage students to stage a literary show-and-tell. Our larger objective was to find social meaning in individual experience—to push students to use their stories as windows not only on their lives, but on society.

There were other objectives. We hoped that through building a collective text, our students—particularly working-class and minority students—would discover that their lives are important sources of learning, no less important than the lives of the generals and presidents, the Rockefellers and Carnegies, who inhabit their textbooks. One function of the school curriculum is to celebrate the culture of the dominant and to ignore or scorn the culture of subordinate groups. The personal writing, collective texts, and discussion circles in Linda's and my classes are an attempt to challenge students not to accept these judgments. We wanted students to grasp that they can *create* knowledge, not simply absorb it from higher authorities.[4]

All of this sounds a little neater than what actually occurs in a classroom. Some students rebel at taking their own lives seriously. A student in one of my classes said to me recently, "Why do we have to do all this personal stuff? Can't you just give us a book or a worksheet and leave us alone?" Another student says regularly, "This isn't an English class, ya know." Part of this resistance may come from not wanting to resurface or expose painful experiences; part may come from not feeling capable as writers; but I think the biggest factor is that they simply do not feel that their lives have anything *important* to teach them. Their lives are just their lives. Abraham Lincoln and Hitler are important. Students have internalized self-contempt from years of official neglect and denigration of their culture. When for example, African-American or working-class history *is* taught it is generally as hero worship: extolling the accomplishments of a Martin Luther King, Jr., or a John L. Lewis, while ignoring the social movements that made their work possible. The message given is that great people make change, individual high school students do not. So it is not surprising that some students wonder what in the world they have to learn from each other's stories.

Apart from drawing on students' own lives as sources of knowledge and insight, an alternative curriculum also needs to focus on the struggle of oppressed groups for social justice. In my history classes, for example, we study Shays's Rebellion, the abolition movement, and alliances between blacks and poor whites during Reconstruction. In one lesson, students role-play Industrial Workers of the World organizers in the 1912 Lawrence, Massachusetts, textile strike as they try to overcome divisions between men and women and between workers speaking over a dozen different languages.

STUDYING THE HIDDEN CURRICULUM

In my experience as a teacher, whether students write about inequality, resistance, or collective work, school is *the* most prominent setting. Therefore, in our effort to have the curriculum respond to students' real concerns, we enlist them as social researchers, investigating their own school lives. My co-teacher and I began one unit by reading an excerpt from the novel *Radcliffe*, by David Storey.[5] In the selection, a young boy, Leonard Radcliffe, arrives at a predominately working-class British school. The teacher prods Leonard, who is from an aristocratic background, to become her reluctant know-it-all—the better to reveal to others their own ignorance. The explicit curriculum appears to concern urban geography: "Why are roofs pointed and not flat like in the Bible?" the teacher asks. She humiliates a working-class youth, Victor, by demanding that he stand and listen to her harangue: "Well, come on then, Victor. Let us all hear." As he stands mute and helpless, she chides: "Perhaps there's no reason for Victor to think at all. We already know where he's going to end up, don't we?" She points to the factory chimneys outside. "There are places waiting for him out there already." No one says a word. She finally calls on little Leonard to give the correct answer, which he does.

Students in our class readily see that these British schoolchildren are learning much more than why roofs are pointed. They are being drilled to accept their lot at the bottom of a hierarchy with a boss on top. The teacher's successful effort to humiliate Victor, while the others sit watching, undercuts any sense the students might have of their power to act in solidarity with one another. A peer is left hanging in the wind and they do nothing about it. The teacher's tacit alliance with Leonard and her abuse of Victor legitimate class inequalities outside the classroom.[6]

We use this excerpt and the follow-up discussion as a preparatory exercise for students to research the curriculum—both explicit and "hidden"[7]—at their own school (Jefferson High School). The student body is mostly African-American and predominately working class. Linda and I assign students to observe their classes as if they were attending for the first time. We ask them to notice the design of the classroom, the teaching methodology, the class content, and the grading procedures. In their logs, we ask them to reflect on the character of thinking demanded and the classroom relationships: Does the teacher promote questioning and critique or obedience and conformity? What kind of knowledge and understandings are valued in the class? What relationships between students are encouraged?

In her log, Elan focused on sexism in the hidden curriculum:

> In both biology and government, I noticed that not only do boys get more complete explanations to questions, they get asked more questions by the teacher than girls do. In government, even though our teacher is a feminist, boys are asked to define a word or to list the different parts of the legislative branch more often than the girls are. . . . I sat in on an advanced sophomore English class that was doing research in the library. The teacher, a male, was teaching the boys how to find research on their topic, while he was finding the research himself for the girls. Now, I know chivalry isn't dead, but we are competent of finding a book.

Linda and I were pleased as we watched students begin to gain a critical distance from their own schooling experiences. Unfortunately, Elan did not speculate much on the social outcomes of the unequal treatment she encountered, or on what it is in society that produces this kind of teaching. She did offer the observation that "boys are given much more freedom in the classroom than girls, and therefore the boys are used to getting power before the girls."

Here is an excerpt from Connie's log:

> It always amazed me how teachers automatically assume that where you sit will determine your grade. It's funny how you can get an A in a class you don't even understand. As long as you follow the rules and play the game, you seem to get by. . . . On this particular day we happen to be taking a test on chapters 16 and 17. I've always liked classes such as algebra that you didn't have to think. You're given the facts, shown how to do it, and you do it. No questions, no theories, it's the solid, correct way to do it.

We asked students to reflect on who in our society they thought benefited from the methods of education to which they were subjected. Connie wrote:

> I think that not only is it the teacher, but more importantly, it's the system. They purposely teach you using the "boring method." Just accept what they tell you, learn it and go on, no questions asked. It seems to me that the rich, powerful people benefit from it, because we don't want to think, we're kept ignorant, keeping them rich.

Connie's hunch that her classes benefit the rich and powerful is obviously incomplete, but it does put her on the road to understanding that the degrading character of her education is not simply accidental. She is positioned to explore the myriad ways schooling is shaped by the imperatives of a capitalist economy. Instead of being just more of the "boring method," as Connie puts it, this social and historical study would be a personal search for her, rooted in her desire to understand the nature of her *own* experience.

In class, students struggled through a several-page excerpt from *Schooling in Capitalist America* by Samuel Bowles and Herbert Gintis. They read the Bowles and Gintis assertion that

> major aspects of educational organization replicate the relationships of dominance and subordinancy in the economic sphere. The correspondence between the social relation of schooling and work accounts for the ability of the educational system to produce an amenable and fragmented labor force. The experience of schooling, and not merely the content of formal learning, is central to this process.[8]

If they are right, we should expect to find different hidden curricula at schools enrolling students of different social classes. We wanted our students to test this notion for themselves.[9] A friend who teaches at a suburban high school south of Portland, serving a relatively wealthy community, enlisted volunteers in her classes to host our students for a day. My students logged comparisons of Jefferson and the elite school, which I will call Ridgewood. Trisa wrote:

Now, we're both supposed to be publicly funded, equally funded, but not so. At Jefferson, the average class size is 20–25 students, at Ridgewood—15. Jefferson's cafeteria food is half-cooked, stale and processed. Ridgewood—fresh food, wide variety, and no mile-long lines to wait in. Students are allowed to eat anywhere in the building as well as outside, and wear hats and listen to walkmen [both rule violations at Jefferson].

About teachers' attitudes at Ridgewood, Trisa noted: "Someone said, 'We don't ask if you're going to college, but what college are you going to.' "

In general, I was disappointed that students' observations tended to be more on atmosphere than on classroom dynamics. Still, what they noticed seemed to confirm the fact that their own school, serving a black and working-class community, was a much more rule-governed, closely supervised environment. The experience added evidence to the Bowles and Gintis contention that my students were being trained to occupy lower positions in an occupational hierarchy.

Students were excited by this sociological detective work, but intuitively they were uneasy with the determinism of Bowles and Gintis's correspondence theory. It was not enough to discover that the relations of schooling mirrored the relations of work. They demanded to know exactly who designed a curriculum that taught them subservience. Was there a committee somewhere, sitting around plotting to keep them poor and passive? "We're always saying 'they' want us to do this, and 'they' want us to do that," one student said angrily. "Who is this 'they'?" Students wanted villains with faces and we were urging that they find systemic explanations.

Omar's anger exploded after one discussion. He picked up his desk and threw it against the wall, yelling: "How much more of this shit do I have to put up with?" "This shit" was his entire educational experience, and while the outburst was not directed at our class in particular—thank heavens—we understood our culpability in his frustration.

We had made two important and related errors in our teaching. Implicitly, our search had encouraged students to see themselves as victims—powerless little cogs in a machine daily reproducing the inequities of the larger society. Though the correspondence theory was an analytical framework with a greater power to interpret their school lives than any other they had encountered, ultimately it was a model suggesting endless oppression and hopelessness. If schooling is always responsive to the needs of capitalism, then what point did our search have? Our observations seemed merely to underscore students' powerlessness.

I think the major problem was that although our class did discuss resistance by students, it was anecdotal and unsystematic, thereby depriving students of the opportunity to question their own roles in main-

taining the status quo. The effect of this omission, entirely unintentional on our part, was to deny students the chance to see schools as sites of struggle and social change—places where they could have a role in determining the character of their own education. Unwittingly, the realizations students were drawing from our study of schools fueled a world view rooted in cynicism; they might learn about the nature and causes for their subordination, but they could have no role in resisting it.

THE "ORGANIC GOODIE SIMULATION"

Still stinging from my own pedagogical carelessness, I have made efforts this year to draw students into a dialogue about the dynamics of power and resistance. One of the most effective means to carry on this dialogue is metaphorically, through role play and simulation.[10]

In one exercise, called the "Organic Goodie Simulation," I create a three-tiered society. Half the students are workers, half are unemployed,[11] and I am the third tier—the owner of a machine that produces organic goodies. I tell students that we will be in this classroom for the rest of our lives and that the machine produces the only sustenance. Workers can buy adequate goodies with their wages, but the unemployed will slowly starve to death on their meager dole of welfare-goodies. Everything proceeds smoothly until I begin to drive wages down by offering jobs to the unemployed at slightly less than what the workers earn. It is an auction, with jobs going to the lowest bidder. Eventually, all classes organize some kind of opposition, and usually try to take away my machine. One year, a group of students arrested me, took me to a jail in the corner of the room, put a squirt gun to my head, and threatened to "kill" me if I said another word. This year, before students took over the machine, I backed off, called a meeting to which only my workers were invited, raised their wages, and stressed to them how important it was that we stick together to resist the jealous unemployed people who wanted to drag all of us into the welfare hole they are in. Some workers defected to the unemployed, some vigorously defended my right to manage the machine, but most bought my plea that we had to talk it all out and reach unanimous agreement before any changes could be made. For an hour and a half they argued among themselves, egged on by me, without taking any effective action.

The simulation provided a common metaphor from which students could examine firsthand what we had not adequately addressed the previous year: To what extent are we complicit in our own oppression? Before we began our follow-up discussion, I asked students to write on who or what was to blame for the conflict and disruption of the previous day. In the discussion some students singled me out as the culprit. Stefani said, "I thought Bill was evil. I didn't know what he wanted." Rebecca concurred: "I don't agree with people who say Bill was not the root of the problem. Bill was management, and he made workers feel insecure that the unemployed were trying to take their jobs." Others agreed with Rebecca that it was a divisive structure that had been created, but saw how their own responses to that structure perpetuated the divisions and poverty. Christie said: "We were so divided that nothing got decided. It kept going back and forth. Our discouragement was the root of the problem." A number of people saw how their own attitudes kept them from acting decisively. Mira said: "I think that there was this large fear: We have to follow the law. And Sonia kept saying we weren't supposed to take over the machine. But if the law and property hurt people why should we go along with it?" Gina said: "I think Bill looked like the problem, but underneath it all was us. Look at when Bill hired unemployed and fired some workers. I was doin' it too. We can say it's a role play, but you have to look at how everything ended up feeling and learn something about ourselves, about how we handled it."

From our discussion students could see that their make-believe misery was indeed caused by the structure of the society: The number of jobs was held at an artificially low level, and workers and unemployed were pitted against each other for scarce goodies. As the owner I tried every trick I knew to drive wedges between workers and the unemployed, to encourage loyalty in my workers, and to promote uncertainty and bickering among the unemployed. However, by analyzing the experience, students could see that the system worked only because they let it work—they were much more than victims of my greed; they were my accomplices.

I should hasten to add—and emphasize—that it is not inherently empowering to understand one's own complicity in oppression. I think it is a start, because this understanding suggests that we can do something about it. A critical pedagogy, however, needs to do much more: It should highlight times, past and present, when people built alliances to challenge injustice. Students also need to encounter individuals and organizations active in working for a more egalitarian society, and students need to be encouraged to see themselves as capable of joining together with others, in and out of school, to make needed changes. I think that all of these are mandatory components of the curriculum. The danger of students' becoming terribly cynical as they come to understand the enormity of injustice in this society and in the world is just too great. They have to know that it is possible—even joyous, if I dare say so—to work toward a more humane society.

TEACHERS AND TEACHER EDUCATORS AS POLITICAL AGENTS

At the outset I said that all teaching should be partisan. In fact, I think that all teaching *is* partisan. Whether or not we want to be, all teachers are political agents because we help shape students' understandings of the larger society. That is why it is so important for teachers to be clear about our social visions. Toward what kind of society are we aiming? Unless teachers answer this question with clarity we are reduced to performing as technicians, unwittingly participating in a political project but with no comprehension of its objectives or consequences. Hence teachers who claim "no politics" are inherently authoritarian because their pedagogical choices act on students, but students are denied a structured opportunity to critique or act on their teachers' choices. Nor are students equipped to reflect on the effectiveness of whatever resistance they may put up.

For a number of reasons, I do not think that our classrooms can ever be exact models of the kind of participatory democracy we would like to have characterize the larger society. If teachers' only power were to grade students, that would be sufficient to sabotage classroom democracy. However, as I have suggested, classrooms can offer students experiences and understandings that counter, and critique, the lack of democracy in the rest of their lives. In the character of student interactions the classroom can offer a glimpse of certain features of an egalitarian society. We can begin to encourage students to learn the analytic and strategic skills to help bring this new society into existence. As I indicated, by creating a collective text of student experience we can offer students practice in understanding personal problems in their social contexts. Instead of resorting to consumption, despair, or other forms of self-abuse, they can ask why these circumstances exist and what can they do about it. In this limited arena, students can begin to become the subjects of their lives.

When Steve Tozer of the University of Illinois asked me to prepare this article, he said I should discuss the implications of my classroom practice for people in social foundations of education programs. First, I would urge you who are teacher educators to model the participatory and exploratory pedagogy that you hope your students will employ as classroom teachers. Teachers-to-be should interrogate their own educational experiences as a basis for understanding the relationship between school and society. They need to be members of a dialogical community in which they can experience themselves as subjects and can learn the validity of critical pedagogy by doing it. If the primary aim of social foundations of education coursework is to equip teachers-to-be to understand and critically evaluate the origins of school content and processes in social context, then the foundations classroom should be a place for students to discuss how their own experiences as students are grounded in the larger society, with its assumptions, its inequities, its limits and possibilities.

As you know, a teacher's first job in a public school can be frightening. That fear mixed with the conservative pressures of the institution can overwhelm the liberatory inclinations of a new teacher. Having *experienced*, and not merely having read about, an alternative pedagogy can help new teachers preserve their democratic ideals. Part of this, I think, means inviting your students to join you in critiquing *your* pedagogy. You need to be a model of rigorous self-evaluation.

The kind of teaching I have been describing is demanding. The beginning teacher may be tempted to respond, "Sure, sure, I'll try all that when I've been in the classroom five or six years and when I've got a file cabinet full of lessons." I think you should encourage new teachers to overcome their isolation by linking up with colleagues to reflect on teaching problems and to share pedagogical aims and successes. I participated in a support group like this my first year as a teacher and our meetings helped maintain my courage and morale. After a long hiatus, two years ago I joined another group that meets bi-weekly to talk about everything from educational theory to confrontations with administrators to union organizing.[12] In groups such as this your students can come to see themselves as creators and evaluators of curriculum and not simply as executors of corporate- or administrative-packaged lesson plans.

It is also in groups like this that teachers can come to see themselves as activists in a broader struggle for social justice. The fact is that education will not be *the* engine of social change. No matter how successful we are as critical teachers in the classroom, our students' ability to use and extend the analytic skills they have acquired depends on the character of the society that confronts them. Until the economic system requires workers who are critical, cooperative, and deeply democratic, teachers' classroom efforts amount to a kind of low-intensity pedagogical war. Unfortunately, it is easy to cut ourselves off from outside movements for social change—and this is especially true for new teachers. As critical teachers, however, we depend on these movements to provide our students with living proof that fundamental change is both possible and desirable. It seems to me you cannot emphasize too strongly how teachers' attempts to teach humane and democratic values in the classroom should not be isolated from the social context in which schooling occurs.

In closing, let me return to Freire's encouragement that we live part of our dreams within our educational space. Teachers-to-be should not be ashamed or frightened of taking sides in favor of democracy and social justice. I hope *your* students learn to speak to *their* students in the language of possibility and hope and not of conformity and "realism." In sum, your students ought to learn that teaching is, in the best sense of the term, a subversive activity—and to be proud of it.

NOTES

1. Paulo Freire and Donaldo Macedo, *Literacy: Reading the Word and the World* (South Hadley, Mass.: Bergin and Garvey, 1987), p. 127.

2. See especially Ira Shor and Paulo Freire, *A Pedagogy for Liberation* (South Hadley, Mass.: Bergin and Garvey, 1983.)

3. See Linda Christensen, "Writing the Word and the World," *English Journal* 78, no. 2 (February 1989): 14–18.

4. See William Bigelow and Norman Diamond, *The Power in Our Hands: A Curriculum on the History of Work and Workers in the United States* (New York: Monthly Review Press, 1988), pp. 15–23.

5. David Storey, *Radcliffe* (New York: Avon, 1963), pp. 9–12. I am grateful to Doug Sherman for alerting me to this excerpt.

6. While most students are critical of the teacher, they should always be allowed an independent judgment. Recently, a boy in one of my classes who is severely hard of hearing defended the teacher's actions. He argued that because the students laughed at Leonard when he first entered the class they deserved whatever humiliation the teacher could dish out. He said the offending students ought to be taught not to make fun of people who are different.

7. See Henry Giroux, *Theory and Resistance in Education: A Pedagogy for the Opposition* (South Hadley, Mass.: Bergin and Garvey, 1983). See especially Chapter 2, "Schooling and the Politics of the Hidden Curriculum," pp. 42–71. Giroux defines the hidden curriculum as "those unstated norms, values, and beliefs embedded in and transmitted to students through the underlying rules that structure the routines and social relationships and classroom life" and points out that the objective of critical theory is not merely to describe aspects of the hidden curriculum, but to analyze how it "functions to provide differential forms of schooling to different classes of students" (p. 47).

8. Samuel Bowles and Herbert Gintis, *Schooling in Capitalist America* (New York: Basic Books, 1976), p. 125.

9. See Jean Anyon, "Social Class and the Hidden Curriculum of Work," *Journal of Education* 162 (Winter 1980): 67–92, for a more systematic comparison of hidden curricula in schools serving students of different social classes.

10. There is an implication in many of the theoretical discussions defining critical pedagogy that the proper role of the teacher is to initiate group reflection on students' outside-of-class experiences. Critics consistently neglect to suggest that the teacher can also be an initiator of powerful in-class experiences, which can then serve as objects of student analysis.

11. Bigelow and Diamond, *The Power in Our Hands*, pp. 27–30 and pp. 92–94. See also Mike Messner, "Bubblegum and Surplus Value," *The Insurgent Sociologist* 6, no. 4 (Summer 1976): 51–56.

12. My study group gave valuable feedback on this article. Thanks to Linda Christensen, Jeff Edmundson, Tom McKenna, Karen Miller, Michele Miller, Doug Sherman, and Kent Spring.

Navigating the Four C's: Building a Bridge over Troubled Waters

Until now, the debate about curriculum has not dealt with the interrelationships among the process of change, the culture of schools, the context of classrooms, and the content of the curriculum. In this article, Ms. Lieberman fills that void.

ANN LIEBERMAN

ANN LIEBERMAN is a visiting professor at Teachers College, Columbia University, New York, N.Y., and a professor of policy, governance, and administration and of curriculum and instruction at the University of Washington, Seattle. She is the executive director of the Puget Sound Educational Consortium.

A CRUCIAL ELEMENT has been missing from our debate about curriculum. No one has discussed the *interrelationships* of what I call the four C's: the process of *change*, the *culture* of schools, the *context* of classrooms, and the *content* of the curriculum.

In the past we dealt with these four C's individually. Reform movements typically focused on curriculum change without regard for such complicating factors as the people who were to make the changes or the institutions in which they were to occur. In the Seventies, during the period of "options, alternatives, and electives," large-scale research on the effects of federal initiatives for school reform revealed for the first time the complexity of the implementation process.[1] The focus on implementation was a powerful breakthrough because it shifted the discussion of school reform to the local site and to the means by which content actually made its way into the social system of the school. This was the first time that

Illustration by Susan Hunsberger

content, culture, and change were discussed within the specific contexts of school districts throughout the country.

CONTENT

The conservative critique pays lip service to the complexity of the changing U.S. culture (poverty, homelessness, a deteriorating urban environment, a growing multicultural population) and the stresses it is putting on the society and the schools. However, when considering how the curriculum should respond to this new set of societal problems, conservatives tend to isolate a single factor: content. Certainly we must struggle with

the essential curricular questions: What knowledge is of most worth, and what should the schools teach? But considering content in isolation is not enough. (Maxine Greene has long reminded us that our multiple perspectives will yield multiple meanings even if everyone is given the same core curriculum.)

RESTRUCTURING AND THE CULTURE OF THE SCHOOL

One way to understand how the four C's interact is to look at the movement to restructure the schools, because it is here that we face head-on such factors as differences among students, changing curriculum demands, and the engagement of teachers. It is the intent of the school restructuring movement to change the roles and relationships of principals, parents, teachers, students, and, in some cases, businesses and community agencies. Issues of structure and governance — such as school-site decision making and the granting of greater authority at the local level — are paramount in this effort, but attempts to rethink the curriculum, to humanize and personalize instruction, to integrate subject areas, and to shift the focus from "teaching" to helping students learn are all part of the movement as well.

Teacher development is a vital part of restructuring, and it is a far more complicated process than previously thought. A study of staff development in California reported that, despite a tremendous amount of money being spent, most staff development made little difference in the way teachers actually worked with students. This large-scale study revealed long-standing differences between the kinds of staff development that teachers said they needed and what was planned by others *for* them.[2]

From *Phi Delta Kappan*, March 1990, pp. 531-533. Reprinted by permission of *Phi Delta Kappan* and the author.

TEACHER UNIONS AND THE CULTURE OF THE SCHOOL

Teacher unions have often been involved in bargaining for such professional improvements as greater participation in decision making and the adoption of programs using mentor teachers, lead teachers, and teacher leaders. Nevertheless, many teachers feel that they have been victims of the reform movements rather than participants in them. In the words of a 20-year veteran who taught at a school actively engaged in reform, "We do not fear change, but we feel emotionally ripped off." Thus it is not enough to make decisions *for* teachers, even when this is done with the best of intentions; teachers themselves must be involved in the decision-making process.

When teachers participate authentically in making decisions about school governance, the culture of the school begins to change. Teachers come to feel that they have a significant stake in decisions concerning the curriculum as well. This attitude energizes teachers' participation in the school as a whole and commits them to greater involvement in issues of curriculum and instruction. Union contracts are important, but strategies to change curriculum content and the nature of the teacher/student relationship must come from within the culture itself, often with help from sensitive outsiders.[3] Teachers must be involved as willing partners in changing their own organizational culture. When the unions are part of school restructuring efforts, they too must work to locate greater authority for decision making at the local level.

But changing the culture of a school is hardly a simple process. Indeed, changing anything in schools is difficult. Those involved in the restructuring movement have found it to be time-consuming, labor-intensive, and fraught with conflict. And these difficulties are not just matters of reallocating resources. Restructuring involves trying to change human relationships that have been the same for decades. And every school differs from every other school in so many ways that standardized formulas make no sense.

TEACHER DEVELOPMENT AND THE FOUR C's

Our understanding of teacher development has grown and changed in recent years. Today we are more aware of issues related to the professionalization of teaching — teacher leadership, increased teacher participation, changes in the career structure, shared decision making,

the growth of colleagueship, and so on. As teachers take on the new roles, they participate more actively in the reshaping of schools.

This kind of experience differs significantly from what teachers have known before. As one teacher leader told me, "On the one hand, this has been one of my most exciting years because of my involvement in this kind of thinking and work — but, on the other hand, the changing student population leaves me so depressed." This combination of exhilaration and discouragement has been documented by others as well. Teachers gain newfound strength and excitement from their participation in the restructuring of roles and relationships, but they become exhausted by the struggle with curricular and instructional issues.[4] For example, it is increasingly difficult to deal with such complex issues as equity for all students when the student population is increasingly poor and at risk.

While some curricular efforts have encountered difficulties, others have succeeded in engaging and exciting teachers, sparking their participation in changing curriculum and pedagogy. When we look at these successful efforts to change the nature of student/teacher relationships, we see that they all tend to combine in some way teachers' experiential learning with learning related to the classroom culture. They rely on networking to provide the kind of support and nonjudgmental help that teachers need as they develop new norms and expectations and take the risks involved in changing their own roles in order to improve student engagement and learning.

A number of programs and curricular innovations — e.g., the process approach to teaching writing, whole-language learning, cooperative learning, and the Foxfire experience — have given us the means to break teacher isolation, to build a sense of community, to look differently at the curriculum, to model experiences for teachers, to support them as they are learning, to celebrate their successes and, in some cases, to provide them with opportunities for leadership. Whether consciously or not, these programs have linked content and pedagogy, sensitivity to the classroom context, teachers' experiential learning, and the necessity for organizational supports to initiate and maintain the process of change. In the best of these programs, a unifying philosophy and a strong set of values underlie the activities and guide the teachers' interactions with their students. These programs and practices are based not on gimmicks or strategies but on a way of

thinking about teaching, learning, and professionalism. This way of thinking sees content, context, and culture as integral to teachers' involvement in new ways of using curriculum and pedagogy and to their participation in making the organizational decisions that most affect their students and themselves.

TENSIONS AND TRADEOFFS IN SCHOOL RESTRUCTURING

Changing pedagogy and curriculum and involving teachers in restructuring efforts are very complicated matters. These two strands of teacher development are not always clearly linked, and the process of change brings tensions and tradeoffs that we are just beginning to understand.

The form that restructuring takes depends on many factors, including who initiates the change, how the restructuring efforts are actually played out, the histories of the particular districts and schools, and the values held by the state and local governments. Decisions about the place of administrative leadership and of teacher leadership, about process and content, about whether to start with students or to start with teachers, and about whether to do something first and analyze it later or to reflect before taking action — all these issues create tensions in the process of restructuring schools. Such tensions and tradeoffs do indeed make the waters of school restructuring treacherous, but they also point out how much we need to build bridges across these troubled waters.

We know more about school change than we knew 20 years ago. We know that we have to attach content to people and institutions, and we know that we have to consider the differences in the cultures of schools. But we cannot hope to influence the restructuring movement unless some of us work more closely with the schools. This means climbing down from our proverbial ivory towers and working with schoolpeople. There are thousands of researchable problems and hundreds of ways to engage in productive work in the schools. If we see ourselves working *with* schoolpeople — not *on* them — we can indeed exert an influence. However, if we continue to distance ourselves from the schools by acting only as critics rather than as participants, we will have little influence.

I once brought a student of mine to the annual meeting of the American Educational Research Association. She dutifully took notes at the many sessions she attended. On the last day I asked her, "So, what do you think of the AERA?" She answered, "You know, if all the schools sank into the Pacific Ocean, I don't think anyone here would blink."

David Cohen has reminded us that we researchers have created a language whose primary users seem to be ourselves. We study one thing at a time, oversimplify it for research purposes, and then become wedded to our conception. Not only are we isolated from the rest of the world, but our own house needs more teamwork, more efforts at developing colleagueship, and more opportunities for cooperation. This cooperation, in turn, might lead us to work more closely with the schools — a development that might help our research, our institutions, and the schools as well. Some few institutions are already involved in such efforts.

Murray Schwartz, dean of the College Arts and Sciences at the University of Massachusetts at Amherst, describes the "boundary anxiety" that exists today in the subject areas. We need to take account of that anxiety in our own work as well. There are exciting changes going on. We need to join in and make our voices heard, but that means that we must think of ourselves as learners as well as teachers. As Seymour Sarason and his co-authors have written, "You have to know and experience in the most intimate and tangible ways the situations which your actions purport to affect."[5]

To affect the current debate about curriculum, we will need to examine our behaviors — both as individuals and as institutions — and to find ways to partici-pate. This means, for example, that we will have to struggle with a larger view of scholarship. There are a variety of ways of knowing and a variety of means to express that knowledge. *Educational Leadership* has as much meaning to its readers as *Educational Researcher* has for us. Can't we contribute to both publications? Instead of mourning our lack of influence, we need to join coalitions with schoolpeople. We can engage in collaborative inquiry and in a collective struggle over tough issues of content, which — in context — will help us to probe the limits and possibilities of change in both schools and universities.

Mechanisms such as school/university collaborations, which help establish networks and coalitions of all kinds, should be created — not for cosmetic reasons ("everybody is doing it") but because they offer us a unique opportunity to become involved with the schools in authentic ways. Establishing professional development schools, working to professionalize teaching, or restructuring schools will force us to deal with the construction of knowledge in its organic relationship to context.

We must shift our thinking about the knowledge base of teaching and learning. It in no way denigrates the university to admit that we have much to learn from the people who work in the schools. We are hampered from doing so because we typically adopt a paternalistic attitude toward schoolpeople and because there is a lack of institutional recognition and support for those professors who are active-ly working in the schools. The university must change its view of scholarship so that it recognizes and rewards active participation in schools (and the research and writing that it generates) as valuable — and time-consuming — scholarly activity.

We must struggle with these issues seriously, so that the university can become the important influence in education policies and practices that it should be. We must not allow ourselves to become increasingly irrelevant to the schools when the opportunity exists to become partners with them in the difficult — but incredibly rewarding — task of reshaping education in our country. To that end, let us navigate the four C's together.

1. Milbrey McLaughlin and David Marsh, "Staff Development and School Change," in Ann Lieberman and Lynne Miller, eds., *Staff Development: New Demands, New Realities, New Perspectives* (New York: Teachers College Press, 1978).
2. Judith Warren Little et al., *Staff Development in California: Public and Personal Investments, Program Patterns, and Policy Choices* (San Francisco: Policy Analysis for California Education and Far West Laboratory for Educational Research and Development, 1987).
3. Myrna Cooper, "Whose Culture Is It Anyhow?," in Ann Lieberman, ed., *Building a Professional Culture in Schools* (New York: Teachers College Press, 1988), pp. 45-54.
4. Marilyn Cohn et al., *Teachers' Perspectives on the Problems in Their Profession: Implications for Policymakers and Practitioners* (Washington, D.C.: U.S. Department of Education, Office of Educational Research and Improvement, 1987).
5. Seymour Sarason, Kenneth S. Davidson, and Burton Blatt, *The Preparation of Teachers: An Unstudied Problem in Education*, rev. ed. (Cambridge, Mass: Brookline Books, 1986), p. xix.

'Those' Children Are Ours: Moving Toward Community

If families make the greatest difference in how children do in school, how can schools help students who might otherwise fail? Redefining schools as a community effort is the essential first step.

PATRICIA GÁNDARA

Patricia Gándara, currently a professor of education at California State University at Sacramento, was until recently director of education research for the Assembly Office of the California Legislature and commissioner of postsecondary education for the State of California. Her research interests have included causes of success among minority students, bilingual education, and the year-round school.

America is experiencing an unpublicized crisis in education. It is not the crisis of mediocrity of which we were warned in 1983, nor is it a failure to keep up academically with the Japanese or the Soviets. In reality, our brightest students are still competitive with any other country's brightest students. America's crisis results from our forgetting, in our headlong race for "excellence," that a significant portion of our children are not on the excellence bandwagon—not, in fact, on any bandwagon at all. The education reform movement has ignored them altogether.

Nearly a quarter of America's children are on an educational path leading nowhere. While test scores appear to be on the rise all over the country, a closer look at the figures reveals that the least successful students are actually losing ground: The gap between their skills and performance and those of their peers is growing wider. These are the children of the poor, who coincidentally are also often ethnic minorities.

The failure of the reform movement to make any positive difference for these children has raised some hard questions: Can schools make a difference for poor and minority children—or is their school performance too closely bound to home and neighborhood experiences? How do some poor, minority parents help their children overcome barriers to school success? What role can a community play in securing these students' educational future?

We know from decades of research that families are critically important to the academic success of all children. Studies have shown that, for most children, the schools they attend make less difference to eventual academic attainment than the families from which they come. Given this evidence, the conclusion would seem to be that schools cannot make the important difference for children's life chances, that this must be the work of parents. But parents are not equally equipped to complement the school curriculum within their own homes. What occurs in homes that provides an advantage to some children? What proves a disadvantage to others? And are these factors changeable, given our social and economic structure?

The first question to address is: Why are the effects of family so powerful? Part of the answer is that parents are a child's first educators. Half of children's mature intellect is formed at home before they even reach school. So are cultural patterns, notions of appropriate behavior, and basic values. And to the extent that these differ from the expectations of the school, the child will be at risk for school problems.

If a child, for instance, has learned behavioral patterns such as avoiding eye-contact with the teacher or being reluctant to answer questions in class, or if the child speaks a different language, the barriers between student and teacher will be high, and the educational prognosis will be dim. Research has demonstrated that even the most well-meaning teachers tend to have lower expectations of the ability of minority children, call upon them less in class, and reinforce their responses less than those of majority culture children. Hence, among the critical, and largely immutable, things that children bring with them from home are their ethnicity, their native languages, and their social status. But this only partly explains the effect of family on school performance.

Families also differ with respect to basic resources, both physical and psychological. Some homes reinforce the school curriculum daily, through the array of ideas and possibilities presented in the normal course of middle and upper-middle class family life. Access to things that enhance academic learning (computers, educational toys) also generally increases with income and education.

Even more important, however, are the psychological resources of middle-class and majority-culture parents, who tend to see the parent-school relationship in employer-employee terms. These parents *expect* the school to educate their children. If it fails, they will demand changes. Poor, minority parents more often *hope* the school will educate their children well, but if it fails, they are less likely to know what to do. Nor may these parents be in a position to evaluate the quality of edu-

cation their children receive.

But the most important psychological resource of middle class parents is their conviction that they and their children rightfully belong in the social order—and that they have the authority to make changes. Poor parents and minority parents, perceiving themselves as marginal to the system, often feel that they lack such authority.

A school does not become part of a community by sending notes home, even carefully translated into the home language.

The Society's Owners

Certainly the greatest advantage an individual can have in any society is the power that accompanies a sense of belonging and a familiarity with the society's unwritten codes. Children from the middle class and from the majority culture are likely to grow up with a belief in their own power to affect their environment. They learn this from parents who "get things done" by knowing the right people, recognizing the right things to say, and understanding the system well enough to know how to make it work for them. These children act out powerful behaviors in school, where they are rewarded for demonstrating leadership skills, and where they will continue to fulfill society's prophecy for them.

A whole body of research has grown out of the study of "locus of control"—of whether people believe they're in control of their own lives. Middle-income students tend to believe their future is in their own hands. Lower-income students more often see their futures as out of their own control. Lower-income students, say researchers, translate this attitude toward life into counterproductive behaviors like not involving themselves in school or even dropping out.

"Externally locused" behaviors are often considered the product of a "culture" of poverty. They are, rather, responses to the reality of poverty and marginality. People on the margin of society rarely have the opportunity to shape their own lives, and they seldom

witness such behaviors within their own environs.

I am reminded of the comments of a friend, a university professor, who suggested he could always tell the difference between the Mexican American students on campus and the university students from Mexico who were just visiting (and who, almost by definition, were middle-class). In terms of physical characteristics the two were indistinguishable, but a few minutes' observation made the differences apparent.

The students from Mexico strode across campus looking as if they belonged there. They didn't hesitate to claim space for themselves in the middle of the cafeteria, or anywhere else an activity was occurring. They had never perceived themselves as second-class citizens.

The Mexican American students, on the other hand, always seemed to huddle in a corner of the room. They didn't stride so much as stoop across campus—carefully staying out of the way of the other students, who "belonged" there. The belief that they are members of the club, invited guests at the banquet, may be the most powerful inheritance of the children of the middle class and the majority culture. Because this is not often possessed by poor and minority parents, they are unable to bequeath it to their children.

The Resources of the Poor

It would be inaccurate, however, to paint a picture of poor and minority families as empty shells, devoid of resources to aid their children. My own work, and that of other researchers, such as Emmy Werner at the University of California, Davis, offers powerful evidence of the importance of the family in the lives of poor and minority children. These families mediate the experience of the outside world. They make the children feel whole again when others suggest that they are different, and possibly inferior.

Within the family, even if not in the outside world, poor and minority children are able to communicate freely in a common language. Within the family, these children most often find the encouragement and support to go on and succeed even when society's expectations are low. Most of the poor, Mexican American students I studied who were successful in school attributed their desire to succeed less to schools or peers who introduced the notion of striving than to mothers who believed in them and encouraged them unwaveringly.

This faith came most often from some experience within the parents' own families of origin. Their parents, or grandparents, or other family members were perceived as powerful individuals. Always, there was the example of family members who had been able to exercise control over their own lives. Within such families is great untapped power. For other minority families, where even the memory of hope is dim, the solution may lie in links with such hopeful families as these.

Needed: Powerful Families

The urgency and importance of empowering parents becomes greater every day. This country's demographics are changing rapidly. A larger percentage of school-age children is coming from poor and minority homes than ever before. In California, a bellwether state for demographic change throughout the nation, 40 percent of the children in the public schools are now Black or brown. In the nation as a whole, one child out of four lives in poverty. For Black, Mexican, and Puerto Rican children, the figure is closer to one in two. All indications are that circumstances are worsening for the poor. Families at the bottom of the economic ladder hold a smaller share of the country's wealth than they did a decade ago.

Even among the middle class, more and more children face potentially handicapping circumstances. Sixty percent of the children starting school today will have lived in a single-parent home by the time they finish high school—if they finish high school. And some research suggests that the most important variable for the eventual academic and economic success of poor children may be the presence of two parents. Then, too, most mothers of school-age children work outside their homes, so even middle-class mothers find it more and more difficult to give their children's schooling the attention that they have traditionally provided, and upon which schools have depended. More and more children are getting lost between school and home.

How do we make it possible for "disadvantaged" families to produce advantaged students? We start by defining our children as an economic re-

source—not through the platitudes behind the creation of remedial programs for *those* children, but in a very personal way, acknowledging them as *our* children, our resource. We should choose to change the course of children's lives not because it is a generous thing to do, but because it is a smart thing to do: a good investment of our resources.

In California, school dropout rates hover around 50 percent in areas where Black and brown students are most heavily concentrated. And for Californians today, as for many other states in the coming decades, the future will depend on the economic productivity of these children—our children.

The reason for redefining *those children* as *our children* is not solely to make them more likely objects of our largess, but to help us redefine ourselves as a community of people whose futures are inextricably linked. We have heard much about the need to increase our level of productivity if we are to ensure our country's eco-

---

The greatest advantage an individual can have in any society is the powerfulness that accompanies a sense of belonging.

---

nomic survival. And rightly so, as industry spends an ever-greater amount of time and money to train underskilled and undereducated workers. But less attention has been paid to the enormous social price that must be paid if large numbers of children are allowed to grow up unskilled and unprepared for participation in our social system. Do any of us wish to thrust our progeny into a world made hostile and divided by deprivation and disillusionment?

The Old School Community

It is unlikely that poor families alone will be able to change the educational and economic futures of their children, but a community of families *can* change the future of *our* children. Veterans of the school desegregation battles of the 1960s and 1970s will re-

call that the object of that social policy was not just to integrate classrooms and thus bring powerful parents together with less powerful parents to create change. School desegregation was an attempt to create a community of self-interest that would benefit all students.

Desegregation efforts have evidently succeeded in strengthening schools and school outcomes in some places. But already established communities have been a chief impediment to more widespread success. Parents and families understood the importance of connectedness. They saw the possibility that their children might lose the benefits of that community by reassignment to different schools, and they rejected that reassignment. Unfortunately, too, in many cases, little or no effort was made to forge a new sense of community in re-formed schools. This, we know, is possible. Private schools and parochial schools located great distances from where children live are frequently characterized by a strong sense of community and common vision. But communities, like other human relationships, require care and nurturing and sharing of both rights and responsibilities. A school does not become part of a community just by sending notes home to parents or inviting them to Open House, even if the notes are carefully translated into the home language.

The question we need to be asking is not, what can poor parents do to aid their children's schooling? but, what can schools and parents do together to create communities that will nurture all our children? Skeptics will immediately interpret this challenge as a suggestion that schools take the lead in solving social ills that are beyond their capabilities and resources. If solutions were limited to tacking on one more social program to the schools' mandate, the skeptics would probably be right. But there are other, better solutions.

The Case for Redefinition

The original purpose of schooling in this country was to transmit a common set of values and information that would allow citizens to participate productively in our social and economic system. Attendance was voluntary, and schools were viewed as supplemental to the instruction that occurred at home, in the community, and in the church.

No doubt because of our democratic traditions and fundamental belief in equal opportunity, public schooling caught on to an extraordinary degree. We began to worry about the social costs of excluding large portions of our youth. We established laws of compulsory attendance.

Required schooling was viewed as a way to avoid large-scale exploitation of an underclass and simultaneously inculcate values that would reduce the likelihood of antisocial behavior. (Of course it was also in some people's interests to keep young people out of the labor market and off the streets—but these, of course, were the most cynical of reasons for requiring schooling.) This attempt to educate so many students from diverse backgrounds and with diverse needs in a single setting has posed enormous challenges for our schools and given birth to controversies seemingly without resolution—over bilingual education, desegregation, equity in financing.

The increasing diversity in the school population, a growing self-consciousness about teaching "values," and a concurrent demand for "relevant" education to prepare youth for the job market have together resulted in the development of school curricula that are anything but equal. A curriculum rich in history, science, the humanities, and the arts, which could prepare students to live in a diverse and rapidly changing society, is conspicuously absent from many of our schools. Their curriculum offers students instead a core of skills and information designed to prepare them for only the most basic level of participation in society. Most important, the message of low expectations that such a curriculum carries probably does more damage to the psyche of these youth than their failure to acquire the subject matter.

Skills of Social Navigation

Ironically, our very diversity, the complexity of our lives and social systems, the explosion of knowledge and options, and the decline in importance of many social institutions that formerly complemented the work of the schools—churches, informal community groups, formal apprenticeships—require that our youth be prepared in more than just basic skills. They must be helped to navigate this complex social system, to understand its unwritten codes, and to make it respond to their needs.

Perhaps in part because we are a young country, composed of immigrants, we have become overly complacent about the process of acquiring the skills necessary to survive in a society like ours. We often think that these skills simply come with time. We are wont to call upon the experiences of our forebears as proof that poverty and marginality are only temporary stages in an inevitable process of becoming middle class. After all, children of the Great Depression went without meals, wore hand-me-down clothes, and eventually saw an end to that economic deprivation. Earlier, at the turn of the century, immigrants flooded into this country, undereducated and unable to speak the language. But few Americans had high school educations, and getting a job depended more on the strength of your back than on the language you spoke. Immigrants managed to enter the mainstream of our society relatively rapidly.

Today, however, the social costs of being poor and undereducated are high. Social and economic mobility are rewards for a superior education, skill, and social contacts. None of these things is readily available in the schools serving the poorest of our students.

The Schools We Need

How, then, shall we redefine schools to better match the needs of our students? We must start with the realization that students are first members of a family. They are daughters and sons, nieces and nephews, before they come to school and when they go home every afternoon. If students are not faring well within the family, they are not likely to fare well in school. If the family is troubled, it will not likely have the resources to support the children in their schoolwork. Every teacher recognizes and can readily identify the students who are not expected to do well in school because of "family situations." Yet we continue to respect a strict dividing line between schools and home.

If schools are to meet the real needs of children, they must meet the needs of the whole child. This may mean vaccinations, nutrition, or family counseling. It may mean a warm jacket for cold days, someone to supervise homework, or someone to care for the children after school. It may just mean someone for an overstressed single parent to talk to about managing a family alone. But it must mean linking parents together in such a way that the hopeful can help the hopeless, and those who expect the most from their schools and their children can encourage those same expectations for other children.

Of course, the school as currently structured cannot take on all of these tasks. But local government and community agencies can be coordinated at the school site. Local community resources can be inventoried, and many needs can be met by community members themselves.

What would such a community school look like? Perhaps it would resemble the one in East Los Angeles where the principal created a sewing room with borrowed and donated sewing machines. The school encouraged parents to come in and help make outfits for the band and curtains for the classrooms. The parents were also al-

> **Parents made a major contribution to the school, so they felt involved. They also created a community within the school.**

lowed to use the machines to make clothes for their children—clothes that would otherwise have been prohibitively expensive to purchase.

Parents—mostly non-English speaking—flocked in. They made a major contribution to the school, which made them feel valued. But they did more than that. They created a community within the school. The principal always had parents to call upon for help, and the parents developed a social network of their own upon which to rely. The children in the school apparently benefited from the close relationship between school and home, because their reading scores rose dramatically.

The community school might also resemble another Southern California school, where the parents aren't asked to sit through tedious advisory board meetings, but where they are asked to contribute the particular skills they have—carpentry, sewing, cooking—to fundraising efforts for the school.

Here the biggest community event of the year is the parent-child appreciation luncheon, which everyone attends, dressed up. All of the children —not just the excelling students—and all the parents are made to feel special. Not surprisingly, by reaching out to all parents in a way that values their particular skills, this school enjoys an extremely high degree of parent participation. The children's level of achievement is notably higher than in surrounding schools.

A community school, by definition, reflects its surrounding neighborhood. Buildings are used year-round and throughout the evening. Community members meet regularly, perhaps over a dinner prepared by parents, to discuss school and other community issues. An office, a trailer, or a portable building is staffed with volunteers as well as local agency personnel. The local school is the first place people in the community turn for help.

Where there is a community school, teenagers who want to earn money or school credits know where to go to find work doing after-school homework supervision, tutoring, recreation supervision, or child care. Senior citizens in the neighborhood can walk to the school to volunteer time and share in the companionship of their community. Because the school meets the needs of all kinds of parents—working parents' needs for homework supervision and after-school care, lower-income parents' needs for health screening and social services—there's no longer a need to plead with parents to come to school. The community school is the place where family needs are met, where the community draws strength and identity.

If we were to turn schools into resource centers for communities, if the terms "school" and "community" began to merge in citizens' minds, then a parent might spend some part of the day in the back of the classroom, not only monitoring the progress of the students and the quality of the education, but also making an unspoken statement that education is crucial and that the people providing that education deserve the respect of the students and the community. Businesses might provide release time for parents—maybe even other community members—to spend a few hours a month in the schools. Their presence would convey a basic message: school is serious business, and communities are partners in that business. The schools might enjoy the support of all sectors of the community. No longer would they be the special interest of that one-quarter of the voting public with children in school.

A New American Community

A few years ago, a very important book appeared. *Habits of the Heart* warned us of the perils of what has often been perceived as our greatest strength as a nation: our unflagging faith in the spirit of individualism. American culture is filled with the legends of people who supposedly pulled themselves up by their own bootstraps and became successful with nothing more than a belief in themselves and the opportunity to pursue their destinies in a land that did not confine them to the limitations of their origins. In America, the son of a janitor can leave his home, leave his community, and become a successful businessman.

Maybe. Statistically, however, the son of a janitor is more likely to leave his home, leave his school, move to a neighborhood not unlike the one in which he grew up, but where he is unknown, and become a janitor. The authors of *Habits of the Heart* suggest that we may have traded the strength and support of our communities for an increasingly elusive personal benefit. We may have traded poverty of body for poverty of spirit. There is no more important place to begin to change that trend than in our schools, where our children learn what we value as a nation, more by what we don't do than by what we do. And there is no better place to create a community of caring than in our schools—the heart of our future.

For Further Reading

Broken Promises: How Americans Fail Their Children. W. Norton Grubb and Marvin Lazerson. Basic Books, 1982. This book challenges Americans to make the welfare of "other people's children" their own concern, suggesting that this may, indeed, be the only way of achieving social justice in our society.

Habits of the Heart: Individualism and Commitment in American Life. Robert N. Bellah and others. Berkeley: University of California Press, 1985. The authors propose a rethinking of the American emphasis on individualism and, borrowing from de Tocqueville, warn of a nation becoming devoid of community.

Parents as Partners in Education. Eugenia H. Berger. Merrill, 1987. This handbook on developing parent-school partnerships devotes considerable attention to school-based and home-based programs to enhance the communication between families and schools.

"Passing Through the Eye of the Needle." Patricia Gándara. *Hispanic Journal of Behavioral Sciences*, no. 2, 1982. This article describes a study of Mexican American youth who possessed background characteristics predictive of school failure, but who "beat the system." The focus is on the things that the young women in the study reported to be central to their success.

School Power. James P. Comer. Free Press, 1980. This story of how one community addressed inadequate school outcomes for its children makes the case for education's being a joint activity of families and schools.

Vulnerable but Invincible: A Longitudinal Study of Resilient Children and Youth. E. E. Werner and R. S. Smith. McGraw-Hill, 1982. This report on a group of children being reared on the margins of society looks at the antecedents, in both homes and communities, to successful outcomes for these youngsters.

A Brief Historical Perspective of the Struggle for an Integrative Curriculum

An historical review of curriculum changes in this country clarifies the reasons for the current confusion. The author points to a way out of the curriculum maze.

Daniel Tanner

DANIEL TANNER is a professor in the Graduate School of Education, Rutgers University, New Brunswick, New Jersey. He has written History of the School Curriculum, *co-authored with Laurel Tanner, Macmillan 1989.*

*T*HE CONTEMPORARY SCENE is marked by a struggle for curriculum renewal following the bankruptcy of the "back-to-basics" retrenchment of the 1970s and 80s, and the realization that curriculum fundamentalism has resulted in a decline in thinking ability and writing proficiency. From the historic record, it was predictable that reducing the curriculum to the lowest common denominator of basic educa-tion would result in a curriculum of poverty with poverty of results.

The rising industrialism of the nine-teenth century was accompanied by efforts to provide for universal elemen-tary education in the three R's in Eng-land and the United States. As a British scholar observed, "the new working class needed enough acquaintance with the three R's to do their jobs properly, and provision for teaching them was reluctantly provided on the cheapest possible basis. But there was all the more reason for seeing that the educa-tion of the masses did not go too far, and that it introduced no unsettling ideas."[1] Early in this century, John Dewey offered these trenchant com-ments condemning the tradition of providing an essentialist curriculum for the masses and a full and rich cur-riculum for the privileged:

> He who is poorly acquainted with the history of the efforts to im-prove elementary education in our large cities does not know that the chief protest against progress is likely to come from successful business men. They have clamored for the three R's as the essential and exclusive ma-terial of primary education— knowing well enough that their own children would be able to get the things they protest against. Thus they have attacked as fads and frills every enrich-ment of the curriculum which did not lend itself to narrow economic ends.[2]

From *Educational Horizons*, Fall 1989, pp. 7-11. Reprinted with permission of *Educational Horizons* quarterly journal published by Pi Lambda Theta national honor and professional association, Bloomington, IN 47407-6626.

Efforts to inculcate the waves of immigrants in the educational rudiments (the three R's) early in this century gave rise to the term *literacy education*. Ironically, this term has been revivified in contemporary proposals for educational reform, despite its rudimentary and archaic origins and functions.

The Curriculum Revolution

Throughout the early decades of the twentieth century, heroic and imaginative efforts were made by progressivist-experimentalist educators to extend educational opportunity to all children through universal secondary education and to reconstruct the curriculum so that it would be attuned to the nature of the learner and the ideals of a free society. They recognized that the tradition of *basic education* or *literacy education* for the masses, and *liberal education* for the privileged was untenable in a democracy.

Embracing the concept of *general education* to meet the function of creating a sense of unity through diversity, progressivist-experimentalist educators devised new integrative curricular designs to replace the fragmented subject curriculum. Systematic efforts were made not only to correlate subjects that heretofore had been treated in isolation, but to provide integrative learning experiences that cut across the traditional subject cocoons and were more life related.

Many progressive-experimentalist schools sought to engage students in what John Dewey called the "complete act of thought," or reflective thinking, through the problem-focused core curriculum. The elementary classroom became transformed from anchored rows of desks and a rigid repertoire of rote and recitation, to a flexible and more attractive physical environment and a more cooperative workplace.

THROUGH THE Eight-Year Study (1933-1941), it was found that the traditional college preparatory curriculum was not the best and only way to prepare students for success in college. The students who were engaged in the more experimental curricular designs, such as the problem-focused core curriculum, demonstrated better attitudes toward learning, greater intellectual curiosity, and higher achievement in college than their peers who had completed the more traditional college preparatory program.[3]

Nevertheless, these notable efforts and attainments were not made without opposition. Following World War II, tax conservatives called for a return to the cheap curriculum of basic education in the elementary school and the traditional academic subject curriculum in the secondary school. The wave of McCarthyism gave rise to the censorship of curricular materials and to the avoidance of controversial issues in the curriculum. The great expectations for integrative curricular designs to meet the need for general education in the postwar years faded quickly with the crisis of the cold war and space race.

Nationalizing Influences on the Curriculum

The Soviet challenge of the 1950s and 60s witnessed an unprecedented billion-dollar federal effort to give priority to the sciences, mathematics, and modern foreign languages in the school curriculum through the National Defense Education Act of 1958 and the National Science Foundation. In effect, the National Science Foundation virtually put the U.S. Office of Education into eclipse as an agency for supporting curriculum reform in our elementary and secondary schools. National curriculum projects in the sciences and mathematics proliferated.

The model for the school curriculum was based on the discipline-centered bias of university specialism. The new national curriculum projects designed by university scholar-specialists stressed the disciplinary doctrine of knowledge purity and abstraction at the expense of knowledge application and synthesis. The nature of the learner was recast in the form of a budding scholar-specialist, while the relevance of the curriculum to the life of the learner and the life of a free society was shunted aside. The new curriculum priority and hierarchy resulted in a perverse fragmentation and imbalance in the school curriculum. Scholars in the social sciences and arts sought to imitate the discipline-centered model of their colleagues in the sciences and mathematics, with the result that social studies and history gave way to the social sciences, while feeble efforts were made to refashion the arts as "academic disciplines."

In the aftermath of the "new math," "new physics," "new chemistry," and so on, it was realized by the mid-1960s that the national discipline-centered projects had failed to deliver what was promised. Students had declined in their ability to make knowledge applications. Their attitudes toward science and scientists were less favorable than their peers who had been exposed to more flexible curricula. Although the nationalistic goal of the discipline-centered curriculum reforms was to produce more scientists, a sharp decline actually occurred in the number of college students majoring in the sciences at a time when college enrollments were mushrooming.[4]

Assessing the handiwork of the university scholar-specialists in developing the discipline-centered curriculum packages for the elementary and secondary schools, Alvin Weinberg, director of the Oak Ridge National Laboratory, commented, "The professional purists, representing the spirit of the fragmented, research-oriented university, took over the curriculum reforms, and by their diligence and aggressiveness, created puristic monsters."[5] In examining the curriculum representing the "new math," the late Richard Feynman, Nobel laureate in physics, found the material to be "an abstraction from the real world...used by pure mathematicians in their more subtle and difficult analyses, and used by nobody else." He went on to attack the "new math" as "full of such nonsense."[6]

Humanizing the School

Just when it was being realized that new integrative curriculum designs were needed which would reveal the interdependence of knowledge and its significance to the life of the learner and the life of a free society, the latter 1960s were marked by the shock waves of student protest and disruption on our college campuses in connection with the civil rights movement and the U.S. involvement in the Vietnam War, with the disruption eventually filtering down into the high schools. The dominant student demand was for curriculum "relevance," but "relevance" proved to be an empty slogan in the absence of a coherent curriculum design for general education. The colleges, followed by the high schools, took the path of least resistance by introducing more and more electives on current topics, while the university scholar-specialists continued to pursue their special interests.

ALTHOUGH there was much talk of "humanizing" the school and college curriculum and developing interdisciplinary approaches to the curriculum, no concerted efforts were made in these directions. For the elementary school, the move was toward the open classroom, presumably patterned after the efforts in Britain to provide for an integrative curriculum in the primary school.[7] However, instead of developing an integrative curriculum by removing the walls of separation marking the traditional subjects in the curriculum, the open classroom was "adopted" by removing classroom walls. Books by radical school critics proliferated on the best-seller lists, advocating an open curriculum or no curriculum at all.[8]

The Fundamentalist Counterreaction

By the mid-1970s, the inevitable counterreaction for the schools was "back-to-basics," coupled with the call for alternative or magnet schools to meet the special interests of special pupil populations. In 1916, Dewey prophetically observed that:

When it is perceived that after all the requirements of a full life experience are not met, the deficiency is not laid to the isolation and narrowness of the teaching of the existing subjects, and this recognition made the basis of reorganization of the system. No, the lack is something to be made up for by the introduction of still another study, or, if necessary, another kind of school...the remedy is to cut off a great many studies as fads and frills, and return to the good old curriculum of the three R's in elementary education and the equally good and equally old-fashioned curriculum of the classics and mathematics in higher education.[9]

The cheap curriculum wrought by the back-to-basics retrenchment of the 1970s through most of the 80s witnessed the wide use of worksheets and workbooks in place of real books. Textbooks were "dumbed-down" to rudimentary exercises in basic skills. Youngsters were exposed to mechanical drill-skill exercises, negating the experience of reading for meaning and enjoyment.

Statewide minimum-competency tests proliferated. Instead of seeking to optimize the educative process, the process of education was minimized. Teachers were pressured to teach the test in order to demonstrate improved test scores. Belatedly, it was realized that during the period of curriculum retrenchment through back-to-basics, "expenditure for textbooks and other instructional materials (had) declined 50 percent over the past 17 years. While some recommend a level of spending on texts of between 5 and 10 percent of the operating costs of schools, the budgets for basal texts and related materials have been dropping during the past decade and a half to only 0.7 percent today."[10]

New Nationalization Influences

In the wake of the "Japanese challenge," national reports on educational reform in the 1980s called for the "new basics"—to refashion the curriculum to meet narrow economic interests. Today, the educational literature resounds with the call for literacy—basic literacy for socioeconomically impoverished children and youth in our inner cities, and every fractionated and confused kind of "literacy" for all others: "cultural literacy," "computer literacy," "scientific literacy," "mathematical literacy," "aesthetic literacy," "political literacy," "economic literacy," "technological literacy," and so on. The confusion of "literacies" augurs for the further fragmentation and isolation of the curriculum, while neglecting education for a full life experience.

In the multitude of "literacies," each form of literacy must compete for priority in the curriculum at the expense of the others. At the same time, the rising generation is divided so that only a rudimentary form of literacy is provided the less privileged. It is indeed ironic that the United Nations General Assembly should proclaim 1990 as International Literacy Year, targeting the goal of literacy for third-world nations while the United States has also embraced this rudimentary educational concept for its own rising generation.

INSTEAD of seeking to treat the curriculum in ecological interdependence, there is the tendency to induce curricular change segmentally by accretion, deletion, injection, and excision, as though each element is independent or at odds with other elements. The result is either curriculum congestion or the removal of important studies in favor of the subject matter that fits the latest educational crisis or fashion. For example, the recent rediscovery of the decline in thinking ability has led to a segmental emphasis on critical thinking rather than seeking to have students engage in critical thinking throughout the curriculum and as a central function of general education. The same problem attends to the college curriculum. Recently, in reaction to the unethical conduct in the American business sector, the Harvard Business School announced that it had received a multi-million dollar donation to establish a course in business ethics. Instead of dealing with problems of ethics throughout the business curriculum, a new course is inserted to take care of ethics while the curriculum remains essentially undisturbed. The consequence is that ethics never becomes part of the working capital of the business curriculum as a whole, but is treated as another subject of special study. As one graduate student commented in response to the problem of ethics and illegal activity in American business, "My view is that all that illegal activity comes with the job, and the point of your job is to be good enough not to get caught."[11]

It seems that at periodic intervals there is inevitably a reawakened demand for citizenship education, with the result that it is inserted segmentally into the curriculum without seeking to build democratic citizenship into the everyday life of the school. To study civics or government as another academic subject, while bias and bigotry are allowed to run rampant on the playing field and in the community—or when books are censored by school authorities, or when controversial issues are avoided—the real curriculum is not the academic subject matter, but the life experience in the school and community.

WHEN nationalistic interests lead to a demand to give priority to the sciences and mathematics, or when the call is for a return to the basics, the "remedy" is to make these shifts while diminishing other studies that make for a full and rich curriculum. In the same vein, when priority is given to the gifted and talented, there is sure to be a counterreaction whenever such priority is taken at the expense of children and youth who are at risk. The point is that a free society requires that the best be done for all children and youth. We need to get away from the dichotomous mindset that treats any gain in one direction as a necessary loss in another direction. In connection with the curriculum, the old tradition of providing a full and rich curriculum for the privileged and rudimentary curriculum for others is untenable in a democracy. An integrative curriculum for general education can provide the needed sense of unity, while diverse needs can also be met through a comprehensive curriculum.

The Way Out of the Curriculum Confusion

We can begin by applying a simple test to any and all areas of study in the curriculum. As explicated by Alvin Weinberg, the measure of any area of study in the curriculum should be determined by its "relevance to neighboring fields" and to "human welfare and values."[12] Or, in the words of Richard Feynman, "The utility of the subject and its relevance to the world must be made clear to the pupil."[13] Alfred North Whitehead put the matter in these words:

The solution which I am urging is to eradicate the fatal disconnection of subjects which kills the vitality of our modern curriculum. There is only one subject matter for education, and that is Life in all its manifestations. Instead of this single unity, we offer children—Algebra, from which nothing follows; Geometry, from which nothing follows; Science, from which nothing follows; History, from which nothing follows; a couple of Languages, never mastered; and

lastly, most dreary of all, Literature, represented by plays of Shakespeare with...substance to be committed to memory. Can such a list be said to represent Life, as it is known in the midst of the living of it? The best that can be said of it is, that it is a rapid table of contents which a deity might run over in his mind while he was thinking of creating a world, and had not yet determined how to put it together.[14]

There is a biological principle that structure determines function, from which is derived the architectural principle that form follows function. This is no less valid for the curriculum. Integrative curriculum designs are needed to counter the isolation and fragmentation of knowledge that plagues the traditional curriculum. There is a powerful heritage in American education in devising integrative approaches to the curriculum to fulfill the need for a universe of discourse, understanding, and competence shared by all members of a free society.

This does not mean a search for a "final solution" to the curriculum problem through a "one best" curriculum, but rather the need to seek ways of building a sense of unity through diversity in meeting the function of general education for a democracy. The metaphor of general education as the "palm of the hand" or "trunk of the tree" from which all forms of specialists reach out, should be vivid to those who seek to reconstruct the curriculum to meet the need for an enlightened citizenry in American democracy.[15] Through the agency of the comprehensive or cosmopolitan high school, the curriculum in general education must be reconstructed to serve an integrative and democratizing function alongside the specializing function of vocational education and college preparation. The separate vocational school,

alternative school, or magnet school has served only to exacerbate social divisions and to isolate our pupil populations.

PROPOSALS for curriculum reform will continue to lead us astray when they are targeted at narrow nationalistic interests at the expense of the wider public interest, when they favor a narrow side of the curriculum at the expense of a full and rich curriculum, and when they favor one pupil population at the expense of another. An integrative core curriculum requires a new recognition of the interdependence of knowledge and its relevance to the life of the learner in a free society.

1. J. Bernal, *Science in History* (Cambridge, Mass.: M.I.T. Press, 1971), p. 1149.
2. J. Dewey, "Learning to Earn," *School and Society* (24 March 1917): 332.
3. W. Aikin, *The Story of the Eight-Year Study* (New York: Harper & Brothers, 1942).
4. See D. Tanner and L. Tanner, *Curriculum Development: Theory Into Practice*, 2nd ed. (New York: Macmillan Publishing Company, 1980), chap. 16.
5. A. Weinberg, *Reflections on Big Science* (Cambridge, Mass.: M.I.T. Press, 1967), p. 154.
6. R. Feynman, "New Textbooks for the New Mathematics," *Engineering and Science* (March 1965): 13.
7. C. Silberman, *Crisis in the Classroom: The Remaking of American Education* (New York: Random House, 1970).
8. W. Engler, *Radical School Reformers of the 1960s*, doctoral dissertation (New Brunswick, N.J.: Rutgers University, 1973).
9. J. Dewey, *Democracy and Education* (New York: Macmillan Publishing Company, 1916), p. 289.
10. National Commission on Excellence in Education, *A Nation at Risk: The Imperative for Educational Reform* (Washington, D.C.: U.S. Department of Education, April 1983), p. 21.
11. S. Salmans, "How Prodigies Perceive Business," *The New York Times*, 3 September 1989, p. F4.
12. A. Weinberg, *Reflections on Big Science*, pp. 75, 76.
13. R. Feynman, "New Textbooks for the New Mathematics," p. 13.
14. A. Whitehead, *The Aims of Education and Other Essays* (New York: Macmillan Publishing Company, 1929), pp. 10-11.
15. Harvard Committee on General Education, *General Education in a Free Society* (Cambridge, Mass.: Harvard University Press, 1945), p. 102.

Striving for Excellence: The Drive for Quality

North Americans have always debated what was the best academic performance one could expect of all non-cognitively handicapped youth in their schools. There has always been tension between "quality" and "equality" of opportunity in the educational policy debate. "Top down" solutions have been traditional to educational problems in the United States, Canada, and the rest of the world. Perhaps this is not avoidable due to the logical necessity of governmental financing of public, tax-supported school systems. However, the "top-down" pattern of national-state (provincial) policy development for schooling needs to be tempered by even more "bottom-up," grassroots efforts at improving the quality of schools such as is now underway in many school systems across the North American continent.

The debate over improving the quality of teacher education programming reflects well the current struggle for excellence in education in the United States. The American Association of Colleges for Teacher Education (AACTE) voted to withhold support for the National Board for Professional Teaching Standards, a Carnegie Corporation-endorsed board that has been meeting for two years to draft national certification standards for teachers. This event demonstrates dramatically the tension and debate over how to achieve excellence in teaching, and the conflicts of interest and value that run through the whole educational reform movement in the United States. The Bush administration has committed itself to facilitating, from its perspective, the implementation of reforms in the quality of elementary, secondary, and teacher education. It remains to be seen whether or not the AACTE and the National Board for Professional Teaching Standards can overcome the impasse they have reached over the academic preparation of teachers and the qualifications of individuals who may apply for National Board certification.

Excellence is the goal: the means to achieve it is the dispute. There is a new dimension to the debate over the assessment of the academic achievement of elementary and secondary school students. In addition, there is a continuing struggle of conflicting academic (as well as political) interests over improving the quality of preparation of future teachers.

Few conscientious educators would oppose the idea of excellence in education; as with motherhood and one's nation, some things are held in deep and generalized reverence. The problem in gaining consensus over excellence in education is that excellence is always defined against some standard. Since there are fundamentally opposing standards for determining what constitutes excellent student and teacher performances, it is sometimes debatable which standards of assessment should prevail. The current debate over excellence in teacher education in the United States clearly demonstrates how conflicting academic values can clash and lead to conflicting programmatic recommendations for educational reform.

The 1980s brought North American educators many important individual and commission reports on bringing qualitative improvement to the educational system at all levels. Some of the reports addressed higher education concerns (particularly relating to general studies requirements and teacher education), but most of them focused on the academic performance problems of elementary and secondary school students. There were literally dozens of such reports. In this area, the activities of the Bush administration and the National Governors' Conference in the United States may foster additional items for the educational reform agenda. There have been some common themes in those reports on school reform sponsored by government, philanthropic, and corporate bodies. There has been some thematic commonality in those reports issued to date by affected groups of educators. However, there are professional teaching organizations that take exception to what they believe to be too heavily laden hidden business and political agendas underlying some of the public rhetoric on school reform. Educators in teacher education are not in agreement either. There is still the debate as to whether academic goals or social goals should control the nature, content, and direction of educational change in North America. Many have always believed that social goals must be secondary to academic ones in schools. Yet there are others who point out civic educational goals are needed to prepare students for their roles as fully participating adults in society. We should avoid false dichotomies between academic and civic or social goals.

Any conceptually adequate educational reform movement must concentrate on the commissioned goals of public schools and develop an integrated strategy for their achievement. Both the manifest (explicit) and the latent (real, identifiable, but implicit) effects of acting on particular educational policy initiatives need to be investigated. Is a just and workable national consensus on these issues possible? I believe it is. The debate over "school reform" in the United States provides an opportunity to clarify and change fundamental national and state educational policies of the past four or five decades.

As the United States and Canada debate the educational tradeoffs involved in alternative strategies for school reform, they can learn which educational attitudes, values, and performance outcomes must prevail. These spirited, generalized public debates over educational policies and programs should produce great learning societies.

The following are types of questions that can be considered when developing policy alternatives for improvement of student achievement. Should schools with different missions be established at the secondary level as they are in some parts of Europe? If specialization is considered desirable or necessary at the secondary level, what specific types of specialized secondary schools should be established? Or should there be a common secondary school curriculum for all secondary school students? If existing American and Canadian elementary and secondary schools are not producing desired levels of academic competency, what specific course changes in school curricula are required? What forms of teacher education and in-service reeducation of teachers are needed? Who pays for any of these programmatic options? Where and how are funds raised or redirected from other budgetary priorities to do these things? Will Americans ever adopt the "streaming" and "tracking" models of secondary school student placement that exists in Europe? How can we best assess (evaluate) academic performance? Will North Americans accept structural realignments in the educational system? How will handicapped learners be scheduled in schools? Is there a national commitment to heterogeneous grouping of students, and to mainstreaming handicapped students in the United States? Many individual, private, and governmental reform efforts have failed to address and resolve the reform agenda issues these questions raise.

Other industrialized nations have championed the need for alternative secondary schools to prepare young people for varied life goals and civic missions. The American dream of the common school translated into a comprehensive high school in the twentieth century. It was to be a high school for all the people with alternative diploma options and its students "tracked" into different programs. What is the next step? What is to be done? To succeed in improving the quality of student achievement, concepts related to our educational goals must be clarified, and political motivation must be separated from the demonstrable realities of student performance. We must clarify our goals. When we do this we come down to getting clearer on "what knowledge is of most worth?" Which educational values and priorities are to prevail?

Looking Ahead: Challenge Questions

Try to identify some of the different points of view on achieving excellence in education. What value conflicts

can be defined?

Do teachers see educational reform in the same light as governmental, philanthropic, or corporate-based school reform groups? On what matters would they agree? On what matters might they disagree?

What can be learned from recent reports on the state of American education? What are your views of the recommendations being offered to improve the quality of schooling?

How could school curricula and instructional practices be modified to encourage excellence in teaching and learning?

What are the minimum academic standards that all high school graduates should meet?

What are the most significant issues to be addressed in the development and use of minimum competency testing?

Is there anything new in the struggle for excellence? What can be learned from the history of efforts to reform education?

Reform In The 80's

Fixing The System *from* The Top Down

By David Hill

David Hill is an assistant editor of Teacher Magazine.

On April 26, 1983, the afternoon papers and evening television newscasts led with a startling story: A federal report released that morning proclaimed that a widespread failure of public schools had placed the nation "at risk." A blue-ribbon panel, appointed by the U.S. secretary of education, decried "a rising tide of mediocrity" in education that was eroding the very foundation of society.

With unusually powerful rhetoric, the 60-page document began: "Our once unchallenged pre-eminence in commerce, industry, science, and technological innovation is being overtaken by competitors throughout the world." And it concluded that "if an unfriendly foreign power had attempted to impose on America the mediocre educational performance that exists today, we might well have viewed it as an act of war."

In 18 months of hearings, debate, and study, the National Commission on Excellence in Education had found little excellence. Instead, it encountered widespread deterioration of student achievement. The report cited, among other evidence, a steady decline in average Scholastic Aptitude Test scores from 1963 to 1980; "consistent declines" in such subjects as physics and English, as measured by College Board achievement tests; and, between 1975 and 1980, a 72 percent increase in the number of remedial mathematics courses taught in public four-year colleges.

To address these ills, *A Nation at Risk* offered specific recommendations, including: strengthening high school graduation requirements; increasing standards and expectations for student performance; lengthening the school day and the school year; and improving the teaching profession through higher standards and higher salaries.

Secretary of Education Terrel H. Bell later recalled the attention given to the release of the report: "Our press-clipping service revealed that the commission's report was on the front page of all the major newspapers in every city—small, medium, and large—across the nation. . . . Phone calls and letters poured in from across the country. We had hit a responsive chord. Education was on everyone's front burner."

Although *A Nation at Risk* is credited with launching the current national effort to reform education, limited efforts had been under way in a number of states since the mid-1970's. And many of them reflected a disenchantment with teachers.

By the end of 1981, 18 states required competency testing for teacher certification, and 13 states required such tests for admission to teacher-training programs. Several months before *A Nation at Risk*, California State Superintendent of Public Instruction Bill Honig announced a basic-skills test to screen prospective teachers. "I realize that this means some candidates won't receive a California teaching credential," he said at the time, "but our children have to come first." Two months later, Honig proposed a sweeping plan that would impose statewide high school graduation requirements, lengthen the school day, provide higher salaries for starting teachers, and loosen procedures for dismissing teachers.

Also in 1983, Lamar Alexander of Tennessee became the first governor to propose a statewide career-ladder plan for teachers—which the legislature passed despite heavy opposition from the Tennessee Education Association (an affiliate of the National Education Association). But the excellence commis-

sion put the topic of school reform on the national agenda, and triggered a frenzied period of reform actions in virtually every state capitol. A 50-state survey conducted by *Education Week* at the end of 1983 found that:

• More than 100 formal state commissions had been established to study public education and make recommendations for improvement. In 1983 alone, 54 state-level commissions were formed to study reform.

• That same year, 33 states considered changes that would increase salaries and status for exemplary teachers. State legislatures in both California

Rethinking Teacher Education

The call for a stronger, more proficient teaching force naturally directed the critical gaze of education reformers to the college and university programs that prepare teachers.

State legislators and policymakers rushed to raise entrance standards for schools of education, toughen program requirements, and mandate competency tests for beginning teachers. However, critics charged that most of the corrective actions were ill-conceived and lacking coherence.

Although a number of groups released reports that addressed teacher preparation, it wasn't until April 1986 that a comprehensive blueprint for change emerged, and it came from an unexpected part of the teacher-training community. The tract, titled *Tomorrow's Teachers*, was the culmination of more than two years of work by the Holmes Group, a coalition of 40 deans of education from some of the nation's leading research universities—institutions that historically have given low priority to teacher preparation.

Because of its wide-ranging scope and controversial recommendations, *Tomorrow's Teachers* jarred the education community and attracted widespread national attention.

The report sharply criticized traditional teacher preparation and called for "radical" changes in teaching and in the education of teachers. Teacher-education programs are "intellectually weak," the deans wrote: "Basically a 'non-

program' at present, professional courses are not interrelated or coherent. The curriculum is seldom reviewed for its comprehensiveness, redundancy, or its responsiveness to research and analysis."

The Holmes Group proposed that prospective teachers major in an academic subject rather than education, receive the bulk of their professional training at the graduate level, and then complete a year-long supervised internship. In what has proved to be the most controversial of their recommendations, the deans advocated the abolition of the undergraduate education major.

They also suggested that the teaching profession be entirely recast into a three-tiered hierarchy that has "career professionals" at the highest level and "instructors," with only a liberal arts degree and limited responsibility, at the lowest.

The recommendations contained in *Tomorrow's Teachers* were directed to all of the approximately 1,250 colleges and universities that train teachers, as well as to the nation's public schools and policymakers. Thus, the group's decision, following the release of its report, to restrict its membership to a select core of roughly 100 research universities was denounced as elitist and exclusionary by a number of teacher-educators.

Although its recommendations remain to be implemented on a wide scale, the Holmes Group—and *Tomorrow's Teachers*—has focused and dramatically influenced the debate over teacher preparation.

and Florida approved career-ladder plans for teachers.

• Seven states—California, Arkansas, Florida, Idaho, Indiana, North Carolina, and North Dakota—had approved legislation to extend instructional time either statewide or in selected districts. Other states had considered extending the school day or requiring that the use of instructional time be improved.

• In states with the most comprehensive reform packages, the changes were championed by governors. Former Govs. Robert Graham of Florida, William Winter of Mississippi, and Richard Riley of South Carolina, for example, worked with their legislatures through several sessions to enact sweeping reforms.

• The *Education Week* survey and a follow-up report by Bell in the spring of 1984 made clear that the reform movement was essentially a "top-down" regulatory effort being driven by governors and legislators.

Many of the state actions seemed predicated on the notion that the main cause of educational failure was laxness, an abandonment of standards and accountability. The response, therefore, was more often than not to get tough: to raise standards, tighten accountability, increase testing, beef up curricular requirements, and demand better teachers and better teaching.

Two years later, another 50-state survey by *Education Week* found that "the drive to improve schools has generated an unprecedented level of legislative and policymaking activity in the states." It took 18 tabloid pages of small type to publish the survey's results. Among its findings: 43 states had raised high school graduation requirements; 15 of those states required an exit test for graduation; 37 states had acted to institute statewide assessments of students; and 29 states had upgraded teacher-education requirements to include a mandatory competency test. In addition to increased accountability for teachers, some states had moved to recognize better teachers with better pay. And 18 states had increased teachers' salaries: Alabama, for example, increased salaries by 15 percent, bringing the statewide average to about $20,000. School reform was sweeping the nation, but not everyone was pleased with the manner in which it was being enacted. Wrote Ernest Boyer, president of the Carnegie Foundation for the Advancement of Teaching: "It's ironic that while American business is beginning to recognize the importance of the worker, in education we still are trying to fix the system from the top down. The time has come to recognize that school renewal should be led, not just by politicians, but by educators, too. Principals and teachers must be given not only more responsibility but more empowerment as well."

High School, Boyer's own critique of secondary education in America, had been published within months after *A Nation at Risk.* And it was soon followed by two other major reports, Theodore Sizer's *Horace's Compromise: The Dilemma of the American High School,* and John Goodlad's *A Place Called School.*

About the only thing that these three books had in common with the Bell Commission report was their criticism of the nation's schools as currently organized and operated. But where *A Nation at Risk* concentrated on tightening standards and increasing accountability, the Boyer, Sizer, and Goodlad books stressed the need for radical restructuring of American education, including the empowering of teachers, to meet the needs of a changing society.

A Nation at Risk and its view of schooling clearly dominated the first phase of the reform movement, but by 1986, many were questioning the effectiveness of top-down reform. And some were beginning to advocate the bottom-up approach to school improvement recommended by Boyer, Sizer, and Goodlad. In this second phase of reform, two major themes were to emerge: the need to give special attention to "at-risk" students, and the need to professionalize and empower the nation's teachers.

The Excellence Commission's report found the nation at risk, but said nothing about at-risk students. That message was left for the National Coalition of Advocates for Students, whose 1985 report—*Barriers to Excellence: Our Children at Risk*—made the term "at-risk students" part of the reform lexicon.

"What the board did was spend the year listening to what people's experiences in schools were and what their worries were," explained Joan McCarty First, director of the NCAS. "We wanted to find out why a large number of children continue to be excluded from schools, why a large number of children in school fail to learn conceptual and problem-solving skills, and why a large number of young people experience unemployment and underemployment in the workplace."

The NCAS report was sharply critical of the top-down regulatory approach to school improvement for overlooking what it deemed the most serious problem facing schools: at-risk students. "Policymakers at many different levels talk of bringing excellence to schools and ignore the fact that hundreds of thousands of youngsters are not receiving even minimal educational opportunities guaranteed under law," said the report, adding: "From the minute they walk into school, many low-income students get the message that society does not really care about their education, that schools expect little from them."

These at-risk children—most often poor, nonwhite, handicapped, or female—cannot possibly benefit from a reform movement that emphasizes quantitative changes over qualitative changes, the report argued. "Schools, indeed, should set high standards," it said. "But schools must also help *all* students meet those standards." Raising standards for students who can't meet even the lower ones they now face simply forces more children to drop out, critics charged.

The NCAS report was followed by several others calling attention to the nation's neediest students and recommending massive efforts to bring them into the educational mainstream. Perhaps the most impassioned in its critique was the report of the Committee for Economic Development—an organization of the nation's largest business corporations. "Clearly, high standards and expectations are necessary if the high school diploma is once again to become a meaningful measurement of educational achievement," said the report, titled *Children in Need: Investment Strategies for the Educationally Disadvantaged.* "Yet . . . raising standards for all students without increased efforts to help children who may not meet those standards will go only partway toward realizing the nation's educational goals. It will leave a significant proportion of the population underskilled and probably unemployable."

What, then, should be done? The report urged "early and sustained intervention into the lives of at-risk children," through prenatal and postnatal care for young mothers, preschool for disadvantaged 3- and 4-year-olds, increased parental participation in education, greater autonomy at the school site, and dropout-prevention programs that combine education with basic work skills.

Business, the report said, should become "a driving force" in the reform of education. "These children need a champion," said Owen Butler, retired chairman of the Procter & Gamble Company and chairman of the subcommittee that produced the report. "Somebody who is accustomed to taking a long-range view of what our society needs has to step in, recognize this problem, and become an advocate for both more money and better programs. We think that businessmen are ideally suited to do that."

Just as *A Nation at Risk* launched the regulatory phase of the reform movement, and *Barriers to Excellence* shifted the spotlight to at-risk children, a major report sponsored by the Carnegie Corporation of New York called the nation's attention to the crucial role of America's teachers.

A Nation Prepared: Teachers for the 21st Century, issued in 1986 by Carnegie's Task Force on Teaching as a Profession, garnered almost as much newspaper space and television time as *A Nation at Risk.* The report stressed the need for a new status and a new role for the nation's school teachers: "If the schools are to compete successfully with medicine, architecture, and accounting for staff, then teachers will have to have comparable authority in

making the key decisions about the services they render," said the report.

"Within the context of a limited set of clear goals for students set by state and local policymakers, teachers, working together, must be free to exercise their professional judgment as to the best way to achieve these goals. This means the ability to make—or at least to strongly influence—decisions concerning such things as the materials and instructional methods to be used, the staffing structure to be employed, the organization of the school day, the assignment of students, the consultants to be used, and the allocation of resources available to the school."

Sharon Batson, an English teacher at Westbury High School in Houston, told *Education Week,* "All of us want this change. People who have not been to a classroom for 10 or 15 years are making decisions for us. They tell us what to teach and how to teach it and they don't even know the children. We know our students' needs. We can develop a curriculum as well as anyone else. I have no qualms about their defining the ends for the children. But they hired me to teach and they should trust me to do that."

Her message—and that of the Carnegie Task Force—was simply that the time had come for teaching to make the transition from occupation to profession. The Carnegie report, prepared by a 14-member task force of business officials, educators, minority-group leaders, and state and national policymakers, laid down a number of specific recommendations, including:

• Creating a National Board for Professional Teaching Standards to certify teachers.

• Restructuring schools to provide a "professional environment" for teachers, giving them autonomy within the classroom while holding them accountable for student progress.

• Introducing a new category of "lead teachers" who would guide and influence the activities of other teachers.

• Requiring that teachers earn a bachelor's degree in the arts and sciences before entering the professional study of teaching.

• Developing a new professional curriculum in graduate schools of education leading to a master's degree.

• Mobilizing the nation's resources to prepare minorities for teaching careers.

• Linking student performance to teacher compensation, and providing schools with the technology, services, and staff necessary for teacher productivity.

• Making teachers' salaries competitive with those in other professions.

The essence of *A Nation Prepared* was that reform begins at home—schools must be restructured to permit teachers and principals to shape and manage them at the local level. Governors, legislatures, and district superintendents, for their part, need to remove regulatory restraints to allow for experimentation and change.

A year after the release of *A Nation Prepared*, there were notable examples across the country that its ideas were taking root and its recommendations were being incorporated into state legislation and school district policy.

A school-reform bill in Massachusetts, for example, was closely modeled on the proposals laid out in *A Nation Prepared*. And in Rochester, N.Y., the superintendent of schools and the president of the local teachers' union painstakingly negotiated a radical three-year contract based on the spirit and recommendations of the Carnegie report.

The Rochester agreement gained national attention and signaled that teachers' unions were ready

Parents Choosing Schools

In his first major speech on education after winning the Presidency, George Bush last January strongly endorsed one of the most controversial issues of the school-reform movement: the right of parents to choose the schools their children attend.

Last year, Minnesota became the first state in the nation to enact a comprehensive open-enrollment plan. Since then, the parental-choice wave has rolled across the country. By last count, some 24 states had adopted some form of choice, or had created task forces or advisory groups to consider such proposals. The Minnesota law allows parents to enroll their children in virtually any public school district in the state. Some 3,700 students asked to tranfer this fall to a new district. Students who transfer take with them roughly $3,300 each in state aid.

Some proponents of choice argue that the most effective way to goad schools into raising quality is to create a free-market situation in which they will have to compete for students. Others contend that choice will promote a diversity of teaching styles and curricular offerings.

"When you make parents actual consumers, you wind up changing the relationship between school districts and parents," says Larry Murphy, chairman of the education committee in the Iowa Senate. "You force the districts to respond to parents' concerns and offer programs that parents want, or they can leave your district."

But others are concerned that the poorest schools (which usually enroll the neediest students) will not be able to compete and will only get worse. "It is naive to believe that a pure market will have the desired effect," says Charles Glenn, who drafted a choice plan for Massachusetts. "Schools are not like other commodities," he adds. "You must have interventions to ensure equity and equality."

The debate over choice is likely to intensify during this year's state legislative sessions. The issue may divide educators, policymakers, and education lobbying groups more than any other reform question.

Even the nation's two largest teachers' unions are on opposite sides of the issue. The National Education Association this summer voted to oppose all state and federally mandated choice plans.

"Choice fosters withdrawal from problems in a neighborhood school, rather than trying to find the answers to them," argues Ed Foglia, president of the California affiliate of the NEA, which is leading the fight against choice proposals in that state.

The American Federation of Teachers, on the other hand, believes that parental choice complements other reforms such as school-based management. Says Albert Shanker, president of the AFT, "School people who view school-based management and shared decisionmaking as their first real opportunity to make some real changes in their schools should be prepared to give parents their first real opportunity to choose their children's school."

Adds Joe Nathan, a former teacher who is now a consultant to several states on choice plans: "The movement for more options among public schools is intended to—and is—expanding opportunities for educators as well as families and students."

to negotiate for school improvement as well as the traditional bread and butter issues. Similar contracts have been forged in cities such as Boston, Cincinnati, Los Angeles, Miami, and Pittsburgh.

The 1980's have probably brought more ferment, more attention, and more change to American education than any other decade in history. But has the school-reform movement really improved schooling in the United States?

There is no shortage of skeptics—including some teachers. According to a survey of 13,500 teachers conducted last year by Ernest Boyer and the Carnegie Foundation for the Advancement of Teaching, the school-reform movement deserved a C. One in five teachers gave it a D or F, and nearly half the teachers believed that morale within the profession had substantially declined since 1983. "We are troubled that the nation's teachers remain so skeptical," wrote Boyer. "Why is it that teachers, of all people, are demoralized and largely unimpressed by the reform actions taken?"

More recently, U.S. Secretary of Education Lauro Cavazos was equally critical in a news conference last spring asserting that the nation's educational performance is "stagnant." "The good news is that the schools are not worse; the bad news is that we are not making progress," Cavazos said. "We are standing still, and the problem is that it's been this way for three years in a row."

Some reform-watchers, however, take a longer view. "I don't think we've gotten to the heart of the problem yet," Theodore Sizer has said. "We're still talking about testing everybody and putting the screws on the existing system even more. The problem *is* the existing system. And until we face up to that unpleasant fact—that the existing system has to change—we're not going to get the kinds of changes that everybody wants."

Just as there is no consensus among reformers and reform-watchers about the accomplishments of the 1980's, there is no consensus about what the 1990's hold for the movement to improve schools. But there is unanimous agreement that the stakes are high—indeed, that perhaps more than ever before America's future is directly linked to the success of its educational system, and that teachers are the key to that success. "What is urgently needed—in the next phase of school reform—is a deep commitment to make teachers partners in renewal, at all levels," says Boyer. "It's time to recognize that whatever is wrong with America's public schools cannot be fixed without the help of those already in the classroom."

Forging A Profession

A new national board defines good teaching and sets prerequisites for certification

For the first time in history, a national body with a teacher majority has defined what every classroom teacher should know and be able to do.

In a few years, teachers who meet this standard may earn higher pay and have greater authority and autonomy on the job. At least that is the hope of the National Board for Professional Teaching Standards, the group that crafted the definition in its effort to forge a national system to certify teachers.

The national board's goal is ambitious: to raise the status of teaching to that of other professions, such as accounting, architecture, and medicine. Many argue that this effort is critical to the future of American education, that dramatic improvements in the nation's schools will only occur through the "professionalization of teaching."

The board has spent two years drawing up the definition of good teaching, and will now spend three more years developing the assessments that teachers will be required to pass to become professionally certified. If it begins to certify teachers in 1993 as planned, the board will have virtually raced from concept to completion.

"Other professions, such as medicine and law, took decades to set their standards," said James Kelly, president of the board. "Our board will attempt to compress this arduous process into one-half of one decade, because we want to influence the quality of the enormous influx of new teachers needed during the 1990's."

Kelly spoke in July at a national forum held near Chicago, where the board released a report outlining the policies that will guide its work. Although general in scope, the document details the mix of skills, knowledge, personal traits, and beliefs that will characterize board-certified teachers. **(See excerpt, next page.)**

The 63-member board plans to create assessments and offer credentials in 29 fields, ranging from early childhood education to vocational education. The fields are clustered under five age-group categories. Within two of those categories, teachers will receive general credentials; within the others, teachers may choose a subject-**area specialty. (See box, last page.)**

All teachers who hold a bachelor's degree from an accredited institution and have successfully completed three years of teaching at one or more elementary or secondary schools will be eligible for national certification.

The creation of the national board was the key recommendation of *A Nation Prepared: Teachers for the 21st Century*, the widely publicized report by the Carnegie Forum on Education and the Economy. The report presented an intricate plan for improving the nation's schools, which hinged on raising the status and authority of teachers. The forum established the board in May 1987, a year after the report's release. Since that time, it has been forging a national certification process for teachers.

Traditionally, teachers have been subject to examinations only for state licensing, which is often mistakenly referred to as certification. A license guarantees the public that a teacher has met a minimum standard of competency set by the state. Board certification, on the other hand, would indicate that a given teacher is an accomplished educator who has met a high set of standards. It will be voluntary and is seen as complementing, not replacing, state licensing.

"For once in this country, we are working out standards for measuring excellence rather than minimum competency," said James Hunt Jr., the former governor of North Carolina and chairman of the board. "The certification process has the potential to transform the current educational system, leverage current investment in teaching, and build a national consensus for increased support of schools."

But before any of that can happen, the board must finish raising approximately $50 million to support its research and the creation of new teacher assessments. To date, it has raised $1.6 million from a corporate fund-raising drive. In addition, the Carnegie Corporation of New York has pledged $5 million during the board's first five years. Proposed legislation that would give the board $25 million in federal aid was still pending in the Congress in late summer.

Even more important, the board's standards and assessments must gain widespread recognition and acceptance among the public and educators, so that teachers will view national certification as something worth pursuing. Participants at the meeting near Chicago frequently raised the question of what incentives teachers will have for becoming board certified.

The board hopes that national certi-

From *Teacher Magazine*, September/October 1989, pp. 12-13, 16. Reprinted by permission of the National Board for Professional Teaching Standards, Detroit, MI.

What Teachers Should Know And Be Able To Do

Following are excerpts from Toward High and Rigorous Standards for the Teaching Profession, *a report issued by the National Board for Professional Teaching Standards:*

The National Board for Professional Teaching Standards seeks to identify and recognize teachers who effectively enhance student learning and demonstrate the high level of knowledge, skills, dispositions, and commitments reflected in the five following core propositions.

1. Teachers are committed to students and their learning.

Board-certified teachers are dedicated to making knowledge accessible to all students. They act on the belief that all students can learn. They treat students equitably, recognizing the individual differences that distinguish their students one from the other and taking account of these differences in their practice. They adjust their practice, as appropriate, based on observation and knowledge of their students' interests, abilities, skills, knowledge, family circumstances, and peer relationships.

Accomplished teachers understand how students develop and learn. They incorporate the prevailing theories of cognition and intelligence in their practice. They are aware of the influence of context and culture on behavior. They develop students' cognitive capacity and their respect for learning. Equally important, they foster students' self-esteem, motivation, character, civic responsibility, and their respect for individual, cultural, religious, and racial differences.

2. Teachers know the subjects they teach and how to teach those subjects to students.

Board-certified teachers have a rich understanding of the subject(s) they teach and appreciate how knowledge in their subject is created, organized, linked to other disciplines, and applied to real world settings. While faithfully representing the collective wisdom of our culture and upholding the value of disciplinary knowledge, they also develop the critical and analytical capacities of their students. Accomplished teachers command specialized knowledge of how to convey and reveal subject matter to students. They are aware of the preconceptions and background knowledge that students typically bring to each subject and of strategies and instructional materials that can be of assistance. They understand where difficulties are likely to arise and modify their practice accordingly. Their instructional repertoire allows them to create multiple paths to the subjects they teach, and they are adept at teaching students how to pose and solve their own problems.

3. Teachers are responsible for managing and monitoring student learning.

Board-certified teachers create, enrich, maintain, and alter instructional settings to capture and sustain the interest of their students and to make the most effective use of time. They are also adept at engaging students and adults to assist their teaching and at enlisting their colleagues' knowledge and expertise to complement their own.

Accomplished teachers command a range of generic instructional techniques, know when each is appropriate, and can implement them as needed. They are as aware of ineffectual or damaging practice as they are devoted to elegant practice.

They know how to engage groups of students to ensure a disciplined learning environment, and how to organize instruction to allow the school's goals for students to be met. They are adept at setting norms for social interaction among students and between students and teachers. They understand how to motivate students to learn and how to maintain their interest even in the face of temporary failure.

Board-certified teachers can assess the progress of individual students as well as that of the class as a whole. They employ multiple methods for measuring student growth and understanding and can clearly explain student performance to parents.

4. Teachers think systematically about their practice and learn from experience.

Board-certified teachers are models of educated persons, exemplifying the virtues they seek to inspire in students—curiosity, tolerance, honesty, fairness, respect for diversity, and appreciation of cultural differences—and the capacities that are prerequisites for intellectual growth: the ability to reason and take multiple perspectives, to be creative and take risks, and to adopt an experimental and problem solving orientation.

Accomplished teachers draw on their knowledge of human development, subject matter, and instruction, and their understanding of their students to make principled judgments about sound practice. Their decisions are not only grounded in the literature, but also in their experience. They engage in lifelong learning which they seek to encourage in their students. Striving to strengthen their teaching, board-certified teachers critically examine their practice, seek to expand their repertoire, deepen their knowledge, sharpen their judgment, and adapt their teaching to new findings, ideas, and theories.

5. Teachers are members of learning communities.

Board-certified teachers contribute to the effectiveness of the school by working collaboratively with other professionals on instructional policy, curriculum development, and staff development. They can evaluate school progress and the allocation of school resources in light of their understanding of state and local educational objectives. They are knowledgeable about specialized school and community resources that can be engaged for their students' benefit, and are skilled at employing such resources as needed.

Accomplished teachers find ways to work collaboratively and creatively with parents, engaging them productively in the work of the school.

Fields Of Certification

The National Board for Professional Teaching Standards plans to develop certificates in the 29 fields listed below. Each certificate will reflect the knowledge and skills that all teachers should possess, the knowledge particular to the developmental level of the teacher's students, and the teacher's content and discipline-area knowledge.

Early Childhood (prekindergarten-grade 3)

Early and Middle Childhood (grades K-6)

Middle Childhood and Early Adolescence (grades 4-9)
Generalist
English
Language
Arts
Mathematics
Science
Social Studies and History

Adolescence and Young Adulthood (grades K-12)
English
Mathematics
Science
Social Studies and History
Vocational Education: Agriculture, Business, Health Occupations, Home Economics, Industry/Technology

Early Childhood through Young Adulthood (grades K-12)
Art
Foreign Language: Spanish, French, Others, Limited-English-Proficient Students
Music
Physical Education/Health
Special Education and Exceptional-Need Students: Moderately Handicapped, Severely and Profoundly Handicapped, Speech Impaired, Hard of Hearing and Deaf, Visually Handicapped, Deaf and Blind, Gifted and Talented

fication may lead to better salaries and more responsibility for teachers. But its report notes that such decisions will be up to individual school districts.

"Unless board certification really means something, I'm not sure teachers will find it worth their while to subject themselves to what is likely to be an anxiety-ridden process," said Joan-Marie Shelley, president of the San Francisco affiliate of the American Federation of Teachers.

But others cautioned against underestimating the teaching force's longing for professional recognition. "National certification will build self-esteem," said New Jersey Gov. Thomas Kean. The governor, who is a board member, said he thinks national certification will "give teachers the power" to improve the quality of their schools.

Now that the board has identified the fields in which it will offer certification, established prerequisites for who can become board certified, and issued its statement of what teachers should know and be able to do, the first phase of its work is done. But the most critical task lies ahead: the development of assessments that will be used to evaluate teachers.

"The actual development of valid and acceptable assessment products will be the most original, costly, and demanding facets of the national board agenda," the report states.

For the certification process to succeed, it notes, these assessments must be "professionally credible, publicly acceptable, legally defensible, administratively feasible, and economically affordable." The board expects them to measure those aspects of teaching that contribute significantly to student learning, and to assess the capacity of teachers to integrate knowledge from several sources and make sound decisions.

To achieve this, the board says it will design an assessment process unlike any teacher examination currently in use. The board expects it to include written essays, multiple-choice tests, portfolios, interviews, samples of student achievement, and classroom observations.

On top of its research and development work, the board intends to support three broad education-reform issues: creating a more effective environment for teaching and learning in schools; increasing the supply of high-quality entrants into the profession, with a special emphasis on minorities; and improving teacher education and continued professional development.

On this last front, the board hopes its rigorous standards for certification will eventually lead to better preparation programs for teachers. Its decision not to require candidates for certification to have graduated from a teacher-training program rankled members of the teacher-education community. They had hoped that graduation from a school of education would be a prerequisite for the board's credential.

Still, those at the Chicago forum expressed the belief that colleges and universities would respond to the professional standards set forth by the board. "It would be anti-professional for the schools of education not to be aiming toward those standards," said Richard Kunkle, executive director of the National Council for Accreditation of Teacher Education, the organization that certifies teacher preparation programs in the nation's colleges and universities.

Rift Over Teacher-Certification Rules Seen Impeding Reform Movement

Education-college group opposes policy of new national board

Beverly T. Watkins

Some teacher educators have objected to the American Association of Colleges for Teacher Education's public opposition to a new certification policy adopted last summer by the National Board for Professional Teaching Standards.

They are concerned that the action, taken by a unanimous vote of the association's directors, may create a rift between teacher educators and the national board that would impede efforts to improve the education profession.

"The A.A.C.T.E. vote does not spell the end of the national board, but it doesn't do anything to cement relations between the two groups, either," said Arthur E. Wise, director of the Rand Corporations' Center for the Study of the Teaching Profession.

Although the association's opposition is not likely to have "major consequences" in the long run, said John R. Palmer, dean of education at the University of Wisconsin at Madison, "it probably does make the effort to improve the quality of teachers and the effectiveness of the schools a bit more difficult."

Prerequisites Termed 'Too Broad'

The directors of the association, which represents more than 700 colleges and universities with teacher-education programs, decided last month not to support the national board's policy on requirements for candidates seeking certification. The association called the prerequisites—a baccalaureate degree in any subject from an accredited institution and three years of teaching experience—"too broad, loosely defined, and permissive" to advance the profession.

The group said that voluntary certification should be linked to the profession's "long-established quality controls," such as graduation from a state-approved teacher-education program, state licensure of graduates, and professional program accreditation.

James A. Kelly, president of the national board, defended its certification requirements, which are part of a broad policy statement that was issued in July.

"The policy on certification was unanimously adopted by the board," he said. "The prerequisites were not a matter of great controversy when the board was developing its policies."

"The policy has not been criticized by the teacher educators on the board," he added.

In chastising the national board for ignoring teacher education, accreditation, and licensing, said Mr. Kelly, "the A.A.C.T.E. is not by any means speaking for the teacher-education community."

Concurrent with the A.A.C.T.E.'s action, the National Council for Accreditation of Teacher Education said it would not take a position on the policy.

"As a professional," said Richard C. Kunkel, the council's executive director, "I am disappointed that the board would look to regional accreditation, which includes the whole university, rather than to professional accreditation of teacher education."

However, he said, "our posture is not to fight about the prerequisites, but to watch how the board develops its standards."

"We're not getting in the middle of the battle," he added.

The council, which accredits 520 of the nation's 1,300 education schools, established a committee to follow the national standards board's activities.

The national board, created in 1987, is developing what will be the first professional-certification process for school teachers. The new credential is intended to be the educational equivalent of certification for other professionals, such as accountants, architects, lawyers, and physicians, attesting to accomplished practice.

Standards Being Developed

The board released its policies in a report called "Toward High and Rigorous Standards for the Teaching Profession." The panel, which includes four teacher educators and three other academics among its 64 members, is now developing standards in various fields and assessment procedures to evaluate teachers.

It expects to issue its first certificates in 1993.

By establishing just two prerequisites—a baccalaureate and three years' teaching experience—for completing the assessment process, the board took the position that certification should be open to as many teachers as possible.

Teacher educators have estimated that about 2 million of the nation's 2.5 million schoolteachers will be eligible to undergo assessment under the board's prerequisites.

A candidate who satisfies the two requirements will already have met some state licensing and accreditation requirements, the board said.

From *The Chronicle of Higher Education*, October 18, 1989, pp. A19, 22, 23. Copyright © 1989, The Chronicle of Higher Education. Reprinted with permission.

3. STRIVING FOR EXCELLENCE

'A Perplexing Requirement'

"As a practical matter," said Mr. Kelly, providing an example, "finishing three years of teaching means that you were employed somewhere. To be employed, you had to meet a state's requirements for teachers."

When it was developing its certification policy, the national board considered requiring licensing and accreditation as prerequisites, said Mr. Kelly. However, the board found so many different opinions among educators and state officials about those requirements that it decided against asking for them.

For example, said Mr. Kelly, accreditation would be "a perplexing requirement," because teacher-education programs at some highly regarded institutions are not professionally accredited.

"Wisconsin is not N.C.A.T.E. accredited. Harvard is not N.C.A.T.E. accredited," he said. Would the board then "prohibit graduates from such institutions from ever becoming certified just because they have not graduated from an N.C.A.T.E. institution?"

Educators who are concerned about the teaching profession hold different opinions about the national board's requirements.

Russell Edgerton, president of the American Association for Higher Education and director of his organization's Presidents' Forum on Teaching as a Profession, said, "It was not an easy call, but the board came down on the right side."

With teacher-education programs in flux and the board's assessments not in use yet, he said, "it's wisest to stay agnostic as to where people come from."

Frank B. Murray, dean of education at the University of Delaware, said the board had made a mistake by not having more requirements and "a phase-in period."

Accommodating everyone now "is the right thing to do," he said, "but in 10 years, we want to be a profession."

Ignoring accreditation, licensing, and teacher education "will not strengthen the profession," said Mr. Murray, who is also co-director of Project 30, a national program to reform the teacher-education curriculum.

"The national board's stance is that you can learn to be a teacher on your own," said Rand's Mr. Wise. "In virtually every other field, you must complete a program in an accredited professional school before you sit for a board examination."

Adding Intellectual Content

If it follows other professions, said Mr. Wise, "the board ultimately will be obliged and will want to recognize the importance of professional preparation."

"As it develops standards and the assessment process, it will be incorporating intellectual content," he continued. "People will find it easier to go to professional school to acquire that knowledge."

In the short run, said Mr. Wise, "the national board is stuck with what it has said."

'We Do Not Go to Mars'

"But it is not up and running yet, so that policy has no effect," he added.

The national board's president has not closed the door to future change.

"I would expect to reconsider policy from time to time," said Mr. Kelly. "We talk to our friends in the teacher-education community regularly. We do not go to Mars in search of advice."

TEACHER PREPARATION
SHOULD IT BE CHANGED?

WILLIS D. HAWLEY

Mr. Hawley is a professor of education and political science at Vanderbilt University.

As the attacks on teacher education have increased, one reform strategy seems to have gained the most adherents: the proposal to require teacher candidates to have at least five years of preservice education rather than the four now typically needed for certification. The five-year teacher preparation movement, which encompasses many programmatic variations, has powerful proponents. Among them are a special task force of the American Association of Colleges of Teacher Education (AACTE), the majority of the members of the National Commission on Excellence in Teacher Education, and the Carnegie Forum on Education and the Economy. The Holmes Group, which includes the deans of schools of education at most of the nation's research universities, publicly calls for would-be teachers to complete five years of college and an internship before teaching full-time. Many leading schools of education (such as those at the University of Chicago and Stanford University, and Teachers College, Columbia University) now offer teacher training opportunities only at the postbaccalaureate level.

Remarkably, this movement to increase the years of preservice education for prospective teachers has been proceeding apace without serious opposition, despite the probability that it could decrease both the number and the quality of teacher candidates at a time when we expect a severe teacher shortage. Moreover, there is no evidence that extended preparation programs make beginning teachers more effective.

One reason that extended programs have not been subject to more criticism is that they come in so many shapes and sizes. Here, I am concerned with any strategy that requires students to take a minimum of five years of college-based coursework (which could include practice teaching) before they are allowed to teach at full salary.

The case for extended teacher preparation programs rests fundamentally on criticisms of undergraduate programs rather than on documented benefits for postbaccalaureate preservice teacher education. Among the attacks on undergraduate programs that appear most to influence demands for this proposed reform are the following:

- Education courses often lack intellectual rigor.
- Teacher education faculty are not as well prepared academically as other university faculty—they are neither up-to-date practitioners nor scholars in their fields.
- There is too much to know about teaching to be learned in four years of college, given the other things students must learn in order to be well-educated professionals.
- The relatively low status of teaching is the product, at least in part, of the fact that the preparation for many other professions begins in earnest after students have a bachelor's degree (law and medicine are usually cited as examples).
- It is difficult to prepare teachers to be practitioners in undergraduate colleges that do not

recognize the importance of career-related education.

If, for the sake of expediency, one were to grant each of these problems with undergraduate teacher preparation, would it follow that more preservice education is an effective solution? On the face of it, extended programs do not address the first two criticisms at all and are likely to be ineffective or very limited responses to the others.

Strategies for improving teacher education are not limited to incremental changes in conventional four-year programs and the adoption of extended programs. There are at least two other general alternatives: basic reforms of undergraduate programs and more radical reforms involving the sharing of the responsibility for teacher preparation with the teaching profession. While the evidence on teaching effectiveness continues to grow, knowledge about how teachers become effective is in short supply. For this reason, and because all proposals for teacher education reform are problematic, this is the time for experimentation and research. In short, it is premature to settle on one best way to prepare teachers, especially when the new model being advocated most aggressively has high costs and uncertain outcomes.

Much of the debate over four- versus five-year teacher preparation programs consists of unsubstantiated claims and assumptions. To some extent, speculation about the probable impact of future policies is inevitable, but it is possible in this case to be more analytical about the costs and consequences of teacher education improvement strategies than we have been thus far.

The problem in making policy is to choose the most cost-effective strategy that can be widely implemented. If the ultimate goal of teacher education reform is to enhance the learning of elementary and secondary school students, the problem faced by policymakers—in government and in institutions of higher education—who are considering the mandating or funding of extended programs is to determine not only whether to invest in one or more promising strategies for improving teacher education but to decide whether such an involvement of money and energy seems to be among the most promising ways to enhance student learning in schools.

RISKS OF EXTENDED PROGRAMS

There are two types of risks that would be incurred if extended programs were required of all teacher candidates: (1) the costs of becoming a teacher would increase and, absent significant improvements in teacher compensation and working conditions, the quality and quantity of candidates in the applicant pool would decline; (2) the costs of implementing extended programs would deny resources to other, more productive educational reforms.

In calculating public and individual costs, I am assuming that new policies would become effective in 1990. All estimates, therefore, use the latest data available and extrapolate recent trends to arrive at the 1990 estimates.

The cost of a five-year teacher preparation program to individuals is of two types. First, the cost of tuition and fees. In the 1990–91 academic year, these annual costs will be about $2,000 at four-year public colleges and universities. The tuition cost to students of adding a fifth year at private colleges and universities is four to five times this amount.

A second type of cost to individuals is earnings foregone. Let us assume that first-year teachers will earn salaries and fringe benefits worth about $21,500. Thus, requiring a fifth year of collegiate education prior to entry into the profession will increase the overall cost of becoming a teacher by $23,500 for the average individual at a public college or university. The costs would be much higher for students attending private institutions.

These are substantial costs to add to the current cost individuals must pay to become a teacher, much higher costs than those alluded to by advocates of five-year programs. The advocates of five-year preservice teacher preparation recognize that there are costs, but they seldom count earnings foregone and, when they do, they often argue that, over time, the five-year teacher will make up the amount by higher salaries. This second argument has two parts. First, it is asserted that the fifth year of study will qualify individuals for a higher place on the salary scale than the bachelor's-degree-only teacher, so that the money lost will be earned back in a short time. But this is not the case. Typically, a master's degree would add about $1,600 to a teacher's annual earnings. While not all five-year programs would lead to a master's degree, let us make that assumption to give the argument for five-year programs the benefit of the doubt.

Second, assuming that the four-year teacher begins to pursue a master's degree in year two of service and completes the degree in three years, going to school part-time, the four-year teacher would "catch up" with the five-year teacher over a period in which the net income advantage of the five-year teacher was about $6,400. But the five-year teacher "lost" more than $21,500 in earnings foregone during the extra year he or she was in college.

These estimates make the unlikely assumption that the individual would not have to borrow money to pursue a fifth year of study. With a 9 percent interest rate on a $5,000 student loan, the five-year teacher will pay about

COSTS

$2,500 in interest over a five-year repayment period.

Arguments that some of the $26,000 of additional costs of becoming a teacher can be amortized over time may be unpersuasive to teacher candidates, many of whom are not sure they want to teach for a very long time. Moreover, if you do not have the $26,000 to invest, the idea that there is a reasonable return on investment (an incorrect assumption in any case) is irrelevant. Historically, teaching has drawn its candidates from those college students least likely to be able to make such an investment.

If we increase the costs of becoming a teacher, the attractiveness of the profession will decline unless these costs are offset by benefits, intrinsic and extrinsic, not now available. Those who will drop out of the pool will come disproportionately from the ranks of those who are brightest, have the best interpersonal skills, are the most imaginative, and for other reasons have broader career options. This proposition is a fundamental assumption made by labor economists and is akin to the idea that we cannot expect to increase the quality of our teachers unless we raise teachers' salaries significantly, an argument often made by advocates of extended programs.

There are those who argue that since teachers are not motivated by money, those who now teach will not take these new costs into account. But the market is now in equilibrium in this regard; that is, we attract those students whose altruism leads them to discount economic benefits. If we raise the economic costs, we shall have to raise the intrinsic rewards teachers get from teaching or a decline in the quality and quantity of teacher candidates will result. Extended programs do not alter the intrinsic rewards of teaching. If we did increase the benefits of being a teacher, without increasing the costs of becoming a teacher, we could enhance the quality of the applicant pool. This reality is evident in the recent increases in numbers and quality of teacher candidates that follow nonincremental increases in teacher salaries.

It would be possible for the public to subsidize the individual's costs of becoming a teacher so that extended programs would not decrease the quality and size of the teacher candidate pool, but let us draw attention to two reasons other than the economic one given that eliminating undergraduate teacher preparation programs, as many proponents of extended teacher preparation advocate, is likely to decrease the quality and quantity of those entering the teaching force. First, national studies demonstrate that college students become increasingly materialistic and concerned with their own welfare as they progress through their undergrad-

TRADE-OFFS

uate studies. It can reasonably be argued that undergraduate teacher education programs can attract idealistic students to the profession by providing them with early opportunities to experience the intrinsic rewards of teaching, have the support of likeminded peers, and be socialized by their professors. Ralph Tyler, in the 1985 *Phi Delta Kappan*, reminded us that there is much to learn from the past in this regard. Tyler draws attention, for example, to the findings of the Commission on Teacher Education, which concluded in its 1944 report that attracting altruistic and able youngsters into teaching was significantly fostered by providing freshmen and sophomores with opportunities to be involved in classrooms from the time they entered college. Experiences with teacher education early in college can also provide students who are really not interested in or suited to teaching with opportunities to change directions at relatively low cost—often at no cost. (The majority of youngsters who say they want to teach, at age eighteen, do not complete a teacher preparation program.) The person who completes the fifth year of studies in preparing to teach who then changes her or his mind, or is found to be unqualified, will have made a big investment for which there is no direct return. (Thirty percent or so of those who complete teacher preparation programs choose not to teach, although this percentage could decline if entry costs were higher.)

Another likely consequence of eliminating teacher certification for persons who do not have a year of postbaccalaureate study will be a substantial reduction in the role now played by liberal arts colleges in the preparation of teachers. One recent study of private institutions in Ohio, by F. R. Cyphert and K. A. Ryan in the 1984 *Action in Teacher Education*, found that only one-third were certain that they would continue to prepare teachers if five-year programs were mandated in that state. It is not clear what the overall impact of this will be on the quality of teacher preparation because the ability of such schools to offer a full and up-to-date curriculum in education varies widely. But it is virtually certain that the number of young teachers educated at selective and high quality colleges such as Swarthmore, Dartmouth, Oberlin, and the University of the South (Sewanee) will decline because such students will be less likely than those with fewer options to explore a teaching career. The same point seems applicable to universities that do not have schools of education but now offer programs of undergraduate teacher certification. Such universities include Brown, Emory, Rice, Tulane, and Washington at St. Louis. This means that the role played by private colleges and universities in the education of the nation's teachers will decline. Aside from the practical consequences of pushing such high-status colleges and universities out of the teacher education business, the symbolic importance of their involvement in the preparation of teachers should not be overlooked. It is not inconsequential that Harvard has recently returned to the business of undergraduate teacher preparation, even though very few teachers will be Harvard graduates.

Some advocates of extended teacher preparation are aware that such programs are likely to have a negative effect on the size and quality of the teaching force. This recognition has led some would-be reformers to the advocacy of significant governmental subsidies for extended programs. How much would it cost to maintain the quality of the teacher candidate pool? Conventional economic analysis would say that we would need to eliminate the added costs of entry to retain the same quality of entrant. If one follows this logic, and if one accepts the National Center for Education Statistics (NCES) estimates that we could require as many as 170,000 new teachers a year in the mid-1990s, the annual costs of subsidies for extended programs to the taxpayers would be over $5 billion.

If subsidies are paid by states, this will place a particular constraint on the teacher labor market because, as is now the case for financial incentive programs for math and science teachers, beneficiaries will almost certainly have to teach in the state providing the funding. This, in turn, will discourage competition for teachers across states reducing the pressure for higher teacher salaries. In times of teacher shortages, interstate competition for teachers is a powerful impetus to increased teacher salaries, as the current pattern of changes in teacher compensation in the southern states indicates.

Whether government subsidies are available or not, extended programs will increase the costs to the taxpayers. Requiring students to attend college for five rather than four years means that we shall require that 25 percent more services must be provided in the form of courses, facilities, and student services. This cost will be reduced in the short run to the extent that students fill out their additional year by attending courses and using facilities that would otherwise be underutilized. In the long run, savings in the public's cost for higher education that could be obtained as a result of the decline of the college-age population would be lost because fifth-year teacher candidates would take up space that could otherwise be used, faculty would be kept on who would not otherwise be needed, and institutions of higher education would be discouraged from seeking new markets—some of which might not be as highly subsidized as is upper-division undergraduate education.

James B. Conant, in his criticism of extended teacher preparation, in *The Education of American Teachers*, focused, in part, on the utility to society of this investment: "The issue between four-year and five-year continuous programs turns on the value one attaches to free electives. And if a parent feels that an extra year to enable the future teacher to wander about and sample academic courses is worth the cost, I should not be the person to condemn this use of money. But, I would, as a taxpayer, vigorously protest the use of tax money for a fifth year of what I consider dubious value."

Data that would allow a good estimate of the cost to the taxpayer, not counting the costs of aforementioned subsidies to individuals, are not available. One can conservatively estimate the average publicly subsidized cost of one year of college for each student who graduates from teacher-education programs to be approximately $5,250. If we take into account the role of private colleges and universities, which would diminish substantially if the costs of re-entry teacher education were significantly increased, the preparation of teachers would cost the taxpayers about $850 million more than if all teachers entered the profession after four years of college. (There would be a proportional cost to private colleges and universities.) If the fifth year counted toward a master's degree, then taxpayers would pay higher teacher salaries for beginning teachers and this cost would be about $6,400 per teacher. Add another billion dollars a year.

If we were to add the institutional costs of extended programs at public colleges and universities, the costs we would have to add to maintain the quality and size of the teacher candidate pool (recogninizing that most observers feel the pool is now inadequate), and the increased salary costs, the annual cost of implementing extended teacher programs nationwide could be close to $7 billion.

The number and assumptions upon which these calculations rest are not beyond question. But if extended programs were not to result in a decline in the quality and quantity of teacher candidates, there seems to be little doubt that the cost would comprise a very sizable share of the funds available for educational improvement. Does anyone believe the society will make a multibillion-dollar investment in preservice teacher education? Does anyone really believe that it should, given that these funds might be used to increase teacher salaries, or improve the skills of those already teaching, or reduce class sizes for children with special needs?

WHAT WILL WE GAIN?

If we recognize that there are considerable

risks and high costs to requiring that teachers have five years of college before they teach, we should expect advocates of extended programs to make a persuasive case that the change they propose will significantly improve the quality of teaching. No evidence to this effect has yet been offered. The proponents of extended programs assert that teachers so prepared will be more knowledgeable and skillful. This argument appears to rest on one or more of the following assumptions about extended programs: (1) there will be gains in the attractiveness of the profession; (2) students will learn more in extended programs about teaching and how to teach; (3) teachers trained in extended programs will be better prepared in their teaching fields; (4) taking more liberal arts courses will make students more effective teachers; (5) what students learn in college about teaching will be reflected in their classroom performance on the job. Let us briefly examine each of these assumptions.

Assumption 1 is that there will be gains in the attractiveness of the profession. Advocates of extended programs have argued that requiring teachers to have an additional year of schooling before they are allowed to teach will actually increase the quality of those entering the profession because extended programs will improve the status of the profession, which in turn will lead to an increase in teachers' salaries. Improved status and higher salaries will attract able students.

QUESTIONABLE ASSUMPTION

Generally speaking, earnings and educational attainment are not closely related once college graduation is assured, especially for women. One can only speculate about the public's willingness to pay teachers more competitive salaries because they have higher degrees. The current market differential for a master's degree is only about $1,600. Teacher salaries declined in the 1970s while increasing proportions of teachers earned master's degrees. (Indeed, teachers are twice as likely as other college graduates to have a master's degree). Moreover, public funds necessary to implement extended programs would diminish the resources available for teacher salary increases.

The salary and status arguments are interrelated. Does the requirement of more education for entry lead to higher status for a given profession? Advanced education is correlated with occupational prestige, but many jobs require no more than a college degree for entry and have higher status than does the job of school teaching, including engineering, journalism, and many jobs in business. Education is only one component of occupational prestige, and its contribution seems related, at least in part, to assumptions about the degree to which higher education separates the intellectually able from the less able and transmits knowl-edge and skills beyond the reach of most people. One reason teachers do not have higher status is that there are so many of them. About ten percent of all college graduates are needed each year to staff the schools.

The tenuous link between postbaccalaureate education and social status for teachers is nicely illustrated by looking at cultures different from our own. Japan, for example, probably accords its teachers higher status than does any other industrialized country. Yet fewer than 4 percent of Japanese teachers have a master's degree and almost all started to teach upon graduation from college or junior college. The relatively low status of teachers in the United States tells us more about the value we place on good teaching and public servants in general than it does about the relationship between social status and the years of college completed after one receives a bachelor's degree.

One way to test the argument that extended programs will lead to higher salaries and higher status is to look at what has happened in California, the one state that has required completion of a fifth year of college before would-be teachers can be fully certified. First, teachers' salaries in California have been similar to those in many nonsouthern states for several years. In 1985–86 beginning teachers' salaries in California took a nonincremental jump to go above the national average. To attribute this salary increase to a requirement that was established more than two decades ago would be wrong. It is much more reasonable to assume that the recent increase in teachers' salaries in California (not so remarkable when the cost of living is taken into account) is the result of concern over the quality and quantity of those who have chosen to teach in that state, given its fifth-year requirements. Many cities in California cannot fill open teacher positions; teaching candidates have ranked very near the bottom of thirty occupations with respect to measures of verbal and quantitative abilities; and close to one-third of the teachers statewide have been hired with temporary credentials because not enough students seek full certification before entry. In short, the lesson to be drawn from California's long experience with extended programs is that they do not increase the status or attractiveness of the teaching profession.

ARGUMENT TESTING

Assumption 2 is that students will learn more in extended programs about teaching and how to teach. A major argument for fifth-year programs is that teachers so educated will know more about teaching. There are two ways in which this might happen. First, teacher candidates might take more professional coursework. Second, teacher applicants in extended programs will take more sophisticated and more demanding courses.

3. STRIVING FOR EXCELLENCE

One-year postbaccalaureate certification programs generally limit students to fewer education courses than they might take in an undergraduate program. Students might be required to take undergraduate electives in preparation for the fifth year, but such requirements would further complicate entry to the profession because they would further extend the time required to prepare to teach for those who decide to teach after graduation from college or late in their college career.

If teachers' initial training in extended programs would result in a master's degree, the total amount of formal professional education the typical career teacher receives probably will be less than it is now. For example, the typical high school teacher certified upon graduation from college will have taken about sixty semester hours of professional coursework by the time he or she receives the master's degree. The person who receives the master's degree upon completion of a one-year postbaccalaureate training program will take half this much coursework. This argument will not be persuasive to those who discount the value of professional education courses, but such persons are presumably not among the advocates of five-year programs.

It might be argued that the "graduate" courses embodied in extended programs will be more intellectually demanding and thus students will learn more about how to teach. Graduate courses required of master's degree candidates in education are not known to be more demanding than undergraduate education courses. Why should they be? They will be taught by the same faculty members. So far as we know, twenty-two-year-olds are not better learners than twenty-one-year-olds. On the other hand, persons pursuing a master's degree or a fifth year of study are likely to be more productive learners if they actually have taught in classrooms because they can then use their experience to frame questions and to organize information. Good teaching involves an enormously complex and demanding set of intellectual tasks. Learning how to perform those tasks is likely to be easier if teachers have a clearer idea about what the process of teaching actually involves.

It seems difficult to argue, either on the basis of existing evidence or on logical grounds, that extended teacher education programs, in themselves, will improve what teachers know about teaching. It may be that extended programs requiring undergraduate education courses could provide teachers with more pedagogical knowledge than four-year programs that insist on a strong liberal arts curriculum and intensive study of the subjects or subject the student will teach. Whether this will make such teachers more effective is a different issue.

INTELLECTUAL RIGOR

Assumption 3 is that teachers trained in extended programs will be better prepared in their teaching fields. Extended programs requiring undergraduate education courses will not open up much room in the curriculum for subject-matter courses. To the extent that they do, or that postbaccalaurate-only programs do free up time for subject-matter courses, this will permit persons training to be elementary school teachers to take more math, science, English, or social studies courses. But extended programs should have little impact on the number of courses in their subject field that secondary teachers take. In most education schools, secondary teacher candidates already complete a disciplinary major or its equivalent.

The content of the courses they take is more important than the numbers, but this point is not relevant to the debate over the length of preservice teacher education. Moreover, there is reason to believe that the amount of coursework in the subject being taught does not contribute to effective teaching. This last point seems counterintuitive, but it may suggest that once one has ten or so courses in one's field, it is not the number of courses, but whether or not one understands fundamental principles and the structure of the discipline or body of knowledge involved. It seems doubtful that most undergraduate course sequences in any particular field produce these understandings among the students who take them. At most colleges and universities, especially those that educate the greatest number of teachers, undergraduate education seems to be something of a random walk during which course selection is often based on convenience and the desire for free time. As a recent report of the Association of American Colleges concludes, the typical curriculum "offers two much knowledge with too little attention to how knowledge has been created and what methods and styles of inquiry have led to its creation."

Assumption 4 is that taking more liberal arts courses will make students more effective teachers. Some advocates of extended programs, in particular those who argue that teacher preparation programs should begin after undergraduate education has been completed, believe that this reform will make teachers better educated and thus more effective.

Let us assume that undergraduate teacher candidates will take, in addition to the education-related courses they must pass to be certified (some of these are liberal arts courses, in most states), an academic major and satisfy general education or distribution (liberal arts) requirements. Thus most students seeking certification in secondary education will take about three-fourths of their courses outside of education departments and colleges. If no increases in the number of education courses ac-

LIBERAL ARTS

companied the implementation of extended programs, requiring five years of college for teacher preparation would mean that students would be freed to take eight to ten electives in lieu of education courses. There is absolutely no evidence that such a change would make students better teachers. The extent to which taking more liberal arts courses would improve teaching would seem to depend importantly on the difference between the intellectual content of the electives and the education courses a student would take. No doubt there are education courses that are undemanding and devoid of the concerns for theory and method of inquiry that characterize the best liberal arts courses, but many students seem to choose their electives on the basis of how undemanding they are. If it is true that many liberal arts courses are more rigorous than many education courses, this speaks to the need to change the content of education courses.

Assumption 5 is that what students learn in college about teaching will be reflected in their classroom performance on the job. The movement toward extended teacher education programs, at least among teacher educators, is motivated in large measure by the rapid growth in knowledge about effective instructional practices and teaching behaviors. The argument is that there is now more to know about how to teach effectively than ever before and that teachers should know this information and be able to use it before they enter the classroom. This argument assumes that what teacher candidates learn before they become teachers is often put to good use in the classroom. There is, however, reason to doubt this presumption. Recent research on how teachers learn to teach indicates that much of what teachers learn in the preservice stage of their career is undone or substantially mitigated during the first year or two of teaching and, perhaps, by the "practice teaching" experience. The implication of this reality is that increasing the amount of information and skills teachers learn in college is an inefficient—and perhaps futile—strategy unless ways are devised to enhance the ability of teachers to use what they have learned on the job. Some advocates of extended programs, such as the Holmes Group, have recognized this problem and have advocated the use of intensively supervised paid internships to facilitate induction to the profession. These internships, however, when added to the extended program, will significantly increase the costs of entry for individuals or the public costs of preparing new teachers.

In short, the possibility that extended programs will reduce the quality and quantity of teachers is high and the likelihood that they will improve teacher performance is not great. This does not mean that we should not experi-

RISKS

ment with extended teacher preparation programs but it does mean that such trials should be carefully evaluated. If the risks of extended programs seem high and the benefits uncertain, other strategies for improving teacher education should be explored more aggressively than they have been. Two such alternatives to both the status quo and the extended college-based programs are the reform of undergraduate programs and postbaccalaureate internships. These two strategies would complement each other and, taken together, would almost certainly be more cost-effective than extended programs.

IMPROVING TEACHER EDUCATION

The idea that five years of preservice education will enhance the quality of teaching is another manifestation of the propensity of social reformers to respond to weaknesses in political institutions by creating new structures rather than reforming the ones found to be inadequate. It is the American way of change but it usually is ineffective because it does not address fundamental problems.

Ideally, significant proposals to change undergraduate teacher preparation would address two conflicting beliefs held by different advocates of five-year programs. On the one hand, such reforms must address the concern of professional educators and education professors that the new teacher will have the knowledge and the skills necessary for effective teaching. On the other hand, they must respond to the belief that a substantial liberal arts undergraduate education is necessary if our teachers are to be well educated. The way out of this conundrum seems to have four stepping stones.

First, recognize that teachers cannot learn all or even most of what there is to know about effective teaching in one year or a year and a half of college. Acceptance of this proposition has important implications for how we structure the teaching profession. No teacher educator would disagree with this assertion, but many are unwilling to make the tough choices about what is to be learned and how. Moreover, the content and modes of instruction embodied in teacher education need to take into account the fact that what is known now will be replaced—in short order if recent history is any guide—with new, more powerful knowledge.

Second, prepare teachers to be learners on the job. If we adopt the view that preentry teacher education should focus on essential professional knowledge and skills, and we recognized that our knowledge about teacher effectiveness will change and inevitably be incomplete, we need to help prospective teachers to be good at learning and applying new information to the solution of the complex and varied problems most teachers confront. Learning on the job would be facilitated most significantly if teachers were better able to (1) manage their classrooms and the teaching-learning process, (2) use theory as a tool for learning and inventing, (3) engage in systematic inquiry about the complicated instructional problems with which they must deal, and (4) engage in collegial learning.

Third, make teacher education more intellectually rigorous. Much of the critique of teacher education is based on the assumption that it is less demanding academically than most other college or university courses of study. The validity of this assumption varies, but it seems all too true. The easy and well-traveled paths to academic rigor are tougher grading policies and increased requirements. More fundamental strategies include the incorporation of new research and significant theory in the curriculum, insistence that students be held to high expectations (in much the same way that good school teachers are taught to relate to their students), and attention to the development of student skills of critical inquiry and clarity of expression. All of these goals can best be achieved when they are pursued by all of an undergraduate's teachers.

Fourth, transfer the responsibility for initial on-the-job training to school systems. Outside the fields of medicine and education, colleges and universities typically do not provide significant preservice clinical or practical education to either undergraduate students or professional students. In teacher education programs, the so-called practice teaching experience often replaces three to five courses and, in general, does little—at best—to facilitate students' transfer of their course-based learning to effective use in the classroom. Eliminating practice teaching from the undergraduate curriculum could focus attention on the need for opportunities to apply knowledge in the context of specific courses. Some of this could take place in schools and much of it could be realistic and complex through the use of computer-driven, video-disk-supported problem-solving exercises.

Simply transferring the responsibility for clinical training to school systems would not facilitate the transfer of knowledge to the actual practice of teaching, but it seems doubtful that much of what the typical teacher now brings to his or her first full-time job would be lost. However, the burden on school systems and the desirability of linking what is taught in college to what is learned on the job suggest the need for a new mechanism for training teachers, such as an internship or what the Holmes Group calls a Professional Development Center.

There is growing agreement among researchers, teachers, and teacher educators that something must be done to make induction into the teaching profession a more rewarding experience so that teachers build upon rather than abandon what they learned in preservice education. Not only do the current forms of induction into teaching (including practice teaching) often result in unlearning of college-acquired knowledge and skills, they often result in a failure to experience fully the intrinsic rewards of teaching, so that new teachers are discouraged from persisting. Between 20 and 25 percent of new teachers leave teaching before they begin their third year. This high rate of attrition results in high costs to school systems, to taxpayers (who must pay for training replacements for the teacher dropouts), and to the children who must break-in the large number of new teachers that the nation's schools recruit each year.

RESPONSIBILITY TRANSFER

The problem of entry to teaching appears to be as great for students who graduate from extended programs as it is for those who enter teaching upon receipt of their baccalaureate degree. Thus, an absolutely essential aspect of any teacher-education reform program is the provision to teachers of significant support as they make the transition from college to independent responsibility for classroom teaching. Depending on how such support is provided, it would be feasible to transfer practice teaching—and perhaps specific methods courses— out of the undergraduate curriculum (or graduate curriculum, for that matter) and to make these part of the induction experience.

TEACHER INDUCTION

The way in which both college-based teacher preparation and teacher induction could be improved is through the establishment of teaching schools or Professional Development Centers (PDC's), which would provide teacher candidates with opportunities for clinical learning and practice that are significantly different from those now available to either education students or new teachers.

PDCs would be the joint responsibility of schools of education and school systems and would be staffed by faculty from both who were selected because of teaching abilities and their existing or potential expertise as teacher educators. PDCs, like teaching hospitals, would serve an array of clients (students) so that the elite laboratory school model for teaching training of the past would not be replicated.

Regular teachers who were especially selected and trained would teach classes, and teacher candidates would assist them, eventually taking full but supervised responsibility for teaching. Specific methods courses would be taught in the PDC during the first part of the academic year, and more advanced subjects would be taught later in the year, perhaps in module formats.

Not every school system would have a PDC. Access to state funds needed to support PDCs over and above the district's per-student expenditures would be competitive and provided on a per-student-teacher basis. In states with career ladder or mentor teacher plans, some teachers reaching the highest step could become teacher educators, so that already appropriated funds could be used to provide partial support for the programs. The PDCs would educate teachers for any school system just as colleges and universities do now. Reciprocal agreements among states could avoid restrictions on the labor markets for teachers. Public and private colleges and universities would be allowed to compete, in collaboration with school systems, for the resources necessary to administer a PDC.

STAFFING

In addition to the classroom teachers staffing the school, college and university faculty as well as senior master teachers would be assigned to the PDC. Classroom teachers could be rotated through the school and, as teacher candidates assumed more responsibility, would be freed to undertake research or other enrichment activities, include preparation for leadership roles in staff development throughout the school system. This is not the place to lay out the details of how a PDC would be organized and financed. It would surely cost more per teacher trained than four-year preparation programs; but it would cost less than extended programs. Whatever stipends were necessary to maintain or increase the quality of the pool of candidates would be no greater than those needed for extended programs—and might be less, since services would be provided to the school system involved.

Is this proposal not just another form of an extended program? Not really. It substantially alters the character of the learning-to-teach experience that teacher candidates now have in extended programs. In particular, a PDC would deal with the weakest characteristics of conventional teacher education, clinical training and induction to the profession. Extended programs by and large do not address these problems in satisfactory ways.

The training that a teacher received in a PDC should be seen as the beginning of a career throughout which there would be recurrent opportunities for professional growth, including graduate study. It seems reasonable to believe that teachers would benefit more from a graduate study after they have taught than before they entered the profession.

Neither the improvement of undergraduate teacher education nor the establishment of Professional Development Centers will ensure effective teaching, but they are, especially if implemented together, likely to be more cost-effective ways of improving the quality of teaching in our schools than are extended college- and university-based teacher preparation programs.

Extended programs will be very costly and their benefits uncertain. Moreover, they seem to dodge or implicitly deny some important criticisms of teacher education, including the lack of curricular rigor, the relative absence of scholarly credentials within the education professorate, and the problem of induction.

It may be that the more one accepts the "more is better" argument of extended-program advocates and the more one considers the implementation problems, the more one is likely to argue for even more extensive preservice programs. The Holmes Group, in wrestling with implementation problems facing extended programs and with the need to alter substantially both the intrinsic and the extrinsic rewards of being a teacher, seeks to resolve these problems by establishing two classes of teachers, one educated at major research universities for extended periods (preservice is just the beginning), and the other educated less rigorously and less extensively at other colleges and universities. In order to encourage the "best and brightest"—or some approximation thereof—to bear the costs of entry and to forgo other occupational options, the Holmes Group would provide access to more prestigious and higher paying roles only to graduates of programs like the ones it advocates. Differences in classes of teachers would, in effect, create an occupational caste system among teachers not unlike the physician-nurse or physician-technician distinctions in the medical professions. Initial eligibility for advanced professional status would be defined by academic ability not by teaching performance. The irony of all this is that the public and private flagship universities would likely lose any claim to a leadership role vis-à-vis those colleges and universities that would end up training the bulk of the nation's teachers.

REASONS FOR DOUBT

I may be overstating the negative consequences of extended programs. But reasons to doubt the contributions that extended programs will make to improved student learning are rooted in (1) current criticisms of teacher education, (2) the experience of California in prescribing five-year programs, (3) conventional assumptions about the relationship between increased costs of occupational entry and a decreased supply of academically able teacher candidates, and (4) sensible conclusions about the limits of public funds available for educational reform. The case for extended programs rests on precarious analogies to other professions that are very differently organized and financially supported and the expert judgement of teacher educators from research universities. The advocates of extended programs are not alone among would-be reformers in their claims that intuition and common sense should determine public policies; but sharing this commitment with other wishful thinkers does not equate one's dreams with the welfare of children.

One might characterize the claims for extended programs as bad theory and bad policy analysis, but this would be imprecise. Proposals for extended programs are wholly devoid of policy analysis. If the types of theory most relevant to arguments for reforming teacher education are those relating to how teachers learn and how organizations change, one will find no such foundations used to construct the case for extended programs.

Murray Edelman has characterized changes in public structures that do not address the fundamental problems that created the demand for change as symbolic politics. One consequence of symbolic politics is that the illusion of substantive change so created induces quiescence because demands for change have the appearance of being met. The establishment of extended programs may be an example of symbolic politics. None of this need be planned and is not meant to question the motives of those who advocate extended pro-

grams. But before we plunge into a commitment to extended programs, it seems sensible to insist that their proponents demonstrate how their proposals would change teachers' capacities and behaviors in ways that will improve student learning.

The truth of the matter is that we know relatively little about how to educate effective teachers. It speaks volumes that there is almost no research on the effectiveness of alternative ways to educate teachers. Before initiating major system-wide changes in the requirements students must meet in order to teach, it seems prudent to experiment with different strategies and curricula and to evaluate their relative effectiveness. This will require collaboration among state education departments, colleges and departments of education, and school systems. It is ironic that a knowledge-based industry such as education has been so little interested in using research to determine how better to perform its function.

At a time when there is so much doubt about the usefulness of teacher education, we need to be deregulating, encouraging innovations, and evaluating the efficacy of alternatives. No doubt, some ways of preparing teachers are better than others. So far as we know, there is no one best way.

HOW DO YOU SPELL DISTINGUISHED?

Peter Arnott

Peter Arnott is professor of drama at Tufts University. He is the author of numerous books on ancient civilizations and on the history of the theater including The Romans and Their World, The Theatres of Japan, The Theatre in Its Time, *and* Public and Performance in the Greek Theatre. *He has also been, for forty years, a director and performer of Greek drama in various media.*

When I heard that N.T. Stonex was dead, my first thought was that I had once nearly killed him myself—not out of malice, though this easily could have been true; rather, out of inadvertence. In the beleaguered, attenuated world of the English private school in wartime, he was my formmaster, my housemaster, my Latin master, and my scout-master, in which diversity of functions he dominated most of my waking hours and not a few of my nightmares. It was in the last capacity that I nearly dispatched him to join his forefathers. He had been teaching bicycle repair and maintenance to the scout troop and foolishly offered his own machine to be experimented on. I disassembled it capably and reassembled it somewhat less capably. Next morning he called me to his study and informed me, more in anger than in sorrow, that on his way home it had fallen to pieces beneath him. He had been coasting down a steep hill at the time. He was compelled, he told me, "to leap into the bushes to avoid oncoming traffic."

He had given names, of course, not merely initials. I knew what they were, and I still do. But after more than forty years, I can no more bring myself to utter them than would a devout Jew spell the true name of his Maker. Our paths first crossed in 1942. I was a new boy, elevated to the glory of my first long trousers, fresh from a parochial school—a brooding, sullen building with an outside lavatory so festering and malodorous that it would have been worth half a chapter to Dickens in one of his grimmer moods. Huddled in air raid shelters dug deep beneath the

playground and lit by minimal blue bulbs, we had scribbled the examinations on which the rest of our lives depended. By some miracle of concentration, I had achieved a scholarship; and here I was, reduced to nothing, adrift in an ocean of strange faces, a flyspeck in the history of a school that went back at least to Cardinal Wolsey and, some claimed, to King Alfred. In the true English tradition of inculcating self-reliance through terror, I had been given no orientation, no instructions. Everyone else knew where he was going, but not I. I did not know which class I was in, or where it met, or what I was supposed to be doing when I got there. I wished I were dead.

AN UNEXPECTED TEACHER

What led me to Stonex, and created a bond of sympathy even when I had cause to hate him most, was that he was an odd man out himself. His oddity began with the fact that he was there at all. In a world at war, he was a conscientious objector. Rumor said his brother had been killed in the fighting, and this had turned him against it. Whether this was true or not, I never discovered. But he must have faced an unusually generous draft board—or, more likely, faced an ordinary board and bullied them; for, while other conscientious objectors were made to drive ambulances or work in factories, he was allowed to continue in his own profession. Thus, he was the only youngish master in the school. His colleagues were either graybeards and baldheads past the age of service or—the ultimate atrocity of war in this male enclave—women, inflicted on us for the duration. These harpies were far more intimidating than any

male I later encountered—so defensive, so prone to imagine slights and insults that they would send us for a beating if we whispered.

Stonex did not beat us. I never saw him lay a finger on a boy. He had other, more effective methods—principally, a vein of acid sarcasm that could flay the skin at twenty paces. In the cosseted, insulated, PTA-controlled world of American public education, he would not last three days. He would be fired, probably sued, and forbidden ever to inflict himself upon the sensitive young again. I first appeared before him with a thick Suffolk accent, one of the ugliest in the British Isles. He ridiculed me out of it. I was fat and awkward; he called me offensive names in Latin. He criticized my clothes, my manners. He drew frequent public attention to the depths of my ignorance. When I made my first stumbling ventures into rugby football—played at a level of ferocity which, even now, causes me to look on the American game as effete—he could be heard laughing ghoulishly on the sidelines, inviting total strangers to witness my discomfiture.

And there was no escape from him. In this world, constrained and hallowed by tradition, parents had no voice. (My parents, in any case, were as frightened of the man as I was.) I could not complain, for there was no one to complain to. The headmaster was an ineffectual cleric who, when he sensed an emergent protest, moved sharply off in the opposite direction and disappeared for days. To survive, I had to anticipate Stonex and forestall him. I lost my accent and some twenty pounds. I spent hours at my books. I even became moderately good at rugby football. And once he had eviscerated me, he began to fill me up again, with his own uncompromising brand of education.

His teaching methods were, like himself, eccentric. Although he was exempted from the war, his hatred for the military devoured him. Often, when the school's Officers' Training Corps was parading in the yard below, shouting belligerent commands in barely broken voices, he would stop the lesson, throw the windows open, and scatter pennies contemptuously at their feet. How he escaped lynching by his bellicose colleagues I shall never know. He would teach nothing that had to do with war and violence. While our peers in other classes were plodding through Caesar's invasion of Britain, we were reading Virgil on beekeeping or Ovid on the climate of the Black Sea. Only in this educational environment, with the notorious English tolerance of eccentricity, could he have survived.

With him, the unusual often turned into the bizarre. Like other teachers at this time, he was expected to plug gaps by teaching outside his own subject. For several years, he taught us English literature and compensated for the dullness of the syllabus by turning literature into drama. We were all assigned parts and acted out what we read.

One of our texts was Robert Louis Stevenson's *The Black Arrow*—a work that I have never been able to face again but which in his hands, assumed exciting —and potentially lethal—proportions. I was given the role of Father Oates, a shifty Catholic priest. In one sequence the action called for me to be praying "like a windmill" in my pew when the ominous weapon of the title flew through the chapel window and stuck quivering in the woodwork beside me. I was called out before the class; an empty desk became my pew; I sank to my knees, read, and prayed; suddenly an old nib pen, blackened and corroded with age, impelled by the fiendish hand of Stonex, whistled across the classroom and stuck in the desk two inches from my right hand. It did not occur to me until much later that I might have died from blood poisoning that day.

Mercifully, weight and the exigencies of casting saved me from a worse fate. The same book called for an escaping hero to be lowered down the face of a cliff. Stonex seized one of my smaller classmates, trussed him like a chicken—using good Scout knots, of course—and lowered him

■ *Eton students in their prescribed uniform.*

(British Tourist Authority)

to the ground from the second-floor window. It was raining hard at the time.

And so, as our acquaintance ripened, he became more Jekyll than Hyde. He was one of only two men of whom I have been genuinely afraid—the other was my tutor in ancient history at Oxford, for very similar reasons—and also the man who first taught me to love *David Copperfield*, which has been one of the joys of my life ever since. It is my favorite book in the English language. Every year I read it again; and I remember how, the first time, under the spell of this loved and hated man, I brought the class to a standstill, and other teachers in to complain, because I was laughing so hard at the chapter called "My First Dissipation."

But Latin was his forte. He loved the language and sought hard to share his love with us. Even the most dimwitted of us realized, I think, that he recognized his subject as more important than he was, or than we were; and if he could force us to comprehend this only at the cost of his own popularity, so be it. I look in vain for this approach to education today. And so, while loathing him, we learned. For the first two years, we memorized. Verbs, nouns, adjectives in their infinite declensions and variety—we knew them all. If not, our names were written on a blackboard, and we relearned them in detention. He rejoiced in what he called "the herring season," when he went trawling for offenders. If one boy failed to conju-

gate a verb, his name was written on the wall of shame and the question passed on to the next boy. Usually, his name went up, too, and the next, and the next; often, by class end, the board was awash with names, and the detention room was crammed with delinquents. But we learned them—so well that, though I have not been a classicist for many years, I can still recite them exactly as I was taught. And in learning them we learned not only Latin but the art of memory as well, which can be applied to anything.

As we grew more capable, he grew more demanding. Once we had acquired a basic vocabulary, he refused to let us touch a dictionary. All translation had to be done sight unseen. He compelled us to look at the structure of language, to break down unfamiliar words into their more familiar components, to make associations with words in other languages that we already knew. And so we learned to analyze and compare, to proceed from the known to the unknown, to make informed guesses based on the evidence available —in short, to use our minds. In this, Stonex was a particularly able exponent of the best qualities of English education of that time. I remain convinced that the enduring prestige of British degrees in the American education system is due not so much to what we know--Americans acquire just as much information, in the end —as to how we came to know it. Whether this will continue to be true under

Margaret Thatcher's new dispensations remains to be seen.

At a more advanced level still, we came to write Latin and to be abused by Stonex because we could not write prose as well as Cicero or dactylic hexameters like Virgil's. Latin prose was the first class on Monday morning, a wonderful beginning for the working week. Stonex would manifest himself promptly at nine and tear to shreds the compositions we had so arduously written the Friday before. There were only two of us left by this time. The rest had run away, or were gibbering in madhouses, or had been sold into the salt mines of Siberia. My friend and I would cower in the cloisters, watching for his approach and praying—literally praying—that he would be stricken by the plague and not come. He always came. He was the healthiest man I have ever met. When I return to my old school now, with a string of degrees and thirty books to my name, I still go up and stand there: It is always Monday morning, and the terror returns.

BETTMANN

■ *A demonstration during Columbia University commencement ceremonies.*

OTHER TIMES, OTHER WAYS

This was the man who gave me my career. I fought him and learned from him; I hated him and cherished him. And in the end, I knew what he had done for me. It grieves me deeply now that, though I saw Stonex periodically after our official ties were severed, I could never bring myself to tell him these things. I did come close. On our last meeting, a couple of years before his death, I said to him, "Sir: I should like you to know that everything you said about me turned out to be absolutely true." "Oh dear!" he replied. "I should hate to believe that."

The past never dies. It merely goes away to hide, and pounces on you when you least expect it. The years slip by, youth wanes into senescence, the instructed has long since been the instructor; and Stonex steps out of the shadows to fix me with that familiar, formidable eye and say:

"Account for yourself, boy. What did you really learn from me?"

And in all honesty, I reply: "Sir, you taught me three things."

"What were they?"

"First, the dangers of too hasty judgments. I never really liked you when I was at school."

"I know it. You have seen the error of your ways, I trust."

"I have. But it took me ten or twenty years to do it. I only saw the drudgery. The hours of homework. The criticism of everything I did. What I didn't see until much, much later was what I was absorbing from you. I built my life, such as it is, on what you taught me. You handed me my career on a plate."

"A vulgar Americanism. Avoid it."

"Well, after all. . . . I *am* a professor at an American university."

"Of Latin?"

"I'm afraid not, sir. My field is drama now."

"You were always frivolously inclined. Why is this relevant?"

"Because this *is* America; and because of certain things that happened in the sixties. There were riots and protests all across the country. Students demanded the right to control their own education, to hire and fire faculty, to have a voice in governing the institution, and to take new kinds of courses, like Creative Photography and the Human Sexual Response."

"Instead of Latin?"

"I'm afraid so. Some of this was bad, but there were good things in it. It brought fresh air into the system. It scared teachers and professors who had spent their lives lecturing from the same old yellowing sheaf of notes. It forced us to defend our subjects."

"And is it still like that?"

"Not really. Things are quieter now. The good things were absorbed into the system. But there are some hangovers. Students expect to comment on their classes. At the end of every course, we hand out questionnaires—forms that the students can fill in with things like 'Was the instructor well-informed?' or 'Was the instructor coherent in class?' or 'How did this course contribute to your education?'"

"This seems to offer unbridled scope for malice."

"It could. But, to be honest, it isn't often used in that way. Sometimes students work off resentment because they know they've done badly, but you can always spot those. No, what bothers me is, how do they know? How can they tell how well-informed an instructor is without knowing more than he does? How do they know how much the course contributed to their education? It's too early to decide that. If I'd been allowed to fill in such a form about you, I'd have sent you to the guillotine on the spot.

"Evaluating a course, it seems to me, is even more difficult than reviewing a book or a play. It isn't—or at least, it shouldn't be—simply the expression of a personal opinion. That's worthless. Reviewing takes a sophisticated, critical mind. Above all, it needs a significant mass of material to use for comparisons. This is what students, almost by definition, don't have. It may be the only course in the subject that they've ever taken. They can't compare it to other people's handling of the same material. And, not being blessed with foresight, they have no way of knowing what will come from this or how it will shape the pattern of their lives. No. Education's too important to be left to the students. All they can say at the moment is whether they enjoyed a course or not. And that's the least important thing about it. All the things I learned that did me the most good I hated at the time."

"Like Latin."

"That was the second thing you taught me. I hated it at first because I wasn't good at it."

"I remember."

"I only got through the first year because the boy sitting next to me was much better than I was, and I had good eyesight."

"I remember him, too. An excellent student. He is still in the same field, I trust?"

"No. In electronics. He lives in Indiana and earns vast sums of money."

"But you improved."

"Because I was damned if I would let you win. That's something else that's gone wrong over here. They have taken out the challenges. They don't try to bring the student up to the level of the course. They drop the level of the course to suit the student. And if students really can't handle it—if they find they have to study hard, read books, and do unpalatable things like that—they're allowed to drop it and do something easier."

"Back to Latin. What did you find to be the use of it?"

"You asked us that on the first day of school. There was the inevitable small boy who piped up, 'Well, sir, if you want to be a doctor, or a lawyer...,' and you soon squashed him. But no one else had any answer at all."

"Why not?"

"Because we'd never asked ourselves the question. We studied Latin because we had to. And there was a general sense that Latin was a Good Thing. It was never 'relevant,' in the current phrase. It had no practical value, although in England we were told, periodically, that a first-class honors degree in classics was a passport to the upper reaches of the civil service or the diplomatic, or that most of the English board of directors of ICI had degrees in Greek and Latin. These things didn't bother us unduly. We did have a sense, though, that Latin was prestigious. Elit-

ist. It separated the sheep from the goats. All the things that are bad words now."

"So snobbery is not a motivation in the United States?"

"No. American students prefer to side with the majority. It's the democratic way."

"But Latin is taught here?"

"Not nearly so widely as it used to be. It was entrenched once, established, just like in England. Then, almost overnight, it ceased to be required. The older generation of teachers, who never needed to make their subject interesting because people had to take it anyway, suddenly found they had to make it interesting, but they didn't know how. The younger teachers, fresh from college, had the interest and enthusiasm but not the authority."

"So what happened?"

"There were two contradictory reactions. In the universities, classicists became defensive. They tried to cling to what they had. Word came down from on high: 'Hoard your speciality, no matter how arcane. Don't pander to the mob. Never compromise.'"

"You make them sound like monks in the Dark Ages."

"Or the memorizers in *Farenheit 451*, each with a different book locked in his mind, awaiting the millennium. It's almost incredible, now, how fiercely they resisted teaching classics in translation. They thought of that as profanation. Vulgar. Not that there were many good translations then. The English was usually more opaque than the original. Good, popular, readable translations didn't begin to appear until later. In some places, the old attitudes still haven't changed. There's still one London college that warns its students to avoid the Penguin Classics as 'too demotic.'".

"And the other reaction?"

"The opposite. This is a country that goes to extremes. There was a desperate movement to make Latin fun—to take the pain out of it, to teach it as a living language and have courses in Latin conversation."

"But it never was a living language."

"Of course not. Not the Latin we have. It was never spoken in the streets. It was a highly sophisticated literary language, used for history, or poetry, or formal speeches. We know what popular Latin was like only from a few scattered sources. The average Roman would no more have ordered dinner in rolling Ciceronian periods than he would have worn a toga while eating it."

"And how did this affect the schools?"

"Latin time was party time—a rash of Roman banquets, where students wore sheets, auctioned slaves, and ran chariot races. But nobody learned very much. All this frenzied activity simply skirted round the real problem."

"Which was?"

"That Latin's difficult. You either learn it or you don't. There's no real way of making it easy. And the schools, like the universities, were coming to think that difficulty was not something to be faced but avoided. May I read you something?"

"Please."

"It's by James Thurber, written about thirty years ago—in an English magazine, as it happens, *Punch*. 'In my day, Latin was taught in high schools to prepare the youthful mind for the endless war between meaning and gobbledegook. But it was a mental discipline; and discipline has become a bad word in America, for the idiotic reason that we identify it with regimentation, and hence damn it as Communistic.'"

"You mean that Latin is avoided because some can do it and some can't? And this imperils the American myth of equality?"

"Exactly. But perhaps we shouldn't put it quite so bluntly."

"What was the third thing that I taught you?"

"Related to the above: the value of compulsion—at least, in education. There was always something that we *had* to do: books to read, essays to write, activities to engage in. We felt put upon at the time. But we were kept so busy that there was no time for problems."

"Americans have problems?"

"Lots."

"What do they do about them?"

"Go to counselors, who find more problems."

"So you were glad we told you what to do."

"In the end, yes. Take Latin. The first few years were never fun. I don't think that beginning a new language ever can be fun. You have to learn the grammar and the syntax first. It's like music. You have to learn scales before you can play music. We started when we were so young that we weren't able to protest. Then, when we were old enough to say we didn't like it, we found we'd done all the donkey work and could start to enjoy it."

"I gather that compulsion's not in favor here?"

"Nobody *makes* anyone do anything any more. A master at one of the more prestigious New England private schools told me, 'We don't require students to go to any assemblies these days. We let them use their own judgment.' But what judgment can you use when you're being offered something totally new to you? If I hadn't been forced to, I would never have learned Latin. I never would have read *Crime and Punishment*, I never would have seen a play by Yeats. In the words of Wodehouse's immortal Gussie Fink-Nottle, education may be a drawing out, not a putting in; but if you don't put in something somewhere along the line, you have nowhere to start from.

"It's strange that compulsion has become a forbidden word in American education because it's the only thing that many students respond to. I once asked a student if she'd read the novels of Thomas Hardy, and she gave me the archetypal American response."

"Which was?"

"'No. I never had to.' The old European joke is quite true, unfortunately. Give American students a reading list of a hundred books, and they'll read a hundred books. Give them a list with one required book and ninety-nine recommended, and they'll read one book."

"What happens when American students go to England?"

"Chaos and confusion. They run around asking for their reading lists; and when their professors tell them, quite properly, 'The library is your reading list,' they don't know how to handle it. Some adjust, but some never recover. Let me tell you a story.

"Thirty years ago, when I was new to the States, I taught a course in classical civilization. Every day I gave a lecture, and at the end I'd say 'I'd like you to read *Oedipus Rex*'; or, 'the second book of Herodotus'; something like that. Then came the first test, and one student failed totally, because he'd obviously never read any of those things at all. When I pointed this

■ *A Harvard demonstration.*

BETTMANN

out to him, he was very angry and said 'But you never said they were *assignments*! You never used the word assignments!!!'"

"Why do you stay here?"

"Because, at a certain level, there's a joyousness about education that we never had. If you have enough motivation, you can do anything you want to. But I think most students would benefit from having to listen to you, at least once in a while. There wouldn't be so many gaps. Fewer of those awful blanks you find even in the best students. Another story?"

"If you wish."

"In my own department, we have a foreign language requirement for graduate students. Most offer French or German. If they failed, I used to tutor them, privately, to get them ready for the next time. Well, we had a graduate student once who seemed to be pretty well-read, but he failed his French. I started working with him, translating a French history of nineteenth-century literature. One morning he pointed at the name of Balzac and

said 'I've never heard of that place.' 'It's not a place,' I said. 'It's a person. A writer. I suppose in a loose sort of way, you might call him the French Dickens.' And he replied: 'Dickens?'"

"Appalling. I think I should go now."

"One more story. I was once visiting a small college in Pennsylvania. My work was done, I was ready to leave, and I was waiting in the office of my faculty host, who was busy somewhere else. There was a knock at the door, and a student came in. He wanted to ask my host a question. I explained that he had gone and asked if I could help. He brightened up. 'Yes,' he said, 'You probably could. I'm applying to graduate school, and I want to tell them that I can make a distinguished contribution to their program.' So I asked what I could do."

"And he said?"

"He answered with the title of this essay."

"Good night."

"Good night sir."

Morality and Values in Education

Major generative inquiry into the status of the moral dilemmas and the moral perspectives of American children is underway. American social values have been under close scrutiny for several decades. Understanding the differing value perspectives of present-day American youth has been significantly expanded by recent surveys on the values of American children. Both "open-ended" and more structured interest now compete for the loyalties of American youth.

Recent studies on American teenagers' values reveal the magnitude of the task of American educators if they choose to teach skills of critical reasoning in moral judgment. Robert Coles and Louis Genevie have recently noted that some young persons are social captives in our highly competitive North American social environment as "cultural literacy" increases, "moral literacy" declines (see Article #18). Surveys of young Americans on how they resolve moral dilemmas sometimes reveal a very different image of the moral situation in American society from what their teachers, parents, and political leaders would like to perceive as true. How can we help children and adolescents to make wise moral choices? How can we help them to develop reasoning skills to handle problematic social situations?

There is a need for teachers to develop principles of professional practice that will enable them to respond reasonably to the many ethical dilemmas they face. The knowledge base on how teachers derive their knowledge of professional ethics is developing. The study of how teachers come to be aware of their basic values and of how these values shape their professional practice is very important. Educational systems at all levels are based on the desirability to teach certain fundamental beliefs and the disciplines of knowledge (however they may be organized in different cultures). School curricula are based on certain moral assumptions (secular or religious) as to the worth of knowledge, and the belief that some forms of knowledge are more worthy than others. Schooling is not only to transmit national and cultural heritage, including the intellectual heritage, of a people; it is also a fundamentally moral enterprise. It is a fundamentally moral enterprise because in curriculum construction, fundamental moral choices are made as to: (a) what knowledge every student ought to know from the accumulated knowledge base of humanity, and (b) what inquiry, experimentation, and knowledge-seeking skills a student should be permitted to acquire. Therefore, "moral bases of education" is the evaluation of choices and the making of decisions on the knowledge and academic skills that deserve to be taught to students, or at least to some students in the case of more selective educational systems.

We see, therefore, that when we speak of "morality and education" there are process issues as to the most basic knowledge-seeking, epistemological foundations of learning. Hence, the controversy over morality in education deals with more than just the tensions between secular and religious interests in society, although to know about such tensions is a valuable, important matter. Moral education is also more than a debate over the merits of methods used to teach students to make morally sound, ethical choices in their lives—although this also is critically important and ought to be done. Thus, we argue that the construction of educational processes and the decisions as to the substantive content of school curricula are also moral issues, as well as epistemological ones having to do with how we discover, verify, and transmit truth.

One of the most compelling responsibilities of Canadian and American schools is the responsibility of preparing young persons for their moral duties as free citizens of free nations. Moral education in public institutions in North America is strongly focused on helping young people define what it means to be a fair, just, and compassionate citizen. North American educators are involved in a continuing dialogue regarding the moral bases of schooling. Free peoples have to help the members of each new generation discover the noblest and best in their civic heritage, as well as teach them principles of rational ethical argumentation as they proceed into the middle and later grades. The Canadian and American governments have always wanted the schools to teach the principles of civic morality based on their respective constitutional traditions. Indeed, when the public school movement began in the United States in the 1830s and 1840s, the concept of universal public schooling as a mechanism for instilling a sense of national identity and civic morality was supported. In every nation, school curricula have certain value preferences imbedded in them.

Significant constitutional issues are at stake in the forms and directions moral education should take in the schools. Both theistic and nontheistic conceptions of what constitutes moral behavior compete for the loyalties of teachers and students. Extremist forces representing the ideological left and right, both religious and secular, wish to see their moral agendas incorporated into school curricula. The pressures from these groups can be extreme. Yet the schools must maintain their autonomy and integrity in the face of these pressures, and retain control of

Unit 4

what is moral education in tax-supported schools.

The cherished civil freedoms of all young people must be protected. These freedoms include the freedom to believe or not to believe matters of doctrine unrelated to the shared civic values that form the basis for our free, democratic social order. These doctrinal matters, including such fiercely controverted social issues as abortion and sexual morality, raise a number of questions. Do teachers have a responsibility to respond to student requests for information on sexuality, sexual morality, communicable diseases, etc.? Or should they deny these requests? For whom do the schools exist? Is a teacher's primary responsibility to his or her client, the student, or to the student's parents? Do secondary school students have the right to study and to inquire into subjects not in officially-sanctioned curricula? What are the moral issues surrounding censorship of student reading material? What ethical questions are raised by arbitrarily withholding information regarding alternative viewpoints on controversial topics? In my opinion, public school teachers are placed in authority by state educational agencies to serve the needs of their students, not the private moral agendas of parents and pressure groups.

Schools cannot avoid reflecting some values because, as noted previously, the values underlying the content of any curriculum are easily identified by most students from the middle grades upward. Likewise, teachers cannot hide all of their moral preferences. However, they can learn to conduct just, open discussions of moral topics without succumbing to the temptation to deliberately indoctrinate students with their own views.

Teaching students to respect all people, to revere the sanctity of life, to uphold the right to dissent on the part of any citizen, to believe in the equality of all people before the law, to cherish the freedom to learn, and to respect the right of all people to their own convictions—these are principles of democracy and ideals worthy of being cherished. An understanding of the process of ethical decision-making is needed by the citizens of any free nation; thus, this process should be taught in a free nation's schools.

The continuing goal of schools is to help each student become an ethical citizen with a sense of personal moral responsibility that cannot be swayed by partisan bigotry, and a commitment to social justice demands a faith in the rights of all to freedom of belief, assembly, speech, and press. We are still debating what constitute the best, or most effective moral education curricula for achieving this noble and necessary objective.

The essays in this unit constitute a comprehensive overview of moral education with considerable historical and textual interpretation. Topics covered include public pressures on schools, and the social responsibilities of schools. The unit can be used in courses dealing with the historical or philosophical foundations of education.

Looking Ahead: Challenge Questions

What is "moral education"? Why do so many people wish to see a form of moral education in schools?

What are the differences in moral education issues in public and private schools?

Are there certain values about which most North Americans can agree? Should they be taught in schools?

Should local communities have total control of the content of moral instruction in local schools, as they did in the nineteenth century? Why or why not?

What are some of the problems with the manner in which ethics and ethical decision-making skills have been taught in schools?

What is civic education? How do states encourage civic education in the schools?

Should schools be involved in teaching people to reason about moral questions? Why or why not? If not, who should do it? Why?

What is the difference between indoctrination and instruction?

Is there a national consensus concerning the form that moral education should take in schools? Is such a consensus likely if it does not now exist?

What attitudes and skills are most important to a responsible approach to moral decision-making?

How can we learn about how teachers' values affect their professional relationships with students?

The Moral Life Of America's Schoolchildren

An Introduction

Is the moral fabric of America's children unraveling? A landmark survey suggests the answer is yes. But if children's values truly are hanging by a thread, restoring moral authority to the schools may put them on the mend.

Jeff Meade

Robert Coles—eminent child psychiatrist, Harvard professor, friend and confidant of the late Robert F. Kennedy, and what some might describe as a member of the liberal intellectual left—recalls, almost wistfully, the good old days when religion was taught in the schools.

In what is perhaps an unguarded moment, he reminisces about the teachers who would lay into him, with parental blessing, at the first sign of disobedience or slackness.

He seems genuinely nostalgic for those long-ago frosty autumn mornings, when the children would line up in the schoolyard—perfectly still little rows of children, like clothespin dolls, with cheeks scrubbed red and clothes clean and patched—and place their right hands over their hearts, and pledge allegiance to the flag of the United States of America. One nation under God. All that.

To assume from these revelations that Robert Coles, M.D., author of the acclaimed *Children of Crisis* series, devoted civil rights advocate and friend to Martin Luther King Jr., is lately taking a turn to the right would be to do him a grievous disservice.

Coles is not, and has never been, an advocate of organized prayer or Bible reading in the nation's classrooms. Nor does he espouse a return to more enthusiastic brutality in the furtherance of children's education. And he has nothing against the Pledge of Allegiance, although he does not regard it as a test of loyalty.

But in the absence of these solid, reliable symbols of authority, Coles senses a void. Something in America's homes and schools is missing, and has been missing for years.

Now, a massive new survey—sponsored by the Girl Scouts of America, the Lilly Endowment, and the Mott Foundation, with Coles as the project director—begins to shed light into that vast, empty space. What appears to be missing, quite simply, is a strong, inarguable notion of right and wrong, good and bad. The survey is the first part of a long-term effort designed to gain a better understanding of the moral development of American children.

In the special report that follows, Coles, along with his colleague, sociologist Louis Genevie, analyzes some of the most significant findings of the survey. Their joint effort raises serious questions about the moral character of children, whom we often see as innocent, frequently brutally honest, creatures utterly without guile.

During the fall of 1989, surveyors fanned out across the country, visiting public, private, and parochial schools, in the cities and in the suburbs. During several weeks, they posed more than 90 probing questions to more than 5,000 children in grades 4 through 12. They asked simple questions: Do you believe in God? And they asked some tough ones: Who has the final say if a teenage girl wants an abortion: the girl or her parents?

Most importantly, they asked: How do you decide what is right and wrong? What system of values informs your moral decisions?

The answers reveal a nation of children who do, in fact, have fairly complicated belief systems. But far more often than not, those beliefs run counter to traditional values.

What's more, there is an unmistakable erosion of children's faith in, and support for, traditional sources of authority. Although children believe parents, teachers, and religious leaders care for them, increasingly they turn to their peers for guidance on matters of right and wrong. Their decisions are sometimes shocking, but from Coles's perspective, both as a teacher and an often sharp social critic, perhaps not unexpected.

"I saw an awful lot of kids," Coles says, "who are bright, but whose conscience is not all that muscular." That this should be so, he believes, reflects in part the moral values of society in general.

In an interview from his home in Concord, Mass., Coles's observations are fairly pointed. "People tend to romanticize children," he says. "So I think this survey will come as a shock."

But, he says, some of the parents who will gasp in horror at the corruption of children's values are, in reality, the inadvertent role models for their children's slippery beliefs. Winning is everything. Me first. Parents—along with some of our more celebrated white-collar thieves—are often the unknowing font of situational ethics.

"What I think we are seeing here is a conflict," he says. "On the one side, kids with a strong belief in the Judeo-Christian religious ethic, and on the other side, [kids] paying very close attention to that 'get ahead at any cost' attitude that they've picked up in their family lives."

This is not to suggest, Coles says, that most children, if given the chance, would lie, cheat, or steal to get ahead. What it means, rather, is that a majority of children have no firm religious or moral code to guide them. Left to their own devices, they may well do the "right" thing. But they may do it because it makes them happy, gets them ahead, or seems best for everyone. Often, they seem not so much to be doing what they think is right, but doing what they think grown-ups expect. As adults themselves, they may learn to do the "right" things, too. But, again, for all the wrong reasons.

"They'll learn control for some utilitarian reasons," he says. "They're going to see that Ivan Boesky got caught, so you could get caught."

For teachers in particular, then, what is the meaning of the survey? That is not an easy question to answer. One survey, no matter how significant, can never tell the whole story, Coles cautions. For one thing, there is often a difference between what survey respondents say they will do and what they actually do. "It's one thing to say on a survey questionnaire that you would cheat, and quite another to actually do it."

Coles also suspects that, as his team of researchers continue to explore in greater depth the issues raised in the survey, they may find that children are not comfortable with their values. "As we start seeing more and more of these kids, they're probably going to tell us about their moral anxiety," he says.

But Coles believes there is an important role for teachers. He is passionate in his support of moral education. "At Harvard, at least until 1902, it was the mission of the college to educate men of character," he says. And, indeed, he adds, moral education is the very heart of education. "Schools," he says, "are for the education of the whole person, and it is the responsibility of the schools to inculcate character."

Schools, Coles says, have to do far more than merely hand out character awards at graduation. "The leadership awards," he notes, "usually go to the best athlete. But character can be defined in a more traditional way, and rewarded."

Character, in the traditional sense, was instilled in Coles at a very early age. Hailing back once again to those golden days, he remembers the 4th grade teacher who, on the first day of school, wrote on the blackboard a poem by Sara Teasdale, from which he recalls one line in particular, about the need to have "a heart that never hardens."

"Not only did she write it on the board and make us memorize it," he says, "but she also explained what it meant." And it has stayed with him—as part of his moral compass—ever since.

The Moral Life Of America's Schoolchildren

Robert Coles and Louis Genevie

Robert Coles, M.D., professor of psychiatry and medical humanities at Harvard University, is the author of The Moral Life of Children *and* The Call of Stories: Teaching and the Moral Imagination.

Louis Genevie, former assistant professor of psychiatry at Albert Einstein College of Medicine, is currently a research associate with Robert Coles at Harvard. He is the author of The Motherhood Report *and* The Samson and Delilah Complex.

Survey research helps us see general trends and patterns of belief or behavior, but conversations with individual boys and girls give us a sense of the complexity and subtlety at work in the minds of these children—the particular, real-life emotional and theoretical issues with which they struggle.

It would be difficult to overstate the significance of the survey findings, summarized here. No such comprehensive national survey of children's moral values has ever been conducted. Children from the 4th through 12th grades, attending public, parochial, and private schools nationwide, responded to more than 90 probing questions dealing with a diverse array of moral issues.

The picture that emerges reminds us that there are substantial differences in the ways our children come to think about what is right and what is wrong, what ought to be done and what ought not to be done. Some of them (16 percent) call upon God, the Bible, church, or synagogue for major guidance. Others (18 percent) essentially fall back upon themselves, their own wishes, feelings, interests, or moods. Still others (25 percent) look to the world around them, to their neighborhood or community, to the nation and its standards. A certain number look to what is useful for them, what seems to work (10 percent) or to what has traditionally been upheld as desirable or undesirable (19 percent). The rest (11 percent) struggle with the moral dilemmas they face with no clear-cut form of moral logic or reasoning to help them decide.

Here, for instance, is a 10th grader who exemplifies the children who rely mainly on what feels right to them personally when they face tough moral choices. The boy, who attends a suburban high school in New England, talks quite candidly about his moral life, including such matters as cheating and lying, as well as sexual activity: "We go to church sometimes, but not a whole lot. My dad tries to do the best he can; he's a businessman. My mom works in an insurance office. They're good folks. They want me to get ahead, and I'll try. I'm no great whiz at school, but I'm no idiot, either—in the middle.

"I decide a lot of things on how it hits me in the gut. It's my instinct, I guess you could say. You have to do what feels right inside you—that's what I've learned: Act upon your true feelings. I don't mean do anything you feel like doing, no." (I had asked.) "I guess I mean this: So long as you don't hurt the next guy, it's basically up to you what you do. When I'm in a bind, I talk to myself: 'Hey,' I say, 'what's going on inside you—what feels right?' That's how I come out on something—me talking to me, and getting the answer from me."

In the same town, however, a boy of similar age and socioeconomic background has quite another point of view: "You have to decide [what's right and wrong] on the basis of the whole town here. In school, too, there's got to be some rules, and they deserve obedience. My dad and mom tell me: 'You're a citizen, so act like one!' I try to be independent; I try to be my own person. But I try to do what's best for everyone concerned. You have to think of others, not just yourself!"

Another student, a 9th grade girl from a Midwestern town, has a much different perspective. She doesn't just think of others; she also calls upon her religious faith. "You have to live up to the Ten Commandments," she says. "You have to remember what Jesus said, when He spoke to the crowds that came to hear Him. If you don't live up to your religion, then it's no use going to church. You should stop yourself, and say: Is this what the Lord wants me to do, or am I falling away [from Him]? It can be hard sometimes, I know, but you have to remember that God has told us what is right, and it's up to us to check with Him before we decide what to do."

Not that all children, by any means, "check" with God, or with themselves and their personal feelings, when they consider a course of action. A good number of children call upon convention—that is, they conform to what they believe is required by tradition. Or they call upon a notion of what is useful for them, or "practical," or what "works"—meaning what helps them in their various objectives, purposes, and plans.

This reliance on the traditional or the utilitarian increases as children grow older, and has, by the high school years, become a firm part of the thinking of many youths—as with this Atlanta girl: "I'm not always sure what to do. I usually decide by saying to myself: 'Do the best you can,' and hope it'll work out. I try not to do something that will get me in trouble. I try to stay with the crowd, I guess. My mom has always told us to be 'practical,' and that's my yardstick, I'd have to say."

A friend of hers, a girl one year older, is also "practical," but she adds this dimension to her justification for what is to be done or not done: "I try to stick by the rules: If you break them, the next thing you know, you're in trouble. I try to be popular, I'll admit—and that affects what you decide. You don't want to be standing alone, with your hand the only one raised in the class. If people have lived a certain way all these years, there must be a good reason for it. I feel that, mostly. I'll admit, I might have my own opinion sometimes, but I'm not one to go running off with them, without checking on how the people next to me are deciding."

As children grow older, and this form of moral reasoning becomes more and more common, their reliance on social and religious authority declines and, not surprisingly, most children begin to turn away from adults as the primary source of advice on moral issues. Increasingly, adult advice takes a back seat to peer influence, so that by high school, the majority (58 percent) rely mainly on their peers for moral guidance. Of course, younger children, more directly dependent on adults, seek out the advice of parents, teachers, and other responsible adults more often.

Age and the maturation process associated with it are not the only factors that differentiate how children relate to moral issues. Boys, for example, tend to be practical utilitarians in deciding difficult moral issues, while girls tend to be more altruistic in their orientation. Wealth and poverty also make a difference. Affluence, it seems, tends to lead to moral uncertainty; the higher the family's income level, the less clear a youngster is about right and wrong.

While these factors are important, a child's relationship to God and religion in general is just as

What Children Worry About

When asked, "Of these problems facing kids today, which one do you worry about most?" the most frequent responses related to the fulfillment of conventional adult expectations. Twenty-four percent said they feel pressure to do well in school or sports, and 17 percent worry about what to do with their lives.

Of the serious social concerns usually expressed by adults, children seem far less worried. Just 6 percent are concerned about teen pregnancy, 3 percent are worried about teen suicide, and 3 percent are troubled about violence in the schools. Only 1 percent care about alcohol abuse. In fact, of all the problems typically associated with growing up in America, only drug abuse drew a response higher than 10 percent: 13 percent expressed concern.

No matter how dangerous the landscape of growth and maturation may seem to adults, it clearly looks less hostile to children. Only 11 percent of the junior and senior high school students reported feeling "a lot" of pressure to have sex. Just 16 percent of all children responding said they feel pressured to drink alcohol, and only 6 percent feel pushed to take drugs. On balance, far more children feel the pressure to "fit in" (38 percent) than to drink, smoke, or have sex.

They feel most pressured to obey parents and teachers (80 percent), to get good grades (78 percent), *not* to take drugs (77 percent), to prepare for the future (69 percent), and to earn money (62 percent). —J.M.

important in understanding the moral choice he or she makes. The various forms of moral logic that children use have an important influence on their moral decisionmaking that transcends age, gender, and class. This logic and the moral assumptions on which it is based function as a "moral compass" that helps children cope with the moral uncertainty and challenges they face. (See "Marching To Different Drummers.") When the basic moral assumptions are oriented toward self gratification or enhancement, similar moral decisions follow. When a real concern for others, or social and religious authority, are at the core of the decisionmaking process, more altruistic decisions emerge.

The results of this first phase of our research reveal a nation whose children are morally divided—by virtue of their ongoing personal development, their sex, their race, and their social and economic circumstances. And, most important, their underlying ethical assumptions all combine to give shape to their notion of what is right and wrong.

What the study reveals is that American schoolchildren do indeed act on moral assumptions, but these assumptions are not uniform and therefore are difficult to address in a uniform fashion. Teachers who try to establish an orderly classroom and try to encourage in their children certain standards of effort and work, certain standards of what is permissible and what is absolutely out of order, will no doubt have to contend with such disparate assumptions. Too often, teachers don't address some of these assumptions or, for that matter, challenge them.

In many respects, teachers cannot be blamed for their reluctance or inability to take a stand. Teachers struggle every day with issues of character, but their hands are tied. They can't say what is absolutely wrong, what is evil, without risking being accused of promoting religion.

Once, teachers were invested with a kind of moral authority. Religion was taught in the schools, and children prayed at the beginning and end of the day. Children stood and saluted the flag.

We're not advocating a return to those days, for clearly the line between church and state had become dangerously blurred. Under such conditions, individual freedom, particularly individual *religious* freedom, can erode very quickly. We must be constantly on guard to make sure the line is not crossed again. But the point remains that when religion was removed from the schools, nothing came along to take its place, and teachers were stripped of the moral authority they once had.

Perhaps, in our haste to redress a constitutional wrong, we didn't stop to think about the repercussions. In effect, we have removed right and wrong from school. And when you do that, you remove discipline. How can you have discipline when *nothing* is wrong?

And it isn't just that we've gotten rid of religion.

To Have And Have Not

Money seems to blur one's moral judgment. For reasons that aren't clear, children from families in the highest tax brackets express greater uncertainty when confronted with a morally ambiguous situation.

For example: When asked what to do when pressured to drink alcohol at a party; whether to advise a pregnant friend to have the baby and keep it, or opt for an abortion; or to suggest who should have the final say over an abortion, the girl or her parents, children whose families earn more than $40,000 a year were much more likely to answer: "Don't Know."

If doubts plague the "haves," self-destructive behavior may condemn many of the "have-nots" to a life of continued poverty. Among the children at the bottom of the economic ladder, the pressure to indulge in immoral conduct is far greater than for other children.

Children from families who receive food stamps, or in which the parents are unemployed, are three times more likely than most children to feel pressure to take drugs, twice as likely to feel pushed into disobeying authority, and four times more likely to feel prodded into joining a gang.

Perhaps the most telling of all, almost 20 percent of the junior and senior high schoolers from the poorest circumstances agreed with the statement: "Suicide is all right, because a person has a right to do what he wants with himself." Most other children in the same age group evidently place a higher value on life, with just 8 percent agreeing that suicide is "all right." —J.M.

The whole society has become self-centered, resulting in the attenuation and the weakening of civic responsibility.

Consequently, a lot of kids have been brought up not to be anxious or to ever feel guilty. Shame, after all, is a moral position, and some of these kids have no language to express this. We find it personally very worrisome that almost 60 percent of the children in our survey rely on moral standards that have, as their main purpose, self-gratification.

A high school teacher in Massachusetts, perplexed at having to deal with students' moral problems, says this: "I have trouble enough getting the work before the students. I guess I have *my* assumptions, too—that they'll want to do the work, and that they will, and that they'll be honest. Of course, I know not all of them live up to that."

Indeed not. Our survey, for instance, shows a disturbing willingness of young people to cheat in school, a willingness that increases with age and with educational experience. In elementary school, 21 percent of the children we interviewed would try to copy answers or glance at another student's test for ideas. That's appalling. But far worse is that an astonishing 65 percent of high school students say they would cheat.

We've all heard kids talk about cheating in school, but we are frankly surprised at the willingness of so many to entertain it as almost a casual alternative. Our hunch is that 20 to 30 years ago we would not have seen such a high percentage of children admitting to behavior that is unquestionably wrong.

This tendency to think of cheating as permissible is not, however, something that emerges independent of a child's moral assumptions. The children whose moral standards are rooted in religion, and in a sense in civic responsibility, show the most resistance to the temptation to violate an extremely important rule—thou shalt not cheat—which every school needs to enforce an honest standard of grading.

Only 6 percent of the children who said they rely on God or scripture to help them decide what is right said they would copy answers from another student, compared with almost one out of five of those children who said they do what makes them feel good when confronted with a moral dilemma.

But perhaps some children merely reflect the values of their society: The notion of "what works" is "what works for me." Given their membership in a highly competitive, SAT-conscious culture, some children can very easily entertain the notion of cheating. It shows the ambitiousness of some of these kids: They're so fiercely committed to using the schools to achieve their own ends. Sadly, as so-called "cultural literacy" grows, what could be called "moral literacy" declines.

This survey really reminds us that we are not one nation indivisible. We have some children who still live up to the Judeo-Christian tradition, or adhere to some civic-oriented sense of duty and responsibility, and others who really don't. We regret to say that, even at Harvard, we see a lot of kids who are bright, but whose conscience is not all that muscular.

In spite of this rather pessimistic assessment, there is in all of this a ray of hope: Almost half of the children, when confronted with the various moral dilemmas posed in our survey, put up a good, stiff fight. In terms of the moral logic, however, only 38

The Wallpaper Factor

Most children (94 percent) believe their parents care for them, and they still go to them for advice (64 percent) when confronted with a problem. However, as kids get older, they turn more often to each other and less often to their parents for advice. By high school, 58 percent of the children say they would be more likely to ask a friend their own age for advice.

Far more disturbing is what survey researchers call "the wallpaper factor"—that is, the clear reluctance of children to take their problems to other traditional authority figures, notably teachers and religious leaders. About a third of the children agree that their teachers care for them, for example, but only 7 percent would turn to them for advice in a matter of personal values. And despite the fact that most of the children (82 percent) believe there is a God, and more than a third have had a significant religious experience that changed the direction of their lives, and nearly 40 percent pray daily, only 3 percent of the children would seek out a member of the clergy for help with a moral problem.

Clearly, what we like to think of as "traditional" sources of authority are no longer taken seriously. When it comes to the truly serious issues of right and wrong in children's lives, teachers and clergy are, much like wallpaper, present—but almost purely decorative.
—J.M.

Hell, No, They Won't Go

When their country calls, an alarming number of young people are likely to put Uncle Sam on hold.

Relatively few of the junior and senior high school students surveyed (22 percent) would be willing to fight for their country under any condition. One out of five, however, wouldn't fight, no matter what. The survey did not seek to determine why they feel as they do, but their views suggest several possibilities: That, for some of these teenagers, war is morally objectionable under all circumstances; that the nation is still paying the price for Vietnam; or that their concern for self exceeds their concern for country.

Equally, if not more, disturbing is the great reluctance among these students to serve in even a noncombatant capacity. Asked if they would be willing to serve a year in an organization like VISTA or the Peace Corps, fully 60 percent said no.

Some of the survey's findings about civic responsibility echo concerns first voiced last year in a survey conducted by People for the American Way. One young man, questioned in that poll about civic involvement, responded: "Well, that's not going to buy me a Gucci shirt. . . . What's in it for me?" Also in that survey, fewer than two-fifths of the respondents had been involved in any community or neighborhood service activity within the past year, fewer than 40 percent would fight to defend freedom of speech, and fewer than half strongly agreed that all Americans owe something to their country. —J.M.

percent rely on traditional religions or social authorities. The rest rely either on what makes them feel good, what works for them, or what would be best for everybody involved.

Perhaps more and more of us who teach will want to consider not only what we require intellectually and morally of our students, but what the sources are for their assumptions and ours: why we believe what we do, what our values, ideals, and principles are. Perhaps, too, we teachers need to explain vigorously what we expect of our students and *why*, and engage them in a spirited discussion of alternative rules or moral standards—*and their consequences*. Maybe this would help clear the air in our high schools, where one assumes moral questions are constantly being put to the test by the various challenges and temptations in and out of the classroom.

We hope that this survey will give teachers the strength to stand up for what teachers have always stood for. And they don't have to resort to the Bible as the source of their authority. They can get it from political theorists and social essayists—from George Orwell, Robert Frost, Leo Tolstoy, John Cheever, and Hannah Arendt.

The challenge for teachers is to address the issue of moral reasoning and logic in a direct way, without violating constitutional standards or community norms. It's important for teachers to remember that they *do* have the tools.

Marching To Different Drummers

From a moral perspective, each child steps to the music he or she hears. No one system of values predominates. Instead, each child is guided by his or her own "moral compass." Although individual moral guideposts may allow a child to be placed in one of the categories listed below, each is obviously a moral composite of several, if not all, of them.

Civic Humanist (25 percent): Children in this group do what's best for everybody— their family, friends, school, community, or the nation at large.

Conventionalist (20 percent): Those in this group defer to authority. They are more likely to follow the advice of a parent, teacher, or youth leader.

Expressivist (18 percent): If it feels good, do it. Kids in this category do what makes them feel happy.

Theistic (16 percent): God makes them do it. These children adhere closely to religious authority, such as their minister or rabbi, or scripture.

Utilitarian (10 percent): If it helps them improve their situation or get ahead, they do it. —J.M.

Teaching Values in School: The Mirror and the Lamp

DAVID NYBERG

State University of New York at Buffalo

Moral education may be a phrase like "wet water." Education is inherently moral in some respects, just as water is inherently wet. This is because any planned, deliberate education, whether in liberal arts or manual arts, is always undertaken for the purpose of rendering the student, or the community in general, better off as a result of that education. Doing something to help improve the circumstances of people's lives is to act with moral purpose, and since education is meant to help people, all education is—whatever else it is—in some ways moral.[1] Not all education is deliberately planned, however, and of course not all of it takes place in schools. As Protagoras saw during his dialogue with Socrates, in society everybody is a teacher of values, each according to his or her abilities, as surely as every Greek citizen is a teacher of Greek. Values, or virtues, as they used to be called, are expressed in what we do, how we behave, and what we say. A lot of "unplanned moral instruction comes about in the very act of speaking, whether one is actually talking about values or not."[2] To change the metaphor a bit, we could say that morality is "as much embedded in the terms of everyday language as the experience of color is in our seeing."[3]

MORAL BUCK-PASSING

The problem as I see it is not whether to teach values—we simply cannot help doing that. The problem is twofold: how to choose wisely what we explicitly teach in the way of values, and how to understand and control the implicit moral education, such as it is these days, in schools and in the communities that support them. Of the two problems, the second is the more neglected and the more formidable precisely because we tend to be unaware of it. What is needed is an awareness of the landscape within which we operate when we set out deliberately to discuss or practice

moral education. Neither teachers nor parents can avoid teaching values through their own words and actions; they can only avoid thinking about *which ones* they actually do teach, *how* they teach them, and how these values compare with the ones they believe they ought to be teaching.

I put parents and teachers together in the last sentence because it is a mistake for either party to think that teachers are mainly or independently responsible for teaching values. They are not. At best they are parents' educational partners. If parents do not contribute to the moral education of their own children, teachers cannot reasonably be expected to make up the deficit.

Yes, teachers must teach values in school, but not alone, and not in opposition to what goes on (or does not go on) at home. Parents who sanction their children's watching five or six hours of television per day, who do not talk to their children about what they watch, and who read little other than what contributes directly to earning money or illustrates yet more ways to spend it cannot seriously expect their children to become interested in the value of education, or any of the values traditionally associated with being an educated person. Though parents may be aware of their implicit teaching of values when they invite their children's friends to share in some festive celebration or outdoor adventure, they must also learn to become aware of the negative messages they convey when they show little interest and less involvement in their children's own activities, including school. Perhaps the first move in rethinking how we teach values in school is to impress on parents that they, and not teachers, are their children's primary educators.

NOBODY KNOWS WHAT VALUES EDUCATION IS

The fact that there is so much persistent disagreement over teaching values—Do we? Should we? Who should? How do we know which ones?—is at once a

From *Teachers College Record*, Summer 1990, pp. 595-611. Copyright © 1990 by Teachers College, Columbia University. Reprinted by permission.

philosophical problem (of definition) and an invitation to philosophical reflection (achieving some new understanding by searching out and clarifying assumptions). We cannot assume, for example, that values education is a well-structured area, like chemistry, with definitely agreed-on characteristics and known procedures for effective teaching.

While the aim in chemistry, as in all science, is reduction of the complex into fewer and simpler laws, our aim in American public education is to cultivate an enlightened pluralism with regard to almost every aspect of our culture(s) and the values we hold, from the kind of democracy we want, to the way we would like our neighborhoods to be, to tastes in entertainment, religious views, what we find fit to eat, and so on. This is our blessing and our curse at the same time, for it means that we will always have to live with conflict; we have no hope at all that everyone will agree on anything really important, and we will probably never get completely organized.

On the other hand, we have the opportunity of using that conflict as a focus for open, public educational debate, and for protecting ourselves against the deplorably oppressive alternative of political, cultural, or religious orthodoxy. If values education were a structured area, it would be reasonable to envision a technology for teaching it. (If you have the raw materials and the specifications for a particular product in hand, you can build a machine to produce it; if you have the raw materials but no fixed idea of how the product ought to look in the end, no machine will do. Therefore, if you prize the ideal of enlightened pluralism in the realm of values, beware of all prepackaged programs for moral education.[4]) Some readers will have noticed that I have been using "enlightened pluralism" as if it were itself a "fixed idea." In fact, I do not take it to be a fixed idea so much as a preferred value. Although I do consider enlightened pluralism a goal for education in democratic society, I am not sure even my parents would agree with me as to where the line should be drawn between "enlightened" and "deluded by sophistication," or between "pluralism" and "lack of strong, essential commitment to anything."

SURVIVING AND FLOURISHING

What is behind our concern to "teach values"? I think at bottom we have two concerns. The first is survival, and the second is thriving or flourishing. Survival is the primary need: Violence, vandalism, drug abuse, teenage depression and suicide, a generation equally indifferent to world history and the future of the planet—these are clear threats to both local and international survival. Survival comes first: We must survive in order to thrive. But then how should we thrive? We need to have some ideal in mind to make the drudgery of hard thinking, work, and sacrifice worthwhile. Life without meaningful vision is no joy; it is a

burden. This is perhaps obvious in the world of labor and politics, but not so obvious in the world of interpersonal relations, or the inner *moral* world, where judgments are made in response to feelings as well as to reasons.

I do not want to state this division too strongly but perhaps survival ultimately will depend on some kind of rationality derived from scientific truth and understanding, while human flourishing will be best nurtured by a better understanding of our sentiments and an appreciation for the role of discretion with the truth in ordinary relations with others.

William James has said some interesting things about this in an essay called "On a Certain Blindness in Human Beings":

> Our judgments concerning the worth of things, big or little depend on the *feelings* the things arouse in us. Where we judge a thing to be precious in consequence of the *idea* we frame of it, this is only because the idea is itself associated already with a feeling. If we were radically feelingless, and if ideas were the only things our mind could entertain, we should lose all our likes and dislikes at a stroke, and be unable to point to any one situation or experience in life more valuable or significant than any other.

Now the blindness in human beings [I am talking about] is the blindness with which we all are afflicted in regard to the feelings of creatures and people different from ourselves.[5]

James goes on to argue that we should try to learn the simple truth that pain in our neighbors throbs the same as pain in ourselves, their joy is no less heartfelt than our own. To see this clearly, to be moved by the insight, is to be unable ever to forget it. Once you know this truth about the universality of human sentiment, you can begin to know your moral duty, which has a lot to do with the way we respond to human suffering.

James's insight does not come easily, however. Most of us have to take considerable trouble to learn it, and we must relearn it throughout our lives. Taking that trouble may be the most important step in moral education; causing that trouble could be the first obligation of parents and teachers concerned with teaching values. To put the point in different words: The most important moral skill we can learn is to think seriously about—and try persistently to feel—what it is like to be somebody else. I am not talking just about sympathy, which is the arousal of appropriate emotion; I am talking about empathy, which is giving up your own point of view for the purpose of seeing the world (an event) as someone else sees it, at least for a while.

TWO MORALITIES: CONVENTION AND AUTONOMY

William Frankena has written a good short book called *Thinking about Morality*, distinctive for its blend of wisdom and modesty. In the book Frankena draws a distinction between two kinds of morality and in so doing points out an ambivalence that we all, especially perhaps we educators, need to think about. The first kind is what he calls a positive, social morality. In John Locke's terms, it is "a law of opinion and reputation." We need it because

> if one is at all realistic, one must admit that very many of us humans are very often ignorant, weak-willed, prejudiced, wayward, easily tempted, thoughtless, inconsiderate, careless, unloving, irresponsible, lazy, self-interested, self-willed, etc., even when we are not hypocritical, mean, cruel, vicious, or wicked, as we also sometimes are. Furthermore, we are all immature for a rather long time; we all have to act quickly on occasion; we are all subject to pressures of various sorts; and we are all capable of self-deception even when we mean to take the moral point of view. For reasons such as these, society should not leave us wholly to our own consciences; even if we have consciences, and not all of us do, we are too likely to go awry in one way or another. Without any external aid or discipline, moreover, our individual consciences may tell us to do very different, and even immoral, things. Society must have a positive social morality of some kind, even if it does not include rules of some of the sorts that new moralists object to.[6]

(For example, some new moralists might object to rules about adult sex and abortion, but would insist on rules about conservation and pollution.)

Of course moral life is too complicated for any one set of rules about it to be complete and satisfactory. On the other hand, life is too complicated for us to live without at least some of them. We need some conventions, and we need to cooperate with some rules that make it possible for people who disagree to get along.

The second kind of morality is concerned with the ability—and the strength of will—to make morally important choices when it simply will not do to follow a particular rule, or some set of rules. Sometimes we need to step back from convention, evaluate it, and make decisions on the basis of personal commitment. It is not unusual to find that two or more principles of conventional morality come into conflict, or are in some other way inadequate to the situation. Should I betray my best friend by turning her over to the law if she has, in a moment of desperation, committed a petty theft in order to feed her child? Or should I hide this truth and betray my implicit promise as a citizen to obey the law and cooperate with its enforcement? In such cases, we are expected to act autonomously, that is, on the basis of some inner value to which we are bound of our own free choosing. Such choice involves some skills in reasoning, but it also involves the will to act independently and do what seems to be the right thing.

This second kind of morality presents a problem for educators. Surely, the will to act independently (moral autonomy) can be an impediment to moral education because—let's face it—we do not feel comfortable with young people, adolescents, deciding for themselves what is right and wrong. Some educators and parents may be particularly threatened by the fact that young people are more likely to ask other adolescents than adults for advice when they are not sure themselves what to do. On the other hand, if we educate a young person merely to conform uncritically to the conventions of our society, and not to think autonomously about those conventions themselves, can we say honestly that we have produced a moral agent, or a morally educated person? I do not think so. Obedience is not the same as moral choice, even when both may lead to the same action. Obedience requires knowing what the rules *are*, but moral choice requires knowing what the rules *mean* and what they are worth and when it is right to disobey them. Perhaps we should not assume that autonomy means "thinking freely for oneself." A better sense of the concept might be "thinking about one's relations to rules (for conduct and for moral reasoning), and what these rules mean personally."

The first kind of morality emphasizes finding *direction* based on social authority; the second is concerned more with *decision* based on independent judgment. The conflict between these two moralities, and our ambivalence about them, is unforgettably dramatized in Sophocles' *Antigone*. The action of the play is straightforward. Creon becomes king of Thebes in troubled times; his duty is to establish order and stability, to get Thebes back on track toward recovery from the devastations of war. Following an attack on Thebes, Creon buries one of his nephews with honor and decrees the other must lie unburied, rotting in the field as a symbol of the king's authority over those who dare threaten the state. His niece, Antigone, defies him and buries her brother. For this, Creon feels he must put her to death. She is willing to die, proud of her loyalty to what she believes most important in the world—her family and her religious beliefs. Early in the play, Ismene tries to reason with her sister, Antigone:

Ismene:
    The law is strong, we must give in to the law
    In this thing, and in worse. I beg the Dead
    To forgive me, but I am helpless: I must yield
    To those in authority. And I think it is dangerous
        business
    To be always meddling.
Antigone:
    I say that this crime is holy: I shall lie down
    With him in death, and I shall be as dear
    To him as he is to me.
    It is the dead,
    Not the living, who make the longest demands:
        We die for ever . . .
    You may do as you like,
    Since apparently the laws of the gods mean nothing
        to you.
Ismene:
    They mean a great deal to me; but I have no strength

To break the laws that were made for the public
  good.
 Antigone:
  That must be your excuse, I suppose. But as for me,
  I will bury the brother I love.

As events unfold, making Antigone's fate clear, she receives this judgment from the chorus:

Reverence is a virtue, but strength
Lives in established law: that must prevail. You have
  made your choice,
Your death is the doing of your conscious hand.

Creon stands for the morality of convention; the young Antigone stands for passionate commitment to values that she believes are beyond the prescriptions of any public morality. Creon's strength lies in his willingness to exercise the authority entrusted to him to look after the welfare of the state, even at the painful cost of his own family. Antigone's strength is defined by her heroic self-sacrifice for what she believes in most deeply. Both Creon and Antigone stand as objects of the wise man Teiresias' caution that "the only crime is pride."[7]

MORAL KNOWLEDGE AND MORAL WILL

To be moral, or to act morally, a person must believe in some values and have the will to act accordingly. When Duty whispers "Thou must!" it is no good for the student to reply, "I know, I know, but I won't." Each of these aspects poses its own question about the proper role of schooling in moral education: (1) Should schools teach particular values, and if so, how is this to be done? and (2) Should teachers be expected to teach the will to act morally, and if so, how is it possible to do this?

Those who fear moral indoctrination and (at least some of those who value moral pluralism believe that the proper educational role of the school is to teach *about* morality in a theoretical and comparative way that is itself morally neutral, but it is decidedly *not* the role of the school to teach people to *be* moral according to any specific point of view. The ground for this belief is roughly that commitment at the level of theory is less personally offensive and therefore more tolerable than commitment to particular values and practices that certainly are not universally shared in a pluralistic society.

Is this belief defensible? There are good reasons to think not.[8]

Education is and always has been about the acquisition of character, which includes expressions of moral attitudes. It is possible to redefine education as something else, as Carl Bereiter did in his book *Must We Educate?* where he argued that teachers are not in any way qualified to shape character because they are trained only to teach discrete skills and they have no right anyway to interfere with anyone's character precisely *because* it is so very important.[9] Short of assuming that kind of radical redefinition, we cannot avoid the commonplace observation that it is impossible for educators to be neutral about character and the expression of moral attitudes. Asking that would be like asking a physics teacher to be neutral about scientific method, or trying to paint a picture without a point of view. So, even if it were to be preferred, it would not be possible for teachers to be morally neutral about education. Still, Bereiter is half right. Teachers are not trained or formally qualified in moral education. Yet they have no choice: They cannot avoid contributing to it anyway, either directly as instructors of prescribed curriculum (as educational authorities), or indirectly as examples or models of lived values.

All that I have said just now applies to teaching within the school culture, which requires a certain shared sense of direction even to operate, and it applies to teaching about the broader society, some ideal of which is inherent in the very idea of education.

As many others have pointed out, we do not learn mathematics merely by learning "about" it; we learn mathematics by working through problems and demonstrating proofs ourselves. Likewise, we do not learn morality merely by being taught about it; we need practice in working through problems in situations that require moral reflection and choice. We need experience in all kinds of learning before we come to know what it is we are trying to know. Knowing what is good or what is right is partly a matter of being there, confronting a moral situation eye-to-eye, and partly a matter of arriving with a stock of sentiments, dispositions, values, and principles that may be called on in formulating a response. Neither knowledge nor will alone is sufficient for moral action. Responsibility, for example, means being *accountable* and in addition it means being *able to respond*. One can know that one is going to be held accountable, but one needs experience to learn whether one is or will be able to respond with a morally right action when accountability becomes an issue.

Anyway, it is a rationalist prejudice to limit what counts as knowledge only to whatever can be expressed as theory or as a set of rules for action. We know much more than we can tell. Aristotle, who has taught us quite a lot about knowledge of many kinds, emphasized the essential role of experience in learning to be moral. He called this kind of experience habituation through training and education. Such experience was important in Aristotle's moral theory because he believed that we *become* just people by *doing* just acts.[10] This might be the most efficient approach to take in attempting to teach the will to act morally. Perhaps today we should stress more the role of early habit training, and back it up with a structure of reinforcements based in motivations children already have, such as their strong interest in playing cooperatively, succeeding at manageable tasks, and avoiding trouble. The point is to show young people that moral action is in their terms profitable (useful and agreeable). It is not true for young people, nor is it true for many adults, that "virtue has its own rewards." If virtue is not useful or agreeable, or both, it carries no reward. The way to get children interested in moral behavior is to *show* them (not just tell them) that it is in their best interest. When we tell them to behave morally even if it means going against their own self-interest, and they demand to know "What's the use?" we had better have an answer. Of course moral principles play a role, but merely learning them and strutting them about has obvious drawbacks. As one (female) character observed of another (male) in Harley Granville Barker's *The Voysey Inheritance:* "That's the worst of acting on principle . . . one begins thinking of one's attitudes instead of the use of what one is doing."[11]

Aristotle's advice on the matter of developing a moral character was to begin early doing what is right—what is both useful and agreeable—in the context of social life as people actually live it, only later learning what principles are involved. Such principles as there are to guide us in moral matters will survive so long as they contribute to the quality of actual human lives. (I wonder whether history could be read as a series of experiments with moral hypotheses: The chief value for Homer was courage; for Kant, it was duty; and today it is either some kind of social utility or personal integrity.)

I have to add a note here about a philosophical problem of aiming directly at the development of moral character. Character may be defined as a stable state productive of choice that results in action. The ideal is intensity, and perhaps consistency, but without strain. The problem in setting out methodically to become a certain kind of character is that the very act of pursuing a model to be emulated undermines the project. It is likely to end in *posing* (like Osmond in Henry James's *Portrait of a Lady*). The problem can be described by comparing two senses of character-based morality. The first is the outward Aristotelian focus on the act itself; one learns to see through oneself what is to be done. The second is the inward literary focus on *becoming* a character who *has* a character of a certain sort; one learns to see through the eyes of the desired character instead of through one's own eyes. While Aristotelian moral education depends more on stories, in the sense that it depends on descriptions of personal choices made in context, than on general principles (which are also necessary but not sufficient), the literary model encourages one *to live an envisioned story as if it were one's own life*. These different uses of "story" may create some confusion between the two senses of character, and therefore between the various "story-based" approaches to education of character. It should

be clear by now that I favor the indirect, experiential, Aristotelian approach over the direct inculcation of moral principles.

BEING YOURSELF AND BEING SOMEBODY ELSE

Since I believe we ought to teach something about morality but we cannot teach everything, what could we point to as the key, the core, the essential minimum in moral education? My nominations are: (1) learning to read one's feelings and one's response-ability through guided face-to-face experiences, and (2) learning to empathize. Notice I do not list my own particular favorite values as objects of knowledge to be learned; nor do I choose the rules of moral reasoning, which are also very important. I choose instead two psychological attributes, or dispositions, or skills, or talents, or intelligences, or whatever they are, as the foundation for all else—including the ability to reason on the basis of rules and principles and values. Like the Enlightenment philosopher David Hume, I believe that morality is a product of human psychology, what he called the sentiments of fellow-feeling. Mark Twain gave life to this theory in his rendering of Huckleberry Finn's friendship with Jim.

LYING TO SAVE YOUR FRIEND

Take, for example, the situation Twain posed in *Huckleberry Finn* as Huck and his friend Jim, a slave, drifted on their raft toward the place where Jim would become legally free.[12]

> Jim said it made him all over trembly and feverish to be so close to freedom. Well, I can tell you it made me all over trembly and feverish, too, to hear him, because I begun to get it through my head that he was most free and who was to blame for it? Why, *me*. I couldn't get that out of my conscience, no how nor no way. . . . I tried to make out to myself that I warn't to blame, because I didn't run Jim off from his rightful owner; but it warn't no use, conscience up and says, every time, "But you knowed he was running for his freedom, and you could a paddled ashore and told somebody."

Huck has a crisis of conscience. The morality he has learned in rural Missouri tells him it is wrong to help slaves escape. It is stealing from the slave's owner, in this case, Miss Watson, who had done Huck no harm. But his morality clashes with his feelings, with his sympathy for his friend.

> My conscience got to stirring me up hotter than ever, until at last I says to it, "Let up on me—it ain't too late, yet—I'll paddle ashore at the first light, and tell." I felt easy, and happy, and light as a feather, right off. All my troubles was gone. . . . When I was fifty yards off, Jim says:
> "Dah you goes, de ole true Huck; de on'y white

gentlman dat ever kep' his promise to ole Jim."

Well, I just felt sick. But I says, I got to do it—I can't get out of it. Right then, along comes a skiff with two men in it, with guns, and they stopped and I stopped. One of them says:

"What's that yonder?"

"A piece of raft," I says.

"Do you belong on it?"

"Yes, sir."

"Any men on it?"

"Only one, sir."

"Well, there's five niggers run off to-night, up yonder above the head of the bend. Is your man white or black?"

I didn't answer up prompt. I tried to, but the words wouldn't come. I tried, for a second or two, to brace up and out with it, but I warn't man enough-hadn't the spunk of a rabbit. I see was weakening; so I just give up trying, and up and says—

"He's white."

We all learn morality in some kind of community, somewhere, and most often what we understand as "the morally right thing to do" is what that community has taught us to understand. In this episode, Huck suffers a conflict between his own natural sympathy and the morality he has learned in rural Missouri, which tells him it is wrong to help slaves escape because it is the same as stealing from the slave's owner, in this case Miss Watson, who had done Huck no harm.

Huck knows what his conscience says is the right thing to do but he feels sick about it. In the end, sympathy—his fellow-feeling for Jim—wins out over conscience and Huck lies to the two men hunting for runaway slaves. Huck believes that in lying he has acted weakly and wickedly. He cares for honesty and gratitude, and this requires him to give Jim up, but his love and compassion struggle against his conscience. He chooses for Jim and the hell that he believes awaits him, on the basis of irrational feeling and against the many reasons he has for giving him up. All the reasons are on the side of conscience. He has no principles or arguments on the side of feeling—he simply sees himself as failing through weakness to do what he believed to be right. Twain's masterful touch of irony shows how weakness sometimes leads to right action—or to put it another way, how morality sometimes requires what it normally forbids.

When sympathies are broad and kind like Huck's, and the morality in question is bad or at least contains principles we deeply disapprove of, then things will work out well. Moral principles can also help us when sympathies are questionable or confused. In this sense, principles that embody our best sympathies can help us when our feelings are not at their best. Sympathies and principles should therefore be thought of as checking and balancing each other—sometimes principles become untenable because of the strength of our feelings; sometimes feelings must be overridden. Experiences will evoke responses that can change the

way we think, and the way we choose to apply the principles we hold. Feelings are vital to moral conduct, but they are not everything. Sometimes they must be subordinated. The same may be said of moral principles. Sometimes we must rise above principle to do the right thing. Without these sentiments a person has no basis for morality, and no motivation to develop skills in moral reasoning. The opposite of morality is not immorality; it is indifference.

EMPATHY AND PREJUDICE

Jane Elliott, then a third-grade teacher in Riceville, Iowa, has given us a stunning example of how children can learn through direct experience about their own sentiments of fellow-feeling.[13] On a Friday in April 1968, the day after Martin Luther King, Jr., had been murdered in Memphis, Jane Elliott determined to teach her third graders a lesson in discrimination that carried far beyond the "sympathetic indifference" toward racism she saw in her all-white, all-Christian community. Her lesson began with a question: "I don't think we really know what it would be like to be a black child, do you? I mean it would be hard to know, really, unless we actually experienced discrimination ourselves, wouldn't it?" The children were puzzled until she explained what they were to do. "Suppose we divided the class into blue-eyed and brown-eyed people. Suppose for the rest of today the blue-eyed people became the inferior group. Then, on Monday, we could reverse it so that the brown-eyed children were inferior. Wouldn't that give us a better understanding of what discrimination means?"[14]

Ms. Elliott was not prepared for what she saw:

By the lunch hour, there was no need to think before identifying a child as blue or brown-eyed. I could tell simply by looking at them. The brown-eyed children were happy, alert, having the time of their lives, and they were doing far better work than they had ever done before. The blue-eyed children were miserable. Their posture, their expressions, their entire attitudes were those of defeat. Their classroom work regressed sharply from that of the day before. Inside of an hour or so, they looked and acted as though they were, in fact, inferior. It was shocking.

But even more frightening was the way the brown-eyed children turned on their friends of the day before, the way they accepted almost immediately as true what had originally been described as an exercise. For there was no question, after an hour or so, that they actually believed they were superior.[15]

The children were carefully led through a debriefing at the end of the day, and through many subsequent discussions in which they had the chance, over and over, to read their own and their classmates' feelings as they reported what they actually felt, wished, and thought they "knew" during the experiment. Jane Elliott had a grasp of the difference between emotional and intellectual learning, and she had the creative will to devise a lesson that she was sure would not easily be forgotten. A reunion of her third graders many years later, when they had become parents and were involved with their own children's moral education, proved her right. Their memories of the experiment were still vivid; their attitudes reflected an understanding of discrimination; their behavior as parents demonstrated a moral will that was connected with, if not rooted in, this dramatic early experience. Their teacher's own perspective remained modest: "I'm not so naive that I think this single exercise is going to change the world—or even Riceville. But we have to start somewhere if we hope to live in a society free of the irrationality of racism. I'm a teacher. I work with children. This is simply where I started."[16] She has gone on to run this experiment with other children and with adults, invariably with the same results. Her aim always has been to develop a truly functional empathy through guided "eye-to-eye" experience.

Both learning your own response-ability and learning to think what it is like to be somebody else, someone likely to be affected by what you do, involve learning about feelings and overcoming the blindness to feeling as the basis for judgment, which James wrote of so eloquently. Life is shot through with values and meanings that we miss through being insensible to our own and others' experiences. In many instances, it is easier for us to read about values than to experience them, or to appreciate others' experiencing them. Not many of us have run across a Jane Elliott in our schooling.

In taking a slightly different tack on the value of face-to-face experience as a means for moral education, Harold Howe, among others, has argued that "youth has been progressively denied the opportunity to be engaged in work that is important to others, and therefore denied the rewards such work produces."[17] Howe has reason to believe in a direct link between community service and the education of feeling and emotion. In a way, it seems strange even to think about moral education without including the element—the requirement?—of community service. What is the point of moral education if not to include the needs of others in one's conscious behavior?

THE MIRROR AND THE LAMP

I do not mean to imply that the answer to our concern about teaching values is all this easy, however. A one-time classroom experiment, or an isolated experience in community service, is not likely to be sufficient for altering moral understanding or shaping moral attitudes in every case. Experiences mix with mind in ways we do not fully understand. People have different capacities, or to use Howard Gardner's terms, different kinds of intelligences, for dealing with experience. Gardner thinks that "an intelligence is the ability to solve problems, or to create products, that are

valued within one or more cultural settings,"[18] and that one of these intelligences has to do with inter- and intrapersonal relations—what I have been calling fellow-feeling and self-understanding.

Key to this kind of intelligence is a refined sense of self. Psychology has given us two plausible perspectives on self. Freud located it within the individual and isolated it as *the* necessary object of introspection. William James and other social psychologists taught us to see self as the individual's relationship to others. Gardner elaborates on this difference:

> On the one side, there is the development of the internal aspects of a person. The core capacity at work here is *access to one's own feeling life*—one's range of affects or emotions: the capacity instantly to effect discriminations among these feelings and, eventually, to label them, to enmesh them in symbolic codes, to draw upon them as a means of understanding and guiding one's behavior.
> The other personal intelligence turns outward, to other individuals. The core capacity here is *the ability to notice and make distinctions among other individuals* and, in particular, among their moods, temperaments, motivations, and intentions.[19]

This distinction is reflected in my subtitle, "The Mirror and the Lamp," which "identifies two common and antithetic metaphors of mind, one comparing the mind to a reflector of external objects, the other to a radiant projector which makes a contribution to the objects it perceives."[20] Perhaps the moral ideal is the person who can alternate between these capacities as reflector and radiant projector and show that in moral life, anyway, they need not be antithetical, at least in the strong sense of being direct opposites. They may be taken together as a whole gestalt of mind—now the lamp is figure and the mirror background, now they switch places and the mirror comes forward only to be illuminated from behind by the lamp. In any case, these metaphors give illustration to the distinction that I have been working at clarifying between reading one's own feelings and empathy for others.[21]

It goes without saying that some people are born with greater capacities for musical understanding and performance, or bodily-kinesthetic activity, logic and math, language, and so on. It may be equally true—and I think it probably is—that we are born with a similar spread of capacities for the inter- and intrapersonal realm as well. If that is the case, then we might expect that some but not others will develop the psychological basis of moral action with ease, some will refine their knowledge with relatively little effort because they can more naturally read their own and others' feelings along with the clues that disguise them. In other words, there may be reason to believe that not everyone is equally capable of learning to be moral in the same ways with the same amount of attention and effort, because individual "profiles of intelligences" vary along this dimension as they do along other dimensions. (I should point out emphatically to avoid any confusion that I am *not* arguing here for some kind of genetically determined moral IQ. Rather, with Gardner, I want to emphasize the multiplicity of intelligence, and the complexity of the relationship between the various intelligences and sentiment in moral behavior. Intelligences as Gardner speaks of them are several in kind, like dispositions; all can be educated, each in different ways; no one is best.) The kind of moral education I have been talking about may be suitable for some—even most—but not all. There are other kinds. It is important always to remember that the realm of values is not a well-structured area, nor is there a definitely agreed-on way of teaching the values we choose as the ones we ought to teach.

Again, let me use the words of William James, this time from an essay called "What Makes a Life Significant," to illustrate another aspect of this important point:

> Every Jack sees in his own particular Jill charms and perfections to the enchantment of which we stolid onlookers are stone-cold. Which has the more vital insight into the nature of Jill's existence, as a fact? Is he in excess, being in this matter a maniac? or are we in defect, being victims of a pathological anaesthesia as regards Jill's magical importance? Surely the latter; surely to Jack are the profounder truths revealed; surely poor Jill's palpitating little life-throbs *are* among the wonders of creation, *are* worthy of this sympathetic interest; and it is to our shame that the rest of us cannot feel like Jack. For Jack realizes Jill concretely and we do not. He struggles toward a union with her inner life, divining her feelings, anticipating her desires, understanding her limits as manfully as he can, and yet inadequately, too; for he is also afflicted with some blindness, even here. Whilst we dead clods that we are, do not even seek after these things, but are contented that that portion of eternal fact named Jill should be for us as if it were not. Jill, who knows her inner life, knows that Jack's way of taking it—so importantly—is the true and serious way; and she responds to the truth in him by taking him truly and seriously, too. May the ancient blindness never wrap its clouds about either of them again! Where would any of *us* be, were there no one willing to know us as we really are or ready to repay us for *our* insight by making recognizant return?
>
> We ought, all of us, to realize each other in this intense, pathetic, and important way.
>
> If you say that this is absurd, and that we cannot be in love with everyone at once, I merely point out to you that, as a matter of fact, certain persons do exist with an enormous capacity for friendship and for taking delight in other people's lives; and that such persons know more of truth than if their hearts were not so big.[22]

This, I think, is close to the heart of the moral matter. To take others truly and seriously, and to be taken truly and seriously ourselves, is to become familiar with the moral sentiment, the fellow-feeling that is the seat, the foundation of all morality. It is also the source of self-esteem, of feeling important to someone for some reason. It is in this way that we come to feel the difference between right and wrong, and to become *interested* in reasoning further when we are not sure what to do. To repeat an earlier point made about character education: Teach moral behavior, not directly, but through care for the context in which you hope to find it. Teach an appreciation for truth-telling, not as formal rules, but rather by showing how to use it in dealing with difficult problems.

POSTSCRIPT: CAN THERE BE MORAL EXPERTS?

Knowing right from wrong does not involve any particular skill or factual information. This kind of knowing is like having a taste, or caring about something. Once you know the difference between fairness and unfairness, or between bad and excellent wine, for example, you may possibly cease to *care*, but you cannot *forget* what the difference is. Likewise, being unselfish or forgiving (i.e., virtuous) is not to be good at *doing* anything; virtues are not skills. They are to be classed with tastes and preferences (educated or cultivated ones to be sure). The point is that cultivated taste for generosity or for poetry might be *lost*, but this is not the same as *forgetting* the difference between good and bad poetry, generosity and selfishness. This kind of learning Gilbert Ryle calls "appreciating" and he says it requires "studiousness, judiciousness, and acuteness" along with caring, which covers a range of feelings and actions. "There is nothing in particular that the honest [person] knows, ex officio, how to do. He is not, ex officio, even a bit of an expert at anything."[23]

If Ryle is right, then although we can get a kind of moral knowledge, we can never become moral experts. That, I think, is just as well. I would rather my son had a teacher with a cultivated taste for moral education, ill-structured as it is, than one who professed to be expert in the area.

NOTES

1. T. F. Devany, "Education—A Moral Concept," in *New Essays in the Philosophy of Education*, ed. Glenn Langford and D. J. O'Conner (London: Routledge & Kegan Paul, 1973).

2. Nancy Gayer, "On Making Morality Operational," in *Readings in the Philosophy of Education: A Study in Curriculum*, ed. Jane R. Martin (Boston: Allyn and Bacon, 1970), p. 265.

3. Ibid., p. 264.

4. Much the same sort of thing can be said about the different aims of socializing and educating, where the image of a "good result" is clear for socializing but not for producing an "educated person." For more on this see David Nyberg and Kieran Egan, *The Erosion of Education: Socialization and the Schools* (New York: Teachers College Press, 1981), especially ch. 8.

5. Reprinted in William James, *Talks to Teachers* (New York: Norton, 1958), p. 149. Emphasis in original.

6. William Frankena, *Thinking about Morality* (Ann Arbor: University of Michigan Press, 1980), p. 36.

7. Quotations are from the Dudley Fitts and Robert Fitzgerald translation of the play in Sophocles, *The Oedipus Cycle* (New York: Harcourt, Brace and World, 1939).

8. I take some of the following discussion from Brian Crittenden, *Form and Content in Moral Education* (Toronto: The Ontario

4. MORALITY AND VALUES IN EDUCATION

Institute for Studies in Education, 1972), especially ch. vii.

9. Carl Bereiter, *Must We Educate?* (Englewood Cliffs, N.J.: Prentice Hall, 1973). For criticism of Bereiter's views see Nyberg and Egan, *The Erosion of Education*, ch. 4.

10. *Nicomachian Ethics*, II i 4.

11. Harley Granville Barker, "The Voysey Inheritance," in *Three Plays by Granville Barker* (London: Sidgwick and Jackson, Ltd., 1909), Act III.

12. Mark Twain, *Adventures of Huckleberry Finn*, 2nd ed. (New York: Norton, 1977). Quoted material is from pages 73–75.

13. Discussed in William Peters, *A Class Divided, Then and Now* (New Haven: Yale University Press, 1987).

14. Ibid., p. 20.

15. Ibid., pp. 24–25.

16. Ibid., p. 104.

17. Harold Howe II, "Can Schools Teach Values?" *Teachers College Record* 89, no. I (Fall 1987): 58.

18. Howard Gardner, *Frames of Mind* (New York: Basic Books, 1983), p. x.

19. Ibid., p. 293. Emphasis in original.

20. M. H. Abrams, *The Mirror and the Lamp: Romantic Theory and the Critical Tradition* (Oxford: Oxford University Press, 1953), preface.

21. For more on the skills involved and a theory of their origin, see Jean Baker Miller, *Toward a New Psychology of Women* (Boston: Beacon Press, 1976).

22. In James, *Talks to Teachers*, pp. 170–71.

23. Gilbert Ryle, "On Forgetting the Difference between Right and Wrong," in *Essays in Moral Philosophy*, ed. A. I. Melden (Seattle: University of Washington Press, 1958), p. 157.

Ethical Decision Making for Teachers

LARRY EBERLEIN

Larry Eberlein is a professor of educational psychology at the University of Alberta in Edmonton, Canada. He is currently a member of the Ethics Committee of the Canadian Psychological Association.

Dian Johnson was an attractive fifteen-year-old student at Kennedy Middle School. She was quite popular with her classmates and well accepted by the teaching staff. Although not at the top of her class, she had been on the honor roll the previous two years. She had no record of difficulties or problem behavior in school.

On Thursday afternoon, she came in a panic to see Janice Waite, the English teacher and part-time guidance counselor. She stated she couldn't come back to school the next day and didn't know what to do. After calming Dian down, Ms. Waite attempted to discover the basis of the problem. Dian replied tearfully that she couldn't go back to her math class again because she was afraid of Mr. Erickson, the math teacher.

When pressed, Dian said that Mr. Erickson had been paying a lot of attention to her in the last few weeks and on a couple of occasions had fondled her breasts. This had upset Dian so much that she didn't know what to do. She wanted to talk to someone about it but was afraid to tell her parents. When she told her friends, they laughed at her. "They just don't take Mr. Erickson very seriously; they say he does that to all the girls!" said Dian.

What should the teacher do in this situation? An impulsive person might pick up the phone and call Dian's parents or the police. Although such a decision might be ethically acceptable, the reflective teacher would consider the matter further. What are Ms. Waite's moral and ethical responsibilities to Dian, her parents, the other girls in Mr. Erickson's class, the school in general, and specifically to Mr. Erickson? To whom does she look for guidance?

A Teacher's Code of Conduct

To be professionals, teachers need to understand the moral aspects of teaching and how to make ethical decisions relating to their profession and the welfare of their students. Professional groups tend to have statements about behavioral expectations rather than a systematic ethical code based on articulated moral principles. The National Education Association (NEA) is better than many professional groups when it offers as ideals the belief in the worth and dignity of persons, truth, and democratic principles. Following these ideals are some behavioral expectations that flow from a commitment to both the students and the profession. For example, teachers are expected to preserve confidentiality, if possible, but make reasonable efforts to protect students from conditions harmful to their health and safety. At the same time, teachers generally are not to disclose information about colleagues.

These standards of conduct do not really provide an ethical rationale for making a decision in the above case. Although Ms. Waite's primary concern should be with Dian and the other students, she also has ethical responsibilities to her profession and to Mr. Erickson. Does any disclosure serve a compelling professional purpose? Does she have a legal duty to report Mr. Erickson's behavior as child sexual abuse? Janice Waite

From *The Clearing House*, Vol. 63, No. 3, November 1989, pp. 125-129. Reprinted with permission of the Helen Dwight Reid Educational Foundation. Published by Heldref Publications, 4000 Albemarle St., N.W., Washington, D.C. 20016. Copyright © 1989.

probably has had little experience in resolving ethical issues. These are not matters that are included in most teacher education programs, although useful material is available (Strike and Soltis 1985).

Some have argued that ethics is the responsibility of management, not of the teaching profession (Liberman 1988). It is true that most teacher groups are in a conflict of interest position when dealing with certain ethical dilemmas. It is my position that although ethical decision making is the primary responsibility of the individual teacher, the teacher must have the help and support of colleagues, management, and the professional association.

What would be useful is a new code of ethics based on moral principles with some guidance in the ethical-decision process. This process may occur very rapidly, especially when noncontradictory, clear-cut guidelines exist. However, when ethical principles are in conflict, a more time-consuming process of deliberation is required. One such possibility is the following code, based on the work of the Canadian Psychological Association (CPA).

A Code of Ethics

In 1986, the CPA Ethics Committee presented a new Code of Ethics that has been widely adopted in Canada. The Code is based upon four moral principles representing those ethical values used most consistently by professionals who responded to the presentation of ethical dilemmas. Each principle is followed by value statements and standards considered to be the most generally applicable and to have consensual validity. When conflicts occur, the higher principle should receive the greater emphasis, except where there is a clear and imminent danger to the physical safety of any known or unknown individual. These four principles are as follows:

Principle I: Respect for the Dignity of Persons
Principle II: Responsible Caring
Principle III: Integrity in Relationships
Principle IV: Responsibility to Society

The result is a code that offers more help to individuals than any existing code. This is true because of the structure; the code is better organized, more coherent, and more directly related to the underlying principles that need to be considered when deciding on ethical action. Each of the four principles is followed by an extensive discussion of the values that are included in, and give definition to, the principle. These are, in turn, followed by the standards appropriate to that principle. "Both minimal behavioral expectations as well as more idealized attitudinal and behavioral expectations" are included in the standards (CPA 1986, p. 6E).

I would propose that these same four principles serve as a focus for a new ethical code for teachers that would have its own educational value (Eberlein 1988). To assist in this endeavor, consider the moral and value rationale behind each of the principles, and see which Janice Waite might consider.

I. Dignity of Persons

In all contacts with students, teachers should accept as fundamental the principle of respect for the dignity of their students. This is the belief that each student should be treated as a person or an end in himself or herself, not as an object or a means to an end. Teachers should acknowledge that all students are entitled to have their innate worth as human beings appreciated and that this worth is not enhanced or reduced by any individual differences. Although teachers have a responsibility to respect the dignity of all persons, they always have a greater responsibility to their students, who are in a more vulnerable position, than to persons indirectly involved (school boards and other teachers, parents, and the general public).

The concept of moral rights is an essential component of respect for the dignity of persons. Rights to privacy, self-determination, and autonomy are of particular importance, including the right of students to provide informed consent to activities that involve them. As vulnerabilities increase (at younger ages), the power of persons to control their environment or their lives decreases. The younger the child, the greater the teacher's responsibility to establish safeguards to protect the student's rights.

This principle also includes the concept of equal justice. All students are entitled to benefit equally from the knowledge and contributions of the teaching profession.

II. Responsible Caring

A basic ethical expectation of any profession is that a practitioner be competent and involved in activities that are not harmful to members of society. Teachers must be concerned about the welfare of any student, family, or group with whom they have a relationship as a teacher. Their greatest responsibility is to protect the welfare of those directly involved in their activities (usually the student); their responsibility to school boards, parents, and the general public is therefore secondary.

Because students are seldom "asked" for their consent to take part in many school activities, there is a greater urgency for responsible caring by teachers to protect the welfare of students under their control. This principle would lead teachers to consider the potential harm and benefits involved in their proposed activities, to predict the likelihood of the risk or benefit occurring, and to choose activities where the potential benefits outweigh any potential harm. In the process, teachers need to use pedagogical methods that minimize harm and maximize benefits and to take responsibility for correcting any harmful effects that have occurred as a result of their activities.

This calls for a self-awareness on the part of the

teacher and a recognition that incompetent action is, by definition, unethical. Competent teachers continue to expand and up-date their knowledge and engage in self-reflection to see how their own values and social position affect their teaching activities. These teachers are concerned about both short-term and long-term physical and psychological factors in their students. These include self-worth, fear, humiliation, and interpersonal trust, as well as physical safety, comfort, and freedom from injury.

Responsible caring recognizes the ability of individuals, families, and groups to care for themselves and each other. However, teachers do recognize that as vulnerabilities increase or as power to control one's own life decreases, they have an increasing responsibility to protect the well-being of the student, family, or group involved.

III. Integrity in Relationships

Relationships formed by teachers with students, families, and other staff members embody explicit and implicit mutual expectations of integrity. These include fairness, impartiality, straightforwardness, avoidance of deception, avoidance of conflicts of interest, and the provision of accurate information.

As these values exist within the context of the first two principles (Respect for the Dignity of Persons and Responsible Caring), there will be circumstances in which honesty and straightforwardness will need to be tempered. At times, full disclosure may not be needed or desired and, in some circumstances, may be a risk to the dignity or well-being of others, especially those in more vulnerable positions.

Professional integrity and teaching accountability imply a responsibility for teachers to maintain competence in their respective fields and require that teachers actively rely on, and be guided by, their professional community and its guidelines and requirements.

IV. Responsibility to Society

Teaching exists as a profession within the context of society. Teachers have responsibilities to the society in which they live and work and to the welfare of all human beings in those societies. Teachers are expected to use their knowledge in the development of social structures and policies that will be used for beneficial purposes—purposes that support and reflect the first three principles.

Teachers acknowledge that many social structures have evolved slowly over time in response to human need, are valued by society, and are primarily beneficial. Teachers convey respect for these social structures and avoid unwarranted or unnecessary disruptions. Suggestions for, and action toward, change or enhancement of such social structures are carried out only through an educational process that seeks to achieve a

consensus within society through democratic means.

On the other hand, some social structures ignore or oppose the principles of respect for the dignity of the person, responsible caring, and integrity in relationships. In extreme cases, it would be irresponsible for teachers to work within these social structures and not to be critical of them. They should be an advocate for change to occur as quickly as possible.

Teachers as a whole need to be self-reflective about the role of education and their own role in society, and about the ways in which they might be contributing to or detracting from beneficial societal changes. Teachers need to engage in even-tempered observation and interpretation of social structure and policies, their effects, and their process of change. Individual teachers must decide for themselves the most appropriate and beneficial use of their time and talents in helping to meet this collective responsibility.

Problem Solving for a Teacher's Ethical Dilemmas

It is difficult to apply a limited set of rules to problems that relate to human relationships. Ethical issues in schools almost always involve some conflict among the values, rights, and responsibilities of the teacher and those to whom he or she relates: students and their families, administrators, and other teachers.

Sometimes, in the area of professional ethics, no single response is very satisfying, although more than one may meet the bare requirements of ethical behavior. On many issues where there is not a strong consensus or a specific standard to be referred to, individuals fall back on their own value systems and their interpretation of the spirit of the code that governs their behavior. In addition, there are conflicts between code provisions, among codes of different professional associations, and between codes and the legal requirements of a particular jurisdiction.

Kitchener (1984) discusses two levels of moral thinking—an immediate (intuitive) level and a critical-evaluative level. The "shoulds" and "musts" tend to reflect the intuitive level, the ordinary or perhaps impulsive moral judgments that may be ethically acceptable. Upon further reflection and consideration of the conflicting values, rights, and responsibilities, open-minded teachers usually will modify or qualify a first response. Kitchener describes this critical-evaluative level as having three components: (1) rules and codes, (2) ethical principles, and (3) ethical theory. Use of this higher level implies attention to ethical principles and the use of a systematic approach to making ethical decisions.

It is essential that teachers develop their own problem-solving approaches and be prepared to face ethical problems, such as that faced by Janice Waite. Several authors have developed models with a common pattern involving identifying alternatives, analysis, choice of action, and evaluation. The CPA model (patterned after Tymchuk 1986) is as follows:

1. Identify ethically relevant issues and practices and all persons or groups that need to be considered.

2. Develop several possible courses of action or alternatives.

3. Consider the short-term, on-going, and long-term consequences of each alternative plus the psychological, social, and economic costs. This in effect provides a risk-benefit analysis of each alternative as it affects each person or group.

4. Choose a course of action after applying existing principles, values, and standards. This is the value orientation step.

5. Take action, with a commitment to assume responsibility for the consequences of the action.

6. Evaluate the action.

7. Assume responsibility for consequences of action, including correction of any negative consequences.

Application of Model

In Ms. Waite's dilemma, use of this model would first identify the persons or groups to be considered. These would include Dian and her family, other students in the school, the staff of the school (including Janice Waite and Mr. Erickson), the teaching profession, and society.

Dian's dignity and right to autonomy, privacy, confidentiality, self-determination, and freedom from harassment are relevant issues. Because Mr. Erickson also has similar rights, responsible caring would consider that public knowledge of the charge could destroy Mr. Erickson's teaching career and have a lasting impact on him and his family. Even if Dian's story is not proved, Mr. Erickson would continue under a cloud. Fairness implies an honest consideration of alternatives; due process implies a chance to be heard.

The principal and other staff have to consider the ripple effect of Mr. Erickson's behavior, the right of society to appropriate behavior from its employees, a possible criminal investigation, and the subsequent reflection on both the school and the profession. Janice Waite becomes a key player and will have to accept responsibility for anything she does.

A final issue of some importance is Dian's family's right to know and be involved in what has happened to her and to have input into the decision process. Society has given parents general control over the upbringing and education of their children, even when parental wishes conflict with the children's desires (Henniger 1987).

With this in mind, what can Ms. Waite do? Several possible alternatives come to mind:

1. Counsel and support Dian but take no further action.
2. Move Dian to another math class.
3. Quietly observe Mr. Erickson's behavior.
4. Call in the other students to verify Mr. Erickson's behavior.
5. Discuss the matter with Mr. Erickson.
6. File a complaint with the teacher's association.
7. Refer the matter to Mr. Erickson's superior or the principal.
8. Call Dian's parents, even against her wishes, and let them decide.
9. Call the child welfare authorities or police.

Some of these alternatives might be quickly discarded or others added, but the list will suffice for Ms. Waite to begin the time-consuming task of examining each of the alternatives and seeing how it will affect the persons involved. Although several alternatives appear to be ethical, none will fully meet the competing demands of the case. Ms. Waite may want to consult and discuss the issues with others but ultimately will have to make a decision on which alternative (or combination of alternatives) to choose. In the process, she may well find another choice of action that is more acceptable than those listed.

Conclusion

The teaching profession has a split personality. On the one hand, teachers—both individually and collectively—see themselves as professionals dedicated to the ideals of education. On the other hand, teachers are part of a trade union that bargains with the school boards over wages and working conditions. For example, in 1988, the NEA adopted forty-four policy resolutions related to teacher welfare and collective bargaining rights. Although much of a teacher's code of conduct is related to the professional aspects of teaching, many provisions are related to the union goal of promoting solidarity within the union. One of the goals is to protect the union leadership and the various committees from undue complaints and criticism. Another goal is to protect individual members from inappropriate criticism and provide them a grievance procedure within the union.

The concern in this paper has been with the professional aspect of the issue. What values and ethical concerns are appropriate to education? Certainly we can assume that all teachers are competent in their chosen subject areas and possess a basic knowledge of pedagogical principles. What additional moral and ethical principles should apply?

Teachers want to behave ethically. Yet many do not recognize the ethical dilemmas they confront each day. For example, is it ethical to keep an entire class from recess because one (unknown) member stole money from the teacher? A teacher's Code of Conduct needs to be placed within the framework of a teacher's Code of

Ethics. A series of ethical dilemmas involving the teaching profession would help define a set of standards that could be incorporated into the four principles discussed earlier. The educational value for the profession would be invaluable.

REFERENCES

Canadian Psychological Association, Committtee on Ethics. 1986. Code of Ethics. *Highlights* 8(1): 6E–12E.

Eberlein, L. 1988. The new CPA Code of Ethics for Canadian psychologists: An education and training perspective. *Canadian Psychology* 29: 206–12.

Henniger, M. L. 1987. Parental rights and responsibilities in the educational process. *The Clearing House* 60: 226–29.

Kitchener, K. S. 1984. Intuition, critical evaluation and ethical principles: The foundation for ethical decision in counseling psychology. *The Counseling Psychologist* 12(3): 43–55.

Liberman, M. 1988. Professional ethics in public education: An autopsy. *Phi Delta Kappan* 70: 159–60.

National Education Association. 1988. The 1988–89 resolutions of the National Education Association. *NEA Today* 7(5): 21–23.

Strike, K. A., and J. F. Soltis. 1985. *The ethics of teaching*. New York: Teachers College Press.

Tymchuk, A. J. 1986. Guidelines for ethical decision making. *Canadian Psychology* 27: 36–43.

Discipline and Schooling

When talking with teachers and prospective teachers regarding what concerns them about their roles (or prospective roles) in the classroom, it is usual that "discipline," the management of student behavior, will rank near or at the top of their list. Knowing what classroom learning environment you want and what interactions you want among students and between students and yourself (the teacher) is the starting point. A teacher needs a clear understanding of what kind of learning environment is most appropriate for the subject matter and age of the students. Any person who wants to teach must also want his or her students to learn well and in a manner that helps them to learn basic values of respect for others and how to become more effective citizens. Human and caring ways to do this are most valuable and effective.

There is considerable debate among educators regarding certain approaches used in schools to achieve a form of order in classrooms that also develops respect for self and others. The dialogue about this point is spirited and informative. The bottom line for any effective and humane approach to discipline in the classroom and the necessary starting point is the teacher's emotional balance and capacity for self-control. This precondition creates a further one—that the teacher wants to be in the classroom with his or her students. Unmotivated teachers have great difficulty motivating students.

Helping young people learn the skills of self-control and self-motivation to become productive, contributing, and knowledgeable adult participants in society is one of the most important tasks that good teachers undertake. These are teachable and learnable skills; they do not relate to heredity or social condition. They can be learned by any human being who wants to learn them and who is cognitively (intellectually) able to learn them. We further know that these skills are learnable by virtually all but the most severely cognitively disabled persons. There is a large knowledge base on how teachers can help students to learn self-control. All that is required is the willingness of teachers to learn these skills themselves and teach them to their students. Some might say that this is a task for specialists in methods of teaching and educational psychology. I profoundly disagree with those who would make such an exclusionary academic claim. No topic is more fundamentally related, to any thorough examination of the social and cultural foundations of education.

There are many sound techniques that new teachers can use to achieve success in managing students' classroom behavior. They should not be afraid to ask colleagues questions and to develop peer support groups. These peer support groups should be composed of those colleagues with whom they work with confidence and trust. Educators at all levels encounter some behavioral problems with some students. Even educators of adults sometimes have behavioral management problems in training activities or educational programs. Young teachers starting out in the elementary and secondary schools are always concerned about how they will manage disruptive, disorderly, or disobedient students.

Few problems influence the morale of teachers more than the issue of managing student behavior in the elementary and secondary schools. School discipline involves many moral, legal, and ethical questions, It is a highly value-laden topic on which there is a great diversity of opinion over what techniques of behavior management are effective and desirable.

Teachers' core ethical principles come into play when deciding what constitutes defensible and desirable standards of student conduct. As in medicine, realistic preventive techniques combined with humane but clear principles of procedure seem to be effective. Teachers need to realize that, before they can control behavior, they must identify what student behaviors are desired in their classrooms. They need to reflect, as well, on the emotional tone and ethical principles implied by their own behaviors. To optimize their chances of achieving the classroom atmosphere they wish, teachers must strive for emotional balance within themselves; they must learn to be accurate observers; and they must develop just, fair strategies of intervention to aid students in learning self-control and good behavior. A good teacher is a good model of courtesy, respect, tact, and discretion. Children learn by observing how other persons behave as well as by being told how they are to behave.

Teachers are demanding the respect to which they believe all working people are entitled. They want safety, peace, security, a sense of pride, and the opportunity to practice their art in environments where their efforts are appreciated. Nothing less than this is satisfactory. The National Education Association (NEA) and the American Federation of Teachers (AFT) are calling for public support of teachers in order to improve the quality of teaching and learning in the schools. Greater respect for teachers, if achieved, would be a major turning point in American education, and it is a goal worth seeking.

Confidence in one's own innate worth and in one's ability to teach effectively goes a long way toward reducing or eliminating discipline problems in educational settings. Teachers often function as role models for their students without even being aware of it. Later in life, they might be told by former students what an impact they had;

these revelations are precious to them. From the first day of the first year of teaching, "good" teachers maintain firm but caring control over their classes by means of continuing observation of and reflection on classroom activities. There is no substitute for positive, assertive teacher interaction with students in class.

This unit addresses many of the topics covered in basic foundations courses. The selections shed light on classroom management issues, teacher leadership skills, the legal foundations of education, and the rights and responsibilities of teachers and students. In addition, the articles can be discussed in foundations courses involving curriculum and instruction or individualized approaches to testing. This unit falls between the units on moral education and equal opportunity because it can be directly related to either or both of them.

Looking Ahead: Challenge Questions

What are good general rules, subject to amendment, which can guide a first-year teacher's initial efforts to manage student behavior?

What reliable information is available on the extent and severity of school discipline problems in North America? What sources contain such information?

What are some of the best means for preventing or minimizing serious misbehavior in school settings?

What types of punishment are defensible in behavior management? Is "punishment" ever defensible?

What ethical issues may be raised in the management of student behavior in school settings?

What are some of the best techniques for helping someone to learn self-control?

What civil rights do students have? Do public schools have fewer rights than private schools in controlling student behavior problems? Why or why not? What are the rights of a teacher in managing student behavior?

Do any coercive approaches to behavioral management in schools work better than noncoercive ones?

Is corporal punishment an appropriate method of discipline? What are your reasons for being for or against it?

Why is teacher self-control a major factor in just and effective classroom management strategies?

What are the moral responsibilities of teachers in managing student behavior?

Take the Lead!

Design a Classroom That Works

Teacher Frank Garcia knows that the best classroom environments don't just happen; they're carefully designed. Here, he shares his do's and don'ts for designing the right kind of learning environment.

JOAN NOVELLI

JOAN NOVELLI *is an associate editor at* INSTRUCTOR.

Quick! Draw a picture of your classroom last year. Are the desks in clusters, rows, facing each other, or maybe shaped like a horseshoe? How far is the furthest child from the blackboard? Where is your desk? How is the rest of the floor space utilized? What about wall space? How is your room like the one next door? What makes it different?

Next think about your teaching style. Do you do a lot of whole-class teaching? Is peer tutoring part of your program? What is the level of student interaction during the course of a day? Is cooperative learning at work in your classroom?

Now look at your drawing again. Does the room's organization reflect your teaching style? If your students frequently participate in small-group activities, will the desk arrangement accommodate those meetings with ease? When it's time for whole class instruction, will there be an easy transition? If direct instruction is your primary teaching method, will some students miss out by being on the outer edge of the seating arrangement?

Finally, consider what you know about the way kids learn and how you will incorporate that knowledge into your classroom. The choices you make in designing this year's classroom can help you put your instructional goals into action. So turn your paper over and plan an environment that will incorporate the floors, walls, and furniture of your classroom into your teaching style.

A TEACHER TELLS YOU HOW

Frank Garcia, a sixth-grade teacher at Dove Hill School in San Jose, California, knows that creating great classrooms takes careful thought. As the Evergreen School District's mentor teacher for classroom environment, Garcia has given workshops and seminars on classroom design and is called on throughout the year to assist teachers in his school and district in setting up classrooms that help make learning happen.

While teachers often experiment with variations in classroom configuration, Garcia points out that universities generally don't prepare teachers to deal with the physical space of a classroom. Garcia believes that with careful planning, reflection on personal teaching style, awareness of curriculum needs, and knowledge of the way children learn, teachers can create classroom environments that are conducive to learning.

One of Garcia's objectives is to make the learning environment an exciting place and, he says, organization and structure are part of this excitement. Garcia recommends beginning with a floor plan locating chalkboards, electrical outlets, sinks, and storage areas. These areas, which are generally stationary, help determine where desks, audiovisual equipment, art materials, and other classroom resources should go.

For example, whether instruction is based on cooperative learning, direct instruction, or a combination of the two, most teachers need to direct everyone's attention to the board at some point during the day. When deciding on a seating plan, Garcia recommends that you think about arranging desks so that as many students as possible have easy access to the board. To encourage self-directed learning in your classroom, use lower storage shelves for materials that students can help themselves to— manipulatives, books, ongoing projects, unfinished assignments, or free-time work. The space around these bookshelves or cabinets makes a versatile, small-group meeting space, with a variety of materials close at hand. What does all of this add up to? Less time getting situated for learning and more time doing it!

WHAT ABOUT WALLS?

Garcia says that walls are the most neglected space in classrooms. "My pet peeve," he says, "is drab classrooms with a few posters tacked up and that's it. Walls have to live!" Some would argue that wall materials are potentially distracting. But knowing that kids are going to look at their surroundings, Garcia believes

From *Instructor*, August 1990, pp. 24-27. Copyright © 1990 by Scholastic Inc.

in creating walls that are sources of enjoyment, inspiration, and learning.

Paula Maciel, a third-grade teacher at Dove Hill School with 21 years of teaching experience, agrees. She always felt something was missing from her classroom and called on Garcia for some advice. Together they looked at parts of Garcia's room that Maciel wanted to implement in her own room. Then they went to work on Maciel's room.

The main problem, Garcia found, was the wall space. He points out that if you want kids to notice materials on walls, the displays have to stand out. In Maciel's room, this meant redoing bulletin boards and creating frames or backgrounds for displayed materials. Step one was creating new bulletin-board borders to replace the standard, prefabricated two-inch corrugated paper strips. Maciel followed Garcia's advice, using some black in every bor-

der, accentuating the contrast between the border and the background to bring out what she wanted kids to see. Continuing with this strategy, Maciel framed other wall displays, including prints, posters, and student work, with black paper.

Garcia, who has been known to change a wall display three or four times before being satisfied, advises stepping back from the area to get the full view. He recalls being taught that certain colors don't mix, but his philosophy is: If it looks good, mix it!

Maciel checked for variety in angle and positioning of materials as well as an overall visually exciting look. The result of this careful attention is a classroom that comes alive. And that's a classroom, Maciel found, where kids are drawn to learn.

Ready to get to work on your classroom? Read the details below and find out how.

The Details...

Smart Seats

Because Frank Garcia's teaching style is a mix of both cooperative learning and direct instruction, he finds clusters of three an optimum desk setup. Clusters of four worked well for group activities but left too many kids with their backs to the board. Whatever the configuration of desks and chairs, Garcia says one thing is certain: You need easy access to every student. That means leaving space around rows or clusters so you can move through the seating area comfortably.

Kids need to be able to move around them comfortably, too. Garcia suggests considering the size of the students when planning seating arrangements. Sixth-grade kids will most likely need more space between rows or clusters than first graders.

Deck the Walls

Other colors just don't bring out material on walls like black, says Garcia. He uses black construction paper to frame everything. This may seem overpowering, but, as Garcia points out, there's very little black in most of what goes on walls.

Interactive and decorative bulletin boards are an important part of Garcia's wall planning, and borders get just as much attention as the displays themselves. He finds that kids don't pay much attention to preformed borders, so he designs his own with

paper patterns, colors, and geometric shapes. Garcia's not afraid to go a little wild here: He's used three-dimensional shapes, reflective tape, even tiny tree lights to create effective bulletin-board borders.

Changing Places

After seating 31 students, Garcia still has room for two small tables. He uses them to give small groups of kids close-up attention and to review lessons with students as needed. Kids use the area to work on projects or just to get a change of scenery.

Nearby shelves hold portable learning centers that children can bring back to the table or back to their desks. Garcia emphasizes that because most teachers don't have the space to use a different part of the room for every activity, versatility is what makes an area like this work.

Test Drive

Is this room ready for action? Garcia recommends a trial run before students arrive for their first day.

Sit in the kids' seats. Is the board visible? Are any seats going to be particularly prone to distractions? For example, is one too close to the door, the sink, or the "in" box? Walk through the aisles. Is there a comfortable amount of space?

Help yourself to materials you'll

encourage kids to get and return on their own. Are they easy to find, reach, and put away?

Look around. Do the walls feel friendly? Are interactive bulletin boards accessible from a child's point of view? If something is meant to be read, is it at a child's eye level?

Now step outside the room. Walk back in, as though it's the first day of school. Is this an exciting place to be?

Software Staples

This software storage strategy doubles as a self-directed learning motivator. Stapling sleeves to the wall keeps titles in full view, making the software easy to select and put away. And unlike a traditional filing system, Garcia says this display reminds students of the variety of software available for their use, encouraging them to try something different.

Personal Touch

In this corner, stuffed animals, plants, and knickknacks invite kids to shelves stocked with books, puzzles, map activities, and more. These decorative additions do more than just keep shelves from becoming overcrowded and inaccessible. They also create a warm, welcoming feeling. And "anytime you're in an environment where you feel good," says Garcia, "good things are going to happen."

ORDER in the CLASSROOM

Some teachers swear by Lee Canter's Assertive Discipline system. But if it's so good, why do critics call it "dehumanizing," "humiliating," even "dangerous"?

DAVID HILL

Linda Darling-Hammond had never heard of Assertive Discipline until her daughter, Elena, entered kindergarten two years ago. When she came home from school, Elena had plenty of stories to tell her mother, but they weren't the kind of stories Darling-Hammond expected to hear. Instead of being about new friends and new things to learn, Elena's accounts of her first days at Takoma Park (Md.) Elementary School focused on which kids in her class were being punished—and how. The teacher, Elena told her mother, wrote the names of the "bad" kids on the blackboard, which meant they could have certain privileges taken away from them. Elena wasn't among the "bad" kids; in fact, she brought home happy-face stickers because she had been "good." Yet she was frightened of what could happen if she played with the kids who had been punished.

"She was so terrified by the prospect of having her name placed on the board, being held in from recess, or being excluded from class activities that she stopped participating in class," says Darling-Hammond, an educational researcher for the RAND Corporation at the time and now a professor at Columbia University's Teachers College.

When Darling-Hammond went to observe her daughter's classroom, she learned that the teacher was using a system called Assertive Discipline, developed in the 1970's by Lee and Marlene Canter and now used in many schools across the country. The highly structured system, a mixture of common sense and behavior-modification techniques, stresses rewards and punishments as a way for teachers to "take charge" of their classrooms. Many teachers and administrators swear by it, but Darling-Hammond was appalled by what she witnessed:

"I saw a group of small children trying hard not to move or speak; a young, inexperienced, and unmentored teacher trying religiously to apply rewards and consequences. The list of names on the board grew

From *Teacher Magazine*, April 1990, pp. 70-73, 75-77. Copyright © 1990 by Editorial Projects in Education. Reprinted by permission.

whenever someone wiggled or spoke. The children appeared unhappy and confused. The stickers did not do much to offset their distress, since many of the children who got them felt bad about the children who didn't. Virtually all of the 'offenders' that day were boys; most of them were black. None of them had done anything that I could term 'misbehaving' during my visit. But they had broken rules forbidding talking and moving; i.e., normal 5-year-old behavior."

Takoma Park Elementary School no longer uses Assertive Discipline. And Lee Canter no longer advocates the discipline technique of writing down names on the blackboard. "People such as Linda Darling-Hammond interpret that as something that could be psychologically harmful to the kids," says Canter. "Personally, I don't think it is, but I have come out in all my latest materials saying that teachers should not use it. I think especially with kindergarten kids, I would not write their names on the board."

Darling-Hammond isn't the only critic of Assertive Discipline. In recent years, many educators and child psychologists have spoken out against the technique, calling it, among other things, "dehumanizing," "humiliating," and "dangerous." Yet it remains popular; Canter says that more than 750,000 teachers have been trained in Assertive Discipline during the last 15 years, and his company, Lee Canter & Associates, has grown from a mom-and-pop operation to a multimillion-dollar enterprise, with 75 full- and part-time employees. Proponents of Assertive Discipline speak of it as if it were the greatest thing since sliced bread. The bottom line, they say, is that it works. One middle school principal who recently began using Assertive Discipline at his school goes so far as to call it "a godsend."

IN A MODEST, WINDOWLESS office in Santa Monica, Calif., Lee Canter is explaining to a visitor the genesis of Assertive Discipline. If Canter were a student, he would no doubt get a happy-face sticker, his office is so tidy. On one wall, between two shelves of neatly arranged books, is a cartoon that depicts the kind of fantasy a teacher might have after an especially bad day. In it, a plump, innocent-looking teacher with glasses faces her wide-eyed students and says: "Good morning, children. My name is Miss Applegate. One false move and I'll kill you."

Despite waking up with a stomach virus, Canter, 43, is animated and energetic, constantly emphasizing his points with his hands. He often gives motivational speeches to teachers and principals, and his speaking experience shows, even in a one-on-one situation.

Canter received a master's degree in social work from the University of Southern California in 1970, and says he got most of the ideas for Assertive Discipline while working as a guidance counselor, helping parents and teachers deal with problem children. "I saw what was going on in the classroom," he says. "I saw teachers coming home every night so frustrated, kids not getting the opportunity they needed to learn, and I just sat down with my wife and said, 'We've got to do something about it.' And we came up with ideas that obviously worked.

"I think they probably worked because they're based upon nothing really new. I get a lot of credit for Assertive Discipline, and I get a lot of blame for it from people who don't like it. But there's nothing really brand new in this program. Throughout history, teachers have told kids what they wanted them to do, have had rules for the classroom, have established consequences if you break the rules, and have had positive consequences when you're good. All I really did was to put it together in a package.

"I watched a lot of effective teachers. I went into classrooms, and I sat down and watched teachers who did not have discipline problems. Number one, they were assertive. That meant they clearly and firmly told their kids what they wanted. They were positive with the kids, very straightforward. When the kids were good, the teachers would give them a lot of positive support. If the kids chose not to behave, the teachers would discipline them."

Canter and his wife, Marlene, a former special-education teacher, published *Assertive Discipline: A Take-Charge Approach For Today's Educator* in 1976. The book, now in its 26th printing, remains the basic text for the discipline technique, but Canter's company also publishes a number of other materials for teachers and parents, such as *Positive Reinforcement Activities*, *Homework Without Tears*, and *Assertive Discipline For Parents*. Canter's 25 instructors offer Assertive Discipline workshops all over the country, and there's something for everyone: teachers (K-12), administrators, parents, paraprofessionals, even bus drivers.

Canter says that, in the past, most of the training was done on a schoolwide or districtwide basis, usually in one-day, inservice seminars. (Teachers at Takoma Park Elementary, in fact, were required to be trained in the Assertive Discipline method.) But recently, he says, there has been increased interest in his five-day graduate-level course called "Beyond Assertive Discipline," for which teachers may earn college credit.

Canter promises results, too. Teachers who take the basic one-day training (at an average cost of $28 per person) are told that they will see "an 80 percent reduction in classroom disruptions," "fewer students in the principal's office," "a calm, positive classroom climate conducive to teaching and learning," and "more success in dealing with parents on behavior problems."

Here's how Assertive Discipline works: "Assertive" teachers should (in Canter's words) establish a "systematic discipline plan that explains exactly what will happen when students choose to misbehave." The key, says Canter, is consistency: "An effective discipline is applied fairly to all students."

Canter suggests that the plan include a maximum of five consequences for misbehavior. "For example, the first time a student breaks a rule, the student is warned. The second infraction brings a 10-minute time out [isolation]; the third infraction, a 15-minute time out. The fourth time a student breaks a rule, the teacher calls the parents; the fifth time, the student goes to the principal." Canter says he initially suggested that teachers write students' names on the board because he wanted to eliminate their need to stop the lesson and issue reprimands.

"Writing a student's name on the board would warn the student in a calm, nondegrading manner," Canter says. "It would also provide a record-keeping system for the teacher. Unfortunately, some parents have misinterpreted the use of names and checks on the board as a way of humiliating students. I now suggest that teachers instead write an offending student's name on a clipboard or in the roll book and say to the student, 'You talked out, you disrupted the class, you broke a rule. That's a warning. That's a check.' "

At the same time, Canter says that teachers should reward those students who obey the rules. He suggests, for example, that teachers drop marbles into a jar every time a student does something positive; when the jar is full, the entire class is rewarded by, say, 10 minutes of free time at the end of the day. Canter suggests that students be rewarded with material objects, such as cookies, ice cream, or even a hamburger from McDonald's.

"An effective behavior-management program must be built on choice," Canter has written. "Students must know beforehand what is expected of them in the classroom, what will happen if they choose to behave, and what will happen if they choose not to behave. Students learn self-discipline and responsible behavior by being given clear, consistent choices. They learn that their actions have an impact and that they themselves control the consequences."

Canter often makes the point that Assertive Discipline is not a cure-all. "This is not a perfect program," he says. "This is not the answer. And I keep saying that, because there are people out there who say, 'This is the answer.' "

Teachers and administrators who use Assertive Discipline *do* tend to gush about its benefits. Charles Warner, principal of Jackie Robinson Middle School in New Haven, Conn., has nothing but praise for the system. "It's fantastic," he says. "We're looking at it as a godsend for us."

Warner says that Jackie Robinson and two New Haven elementary schools (which "feed" students into Jackie Robinson) began using Assertive Discipline last

September. The middle school, he says, is located in a neighborhood with a lot of drug activity, an atmosphere that created "a fair amount of discipline problems" and "hostile children." Teachers at the school used to have their own individual discipline plans. "But we felt that we needed to do something different," says Warner.

Now, students at all three schools know exactly what is expected of them—and what will happen to them if they disobey the rules. "Assertive Discipline gave us consistency," Warner says. "That's one of its highlights." He says there has been "a drastic decrease" in discipline problems since the plan was implemented. "I'm sold on it. I had my reservations at first. I thought it was just another thing to spend money on. But once we had our first training session, I realized it was worth doing."

Henry Rhodes, who teaches 7th grade social studies at Jackie Robinson, agrees. "I couldn't wait to try it," he says. "It's easy to use. It's all spelled out for you."

Critics, however, contend that Assertive Discipline is harmful—to students *and* to teachers—precisely *because* of its apparent simplicity. "It totally dehumanizes the teacher by putting the control into a system," says educator Richard Curwin, co-author (along with Allen Mendler) of *Discipline with Dignity*. "Where's the teacher's judgment? For teachers who are insecure, it has a lot to offer."

Assertive Discipline's main objective, say Curwin and Mendler, is to teach kids to be obedient, not to be responsible for their actions. In their book, they write: "We define obedience as following rules without question, regardless of philosophical beliefs, ideas of right and wrong, instincts and experiences, or values. A student 'does it' because he is told to do it. In the short term, obedience offers teachers relief, a sense of power and control, and an oasis from the constant bombardment of defiance. In the long run, however, obedience leads to student immaturity, a lack of responsibility, an inability to think clearly and critically, and a feeling of helplessness that is manifested by withdrawal, aggressiveness, or power struggles. . . . Obedience models are far more interested in keeping students in line rather than maintaining their dignity."

(Curwin also says that the use of Assertive Discipline is "dying out," a charge that Canter disputes. "Every year, more and more teachers go through the program," Canter says. He estimates that his company will train 85,000 teachers this year; 50,000 of them will take the one-day seminar, while 35,000 of them will take the five-day graduate-level course.)

Linda Darling-Hammond believes that Assertive Discipline is especially harmful to children in the early grades, when they are still developing self-regulatory behavior and social skills. For one thing, she says, the rules Canter recommends are "inappropriate for young children" because "they suggest a curriculum in which conversing and moving about in the classroom are inappropriate and punishable activities." In addition, she says, "Designating children's behavior as 'bad' results for young children in them believing they themselves are bad. Under the age of 11, children cannot generally separate attributions about their behavior from attributions about themselves."

Darling-Hammond also cites research showing that the use of rewards actually *decreases* intrinsic motivation among students. Assertive Discipline, she concludes, "replaces the teaching of values and the development of intrinsic motivation for learning with a control-oriented system of rules and penalties stressing compliance, sanctions, and external motivation."

Canter is accustomed to such criticism. "The whole *point* of Assertive Discipline," he says, "is teaching children responsibility. The way you teach kids to be responsible is by telling them exactly what is expected of them and then giving them a choice. One thing that I've always talked about in my work is that children need to be given a choice." He pauses, assumes the role of an assertive teacher, and addresses me as a student. "Dave, you have a choice. If you choose to yell and stop me from teaching someone else, you choose to have this consequence. On the other hand, if you choose to behave, I will recognize that behavior."

He continues: "So Assertive Discipline is based upon choice. Curwin can say that he views it as an obedience model, but I think it's clearly spelling out to kids what's expected and then giving them a choice. Because how else do you learn responsibility but by making choices, and realizing there are choices in life, and that we have to be responsible for our actions?"

The concept of student choice in Assertive Discipline, contends Vincent Crockenberg, professor of education at the University of California-Davis, is "utterly muddled. It is fraudulent." In a 1982 article in the *California Journal of Teacher Education* titled "Assertive Discipline: A Dissent," Crockenberg pointed out that the notion of "choice" is distorted when children have only two options. "The Canters simply stack the deck in favor of the teachers. They give teachers a simple way out of their difficulties, but at the price of miseducating children by deeply misrepresenting to them what it means to choose to do something which affects others, what it means to act morally."

Crockenberg concluded: "Assertive Discipline is too simple. It 'works,' if it works at all, only by distorting moral language, by pandering to the defensiveness of teachers about their work, and by ignoring or even denying that children have any significant rights or needs that are independent of the needs of the adults who are their teachers. That is just too high a price to pay for order in the classroom."

"The thing that I've found," responds Canter, "is that kids need limits. It's not like you're doing something to harm a child when you give him some structure. We're not talking about hitting kids. We're not talking about verbally degrading kids. We're not talking about saying to kindergarten kids, 'You're

going to sit on the rug for an hour.' We're saying there should be some general rules so the kids know there's an adult there who really cares about them. That's what we're after."

Canter claims that Assertive Discipline is "based solidly on techniques that have been shown to work in the classroom," and he even distributes a publication titled *Abstracts of Research Validating Effectiveness of Assertive Discipline*. One study cited, for example, surveyed 129 teachers and 12 principals at three Indiana schools during the 1982-83 school year. Of the respondents, 86 percent said that they liked using Assertive Discipline, and 82 percent said that student behavior at the schools had improved. Yet critics contend that such evidence is scant and, further, that Canter has selectively reported it.

Gary Render, a professor of education at the University of Wyoming, along with Ph.D. candidates Je Nell Padilla and Mark Krank, conducted a study of the existing research on Assertive Discipline and found "a surprising lack of investigation of a program that is being so widely used. The literature supporting Assertive Discipline is not strong or generalizable. Much of it is based on perceptions of teachers, students, parents, and administrators." Their conclusion: "We can find no evidence that Assertive Discipline is an effective approach deserving schoolwide or districtwide adoption."

One of the most troubling aspects of Assertive Discipline is its abuse by some teachers and school districts. In 1983, parents of five children attending Germantown Elementary School in Annapolis, Md., sued the Anne Arundel County Board of Education for $17.3 million, claiming that their children's civil rights were violated when they were placed in solitary confinement for misconduct in 1980 and 1981. One student, 11-year-old Michyle Davis, testified that she was confined for five consecutive days during school hours in a "storage room" with a desk, after she was accused of laughing in class and throwing a chair. The suit also alleged that the children, aged 7 to 12, were discriminated against because they are black.

Ralph McCann Jr., the elementary school's principal at the time, testified that his policy of confining unruly children in isolation rooms was part of Canter's Assertive Discipline program, implemented in 1980 to stem runaway discipline problems at the school. Canter, however, said at the time that Assertive Discipline does not recommend isolating students without adult supervision. When an attorney for the children asked the principal, "Didn't you know that Lee Canter recommended no more than two consecutive hours of in-school suspension for elementary school students?" McCann replied, "No, sir." He also said that he had used Canter's basic concepts but had modified them to "suit our particular needs."

A $30,000 out-of-court settlement was reached in 1984. As part of the settlement, school officials agreed that students placed on in-school suspension would be supervised by an adult at all times.

Milton Shore, a Silver Spring, Md., child psychologist who testified on behalf of the five children, says that he asked Canter to testify in court that the Maryland school was using a "distortion" of his system, but Canter said his lawyer had told him he had "nothing to gain" by doing so. "His comment to me was, 'I wouldn't have approved it,' " Shore says. "Why he wouldn't say it in court is something I've never been able to understand."

Canter says that *both* sides wanted him to testify in the case, and that he was ready and willing to testify on behalf of the children. "Absolutely," he says. "What went on in that district was unconscionable." His lawyer, however, told him not to get involved. "He said, 'Don't get caught in the middle of this thing. You are being set up.' "

Canter admits that Assertive Discipline has taken on a life of its own. "It has become a generic term, like Xerox or Kleenex," he says. "A number of educators are now conducting training in what they call Assertive Discipline without teaching *all* the competencies essential to the program. For example, I have heard reports of teachers who were taught that they had only to stand in front of their students, tell them that there were rules and consequences, display a chart listing those rules and consequences, and write the names of misbehaving students on the board. That was it. Those teachers were never introduced to the concept that positive reinforcement is the key to dealing with students."

To Canter, the problem isn't with the system; rather, it's with the people who don't understand how to use it: "Negative interpretations have also come from burned-out, overwhelmed teachers who feel they do not get the support that they need from parents or administrators and who take out their frustrations on students. Assertive Discipline is not a negative program, but it can be misused by negative teachers. The answer is not to change the program, but to change the teachers. We need to train administrators, mentor teachers, and staff developers to coach negative teachers in the use of positive reinforcement. If these teachers cannot become more positive, they should not be teaching."

At the same time, Canter insists that the teachers who most effectively use Assertive Discipline are the ones who mold the system to their individual teaching styles. "That's fine," he says. "I don't want the legacy of Assertive Discipline to be—and I don't want teachers to believe they have to use—names and checks on the board or marbles in a jar. I want

teachers to learn that they have to take charge." Or, as he also has said: "The children must know that something will happen when they break a rule. The form it takes is not as important as the reality of a negative consequence."

In other words, don't take Canter's suggestions too literally. When Canter's son, Josh, was 13, his father sent him to his room after he had misbehaved. "An hour later," Canter says, "he comes out reading *Assertive Discipline for Parents*, and he says, 'Dad, how many times did you warn me about yelling and screaming?' And I said, 'Two.' And he said, 'But in your book, it says two warnings, maximum half-hour in the room. You sent me in for an hour! You can't even follow your own program!' " Canter laughs about the incident: "It's very hard to practice what you preach."

Linda Darling-Hammond wasn't the only parent upset over the use of Assertive Discipline at Takoma Park Elementary and other schools in the Montgomery County (Md.) school district. When a group of them began voicing their concerns about the system, they found an ally in school board member Blair Ewing, who had done some research of his own. "I thought [Canter's] materials were dreadful," he says. "Assertive Discipline doesn't examine the reasons *why* children are misbehaving. It values conformity above everything, and that's dangerous."

Ewing says he raised the issue "over and over" with School Superintendent Harry Pitt, who eventually issued a policy statement recommending that prepackaged discipline systems not be accepted wholesale by the district. "Assertive Discipline is not prohibited, but it's understood that it's not to be used," says Ewing. "I haven't seen it rear its ugly head again."

Darling-Hammond didn't wait around to see what would happen; she removed her daughter from the school. When she took her to look at another school, one that didn't use Assertive Discipline, Elena said, "Mom, I want to stay in this school, because they don't punish the kids."

'I Cried In Front Of Fifth Period. . .'

The following vignette about Christine Emmel's first year of teaching is excerpted from The Intern Teacher Casebook, *edited by Judith Shulman and Joel Colbert (1988). Following Emmel's story is a reaction by an experienced teacher. Emmel, who describes herself as having been raised in the tradition of white, middle-class values and Catholic schools, taught five life-science classes to noncollege-bound students in an inner-city, primarily black and Hispanic Los Angeles high school. She was emergency certified as part of the Los Angeles Unified School District's teacher intern program.*

I prefer to regard myself as a "first-year veteran," having pulled through the horrendous initiation that Maywood [High School] had in store. Gang violence, vandalism, overwhelming rates of teen motherhood, phenomenal records of truancy, student fights, theft, and extreme student hostility in the classroom were just a few of the charms of this particular institution.

I knew I'd be O.K. . . . if I could just turn in my fifth period to the deck and get a new hand. Fifth period was to be my point of surrender—surrender to the frustration of feeling totally powerless over their behavior, surrender to my own feelings of self-doubt and inadequacy.

In the face of my problems with this class, I decided to try "relating" to the students humanistically; this was a suggestion gleaned from several more experienced teachers.

I told the students that I wanted to talk something over with them, meanwhile easing myself into what I hoped was a nonthreatening "I'm your friend" stance. I proceeded to explain, or rather purge, my feelings—how I felt as though they were pitted against me and resistant to

what I was trying to teach them, how I felt "real bad" about it and wished we could have a friendlier and more enjoyable class. I finished by "relating" my need for their cooperation, since I wanted to help them, and couldn't under the current terms of our relationship.

What a feeling to finally speak the truth of my feelings—and to them! I looked into their faces, trying to gauge their reaction. Feeling so good about opening up myself, I could only hope for the best. Alas, as usual, reality corrected my forever idealistic expectations, in the form of [her student] Geri's comment: "Well, if you weren't such a bad teacher . . ." This cutting remark, in the face of my vulnerability, plus a few smirks and other unsympathetic comments, were enough to push me past my limit.

And so, I cried in front of fifth period—something I never dreamed I'd do and certainly one of my more horrible imaginings. I'd never let them know I could be pushed that far—and yet, here I was, uncontrollably watering the dirty tile floor! I quickly exited to the hallway, to attempt to regain some equanimity. I hoped no other teachers had decided to keep their doors open that day. After a few moments of agonized "I blew it" thoughts in the empty corridor, I stepped back into my room, heart pounding. In the first second of opening the door, I heard the sound of fake sobs from within. So much for the damned "humanistic" approach! Clearly, neither I nor my students were at a point where this tactic could succeed.

What I learned from this experience is still not altogether clear to me. Once again, however, I was permitted to see that school, just like life, goes on no matter what. I felt I had lost a battle that day and had

admitted total defeat in an utterly humiliating way. But a new day of school and fifth period would dawn again . . . and it did. Nothing is irrevocable, and my striving for successful classroom management continued, even though I thought that one day was "The End."

Patricia Norton, a health teacher for more than 20 years and a mentor teacher, offers this reaction:

First of all, I needed to calm down from the outrage I felt upon learning that Christine, with her background and total lack of experience, was sent to such a difficult situation in the first place! I know of no other business where the employers show such a lack of concern about a person's suitability to a particular job. I was beginning to think that the sink-or-swim attitude in education was phasing out with the advent of mentor programs, but I see, as in Christine's dilemma, that the mentality is still alive and well.

Certainly, in a situation like Christine's, a mentor teacher from that school—one who knows the students and the problems—should have spent time with her initially. It was terribly unfortunate that she came to the point of surrender and helplessness.

As to the advice by Christine's colleagues about solving the fifth-period problem by "showing her human side," I think that the interpretation of what that meant needed more defining. An approach that comes from weakness, as hers was interpreted by the students, never works. She needed to come from whatever strength she had left.

I admire Christine's tenacity to hang in there and learn that experience helps. It sounds as if she really has what it takes to be a teacher.

CHARM SCHOOL FOR Bullies

Aggressive kids are learning to negotiate instead of throwing tantrums and punches.

Deborah Franklin is a staff writer.

NATHAN'S A SLAMMER. He'll stomp out of class when somebody crosses him, banging the door behind him. Though bright, the burly fifth-grader taunts and teases to get what he wants. He hates his classmates and they hate him.

Unlike Nathan, who seeks a spotlight, Joe keeps mostly to himself. But when he feels he's been pushed too far—which happens several times a day—he comes back swinging. It's usually the nose of a smaller, weaker kid that gets in the way.

While Nathan and Joe are equally agile in terrorizing their classmates, they don't ordinarily collaborate. But once every week during a recent quarter, Harvard University psychologist Robert Selman brought the two bullies together for a little experiment. Under his tutelage in a counseling office at their Cambridge, Massachusetts, elementary school, the boys learned and practiced socially acceptable methods of manipulating each other.

In each session, Selman would hand Nathan and Joe a construction set, and tell them to play *together*. If they shared the blocks, they could build a space station or castle, complete with turrets and a working drawbridge. Working alone, they would have only enough time and resources to build irregular piles of interlocked plastic.

In their first encounter, the boys ignored each other; Nathan tipped his chair back at one end of the table giving loud Bronx cheers, while Joe, his jacket zipped to his chin, a wedge of rusty hair hiding his eyes, worked silently at the other end. But by the third session, Joe began to perk up. He put a few pieces together and zoomed them around like a jet, loudly bombing invisible enemies. "Do you like my aircraft, Nathan?" he asked, still not looking at the other boy. No response. Nathan was working on his own project, and was missing a piece. He eyed the tail of Joe's jet.

"If I had a piece like you have," Nathan said, "I could sure use it." No response. Nathan began fishing around in a box of 80 or 90 loose pieces. "Help me find one of those things, Joe," he said without looking at him. "I could use it." Joe continued to fly his jet in sweeping arcs, and the bombing grew more intense. Nathan scowled. "If you asked *me* for help, Joe, I'd give it to *you*," he said. A loud buzzer signaled the end of the play period.

Selman, who had silently watched the interaction from a few feet away, wasted no time getting to the point. "So, you guys did a good job of playing today, but it seemed as though you had a problem." He walked through the conflict, getting Nathan to explain what he'd wanted. "You know," Selman said, "I bet that if you guys worked together on a project you could make something really cool."

Nathan nodded his head, and seemed interested. Joe tucked his chin and stared at the floor. "I'd rather each build our own stuff," he said quietly. "When we work together, we get into fights."

Selman nodded. "Yeah, I know that happens sometimes," he said. "But maybe it's worth *trying* to work together, so that you could make the spaceship."

Such odd little scenes of confrontation and mediation are unfolding at a handful of "charm schools" for bullies around the country. The underlying theory of these experimental programs, based on the research of developmental psychologists in the last decade, is that most bullies are made, not born. Search the past of a teenage extortionist, and you're likely to find a fourth-grader who never learned to negotiate. Help the troubled fourth-grader brush up on his social skills, and you may nudge him away from the joys of intimidation—and maybe even toward an appreciation of the other guy's perspective. But in order to learn these skills, all children—especially bullies—need a safe place for lots of practice.

"We would never expect a kid to learn to read or write just from hearing a lecture," says Steven Brion-Meisels, a Cambridge educator who has adapted some of Selman's techniques for use by teachers in the classroom. "And we shouldn't expect them to learn social skills that way either."

If all this sounds like the finely spun theory of naive academics, consider one view from the trenches. Stella Sadofsky has been a social worker in New Jersey schools for 22 years, and knows an educational fad when she sees one. This time she thinks the academics are on to something.

"Teachers are already spending inordinate and increasing amounts of time dealing with kids' social problems," Sadofsky says. "Separating kids and breaking up fights takes time, too. Instead, in the same amount of time, we can teach children to solve their own problems. They start to see that there are many solutions that don't involve slugging it out."

Children don't outgrow aggression. Of 11,000 junior high and high school students surveyed nationally in 1987, almost half the boys, and more than one-fourth of the girls, reported having taken part in at least one fight during the previous year that involved fists or weapons. More than a third had been physically threatened, 14 percent had been robbed, and 13 percent had been attacked while at school or on a school bus. Even students who haven't been beaten up are scared: One-fourth of the students in a similar survey said that the possibility of being bullied is one of their biggest fears.

In the long run, bullying may hurt the aggressor even more than the victim. One study that followed nearly 600 children from age eight to 30 showed that those who bullied in elementary school—acted rudely to the teacher and other children, started fights over nothing, took classmates' toys without asking—were five times more likely than their less belligerent classmates to have been convicted of crimes by age 30. They were also much more likely to have low-paying jobs, to be abusing their spouses, and to be raising contentious children of their own.

"It's unquestionably in the best interests of these kids and society to intervene early," says Selman. He and others who run similar programs focus on children who are not hardened criminals, but who simply spend most of their school hours on the edge of aggression.

Some teachers and parents might question the value of teaching these children Machiavellian reasoning—telling Nathan and Joe, for instance, that sharing is good because it helps *you* get what *you* want. But Selman defends his tactics. "If you try more sophisticated reasoning on kids before they're ready, they'll flat out ignore you," he says. "Recognizing that the other guy has rights independent of your own is a concept that many teenagers and even adults have trouble with." For most bullies, there are only two ways to resolve conflicts: fighting or running.

That's not surprising if you look at the first place children learn about conflict, the family. Leonard Eron, a psychologist at the University of Illinois in Chicago, found that the parents of aggressive children he studied tended to punish their offspring both harshly and capriciously, alternately blowing up at them for minor infractions and ignoring them for long stretches of time. Other researchers say that such parents punish more according to their own moods than in response to the child's behavior.

After these early lessons in erratic parental attacks, some children naturally become wary and misinterpret the actions and intentions of others. Vanderbilt University psychologist Kenneth Dodge says about half the aggressive boys he studies see slights or hostilities where none are meant—even in videotaped scenes of conflict involving other children. "This is the kid who gets angry easily, has temper tantrums, and might get into a lot of fights, but doesn't necessarily start them," says Dodge. "Somebody calls him a name or jostles him in the hallway and instead of tossing it off with a joke as other children do, he overreacts."

To help fifth- and sixth-grade boys who fit that description, psychologist John Lochman of Duke University holds weekly sessions in the Durham, North Carolina, public schools. In role-playing sessions, one kid becomes the bully, another the victim; just before the conflict's climax, the boys freeze, and one group member interviews each actor about when he first noticed a problem, what he was thinking and feeling as the conflict escalated, and what he was likely to do next. Afterwards the group discusses alternate solutions that might have helped both boys get what they wanted without violence. Other exercises are spiced-up versions of counting to ten before blowing your stack: One child holding a puppet concentrates on reciting the alphabet, while five other children taunt the puppet.

Initially, instead of trying to change a bully's desire to dominate, Lochman builds on it. "We'll tell a child, 'Look—if you let those guys get to you, *they're* controlling *you*. They like it when you act out and get in trouble.'" Only later, after the child has mastered staying cool under fire, will Lochman suggest that there might be rewarding alternatives to intimidation.

Of course, not all school districts can afford to pull aggressive children out of class once a week for an hour of intensive training in negotiation. But proponents of these charm schools suggest that teachers can provide some of the same kinds of practice during class meetings held once or twice a week. There, for 30 minutes or an hour, children can have a chance to air complaints and to see that others often have a different viewpoint. Gradually they'll learn that they can take and give criticism without bringing the world down around their ears. Brion-Meisels recalls one such meeting of sixth-graders in Boston: "Rules come up a lot in these meetings, and this particular day, the kids wanted to discuss the rules we should have about swearing." In the midst of the discussion, Eddie, the class bully, said he thought he alone should be allowed to swear, and anyone else who did should be kicked out of class.

"Most of the other kids groaned and called him a jerk," Brion-Meisels says. "But Donald, a kid he sort of admired, spoke up and said, 'Wait a minute, man. You mean that if I swore you'd think I should be kicked out?' Eddie thought about it and said, 'No, I don't know as you'd have to leave. You and I could swear, and that'd be okay.'

"That's a beginning," says Brion-Meisels, "just a tiny chink in the armor on which you can build." The following week in reading group, Eddie's teacher coaxed him to note the perspectives of different children in the story, and paired Eddie and Donald together to work on an art project—small steps in learning to collaborate. "I could have lectured Eddie for a week about the importance of thinking about the other guy, and he wouldn't have gotten it," says Brion-Meisels. "He didn't get it until he started practicing."

Eight weeks into their sessions in Cambridge, Joe and Nathan quietly reached their own milestone. Bored with the simple toys they'd managed to construct individually, the boys decided for the first time to pull together and attempt the space station. As Nathan perspired over the instruction sheet, he crowded Joe, reaching across him for a particular piece. This time, Joe didn't withdraw or, as he had in one previous session, strike back. Instead, he tried to negotiate.

"We don't *need* that part for the next step, Nathan," he said. "This time let *me* put it together."

Nathan backed off, a little surprised, a little relieved. "Okay, we'll take turns, and the next time I'll do it," he said, handing over the half-built toy.

Selman was jubilant. "We had them talking," he says. "That's a big deal for these kids.

"We're not saying that ten weeks like this can turn these kids completely around," Selman adds, "or that it's enough for every child. Some kids have serious emotional problems, and need in-depth counseling." It's also too soon to tell whether the lessons Nathan and Joe have learned will stick. But a study that Lochman has just finished on his aggressive kids in North Carolina is encouraging: Several years after their negotiation sessions ended, the children had more self-esteem, better problem-solving skills, and lower rates of drug and alcohol abuse than similar children who hadn't been in the program.

By the end of the term, Nathan still took the noisy lead in any decision, while Joe's first impulse was to sulk. But gradually, they got better at dreaming up solutions to problems. During the last session, the boys finally built the space station, and both wanted to take it home. Instead, they agreed to keep snapshots of the project. The two class bullies stepped close together behind the structure, swung their arms around each other, and hammed for the camera.

Equal Opportunity and American Education

The problems of inequality of educational opportunity are still of great concern to American educators. One in four American children do not have all of their basic needs met and live under poverty conditions. Almost one in three live in single-parent homes, not that this is necessarily a disadvantage, but under conditions of poverty it often is. More and more concern is expressed over how to help children of poverty. The "equity agenda" of our time has to do with many issues related to gender, race, and ethnicity. All forms of social deprivation or discrimination are aggravated by great disparities in family income and accumulated wealth. How can children and adolescents be helped to have an equal opportunity to succeed in school? We have wrestled with this great practical and moral dilemma in educational policy development for decades. How can we advance the just cause of the educational interests of our children and adolescents more effectively? Throughout North American society, fair-minded persons discuss this problem.

We are several decades into one of the greatest human rights movements in human history, and the international situation has led to the apparent end of the cold war with the Soviet Union. However, other grave and pressing economic and military challenges still divert previous economic resources from the need to create more effective opportunity structures for the young. I cannot imagine a more worthwhile use of precious national resources than for the health, education, and safety of our children and young adults. Discrimination on the basis of sex and race is still a great challenge to North American societies in spite of the great progress we have made. We must resolve never to stop the just and right struggle to secure equal rights for all our youth.

Some of us are still proud to say we are a nation of immigrants. There are powerful demographic and economic forces impacting on the makeup of the populations of Canada and the United States. In addition to the traditional minority-majority group relationships in the United States, new waves of immigrants are making concerns for achieving equality of opportunity in education as important as ever. The new immigrations from Asia and Latin America reemphasize the already pre-existent reality that we are a nation forged from many cultures. Both Canada and the United States are deeply committed to improving intercultural relations in education and the society at large. The sociological and demographic changes in North American population development are very significant, and they represent trends that assure that we will remain multicultural democracies.

The social psychology of prejudice is something North American psychiatrists, social psychologists, anthropologists, and sociologists have studied in great depth since the 1930s. Tolerance, acceptance, and a commitment to the unique worth of every person are teachable and learnable attitudes. The dream of the founders and of the martyrs for human rights lives. It will never die.

The struggle for equality of opportunity is an endless challenge; poverty reduces windows of opportunity for those affected by it. A just society is constantly challenged to find meaningful ways to raise human aspirations, to heal human hurt, and to help in the task of optimizing every citizen's potential. Education is a vital component of all efforts to alleviate, or even eradicate, the causes of poverty. Yet poverty is not the only obstacle to equality of opportunity. Any form of discrimination against persons because of their identity or socioeconomic status is an impediment to democratic social aspirations. Educational systems and the teachers who labor within them can be a bulwark and a source of hope for those who struggle to overcome these impediments and fulfill the full promise of their humanity.

The fulfillment of the full promise of humanity is what democracy is all about. The freedom to teach, the freedom to learn, the freedom to become the best we can be—that is what the schools of free peoples provide. Teachers have enormous opportunities to reach out to their students as examples of justice and fairness in their day-to-day instructional activities. They can incorporate into their lessons an emphasis on acceptance of difference, toleration of and respect for the beliefs of others, and the skills of reasoned debate and dialogue.

The civil rights of students and teachers in schools is a question that is often raised before state and federal courts. The equal treatment of students under national constitutional guidelines is of great importance. Many decisions made by the courts concern issues that affect students and teachers, including the study of religion in schools, prayer and scripture reading in schools, racial desegregation, bilingual education, and academic freedom. The federal judiciary in the United States has established important precedents in all of the above areas. In both Canada and the United States, great importance is attached to the development of workable opportunity structures in national educational systems. The interpretation of these opportunity structures has evolved over many years, as reflected in the evolution of lines of argument in the courts on these matters.

Equality of the interests of citizens of democratic societies is based on the belief that, in any free society, a plurality of interests must be protected. In addition, the dignity and opportunity of each individual citizen must be protected. The unjust limitation of freedom of expression or the limitation of the opportunity to become adequately educated are intolerable in a democratic state.

Americans have witnessed one of the greatest struggles for equality before the law in all of human history. That struggle is especially well known to educators. More than 30 years ago, the Supreme Court of the United States arrived at the first in what was to be a long chain of decisions affecting majority-minority relations in American schools. The famous 1954 decision of the United States Supreme Court in *Brown v. Board of Education of Topeka* expanded equality of educational opportunity to include women, linguistic minorities, cultural minorities, the aged, and the defenseless. This and other decisions constitute a triumphant testimony to the possibility of social justice under the law. Future generations of Americans and other free peoples will forever look with awe at the struggle for civil rights in American schools from 1954 to the closing years of the present century. Rarely have free people asserted their rights under the law as forcefully and effectively as the American people have on the question of equality of educational opportunity.

The closing years of this century can be approached with renewed hope and confidence in regard to the issue of educational opportunity. A vast body of research on this issue has evolved from the many federal court decisions since 1954. Problems of inequity in the schools have been well documented, and the nation is developing increased sophistication and effectiveness in finding solutions to these problems. The desegregation of American schools has been forcefully initiated throughout the nation, and progress is continuing in majority-minority relations in the schools. It is not only cultural minorities who have benefitted from the federal school desegregation cases, however. Affirmative action in employment and admission to professional schools, the students' rights issue, and the rights of women and the aged have been based on the same constitutional arguments and precedents established in the major school desegregation cases and the Civil Rights Act of 1964. The right of linguistic minorities to learn the English language in public schools has been based on these same constitutional principles. Every American has benefitted, either directly or indirectly, from this triumph of constitutional law over racist tradition.

Looking Ahead: Challenge Questions

What do you know about how it feels to be poor? How do you think it would feel in school? How would you respond?

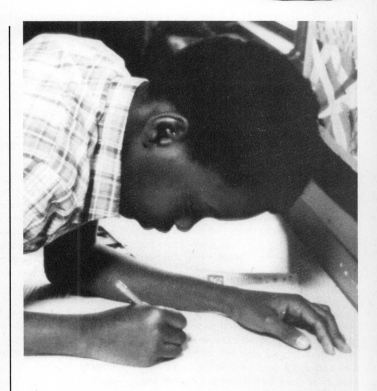

If you are a girl, have you ever felt that you were discriminated against, or at least ignored?

If you are a boy, have you ever felt that you were being favored?

How can schools address more effectively the issue of gender bias?

How do children learn to be prejudiced? How can they learn tolerance?

What were the constitutional precedents for the school desegregation cases?

What academic freedoms should every teacher and student have?

What do you understand to be the interrelationship between the effects of poverty and racial or sexual discrimination?

How can a classroom teacher help his or her students adopt tolerant multicultural perspectives?

POVERTY
CHILDREN OF
THE STATUS OF 12 MILLION YOUNG AMERICANS

Sally Reed and R. Craig Sautter

SALLY REED and R. CRAIG SAUTTER are writers and editors based in Chicago.

IT IS 9 a.m. on a November morning, and Terrence Quinn, principal of Public School 225 in Rockaway, Queens, New York, is serving breakfast. But he's not in the school cafeteria. He's in the lobby of a ramshackle welfare hotel where homeless parents and their children have come to seek shelter. With a social worker in tow, Quinn has cruised the hotel corridors, knocking on doors, inviting what is an ever-changing group of parents to share coffee and break bagels and doughnuts with him while he tries to persuade them to send their children to his elementary school six blocks — and a world — away.

Quinn first tried his pied piper approach to drawing poor children into his school in November 1988, and he repeats the effort periodically. His aim is to make the parents and children feel welcome in his school. Last spring, Jacqueline, a sixth-grader who had lived at the hotel, was selected as the school's valedictorian. One month before the official announcement, she entered Quinn's office and asked to speak to him in private.

"Can someone on welfare actually be the valedictorian?" she asked.

Quinn reassured Jacqueline, a youngster who has overcome many obstacles. Each day millions of others like her are trying to do likewise. And it's not fair. While the last decade became known in the media for its rampant greed, it left millions of poor people (and their children) literally out in the cold. The outcomes are heartbreaking. Why should a child such as Jacqueline feel so humiliated and ashamed of her predicament?

Jacqueline doesn't know it, but she's not alone. We've all been numbed by the horror stories we've heard of late — stories of homeless families sleeping in cars and of crack babies abandoned to hospital nurseries. Meanwhile, the mind-boggling statistics paint a dreadful picture of what life in this nation is like for far too many children. Once you gather all the figures — from conferences, from government agencies, and from scores of reports — the result is frightening. As a nation we're talking about setting goals for fire safety while a wildfire rages out of control all around us. What can educators, politicians, and individual citizens do? People's lives are at stake, and we can't wait any longer.

WAR WITHOUT END

A generation after President Lyndon Johnson declared an official War on Poverty, nearly one-fifth of America's youngest citizens still grow up poor; often sick, hungry, and illiterate; and deprived of safe and adequate housing, of needed social services, and of special educational assistance. Millions of these youngsters are virtually untouched by the vast wealth of the nation in which they begin their fragile and often painful lives.

It didn't take long to lose the War on Poverty. Only a decade after President Johnson's bold declaration, his antipoverty offensive had been lost for millions upon millions of children. By 1975, after the cutback of the Great Society programs by the Nixon and Ford Administrations and after spiraling inflation hit the economy, the interests of children slid lower on the list of economic priorities than even the interests of the elderly. The youngest Americans became the poorest Americans.

During the Great Depression, most Americans were poor. At the end of World War II, about one-third were still poor, but the industrial output of the U.S. was rapidly expanding. By August 1964, when the first antipoverty legislation was enacted, 32 million Americans (about 15% of the population) were materially impoverished. About 13 million of those poor people were children. More of them were elderly.

The one front that has at least received sustained reinforcements since the War on Poverty was scaled back is the fight to improve the lot of the elderly poor. By 1990, 90% of the elderly poor were receiving significant benefits through Social Security cost-of-living adjustments, through housing assistance, through Medicaid, and through other federal and state safeguards.

As a result of this triumph of social policy for senior citizens, many child advocates, including educators and politicians, insist that we can do the same for our most vulnerable citizens, our children. This persistent band is finally making progress toward changing the way society treats youngsters who are the innocent victims of accidents of birth or family misfortune.

But the scale of the problem is overwhelming. Over the past 15 years the incidence of poverty among children has increased and become complicated in ways that portend catastrophic consequences, not only for the children themselves, but also for our schools, our economy, and our social well-being.

Since 1975 children have been poorer than any other age group. By 1989 young people accounted for 39.5% of America's poor. The official U.S. poverty rate for all citizens in 1989 edged slightly downward to 13.1% — only a 2% decline from the Johnson era. Yet in raw numbers more Americans are poor today than before the War on Poverty. Nearly 40 million people of all ages live in families with income levels below the official poverty line of $7,704 for a family of two, $9,435 for a family of three, and $12,092 for a family of four. The current poverty rate is higher than during the worst recession years of the 1970s.

Actually, the real crisis for children and families is even worse than it first appears. Income for the average poor family in 1988 was $4,851 *below* the poverty line. For poor families headed by females, that gap was $5,206. Levels of family income this low mean that some serious family needs — such as food, clothing, medicine, early learning assistance, and housing — are not being met. The result for the children of these families is sickness, psychological stress, malnutrition, underdevelopment, and daily hardship that quickly takes its toll on their young minds and bodies.

Even though the postwar baby boom has long since subsided, nearly as many young people are poor today as when the War on Poverty was launched. However, the percentage today is higher. More than 12.6 million U.S. youngsters — nearly 20% of all children under the age of 18 — are poor.

From *Phi Delta Kappan*, June 1990, pp. K1-K12. Reprinted by permission of *Phi Delta Kappan* and the authors.

Thus one in five American children goes to bed hungry or sick or cold.

And when these children wake each day, they face little prospect that the economic plight of their families will improve enough to make their lives better. Often they internalize the bleakness of their situation and blame themselves for it. Their lives become bitter and humorless or filled with anxiety and fear. Of course, many poor children retain their dignity, and their character is tempered by the Spartan battle for subsistence. But millions of others, permanently damaged, are unable to recover and fall victim to the vicious social pathology of poverty.

And the future seems even grimmer. U.S. Secretary of Education Lauro Cavazos has estimated that, by the year 2000, "as many as one-third of our young people will be disadvantaged and at risk."

Some American youngsters will never even have the chance to see the turn of the century. As has happened in other wars, they will perish. More than 10,000 children in the U.S. die each year as a direct result of the poverty they endure. Often they die during the first weeks of their lives because simple and inexpensive prenatal health care was unavailable to their mothers.

The U.S. has the highest rate of child poverty among the industrialized nations, nearly three times that of most other economically advanced nations. Moreover, the Children's Defense Fund, a leading Washington-based child advocacy group, has sadly noted that only the U.S. and South Africa, among the advanced industrial nations, do not provide universal health coverage for children and pregnant women and do not provide child care to foster early development.

THE YOUNGER, THE POORER

And the picture gets worse. The younger a child is in America today, the greater are his or her chances of being poor. According to the U.S. Census Bureau, the Americans most likely of all to be poor are those age 3 and under. Officially, 23.3% of this age group are poor. During the early years so critical to development, nearly one-fourth of U.S. children lack medical, nutritional, and early-learning assistance. Thus many poor children are needlessly condemned to physical and psychological deficiencies for the rest of their lives.

Further down the road, the social cost of this neglect will almost certainly be extravagant. Physical and mental damage that could have been prevented by inexpensive prenatal checkups or by nutritional programs in early childhood haunts our society in expensive educational, medical, welfare, and correctional costs that can reach into the hundreds of thousands of dollars.

For example, 11% of children end up in special education classes because of cognitive and developmental problems, many of which could have been prevented by prenatal care. Even a pragmatist can count. The willful neglect of America's poor children is not only immoral; it is just plain stupid.

Children of poverty who make it through their earliest years relatively unscathed face new hardships later on. Nearly 22% of 3- to 5-year-olds are poor. Then, after six years of material want, most poor children enter school and make their first significant contact with a social institution. Indeed, the largest group of poor children ranges between the ages of 6 and 11. More than four million of these children — 19.9% of the age group — continue to grow up in unremitting destitution.

Schools should be equipped to help these children gain skills to cope with and ultimately to escape from their economic circumstances. But far too many schools fail far too many poor children. And poor communities tend to get stuck with poor schools as patterns of taxation make a bad situation worse.

Only as children enter their teenage years — and begin to confront a new set of social and biological problems — does the poverty rate actually dip. But even among young people between the ages of 12 and 17, more than 16% live below the poverty line. That figure is higher than the poverty rate for the general population.

The Carnegie Council on Adolescent Development has emphasized that, between the ages of 10 and 15, young people are extremely volatile. For poor teens, the match is even closer to the fuse, since these youngsters are often besieged by problems of school failure, pregnancy, substance abuse, and economic stress.

These young people suffer not only the immediate physical and psychological damage of economic and social adversity; the long-term effects of their childhood deprivation and neglect also manifest themselves in a growing complex of social ills. One-fourth of young black men are reported to have trouble of some kind with correctional authorities. Illiteracy among poor dropouts is endemic. And the personal tragedy of broken homes and a future of perpetually low-paying jobs feeds young black men into the drug trade — and the morgue. The popular appeal of Jesse Jackson's slogan, "Up with Hope," demonstrates just how many young people are growing up in the hopelessness that poverty breeds.

YOUNG FAMILIES, POOR CHILDREN

Then there is the matter of family circumstances. Almost 50% of all U.S. children liv-

ing in a family headed by a person 25 years of age or younger are poor. One-third of all children living in a family headed by a person 30 years of age or younger are poor. In fact, while the nation's overall poverty rate slowly declined from 1967 to 1987, the poverty rate for children living in a family headed by a person 30 years of age or younger shot up from 19% to 35.6%.

Likewise, if a child lives in a family headed by a woman, the chances are better than 50/50 that the child is poor. More than 56% of families headed by single black women are poor. The poverty rate for families headed by Hispanic women is 59%. Yet single-parent families do not necessarily cause poverty. Half of the nation's poor children live with both parents.

Contrary to popular perception, child poverty is not a phenomenon confined to the inner cities. Fewer than 9% of America's poor people live in the nation's core cities. The largest number of poor people still live in semi-isolation in towns and hamlets across the country. About 17% of these people are hidden in rural America. Just as in the inner cities, poverty rates in some rural areas have reached 50% and higher. And some rural regions have been poor for generations. Surprisingly, 28% of America's poor struggle amidst the affluence of suburban communities, shut out from most of the benefits that their neighbors enjoy. Westchester County, New York, one of the 11 wealthiest suburban areas in the country, now has more than 5,000 homeless people looking for shelter.

Another inaccurate perception about poverty is that being poor is directly related to race. Two-thirds of poor Americans are white. The Children's Defense Fund calculates that one white child in seven is poor. However, the rate of poverty is considerably higher for minorities, who are fast becoming majority demographic groups in the 10 largest states. Four out of nine black children are poor; three out of eight Hispanic children are poor. Poverty in America knows no racial boundaries, no geographic borders. The only common denominator for the children of poverty is that they are brought up under desperate conditions beyond their control — and, for them, the rhetoric of equal opportunity seems a cruel hoax, an impossible dream.

THE FLIP SIDE OF PROSPERITY

During the "get-rich-quick" decade of the 1980s, when the number of U.S. billionaires quintupled, child poverty jumped by 23%. More than 2.1 million children tumbled into poverty as the stock market first soared, then plummeted, and finally rebounded. The bull market, with its leveraged buyouts, $325 billion savings-and-loan ripoffs, tax cuts for the wealthy, and junk bond scams, did little to drive up the value of children on the domestic agenda.

"The story of child poverty has become a story of American decline," a congressional staffer who works on poverty-related legislative issues recently lamented. "People have a vague sense that we are doing something wrong nationally, that we are going to be in trouble in the near future. The plight of children is related to this feeling. In addition to being immoral, our treatment of children is profoundly shortsighted. It is economically and socially shortsighted to allow children to grow up with unhealthy bodies and lousy educations and poor nutrition and inadequate health care. We all know that, but now it looks like it will kill us in the 21st century."

What makes matters worse is that the poor are getting poorer. According to the U.S. House of Representatives' Select Committee on Children, Youth, and Families, the income gap between families with the highest incomes and those with the lowest was wider in 1988 than in any year since 1947. The poorest 20% of families received less than 5% of the national income, while the wealthiest 20% received 44%, the largest share ever recorded. Maurice Zeitlin, a sociologist at the University of Caliornia, Los Angeles, recently concluded that the richest 1% of families own 42% of the net wealth of all U.S. families — a staggering proportion that has changed little since the 19th century. This super-rich elite owns 20% of all real estate, 60% of all corporate stock, and 80% of family-owned trusts. These huge disparities make the familiar excuses about budget deficits and tax burdens standing in the way of helping children seem feeble at best.

The vast and ongoing transformation of the U.S. economy from manufacturing to service jobs and from local to global markets has also harmed poor families. When the unemployment of the recession of the 1980s finally began to ease, many of the new jobs were service jobs that paid half as much as manufacturing jobs. According to Michael Sherraden, a professor at Washington University in St. Louis, "The overwhelming reality is that most new jobs being created today are very low-skilled service jobs with low pay and no benefits, not high-tech jobs."

Statistics from the U.S. Department of Labor show that, although the unemployment rate has fallen steadily since 1983, the poverty rate has remained high. Since 1983 unemployment has dropped by 4%. Meanwhile, the overall poverty rate has fallen only 2% — and has actually increased for children.

WORKING HARDER, GETTING POORER

U.S. Census Bureau figures reveal that nearly half of the heads of all poor households are employed. In 1988 the proportion of poor heads of households who worked full-time increased by 1.8%. But that was accompanied by a decline in the average earnings of full-time male workers. A low minimum wage offers one explanation for this stubborn trend. For example, full-time work at the minimum wage by the head of a family of three leaves that family $2,500 below the poverty line.

In nearly 42% of poor households headed by females, the women are employed. About 10% work full-time, year-round. And 87% of poor children live in a family in which at least one person is employed at least part of the time. However, from 1979 to 1987 income for young families with children dropped by nearly 25%.

"The public has a misconception about who the poor are," Sherraden observes. "Most people who live below the poverty line are not welfare recipients and members of the underclass. They are people who have jobs or are members of a household in which someone has a job." He adds, "What kind of message are we delivering if people work hard and still do not make it?"

Some of the workers in poor families are children and teenagers. In 1989 the U.S. Department of Labor discovered 23,000 minors working in violation of the Fair Labor Standards Act. In fact, child labor violations have doubled in the last five years. Most such violations have involved young teenagers working too many hours or under unsafe conditions. Unlike the sweatshops of the past, many violators of child labor laws today are hamburger joints and fast-food establishments. Many teenagers work long hours because they must do so in order to survive, not because they are trying to buy designer jeans or are exploring future careers in food services. And, as teachers know, working often becomes a reason for classroom failure.

CUTBACKS AND REDUCTIONS

To add to an already bad situation, government cutbacks and the perpetual budget crisis have increased children's woes. The House Select Committee on Children, Youth, and Families found that, since 1970, the median grant through Aid to Families with Dependent Children (AFDC) has fallen 23%, from $471 to $361 in constant dollars. In 1987 AFDC reached only 56% of children in poverty, a lower proportion than

in 1964 when the first volley was fired in the War on Poverty.

"Child poverty is Ronald Reagan's legacy to the 1990s," according to Rep. George Miller (D-Calif.), who chairs the Select Committee on Children, Youth, and Families. Between 1980 and 1988, during President Reagan's military build-up, the U.S. government spent $1.9 trillion on national defense, while cutting $10 billion from programs aimed at protecting poor children and families.

According to the Center for the Study of Social Policy, AFDC benefits and food stamps for a family of four amounted to only 66.3% of the 1988 poverty line, down from 70.9% in 1980. Meanwhile, participation in the food stamp program has declined 14% since 1982.

At the same time, federal assistance for low-income housing tumbled 76% when adjusted for inflation. In *The Same Client: The Demographics of Education and Service Delivery Systems*, a recent report from the Institute for Educational Leadership, Harold Hodgkinson concluded that many dropouts and school failures can be attributed directly to such basic factors as the high cost of housing that eats up most of a family's available and limited income. Children living on the edge of homelessness are prevented from finding the stability that usually makes successful schooling possible.

"If low-income children were living in economically and socially secure housing with some rent protection, there is little doubt that most of them could stay out of poverty and in school, while their parents stay on the job and off welfare," Hodgkinson advised in the report. He argued that national housing strategies to increase the availability and reduce the cost of housing are essential, if we wish to limit poverty. So are preventive social strategies that help people who are facing financial emergencies to stay out of poverty.

NO PLACE TO CALL HOME

Poor housing or no housing — those seem to be the options facing most poor children. Homeless children are one more distressing by-product of the new poverty that plagues this nation. The U.S. Department of Education estimates that 220,000 school-aged children are homeless and that 65,000 of them do not attend school. About 15,600 homeless children live in publicly operated shelters, 90,700 live in privately operated shelters, 55,750 stay with relatives or friends, and 63,170 live "elsewhere." The greatest number of homeless children live in Los Angeles, New York, Chicago, Minneapolis, and Houston. Homelessness among children in the nation's capital has increased by a factor of five in recent years.

A report from the General Accounting Office estimated that, on any given night, 186,000 children who are not actually homeless are "precariously housed," living on the verge of homelessness. The Department of Health and Human Services calculates that, over the course of a year, as many as one million youngsters under age 18 lack a permanent home or live on the streets.

Despite the $1.7 billion in federal funds expended through the Stewart B. McKinney Homeless Assistance Act of 1987 and the millions more spent through the Runaway and Homeless Youth Act of 1974, homelessness continues to grow — a disturbing reminder that not all is well in the land of the free.

The future also looks bleak for those categories of young people who no longer live at home, according to the House Select Committee on Children, Youth, and Families. Its late 1989 report, *No Place to Call Home: Discarded Children in America*, concluded that by 1995 nearly a million children no longer living with their parents will cause serious problems for the schools. The study found that between 1985 and 1988 the number of children living in foster care jumped by 23%, while federal funding for welfare services for children rose only 7%.

Foster children are only one of the categories of displaced children, most of whom come from poor families. The number of children in juvenile detention centers rose 27% between 1979 and 1987, while funding fell from $100 million to $66.7 million. The number of children in mental health facilities also soared by 60% between 1983 and 1986. Meanwhile, federal block grants for mental health services declined by $17 million.

Drug and alcohol abuse by parents contributed to these dangerous trends. From 1985 to 1988 the number of children born with drug exposure quadrupled, reaching 375,000 in 1988. Add to that the number of abused or neglected children, which climbed 82% between 1981 and 1988. Of course, not all of these children are poor, but needy children fall into these categories much more frequently than their not-needy counterparts.

Rep. Miller warned that the nation's schools could be "overwhelmed" by such problems in the 1990s. He noted that teachers, counselors, and social workers are already overworked and that none of them "receives the training needed to deal with the complex and difficult problems confronting children and families today."

Clearly, no social problem operates in isolation. Poverty breeds personal and social disintegration. Difficulties in the areas of health, housing, and education are all linked. For example, significant numbers of homeless children suffer a wide range of health disorders. Many risk hearing loss because of untreated ear infections. That in turn leads to serious learning problems. In many homeless shelters, such infectious diseases as tuberculosis and whooping cough run rampant among uninoculated youngsters. Poverty is more than a social label; it is a disease that weakens and often destroys its victims.

HEALTHY GOALS, UNHEALTHY RESULTS

At first glance, it seems that the U.S. has a comprehensive health-care system. For example, we spent $551 billion on health care in 1987. But 37 million Americans, including more than 12 million children, have no health insurance. Uninsured children have a 20% greater chance of poor health and are less likely to have proper immunization against infectious diseases.

Nearly half of all poor children do not receive benefits from Medicaid, despite recent congressional action ordering states to provide more extensive coverage to poor children and pregnant mothers. The National Commission to Prevent Infant Mortality has found that the U.S. ranks 20th among the nations of the world in infant mortality and has urged Congress to take over Medicaid to insure that it reaches *all* infants and pregnant mothers.

This year the Pepper Commission, a bipartisan group of congressional representatives, urged a massive overhaul of the national health system, which is "in total crisis." Among other reforms, the commission called for universal protection for poor children and families. But the $66 billion a year price tag has scared off many potential supporters.

One pregnant woman in four receives no prenatal care during the critical first trimester. Such a mother is three to six times more likely to give birth to a premature, low-birth-weight baby who will be at risk for developmental disability or even death. Ultimately, 10.6 of every 1,000 newborns in the U.S. die — the highest rate in the developed world.

In 1980 Dr. Julius Richmond, then surgeon general of the U.S., published a list of 20 health-care goals for infants and children to be achieved by 1990. Like the recent list of educational goals promulgated by President Bush and the National Governors' Association, the health-care targets were ambitious and essential to heading off social and economic crisis. But by late 1989 the American Academy of Pediatrics, an organization of 37,000 experts on children's medical health, concluded that only one of the 20 goals had been achieved.

That one success was in reducing neonatal mortality: the death rate for infants in the first 28 days after birth has dropped from 9.5 to 6.4 deaths per 1,000. However, other goals, such as improving birth weights and prenatal care and narrowing the gap between racial groups in infant mortality, remain unfulfilled. The mortality rate for black infants is still twice that for white infants, about the same as it was 26 years ago; the infant mortality rate for the entire U.S. population stands at 10.1%, while the rate for African-Americans is 17.9%. (By contrast, the infant mortality rate in Japan is just 4.8%.) Moreover, surviving black infants have nine times more chance than white infants of being neurologically impaired.

Dr. Myron Wegman of the University of Michigan School of Public Health, who conducted the study for the pediatricians, discovered the existence of two separate medical nations within this land. One nation is prosperous, with the latest in health technology and knowledge at its disposal; the other nation is deprived, with death rates and health problems that match those commonly found in the Third World. Dr. Wegman blamed government cuts in health programs and social services during the Reagan Administration for a slowdown that prevented reaching the goals.

IMPACT ON SCHOOLS

What do the mountains of statistics and a heritage of damaged lives mean for educators in the public schools? Surveys of teachers have found disturbing news. The Metropolitan Life Insurance Company's annual *Survey of the American Teacher* discovered that in 1989 American teachers were greatly alarmed at the health and social problems of their students.

Other surveys show that teachers worry about constant pupil turnover, about students' health problems, and about students' preoccupation with family problems. Once again, such concerns are more common among teachers of children from low-income families. Guidance counselors report that, even at the elementary level, they find themselves "dealing with one crisis after another" in a child's life.

Teachers also report that they are seeing more children with learning disabilities. In fact, over the last 10 years the number of children diagnosed as learning disabled has increased 140% — to about 1.9 million children. While educators argue over the meaning of the term and debate possible reasons for the increase, veteran teachers claim that they have never before seen so many children with problems of comprehension and basic skills in their classes.

According to Verna Gray, a veteran teacher in the Chicago schools, poverty leads to more problems than just the lack of the basic academic skills needed to succeed in school. "Many of these youngsters don't have any self-esteem or even the belief that they can achieve," she notes.

The effects on the schools of increasing numbers of children living in poverty may not be completely clear, and the details are certainly debatable. But no one disputes that there are serious effects — or that the effects are negative.

WHAT SOCIETY MUST DO

No single individual or group can successfully tackle all the factors that contribute to child poverty. The lack of jobs that pay a decent wage, for example, is the biggest contributor to poverty in small towns, cities, and suburbs. Clearly, this is a national problem that can be addressed only by a comprehensive economic policy that gives top priority to the creation of jobs that pay a living wage. A number of family experts believe that an even greater increase in the minimum wage than the one recently passed by Congress is essential to help the working poor escape a lifetime of poverty.

Some effective programs already exist to deal with almost every aspect of the cycle of child poverty. But the programs that work have never been properly funded. Head Start is the classic example. Head Start was created by the antipoverty legislation of the 1960s, and a number of studies have documented its positive impact. One study found that nearly 60% of the Head Start graduates were employed at age 19, compared to just 32% of a control group. Only 49% of the control group had graduated from high school, while 67% of the former Head Start students had earned high school diplomas. Nearly 40% of the Head Start graduates had taken some college courses, while just 21% of the control group had taken any coursework beyond high school.

Such statistics add up to lives and money saved. One dollar invested in Head Start saves $7 in later social services that are not needed. Numbers of this kind have convinced many, but Head Start, which celebrates its 25th birthday this year, still serves only one in five eligible students.

That situation might be about to change. There are hopeful signs that some basic services for poor children could improve in the next few years if the federal government reasserts its leadership in child care, health coverage, and education.

Major political players are lining up in favor of a vastly extended support system

for early care and education. The National Governors' Association has made early childhood learning a top goal, and President Bush's education budget called for a modest increase of $245 million for Head Start. Most important, the mammoth child-care bill hammered out by Congress over the last two years will bolster Head Start by as much as $600 million over the next five years. At press time, only a veto by President Bush, who wishes to shift to the states more of the burden of funding the program, can block what has become the most important piece of antipoverty legislation in the last 25 years.

Educators worry that, as the number of children in poverty grows, education for those children — without sharp increases in funding for Chapter 1 and Head Start — can only get worse, not better. Susan Frost, executive director of the Committee for Education Funding, says that "there is no alternative to Chapter 1 and Head Start, which are estimated to serve only one-half and one-fifth respectively of eligible children." The needs of such children, she adds, are not going to be met by restructuring.

Meanwhile, there is growing public support for offering a wider array of social and health services in the schools. In September 1989 a survey by the *Washington Post* and ABC News found widespread support for a variety of nontraditional services in the schools: the dissemination of information about birth control, counseling for psychiatric and drug-related problems, more nutrition information, and so on. Likewise, the 21st Annual Gallup Poll of the Public's Attitudes Toward the Public Schools (published in the September 1989 *Kappan*) found 74% of the public willing to spend more tax dollars to screen children for health programs, 69% willing to spend more money for Head Start, and 58% willing to spend more for day care for young children whose parents work.

WHAT SCHOOLS CAN DO

The prevalence of child poverty in the U.S. is enough to make any educator shudder — and not just because of the damage to the children. All too often the public schools are given the burden of overcoming economic and social inequities, usually without adequate resources to confront these difficult problems. Indeed, children who have been maimed by such new social epidemics as homelessness and crack use by pregnant women are already testing the resources and tolerance of the schools. Many reformers believe that, instead of another add-on program, the schools need a coordinated and concerted societal effort to deal with these problems.

Still, all across the nation, educators are

struggling to meet the crisis with innovative solutions and more of their legendary dedication. The many examples of their efforts fall into two major categories: mobilizing parents and integrating community and health resources into the school.

PARENT INVOLVEMENT

Some educators are reexamining the roles parents can play in the schools. But poor parents face significant obstacles to becoming involved. According to the National Committee for Citizens in Education, "A parent who speaks limited English or who was herself a school dropout is unlikely to volunteer as a member of a school improvement council. A poor parent who has no automobile may not be able to send his child to a better public school located outside the attendance area — even when the option is available — unless transportation is provided by the school district. These barriers to full participation can be removed with training, encouragement, and resources that insure equal access."

Nevertheless, many educators are putting their energies into parent solutions — and getting results.

• The Center for Successful Child Development, known as the Beethoven Project, is a family-oriented early childhood intervention program at the Robert Taylor Homes, a public housing project on the south side of Chicago. Sponsored by the Chicago Urban League and by the Ounce of Prevention Fund, the Beethoven Project opened in 1987. Some 155 families now benefit from a variety of educational, social, and medical services for young children who will ultimately enroll in the Beethoven Elementary School.

• In Missouri, Parents as Teachers combines an early childhood component with an education program for parents. It began as a pilot program in 1981, and today all 543 Missouri school districts are required to provide certain services to families, including parent education, periodic screening through age 4 to detect developmental problems, and educational programs for those 3- and 4-year-olds who are developmentally delayed. The program is not restricted to poor children, but it can catch their problems early, and results have been encouraging.

• James Comer, director of the School Development Program at Yale University, is working with 100 inner-city schools across the country to create management teams made up of parents, teachers, and mental health professionals. The aims are to improve the teachers' knowledge of child development, to involve parents, and to provide children with community resources normally found outside the school.

• In California and Missouri a new approach, known as the Accelerated Schools Program, is trying to change parents' attitudes toward their children. The Accelerated Schools Program attempts to raise parents' expectations about what their children can do, while it also focuses on giving literacy training to the parents. The goal is to empower parents so that they can become involved in their children's education. The program currently operates in two schools in California and in seven schools in Missouri.

A number of researchers and scholars have endorsed the idea of parent involvement. For example, Harold Stevenson of the University of Michigan released a study in 1989 that found that, contrary to popular belief, black and Hispanic mothers are keenly interested in their children's education and want to be involved despite the economic and social barriers to their doing so.

Parents can play a key role in many aspects of a school, providing a sense of community that can nurture as well as protect children in a school setting. During a cold Boston winter, for example, parents noticed that some children at David A. Ellis School in Roxbury did not have warm jackets. The parents established a clothing exchange to make sure that the children were warm on their way to school.

"The parents are part of the everyday life of the school," says Owen Haleem of the Institute for Responsive Education (IRE) at the Boston University School of Education. Two years ago the IRE organized a Schools Reaching Out Project. In January 1990 it organized a national network to increase parent and community involvement in urban public schools serving low-income communities. Known as the League of Schools Reaching Out, the network now includes 37 schools in 19 urban school districts.

"New relationships with low-income parents must be fashioned in order to break the link between poverty and school failure," according to Don Davies, president of the IRE. Two schools were part of a two-year pilot study of ways to develop these new relationships. The David A. Ellis School in Roxbury and Public School 111 in District 2 on the west side of Manhattan each converted one classroom near the principal's office into an on-site parents' center and initially paid a full-time "key teacher" to serve as a link between the school, the students' families, and the community. P.S. 111 offered classes in English as a second language (ESL) for Spanish-speaking parents and organized a lending library for educational toys and games. Parents at Ellis

School offered ESL and formed a support group to study for the high-school-equivalency exams. Both schools send trained parents and community members to visit other parents at home and organize collaborative projects between teachers and parents.

The IRE pilot study was modeled, in part, on a similar program in Liverpool, England, where each school has a coordinator of social services. The IRE programs at P.S. 111 and at Ellis School try to combat the idea that parents need only to come to school for meetings. According to Haleem, "Our goal was to work with regular public schools to build fundamentally different relationships with low-income parents." And both schools have recorded achievement gains, which, Haleem notes, may not be connected to the parent involvement program. But then again they might be.

To some child advocates, *family* literacy is the key both to involving parents and to improving student achievement. A Department of Defense study conducted in the 1980s found that the most important variable in determining the educational attainment of 16- to 23-year-olds was the educational level of their mothers. Indeed, Thomas Sticht of Applied Behavioral and Cognitive Sciences, Inc., in San Diego argues that federal programs need to work with families.

Next year the Department of Education will spend $10,477,000 for Even Start, a program of financial assistance to local agencies that conduct projects in family-centered education. Privately funded and family-centered literacy projects, such as the Kenan Family Literacy Project in Louisville, Kentucky, also teach basic skills to parents while their children attend a preschool. Operating in seven schools in Kentucky and North Carolina, the Kenan Family Literacy Project teaches parents to read and to teach their children to read. This program was a model for the Foundation for Family Literacy, initiated by First Lady Barbara Bush.

For poor children whose parents remain uninvolved, schools may have to come up with other answers. An increasing number of social scientists argue that just one relationship between an adult and a disadvantaged child in stressful conditions can make a significant difference.

Public/Private Ventures, a nonprofit organization based in Philadelphia, examined five programs involving adults in the community and at-risk students. It found that the bonds that formed between the generations helped the youngsters weather crises, gave them a sense of stability, and improved their sense of their own competence.

SCHOOLS AS SOCIAL CENTERS

Indeed, many educators feel that they'll be able to address the needs of poor children only if the community works with the schools.

"The most urgent task is to regenerate families deep in the inner cities," Roger Wilkins, a professor of history at George Mason University, argued in the *New York Times* last year. "While employment, early childhood education, and child-care programs are critical parts of such an effort, it is essential that the public schools become the focus of special remedies," Wilkins asserted. "In addition, the schools would become centers of the community for the children they serve and for their parents and grandparents."

Indeed, more and more schools are designing programs that link social services and academic programs. But such ventures require schools and communities to overcome the instinct to protect their own turf and to agree to work together as one entity.

A number of states — including New York, Oregon, South Carolina, and Florida — have initiated new efforts to coordinate services for children. The problem is that child services are so spread out. In California, for example, 160 state programs for children operate out of 45 agencies. Schools must organize the services in ways that funnel them directly toward the complex needs of poor youngsters.

One initiative that helps not only poor children but all children coming of age today was started by Edward Zigler, Sterling Professor of Psychology and director of the Bush Center in Child Development and Social Policy at Yale University. Zigler has touted "Schools for the 21st Century" — schools that function as community centers, linking a host of family-support services to help children overcome social, psychological, and health problems. The approach includes home visitations, assistance for parents with infants, day care for 3- to 5-year-olds, before- and after-school care for school-age children, teen pregnancy prevention programs, and adult literacy classes. Zigler's program began in Independence, Missouri, and has spread to five states.

One educator who agrees that the school needs to take on a broader role in the lives of children is Allan Shedlin, Jr. In 1987 the Elementary School Center that Shedlin directs called for a reconceptualization of the elementary school as the locus of advocacy for all children.

"Traditional sources of support for the child — the family, the neighborhood, schools, social and religious organizations, nutritional and health care programs — are fragmented or do not exist at all for many children," says Shedlin. School has become the only agency that deals with every child, every day. Thus the school should serve as the center of advocacy for children.

The National School Boards Association (NSBA) argues that school officials cannot wait until all the desired elements are in place before taking action, and it suggests a number of remedies. Schools should:

• establish a local policy to help all children learn — perhaps by means of counseling programs, tutoring programs, or parent involvement;
• examine the needs of a community and determine whether parents need day-care services, health services, job skills, or the help of volunteers;
• develop a demographic profile of the school system — find out whether families are in poverty and whether there are single-parent families, migrant families, immigrant families — and communicate this information to all people in the school system;
• define and identify all youth at risk — considering such factors as student absenteeism, poor grades, low test scores in math or reading, chemical dependency, boredom, and family mobility;
• follow student progress in school by keeping comprehensive records;
• evaluate programs that have already been implemented;
• give administrators and teachers flexibility in helping students at risk and make use of student mentors, faculty advisors, teaching teams, and tutoring;
• involve parents in children's schooling; and
• work with local businesses, agencies, and organizations to develop and fund programs.

Carol Pringle didn't believe that she could wait any longer to help the poor children in her Seattle community. In April 1989 the mother of three and former schoolteacher organized a two-room schoolhouse called First Place. It is now one of a dozen programs in the country designed for homeless children. Technically it is a nonprofit agency, but it works in cooperation with the Seattle School District, which provides buses each day to round up children (kindergarten through grade 6) from homeless shelters all over the city.

Two salaried teachers and a number of volunteers have adapted the regular school curriculum for this new clientele. But the school also finds shoes for the children and, in addition to basic academics, provides breakfast, lunch, and a safe environment. Students stay an average of four to five weeks, but some attend for only a single day. They come from shelters for battered women or live with mothers who can't afford housing. Some are from families that move constantly in an effort to find work.

Other school systems have different programs. The Harbor Summit School in San Diego is near the St. Vincent de Paul Joan Kroc Center. The Tacoma (Washington) School District and the Tacoma YWCA run the Eugene P. Tone School.

However, some school officials believe that homeless children should not be placed in separate programs. Yvonne Rafferty, director of research with Advocates for Children, claims that all children should be in regular programs. New York City prohibits any separate programs for homeless children, and Minneapolis tries to provide homeless children with transportation to their former school.

Essentially the solution to the problem of schooling for homeless children is a state responsibility. The McKinney Act of 1987 grants money to states to develop plans so that homeless children can gain access to the schools.

Like Carol Pringle, Carol Cole couldn't wait any longer. Just as the first wave of crack babies was hitting school systems across the nation, she was hard at work creating a special program for such children. The Salvin Special Education School in Los Angeles is a two-year-old program designed to aid children born to crack-addicted mothers. Eight 3- and 4-year-olds work with three teachers, who give the children as much individual attention as possible. The school has a pediatrician, a psychologist, several social workers, and a speech and language specialist. According to Cole, the home lives of the children are "chaotic." Salvin School reaches only eight children at a time. But 375,000 drug-exposed babies are born annually.

A survey released by the NSBA in February 1990 found that urban school districts face an "awesome challenge" in trying to provide more social services when federal aid for such programs has declined in real dollars. The survey of 52 urban school districts found that the proportion of resources devoted to attacking social and health programs puts "a severe strain on local school districts' budgets, draining their coffers."

Jonathan Wilson, chairman of the NSBA Council of Urban Boards of Education, argues that local resources are running dry. If urban schools are to improve their performance, he maintains, they need dramatic hikes in state and federal funding and in Chapter 1.

N THE END the Children's Defense Fund calculates that the key investments to help rescue children from poverty are not prohibitively expensive. The CDF estimates that universal health care for children and pregnant women is a relatively inexpensive prevention measure and is a far better social policy than trying to remediate social ills later. In addition, the CDF figures that the costs of eliminating poverty and child poverty are not as high as many people think. Good nutrition, basic health care, and early education can make a big difference.

"We must shed the myth that all poor children need massive, long-term public intervention," Marian Wright Edelman told those attending the annual meeting of the CDF in Washington, D.C., in March 1990. "Certainly, some children are so damaged that they need such help," Edelman allows. "But millions of poor children need only modest help. They need child care, not foster care; a checkup, not an intensive-care bed; a tutor, not a guardian; drug education, not detoxification; a scholarship, not a detention cell. But it has been hard to get them what they need — even when we know what to do and when it saves us money."

According to CDF estimates (based on 1987 figures), the cost of eliminating child poverty is $17.22 billion; the cost of eliminating poverty in families with children, $26.874 billion; the cost of eliminating poverty among all persons, $51.646 billion. That last figure is equivalent to only 1% of our gross national product. Eliminating poverty in families with children would cost only about 1.5% of the total expenditures of federal, state, and local governments combined.

Indeed, if the nation's largest bankers are capable of writing off billions of dollars in debts owed by developing nations, if the U.S. Congress can almost nonchalantly commit $325 billion dollars to bailing out the unregulated and marauding savings-and-loan industry, if the public can live with military excesses and a variety of foreign affairs ventures, then surely we can renegotiate the terms of the escalating human debt embodied by the children of poverty.

Congress, the states, and local communities must rewrite the options of opportunity for all our children, but especially for our poor children. We must be willing to write the checks that guarantee poor children a real chance of success from the moment they are conceived until the moment that they receive as much education as they can absorb. Only then will the tragedy of children deprived from birth of a dignified life be banished forever from this land.

A Resource Guide

Numerous organizations, foundations, and education groups are currently focusing on the plight of children in America. Listed below are a few sources of more information on the subject.

ORGANIZATIONS

Children's Defense Fund is a private, nonprofit child-advocacy group that offers extensive research, information, and publications. Among the CDF publications are: *CDF Reports* ($29.95 a year); *Children 1990: A Report Card, Briefing Book, and Action Primer* ($2.95); and *The Health of America's Children* ($12.95). For a free listing of materials, write to: CDF, 122 C St. N.W., Washington, DC 20001.

Family Resource Coalition is a national membership organization that publishes a variety of materials. Individual membership is $30; agency/organization membership, $60. For information, write to: Family Resource Coalition, 230 N. Michigan Ave., Suite 1625, Chicago, IL 60601.

Hispanic Policy Development Project publishes the *Research Bulletin*, a free newsletter. To obtain a copy, write to: Hispanic Policy Development Project, Suite 310, 1001 Connecticut Ave. N.W., Washington, DC 20036.

Institute for American Values is a nonpartisan, nonprofit policy organization concerned with issues affecting the American family. It publishes *Family Affairs*, a free newsletter. To obtain a copy, write to: Institute for American Values, 250 W. 57th St., Suite 2415, New York, NY 10107.

Institute for Responsive Education is a 17-year-old nonprofit public interest group that publishes a variety of reports, as well as the magazine *Equity and Choice* (one-year subscription, $15) and *Building Parent-Teacher Partnerships: Prospects from the Perspective of the Schools Reaching Out Project,* by Jean Krasnow ($6). For more information, write to: Institute for Responsive Education, 605 Commonwealth Ave., Boston, MA 02215.

National Committee for Citizens in Education is a 16-year-old nonprofit organization dedicated to parent involvement and local action. It produces and distributes publications and operates a toll-free hotline (800/Network). For more information, write to: NCCE, 10840 Little Patuxent Parkway, Suite 301, Columbia, MD 21044.

Southern Education Foundation publishes studies on southern states. For more information, write to: Southern Education Foundation, 135 Auburn Ave., Atlanta, GA 30303.

Youth Policy Institute publishes *Youth Record*, a semimonthly report on federal policy ($75 a year). For more information, write to: Youth Policy Institute, 1221 Massachusetts Ave. N.W., Suite B, Washington, DC 20005.

BOOKS AND ARTICLES

Jonathan Kozol, *Rachel and Her Children: Homeless Families in America* (Crown Publishers, 225 Park Ave. S., New York, NY 10003, 1988).

Lisbeth B. Schorr, *Within Our Reach: Breaking the Cycle of Disadvantage* (Doubleday, 666 Fifth Ave., New York, NY 10103, 1989).

James P. Comer, "Educating Poor Minority Children," *Scientific American*, November 1988, pp. 42-48.

REPORTS

An Imperiled Generation: Saving the Urban Schools (Princeton University Press, 3175 Princeton Pike, Lawrenceville, NJ 08648, 1988). The price is $7.50.

A Proper Inheritance: Investing in the Self-Sufficiency of Poor Families (Center for Social Policy Studies, George Washington University, 1730 K St. N.W., Suite 701, Washington, DC 20006, July 1989). The price is $2.05 for postage; include a 9" x 12" self-addressed envelope.

A Survey of Public Education in the Nation's Urban School Districts, 1989 (Special Program Services Department, National School Boards Association, 1680 Duke St., Alexandria, VA 22314, 1990). The price is $35.

Children in Need: Investment Strategies for the Educationally Disadvantaged (Committee for Economic Development, 477 Madison Ave., New York, NY 10022, 1988). The price is $10.50 plus $3 postage.

Conditions of Children in California (Policy Analysis for California Education, School of Education, University of California, Berkeley, CA 94720, 1989). The price is $20.

Family Support, Education, and Involvement: A Guide for State Action (Council of Chief State School Officers, Resource Center on Educational Equity, 379 Hall of the States, 400 North Capitol St. N.W., Washington, DC 20001, 1989). The price is $10.

Kids Count: Data Book, State Profiles of Child Well-Being (Center for the Study of Social Policy, 1250 I St. N.W., Washington, DC 20005, 1990). The price is $10.

Making the Grade: A Report Card on American Youth (National Collaboration for Youth, 1319 F St. N.W., Suite 601, Washington, DC 20004, 1990).

Our Future and Our Only Hope: A Survey of City Halls Regarding Children and Families (National League of Cities, Publications Sales, 1301 Pennsylvania Ave. N.W., Washington, DC 20004, 1989). The price is $10.

Partners in Growth: Elder Mentors and At-Risk Youth (Public/Private Ventures, 399 Market St., Philadelphia, PA 19106, 1989). Single copies are free.

State of Black America (National Urban League, Communications Department, 500 E. 62nd St., New York, NY 10021, 1989). The price is $19.

William Braden et al., "The Critical Years: City Kids Left Behind at the Start." This is a five-part series that ran in the *Chicago Sun-Times* from 26 June through 30 June 1988; it is available through ERIC.

William T. Grant Foundation Commission on Work, Family and Citizenship, *The Forgotten Half: Pathways to Success for America's Youth and Young Families* (William T. Grant Foundation Commission on Youth and America's Future, Dept. K, Suite 301, 1001 Connecticut Ave. N.W., Washington, DC 20036, 1988). Single copies free.

Harold L. Hodgkinson, *The Same Client: The Demographics of Education and Service Delivery System* (Institute for Educational Leadership, Publication Department, 1001 Connecticut Ave. N.W., Suite 310, Washington, DC 20036, 1989). The price is $12.

Michael A. Sherraden and Isaac Shapiro, *The Working Poor: America's Contradiction* (George Warren Brown School of Social Work, Washington University, St. Louis, MO 63130, 1990).

VIDEOS

"Joining Forces: Educating Every Child for a Healthy and Productive Future" is a videotape of a teleconference held on 21 February 1990. It is available from the National Association of State Boards of Education, 1012 Cameron St., Alexandria, VA 22314. The price is $65.

"Learning to Change: Schools of Excellence for At-Risk Students" is a videotape released in 1990 about schools serving low-income students that have turned themselves around. It is available from the Southern Regional Council, 60 Walton St. N.W., Atlanta, GA 30303-2199. The price is $30.

Welfare Reform: Serving America's Children

Daniel Patrick Moynihan

United States Senate

Senator Moynihan restates the critical problems of family, children, and poverty in America that have been his driving concern for decades both as an academic and as a politician. He urges us to view welfare reform as the art of the possible and to develop policies that will save our children.

A quarter of a century has elapsed since Lyndon Johnson's initiative against poverty in America. About one American in six was poor in 1964. About one in six is poor today. In 1964, poverty was essentially a problem of the aged. In contrast, we look up today to find that not only are there more poor Americans than there were a quarter of a century ago, but that the poorest group in our population, one in five, are children (see Table 1).

This is a condition that has never before existed in our history.[1]

Table 1. Percentage below Poverty Level

Age group	1986
Under 18 years	19.8
18–64	11.1
65 and over	12.4

Source: Current Population Reports, Consumer Income, Series P-60, No. 157, *Money, Income and Poverty Status of Families and Persons in the United States: 1986* (Advance data from the March 1987 Current Population Survey, U.S. Department of Commerce, Bureau of the Census).

How has this come about? At one level the answer is simple. It is, as Samuel H. Preston put it in the 1984 presidential address to the Population Association of America, "the earthquake that shuddered through the American family in the past 20 years"[2]—the twenty years, that is, from the beginning of the poverty program.

This is to say that a new dimension of poverty has emerged. As the 1986 census reported, nearly one in every four children (23.5 percent) lives with only one parent, two and one-third times the proportion in 1960 (see Table 2). the vast majority (89 percent) of these 14.8 million children live with their mothers. These include 18.3 percent of all white children, 53.1 percent of all black children, and 30.4 percent of all Hispanic children.

Table 2. Children under 18 Living with One Parent

(Percent)

	1986	1960
Total	23.5	9.1
White	18.3	7.1
Black	53.1	21.9
Hispanic	30.4	(NA)

Source: Current Population Reports, Population Characteristics, Series P-20, No. 418, *Marital Status and Living Arrangements: March, 1986* (U.S. Department of Commerce, Bureau of the Census), p. 8.

Estimates of the number of children who will live with a single parent at some point during childhood are yet more striking. Arthur Norton of the U.S. Bureau of the Census predicts that 61 percent of children born in 1987 will live for some time with only one biological parent before reaching the age of eighteen.[3] Inevitably, large numbers of these children will require some form of public assistance.

We do have programs to provide public assistance: Survivors' Insurance (SI) and Aid to Families with Dependent Children (AFDC). The Aid to Dependent Children (ADC) Program was created in 1935, as Title IV of the Social Security Act, to replace the widows'

From *Teachers College Record*, Spring 1989, Vol. 90, No. 3, pp. 337-341. Copyright © 1989 by Teachers College, Columbia University.

pension programs then operating in all but two states. Just as old age assistance was meant to serve as a temporary bridge until the Old Age Insurance Program matured, ADC was meant to tide over poor widows and orphans who were not yet entitled to receive the survivors' insurance benefits added to the Social Security Act in 1939.

In the 1930s, it was assumed that children lived in two-parent families, that one parent worked and the other kept house. It was further assumed that things would remain so. So long as and to the extent that the assumption was true, the transition from ADC to Survivors' Insurance worked smoothly. In 1986, a fully mature SI Program paid benefits to 3.3 million children. The program for dependent children, by now renamed Aid to Families with Dependent Children (AFDC), did not, however wither away as expected. Rather it grew and grew as it was extended to single-parent families. The program now supports some 7 million children, twice the number of children receiving insured benefits under SI.

The characteristics of the populations served by these two programs are quite different. The majority of the children receiving SI are white. The majority of the children receiving AFDC are black or Hispanic (see Table 3). The figures presented in Table 3 show that our

Table 3. Racial Composition of AFDC and Survivors' Insurance Caseloads

(Percent)

	SI	AFDC
White	66	40
Black	22	41
Hispanic	8	14
Other	4	5

Source: Social Security Administration and Family Support Administration; AFDC data are for 1986; SI data are estimated for 1985.

public assistance programs seem to have created an extraordinary institutional bias against minority children. Since 1970, we have increased the real benefits received by children under SI by 53 percent. We have, in effect, cut the benefits of AFDC children by 13 percent by failing to index them to inflation. The federal government, the American people, now provide the average child receiving SI benefits almost three times what we provide a child on AFDC (see Table 4). The average provision for children under SI has been rising five times as fast as average family income since 1970, thus giving the lie to those who say we do not care about children. We do care about some children—majority children. It is minority children (not only but mostly) who are left behind.

This institutional bias extends to employment opportunities and economic-improvement options available to minority single-parent families. Seventy-two percent of all mothers with children between the ages

Table 4. Average Monthly AFDC and Survivors' Insurance Benefits Payments

(Per recipient payment, in constant 1986 dollars)

	SI	AFDC
1970	$222	$140
1986	339	122
Percent of change	+53	−13

Source: *Background Material and Data on Programs Within the Jurisdiction on the Committee on Ways and Means,* Committee on Ways and Means, U.S. House of Representatives, 100th Congress, 1st Session, 1987 edition, March 6, 1987. (*Note:* CRS put the numbers in current dollars. These do not appear in that form in the source book.)

of six and eighteen are in the labor force. Over half of all mothers with children under the age of three are in the labor force. This marks a great change in the position of women in American life. The only women who have not participated in this change are the heads of AFDC families, of whom fewer than 5 percent work part time or full time.

How has this institutional bias against minority children and families emerged in our public assistance programs? I believe we know how. Welfare has become a stigmatized program, and the children dependent on it (as many as one child in three before reaching eighteen) are stigmatized by association. I believe we must get rid of that stigma by emphasizing child support, support to families, and the education and training adults need to get off welfare. Such a definition must occur at the federal level first. There has been a great deal of talk about both increasing child support and enabling adults through education and training, but the federal government has really never backed either. Once that stigma is gone, or diminished, states will once again feel the moral obligation to maintain and even increase AFDC payments to dependent children. The states are free to do so now. With but two exceptions, they do not. We must change this. AFDC should be a national program, with national benefits that keep pace with inflation, in exactly the same way that Survivors' Insurance is a national program with national benefits.

A child should never be neglected, even in a society brimming with children. How much more careful we ought to be then as children become a scarce resource. The U.S. birthrate dropped below the replacement level fifteen years ago. As a result, the number of young adults—age eighteen to twenty-four—as a percentage of the population will decline 23 percent by the year 2000. As this age group shrinks, there will be fewer adolescent mothers, fewer such mothers seeking public assistance and work training, and—perhaps most important—fewer young adults entering the labor force. The plain fact is that America has no children to waste. Yet, at present, we suffer the impoverishment of 20 percent of our children. Do we expect children growing up in misery to mature into adults capable of maintaining, much less improving, American society? Do we expect poor, ill-educated children to manage the American economy? It ought not to be left to chance.

Still, the conditions that have developed over a generation will not change overnight. It is possible, however, to change direction. We can and we must set a new trend in place by creating a new system of child support that, without abandoning ultimate security, puts its first emphasis on earned income, and that, without giving up on the problems of deeply dependent families, extends coverage to all needful ones.

Welfare reform must become the art of the possible, or it will become a diversion of the essentially unserious.

NOTES

1. New poverty data suggest this condition *has* existed in other nations. See Current Population Reports, Consumer Income, Series P-60, No. 157, *Money, Income and Poverty Status of Families and Persons in the United States: 1986* (Advance data from the March 1987 Current Population Survey, U.S. Department of Commerce, Bureau of the Census).

2. Samuel H. Preston, "Children and the Elderly: Divergent Paths for America's Dependents" (Presidential Address, Population Association of America, 1984).

3. Arthur Norton, Assistant Chief of Population Division, U.S. Bureau of the Census, search Note, March 1987.

Gender Issues in Teacher Education

M. Gail Jones

Jones is Assistant Professor, The University of North Carolina.

Jones examines the influence of gender bias on classroom interactions. Sixty teachers were observed using the Brophy-Good Teacher-Child Dyadic Interaction System to code classroom interactions. Teacher experience was then analyzed in relation to gender differences in classroom interactions. Teachers of all levels of experience were found to interact more with male students than with females. The nature of and differences in interactional patterns are examined. Reform in teacher preparation with regard to educational equity is discussed.

Social science research has revealed the gender inequities that have existed in the schools for many decades. In 1972, the U.S. Congress recognized the seriousness of educational equity by passing Title IX legislation requiring sex equity in all educational institutions receiving federal assistance. But even in the 16 years since Title IX was passed, teacher education programs have failed to meet the challenge of preparing teachers to confront their own biases and to recognize the impact that differential expectations can have on their students.

Societal sex roles have changed tremendously in the last 25 years. The majority of women in the United States now work outside the home, and more are entering the workforce daily. Women are now employed at all levels of managerial, business, and technical fields and clearly are no longer relegated to support or service positions. Although women currently are achieving equitable job opportunities, they continue to be prepared in an educational system that promotes institutional sexism. When prospective teachers exit their teacher education programs with differential expectations for their students based on gender, their subsequent classroom behaviors reflect these subtle biases (Becker, 1982; Jones, 1987; Sikes, 1972).

An examination of the history of education provides insight into the issue of gender and schooling. Coeducation has made dramatic progress despite the sage pronouncements of Plato and Aristotle, who believed that women were morally, intellectually, and physically weaker than men (Smith and Farina, 1984). At one point in history it was even believed that if a woman studied college material her health would be ruined, since the body would lack enough oxygen to both think and reproduce (Smith and Farina, 1984). In America, however, coeducation became the norm with little debate or comment; even when coeducation was questioned, the controversy had little impact on educational policy:

Consider . . . the question of how schools have responded to the social diversity of the American population. If one looks at some of the basic dividing lines in American society, such as race, class, ethnicity, religion and gender, one finds that some social differences have given rise to abundant policy discussion whereas others have not. People have openly debated, for example, issues of race (segregation and access); of ethnicity ('Americanization' or cultural pluralism); and of religion (Bible reading and prayer or public aid to sectarian schools) . . . But other social differences, though powerful and prevalent, such as class and gender, have rarely been prominent on the agenda of public discussion of education. (Tyack and Hansot, 1988, p. 33)

Early in the 19th century, women began entering schools. Children of both sexes attended the many one-room school houses that dotted the American landscape. Tyack and Hansot maintain that coeducation grew gradually, not as a policy direction, but rather as a series of small decisions made by tens of thousands of local school districts. Certainly issues such as vocational education, mathematics, and science enrollments have arisen in recent years, but Tyack and Hansot have pointed out that policy discussion about gender has "tended to focus on only the part of the complex realities of gender in public schools and has often failed to recognize or alter underlying continuities of gender relationships" (p. 34).

Preschool & Elementary Classrooms

In the early childhood years, the teacher plays an important role in shaping behavior. Ebbeck (1984) has shown that teachers may channel children into sex-stereotyped activities as early as the preschool level. Ebbeck observed 30 early childhood teachers and found seri-

From *Journal of Teacher Education*, January/February 1989, pp. 33-38. Copyright © 1989 by the American Association of Colleges for Teacher Education.

ous imbalances in participation of girls in block play, sand play, climbing, and construction behaviors. Ebbeck suggests that each of these types of play offers opportunities for the development of the mathematical, scientific, and spatial skills that females often lack later in life. Overall, teachers in the Ebbeck study spent 60 percent of their time with males and 40 percent with females.

The differences in time spent with male and female students may not appear to be that great initially; however, Kelly (1986) estimated in her meta-analysis of gender differences in teacher-pupil interactions that teachers spend, on the average, 56 percent of their time with males and 44 percent with females. Over the length of a student's school career (about 15000 hours), males would average 1800 more hours with the teacher than females. When that attention is divided up among 30 students, the average girl would end up with 60 fewer hours of individual attention than the average boy. Kelly suggests that such a discrepancy should be taken very seriously by the teaching profession.

In another study of preschool classes, Serbin, O'Leary, Kent, and Tonick (1973) noted that boys received more responses to solicitation, more detailed instruction, and more praise and hugging than girls. The investigators reported that girls are more likely to be ignored, except when physically located directly beside the teacher.

In a study of first-grade classes, Simpson and Erickson (1983) found that teachers gave more verbal and nonverbal criticism, as well as more verbal and nonverbal praise to male students. Meyer and Thompson (1956) investigated the distribution of approval and disapproval among sixth-grade students and found that boys received significantly more disapproval contacts than the girls in the class. Disapproval contacts, although negative, are another form of attention for male students. In a review of elementary school studies, Brophy and Good (1974) indicated that consistent differences in teacher behavior appear across the studies. Curran (1980) explains the implications of these gender inequities:

It is not enough merely to avoid discriminating on the basis of sex. Boys and girls learn, through the family, mass media and peer group pressures, which activities are appropriate for their sex. Boys are more likely to play with mechanical and scientific toys and to gain practical spatial (three-dimensional) experience outside school — helping dad with the car, carpentry, chemistry . . . Girls are more likely to lack experience of handling concrete objects, which leaves them at a disadvantage for scientific work.

If girls are to get a fair chance later, it is essential that teachers not only *refrain* from further disadvantaging them, but recognizing that they are disadvantaged by our sexist society, and practice positive discrimination; that is, provide girls with the mechanical and spatial experiences that boys pick up informally at play and at home. (p. 31)

Middle & Secondary Classrooms

The pattern of sex-typed behaviors continues beyond the elementary school into the middle and high school. In a study of fourth-, sixth- and eighth-grade classes, Sadker, Sadker, and Thomas (1981) reported that boys were eight times as likely to call out in class as girls. When girls in the study did call out, they were commonly told by their teacher to raise their hand before talking in class. The trend for boys to call out more frequently has been reported in several studies (Baker, 1986; Becker, 1982; Jones, 1987). In a study of geometry classes, Becker (1982) reported that males made 67 percent of the call-outs compared to 33 percent by females. Becker also reported that females received fewer opportunities to respond, received less praise and criticism, encouragement, and individual help, and were less frequently involved in joking and conversation. Overall, Becker indicates that males received more teacher attention and reinforcement.

Sikes (1972) observed 16 math and social studies classrooms for a total of 10 hours. This study reported some consistency among male and female teachers in their unequal treatment of male and female students. Teachers interacted more with male students. Sikes reports that the teachers in the study tended to ask male students more higher-order questions and female students more lower-order questions.

Jones (1987) reported that male students received more of every type of interaction. Male students received significantly more praise and behavioral criticism, and males asked significantly more procedural questions of teachers. In this study, Jones also reported that teachers sex-type occupations and use sex-typed language. Teachers tended to ask more males than females to carry out experiments and to demonstrate equipment. Baker (1986) also reported significant differences (in favor of males), for type of question, type of feedback, and quantity of interactions held with high school teachers.

Data from the 1976-77 National Assessment of Educational Progress were analyzed by Kahle (1983). This report indicated that females aged 13 and 17 report fewer classroom experiences with common experimental materials and instruments. Young women also report having had fewer classroom and extracurricular science activities than males. Kahle points out the effects of gender-biased differences on the science education of males and females:

[T]he most critical difference in the science education of boys and girls occurs in the science classroom. Research shows that girls have fewer experiences with the instruments, materials, or techniques of science. This difference must be addressed by every science teacher in every science classroom to eliminate the inequalities in science education. As long as the majority of our citizens have fewer opportunities to observe natural phenomena, to use scientific instruments, to perform scientific experiments, or to go on science-related field trips, they are disadvantaged in terms of their science education. (Kahle, 1983, p. 1)

Many of the recent research studies on classroom interactions have focused on mathematics or science because these subjects often have differential enrollment patterns in the higher courses, such as physics and calculus. Nationally, there are significantly more males employed as engineers and or physical scientists. Mathematics has been called a "critical filter" (Sells, 1978) that operates to deny women access to undergraduate majors in the sciences and hence to related career opportunities. The data emerging about teacher-student behavior reveal that mathematics and science classrooms may be hostile climates for young women. This climate can be controlled or altered by the expectations and behaviors of the teacher. The teacher plays a critical role in breaking the traditional pattern that suggests that mathematics and physics are subjects for boys.

The language teachers use can communicate very subtle messages about gender to students. Teachers continue to use the generic "he" to refer to both males and females (Jones, 1987). Although teachers believe that students understand that they mean "he" to include both genders, students may be receiving a different message. Stericker (1981) had male and female undergraduates read six job descriptions referring to the job holder as either "he," "he or she," or "they." Students were asked to indicate after reading each description how difficult it would be for people of various races, sex, or age to get the job. The data revealed that the use of the masculine pronoun reduced the estimated chances of a female getting the job. In another study, Harrison and Passero (1975) asked third-graders to match a picture with a description of an activity. When masculine generic terms were used, children selected male pictures to match the activity, making a literal interpretation of the descriptions.

In the study by Kiefer (1983), teachers were asked to grade unknown student essays. Those essays that had male names or no names attached were consistently rated as better than those with female names.

Preservice Education

In a survey of the beliefs of preservice teachers, Smith and Bailey (1982) reported that future teachers have beliefs rooted in traditional sex stereotypes. This survey of students in a teacher preparation program revealed that although future teachers believe that women have equal opportunities to assume equal leadership roles in education, they also believe that men are more dedicated teachers than women. The survey respondents, 98 percent of whom were women, also indicated that 78 percent believed that students prefer men teachers to women. Smith and Farina (1984) suggest the possibility "that women have internalized the idea that men are better. It is likely that they will unconsciously model this attitude as teachers" (p. 31).

Although sex equity has become an issue in current public school textbook selection at the precollege level, this same progress has failed to carry over into teacher education. Sadker and Sadker (1981) surveyed 24 leading teacher education textbooks and reported startling results:

- None of the surveyed texts provided future teachers with curricular re-

sources or instructional strategies to counteract sexism in the classroom.
- Twenty-three of the twenty-four texts gave less than one percent of space to sexism in education.
- One third of the texts failed to mention sexism at all. The texts in math and science education were the most guilty of this oversight.
- There was an average of five times as much content space allocated to males as to females in the foundations of education texts analyzed.
- In the science methods texts, an average of seven times more space was allocated to males than females.
- Sexism was not mentioned in any of the math methods texts analyzed.
- Continued stereotyping was noted in language arts texts. For example, the Sadkers reported one text indicated that girls would read boys' books, but boys would not read girls' books; therefore libraries should buy two boys' books to every one girls'.

If the texts are indicative of what is being taught in teacher education programs, then it is time for serious reform in teacher preparation.

> There now exists a comprehensive body of research indicating how sexism operates in our elementary and secondary schools — in curricular materials, teacher interaction patterns, vocational education, physical education, athletics, employment practices, and many other areas of school life. There is also a good deal of information on the contributions women have made, individually and collectively, to the field of education. Future teachers should have the opportunity to learn about these issues. If the 24 texts analyzed in this study were at all representative, it is an opportunity not yet available to our nation's prospective teachers. (Sadker and Sadker, 1981, p. 332)

The challenge is there for reform in teacher education. O'Reilly and Borman (1985) argue that schools still foster sexism:

> Despite the passage of Title IX there is ample evidence that girls and young women in this country are still receiving a second-class education. Following the pattern of sexism inherent in this society, schools reward sex-role conformity, socializing girls for motherhood and boys for work leadership. . . . Teacher education in most institutions of higher learning reinforces the already existing sexist attitudes for many undergraduates. Most graduates go forth from their teacher education programs with a sex-role ideology firmly in place that will perpetuate the status quo . . . non-sexist teachers are not

born and their undergraduate teacher education programs do little, if anything to help them develop non-sexist attitudes either about themselves, or about the children they are preparing to teach. (p. 111)

Some researchers have questioned whether the role of our schools should involve altering the status of women or any other minority group (Kelly, 1986). Levy (1972) points out that although schools do not dramatically improve the lives of the oppressed or disadvantaged, they do maintain the status quo and thus exert control passively.

Teachers also question the role of schools in changing gender stereotypes. An interview of 30 Ontario teachers revealed that teachers believed that boys and girls behaved differently in school, that students expected to be treated differently, and that teachers had neither the right nor the responsibility to influence sex roles of students (Ricks and Pyke, 1973).

Other educators, however, have called for an examination of values in teacher education: "Many Americans would argue that equality of treatment should be an important educational and societal value. To those who accept this value, it seems clear that research evidence showing that (some) teachers treat boys and girls unequally requires efforts to change those teacher behaviors" (Bank, Biddle, and Good, 1980, p. 128).

Can teachers alter their behavior to reflect sex equity? The research suggests a tentative yes. Inservice training with elementary and secondary teachers has proven effective in altering classroom behavior. Sadker and Sadker (1985) used videotapes and modified microteaching to provide teachers with practice and feedback on their own interaction behaviors. These teachers were able to change both their attitudes and behaviors. The Sadkers have also reported that when teachers become sensitized to their inequitable interaction patterns, their subsequent classroom interactions become more equitable.

Sadker and Sadker found that most teachers were not conscious of their patterns of interaction and welcomed the opportunity to change them:

> From our experience in conducting workshops and training sessions across the U.S., we have become convinced that teachers simply have very little insight

into their own patterns of responding to students. Most teachers are surprised to learn that male students receive more attention than female students. When alerted to this disparity, they want to change their teaching so it becomes more equitable. (Sadker and Sadker, 1985, p. 361)

Whyte (1984) has also used classroom observation techniques along with observer feedback to shift student-teacher interactions to more equitable patterns.

Teacher Experience and Classroom Interactions: A Study

This study was a component of ongoing research on gender differences in student-teacher interactions in science classrooms (Jones, 1987). The relationship between teacher experience and gender differences in student-teacher interactions was examined. It was hypothesized that recent graduates from teacher education programs would tend to show fewer sex-typed interactions than those teachers who had many years of classroom experience. The hypothesis was based on the premise that newly prepared teachers would have different perceptions regarding the rapidly changing role of women in the job market because of their personal experience as well as their exposure to research on gender and education. If teacher education programs are in fact providing graduates with information about gender and education, then presumably these more informed but less experienced teachers should show fewer sex-typed interaction patterns.

Subjects

Teachers were selected from a pool of physical science and chemistry teachers who volunteered to be observed. Thirty physical science (11 male and 19 female) teachers and thirty chemistry teachers (6 male and 24 female) were observed for one class period. The teachers were blind to the experimental hypotheses. The study involved 1332 students from four eastern North Carolina counties.

Methodology

An observer recorded every interaction that occurred between a teacher and a student, using a modified version of the Brophy-Good Teacher-Child Dyadic Observation Instrument (Brophy and Good, 1969). This instrument involves using 43 categories to record classroom interactions. The instrument was first developed for use with elementary schools but has since been adapted for use in secondary classrooms for examining sex differences in particular (Becker, 1982; Sikes, 1972). The instrument allows for the recording of dyadic interaction only, that is, those interactions that occur between the teacher and an individual student. Not all interactions that occur in a classroom are recorded. For example, the coding system does not record peer-peer interactions or interactions that occur between the teacher and the whole class. The following are the types of behaviors coded with the instrument: type of contact, type of question, quality of the student's response, teacher's terminal feedback, teacher's sustaining feedback, child-created private contacts, teacher-afforded nonacademic contacts, and teacher-afforded academic contacts.

Each classroom was observed using the Brophy-Good Teacher-Child Dyadic Observation Instrument for a period of 30 minutes. Observations were made by the investigator, with a second observer present and coding for three classes as a check on observer reliability. The intercoder reliability was .79. In addition, the investigator-observer was checked against another researcher experienced in using the Brophy-Good Teacher-Child Dyadic Observation Instrument, for which the intercoder reliability was .82. Seating charts indicating student sex and location in the classroom were made for each class using a numbering system for each student. Audio recordings were made and analyzed.

Categories of student-teacher interactions were combined, frequencies were obtained, and eight were selected as dependent variables (listed in Tables 1 and 2). In addition, all interactions were combined and analyzed to represent the total number of interactions that occurred in the classroom for each student.

The study consisted of a two-level analysis of variance. The first level included the classification variables teacher sex, experience, and teacher sex by experience. The second level included student sex, teacher sex by student sex, experience by student sex, and teacher sex by experience by student sex. Student sex is nested within each class session.

Limitations

The observation instrument limited the types of interactions that could be recorded in the study. Only those interactions that occurred between the teacher and an individual student were recorded. If a student raised his or her hand to respond, but the teacher did not call on the student, the hand raising was not recorded. Further, nonverbal interactions were not recorded. Teachers often use facial expressions, eye contact, and body language to communicate subtle information.

Only science classes were observed in this study. Different results may be obtained by observing different subjects; however, the literature supports the trend in inequitable interactions in other subjects (Becker, 1982; Sikes, 1972).

One of the underlying assumptions of this study is that the quality of classroom interactions affects individual achievement. However, achievement was not measured in the current study. It is not fully known which types of interactions are most beneficial to achievement. It is also not known if interactions that benefit males equally benefit females. Males and females may learn better with different teaching styles.

Results

The analysis of variance revealed seven of the eight variables had significant student sex variables (Tables 1 and 2). Teacher experience was significant for only two variables, procedural questions and conversation (Table 3). Teachers with 4-5 years of experience had the most instances of conversation with students, whereas teachers with 0-3 years of experience had the fewest instances of conversation. Students asked teachers with 4-5 years of experience the most procedural questions and teachers with 21-35 years the fewest procedural questions. One interpretation is that those teachers with the most experience would be able to predict procedural questions that students are most likely to ask and could structure lessons to ensure that most students understood the task, while less experienced teachers may be less likely to predict or understand the procedural questions that students may ask.

The interaction of teacher experience and student sex was examined to

Table 1
Variable Means for Student Sex

Student Sex	Mean Interactions Per Student				
	Total***	Direct* Questions	Open Questions	Praise*	Procedural**
Female	4.640	0.540	0.073	0.077	0.065
Male	6.633	0.740	0.101	0.141	0.079

*significant at p<.05.
**significant at p<.01.
***significant at p<.001.

Table 2
Variable Means for Student Sex

Student Sex	Mean Interactions Per Student		
	Conversation**	Behavioral* Warnings	Teacher Afforded* Private Contacts
Female	0.021	0.023	0.177
Male	0.048	0.083	0.242

*significant at p<.05.
**significant at p<.001.

Table 3
Variable Means for Teacher Experience

Teacher Experience		Procedural Questions*	Conversation*
0-3 YEARS	N = 18	0.104	0.024
4-5 YEARS	N = 2	0.358	0.153
6-10 YEARS	N = 21	0.081	0.059
11-20 YEARS	N = 17	0.045	0.025
21-35 YEARS	N = 12	0.020	0.029

*significant at p<.001.

test the hypothesis that more experienced teachers would tend to interact more with male students than with female students. The ANOVA results revealed that none of the variables had significant interactions of teacher experience and student sex. That is, teachers of all levels of experience tend to interact more with male students than females. These results indicate that both newly prepared and experienced teachers lack the skills needed to alter their gender-biased behaviors.

Summary and Discussion

The literature reviewed in this article indicates that teachers continue to channel young children into sex-typed activities as early as preschool. At all educational levels, teachers give male students more praise, criticism, and overall attention. Research also shows that the classroom experiences of males and females (particularly mathematics and science) are often very different. Males have more opportunities than females to use equipment, perform experiments, and carry out demonstrations.

The author's study of teacher experience and student-teacher interactions indicates that teacher experience is unrelated to the amount of interaction that teachers have with male or female students. Results showed that teachers in the study gave significantly more praise, conversation, private contacts, behavioral warnings, and direct questions to male students. In addition, male students asked significantly more procedural questions than female students.

The evidence presented in this paper suggests that a reconceptualization of practice is needed with respect to the curriculum and the teacher behavior evidenced in schools. Preservice teachers should be exposed to a foundations of education course that examines the social structure of American society, including gender socialization and the evolution of coeducation in education. Educational and adolescent psychology courses should provide future teachers with an understanding of the differences in the psychological development of males and females and the interaction of socialization with the development of gender identity. Methods courses should discuss reflective teaching and microteaching so that students can examine their own instruction for sex bias. Methods courses can not only provide the needed pedagogical skills for introspection but can also provide preservice teachers with the research evidence that establishes the harmful effects of biased instruction. University instructors must also model equitable teaching behaviors to ensure that teachers perceive the importance of educational equity.

Further research is needed to better understand the way in which gender roles are developed in young boys and girls. Researchers are only beginning to unravel the complex influences that steer girls away from careers in mathematics and science. The financial and societal changes in the family structure now dictate that our educational system prepare females to assume equal roles in the workforce. Teacher educators must take the first steps to ensure educational equity.

References

Baker, D. R. (1986). Sex differences in classroom interactions in secondary science. *Journal of Classroom Interaction, 22* (2), 212-218.

Bank, B., Biddle, B., & Good, T. (1980). Sex roles, classroom instruction and reading achievement. *Journal of Education Psychology, 72,* 119-132.

Becker, J. R. (1982). Differential treatment of females and males in mathematics classes. *Journal for Research in Mathematics Education, 12* (1), 40-53.

Brophy, J., & Good, T. (1969). *Teacher-child dyadic interaction: A manual for coding classroom behavior.* (Report Series No. 27). Austin: The University of Texas, Research and Development Center for Teacher Education.

Brophy, J., & Good, T. (1974). *Teacher-student relationships: Causes and consequences.* New York: Holt, Rinehart & Winston.

Curran, L. (1980). Science education: Did she drop out or was she pushed? In L. Birke, W. Faulkner, S. Best, D. Johnson-Smith, & K. Overfield (Eds.), *Alice through the microscope: The power of science over women's lives* (pp. 22-41). London: Virago.

Ebbeck, M. (1984). Equity for boys and girls: Some important issues. *Early Child Development and Care, 18,* 119-131.

Harrison, L., & Passero, R. (1975). Sexism in the language of elementary school textbooks. *Science and Children, 12,* 22-25.

Jones, M. G. (1987). *Gender differences in student-teacher interactions in physical science and chemistry classes.* Doctoral Dissertation, North Carolina State University, Raleigh, North Carolina.

Kahle, J. B. (1983). *The disadvantaged majority: Science education for women.* AETS Outstanding Paper for 1983, Carolina Biological Society, Burlington, NC.

Kelly, A. (1986). *Gender differences in teacher-pupil interactions: A meta-analytic review.* Manuscript submitted for publication.

Kiefer, N. (1983). *Sex discrimination in the evaluation of students' written composition.* Unpublished Master's Thesis, Kansas State University, Manhattan, Kansas.

LaFrance, M. (1985). The school of hard knocks: Nonverbal sexism in the classroom. *Theory into Practice, 24* (1), 40-44.

Levy, B. (1972). Do teachers sell girls short? *National Educational Association Journal, 61* (9), 27-29.

Meyer, W. J., & Thompson, G. G. (1956). Sex difference in the distribution of approval and disapproval among sixth-grade children. *Journal of Educational Psychology, 47,* 385-396.

O'Reilly, P., & Borman, K. (1985). Sexism and sex discrimination in education. *Theory Into Practice, 24* (1), 110-116.

Ricks, F., & Pyke, S. (1973). Teachers' perceptions and attitudes that foster or maintain sex-role differences. *Interchange, 4,* 26-33.

Sadker, M., & Sadker, D. (1981). The development and field trial of a non-sexist teacher education curriculum. *The High School Journal, 64,* 331-336.

Sadker, D., Sadker, M., & Thomas, D. (1981). Sex equity and special education. *The Pointer, 26* (1), 33-38.

Sadker, D., & Sadker, M. (1985). Is the o.k. classroom o.k.? *Phi Delta Kappan, 66,* 359-361.

Sells, L. W. (1978). Mathematics — a critical filter. *The Science Teacher, 45* (2), 28-29.

Serbin, L. A., O'Leary, D. K., Kent, R. N., & Tonick, I. J. (1973). A comparison of teacher response to the pre-academic and problem behavior of boys and girls. *Child Development, 44,* 796-804.

Sikes, J. N. (1972). Differential behavior of male and female teachers with male and female students. *Dissertation Abstracts International,* 217A (University Microfilms No. 72-1967).

Simpson, A. W., & Erickson, M. T. (1983). Teachers' verbal and nonverbal communication patterns as a function of teacher race, student gender, and student race. *American Educational Research Journal, 20,* 183-198.

Smith, N., & Bailey, G. (1982). *Preservice teachers' perceptions of sex roles in education.* Unpublished Manuscript.

Smith, N., & Farina, R. (1984). Beneath the veneer of sex equity in education. *Educational Considerations, 11* (2), 29-33.

Stericker, A. (1981). Does this "he or she" business really make a difference? The effect of masculine pronouns as generic on job attitudes. *Sex Roles, 7,* 637-641.

Tyack, D., & Hansot, E. (1988). Silence and policy talk: Historical puzzles about gender and education. *American Educational Research Journal, 17* (3), 33-41.

Whyte, J. (1984). Observing sex stereotypes and interactions in the school lab and workshop. *Educational Review, 36* (1), 75-86.

Race and Ethnicity in the Teacher Education Curriculum

William Trent

University of Illinois at Urbana-Champaign

William Trent presents a series of arguments for his proposal that the importance of race and ethnicity in education should become a primary area of study for the prospective teacher. Trent notes recent research showing that blacks and Hispanics are among those groups least well served by schooling in the United States, yet these groups will constitute an ever-increasing proportion of students. The problem is exacerbated, in Trent's view, by the opposite trend in the proportion of minority students who will be teachers, necessitating new understandings and new approaches for majority-population teachers who will be called on to teach increasing numbers of minority youth.

It seems unnecessary today to write an article addressing the need for the explicit, informed treatment of the issues of race and ethnicity as a part of the curriculum in the preparation of the nation's teachers. We are, after all, thirty-five years beyond the Brown decision, twenty-five years beyond the 1964 Civil Rights Act; we have fair housing laws and we have affirmative action legislation. Time does not heal all wounds, however, nor does time erase centuries or years of lived history, and change has been painfully slow.

It is out of respect for the lived history of minorities in America that I argue for the necessity of including scholarship on race and ethnicity as a core part of the preparation of teachers. There are five compelling reasons that support this recommendation. The first is demographic: We are going to have an increasingly diverse nonwhite student population. Second is an economic incentive: We cannot compete in the modern world if we ignore the educational needs of a third or more of our future labor force. Third is the trend in the composition of the teaching force, which is increasingly female and white. Fourth is the idea of competence; no occupation should lay claim to the title "profession" if its treatments fail for a third of its clients or if the incumbents believe themselves to be unable to treat more than a third of its potential clients. Fifth, and in my estimation most important, is the imperative to protect the human and civil rights of the clients. In this article, I will elaborate these reasons

with evidence gathered from a variety of research efforts (my own and those of others) following a few prefatory comments.

SELECTED FEATURES OF THE SOCIAL CONTEXT

Despite the positive advances of the late sixties and early seventies, which created a very narrow window of opportunity, we have also had benign neglect of minorities: the Bakke and Weber legal decisions, which weakened affirmative action efforts; a declining rate of postsecondary enrollment for blacks; limited advances in enrollment of Hispanics and American Indians; a Justice Department bent on dismantling any efforts aimed at affirming civil rights; the recent demonstrations of overt racism brought to mind by names such as Howard Beach, Willie Horton, and skinheads; and finally a Supreme Court apparently constituted along ideological lines, decisions of which have substantially constrained, if not crippled, affirmative action. The past forty-five years have brought about more school desegregation, but not substantially more societal desegregation and certainly not the pervasive integration that many assumed would occur. Inequality in educational and employment opportunity is still a reality.

In many ways the conditions we confront in examining the nation's minority community are far more complex than was the case when the war on poverty was launched, due to the even more diverse composition of that community. The racial and ethnic composition of the minority community is today more diverse in national and geographic origin, political history, social and cultural history, language, and political and social vision. Each of these sources of diversity is further complicated by past and current conditions of social class and gender unique to each group.

One result of these aspects of social context is an increasing awareness of the embeddedness and pervasiveness of racism. There is also a growing understanding that the differences among and between us require special recognition and treatment. Research illuminating the latter point makes clear the need to prepare teachers differently if they are to handle diversity better.

Research by sociologists modeling the status-attainment process has shown explicit differences among the experiences of blacks, Hispanics, and whites.[1] Results of such studies have consistently revealed that the fairly logical socialization-based, contest-type model (which assumes a meritocratic process) has not held for blacks and Hispanics as it has for whites. Rather, a sponsorship type of explanation seems to best characterize the attainment process for them. For example, socioeconomic status does not have the intergenerational significance among blacks and Hispanics that it does for whites. Nor does the role of significant others. Instead, avoiding disciplinary problems, adopting the right attitudes, and performing well seem to identify blacks for "sponsorship," or selection for upward mobility.[2]

These results, from quantitative studies of attainment, have been made clearer by the qualitative work of Cicourel, Rist, and others pointing to the ways in which teacher-held conceptions of capable students vary by race, ethnicity, and social class.[3] These latter works have heightened our attentiveness to teacher expectations as a critical factor in the educational success of different groups of students. Finally, European social scientists and others have led a sustained challenge to the meritocratic characterization of the educational process in Western, capitalist societies.[4]

The combination, then, of the continuing societal inequalities and the research underscoring the ways in which schooling contributes to their persistence suggests a compelling argument for changing the way teachers are prepared to handle racial, ethnic, and gender diversity. This argument becomes even stronger when demographic, economic, professional, and ethical dimensions of the current situation are made explicit.

DEMOGRAPHIC CHANGE

If the preceding depiction of inequality and schooling is an accurate one, the demographic realities we confront are cause for major concern. Writing in 1985, Hodgkinson reported that

> today we are a nation of 14.6 million Hispanics and 26.5 million blacks. But by 2020 we will be a nation of 44 million blacks and 47 million Hispanics—even more if Hispanic immigration rates increase. . . . At the moment . . . [Asian Americans] are a much smaller group than Blacks or Hispanics (about 3.7 million in 1980), but their growth potential from immigration is very great for the next decade—they currently represent 44% of all immigrants admitted to the US. However their diversity is very great.[5]

It is not the population mix itself but what it portends for schools that captures our attention. In 1984 there were sixteen states in which minority public school enrollment exceeded 25 percent. Ten of those states had the highest dropout rates during that period, ranging from a high of 43.7 percent to a low of 35.4 percent. Simply put, minority students are now, and

seem increasingly likely to be, those who experience the least success in our schools. Failure to prepare teachers responsibly for the existing conditions will at least perpetuate if not exacerbate the current conditions of high dropout rates and low levels of educational attainment or achievement that characterize the minority educational experience.

At the very least, prospective teachers need to understand why the school classroom composition they envisioned is less likely to be available to them now or throughout their careers in teaching. Not just central city urban schools but also suburban schools are increasingly diverse in racial and ethnic terms. In many instances the diversity is more complex due to the added factors of poverty, single-parent female-headed households, and language differences. The content of instruction in teacher education, moreover, must be very clear with regard to the distinctive groups of students, for few generalizations will hold either within or between groups. No single set of assumptions about student learning, and no one instructional approach, will adequately serve the learning needs of all students in our schools. Fundamental to the content of instruction in teacher education will be the knowledge and experience necessary to enable teachers to envision and implement a model of excellence to which all students are entitled.

ECONOMIC CONSEQUENCES OF AN UNDEREDUCATED POPULATION

Almost without exception, the economic necessity of better preparing a broader group of students follows closely on the heels of the presentation of the demographic realities. It is a return to the theme of enlightened self-interest stated so clearly in *A Nation at Risk*, which, despite its narrow ideological framework, merits our attention.[6] Because of the historical patterns of economic discrimination against minorities, combined with the declining ratio of earners to retirees, we now entertain arguments that make minority human capital a greater resource in constructing the nation's market competitiveness and hence our quality of life. This is not a new condition. It has always been the case that minorities have been a core supply of labor even if only in the tertiary or reserve labor pool.[7] Support for the education of minorities, particularly blacks, has often been cited as a quality-of-life issue for this nation,[8] but only in recent times have the demographic data become so compelling as to require that we address their educational needs from the standpoint of inclusion in the primary labor force. This necessitates examining the adequacy of teacher preparation in equipping teachers for this task. It should be done, however, so as to avoid the traditional mistake of assuming that vocational education is the solution to the educational problems of minority students. If Weisberg is correct in his finding that "general literacy skills are more likely than any other factor to yield success in the labor market,"[9] then the economic imperative, too, suggests that new ways must be found to facilitate all students' learning in communication and computational skills.[10] To teach teachers that high schools are a place for minority students to learn specific job skills in an increasingly service-oriented economy is to divert attention from the basic educational needs that will have the best "pay-off" for all students in the future.

TRENDS IN THE COMPOSITION OF THE TEACHING FORCE

The third reason for preparing teachers to understand race and ethnicity centers on who our teachers will be, based on studies of the composition of the teaching force, college enrollment, and degree attainment. Schlecty and Noblit are most often cited for their finding that the best and the brightest leave teaching sooner and at a greater rate than their peers. They also reported that the teaching force will increasingly be comprised of young white females.[11] With declining black enrollment in higher education and fairly stable Hispanic and American Indian enrollment, combined with fewer students choosing teaching as a career, it is imperative that nonminority teachers be better prepared to address the educational needs of minority students.

General patterns with regard to degree attainment indicate that bachelor of arts degrees in education have been declining overall, and sharply for selected groups of students:

> From 1976 to 1981 the total number of bachelor degrees awarded in education went from approximately 151,000 to 105,000 a 31 percent decline.[12]
> Females continue to dominate among education degree recipients both in total number and in percentage across all major fields.[13]
> Consistent with the forecast of low numbers of minority teachers by the year 2000, blacks show a greater rate of decline in their concentration in education from 1975 to 1981 compared with whites, and black and Hispanic females show a greater rate of decline during that period compared with white females.[14]

Combining these trends with the renewed emphasis on teacher competency as determined by the National Teacher Examination and state testing procedures, the predictable results are that the teaching force will be both more female and more white than Schlecty and Noblit speculated.

Even without regard to race, ethnicity, or gender, the need for better preparation of the future pool of teacher candidates is clear. Especially because of the disparity between the demographics of students and those of teachers, race and ethnic differences and their consequences for education must receive more explicit treatment in the teacher education curriculum. At the same time, we need to redouble our efforts to increase the supply of minority educators. This should not be taken to mean that the minority educator, male or female, will necessarily be a better teacher without a reformed curriculum and other changes needed in the public schools. Minorities too harbor misconceptions and stereotypes. Thus if the implicit assumption is that minority teachers will "naturally" do better, then I think the evidence for that is less than clear.[15] Nor should it be held that hiring minority educators will absolve others of responsibility for educating minority children, an attitude that in itself reveals the need for a reformed teacher education curriculum.

PROFESSIONAL COMPETENCE

The fourth reason undergirding the recommendation for change results from ongoing research focusing on problems in the teaching profession and the perceived consequences of selected teaching reform policies for minority educators. A pilot of a recent national survey revealed that teachers report their belief that their competency with blacks and other minorities is limited.[16] Inadequate undergraduate exposure to course content familiarizing them with the experiences of minorities and limited cross-race contact or multicultural experiences in or outside of school were given as primary reasons for this belief. In other research we were able to identify "training in sociocultural understanding" as a major area of need for teachers.[17] Each of these tentative findings underscores the need to improve the sense of competence that teachers bring to their work.

Earlier I introduced the idea that no occupation merited the status of a profession if its practices were unsuccessful for a third of its clients. While such a statement may sound alarmist, the statistics that are regularly cited suggest that it may be an understatement. For example, the following are reported in *Barriers to Excellence: Our Children at Risk:*

> Studies conducted in urban high schools have revealed dropout rates as high as 85 percent for native Americans, and between 70 and 80 percent for Puerto Rican students.
> The national dropout rate for blacks in high school is nearly twice that of whites.
> Black students are more than three times as likely to be in a class for the educable mentally retarded as white students, but only half as likely to be in a class for the gifted and talented.
> At the high school level, blacks are suspended three times as often as whites; while minority students are about 25 percent of the school population, they constitute about 40 percent of all suspended and expelled students.
> In our own research focusing on black male students, we find limited evidence of the "criminalization" of these students, a process whereby teachers are at least implicitly communicating their fear of black males.[18]

These "educational" experiences of black and other minority students suggest that our current strategies for treating their educational needs consist largely of removing the students from what we would consider an effective learning environment. Paraphrasing the often cited declaration in *A Nation at Risk*, these conditions amount to a declaration of war against minority students. It is clear from these conditions that our current preparation of teachers falls far short of most definitions of adequate.

It is interesting to note that the debate over professionalism seldom addresses the transportability of teaching skills. Most education graduates seem to envision themselves returning to the schools they know, not just to any school where the jobs and need for their services exist. I contend that preparing teachers to apply their skills in a wide range of contexts will both improve their sense of personal competency and reduce the stress related to teaching in racially diverse school contexts.

THE RIGHTS OF STUDENTS

My fifth and final reason for urging systematic attention to race and ethnicity in teacher education programs is that it is the only way to protect the human and civil rights of the students in our schools. In a recent study I interviewed administrators from my hometown school district in Virginia who reminded me of the mission-like and visionary quality of the teachers in my segregated school system. I have since wondered what it was that sustained their ability to teach us despite the overt racism of the separate but (un)equal system and their ability to inspire us to aspire to and prepare for careers that were effectively closed to us. While I have no evidence to substantiate it, I am increasingly convinced that their knowledge of our circumstance and conditions fueled their hopes and aspirations for us, which shaped how they taught us. In many instances these educators were victims of racism and discrimination and had personally experienced denied opportunity despite having fully prepared themselves for excellence. Their intimate understanding of the community, its strengths and constraints, provided them the insights to student needs and potential out of which they taught and with which they nurtured success. Much has changed in the past thirty years, including many human rights accomplishments. Nonetheless, as one respondent put it, "We don't seem to demand as much from or want as much for our students as we did with your group."[19]

Teachers do have a vision for minority students today but it is not one shaped by an informed and intimate knowledge of the students and their circumstances. If we are to change that vision in a positive way, to one that will nurture and sustain aspirations for and commitment to excellence, we must provide teachers with a far clearer and more intense curricular experience focused on race and ethnicity and their implications for education.

NOTES

1. See, for example, Alan Kerckhoff, "The Status Attainment Process: Socialization or Allocation?" *Social Forces* 55, no. 2 (1976): 368–89; idem and Richard Campbell, "Race and Social Status Differences in the Explanation of Educational Ambitions," *Social Forces* 55 (1977): 701–14; idem, "Black-White Differences in the Educational Attainment Process," *Sociology of Education* 50 (January 1978): 15–27; Alejandro Portes and Cynthia Truelove, "Making Sense of Diversity: Recent Research on Hispanic Minorities in the United States," *Annual Review of Sociology* 13 (1987): 359–85; Alejandro Portes and K. L. Wilson, "Black-White Differences in Educational Attainment," *American Sociological Review* 41 (June 1976): 414–531; W. Tenhouten et al., "School Ethnic Composition, Social Context and Educational Plans of Mexican-Americans and Anglo High School Students," *American Journal of Sociology* 77, no. 1 (1971): 89–107; and G. E. Thomas, "Race and Sex Differences and Similarities in the Process of College Entry," *International Journal of Higher Education* 9 (1980): 179–202.

2. Kerckhoff and Campbell, "Black-White Differences in the Educational Attainment Process."

3. See Aaron V. Cicourel and John I. Kitsuse, "The School as a Mechanism of Social Differentiation," in *Power and Ideology in Education*, ed. J. Karabel and A. Halsey (New York: Oxford University Press, 1977), pp. 282–92; and Ray C. Rist, "On Understanding the Processes of Schooling: The Contributions of Labeling Theory," in ibid., pp. 292–305.

4. See, for example, Michael Apple, Pierre Bourdieu, and Jean-Claude Passeron, *Reproduction in Education, Society, and Culture* (London: Sage Publications, 1977); Samuel Bowles and Herbert Gintis, *Schooling in Capitalist America* (New York: Basic Books, 1976); Henry Giroux, *Theory and Resistance in Education* (South Hadley, Mass.: Bergin and Garvey Publishers, 1983); Paul Willis, *Learning to Labour* (Lexington, Mass.: D. C. Heath, 1977); and Michael F. D. Young, *Knowledge and Control* (London: Collier-Macmillan, 1971).

5. Harold Hodgkinson, *All One System* (Washington, D.C.: Institute for Educational Leadership, Inc., 1985).

6. The National Commission on Excellence in Education, *A Nation at Risk* (Washington, D.C.: U.S. Government Printing Office, 1983).

7. See, for example, William Julius Wilson, "Segregation and the Rise of the White Working Class," in *The Declining Significance of Race* (Chicago: University of Chicago Press, 1978); and James D. Anderson, *The Education of Blacks in the South, 1865–1935* (Chapel Hill: The University of North Carolina Press, 1988), esp. ch. 1.

8. Anderson, *The Education of Blacks*, pp. 27–32.

9. A. Weisberg, "What Research Has to Say about Vocational Education in the High Schools," *Phi Delta Kappan* 64, no. 5 (1983): 59.

10. The National Commission on Excellence in Education, *A Nation at Risk*.

11. Philip C. Schlechty and George W. Noblit, *Policy Research*, Vol. 3 of Research in Sociology of Education and Socialization (Greenwich, Conn.: JAI Press, 1982), pp. 283–306.

12. William T. Trent, "Equity Considerations in Higher Education: Race and Sex Differences in Degree Attainment and Major Field from 1967 through 1981," *American Journal of Education* 92, no. 3 (1984): 280–305.

13. Ibid.

14. Ibid.

15. For an insightful discussion of this point, see Lisa Delpit, "Skills and Other Dilemmas of a Progressive Black Educator," *Harvard Educational Review* 56, no. 4 (1986): 379–85; and idem, "The Silenced Dialogue," *Harvard Educational Review* 58, no. 3 (1988): 280–97.

16. Harry Broudy, Steven Tozer, and William Trent, "The Illinois Project on Professional Knowledge in Teacher Education: A Pilot Study of Core Problems in Teaching" (Unpublished Report, University of Illinois College of Education, Champaign, Ill., 1986).

17. William Trent, "The Implications of Reform for Minority Educators" (A presentation to the American Educational Research Association, Washington, D.C., 1986).

18. *Barriers to Excellence: Our Children at Risk* (Boston: National Coalition of Advocates for Students, 1985); see also Broudy, Tozer, and Trent, "The Illinois Project."

19. Trent, "The Implications of Reform for Minority Educators."

Social Class, Race, and School Achievement: Problems and Prospects

Allan C. Ornstein
Daniel U. Levine

Ornstein is Professor, Loyola University of Chicago; Levine is Professor, University of Missouri, Kansas City.

Ornstein and Levine provide documentation regarding the relationship between the socioeconomics of students' lives and their subsequent capacity to perform effectively in school contexts. Research aimed at understanding and prescribing methods of overcoming the problems of urban low achieving students is discussed in the form of classroom and extra-classroom realities. The authors then suggest selected reform measures for ameliorating those realities that plague urban schools.

Today, the term *working class* is more widely used than *lower class,* but social scientists still generally use measures of occupation, education, and income to describe three to six levels of socioeconomic status (SES) ranging from upper class at the top to lower working class at the bottom. The UPPER CLASS is usually defined as including very wealthy persons having substantial property and investment; the MIDDLE CLASS includes professionals, managers and small business owners (upper middle) as well as technicians, sales personnel, and clerical workers (lower middle). The WORKING CLASS is generally divided into *upper working class* (skilled manual workers such as construction workers) and *lower working class* (unskilled manual workers such as those at hamburger restaurants). Skilled workers may be either middle class or working class, depending on their education and

other considerations such as the community in which they live. In recent years, a number of observers also have identified an *underclass* which to some extent resembles the lower working class, but appears to be locked more permanently in a cycle of poverty and social disorganization (Auletta, 1988; Gelman, 1988; Vroman, 1988). Usually concentrated in the core slums of cities or in deteriorated rural poverty areas, members of the underclass frequently have little or no hope that their economic and social situation will ever improve. A large percentage are minority — mostly black and Hispanic.

Studies on Social Class and School Success

One of the first systematic studies investigating relations between class and achievement in the educational system was the Lynds' (1929) study of "Middletown" (a small midwestern city). The Lynds concluded that parents, regardless of social class level, recognize the importance of education for their children; however, working-class children do not come to school academically equipped to deal with the verbal skills and behavioral traits required for success in the classroom.

Thousands of studies have since documented the close relationship between social class and achievement in the educational system. For example, as reported by the National Assessment of Educational Progress and shown in Table 1, only 41 percent of students whose parents had not graduated from high school (which is one measure of social class) had reading proficiency on scores at or above the "intermediate" level, compared with 72 percent of students whose parents had attended post-

secondary institutions. Furthermore, the average proficiency score of seventeen-year-old students whose parents had not graduated from high school was almost identical to the average score of thirteen-year-old students whose parents had attended postsecondary institutions. Only 20 percent of seventeen-year-old students whose parents did not complete high school scored at or above the "adept" level, compared with 52 percent of those whose parents had a postsecondary education. Similar patterns were reported for science (NAEP, 1985, 1988).

School achievement also is correlated with type of community, which reflects the social class of persons who reside there. Also shown in Table 1, for example, the average reading score of thirteen-year-old students in high-status metropolitan (middle-class, suburban) locations is much higher than that of other students, and the average score of students in low-status metropolitan locations (with a high concentration of lower working-class and underclass families) is much lower. Students in mixed-class communities, such as rural areas and medium-sized cities that include substantial proportions of both working-class and middle-class families, have average scores in between those of wealthy, suburban, and inner-city, poverty communities. Similar patterns were found for science. Further evidence of the relationship between social class and school achievement can be found in studies of poverty neighborhoods in very large cities. Data on the performance of students in such neighborhoods have provided an almost unremittingly bleak picture of ineffective schooling for the past three decades (Levine and Havighurst, 1988; Ornstein, 1982).

From *Journal of Teacher Education,* September/October 1989, pp. 17-23. Copyright © 1989 by the American Association of Colleges for Teacher Education.

Many educators also are particularly concerned about the achievement of low-status rural students, especially those who live in pockets of rural poverty. Although the average achievement of rural students is generally at about the national average, research indicates that poverty and inequality hamper the achievement of many rural students (Arends, 1987; DeYoung, 1987).

Race/Ethnicity and School Success

Patterns involving social class and educational achievement in the United States are further complicated by interrelationships among these variables and those of race and ethnicity. (The term "ethnicity" refers to shared culture and background.) The nation's largest racial minority group — black Americans — is much lower in social class than is the white majority. Several other major ethnic groups — Mexican Americans and Puerto Ricans — are also disproportionately in the lower working class and under-class. In line with their lower social class standing, these racial and ethnic minority groups are also low in academic achievement, high school and college graduation rates, and other measures of educational attainment.

The close association among social classes, racial/ethnic minority status, and school achievement is shown in Table 2, which represents average reading scores obtained by a nationally representative sample of high school students in 1980 and 1982. As shown in the table, black and Hispanic students have the lowest SES scores and also the lowest language, math, and science scores; non-Hispanic whites are highest on nearly all of these measures. Except for math scores among Asian-Pacific Americans, achievement scores parallel scores on socioeconomic status; the higher the SES score, the higher the academic scores. Black students, Hispanic students, and Native American students are much lower in SES than are non-Hispanic white and Asian-Pacific students and have much lower academic achievement scores.

However, data collected by the NAEP (1985) also indicate that black and Hispanic students have registered gains in reading, science, and math since 1971. Whereas proficiency scores for white students in these subject areas have remained "flat" or "constant," black and Hispanic students have regis-

Table 1
Reading and Science Scores of Thirteen-year-old Students by Social Class, 1977 and 1984

Parental Education	Average Percent Correct in Science, 1977	Percentage Reading at or above Intermediate Level, 1984*
Not graduated high school	53	41
Graduated high school	59	56
Attended postsecondary school	66	72

Type of Community	Average Percent Correct in Science, 1977	Average Reading Proficiency Score, 1984
Rural	56	254
Low-status metropolitan	48	237
High-status metropolitan	67	274
Main big city	57	253
Urban fringe	63	261
Medium city	61	257
Small communities	60	256

* Note: A reading proficiency score of 250 is considered "intermediate" (the student is able to recognize paraphrases of what he or she has read), and a score of 300 is considered "adept" (the student is able to understand complicated passages). "Low-status metropolitan" refers to urban areas with a low proportion of professional or managerial workers in cities of more than 200,000 population. "High-status metropolitan" communities in such cities have a high proportion of professionals and managers. "Main big city" communities also are in these large urban areas and are moderate in proportion of professionals and managers. "Medium cities" have between 25,000 and 200,000 residents, and "small communities" are urbanized areas with less than 25,000 persons.

Source: *The Condition of Education 1986* (p. 212), compiled by U.S. Government Printing Office, (1986), Washington, DC.

Table 2
Language, Math, and Science Scores of High School Sophomores and Seniors, by Racial and Ethnic Group, 1980 and 1982

Racial/Ethnic Group	Language Skills Score	Math Score	Science Score	Percent in Lowest 25%	Percent in College-Bound Program
Black	14.5	6.5	6.4	45	29
Hispanic	15.6	7.7	7.4	43	23
Native/American	18.5	7.8	8.8	36	23
Asian Pacific	25.2	16.6	11.0	22	47
White (non-Hispanic)	27.8	15.5	11.2	18	37

Note: Language scores are a combination of scores in vocabulary, reading, and writing. The maximum scores for language, math, and science skills were 57, 38, and 20, respectively. Social class is a composite measure of father's and mother's education, father's occupation, parental income, and types of items in the home. Language and math scores are for 1980 sophomores; science scores are for 1982 seniors.

Source: *High School and Beyond Study* (p. 56), compiled by U.S. Government Printing Office (1980), Washington, DC; *The Condition of Education 1985* (p. 58), compiled by U.S. Government Printing Office (1985), Washington, DC.

tered about 10 to 15 percent increases over a 15 year period in reading (Rothman, 1988; U.S. Government, 1986). Some observers attribute these improvements partly to the effects of the federal Chapter 1 programs and/or some increase in school desegregation (Koretz, 1987). On the other hand, black and Hispanic students still score far below whites in reading and other subjects, and black and Hispanic seventeen-year-old students still have average reading scores at about the same

level as the average white thirteen-year-old students.

In line with the achievement and social-class data shown in Table 2, non-Hispanic whites and Asian students (other than Vietnamese Americans) are much more likely to complete high school than are black and Hispanic students. As shown in Table 3, high school completion rates for black students have been rising since 1975, and rates for Hispanic students only have increased since 1983. (Cautions in interpreting the Hispanic scores are noted in the table.) Graduation rates for Asian students are higher than whites (Yao, 1987), but are not reported because they were not identified by the population survey data of the table.

In addition, high school dropout rates are still very high among black and Hispanic students in big-city poverty areas. Knowledgeable observers estimate that dropout rates range from 40 to 60 percent in some big cities and sometimes exceed 75 to 80 percent at schools enrolling mostly underclass students (Hahn, Danzerger, and Lefkowitz, 1987). Inasmuch as high school dropouts have rapidly diminishing opportunities to succeed in the economy, these considerations indicate that dropping out of urban schools has become a major problem in U.S. society, particularly among minority students.

Regardless of whether an assessment of the situation in the inner city emphasizes poverty, segregation, social disorganization, or other social indicators, it is clear that educational achievement and attainment levels of inner-city children and youth are typically low. The exent of this ineffectiveness was underlined in an analysis of scores on the American College Testing (ACT) exam among high school seniors in the Chicago metropolitan area (Ornstein and Levine, 1989). After randomly selecting one-third of the schools for which data were available, the authors found that all but two of the twenty-six city high schools had average ACT scores below 15, and all but one of the thirty-six suburban schools had average scores above 15. Income and minority status accounted for a substantial portion of the outcomes; only three out of 36 suburban schools had more than 25 percent low-income students, whereas twenty of the city schools had more than 25 percent low-income students. (In addition, most of the city high schools were more than 75 percent black and/or Hispanic.)

The ACT is not a good measure of what has been learned in school, but it does provide a useful prediction of whether students are likely to succeed in traditional, four-year colleges. Thus, the overall pattern indicated that the large low-income population of seniors in Chicago high schools generally is not adequately prepared to succeed in traditional colleges, even though most

Table 3
High School Completion by Ethnic Origin, Persons 18 to 19, 1975 to 1985

Year	Total	White	Black	Hispanic (a)
1975	73.7%	77.0%	52.8%	50.0%
1977	72.9%	75.7%	54.9%	50.7%
1979	72.8%	75.3%	56.4%	53.7%
1981	72.5%	74.8%	59.6%	47.2%
1983	72.7%	75.6%	59.1%	50.3%
1985	74.6%	76.7%	62.8%	59.8%

Note: a = Year to year differences in completion rates for Hispanic are not statistically significant due to small size of the Hispanic sample and to the fact that Hispanic students sometimes categorize themselves as white. Also, the number of immigrant Hispanic students steadily increases — perhaps masking real gains of American Hispanics who have been in the country for several years or even for second and third generations.

Source: *The Condition of Education 1987* (p. 26), compiled by U.S. Government Printing Office (1987), Washington, DC: Author.

of their lowest-achieving students already have dropped out or do not take the ACT. Comparable patterns undoubtedly would be found in many other metropolitan areas in which data are collected by city/suburban location.

Because social class, race/ethnicity, and school achievement are so closely interrelated, researchers frequently ask whether race and ethnicity are associated with performance in the educational system even after one takes into account the low socioeconomic status of blacks and other disadvantaged minority groups. In general, the answer has been that social class accounts for much of the variation in educational achievement by race and ethnicity. That is, if one knows the social class of a group of students one can predict with a good deal of accuracy whether their achievement, ability scores, and college attendance rates are high or low. This generalization also means that working-class and underclass white students as a group are low in achievement and college attainment (although their problems are often ignored because they are not well organized as a group and are not deemed newsworthy by the media).

Reasons for Low Achievement: Some Realities

Much research aimed at understanding and overcoming the problems of low-achieving students has been conducted during the past forty years, and a variety of explanations has been advanced to explain the academic deficiencies of low-achieving students in general and low-achieving, lower work-

ing-class, and underclass students in particular. The reasons can be categorized, at least for our purposes, as teacher-related (the first five reasons) and nonteacher-related (the last five reasons).

Reality 1: Differences in teacher/student backgrounds

Teachers with middle-class backgrounds may experience particular difficulties in understanding and motivating their working-class and lower-class students. Problems of this nature may be particularly salient and widespread in the case of white teachers working with disadvantaged minority students, in part because differences in dialect and language background make it difficult for middle-class and/or nonminority teachers to communicate effectively with minority students, and even to reject the students' lifestyle and culture.

Reality 2: Teacher perceptions of student inadequacy

Based on low levels of achievement in their classrooms, many teachers in working-class schools reach the conclusion that large numbers of their students are incapable of learning. This view becomes a self-fulfilling prophecy because teachers who question their students' learning potential are less likely to work hard to improve academic performance, particularly since improvement requires an intense effort that quickly consumes virtually all of a teacher's energy. Because students are influenced by their teachers' perceptions and behaviors, low teacher expectations generate further declines in students' motivation and performance.

Reality 3: Low standards of performance

The end result of this series of problems is that by the time low-achieving students reach the upper elementary grades or the junior high school, they are required to accomplish very little — low performance has become acceptable to their teachers. Whether in a lower working-class or a mixed-status school, many working-class students make little or no effort to meet demanding academic requirements by the time they reach the secondary level. Not only do teachers add to the situation by expecting little from such students, they sometimes wind up praising them for below grade work and meaningless work so as not to foster hopelessness.

Reality 4: Ineffective instructional grouping

Educators faced with large groups of low achievers frequently address the problem of setting them apart in separate classes or subgroups in which instruction can proceed at a slower pace without detracting from the performance of high achievers. Unfortunately, both teachers and the students themselves tend to view concentrations of lower achievers as "slow" groups or just plain "losers" for whom learning expectations are minimal.

On the other hand, individualized instruction in heterogeneous classes might make it possible for each student to make continual progress at his or her own rate, but individualization is extremely difficult to implement effectively and probably requires such costly and systematic change in school practices as to make it nearly impossible or impractical. Thus, teachers confronted with large heterogeneous classes in inner-city schools generally have not been able to work effectively with the low achievers in their classrooms.

Reality 5: Difficulty of teaching conditions

As lower working-class and underclass students fall further behind academically, and as both teachers and students experience frustration and discouragement, behavior problems increase in the classrooms, and teachers find it still more difficult to provide a productive learning environment. The terms "battle fatigue," "battle pay," and "blackboard jungle" have been used in the literature to describe the teaching conditions in some inner-city schools. One frequent result is that some teachers eventually give up trying to teach low achievers or seek less frustrating employment elsewhere.

Reality 6: Differences between parental and school norms

Lower working-class and underclass parents typically use physical punishment when their children actively misbehave or do not follow instructions; schools, on the other hand, tend to stress the middle-class approach, which emphasizes internalization of norms through inner controls and feelings of shame and guilt. Although the latter approach may be more productive in helping children internalize rules and expectations, differences between the home and the school make it difficult for many lower working-class students to follow rules and procedures when sanctions are not consistent with those imposed at home. In addition, even more than is the case among middle-class families, some working-class parents lack interest or are too preoccupied with their own lives to provide effective support for teachers.

Reality 7: Lack of previous success in school

Lack of academic success in the early grades not only detracts from learning more difficult material later, but also damages a student's perception that he or she is a capable learner who has a chance to succeed in school and in later life. Once students believe that they are inadequate as learners and lack control over their future (two characteristics of low-achieving students), they are less likely to work vigorously at overcoming learning deficiencies.

Reality 8: Negative peer pressure

Several researchers have studied peer influences in predominantly inner-city schools and reported that academically oriented students frequently are ridiculed and rejected for accepting school norms. Strong antischool peer influence is attributed to black students as a "coping lifestyle" that is reinforced when children become disillusioned about their ability to succeed, less interested in or motivated by school, and less willing to exert the effort necessary to do well in school.

Reality 9: Inappropriate curriculum and instruction

Curriculum materials and instructional approaches in the primary grades frequently assume that students are familiar with vocabulary and concepts to which lower working-class and underclass students have little or no exposure. As students proceed through school, terminology and concepts become increasingly abstract, and many lower working-class and underclass students fall further behind because their level of mastery is too rudimentary to allow for fluent learning. After grade three, much of the curriculum requires an increasing degree of reading skill that many low-achieving students have not yet attained; hence, they fall further behind in other subject areas.

Reality 10: Delivery-of-service problems

The problems we have described suggest that it is very difficult to deliver educational services effectively in classes or schools with a high percentage of low achievers. If, for example, a teacher in an inner-city school has ten or fifteen low-achieving students in a class of twenty-five, the task of providing effective instruction is many times more difficult than that of a teacher who has only four or five low achievers in a middle-class school. Not only do teachers in the formal situation need to spend virtually all their time remediating low achievers' learning problems, but the negative dynamics that result from students' frustration and misbehavior make the task that much more difficult.

Basically, the same observation can be offered regarding the functioning of inner-city administrators, counselors, and other specialized personnel in such schools: so much time is spent dealing with the frequent occurrence of learning and behavior problems that little time may be left for delivering improved services for students. From this point of view, the working-class and especially underclass school can be called an overloaded institution in which a higher incidence of serious problems makes it very difficult for educators to function effectively. Indeed, in housing, private industry, and the military when conditions become too difficult the institution or operation is abandoned; in many schools, they just get worse.

Improving the Preparation of Teachers: Some Reforms

Given the difficulties teachers encounter in trying to enhance the performance of lower working-class and particularly underclass children and youth in big-city poverty areas, substantial improvements are imperative in preparing new teachers for success in overcoming the achievement patterns and problems described in the preceding pages. Possibilities for helping to bring about such improvements are discussed briefly in the remainder of this paper. They are geared only toward the first five teacher-related realities discussed in the previous section.

Increase the number of minority teachers. (Helps resolve problem reality #1.)

Only 10 percent of the current teaching force is black and Hispanic (NEA, 1987), and only 6 percent of the current teacher education majors are from these minority groups (Evangelauf, 1988). On the other hand, the percentage of black and Hispanic students in public schools has increased to 30 percent and is expected to exceed 35 percent by the year 2000 (Ornstein, 1984). Minority teachers will be increasingly underrepresented relative to the minority school population in the future. The problem is compounded by the fact that most of the states have introduced requirements that prospective teachers pass proficiency tests in basic skills, subject area specialization, and/or professional knowledge — in which black candidates fail more than twice and Hispanics 1½ times the rate of white candidates (Ornstein and Levine, 1989). Although the courts have upheld these tests as valid, the Educational Testing Service has announced that in 1991-92 it plans to replace the National Teacher Examination (now used by 30 states for licensing school teachers), and will rely less on pencil-pen tests and more on computer simulations and interactive videos. However, it will still require prospective teachers to take a test in reading, writing, and math during their sophomore year (Watkins, 1988).

In this connection, new programs should be initiated by the NEA and AFT in conjunction with colleges of education to attract minorities, including loans and scholarships, as well as compensatory and tutoring programs to enhance the number of well-prepared minority teacher education candidates.

Build in knowledge components focusing on effective instruction for low achievers. (Helps resolve problem realities #2,3,4.)

As researchers have pointed out, much has been learned concerning provision of success experiences, utilization of wait-time, direct or explicit instruction, introduction of cooperative learning, and mastery learning (Ornstein, 1987; Rosenshine, 1987; Slavin, 1988), and other approaches for improving the performance of low achievers, but many or most teacher education programs do little to help future teachers acquire knowledge of what works so they can use an appropriate repertoire of these techniques effectively in real-world schools. Preservice coursework would be more effective if research and theory were blended with laboratory settings that can offer sufficient opportunity to practice and master appropriate techniques (Berliner, 1985; Goodman, 1988).

Improve practice teaching by making opportunities to practice a systematic part of a larger learning experience. (Helps resolve problem realities #2,3,4.)

Reviews of research on practice teaching in general and student teaching in particular have concluded that these experiences frequently are too fragmented and isolated to allow for reliable acquisition of requisite teaching skills (Killian and McIntyre, 1988; Lanier and Featherstone, 1988). Even those student teachers who have had productive methods have had little opportunity to develop their skills in a practical situation. Efforts should be made to help them negotiate the negative influences that sometimes function in the classrooms of cooperating teachers. More efforts are needed, according to researchers (Bunting, 1988; Evertson, 1986), in the training of cooperating teachers in the strategies being taught at the teacher preparation level.

Provide much greater assistance to teachers during their first years of teaching. (Helps resolve problem realities #4,5.)

One reason why many new teachers are unable or unwilling to utilize potentially effective techniques is because they become dependent on trial-and-error approaches acquired in isolation at the start of their teaching careers (Corcoran and Andrew, 1988; McLaughlin, 1986). Such methods have been demonstrated to be particularly ineffective in working with low achievers. New teachers who work in inner-city schools would receive greater and more meaningful assistance in the future through the initiation of projects that assign successful teachers to work as mentors or coaches (Anderson, 1987; Maeroff, 1988).

Improve class management strategies for teachers. (Helps resolve problem reality #5.)

Of all the problems that concern beginning inner-city teachers and cause anxiety and stress, the foremost is related to discipline. Discipline has been considered the most important school problem with which public school teachers must deal with in the last 12 out of 15 public surveys conducted by the Gallup organization for Phi Delta Kappa; it was second the other three times (Gallup and Elam, 1988). Furthermore, in only 39 percent of the public schools do teachers feel that student behavior is positive, and in only 66 percent of the schools do they feel in control of the classrooms (Ornstein, 1989b). Moreover, the percentages are worse for inner-city teachers.

Beginning teachers must be educated in managing students and classrooms, especially in how to evoke preventive disciplinary measures and coping strategies when necessary. A research-based consensus of expert opinion on classroom management is evolving, and it must be incorporated into preservice and internship programs (Brophy, 1986; Brophy, 1988).

Consider several teacher effectiveness models in preservice and inservice education. (Helps resolve problem realities #4,5.)

The current research on teacher effectiveness tends to focus on a host of business-like, structured, and task-like behaviors, sometimes called teacher competencies. These behaviors are product oriented and easy to measure, yet they fail not only to consider different types of effective teachers, but also the fact that many effective teachers do not exhibit such direct behaviors (Ornstein, 1989a; Unks, 1986). Many experts jumped on this educational bandwagon, and many state departments and local school districts have developed "master teacher" and "merit pay" plans on the basis of these explicit behaviors. Even more questionably, teachers who do not exhibit these business-like and structured behaviors are often penalized, labeled as "marginal," and in some cases find their jobs are at stake (Conley, 1986; Holdzkom, 1987; Ornstein, 1988).

We must learn to accept that not all aspects of teaching are easy to measure. Teaching is part science and part art, and good teaching involves experience, values, insights, imagination, and appreciation. Much of teaching also involves creative ideas and inquiries, as well as artistic and philosophical appreciation, the kind of "stuff" that cannot be easily observed or quantified but corresponds with other research-based patterns of effective teachers: such as the warm-democratic, the creative-imaginative, and the problem solving-critical thinking teacher. The need is to recognize various types of "good" or "successful" teachers for inner-city schools as well as schools in general. When everyone involved with the schools can strip away the titles and come to realize that teaching and learning are a matter of people relating to each other and not a matter of tiny or sequenced prescriptions, we will have come a long way in training teachers and characterizing effective teaching.

Conclusion

The preceding analysis makes it clear that lower working-class and especially underclass students are educationally and economically disadvantaged, and that the interrelationships produce a host of problems for the schools. While some of these students are successful in the educational system, the general pattern has led some social scientists to question whether schools can indeed make any difference. Of course they can, but that will happen only when we provide improved preparation that helps teachers learn to deal with the problems and considerations that generate low achievement patterns among economically and socially disadvantaged students.

References

Anderson, L. W. (1987). Staff development and instructional improvement. *Educational Leadership, 44* (5), 64-66.

Arends, J. H. (1987). *Building on excellence: Regional priorities for the improvement of rural, small schools.* Washington, DC: Council for Educational Development and Research.

Auletta, K. (1982). *The Underclass.* New York: Random House.

Berliner, D. C. (1985). Laboratory setting and the study of teacher education. *Journal of Teacher Education, 36* (6), 2-8.

Brophy, J. E. (1986). Classroom management techniques. *Education and Urban Society, 18* (2), 182-194.

Brophy, J. E. (1988). Educating teachers about managing classrooms and students. *Teaching and Teacher Education, 4* (1), 1-18.

Bunting, C. (1988). Cooperating teachers and the changing views of teacher certification. *Journal of Teacher Education, 39* (2), 42-47.

Conley, D. T. (1986). Certified personnel evaluation in Colorado. Unpublished doctoral dissertation, University of Colorado, Boulder.

Corcoran, E., & Andrew, M. (1988). A full year internship: An example of school-university collaboration. *Journal of Teacher Education, 39* (3), 17-24.

DeYoung, A. J. (1987). The status of American rural educational research. *Review of Educational Research, 57* (2), 123-148.

Evangelauf, J. (1988, January 3). Plan to encourage minority students to pursue teaching careers is proposed. *Chronicle of Higher Education,* p. 2.

Evertson, C. M. (1986). Do teachers make a difference? *Education and Urban Society, 18* (2), 195-210.

Gallup, A. M., & Elam, S. E. (1988). The 20th annual Gallup poll of the public's attitude toward the public schools. *Phi Delta Kappan, 70,* 33-46.

Gelman, D. (1988, March 7). Black and white in America. *Newsweek,* pp. 18-23.

Goodman, J. (1988). The political tactics and teaching strategies of reflective, active preservice teachers. *Elementary School Journal, 89* (1), 24-41.

Hahn, A., Danzerger, J., & Lefkowitz, B. (1987). *Dropouts in America.* Washington, DC: Institute for Educational Leadership.

Holdzkom, D. (1987). Appraising teacher performance in North Carolina. *Educational Leadership, 44* (7), 40-44.

Killian, J. E., & McIntyre, D. J. (1988). Grade level as a factor in participation during early field experiences. *Journal of Teacher Education, 39* (2), 36-41.

Koretz, D. (1987). *Educational achievement: Explanation and implications of recent trends.* Washington, DC: Congressional Budget Office.

Lanier, J. E., & Featherstone, J. (1988). A new commitment to teacher education. *Educational Leadership, 46* (3), 18-22.

Levine, D. U., & Havighurst, R. J. (1988). *Society and education,* (7th ed.). Needham Heights, MA: Allyn and Bacon.

Lynd, R. S., & Lynd, H. M. (1929). *Middletown: A study in American culture.* New York: Harcourt, Brace.

Maeroff, G. I. (1988). Withered hopes, stillborn dreams: The dismal panorama of urban schools. *Phi Delta Kappan, 69,* 632-638.

McLaughlin, M. W. (1986). Why teachers won't teach. *Phi Delta Kappan, 67,* 420-426.

National Assessment of Educational Progress. (1985). *The reading report card.* Princeton, NJ: Educational Testing Service.

National Assessment of Educational Progress. (1988). *Who reads best.* Princeton, NJ: Educational Testing Service.

National Education Association. (1987). *Status of the American public school teacher 1985-86.* Washington, DC: Author.

Ornstein, A. C. (1982). The education of the disadvantaged: A 20 year review. *Educational Research, 24* (3), 197-211.

Ornstein, A. C. (1984). Urban demographics for the 1980s. *Education and Urban Society, 16* (4), 463-477.

Ornstein, A. C. (1987). Emphasis on student outcomes focuses attention on quality of instruction. *National Association of Secondary School Principals, 71* (495), 88-95.

Ornstein, A. C. (1988). The changing status of the teaching profession. *Urban Education, 23* (3), 261-279.

Ornstein, A. C. (1989a). For teachers,

about teachers. *Peabody Journal of Education,* in press.

Ornstein, A. C. (1989b). Private and public school comparisons: Size, organization, and effectiveness. *Education and Urban Society, 21* (2), 192-206.

Ornstein, A. C., & Levine, D. U. (1989). *Foundations of education* (4th ed.). Boston: Houghton Mifflin.

Rosenshine, B. (1987). Explicit teaching and teacher training. *Journal of Teacher Education, 38* (3), 34-36.

Rothman, R. (1988, May 4). Black achievement in science and math up during 80s: Board finds. *Education Week,* p. 5.

Slavin, R. E. (1988). Cooperative learning and student achievement. *Educational Leadership, 46* (2), 31-34.

Unks, G. (1986). Product oriented teaching: A reappraisal. *Education and Urban Society, 18* (2), 242-254.

U.S. Government Printing Office. (1980). *High school and beyond study.* Washington, DC: Author.

U.S. Government Printing Office. (1985). *The condition of education 1985.* Washington, DC: Author.

U.S. Government Printing Office. (1986). *The condition of education 1986.* Washington, DC: Author.

U.S. Government Printing Office. (1987). *The condition of education 1987.* Washington, DC: Author.

Vroman, W. (1988). Relative earnings of black and white men: What will close the gap? *Urban Institute Policy and Research Report, 18* (2), 9-10.

Watkins, B. T. (1988, November 2). Educational Testing Service to replace National Teacher Examination by 1992. *Chronicle of Higher Education,* p. A32.

Yao, E. L. (1987). Asian immigrant students: Unique problems that hamper learning. *National Association of Secondary School Principals, 71* (503), 82-88.

Serving Special Needs and Humanizing Instruction

The range of profoundly serious special problems confronting North American students has seldom been broader or more complex than it is today due to severe societal imbalances in the struggle for economic, cultural, and personal survival. "Survival" is not an inappropriate indicator if we mean to imply the ability of students to achieve their highest potential. Helping to make schools a place where teachers and students engage in cooperative learning activities is now a well-established focus in the knowledge base on teaching. Helping people learn on their own and with peers is a major educational objective. The moral and legal issues created by dramatically changed national social conditions require special attention from educators. So many present-day societal problems have invaded some schools that it is difficult for educators to maintain effective and humane environments for effective learning.

Several specific issues have had a particularly severe impact on individual students' lives. Problems of addiction, teenage parenthood, social alienation, sexually transmitted diseases, insufficient employment opportunities for the poor and the working middle classes, and disaffection with the whole idea of going to "school" at all, are some of the major problems that affect many youths of our time. Every school system is struggling to address these and similar issues. But there are specific curriculum and instruction issues in schools related to the fashion among some educators in recent years to use the old approach of grade retention to attempt remediation of students' school performance. These policies are now under critical scrutiny by some researchers and scholars. Anything students experience while they are in school can, and often does, have long-term emotional and intellectual consequences. Therefore, how we address the special needs of students is very important.

Some issues that confront teachers and their students are unique to the teacher-student relationship. Other issues that affect teachers in their work with students have their origin in the problems of society at large. These problems impact on teachers because students bring these social problems to school with them. Since first issued in 1973, this anthology, has aimed to provide discussion of special social or curriculum issues affecting the teaching-learning conditions in schools. Fundamental forces at work in North American culture during the past several years have greatly affected millions of students. The social, cultural, and economic pressures on families have produced several special problems of great concern to teachers. There is demand for greater degrees of individualization of instruction and for greater development and maintenance of stronger self-concepts by students. The number of students who are either in single-parent situations or who have both parents working and maintaining careers has been growing. School systems and the teachers who work within them have been confronted with student populations that experience many problems that, traditionally at least, they were not expected to address. Teachers have an opportunity to shape the lives of young people by being good examples of stable personalities themselves, and through individualizing interactions with their students. Children and adolescents do not all have the same opportunity to be exposed to untroubled and stable men and women.

A teacher needs to see the work of the school as integrated with the activities of the general society that created and sustains it. There is too much superficial conceptualizing of schooling as not related to, or somehow separated from, the rest of the world. Teachers need to be good observers of the learning styles of their students. They should be willing to modify instructional planning to provide learning experiences that are best for their students. It is a reality of the current social foundations of education that in the past 20 years (or more) special problems have emerged in the national culture that have affected teacher-student relations. These include development of "mainstreaming," problems of drug abuse among youth, increase in the rate of teenage suicide, collapse of the traditional American family unit (except among the most conservative religious and social groups), the women's rights movement, and the evolution of nontraditional parenting patterns. To elucidate these problems is to gain a sense as to how teachers are facing the special instructional needs of students living in a time of economic and social upheaval without traditional family support systems.

Teachers should become aware of the extraordinary circumstances under which many children and young adults strive to become educated. Teachers are interested in studying their options to respond constructively to the special needs of their students. They want to know how they can help build self-confidence and self-esteem in their students, and how they can help them to want to learn in spite of all of the distracting forces in their lives. There are even those who argue that all teachers can benefit from practicing certain "parenting" skills in their interactions with students. Development of constructive, positive student-teacher relationships to assist students in facing difficult life situations is a common theme in talk about curriculum and instruction.

We are all human beings sharing the same universe and the common heritage of our species; yet, marvelously, each of us is exceptional in some way. We all have special gifts and special limitations. The ancient Greeks believed every person could be educated to the optimum extent to perfect his or her excellent qualities. To a certain degree, we can also be educated to compensate for disabilities. Children are born into many special circumstances and different social atmospheres. Some must fight to survive and maintain their sense of dignity and self-worth. What constitutes the most appropriate learning atmosphere for each student has become a serious legal and moral question in recent years.

The special needs and abilities that people possess are often called exceptionalities. Exceptionalities of certain kinds, whether they be physical or cognitive (mental), sometimes require special intervention or treatment skills. How can education address the unique needs, interests, abilities, and exceptionalities of students? How can teachers best serve their students' needs for attention and intellectual stimulation, demonstrate concern for the students, and also meet regular instructional responsibilities? Many children are not aware of their special needs and academic and social capabilities. School systems must find ways to help students discover these needs and potentials, and they must create conditions for students to progress both academically and socially.

The Education of All Handicapped Children Act of 1975 (PL 94-142) was passed by Congress to address the special needs of handicapped learners by placing them in least restrictive learning environments. This law has increased sensitivity to the educational requirements of exceptional students. Gifted persons are exceptional, too, and their least restrictive learning environments can require special intervention strategies. Herein lies one of the dilemmas of special education: there are many special and exceptional students, and they all need carefully planned and individualized educational strategies. A liberating classroom climate for one student may be a stifling and boring climate for another. The nation's schools are called upon to address a range of special needs so vast that the schools are financially and professionally stressed to their limits.

Mainstreaming is an educational policy response to the 1975 federal legislation regarding the handicapped. There is a big gap between the hopes and expectations for mainstreaming and the realities of implementing it. The debates between proponents and opponents of mainstreaming as a required educational policy in the United States have grown more intense. Many teachers complain that the inadequate implementation of the policy in many school systems and the difficult teaching conditions cre-

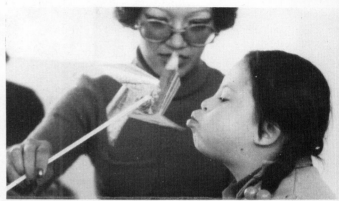

ated by the policy prevents quality teaching for all students from occurring.

The issues discussed in this unit are ones that critically impact the working conditions of teachers. These issues have been produced either by social forces outside of the schools, or by the thought of improving how we serve students' needs as a profession. They are relevant to the social foundations of education when the cultural foundations of learning are comprehensively conceived. These concerns are likewise relevant to the study of issues in curriculum and instruction and curriculum construction.

Looking Ahead: Challenge Questions

What would be a philosophical justification for improving "self-esteem" as a general claim of education?

What ought to constitute a teacher's attitude toward learning?

How could a mainstreaming program in a school be legal but not educationally viable?

What is meant by least restrictive placement? What would be an example of such placement for a handicapped child? For a gifted child?

What is meant by individualization of instruction? How can it be accomplished? Do elementary and secondary teachers encounter different problems when it comes to individualizing instruction?

What is the present state of drug use or chemical dependency in the United States?

What are the best strategies for helping teenagers who become parents? Why do some people leave school altogether?

How can teachers help students with AIDS? What have been the effects of the AIDS crisis on teachers and students?

Why might grade retention not be a good curriculum policy? Why is it being debated?

The ABC's Of Caring

A California experiment replaces traditional classroom approaches with methods aimed at teaching children to be more cooperative and compassionate

Alfie Kohn

Alfie Kohn is the author of The Brighter Side of Human Nature: Altruism and Empathy in Everyday Life, *published by Basic Books, and* No Contest: The Case Against Competition, *published in paperback by Houghton Mifflin. He lives in Cambridge, Mass., and lectures widely on educational issues.*

RUBY TELLSWORTH STILL TALKS about the day she returned to her classroom after a break to find her 2nd graders sitting in a group, earnestly discussing something. When she asked what was going on, they told her a problem had come up during recess and they had convened a class meeting to work it out. They proceeded to resolve the problem on their own while she finished her coffee.

Tellsworth's students did not drop out of some teacher heaven. They had come to care about each other—and to take responsibility for what went on in their classroom—because of her patient efforts, day after day, to elicit just such attitudes. Those efforts result from her participation in a landmark study in social, moral, and academic education that has been under way in California's San Ramon Valley since the early 1980's. It is a study designed to discover whether schools can help children learn to look out for others instead of just for themselves.

For the last seven years, the educators and psychologists involved in this pioneering effort, known as the Child Development Project, have been training teachers, designing schoolwide activities, and reaching out to parents. Supported by a grant of roughly $1-million each year from the William and Flora Hewlett Foundation, CDP has suggested changes in what is taught, how it is taught, how classrooms operate, how discipline is conceived, and how teachers regard their task and relate to students and to each other. It is by far the most ambitious program of its kind ever attempted—and it seems to be working.

"I've watched a variety of character education fads sweep through the schools," says Bill Streshly, superintendent of San Ramon Valley Schools. "Most of them have been little add-on programs for whatever the social problem is: sex, drugs, patriotism, kindness to animals. They're not part of the basic mission of the schools, and they fade out. But CDP incorporates its ethical mission in every part of the school day."

In some schools where CDP is not in place, Streshly continues, an occasional class period is devoted to values education. "Then it's, 'take out your math books, do the problems, first one through gets an M & M,' " he says. "That is when the real values come out." Those values aren't always obvious, but they are potent nonetheless. Students are implicitly taught that other people are to be regarded as obstacles to their own success. They also get the message that their achievement, like their behavior, is a function of external rewards and punishments.

CDP, by contrast, is based on the idea that "we need to get them to internalize ethics," Streshly says. "There aren't enough M & M's to keep people on track, to manipulate behavior once they leave the high-surveillance school setting." Project teachers, he adds, "teach cooperation because cooperation is a part of citizenship that we want."

The actual program being implemented in the San Ramon schools has several distinct components. First, there is its approach to classroom management. In place of authoritarian, sit-down-and-shut-up discipline or gimmicks to reward obedience, CDP teaches teachers to work together with children to decide how the classroom should be organized and how behavior problems should be handled. Instead of wondering, "What rules am I supposed to follow?" a child is encouraged to ask, "What kind of classroom do we want to have?" Teachers also are urged to develop warm and respectful relationships with students—and to avoid attributing unnecessarily negative motives to their actions—so there will be fewer behavior problems that have to be solved.

That explains why, when some of Tellsworth's 2nd graders at Rancho Romero School were rude to her, she took them aside, reminded them that she had never treated them like that, and let them know how awful they had made her feel. (They have been more considerate ever since.) And when one of Mary Korzick's 1st grade students at the Walt Disney School threw a rock during recess, she solicited the class's opinion on whether a prohibition on rock throwing was a reasonable rule, and why. (They decided it did make sense.)

The second part of the program emphasizes cooperative learning: Children spend part of the day working on assignments with a partner or in larger groups. With respect to both achievement and social skills, CDP staff members believe that allowing children to jointly devise problem-solving strategies makes at least as much sense as either of the two dominant American classroom models—working against each other (competition) and working apart from each other (individualized learning). Hundreds of studies have shown that cooperative learning helps students feel more positive about themselves, each other, and the subject matter. It also has been found to boost academic achievement regardless of the child's ability level or age—perhaps because, in the words of 10-year-old Disney student Justin Wells, "It's like you have four brains."

Joel Thornley, superintendent of the neighboring Hayward school system, where CDP began the second phase of its program in 1988, overcame his doubts about cooperative learning only after watching it in practice. "Once we saw the kinds of responses they get in San Ramon, we had no reservations," he explains. "Cooperative learning works. If there's a single bet we've missed over the years, it's making kids sit quietly at their desks instead of letting them work with each other."

CDP's third component is a curriculum designed to display and reinforce what psychologists call "prosocial" values: caring, sharing, and helping. Students learn to read by being immersed in works of literature whose themes and characters get children to think about how other people feel and to respond empathetically.

Today, for example, Ann Cerri's 6th graders are discussing a story about a white boy who meets his first black—an entirely realistic premise in the predominantly white schools of San Ramon Valley. The story's narrator worries that his new acquaintance will be insulted if asked whether his forebears were slaves.

Cerri puts down the book and asks her students whether this is a reasonable concern. It depends on whether or not they actually were slaves, one girl suggests. It depends on how the question is asked, says a boy. It depends on the area of the country they're in, someone else offers. Soon the whole class is discussing the matter animatedly, imagining themselves in the position of the narrator and of the black man. One student recalls how he felt when people kept asking him about his grandfather's death.

Beyond the individual classroom, CDP has arranged for the schools to provide activities that give children practice at being helpful to, taking responsibility for, and learning about others. Each child is assigned a buddy in another class, for instance, so a 5th grader and a 2nd grader periodically have a chance to work together or socialize, and older children can set an example.

Eric Schaps, CDP's director, is especially proud of this part of the project. He shows a visitor a photograph of a bus full of children returning from a field trip. A 1st grader in the foreground has fallen asleep, his head resting on his 5th grade buddy's shoulder. "What 5th grade kid do you know who would do this?" he asks. American schools have "systematically deprived kids of this kind of cross-age interaction. It's the experience of caring about another person, not being responsible for cleaning the erasers, that makes one a kind, nurturing person," he says. And the younger child, Schaps adds, learns that he is cared for.

Schaps ticks off some of the other elements of the program. Older students can give up some free time to tutor younger children—and many do. Classes don't just collect toys for something called "charity": each adopts one needy family, whose names are withheld but whose circumstances are described to the children in detail. Students hear firsthand about the experiences of people who are handicapped or from different cultures.

Then there are the aspects of CDP that follow students home. Some homework, for example, is specifically designed to be done with parents. A 2nd grader may bring home a poem about a child who is teased by a sibling. Parents are invited to share their own childhood memories, to help their child compose a poem or story on the same subject.

By themselves, reflects 6th grade teacher Bob Brown, none of these components were "foreign or shocking or new." He notes, however, that CDP "brought several elements together" that added up to a significant change "in the way you look at kids and the way kids learn."

THE CHILD DEVELOPMENT PROJECT WAS born in the mind of Dyke Brown, now 74, who, three decades after helping to start the Ford Foundation, was troubled by what he calls the "increasing degree of self-preoccupation in our students." Drawing on solid research showing that cooperative learning promotes higher achievement than individualized or competitive approaches, that attention to social skills or moral values doesn't have to come at the expense of academics, and that children are more likely to follow rules when they know the reason for them or have had a hand in creating them, he developed the CDP concept. After securing a massive seven-year grant from the Hewlett Foundation in 1980, Brown found Schaps, a social psychologist who had enough experience working with educators to successfully run a program and who had the methodological expertise to evaluate whether it was doing any good.

Schaps hired a staff, designed a program and a research plan, and then began looking for some receptive schools in which to try them out. They eventually set up shop in San Ramon Valley, a cluster of suburban communities about an hour's drive east from San Francisco. There they chose six of the district's 13 elementary schools—two groups of three, carefully matched for size and socioeconomic status—that seemed especially eager to be part of the project. A coin was ceremoniously flipped to determine which three would be the program schools (Walt Disney, Rancho Romero, and Country Club) and which would be the comparison schools to serve as a control group.

They started training teachers in 1982. The training began—as it has each year since then—with a one-day introduction in May, followed by a full week in August, and then one day each month throughout the next school year. Teachers meet in groups of about 13 and get some hands-on practice working together. This serves the dual purpose of reducing their professional isolation and giving them a taste of the approach they will be using in their own classrooms. Someone from the CDP staff observes each teacher weekly and offers advice on how to handle a disruptive child, how to run a class meeting, how to structure cooperative learning, and how to make the best use of texts to promote prosocial values.

The staff now admits to having made mistakes in its early training procedures. CDP worked with kindergarten teachers the first year, 1st grade teachers the next year, and so on. But it took too long to involve the whole faculty that way. Moreover, teachers were expected to master the new concepts and skills almost immediately.

Since then, various aspects of the program have been changed, many based on suggestions from teachers. Some experienced teachers, in fact, have been hired to coach their colleagues and bring the program to other schools in the area. Says Schaps,

"Our hope is that the district eventually will spread this on its own, using these teachers to do it."

Indeed, most San Ramon teachers—even some of those who had misgivings in the beginning—have become believers. "I couldn't see it at first and I found it very difficult" to learn, says Phil Wallace, who traces his traditional approach to classroom discipline to his military background. But now, having just retired from teaching 4th grade, Wallace works part time as a substitute and sometimes runs across his former students.

"There's a tremendous difference" between those taught by CDP-trained teachers and the other children, he says. "It's a wonderful thing to see; these kids are helping each other, caring for each other. I said to myself, 'Holy Mackerel! Don't tell me this actually works!'"

Because the main group of children being tracked by CDP experimenters are now in junior high school, the research doesn't require that the original batch of teachers keep using the project's approach. Many, however, have no intention of going back to the way they used to do things.

"I'll be using this as long as I teach," says Tellsworth. "It's a way of life now. If I was put in a school where I had to use Assertive Discipline [a currently fashionable approach in which teachers use a system of rewards and penalties to enforce rules that they alone specify], I would leave."

THIS, OF COURSE, DOESN'T MEAN THAT THE CDP approach was easy for teachers to master. It requires them to abandon the idea that a "good" classroom is a quiet roomful of children who passively absorb information, obey someone else's rules, and keep their eyes on their own work. It means agreeing to question the assumption that bribes or threats—even if called by fancier names—will induce students to care about learning or about each other.

Janet Ellman, a 1st grade teacher at the Longwood School in Hayward, Calif., laughs as she recalls her occasional frustration when she first tried out CDP's suggestions for classroom management last year. "Sometimes they just wouldn't shut up. It was tempting to fall back on external kinds of reinforcement for quiet behavior. But this year, it has been much easier for me to get quiet from my children by bringing them into the process and showing them how it's difficult to learn sometimes when there's talking going on."

Not all teachers remain open to these unsettling proposals long enough to make them work. "Some people were very opposed to CDP because it was very frightening to them," says Sharon Kushner, a 3rd grade teacher at Disney. "After you teach for a number of years, you fall into a pattern and do things automatically. It doesn't get changed very easily."

That was the case for Ann Cerri at first. "A lot of us felt that the structure was being pulled out from under us" when traditional beliefs about discipline were challenged, she says. "I remember feeling a little overwhelmed. [The CDP approach] wasn't a formula that you tried out and everything was hunky-dory from then on. It was hard work. But in my gut I thought it was the right way to work with kids. I like the way the class feels now, the way the kids and I relate to each other."

Tellsworth tells a story that illustrates another side of the program. A mother was concerned that her daughter didn't stand up for herself with her peers. But midway through a school year, the mother overheard her talking on the phone with a bossy classmate and was amazed to find that her daughter was explaining why she didn't want to play with the other girl, enumerating the behaviors that bothered her, and making it clear that they would get together only if the girl controlled them.

Such tales don't surprise Schaps, the project's director. Getting kids to stand up for themselves is part of what the project is after, he points out. "We're looking for a healthy balance of concern for self and concern for others. We don't want to turn kids into doormats." In fact, results of CDP's tests show that children in the program schools are more likely to stand up for their own views than those in other area schools.

The project teaches children that "you shouldn't please your peers at the expense of your integrity and what you think is right," says Marilyn Watson, who is in charge of the teacher training component. Social problem-solving is encouraged, she explains, as is "articulating dissenting opinions"—and there is nothing about caring for others that conflicts with these goals.

Watson, who used to teach education at Mills College in Oakland, Calif., burns calories just having a conversation; her head, hands, and shoulders are always in motion. "We're not saying there's no self-interest," she emphasizes. "We're saying there's more to work with than just self-interest."

TODAY, WATSON IS SERVING AS AN INFORmal tour guide through one of San Ramon's non-program schools. It is typical of affluent, suburban elementary schools. In the back of a 1st grade classroom is a box of books, one of which, *Being Destructive*, is packed with "do nots" and "you shoulds." The book informs readers, "If you are destructive because you do not care, you may need to be punished."

In the front of the room, the teacher is speaking in a sharp voice and snapping her fingers. "Boys and girls, when I get to zero, you must be looking at me. Five . . . four . . ." She points ominously at "CLASS WARNING" written on the blackboard. "You must stay in your seats!" she insists. "If you raise your hand, I will come to you." She lines the children up so they can look at a map one at a time. She often refers to herself in the third person.

Watson later points out how this teacher, presum-

ably well-meaning and well-trained, is making the children compete with each other rather than learning to work together, how she is encouraging them to depend on her rather than taking responsibility for their own learning and behavior, and how she keeps herself distant from them at the same time.

In a 5th grade room down the hall, only the A plus papers are tacked to the wall. The teacher's disciplinary approach is traditional, yet the room is far more chaotic than CDP classrooms. "I'm waiting!" she yells to a group of oblivious 10-year-olds. "Anyone talking now will be sure their name won't get in the paper."

Next door, a teacher proudly shows off her "checking account" system of class control: A poster board lists how much a student "pays" for late work or a messy desk and how large a deposit he or she will get for an A on a test.

Afterward, Watson concedes that such a system may produce quiet classrooms and perhaps it might even result in higher test scores in the short run. "But you're aiming for the long run, for them to do it because they want to learn, not because they want money," she explains. "You can get the [desired] behavior this way. What you can't get is a commitment to the behavior, a sense that 'I'm in charge,' a sense of personal responsibility."

The shift in focus that Watson advocates is beginning to generate considerable excitement among educators. The Child Development Project has been honored by the American Association of School Administrators and the National Council for the Social Studies and has been certified by the U.S. Department of Education's Program Effectiveness Panel. Hundreds of requests for information about the project have been rolling in from schools and school districts, many of which are eager to begin adopting it.

Closer to home, a visitor has to look hard to find any critics of CDP in San Ramon Valley. Bob DuPont, part of a solid conservative majority on the local school board, says he knows of no opposition to the project. "We can—and have to—provide the basic values of positive citizenry in the schools," he says. "What's the alternative? If the schools don't do it, no one will."

Some parents were nervous when the idea was first presented to them. Fred Messreni, a 44-year-old corporate manager who is on the city council, remembers asking, "What is this program that's going to be experimenting with the behavior of my [daughter]?"

But, he says, "the concern rapidly evaporated and became excitement about the opportunity she was given. It's difficult to argue with constructive, positive influences that bring results."

Another family, the Greningers, say they have modified their approach to parenting after watching what the project has done for their three children at Disney. "We've incorporated it into our home," which means holding family meetings to resolve conflicts, says Barb Greninger. "Every time we've included [the children] in the decisionmaking process, it has worked out better."

"I swear," her husband, Dave, a Little League coach, chimes in. "The kids who are the troublemakers around here"—he waves at the neighborhood beyond his sliding glass doors—"don't go to Disney."

One teacher who does express reservations about CDP is Bill Randall, who recently completed a year of training for his 6th grade classroom. "It takes an undue amount of time," he says. "People in education are giving so much. You have to ask yourself, 'Why am I here? To teach study skills or to teach behavior skills?' But my main concern is, Does it last? Does it stick in the kids? Is there really a noticeable difference? The ideals sound fine, but what's the reality?"

The CDP researchers asked the same questions, unsatisfied with mere anecdotal accounts of success. Not all the tests administered to children—or the systematic monitoring of 67 classrooms each spring by observers who weren't told what the study was about—have shown consistent and statistically significant differences between the program schools and the comparison schools.

One possible explanation—which does not call into question the fundamental soundness of the CDP concept—is that some teachers were less effective at grasping and implementing the principles of the program. Another is that all of the comparison schools have independently become convinced of the value of cooperative learning and have begun encouraging their own teachers to use it—making a true test of CDP's comparative effectiveness difficult.

Nevertheless, some of the results are striking. Children in CDP classrooms are more likely to be spontaneously helpful and cooperative, better able to understand conflict situations, and more likely to take everyone's needs into account in resolving them than their counterparts in other schools. Newer research with a group of younger children in the project schools also shows some positive effects, which means that at least some of the teachers who were trained are continuing to use CDP techniques on their own.

These findings also have apparently impressed the Hewlett Foundation. "If the hypotheses hadn't been borne out, we'd be folded up by now," says Dyke Brown, the father of CDP. Instead, the grant was extended for an extra three years so that two critical questions can be answered: First, will the positive effects persist now that the students have moved on to junior high school and begun to mix with children who haven't been taught to care and cooperate? And, second, will such a program work in a less affluent, more ethnically heterogeneous school district—a district such as Hayward?

There are no data yet to answer the first question, and it's too soon to know for sure about Hayward. Initial signs regarding the latter are promising enough, however, that director Schaps wants to go even further. He will soon be seeking funding to take the program beyond California. If all goes well, 10 sites around the country will be chosen to receive CDP training over a period of four years. Ideally, teams of teachers and administrators in those districts will then be qualified to train still others.

Can teachers just adopt the program on their own? Some aspects—pairing buddies from different classes, for example—could be put into place tomorrow in any school. But other parts, such as the approach to discipline, are more difficult to implement than it might appear. Teachers need extended guidance and support, says Schaps, and they would have particular difficulty making major changes in classroom management without the backing of their colleagues and principal.

Project teachers tend to agree with this. At first, says Kushner, "the classroom was so noisy and I worried about what other people would think. I can't imagine trying to do this without other people in the school knowing that the kids aren't going to be sitting down in rows."

Implementing the program requires intensive teacher training, concedes Paul Mussen, a developmental psychologist who served on the CDP's advisory board. "It does present real practical problems," he says. "But the project proves that one can, with great effort, make great differences in how kids interact with each other. It shows that schools can have an effect."

Honig v. Doe: The Suspension and Expulsion of Handicapped Students

ABSTRACT: *Public Law 94-142 provides for a free appropriate public education for all handicapped children, but does not address the issue of disciplining handicapped students. The result has been confusion and uncertainty, particularly concerning expulsion and suspension. The courts have been forced into this vacuum, acting as arbiters. The Supreme Court's ruling in* Honig v. Doe *will help to delineate the proper role of educators in the suspension and expulsion of handicapped students. This article examines that role and offers recommendations for school policies regarding the discipline of handicapped students.*

MITCHELL L. YELL

MITCHELL L. YELL *is Doctoral Candidate, Special Education Programs, University of Minnesota, Minneapolis.*

☐ Public Law 94-142 and regulations implementing the law provide for a free, appropriate public education for handicapped children. However, neither the law nor the regulations address the issue of the discipline of handicapped students. The result has been confusion and uncertainty among special educators and administrators concerning their rights and responsibilities in the area.

The courts have been forced into this vacuum, acting as arbiters, having to balance the rights of the handicapped with the school's duty to maintain order and discipline and to provide an appropriate education for all children. A substantial body of litigation has emerged concerning these issues, especially regarding the suspension and expulsion of handicapped students. In interpreting existing laws and regulations, the courts have fashioned a body of common law (law based on court decisions rather than legislatively enacted law) which has helped to clarify this balance. The issue remains unclear, however, because much of this litigation has been contradictory and the decisions by the courts apply only to their particular jurisdiction (e.g., decisions by the 9th Circuit Court apply only to the ninth circuit). On January 20, 1988, the Supreme Court issued a ruling in *Honig v. Doe* that should serve to remove the confusions and uncertainty surrounding these issues. Supreme Court rulings become the law of the land; therefore, this ruling is binding on all schools in the United States.

The purpose of this article is to explicate the rights and responsibilities of special educators and administrators in the suspension and expulsion of handicapped students from school. In addition to a discussion of *Honig v. Doe*, this article presents the common law principles

that have been developed in federal litigation. Principles developed in these cases are examined, rather than the cases themselves. Further details can be found in a number of excellent reviews (Barnette & Parker, 1982; Hartog-Rapp, 1985; Leone, 1985; Osborne, 1985, 1987; Ratwick, 1983; Rothenberg, 1986).

COMMON LAW PRINCIPLES

Common law is defined in Barron's Law Dictionary (Gifis, 1984) as a system of law "which is based on judicial precedent rather than statutory laws, which are legislative enactments" (p. 81). It is derived from principles based on judicial reasoning and common sense, rather than rules of law. These principles are determined by social needs and have changed in accordance with changes in these needs. The body of common law dealing with the suspension and expulsion of handicapped students has been developed in a number of federal cases. These cases, citations, and major rulings (including *Honig v. Doe*) are listed in Table 1.

The common law principles developed from the cases listed in Table 1 are instructive and can guide the development of school disciplinary policies with handicapped students. These principles retain their significance after *Honig v. Doe* because the Supreme Court's ruling did not address all pertinent issues.

Principle 1. Temporary suspensions are available for use in disciplining handicapped students. Schools have a right and duty to maintain discipline and order. The courts have consistently held that short-term suspensions (of less than 10 days) are neither changes in educational placement nor a cessation of educational services and that these suspensions are therefore available for use with handicapped students. Serial, indefinite, or lengthy suspensions (of more than 10 days), however, are not permitted. In a number of cases in which

From *Exceptional Children*, Vol. 56, No. 1, September 1989, pp. 60-69. Copyright © 1989 by The Council for Exceptional Children. Reprinted with permission.

TABLE 1
Federal Cases Involving the Suspension and Expulsion of Handicapped Students

Court Case	Citation	Rulings
Stuart v. Nappi (1978)	433 F.Supp. 1235	1. P.L. 94-142 prohibits the expulsion of handicapped students. 2. Short-term suspensions of handicapped students are permissible. 3. Changes in placement and determination of the appropriateness of an educational placement must be made by a team of educators and parents. 4. Handicapped children are not immune from a school's disciplinary procedures.
Doe v. Koger (1979)	480 F.Supp. 225	1. P.L. 94-142 does not prohibit the expulsion of all disruptive handicapped children, only the expulsion of those who misbehave because of their handicap. 2. When a student cannot be expelled, the school may transfer the child to a more appropriate educational setting.
Mrs. A.J. v. Special School District No. 1 (1979)	478 F.Supp. 418	1. A school's duty to a handicapped child begins after the identification process, not before. 2. A school system is not required to provide a formal hearing process in the case of a short-term suspension.
Sherry v. New York State Education Department (1979)	479 F.Supp. 1328	1. Indefinite suspensions are to be considered a change in placement which triggers the procedural safeguards of P.L. 94-142.
S-1 v. Turlington (1981)	635 F.2d 342	1. Handicapped children cannot be expelled for misconduct which is a manifestation of their handicap. 2. School officials must make this determination. 3. The determination must be made by a group of individuals who possess the necessary expertise to make such a determination. 4. Expulsion is allowable if there is no relationship between the misbehavior and handicapping condition.

Continued on next page

suspensions of a lengthy nature were used, the courts have considered them to be expulsions. Attempts to obfuscate expulsion by using suspensions in this manner have not been tolerated by the courts.

Principle 2. Expulsions and lengthy suspensions are changes in educational placement which trigger the procedural safeguards of P.L. 94-142. The courts have stated that expelling or suspending a handicapped student for a lengthy period of time (more than 10 days) is tantamount to changing his or her educational placement. According to P.L. 94-142, the educational placement of a handicapped child cannot be changed unless certain procedural safeguards are followed.

Principle 3. A trained and knowledgeable group of persons must determine whether a causal relationship exists between a child's handicapping conditions and the misbehavior. Only if no relationship exists can a handicapped child be expelled. The courts have recognized that schools have a limited right to suspend and expel handicapped students. Before schools take an action of this nature, however, a trained and knowledgeable group of persons must determine whether a causal relationship exists between the student's handicapping condition and the misbehavior. This group must possess specialized knowledge about the student's handicapping condition. The decision concerning the relationship of the behavior and the handicap must not be a unilateral administrative decision, and cannot be made by persons not knowledgeable about the student's handicap (e.g., a school board).

If a relationship is determined to exist, expulsion is not allowable; however, in the absence of this relationship, expulsion is permitted. Theoretically, expulsion of handicapped students remains available as a disciplinary tool.

In cases in which suspension or expulsion

TABLE 1 *Continued*

Court Case	Citation	Rulings
		5. Expulsion is a change in placement which triggers the procedural safeguards of P.L. 94-142.
		6. During a period of expulsion, schools have to continue educational services to the child.
Board of Education of Peoria v. Illinois Board of Education (1982)	531 F.Supp. 148	1. Short-term suspensions are available for use with handicapped students even if the misbehavior is a manifestation of the handicapping condition.
Kaelin v. Grubbs (1982)	682 F.2d 595	1. Expulsion is a change of placement.
		2. Expulsion is available only when it is determined that the misbehavior leading to it and the handicapping condition are not related.
		3. During periods of expulsion, educational services must be provided.
		4. Suspension is available as long as children receive the procedural safeguards set forth in *Goss v. Lopez.*
Lamont X v. Quisenberry (1984)	606 F.Supp. 809	1. A change in placement of a handicapped student cannot take place without following procedures mandated by P.L. 94-142.
Victoria L. v. District School Board (1984)	741 F.2d 369	1. Schools have the responsibility to provide a safe school environment, and when a handicapped student's behavior presents a threat to peers and school officials the student's program status may be changed.
		2. Regulations support a transfer to a more restrictive setting. When the behavior of handicapped students interfere with the education of other students, placement may be changed.
		3. Placement may be changed immediately if the behavior is dangerous to others.
Jackson v. Franklin County School Board (1986)	806 F.2d 623	1. When a handicapped student presents a substantial danger to himself or others, immediate removal from the classroom may be justifiable.
School Board v. Malone (1985)	762 F.2d 1210	1. Expulsion of a handicapped child is a change in placement which triggers P.L. 94-142 procedural safeguards.
Doe v. Maher (1986)	793 F.2d 1470	1. P.L. 94-142 prohibits expulsion for misbehavior which is related to a student's handicap.
		2. Short-term suspensions are permitted.
Doe v. Rockingham County School Board (1987)	658 F.Supp. 403	1. Handicapped students must remain in their current educational placement pending review of such placements.
Honig v. Doe (1988)	56 S.Ct. 27	1. P.L. 94-142 prohibits schools from unilaterally excluding handicapped children from the classroom for dangerous or disruptive conduct growing out of their disabilities.
		2. Regulations allow the use of normal nonplacement-changing procedures including temporary suspensions for 10 school days in disciplining handicapped students.

is considered, it is clearly the duty of the schools to convene the Individual Educational Program (IEP) team or the team responsible for determining the appropriate educational setting of the child, and determine whether the child's misbehavior is a manifestation of the child's handicapping condition. The issue of how this determination is to be made is examined in a later section of this article. At present, however, even though the courts have agreed that this is mandatory when considering suspension or expulsion, no judicial guidelines for doing so have been forwarded.

If the team determines that the student's misbehavior and the handicapping condition are not related and the student is expelled, the school district must continue to provide special education services.

Principle 4. Due process procedures are required when suspending or expelling handicapped students. According to the Supreme Court in *Goss v. Lopez* (1975), a student's education is a property right that is protected by the 14th amendment. The court ruled that these rights cannot be taken away for misconduct without adherence to due process procedures. Stating that discipline is essential to the educational process, the court found that behaviors which require immediate and effective disciplinary action may subject the misbehaving student to suspension. The court held that suspension is not only a necessary tool to maintain order and discipline, but also a valuable educational device. Even when students face minimal suspensions of 10 school days or less, however, they *must be* afforded a hearing in which they are presented with the evidence against them, and they must be given an opportunity to present their side of the story. With the exception of an instance in which the student poses a threat to other students or to the educational process, they must be afforded these due process procedures.

Although this case did not involve handicapped students directly, the ruling pertains to them. When imposing suspension or expulsion on handicapped students, school officials will be held to the more extensive due process procedures of P.L. 94-142.

Principle 5. An option open to schools is to transfer a disruptive student to a more restrictive setting. The courts have consistently stated that when a handicapped student is extremely disruptive to the educational process, an option open to the school is to change the student's educational placement by moving him or her to a more restrictive setting. The U.S. Court of Appeals, 11th Circuit (*Victoria L. v. District School Board*, 1984), held that not only was the option of transferring a student to a more restrictive placement available, but that it could even be made unilaterally if necessary (e.g., the student's behavior poses a danger to others or impairs the education of other students). When a change in placement is made, the requirements of P.L. 94-142 must be adhered to.

SUMMARY

These principles delineate the school's responsibilities when suspending or expelling a handicapped child. The courts have consistently held that there is a difference between suspensions and expulsions. Short-term suspensions, of up to 10 school days, are allowed. Expulsion, which is the removal of a student from school for a lengthy or indefinite period of time, is allowed only if certain procedures are followed. The first step is to convene the group of persons knowledgeable about the handicapped student (this should be the child's IEP team). It will be the team's task to determine if the child's misbehavior is a manifestation of his or her handicapping condition. If a relationship is determined to exist, the child cannot be expelled. If the misbehavior poses a threat to others or disrupts the educational process, however, the child may be suspended on a temporary basis. The suspension must not last more than 10 days, and the student must be afforded due process rights. If it is determined that there is no relationship between the misbehavior and the handicap, expulsion theoretically remains an option. In cases in which the child is expelled, it is the school's duty to continue providing educational services; therefore, the school will be required to provide an alternate educational program. Because expulsion is considered a change in placement, the school must follow the change-in-placement requirements of P.L. 94-142. An option always available to schools is to transfer the child to a more restrictive placement if he or she cannot be educated in the current placement.

HONIG V. DOE

Honig v. Doe was a case involving the suspension of two emotionally handicapped students enrolled in the San Francisco Unified School District. The students, who were identified as John Doe and Jack Smith in the judicial opinion, were both identified as emotionally disturbed and were receiving special education services.

Student Doe had been placed in a developmental center for handicapped students. While attending school, he assaulted another student and broke a window. When he admitted these offenses to the principal, he was suspended for 5 days. The principal referred the matter to the school's student placement committee with the recommendation that Doe be expelled. The suspension was continued indefinitely as permitted by California state law, which allowed suspensions to extend beyond 5 days while expulsion proceedings were being held.

Student Smith's IEP stated that he was to be placed in a special education program in a regular school setting on a trial basis. Following several incidents of misbehavior, the school unilaterally reduced his program to half-day. His grandparents agreed to the reduction; however, the school district did not notify them of their right to appeal. A month later Smith was suspended for 5 days when he made inappropriate sexual comments to female students. In accordance with California law, Smith's suspension was also continued indefinitely while expulsion proceedings were initiated by the school placement committee.

Attorneys for the students jointly filed a lawsuit in U.S. district court. The lawsuit challenged the indefinite suspensions and, in Smith's case, the reduction to a half-day program. The district court issued an injunction preventing the school district from suspending any handicapped student for misbehavior related to his or her handicap. Appeals were filed, and the case was heard by the U.S. Court of Appeals, Ninth Circuit, on October 9, 1986 (*Doe v. Maher*). In a lengthy and comprehensive judgment, the court arrived at a number of conclusions that essentially mirrored the aforementioned principles of common law. The court held that:

1. P.L. 94-142 prohibits the expulsion of handicapped students for misbehavior that is a manifestation of his or her handicap.

2. Whether or not the misbehavior is handicapped related, expulsion constitutes a change in placement, triggering the procedural safeguards of P.L. 94-142.

3. Informal and reasonable punishments traditionally used to maintain order in the classroom (including short, fixed-term suspensions) may be used with handicapped students.

4. Before an IEP team can recommend a handicapped student for expulsion, it must consider the results of an independent evaluation.

5. P.L. 94-142 does not compel localities to place handicapped students in regular educational classrooms, but only in the least restrictive setting consistent with their needs and the needs of other students.

6. If the misbehavior of a handicapped student is not a manifestation of his or her handicap, the student may be expelled; and the school district may cease providing all educational services. (Note: This conclusion by the court is at odds with a number of prior decisions concerning the continuation of educational services during expulsion.) This portion of the Appeals Court's ruling was not addressed by the Supreme Court.

Appeals were filed; and on November 9, 1987, the Supreme Court heard oral arguments.

The case was renamed *Honig v. Doe*. The court issued its ruling on January 20, 1988. The ruling dealt with two issues raised by Bill Honig, California Superintendent of Public Instruction and petitioner in the case. The first issue involved the "stay-put" provision of P.L. 94-142. This provision prohibits state or local school authorities from unilaterally excluding handicapped children from the classroom for dangerous or disruptive conduct during the pendency of IEP review proceedings. The second issue that the Supreme Court addressed involved the decision in *Doe v. Maher* that the state must provide direct services to all handicapped children not provided educational services by the local school district. This portion of the court's ruling is not examined here.

The petitioner had sought review in the Supreme Court of the Court of Appeals interpretation of the "stay-put" rule. The appeals court had interpreted this provision literally, holding that no handicapped student could be excluded during the pendency of the review regardless of how dangerous his or her behavior was. The petitioner contended that the court's interpretation of the provision conflicted with the interpretation held by several other federal courts of appeal (*Jackson v. Franklin County School Board*, 1986; *Victoria L. v. District School Board*, 1984; *S-1 v. Turlington*, 1981) that had recognized a "dangerousness exception" to the "stay-put" provision. According to this exception, handicapped students who present a danger to others can be removed from the classroom during pendency of the sometimes lengthy review procedures. Honig argued that Congress could not have intended that the "stay-put" provision be read literally. His contention was based on a common-sense proposition that a literal reading of the provision would put schools in the untenable position of having to return violent or dangerous handicapped students to the classroom although this might expose other students to a dangerous situation.

Justice Brennan, writing for the the majority, stated that the "stay-put" provision demonstrated that Congress had indeed intended to strip schools of the unilateral authority that they had been using to exclude disabled students from the school. The court found the language unequivocal, holding that during the pendency of any review meetings the child must remain in his or her current educational placement unless the school officials and the parents agree otherwise. Exclusion is a change in placement, and schools may not unilaterally change a handicapped child's placement, regardless of the degree of danger presented by the student.

According to the court, however, schools could still use normal disciplinary procedures with handicapped children. Permissible procedures listed by the court include study carrels, timeout, detention, the restriction of privileges, and temporary suspension of up to 10 school days. The court's opinion stated that the suspension authority ensures that schools can protect the safety of others by promptly removing dangerous students from the classroom. It also provides a cooling-down period during which the school can initiate IEP reviews to seek interim placement for the child. In cases in which the parents refuse to permit a change in placement, the 10-day period gives school officials time to enlist the aid of the courts.

The decision in *Honig v. Doe* is in agreement with the majority of the past decade of common law that deals with the discipline of handicapped students, with one significant difference. The Supreme Court rejected the "dangerousness exception" to the "stay-put" provision which had been advanced by a number of courts. Although an analysis of the *Honig v. Doe* ruling seems to preclude the use of expulsion with handicapped students, it might be argued that the Supreme Court left the door slightly ajar when it agreed with the appeals court that expulsion of handicapped students for *conduct attributable to their disability* deprives students of their congressionally mandated right to a free appropriate education. This language might be interpreted as the Supreme Court's tacitly agreeing that a handicapped child can be expelled for conduct not attributed to his or her disability.

Determining the Relationship of the Handicap to the Misbehavior

An analysis of the *Honig v. Doe* decision leads the author to conclude that using expulsion to discipline handicapped students or to exclude a potentially dangerous handicapped student from a classroom is no longer an option available to schools. The Supreme Court, however, quoted the line from *Doe v. Maher* (1986) stating that a handicapped student cannot be expelled for misbehavior that is attributable to the disability. Thus, one might assume that to expel a handicapped child for conduct not attributable to his or her handicapping condition is permissible. This is a tenuous assumption at best. If a school were to adopt this position and expel a handicapped student if the IEP team determined that no relationship existed between the handicap and misbehavior, the school officials would be putting themselves in a legally precarious situation. Given the *Honig v. Doe* decision and existing case law, a good attorney could probably convince a court that misbehavior is always related to the handicapping condition. School districts expelling handicapped students would certainly be

inviting administrative reviews and potential litigation (both expensive procedures). Precedence suggests that in such actions school districts would very likely lose, in which case they would open themselves to being sued for attorney's fees. Ignoring the ethical problems inherent in the exclusion of handicapped students from school, the above considerations must lead to the conclusion that the loss of expulsion is really not a great loss. Normal school disciplinary procedure, suspension, and transfer to a more restrictive setting will remain available.

In virtually every case dealing with these issues, the courts have held that it is the responsibility of the school to determine if the student's misbehavior is a manifestation of his or her handicapping condition. Courts have also repeatedly held that this determination can be made only by a trained and knowledgeable group of persons familiar with the student's handicapping condition (the IEP team). As difficult as this determination might seem, special educators and administrators must assume this responsibility. In *Doe v. Maher* (1986), the court recognized the difficulty in making this distinction, but noted that states must assume this burden because they accept federal funds: "Those who accept the sovereign's pay cannot complain of his terms of acceptance" (p. 1483).

The courts have unanimously held that if the misbehavior is a manifestation of the handicapping condition (that is, the handicap significantly impairs the student's ability to control his or her behavior), the student cannot be expelled. The courts have also made it clear that it is the obligation of the school district to make this determination before making a decision to suspend or expel. Unfortunately, courts have provided no legal criteria for guiding schools in making this determination. Examination of the case law reveals that the courts that have attempted to provide some guidance have been reaching contradictory conclusions.

In *Doe v. Maher* (1986), the court held that the relationship between the handicapping condition and misbehavior must be significant if the misbehavior is determined to be a manifestation of the handicap and does not exist in instances where there is only an attenuated relationship. The court gave an example of an attenuated relationship as one in which the handicap causes low self-esteem, which leads the child to misbehave to gain attention or win approval. The U.S. Circuit Court of Appeals Fourth Circuit (*School Board v. Malone*, 1985), however, held that a learning disabled student who had been expelled for participating in a drug transaction did so because his learning disability had caused him to have a poor self-image. According to the court, the lowered self-esteem caused the student to seek peer approval, which he felt he could gain through the drug transaction. Additionally, the court felt that the student's learning disability prevented him from understanding the long-term consequences of his actions. The student's IEP committee had found no causal relationship between the handicap and the misbehavior. The court disagreed and stated that the student could not be expelled. These two decisions are indicative of the lack of judicial guidelines in the determination of the degree of relationship between the handicap and the misbehavior.

A few cases have dealt with the category of the handicapping condition and the degree of relationship. In *Doe v. Maher* (1986), the court noted that the misbehavior of an emotionally handicapped student will always be related to the handicapping condition. In two cases (*S-1 v. Turlington*, 1981; *School Board v. Malone*, 1985) school districts contended that a relationship between a student's handicap and misbehavior did not exist the child was identified as handicapped, but not emotionally. In both cases the courts disagreed with this argument. The courts have held that the category of handicapping condition has no bearing on whether or not the misbehavior that led to suspension or expulsion is a manifestation of the handicap. Therefore, if schools maintain that a child's handicap is not emotional and that there can be no relationship between the handicap and misbehavior, these schools are treading on exceedingly thin ice.

Another indication contributes to the lack of clarity in the area: The courts have stated that a group of specialized persons must determine the nature of this relationship, yet the courts have often overturned decisions by the specialized teams when the courts have not agreed with such decisions.

Leone (1985) suggested that the process of clarifying the relationship involves a systematic review of the child's behavior, deliberation, and professional judgment. An initial step in such a review would be an examination of the child's academic and disciplinary record. Trends and patterns in this record provide useful information. Leone contends that steady academic progress for a length of time (several years) followed by little or no academic growth and accompanying behavior problems suggests that a relationship between the handicap and the misbehavior does exist. A pattern of misbehavior that indicates a lack of judgment and deficient social skills over time may also indicate the existence of a relationship. However, serious acts of misbehavior that are atypical for the child in question and that do not follow changes in placement may suggest no relationship.

Given the necessity of making this determination in cases of expulsion, the lack of guidelines by which to do so, and the possibility that the decision may be overturned in administrative or judicial review, it may be advisable to consider that a child's misbehavior is always related to his or her handicapping condition. There is legal authority for making this assumption from litigation and decisions of the Office of Civil Rights (Hartog-Rapp, 1985).

School officials and IEP team members might be well advised when considering the discipline of a handicapped child to always conclude that there is a relationship between the misbehavior and the handicapping condition and to then make the determination as to the appropriate disciplinary technique without consideration of expulsion. The *Honig v. Doe* decision clearly states that the removal of handicapped students from their educational placements can only be accomplished with parental permission or, as a last resort, with the permission of the courts. If, however, a school district wishes to establish that there is no relationship between the handicap and misbehavior, it is extremely important that the process be handled properly.

Unanswered Questions

Though the *Honig v. Doe* decision answered a number of important questions concerning the suspension and expulsion of handicapped students, it left a number of questions unanswered. An important question concerns how handicapped students can be disciplined in light of this decision. Despite Justice Brennan's assurance that educators will not be "hamstrung" in disciplining handicapped students and that schools may employ normal disciplinary procedures, the matter is far from settled. The first question is: What is a normal disciplinary procedure? What is the status of procedures such as timeout or in-school suspension?

A second unanswered question concerns the court's ruling concerning the interim placement of a handicapped student. According to the court, if a child is a danger to others the school may suspend him or her for up to 10 school days. During this period the school may initiate an IEP review and seek to convince the parents to agree to an interim placement. If the parents refuse the change in placement and the child is "truly dangerous," the school may appeal directly to the courts for relief. The burden of proof would rest on the schools in an appeal of this nature. What would the schools have to prove in such cases?

FIGURE 1
Policy Models for the Discipline of Handicapped Students

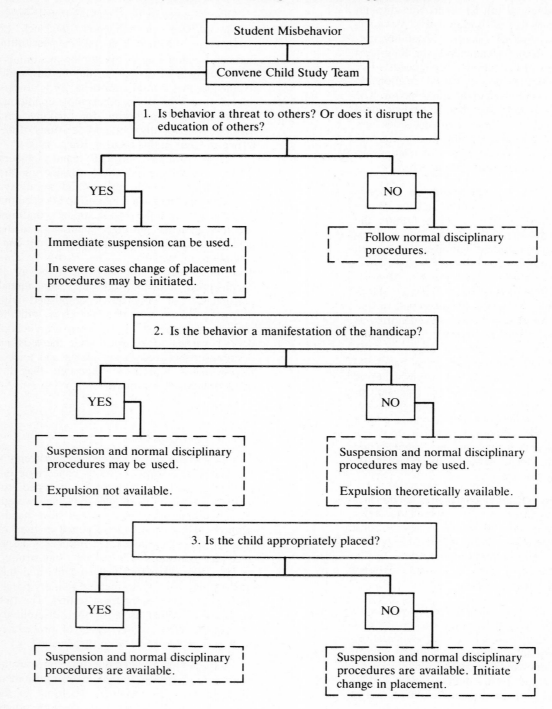

A third unanswered question concerns the court's ruling that 10-school-day suspensions are allowable. Does this refer to 10 consecutive or 10 cumulative school days? The Office of Civil Rights stated that suspensions of handicapped students which total more than 10 cumulative days in a school year violate the Rehabilitation Act of 1973 (Sarzynski, 1988). Whether the courts will agree to this interpreta-

tion is uncertain. The Supreme Court did not answer these questions; future litigation will probably do so.

MODEL FOR POLICY FORMATION

According to Leone (1985), administrators, parents, and teachers must possess the following information to review and monitor disciplinary codes for handicapped children: an understanding of the rights granted to the handicapped children and their parents by P.L. 94-142, an understanding of court decisions involving the discipline of handicapped students, and a series of procedures for guiding their deliberations.

When considering the use of disciplinary procedures with handicapped students, school officials must address the following issues:

1. Is the behavior a threat to the student or others?

2. Is the misbehavior a manifestation of the handicapping condition?

3. Is the handicapped student's current placement appropriate?

These questions must be answered by the student's IEP team (or a similar specialized group of persons), and must not be answered by a school board, principal, or anyone acting unilaterally. The parents must be involved. A model for considering the discipline of handicapped students is presented in Figure 1.

CONCLUSION

Because P.L. 94-142 and the regulations implementing it do not address the discipline of handicapped students, the issue has become one of great controversy and confusion. In the absence of statutory law, the courts have fashioned a body of case law. It is important, as the cases illustrate, that special educators and administrators be familiar with the principles of this law to guide them in formulating policies for the discipline of handicapped students. In establishing these policies it is important that the rights of handicapped students are not abridged. Educators should not avoid disciplinary procedures because a student is handicapped. The principles fashioned by the courts place restrictions on actions of the school, but do not prohibit them.

The purpose of discipline is to teach. If students, handicapped and nonhandicapped alike, are to learn their roles and responsibilities in school and society, they must understand the purposes of rules and the consequences of not adhering to those rules. To shelter handicapped students from disciplinary sanctions would be to shelter them from the realities of life.

REFERENCES

Barnette, S. M., & Parker, L. G. (1982). Suspension and expulsion of the emotionally handicapped: Issues and practices. *Behavioral Disorders, 7,* 173-179.
Board of Education of Peoria v. Illinois Board of Education, 531 F.Supp. 148 (C.D. III, 1982).
Doe v. Koger, 480 F.Supp. 225 (W.D. Ind. 1979).
Doe v. Maher, 793 F.2d 1470 (9th Cir. 1986).
Doe v. Rockingham County School Board, 658 F.Supp. 403 (W.D. VA. 1987).
Gifis, S. H. (1984). *Barron's law dictionary* (2nd ed.). New York: Barron's Educational Services Inc.
Goss v. Lopez, 419 U.S. 565 (1975).
Hartog-Rapp, F. (1985). The legal standards for determining the relationship between a child's handicapping condition and misconduct charged in a school disciplinary proceeding. *Southern Illinois University Law Journal, 2,* 243-262.
Honig v. Doe, 56 S.Ct. 27 (1988).
Jackson v. Franklin County School Board, 806 F.2d 623 (5th Cir. 1986).
Kaelin v. Grubbs, 682 F.2d 595 (6th Cir. 1982).
Lamont X v. Quisenberry, 606 F.Supp. 809 (S.D. Ohio 1984).
Leone, P. E. (1985). Suspension and expulsion of handicapped pupils. *The Journal of Special Education, 19*(1), 111-121.
Mrs. A. J. v. Special School District No. 1, 478 F.Supp. 418 (D. Minn. 1979).
Osborne, A. G. (1985). Disciplining handicapped students. *West's Education Law Reporter, 30,* 1009-1015.
Osborne, A. G. (1987). Discipline of handicapped students revisited. *West's Education Law Reporter, 37,* 753-761.
Ratwick, P. C. (1983). Discipline of handicapped students—has expulsion been abolished? *West's Education Law Reporter, 7,* 757-768.
Rothenberg, H. A. (1986). Suspension and expulsion of handicapped children: An overview in light of *Doe v. Maher. Western State University Law Reviewer, 14,* 341-352.
S-1 v. Turlington, 635 F.2d 342 (5th Cir. 1981).
Sarzynski, E. J., (1988). Disciplining a handicapped student. *West's Education Law Reporter, 46,* 17-26.
School Board of Prince County v. Malone, 762 F.2d 1210 (4th Cir. 1985).
Sherry v. New York State Education Department, 479 F.Supp. 1328 (W.D. N.Y., 1979).
Stuart v. Nappi, 443 F.Supp. 1235 (D. Conn. 1978).
Victoria L. v. District School Board, 741 F.2d (11th Cir. 1984).

The author wishes to thank Frank Wood, Christine A. Espin, and Bonnie Ridley for their assistance in the preparation of this paper.

■ TEEN-AGE PREGNANCY

The Case for National Action

FAYE WATTLETON

Faye Wattleton is president of Planned Parenthood Federation of America.

In 1983 a 25-year-old woman with a 9-year-old daughter gave the following testimony before Congress:

> In the tenth grade, my girlfriends and I were all sexually active, but none of us used birth control. I had hopes of a career and I wanted to go to college. One day my mother said, "Towanda, you're pregnant." I asked her how she knew. She said, "I can just tell."
>
> My mother wouldn't even consider abortion. I had nothing to say about a decision that would alter my entire life. A few weeks after the baby was born, my mother said, "You'll have to get a job." The only job I could get was in a bar.
>
> I spent two years dealing with the nightmare of welfare. Finally I went to the father of my child and asked him to take care of her while I went back to school. He agreed.
>
> I am now making some progress. I went to business school and I now have a job working in an office in Washington. But my life has been very difficult. . . . I had ambitions as a child, but my hopes and dreams were almost killed by the burden of trying to raise a child while I was still a child myself.

This young woman's story is relived around us every day. The United States has the dubious distinction of leading the industrialized world in its rates of teen-age pregnancy, teen-age childbirth and teen-age abortion. According to a study of thirty-seven developed nations published by the Alan Guttmacher Institute in 1985, the teen pregnancy rate in the United States is more than double the rate in England, nearly triple the rate in Sweden and seven times the rate in the Netherlands. Throughout the 1970s, this rate rose in the United States, while it declined in such places as England, Wales and Sweden. Each year, more than 1 million American teen-agers become pregnant; about half of these young women give birth.

Teen pregnancy is both cause and consequence of a host of social ills. The teen-agers likeliest to become pregnant are those who can least afford an unwanted child: those who are poor, those who live with one parent, those who have poor grades in school and those whose parents did not finish high school. As the National Research Council points out, teen mothers face "reduced employment opportunities, unstable marriages (if they occur at all), low incomes, and heightened health and developmental risks to the children. . . . Sustained poverty, frustration, and hopelessness are all too often the long-term outcomes." Compounding the tragedy is the fact that children of teen-age mothers are more likely to become teen parents themselves. The burden is felt by the entire society: The national costs of health and social service programs for families started by teen-agers amount to more than $19 billion a year.

Media accounts have tended to represent teen-age pregnancy as primarily a problem of the black community, and implicitly—or explicitly, as in the case of the 1986 CBS Special Report on the "vanishing" black family by Bill Moyers—they have attempted to blame the problem on the so-called degeneracy of the black family. Such distortions of fact are particularly dangerous because they coincide all too neatly with the insensitivity to blacks and the blame-the-victim ideology that the Reagan Administration so disastrously fostered.

High rates of teen pregnancy actually are as all-American as apple pie. Even when the figures for "nonwhite" teens were subtracted from the calculations, the rate of teen pregnancy in the United States in 1981 (83 per 1,000) far exceeded the teen pregnancy rates in all other major industrialized nations. In England and Wales, our closest competitors, the rate for teens of all races was just 45 per 1,000.

The fact of the matter is that teen-age pregnancy rates in the United States have a great deal more to do with class than they do with race. The majority of poor people in this country are white, and so are the majority of pregnant teenagers. In a report published in 1986, the Guttmacher Institute examined interstate differences in teen pregnancy rates.

It found that the percentage of teens who are black is relatively unimportant as a determinant of overall state variations in teen-age reproduction. It is states with higher percentages of poor people and of people living in urban areas—whatever their race—that have significantly higher teen pregnancy and birth rates.

Teen pregnancy is as grave a problem within many black communities as are poverty and social alienation. One-third of all blacks, and one-half of all black children, live in poverty. And today the pregnancy rate among teens of color is double that of white teens. One of every four black children is born to a teen-age mother; 90 percent of these children are born to unwed mothers. Such patterns can only intensify the problems already facing the black community. Disproportionately poor, blacks are disproportionately affected by the social and economic consequences of teen-age pregnancy.

We need only look to other Western nations to recognize both the cause and the solutions to our teen pregnancy problem. American teens are no more sexually active than their counterparts in Europe; and teen-agers abroad resort to abortion far less often than do those in the United States. There is a major cause for our higher rates of teen pregnancy and childbirth: the fundamental discomfort of Americans with sexuality. Unlike other Western societies, we have not yet accepted human sexuality as a normal part of life. The result is that our children, and many adults as well, are confused, frightened and bombarded by conflicting sexual messages.

Most parents recognize their role as the first and most important sexuality educators their children will have, providing information and sharing family values from the time their children are born. Nevertheless, many parents are unable to talk with their children about such sensitive issues as sex and human relationships. Schools do not fill the gap. Only seventeen states and the District of Columbia mandate comprehensive sex education. As a result, many teen-agers are abysmally ignorant about their reproductive functions.

The mass media, particularly television, only exacerbate the problem. Many teen-agers spend more time in front of the television than they do in the classroom, and their sexual behavior in part reflects what they have learned from this thoroughly unreliable teacher. Nowhere is it more apparent than on television that America suffers from sexual schizophrenia: We exploit sex, and at the same time we try to repress it. Programs and advertisements bombard viewers with explicit sexual acts and innuendo. One study indicates that in a single year, television airs 20,000 sexual messages. Yet rarely is there any reference to contraception or to the consequences of sexual activity.

A substantial number of teens believe that what they see on television is a faithful representation of life. Many believe that television gives a realistic picture of pregnancy and the consequences of sex. And large numbers of teens say they do not use contraceptives because they are "swept away" by passion—surely a reflection of the romanticized view of sex that pervades the mass media.

Network executives, though they apparently have few qualms about exploiting the sexual sell twenty-four hours a day, have the hypocrisy to claim that good taste forbids them to carry ads for contraceptives. Some of the networks recently decided to accept condom ads, though not during prime time, and those ads promote condoms only as protection against AIDS, not against pregnancy. It should not surprise us, then, that America's youths are sexually illiterate, or that 67 percent of sexually active teens either never use contraceptives or use them only occasionally.

We have not failed to resolve this problem for lack of majority agreement on how to do it. A 1988 Harris public opinion survey done for Planned Parenthood found a strong consensus about both the severity of the teen pregnancy problem and about how to solve it:

§ Ninety-five percent of Americans think that teen-age pregnancy is a serious problem in this country, up 11 percent from 1985.

§ Seventy-eight percent of parents believe that relaxed discussions between parents and children about sex will reduce unintended teen-age pregnancy.

§ Eighty-nine percent endorse school sex education.

§ Eighty percent support school referrals of sexually active teens to outside family-planning clinics.

§ Seventy-three percent favor making contraceptives available in school clinics.

School-linked clinics that offer birth control as part of general health care are growing in number in many areas of the country. Community support and involvement are crucial to their development, to insure that the programs are consistent with community values and needs.

Clearly the vast majority of Americans, regardless of racial, religious or political differences, strongly supports the very measures that have proven so effective in reducing teen pregnancy rates in other Western nations. Unfortunately, an extremist minority in this country has an entirely different outlook on sexuality—a minority that has a level of influence out of all proportion to its size. Eager to cultivate the anti–family planning, antiabortion fringe, the Reagan-Bush Administration and its cohorts in Congress sought to whittle down Federal funds for domestic and international family planning, limit sex education in the schools, eliminate confidentiality for birth control and abortion services and block the development of school-linked clinics. These vocal opponents object to everything that has proven successful elsewhere in the industrialized world. Their one and only solution to the problem of teen-age pregnancy is, "Just say no!" But just saying no prevents teen-age pregnancy the way "Have a nice day" cures chronic depression.

There is nothing inherent in American life that condemns us permanently to having the highest teen pregnancy rate in the Western world—nothing that Sweden, England, France, the Netherlands and Canada have been able to do that we cannot.

Parents must talk with their children about all aspects of sexuality—openly, consistently and often—beginning in early childhood. Every school district in the country should provide comprehensive sex education, from kindergarten through twelfth grade. Community groups need to support the development of school-linked health clinics. The media must present realistic, balanced information about relationships and the consequences of sex. Television, in particular, must end the restrictions on contraceptives advertising. Government—at the local, state and Federal levels—must live up to its obligation to eliminate any financial barriers to family-planning education and services and to foster a community environment in which our children can flourish and aspire to a productive and fulfilling life.

But we must also recognize that the teen pregnancy problem cannot be solved through sexuality education and family-planning services alone. If our efforts are to succeed, society must provide all our young people with a decent general education, tangible job opportunities, successful role models and real hope for the future.

It is only by placing such a comprehensive national agenda at the top of the priority list that our society can protect the creative and productive potential of its youth.

HOME REMEDY

A Mom's Prescription for Ailing Schools

VIRGINIA SEUFFERT

VIRGINIA SEUFFERT *lives with her husband and seven children in Oak Park, Illinois.*

What do Wolfgang Mozart, Thomas Edison, Leo Tolstoy, Abraham Lincoln, and the Seuffert kids of Oak Park, Illinois, all have in common? They all received a significant part of their formal education at home. Home-schoolers maintain a low profile, but experts estimate that as many as one million American families are teaching their children at home.

This trend is understandable in view of the sorry results of our nation's public school system. Well-heeled families can turn to private and parochial schools, but those of more modest means or from rural areas with no access to alternative schooling usually have to work with the entrenched National Education Association bureaucracy.

Our family's solution has been to provide our children with their elementary education at home. I am their teacher. And although I am no genius and completed only one year of college, the children's academic progress has been, by modern American standards, excellent. My five-year-old, Mark, is learning to add and subtract and can read simple stories. In five months, six-year-old Katie had completed a challenging first-grade program and is beginning second-grade work. Third-grader John is studying the history of major civilizations (prehistoric, Greek, Roman, and medieval), world geography, and Latin. My fourth-grade student, Carol, who is learning French and studying the five classes of vertebrates, will soon be starting fifth-grade math. Most days, lessons are accomplished in three hours. Work is assigned four days per week.

There have been tremendous personal rewards for me as well. School-age children are not nearly so pesky as toddlers and I find myself genuinely enjoying the extra time with my kids. I am getting an opportunity to study subjects I missed while in school—John and I are learning Latin together. Our family life-style is more relaxed now that we don't have to adhere to a school calendar. When we had out-of-town guests, lessons were dismissed for three days while we showed our friends the sights and toured Chicago's museums.

My greatest reward, however, is knowing that our children's characters are being shaped in our home and influenced by our values and religious beliefs. A home-schooled child is generally free of the dependency on peer approval so common in our nation's classrooms. My children spend more of their time with responsible, hardworking adults who love them and have their best interests at heart. Conventionally schooled students spend the majority of their days with other children who may ridicule or bully them, and they quickly learn to conform to the rules of the tribe. Character formation is not so easy to measure as academic progress, but is even more crucial.

From Home School to Harvard

Home-schooling has a long and honorable history. Famed 19th-century British philosopher and economist John Stuart Mill was educated at home by his father, James Mill. He studied Greek when he was three years old, reading Herodotus and Plato in the original before he started Latin studies at eight. That same year he began to supervise the instruction of his younger siblings. He had a passion for history, studied logic "seriously" at the age of 12, and went through a complete course in political economy at 13. He later wrote that his home education was an "experiment" that proved the ease with which young children may be taught advanced work: "If I had been by nature extremely quick of apprehension, or had possessed a very accurate or retentive memory, or were of a remarkably active and energetic character, the trial would not be conclusive; but in all these natural gifts I am rather below than above par; what I could do, could assuredly be done by any boy or girl of average capacity and healthy physical constitution...."

In our own time, Mary Pride was "afterschooled" by her father, a philosophy professor, while she attended conventional schools. As he had taught her to read when she was five, she found herself double-promoted when her first-grade teacher caught her reading *Jane Eyre*. Two years later, her father taught her the full eight years of elementary school math during one summer vacation. She skipped one year of high school and another in college. Presently Mrs. Pride teaches her own children and has become a noted author on what she refers to as "schoolproof" education.

Living on a remote homestead in California, David

and Micki Colfax have been teaching their four sons at home since 1973. Their oldest son, Grant, graduated from Harvard with high honors and is a recipient of a Fulbright Scholarship. Two younger brothers are presently undergraduates at that same university. The Colfaxes claim that their sole educational theory is that "children will learn, will aspire to excellence, if we recognize and respect their different interests and abilities and give them a chance to develop them...this is denied every day, in word and in action, in our schools."

Tedium at Public School

Naturally, not every home school will obtain such spectacular results, and not every parent finds conventional schooling as repressive as the Colfaxes do. My husband and I were very satisfied with the modest parochial school our children attended in upstate New York. At that small school, a dedicated staff, constantly trying to improve the curriculum, delivered a first-rate education in mixed-grade classrooms on a shoestring budget. The children were held to high standards of courtesy and personal morality as well as academic excellence. I found it ironic when my daughter's Brownie leader reported that Carol was the only six-year-old girl in the troop who could read the Brownie handbook. All the other girls attended the well-funded public elementary school. The experience my children had was not unique. Many graduates of this tiny New York elementary school excelled in high school and went on to study at top-flight colleges.

When our family moved to suburban Chicago in the summer of 1988, we settled one block from the local parish school, fully expecting that it would offer the same solid education. We soon discovered that mediocrity, so prevalent in the public schools of our nation, was seeping into the parochial system as well.

We found that the students' days were filled with mindless workbook assignments and other busywork. In contrast to the individual attention my children were accustomed to, this school offered a homogenized curriculum that made no allowances for pupils who were clearly in need of more intellectually challenging assignments. By the end of October, despite the children's high grade-point averages, we knew we needed an alternative.

The search for a new school illustrated to me what is wrong with modern American education. The local public schools have beautiful facilities, dedicated teachers, state-of-the-art equipment, and the nicest playgrounds I have ever seen, all of this funded by the highest property tax rate allowed under Illinois law. But 30 years after *Why Johnny Can't Read*, they still teach reading by the look-say method. Each class has only one reading group and spends the academic year studying unchallenging material of dubious literary value. The rest of the curriculum is equally uninspiring.

One typical second-grade social studies text talks about how people live in "communities" or "neighborhoods," and the people who live there are called "neighbors." It explains that some people live in single family "houses" and others live in "apartments." There's a chapter on neighborhood helpers: fire fighters put out fires, mail carriers deliver the mail, doctors and nurses help people who are sick, and so on. Based on this text, my kids had mastered second-grade social studies before they started kindergarten. I couldn't subject them to this tedious and pointless curriculum.

The children finished the year at a local Montessori school but we were still dissatisfied. Although we located a challenging junior-senior high school for our oldest son, we had four other school-age children and no acceptable alternative school within our budget. At this point, another mother who shared many of my concerns mentioned that she was considering teaching her children at home.

The idea of home-schooling the children initially seemed like an awfully radical solution. From the little I knew about this alternative, my vague impression was that home-schooling appealed to ultraconservatives who didn't want their children to learn about evolution or

---

Why am I, a college dropout, able to teach in three hours a day what the public schools are not able to do in six?

---

read *The Wizard of Oz*. Still, I was getting desperate and was anxious to avoid moving my children to yet another school that would not meet their needs. Home-schooling seemed worth looking into. I soon learned that, unlike conventional schools, which all seek to provide the same service with varying degrees of success, home-learning is based on diversity. The great variety of options available assure that motivated parents can find, or design, an educational program that will satisfy their children's needs.

Curricula Available

In her book, *The New Big Book of Home Learning*, home-school mom Mary Pride classifies home-based curricula by their general philosophies. I discovered that religiously conservative parents who home-school often use a strong "back-to-basics" approach. The Christian Liberty Academy, with an active enrollment of 20,000 home-study students in grades K-12, typifies this style. It is three-R's oriented, patriotic, and emphasizes Bible studies.

Many parents have been asking the public schools to return to unadorned academic studies, pointing out that, until recently, American education routinely produced excellent results using simple repetition and drill methods. The typical home-school back-to-basics program is free of sex education and substance abuse programs, AIDS education, values clarification, self-esteem exercises, and such nonsense as asking the children to write their own version of the Declaration of Independence without ever reading Jefferson's original. Most

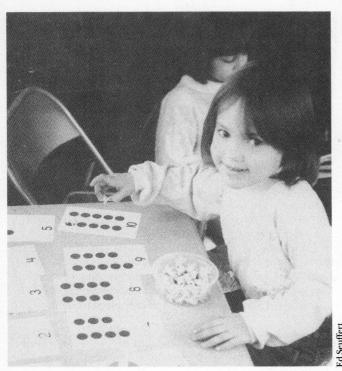

Home preschool: Claire spends the morning with "hands-on" material.

Ed Seuffert

progress. At the appropriate time, the parent introduces new concepts using materials unique to Montessori education. These might include beads (on chains, or formed into bars or cubes), various wooden shapes and puzzles, and cards that match pictures to concepts, all displayed in a manner designed to attract the young scholar. The necessary didactic materials are not inexpensive; I have a friend who has spent at least $10,000 outfitting her Montessori home. Her heavy investment does make sense in the long term, however, when compared with the cost of private education for her six children. This mother is very pleased with a Montessori home education as all of her children are years ahead of their contemporaries academically.

The Oak Meadow School of Ojai, California, which bases its curriculum on Rudolph Steiner's Waldorf School, offers a home-based program that would appeal to New Age, save-the-whale type parents. Steiner (1861-1925) wrote, "One should not ask, 'what does a person need to know and be able to do for the existing social order?' but rather, 'What gifts does a person possess and how may these be developed in him?'" The stress is on imagination, self-awareness, and closeness to Mother Earth. Younger students play more than work. Even after fifth grade, much of the learning is "hands on" and experiential in nature.

Hooked on Classics

We found what we were looking for in yet another category, loosely defined as classical learning. This is a fact-rich, "Great Books" type of curriculum with an emphasis on memorization and the student's ability to think logically and express his ideas effectively. While I found no current home-school program offering a truly classical approach (Latin, Greek, and classical literature in the early grades), I examined two pre-packaged programs that incorporate the classics.

The Calvert School has a prestigious reputation and appeals to those parents who would like their offspring to have a prep school education for a fraction of the cost. It is often used by missionary and diplomatic families because it provides all necessary materials. Along with textbooks and lesson plans, the school sends pencils, rulers, protractors and everything else needed to complete the assignments. Academically, Calvert is among the best, and several graduates (the school was founded in 1897) have gone on to distinguished careers. Calvert students study history, geography, classical literature, and the fine arts starting in the early grades. According to Mary Pride, "A child can graduate from Calvert's eighth-grade course, take a few achievement tests, and go straight to the college of his choice."

The Seton Home Study School places primary emphasis on turning out students who are well grounded in Catholic doctrine and practice, as they receive superior academic preparation. I was very attracted by its flexibility. The school stresses that its lesson plans are only to be used as guidelines, and if a child has mastered a particular concept, he or she moves on and does not complete endless, useless workbook pages. Seton is also willing to customize a program to suit individual needs and abilities, a feature not offered by every school.

programs teach reading phonetically, use fact-rich history, geography, and science texts, and insist on solid preparation in math and English grammar. (John Saxon's math texts, which stress drill in basic arithmetic, are gaining in home-school popularity.)

Another popular direction in home learning is the "unschooling" approach advocated by the late John Holt and, to a lesser degree, by Raymond Moore and Maria Montessori. Holt believed that children, left to their own devices and without adult interference, will want to learn and need only be allowed the freedom to pursue their interests. His followers shy away from all pre-packaged educational programs. They favor an approach where the parent provides educational resources, such as encyclopedias, dictionaries, and atlases, as well as such learning opportunities as museums or home gardens.

Moore and his associates are leaders in the home-schooling movement and base their recommendations on decades of solid research. They believe that all formal education should be delayed until the child is at least eight to 10 years old. Before children learn to read, write, and cipher, Moore suggests they develop strong personal traits of hard work, self-confidence, and community responsibility. After that he recommends a "project" or "integrated" approach where children learn the three R's while being heavily involved in community service, regular household chores, and home-based businesses.

Although most Montessori education occurs in a school setting, parents have found that this method can be transplanted to the home. This system allows the child to set the pace and study whatever is appealing, in a controlled environment. The role of the parent is to prepare the specialized classroom and observe individual

We settled on Seton for its flexibility and its religious training. When the books and lesson plans arrived over the summer I knew we had made the right choice. They have a pioneer, can-do attitude at Seton that makes you want to stand up and cheer. Obviously sharing my distaste for the "Juan and Amy meet Abe Lincoln" school of social studies, Seton's staff has written its own history texts for first and second grade. Six- and seven-year-olds read about famous people and events from America's past, beginning with the voyages of discovery. My first-grader loves it.

Typically, the science curriculum for the early elementary grades emphasizes the human body, good health habits, and other topics young children can relate to. In conventional schooling this translates to a workbook page on the five senses where the student has to color things you see blue, things you taste green, and so on. My Katie's first-grade science book, again written by the Seton staff, explains the workings of the actual organs and gives the child a diagram to color. My lesson plans explain that the student is not expected to retain all the details (the kids aren't tested at this level in science anyway) but they will come away with an understanding that the five senses and other physical functions originate in parts of the body, and that they can be studied and understood. Not bad for first grade!

The older grades use a variety of textbooks, and the excellence of the readers, for example, is obvious to any parent familiar with more modern versions. Most of the selections have been written by famous children's authors, not a committee of reading experts, so they are good literature. The stories were clearly collected with moral formation in mind. They stress traditional values of honesty, obedience, and kindness, and encourage the children to develop personal qualities of hard work and individual initiative.

Immediate Feedback

Last summer, the children and I set up our classroom on a winterized porch. We purchased used desks, globes, and puzzle maps, some Montessori materials, flash cards, and, quite frankly, anything else I could think of. I was convinced that we had found our educational alternative and determined to make home-schooling a success.

I attempted to predict potential problems and plan for them in advance. One concern was my baby, who was nine months old last September. We resolved to wake her up with the rest of the family at 6:00 A.M., so she would be ready for her morning nap at 8:30. This gave me almost three hours, while she slept, to review the children's assignments with them. Unlike conventional classrooms, which are burdened with administrative tasks and classroom management, in home schools three hours is usually sufficient.

We begin each morning with the Pledge of Allegiance and a brief prayer. The three oldest students (Carol in fourth grade, John in third grade, and Katie in first grade) begin the daily assignments I have written for them in a weekly lesson planner. Independent work is encouraged. If needed, I explain the directions or the concept of the lesson. As the children complete their assignments, I correct them and give immediate feed-

Mark, John, teacher, and Claire. "My greatest reward is knowing that our children's characters are being shaped by our values and religious beliefs."

Ed Seuffert

back—one of the greatest advantages of home-schooling and virtually impossible in the traditional schoolroom of 20 or more students.

My actual teaching is divided into two categories. First I work with a specific child on a problem area. John, for example, is a whiz at most subjects, but is bored and impatient with rote math. It is far more effective for me to give him oral problems or flash card review than to assign a textbook page that he will moon over for half the morning. Carol is a meticulous student but lacks spelling skills. I give her word dictation, based on phonetic rules, and I am seeing fine improvement.

Naturally, there is also some subject matter that is best taught directly to the children, at least in the initial stages, and other learning that should be regularly monitored. This is my second category of teaching. Katie and I spend 15 minutes each day with her reading book. By November of first grade, she was in the second-grade reader. John and Carol, both in fourth-grade reading, typically have longer assignments that they read silently. Once or twice a week they read poetry or a short story to me and we discuss the content and the style of the piece.

After the older children are working steadily, I start with Mark, my kindergarten student. He has phonics drill, completes some workbook pages in phonics, visual discrimination, penmanship, or math, and his formal studies are finished for the day, all in about one hour. Mark and his three-year-old sister, Claire, will often spend the remainder of the morning playing with some of our "hands on" material, math manipulatives, sandpaper letters and numbers, sea shells, or Montessori materials. Sometimes they look at picture books—I have some wonderful nature books—or they color and draw. By December, Mark had learned all his basic consonant and short vowel sounds and had begun to read. He can recognize as well as add and subtract numbers up to 10.

If it sounds simple, that's because it is. While I do work hard, teaching is interesting and rewarding and not

Fourth-grader Carol. The typical home-school back-to-basics program is free of sex education, values clarification, and self-esteem exercises.

particularly complicated. In addition to spending my mornings in the classroom, I devote a few hours each weekend to my lesson plans and the minimal record keeping required by Seton.

Cost for Four Kids, $2,300

The cost of home-schooling is modest when compared to other public-school alternatives. My tuition and book bill from Seton (just under $1,300 this year for four children) is about half of what I was paying the local parish school and one-fifth of the Montessori school tuition. I have cleaning help, practically a must for a family of nine people with the equivalent of a working mother. This costs $70 per week, but I am saving on the extra expenses associated with more traditional education such as uniforms, club fees, bag lunches, and transportation. I have probably spent another $1,000 on enrichment materials, but much of this is discretionary— a more cost-conscious parent could just as easily make flash cards as buy them, for example. Educational catalogs are filled with textbooks, interesting learning games, science projects and equipment, and early education manipulatives. I admit, I have no sales resistance.

Even without the catalogs, the possibilities for enrichment are endless. Most weeks, my children have only four days of formal lessons and spend Fridays on field trips. We have spent numerous days at the Field Museum

of Natural History, the Museum of Science and Industry, the Shedd Aquarium, the Brookfield Zoo, and the Adler Planetarium. Additionally, we are planning trips to our state capitol in Springfield and to Washington, D.C.

I try to take advantage of the flexibility allowed by the Seton staff to supplement their lessons. For example, although my first-grader, Katie, reads above grade level, she can still benefit by daily phonics review to develop her reading and spelling skills. I found a textbook that reviews phonics as the child learns to type. She's enjoying an otherwise tedious review as she learns a valuable new skill. Carol and John are also learning to type and are more cooperative in completing their written assignments on our word processor than on looseleaf paper.

In our modern world, study of a foreign language is crucial but all too often delayed or ignored in our public schools. Carol and Katie are learning French using a combination of textbooks, workbooks, and cassette tapes. Third-grader John was attracted to a workbook that teaches Latin grammar and shows the relationship between that language and English.

The abbreviated school day allows the children more time for extracurricular activities. "Gym" is figure skating lessons during the winter and the children get plenty of free ice time. When spring comes, we start Little League baseball and, in the fall, John plays soccer and the girls are cheerleaders. "Music," predictably, involves instrumental instruction. All the children are involved in church activities.

Considering their busy life-styles, it amazes me how often I am questioned about my children's ability to interact socially with their peers. I have a growing suspicion that the importance professional educators are placing on socialization skills is directly linked to the public outcry about their failure to develop intellectual skills. To become socially competent adults, my children must associate with individuals of different ages and backgrounds. The arbitrary grouping of children according to age can lead to an unfortunate peer dependence that will do little to foster desirable social traits.

Not for Everyone

Of course, home education is not without drawbacks. One friend, who started when I did, already has her children back in the classroom. Home-schooling dominates your time and demands a certain energy level that not everyone has. It would be difficult for a working mother to teach her children, and many women are unable or unwilling to delay their return to the work force. Other mothers eagerly anticipate their youngest child's school entry so they can pursue organizational work, hobbies, or even finish their own education. The tuition and book expenses, although generally reasonable, are still out of the question for some low-income families.

One worry of potential home-schoolers, their legal status under compulsory education laws, seems to be less of a problem in recent years. The situation varies from state to state. I am fortunate that Illinois is very friendly to home-schoolers and there are virtually no regulations currently being enforced with any rigor. Seton's director, Mary Kay Clark, feels New York state is at the other extreme of home-school tolerance, requiring monthly progress reports from home-school families. Still, Clark is optimistic about the legal position of home education in general, and religious-affiliated home schools in particular. Many of the court cases challenging compulsory education requirements have involved religious denominations. So far, courts seem to agree that parental authority is paramount regarding rearing children according to the dictates of their faith.

Preliminary Report Card

The Seuffert Home School has completed only its first semester, so it is premature to make any long-term judgments about its effectiveness. Most of my children's accomplishments are self-evident in the home setting; *i.e.*, if a fourth-grader completes a Level 4 math assignment with ease and accuracy, you know the skills are being mastered. Seton provides me textbook answer keys and teacher's manuals to guide my expectations and grading. They also provide quarterly exams, which they correct. More important, their professional teachers grade a number of required written compositions, giving me a more objective and experienced opinion. Finally, once each year, Seton sends me the Stanford Achievement Test, a nationally recognized standardized test to help me gauge the children's progress. So far, their achievements have been well above average.

The most self-evident question is: Why is a college dropout able to accomplish, with relative ease on a heated porch, what a well-funded, beautifully equipped modern school, staffed by highly educated professionals, backed by over a century of educational research, seems incapable of doing? Are administrative and custodial functions of the public schools so time-consuming that I am able to accomplish in three hours what they are not able to do in six?

The answer might very well be a simple matter of goals. The typical public school tries to be all things to all parents (and children), whereas the home-school teacher can concentrate on exactly what she wants. Briefly, my children must be morally and intellectually prepared to meet with confidence whatever challenges they may face as adults. Learning to color within the lines or understanding the meaning of Mother's Day do nothing to forward my aim; solid academic preparation and strong character formation do. Our home life and their time spent in school are wasted when this goal is not pursued.

Modern educators seem to have forgotten what children are capable of—the real possibilities. *The Elson Reader*, printed in 1926 for sixth grade, insisted that a text for that level must score high when tested for quality, variety, organization, and quantity of literature, and that "the foundation of the book must be the acknowledged masterpieces of American and British authors." The student is shown the works of Audubon, Emerson,

Wordsworth, James Russell Lowell, Kilmer, Longfellow, Washington Irving, Dickens, Tennyson, Whittier, and Hawthorne, among others, as well as Theodore Roosevelt, Abraham Lincoln, Benjamin Franklin, and Woodrow Wilson. Additionally, the students read excerpts from the *Iliad* and the *Odyssey*. Consider the effects of exposure to these thoughts before the turmoil of adolescence begins.

Today, in sharp contrast to this, much of the information our children are taught in the public schools is frivolous, unpatriotic, anti-religious, and anti-traditional, and too often schools are downright unsafe. Public schools are dismally failing to impart to our children the basic knowledge they will need to be the future leaders of our nation.

The Gallup Organization recently surveyed children from 10 nations on their knowledge of geography. As usual, American youth came in dead last. My home-schooled third-grader, John, without any warning or preparation, outscored the top-ranked Swedes. Last May,

---

My vague impression was that home schooling appealed to ultraconservatives who didn't want their children to learn about evolution or read *The Wizard of Oz.*

---

when the National Geographic Society held the first National Geography Bee, first prize went to a 15-year-old boy from a Seventh-Day Adventist School with a total enrollment of seven.

It is the responsibility of parents, not the federal government nor the local school superintendent, to ensure that children receive the best possible education. Unfortunately, parents have delegated this responsibility and should recognize that their trust has been misplaced. Parents and children cannot afford to wait 10 years to see if the current educational reform movement returns excellence to our schools.

Many concerned parents are already giving several million American children a far superior education outside the nation's public schools, despite legal and financial obstacles. It is time to remove these barriers and formulate policy that encourages alternative learning and makes it financially possible for even the neediest Americans to give their children a quality education.

ADOLESCENCE:
Path to a Productive Life or a Diminished Future?

The Carnegie Council on Adolescent Development: Work in Progress

Most American adolescents come through the critical years from ages ten to twenty relatively unscathed. With good schools, supportive families, and caring community institutions, they grow to adulthood meeting the requirements of the workplace, the commitments to families and friends, and the responsibilities of citizenship. Even under less-than-optimal conditions for healthy growth, many youngsters manage to become contributing members of society. Some achieve this feat despite threats to their well-being that were almost unknown to their parents and grandparents.

But there are other adolescents for whom poverty, racial prejudice, parental unemployment, family breakup, or disintegrated communities can mean the defeat of aspiration and hope. The obstacles in their path can impair physical and emotional health, destroy motivation and ability to succeed in school and jobs, and damage personal relationships and the chance to become an effective parent.

Across all social groups, there are young people who drop out of school, commit violent or otherwise criminal acts, become pregnant, become mentally ill, abuse drugs and alcohol, attempt suicide, or die or become disabled from injuries.

These two groups of adolescents — the majority who appear to be making a reasonably successful transition to adulthood and the struggling minority for whom meaningful options can fade by the age of fourteen or fifteen — are the urgent concerns of the Carnegie Council on Adolescent Development, an operating program of Carnegie Corporation. The Council was established in 1986 to place the challenges of the adolescent years higher on the nation's agenda for action. It seeks to stimulate broad-based understanding of this vulnerable age and to generate concerted public and private interest in facilitating the transition of youth to adulthood.

Composed of national leaders from education, law, science, health, religion, business, the media, youth-serving agencies, and government, the Council is chaired by David A. Hamburg, the Corporation's president. Through task forces and working groups, meetings and seminars, commissioned reports, sponsored studies, and other activities, the Council seeks to break through disciplinary and professional barriers, to synthesize the best knowledge and wisdom about the adolescent experience in America, and to map uncharted territory for further exploration.

During its first year, the Council chose to work in two major areas: the untapped potential of the school as an education- and health-promoting environment for young adolescents and the assessment of preventive interventions for serious adolescent problems. The first activity resulted in *Turning Points: Preparing American Youth for the 21st Century.* Issued in June this report helped to mobilize public and professional attention toward a neglected level in recent educational change efforts — the middle grades. For most American youths, the biological, psychological, and cognitive changes of early adolescence are accompanied by a dramatic shift to a new school environment, with different teachers and peer groups. The new environment can have a crucial impact on adolescents' continued engagement with education and thus have consequences for their entire lives. For many, middle school is literally a turning point toward a diminished future.

Turning Points concluded, among other things, that "a volatile mismatch exists between the organization and curriculum of middle-grade schools and the intellectual, emotional, and interpersonal needs of young adolescents." Many large middle grade schools, the report noted, "function as mills that contain and process endless streams of students." The report's many recommendations include creating smaller learning environments for students; dividing teachers and students into teams to provide an atmosphere and structure conducive to learning; and ways to foster the development of critical thinking skills. The report urged a transformation of the curriculum to emphasize a core of common knowledge that places renewed emphasis on responsible citizenship and the development of healthful life styles.

A follow-up effort to *Turning Points* is the Middle Grade School State Policy Initiative. A grant program sponsored by the Corporation, it is intended to foster cooperation among various state agencies in the quest for improved middle grades education.

All adolescents have basic human needs that must be met if they are to negotiate safe passage to adulthood. Among these are the need to have caring relationships with adults, to receive guidance in facing sometimes overwhelming challenges, to be a valued member of a constructive peer group, to become a socially competent individual who has the skills to cope successfully with everyday life, and to believe in a promising

(WHO photo by J. Mohr)

Families are the most important support system in the life of an adolescent. Today, however, parents are often not available, and teenagers are left to fend for themselves or fall into peer pressure groups that can be negative to their development.

future with real opportunities. These principles underlie Council members' belief that, with the social and economic transformations under way in American life, major changes must be made in the preparation of young people for adulthood.

As its second activity, therefore, the Council established a steering committee to search for generic approaches to the prevention of a wide range of problems in adolescent health and education. The committee chose to focus on two kinds of constructive intervention in early adolescence — life skills training and social support networks. Work thus far has resulted in two reports, *School and Community Support Programs that Enhance Adolescent Health and Education*, and *Life Skills Training: Preventive Interventions for Young Adolescents* (both published in April of 1990).

As an essential building block for these activities, the Council commissioned a synthesis of current research on adolescent development, which is the focus of this issue's main story. To be published in the fall of 1990, *At the Threshold: The Developing Adolescent* is intended in part to stimulate research on aspects of adolescent development that have hitherto been slighted, such as the experience and developmental processes of adolescence among ethnic minorities. Meetings of public and private funders will be convened to discuss the findings and implications for research support in key areas identified in the volume.

During its second year, the Council considered ways to address the health status of adolescents. Adolescence is generally considered to be a period of good health, but the relationship between health status and behavior points to a need for greater attention to adolescent health needs. Stimulated by

congressional members of the Council, the Corporation is cooperating with the Office of Technology Assessment of the U.S. Congress in the first national-level, comprehensive assessment of the health of American adolescents. After the report is released in 1991, it is expected that Congress will hold hearings to highlight the report's findings.

The Council itself is sponsoring a major assessment of the current state and future directions of adolescent health promotion efforts. Knowledge about adolescent health promotion is fragmented among several disciplines. Furthermore, it is not reaching those involved in developing and implementing adolescent health promotion programs. This new volume will bring together theoretical and empirical research, assess gaps in research and practice, and identify promising approaches to adolescent health promotion.

Throughout the Council's history, sustained interest has been expressed in the potential of visual, auditory, and print media to play a constructive role in the lives of adolescents. Through a consultant based in Los Angeles, the Council and key media organizations have cosponsored a series of seminars and other meetings linking scholars knowledgeable about adolescents with professionals in the news and entertainment industry. The aim is to enhance the ability and commitment of the media to engage public concern about adolescence and to deepen understanding of these critical years. Two commissioned papers on the influences of the media on adolescent development have resulted in the reports, *Strategies for Enhancing Adolescents' Health through Music Media*, and *Popular Music in Early Adolescence*.

Another initiative of the Council is an examination of volun-

tary organizations in the neighborhood and community —
youth agencies, religious youth groups, senior citizens groups,
libraries, museums, recreation and sports programs, and after-
school programs — that can provide supportive environments
for young people. The lack of these supports is serious in low-
income and very poor communities, but it is also a problem
throughout the country. Existing research points to the powerful beneficial influences that community organizations can have
on disadvantaged youth.

Through such activities as these, new territories that are
fundamental to understanding and preventing adolescent casu-
alties are being explored. For example, a grant has been made
for studies of adolescent decision making, resulting in the
working papers, *Risk Taking in Adolescence: A Decision-
Making Perspective*, and *Adolescent Health Care Decision
Making: The Law and Public Policy*. The hope is to find better
ways of understanding how adolescents make decisions about
risk-taking behaviors and to develop curricula and other interventions that are well grounded in evidence.

Families are the most important support system in the lives
of adolescents, and young people report that their parents are
the people they turn to first for moral guidance. Yet parents are
frequently unavailable to them, physically and psychologically.
Very little is known about the diversity and efficacy of efforts
aimed at reengaging families in the education and health of
American youth or at informing and supporting families with
adolescents. In contrast to the early childhood years, there are
few networks or associations of family support groups for this
age group. Teachers and mental health professionals are not
trained to work with families with adolescents. The Council
commissioned an informal survey of family support programs
during adolescence, now published in the report, *Preventive
Programs that Support Families with Adolescents*.

Despite many opportunities for constructive public and private action toward adolescents, they remain a relatively
neglected focus of social policy. Creating a favorable policy
environment for adolescents at different levels of government
and in the voluntary sector, along with broad public education
about adolescents, will receive the highest priority from the
Council in the coming years. The article in this issue represents
the first *Quarterly* report on some of the work and concerns
of the Council.

First Place in Seattle is one place a homeless child knows won't move on him

When School Is A Haven

Deborah Berger

AT FIRST GLANCE, THE students at First Place look like children in any elementary school. They study reading, writing and math. Some have to be reminded to pay attention when the teacher is talking. And they can make quite a racket at recess.

But look closer: Notice the two girls bundled into heavy winter jackets, which they are afraid to remove—even in a warm classroom —because, they say, "we might lose them." Listen to Alexius and Alexandria Slider, 8-year-old twins, describe their home: a single, cramped motel room they share for the time being with their mother and younger sister. "It's horrible," says Alexius. "There are roaches," adds Alexandria, "and people fight, and we can't have pets." Take a seat at the lunch table and hear the kids compare notes on different shelters: "Where I live, it's worse," 10-year-old Brian Davis tells Alexandria. "The police are there every night, and people are always fighting."

These students are homeless. And First Place, in Seattle, Wash., is one of a handful of programs around the country designed to meet the educational and emotional needs of homeless children.

No one knows the exact number of homeless children not in school. The U.S. Department of Education, relying on figures from 42 states, puts the total at about 67,000. The National Coalition for the Homeless cites 200,000 as a more accurate estimate.

What keeps these children out of school? When a family becomes homeless, parents usually find it impossible to transport their children to the school that they originally attended. The red tape that is involved in enrolling them in a public school near the shelter can be difficult and intimidating for adults focusing chiefly on daily survival. Homeless parents also often delay enrolling a child in school because they don't expect to be without a permanent address for more than a couple of weeks. Several months later, however, the family is still homeless, and the child has missed a lot of school.

Carolyn Pringle did not wait for the government to solve the problem of educating homeless kids. In a few hectic months, this mother of three—a former schoolteacher—assembled a staff, solicited contributions from major companies and foundations, incorporated First Place as a nonprofit agency and then arranged for the Seattle School District to provide buses to pick up children from shelters all over the city. Last April, First Place opened its doors. The program, which occupies two classrooms in a graffiti-scarred brick building, is for children in kindergarten through sixth grade.

Going to a regular school can be devastating for a homeless child. At First Place, however, kids don't worry about coming to school without shoes; someone here will find them a pair. They don't have to explain to classmates why they can't invite them over to their house to play. Or why they have moved again.

For children who may not know from one week to the next where they'll be living, First Place is an anchor in a sea of change. Transient parents can keep their child here until they find a permanent home. Getting a child into the program is simple. It took just one phone call for Helen Thompson to enroll her sons, 11-year-old Christopher and Jimmy, 8.

"Moving from school to school is a great stress on my boys, and they have had enough stress in their lives," says Thompson, who worked in a factory until she suffered a stroke seven years ago. Last summer, Thompson gave up her apartment. When her plans to move into a rental house didn't work out, she and her boys found themselves homeless. Nevertheless, the 35-year-old mother was determined that her sons would not miss school. She moved her family from a shelter in the suburbs to emergency housing in Seattle so Christopher and Jimmy could attend First Place.

Five mornings a week, the Thompson boys board a yellow school bus in front of the Broadview Emergency Housing Shelter. By 9:30 a.m., Christopher, Jimmy and the other kids pile off the bus and race into First Place. Their school day includes breakfast, academic work, lunch and quiet time for reading.

Every day, a handful of volunteers assist the two salaried teachers, Kelley Clevenger and Mónica Ferro. Knowing that students stay, on average, four to five weeks (some attend for only a few days; others stay much longer), the two women teach an adapted form of the public-school curriculum. One morning, 12 students can be found printing and illustrating their own books. The classroom—filled with books, toys and colorful posters—is amazingly quiet. Clevenger, who possesses that essential ingredient of all masterful teachers—eyes in the back of her head—moves from child to child, administering praise, offering suggestions, making corrections when necessary. "Miss Kelley!" cries one young boy. "I finished first!" His faces glows as Clevenger reads his work aloud to the class. She rewards him with a certificate for a free meal at a local fast-food eatery. This is just one of the many items—including sneakers, books and furniture—that have been donated to First Place.

Despite the hardships they've suffered, some students do extremely well. At his old school, Christopher Thompson was an A student in the fourth grade and a gifted artist. At First Place, he's doing sixth-grade work. Clevenger is so impressed with his illustrations that she wants to get his book published. Alexius and Alexandria Slider work at or above their grade level. "We talk about them going to college," says their mother, Marva Slider. "I don't want them to have my heartaches."

Some educators believe that homeless children belong in regular public schools. "Children should not be segregated," says Yvonne Rafferty, Ph.D., director of research for Advocates for Children and co-author of a report on the education of homeless children in New York. (New York City law prohibits any sort of separate program for its homeless children.) The staff at First Place points out, however, that these youngsters often need individual attention, counseling and help in catching up with the schoolwork they have missed while being uprooted. "What we offer is an option for families who need extra support," says Deb Brinley-Koempel, the social worker at First Place. "Our goal is to mainstream the kids once they're stabilized. We're not a program for forever and ever."

About half of the students at First Place come from families racked by violence and abuse. Some live in shelters for battered women, the locations of which must be kept secret. That's where 5-year-old John Michaels and his mother, Brenda, lived for a time

last summer. (Both names have been changed to ensure their protection.) "I never thought that we would be living in emergency housing or be on welfare," says Brenda Michaels. "I've always worked." But a combination of abuse from her husband, a lack of child support and the inability to afford day care on her office-worker's salary took their toll.

Fridays at First Place are particularly difficult. "We give the children books and stuffed animals to take home," says Kelley Clevenger, "but it's hard for the kids to leave for two days. We try to love and nurture them. To help sustain them. After a while, they learn that we can be trusted." The teacher pauses. "Not all have given up. They *can* have a good future."

As we go to press, most of these students have moved and been enrolled in regular schools. Their places have been filled by other homeless children.

Helping Homeless Children

THE LAW IS ON THE SIDE OF THOSE who want to keep homeless children in school. The Stewart B. McKinney Homeless Assistance Act, passed by Congress in 1987, provides money for states to set up an office or authority to help implement their plans for educating these children. (All states except Hawaii have submitted plans and are to report their progress to the federal government by April.) The McKinney Act will *not*, however, finance the school programs; that is each state's responsibility.

Meanwhile, communities across the nation are struggling to meet the educational needs of children of the homeless. Here are some examples:

- In San Diego, the Harbor Summit School sits just a few steps from the St. Vincent de Paul Joan Kroc Center, which helps the homeless.
- In Tacoma, Wash., the Eugene P. Tone School is a joint effort of the Tacoma School District and the Tacoma YWCA.
- In Los Angeles, homeless kids receive extra tutoring and health services at Coeur D'Alene Elementary School, thanks to a $70,000 grant from the Greater Los Angeles Partnership for the Homeless.
- In Minneapolis, homeless children attend the public school where they were formerly enrolled—and the school district provides transportation wherever possible. Kids new to the area have tutoring in the morning and a special program at a nearby elementary school in the afternoon.

For more information on First Place, send a business-sized SASE to: First Place, Dept. P, P.O. Box 15112, Seattle, Wash. 98115-0112.

AIDS PREVENTION THROUGH EDUCATION

Is Your School Ready For AIDS?

y name is Michael. I am a teacher in Seattle, and I have AIDS.

With these simple words, a teacher begins an open letter to educators on the impact of AIDS—the real price not just of the disease, but of the anonymity it requires.

I want to tell the administrators at my school that I have AIDS, because there are times when I could use their support. I would like my faculty to know that I am living with AIDS, to help break down the myths and the fears about this disease.... I would like to take my educational skills beyond the classroom—to do public speaking about what it is like to live with AIDS....I cannot, because to do so would very likely jeopardize my right to teach, and I love my work....

You walk into your classrooms day after day thinking that you know no one with AIDS, while I stand in the classroom next door, a living resource I can't even tell you exists. So I lose your support. And you lose my example. But even more tragic than that, our students lose.

Although Michael is a teacher, he could just as easily be a student. And though Michael writes from Seattle, it could just as easily be your city, your school, your classroom. With an estimated 1.5 million Americans infected

with the virus that causes AIDS, sooner or later someone with AIDS—a student or a staffer—will arrive at your school, hoping for your support, fearing your reaction. Are you ready?

To help you, NEA's Health Information Network has created an imaginative AIDS awareness and education workshop. The HIV Education and Training program is designed to prevent the spread of HIV (the Human Immunodeficiency Virus, which causes AIDS) and to protect the rights of those afflicted. Comprehensive in scope, the two-day workshop combines information with policy guidelines and the opportunity to examine the public and personal issues surrounding the spread of this

deadly disease. The "open letter from Michael" in its entirety is a component of this program.

"Many educators don't appreciate how extensive a problem AIDS is. They don't see it as an epidemic," says Jim Williams, director of NEA's Health Information Network. "Unless they know an HIV-positive child or teacher in their school, the idea of an AIDS epi-

demic doesn't hit home. This project brings it home to them."

Fred Gould is a veteran UniServ representative in Chatsworth, Ga. When he first sat down in the NEA AIDS workshop this fall, he expected just another service workshop. "I felt I knew a great deal about AIDS," says Gould, "and I wondered how this would help my efforts in the field.

"But as I sat through the training, its value became clear," adds Gould. "What I hadn't realized was the severity and magnitude of this epidemic. It isn't confined to inner cities or specific populations. There's no miracle cure— not even any comprehensive programs or policies. Education is the only weapon

against AIDS, and that's why this program is necessary, not only for us but for everyone in education."

Gould is one of dozens of UniServ representatives and staff members who have participated in the NEA program. Once trained, staffers continue the awareness effort by conducting training workshops for Association leaders, schools, and members.

In the 1990s AIDS will spare no school. What will happen when you and your colleagues face a student—or a staffer—with AIDS? NEA has developed guidelines and an imaginative training program to help every school cope with America's number one public health challenge.

An AIDS Quiz

Ignorance and misinformation about AIDS can be dangerous—even deadly. Find out how much you know about AIDS: True or false?

1. A few people have become infected by the virus that causes AIDS by touching the tears or saliva of a person with AIDS.
2. Women can transmit HIV to their sex partners.
3. A positive HIV antibody test result means a person has AIDS.
4. Needle-sharing has caused most of the cases of AIDS in women and infants.
5. Sexual experimentation and crack cocaine use are causing a dramatic increase in AIDS cases among teenagers.
6. HIV is transmitted by casual contact, e.g. by touching drinking fountains, toilet seats, and eating utensils handled by HIV-infected persons.

Answers

1. *False.* The virus has been found in tears and saliva, but there have been no reported cases of transmission of HIV this way. AIDS is transmitted only through unprotected sexual intercourse, direct introduction into the bloodstream (needles), or from mother to child during pregnancy or delivery.
2. *True.* HIV can be transmitted from an infected woman to a man—or vice versa.
3. *False.* A positive HIV antibody test result indicates that a person has been infected with HIV. It is still unclear what percentage of HIV-infected people will develop AIDS or AIDS-related illnesses.
4. *True.* Just over half the women who've contracted AIDS had shared IV drug needles. Many of the rest were infected by sex partners who'd shared needles. Nearly 80 percent of all children with AIDS were infected by their mothers during pregnancy or delivery.
5. *True.* Crack, which can lead to promiscuity and sex-for-drugs trades, is partly responsible for the increase in teen AIDS cases.
6. *False.* CDC says HIV cannot be transmitted through casual contact, including shaking hands, coughing, and sneezing. You also cannot become infected with the virus through eating utensils, drinking fountains, or toilet seats.

Supported by the U.S. Centers for Disease Control (CDC), this ambitious five-year AIDS prevention project—begun in 1988—is designed to teach local communities a critical lesson: it's never too early to develop comprehensive health education programs and policies to deal with the gravest public health crisis facing our nation.

A simple set of statistics testify to the urgency of this effort. According to CDC, an estimated 1.5 million Americans have tested positive for HIV. As of September 1989, 110,000 Americans had AIDS; by 1993, an estimated 450,000 will have been diagnosed with the disease. Even more startling, between June 1988 and August 1989 the number of teenagers with AIDS jumped by 43 percent. The increase substantiated early warnings by such experts as former U.S. Surgeon General C. Everett Koop that risky sexual practices by teens are precipitating a wave of HIV infection among our nation's youth.

"Behavioral scientists and medical experts alike say AIDS education must start early and continue throughout a child's education if it's to have any impact," says Williams. "To achieve that, we must work among ourselves and in our communities.

"This training project is only the beginning of the NEA effort," adds Williams. "We're also setting up an HIV Education and Training project that addresses the specific needs of minority students. In the spring we plan to have another component ready—an educational training package complete with a video showing veteran teachers as they carry out successful AIDS teaching strategies. The package will also include resources and discussion guides to help members develop their own teaching programs.

"Education is the best method we have," says Williams, "to stop this disease from killing our colleagues and our students." In the closing words of Michael's letter:

I invite each of you to continue the process of education that will allow you to release your fear of AIDS and of people with AIDS...I invite you to open your minds and your eyes and your hearts so that when the teacher with AIDS in your school looks around, hoping to find someone to trust, you will be there...then share your example with your students. This is not only a personal issue. It is an educational imperative.

—Anita Merina

RESOURCES

Responding to HIV and AIDS, a booklet available from the NEA Health Information Network, 100 Colony Square, Suite 200, Atlanta, GA 30361.

Teaching Strategies for AIDS Prevention: Helping Teachers Get Started. An educational training package for teachers, including a curriculum guide and video show. Scheduled for release in the spring by the NEA Health Information Network.

Infection, Your Immune System and AIDS. A high school and college HIV/AIDS education program with excellent graphics and detail, published by the Enterprise for Education and the Massachusetts Medical Society. Enterprise for Education, 1320-A Third Street, Santa Monica, CA 90401.

Hotlines
The National AIDS Hotline:
   1-800-342-AIDS
Spanish language: 1-800-344-SIDA
Hearing impaired: 1-800-AIDS-TTY
National Gay and Lesbian Task
   Force Crisisline: 1-800-221-7044

AIDS Cases in the U.S. Reported to the Centers for Disease Control, 1981–89 (cumulative), with Projections to 1993

Year	Number of Cases
1981	372
1983	4,311
1985	20,800
1987	61,043
1989	109,167
1992	365,000
1993	450,000

Source: U.S. Centers for Disease Control

Rethinking Retention

Holding students back may do more harm than good

SUMMER BREAK WAS just around the corner, but middle school teacher Sharon Lee's thoughts were not yet on vacation. First she had to face an annual dilemma: whether to retain her slow learners or promote them to the next grade.

"June is a day away, and retention and promotion are on our minds," Lee said last spring as she was winding up the school year at Boston's Martin Luther King Jr. Middle School. "If a child ekes by—passing with a D minus—I feel in a quandary about what to do. Am I helping or hurting this child if I pass him or her on to the next grade?"

The dilemma is one that many thousands of the nation's teachers grapple with each year. And the issue is becoming even thornier now that new research suggests the downside of retention may be even worse than people once thought.

Most teachers and administrators have traditionally supported holding students back a year for a number of reasons. They assumed that by forcing slow learners to repeat a grade, the students would mature, master deficient skills, and be less likely to fail when they reached the next grade. In this way, retention supporters argued, the dropout rate would actually be lowered. In addition, many educators have seen retention as a way to ensure the competence of high school graduates and bring standards and accountability to the educational system.

Support for retention became even stronger in the early 1980s. The first wave of educational reformers, driven by horror stories of illiterate high school graduates, took a get-tough stance, setting rigid guidelines that required low-achieving pupils to repeat a grade. Policies that tie promotion to test scores have been particularly common in reform-minded Southern states, such as Arkansas, Georgia, and North Carolina.

A growing body of research, however, challenges the assumption that retention helps students. In fact, research suggests the practice may actually cause them to drop out. As a result, a number of educators and policymakers have begun to reassess retention policies.

• In a report released in April, the Massachusetts commissioner of education urged school districts to cease holding back low-achieving students; he cited research showing that the practice does not work. And a report by the Massachusetts Advocacy Council recommended that the Boston school system stop linking promotions to students' standardized test scores.

• In May the chancellor of the New York City school system announced that he would end a mandatory, citywide policy that automatically holds students back in grades 4 and 7 if they score poorly on standardized tests.

• The Chicago school system is reevaluating its promotion policy as part of a systemwide reform effort mandated by the state legislature.

• And in June, Florida lawmakers became among the nation's first to adopt a measure encouraging districts to abolish retention in the early grades.

There are no reliable national data on the number of public school students retained each year. But Lorrie Shepard, the co-editor of a 1989 book on retention, estimates that as many as 2.4 million—or 6 percent of K-12 pupils—are held back annually. By the 9th grade, says Shepard, a professor of education at the University of Colorado–Boulder, approximately 50 percent of all U.S. students have failed at least one grade or are no longer in school. She estimates that districts collectively spend nearly $10 billion annually to pay for the extra year of school necessitated by holding so many back.

Retention rates vary widely. A study of 29 urban school systems found that nonpromotion rates for 1st graders ranged from a low of 1 percent to a high of 23 percent. For 9th graders the rate ranged from 1 percent to 63 percent. The study, conducted by the Council of the Great City Schools, also found that the poorest districts were twice as likely as their wealthier counterparts to fail students.

Recent research raises serious questions about the benefits of this practice. A 1989 analysis of 63 controlled studies—in which retained students were followed and compared with children of similar achievement who went directly on to the next grade—found that youngsters who were held back actually performed worse than those who were not. Their behavior, school attitudes, and attendance were also poorer.

The research indicates that most children perceive "staying back" as punishment, which makes them feel sad, bad, upset, or embarrassed—emotions that may be manifested in later behavioral difficulties.

"The other children called me 'burro,' slang for dumb," recalls a school administrator in Arizona who was held back as a child. Watching them go to the next grade without him was painful, he told The Arizona Republic, asking that he not be identified. "There's always this gnawing feeling that something is wrong with you. It's something that still lingers. It never really leaves you."

For many children, the problems associated with retention culminate in the students' quitting school, critics of the practice assert. A 1986 New York City study found that 40 percent of the city's children who were retained dropped out before the end of high school, compared with 25 percent of students with comparable reading levels who had not been held back. Similar findings have emerged from research in Chicago, Boston, and Dade County, Fla.

But among educators there is still no general consensus on whether retention is good or bad. Teacher Sharon Lee, like many others, is torn over the issue. "If we don't have standards and just pass kids along, are we perpetuating [a situation in which] students graduate from school illiterate?" she asks. At the same time, she worries: Will just "following guidelines and retaining children" cause them to drop out down the road?

Teacher Beatrice Mitchell doesn't have such doubts. She believes that retaining children—especially young children—benefits them, and she

'If we pass kids along, are we perpetuating a situation in which students graduate illiterate?' one teacher asks.

holds back one or two pupils a year. "At first the kids who are retained feel bad," says Mitchell, a 1st grade teacher at Hearst Elementary School in Washington, D.C. But she says she works hard at boosting their self-esteem and finds that "matu-

rity—just being one year older—makes them do better."

At least one survey has found that a majority of teachers agree with Mitchell. Researchers Deborah Byrnes of Utah State University and Kaoru Yamamoto of Arizona State University polled 145 Arizona elementary teachers, 65 percent of whom said they believe students who do not meet the requirements of the grade should usually or always be retained.

From personal interviews with 25 of the teachers, Byrnes and Yamamoto also discovered that many teachers feel pressure to retain students from their colleagues in the next grade. Writing in *The Journal of Research and Development in Education*, the researchers reported that the teachers "felt that the next grade teachers would not be able to accommodate the child's level of skills or emotional development and the child would experience even more failure. They also feared being ridiculed by the teachers of the following grade for creating more work for them by sending such ill-prepared students."

Shepard and other critics of traditional retention practices argue that the alternative to retaining students is not simply to promote them, but to promote them while providing additional support, such as tutoring and mentoring. "Instead of 'social promotion,' which is sort of 'promote them and don't pay any attention to their lack of skills,'" she says, "we talk about normal grade-promotion plus."

The growing skepticism about the value of retaining students is prompting some schools to change their policies, especially in the early grades. In recent years states such as

Georgia have backed away from the controversial practice of making children repeat kindergarten because of low test scores. And wide-ranging school reform legislation in Kentucky has replaced grades K-3 with an ungraded primary program in which children will progress at their own pace. Mississippi is also experimenting with ungraded classrooms in grades 1-3.

Despite such stirrings, many educators note that changing the public's belief in the efficacy of retention may prove difficult. According to a 1986 Gallup poll, 72 percent of citizens surveyed favored stricter promotion standards.

Another problem, according to Shepard, is that most alternatives to retention cost money, which must be requested in a district's budget on a line-item basis. In contrast, the cost of retention is hidden in a district's education budget and billed to the state in the form of per-pupil costs.

Regardless of the arguments for and against current retention policies, another observer suggests, the prevalence of the practice points to the deficiencies in the education afforded many students.

"Anyway you look at it," notes Lynn Cornett, vice president of the Southern Regional Education Board, "the retention rates do tell us that there are large numbers of students who are not prepared to move on to the next grade, and that seems to be what is important about it."

—**Lynn Olson,** *Education Week*

Teacher Magazine *Editorial Assistant M. Dominique Long also contributed to this report.*

The Profession of Teaching Today

Recent research by teachers and teacher educators on their professional practice in classrooms is greatly enriching our knowledge base on the teaching-learning process in schools. Many issues have been raised by basic ethnographic field observations, interviews, and anecdotal record-keeping techniques to more precisely understand how teachers and students interact in the classroom. There is a rich dialectic developing among teachers regarding the description of classroom teaching environments. The methodological issues raised by this research into the day to day realities of life in schools is transforming what we know about teaching as a professional activity. These developments are relevant to the concerns of all teachers regarding how to best advance our knowledge of effective teaching strategies.

Likewise, there is also vigorous debate among curriculum theory and construction specialists as to how we should revise our ideas concerning what students study in schools. The vitality and variety of curriculum perspectives vying for influence in the area of curriculum and instruction is really informative. The issues of "what makes a good teacher" and "what would go into a good curriculum" are fascinating to consider. There is more and more collaborative inquiry on teaching practice being jointly conducted by classroom teachers and university-based scholars. From these collaborative efforts we are building bridges of communication between the universities and the elementary and secondary schools. This is a long overdue emphasis that is now building up momentum all across the continent. Ethnographic research techniques developed by anthropologists and sociologists are making this transformation of the knowledge base on teaching possible. Teachers are adapting the "oral history" techniques used by some social historians and folklorists, as well as the closed and open-ended interview techniques first developed in anthropological field studies. The results are sparklingly informative as to the feelings of both teachers and students. Teachers are being encouraged to reflect seriously on their own teaching, and a new genre of knowledge on the problems of teaching is coming from this reflective activity.

The debate over "accountability" for teachers is continuing, with the profession still at odds in its search for a national consensus within the profession as to what that should mean. The debate over national certification of teachers is heating up. Most of the state departments of education (or public instruction) are proceeding with behaviorally focused new standards for the assessment of teaching performance. In some states the implementation of competency testing for initial certification and proposed systems of "tiered" diplomas are putting more pressure on teachers in terms of narrowing the range of freedom open to classroom teachers in their daily practice. Modifying practice in the classroom becomes necessary as teachers may be held accountable for the performance of their students on standardized achievement tests. Issues relating to the academic freedom of teachers and the range of opportunity for creative classroom performance are presented by the nature of new state-sponsored standards of practice. This is not a tranquil time in the profession. What the Bush administration will do, in terms of specific programmatic recommendations, is still uncertain. There have been several models of accountability for teachers discussed in recent months. Many feel that a truly professional model of accountability in teaching must be client-oriented and knowledge-based. There is a large knowledge base on teaching, but there are still serious controversies regarding what parts of that knowledge base demonstrate teacher competence (or lack of it), and how assessment of teacher competence should be conducted.

Creative, insightful persons who become teachers usually find ways to network their interests and concerns with other teachers. There are many opportunities for creative professional practice in teaching in spite of external assessment procedures. President Bush and other political leaders, as well as leaders in the corporate sector, are urging teachers to consider more creative ways to emphasize basic academic standards in written composition, computer literacy, and applied mathematics. The dispute over "alternative approaches" to teacher certification has hampered efforts to gain a consensus on minimum academic qualifications for beginning teachers.

We have often heard it said that teaching is both an art and a science. The science of teaching involves the observation and measurement of teaching behaviors. The art of teaching involves the humanistic dimensions of instructional activities. Interesting and original conceptions of teaching as a humanistic activity are still being developed. We continue to rediscover older methods of relating what is taught to the interests of students. The art of teaching involves not only alertness to the details of what is taught, but equal alertness to how students receive it. Teachers often guide class processes and formulate questions according to their perceptions of how students are responding to the material.

We are in the midst of a period in which fundamental revisions in the structure of the professional roles and status of teachers are being considered and developed. Teachers want more input into how the profession is to be reformed. It will be interesting to see how many of the new proposals for "career ladders" for teachers will be implemented, and how the teaching profession responds to the recommendations for licensure by the new national board for certification of teachers. I believe the idea of national board certification of teachers is a sound one. It will stabilize the system, focusing attention on a national set of standard qualifications for teaching at different levels and in different subject areas. We look forward to the emergence of a national consensus within the teaching profession on the qualifications for teaching. In the past 18 years, we have seen the introduction of increased field experience and clinical experience requirements for pre-service candidates for the teaching profession. It is a very interesting time to be part of this profession.

Though major changes have occurred in teacher education over the past 15 years, recent developments indicate that even greater change can be expected in the next few years. The nation's teachers are confronting new proposals each year that directly affect their morale and security. Difficult teaching conditions, created to a large extent by phenomena such as mainstreaming and competency testing, are intensifying pressures on teachers. They are being asked to do and know more, while they are receiving less assistance in meeting the normal demands of the classroom. In addition, teachers are deeply affected by frustration caused by the decline in their real wages and purchasing power in recent years. The President's Commission Report and others have called for higher pay and career ladders for teachers, as well as for merit pay to attract more academically talented young people into the profession. But, so far, little has been done by either the national or the state legislatures to fund such efforts, and most local communities are unable to do so.

How does a nation achieve a dramatic qualitative advance in the field of education if it is unwilling to pay for it? Blaming most of the problems in education on teacher incompetence is like blaming the victim. Some ways to improve the quality of teaching include the funding of inservice education for teachers, revisions in funding so that teachers can earn wages appropriate to their levels of professional preparation, and the implementation of a method for demonstrating teacher competency.

According to the Rand Corporation and other research groups, serious shortages of teachers already exist in mathematics, the sciences, foreign languages, and in the education of children of linguistic minorities. Shortages are expected to develop in most, if not all, areas of teaching in the next 10 years. Children will always need well-educated and competent teachers. However, the pro-

fession may not be able to provide them unless more academically talented people can be attracted to the field.

To build their hope as well as their self-confidence, teachers must be motivated to an even greater effort for professional growth. Teachers need support, appreciation, and respect. Simply criticizing them and refusing to alter those social and economic conditions that affect the quality of their work will not solve their problems, nor will it lead to excellence in education. Not only must teachers work to improve the public's image of and confidence in them, but the public must confront its own misunderstanding of the level of commitment required to achieve excellence. Teachers need to know that the public cares about and respects them enough to fund their professional improvement and to recognize them for the important force they are in the life of their nation.

The articles in this unit consider the quality of education and the status of the teaching profession today.

Looking Ahead: Challenge Questions

List what you think are the five most important issues confronting the teaching profession today (with number one being the most important and number five the least important). What criteria did you use in ranking the issues? What is your position on each of them?

Does teaching have some problems that other professions do not seem to have? If so, what are they? What can be done about them?

What appears to be the major issues affecting teacher morale?

What are the best reasons for a person to choose a career in teaching?

What are the most critical social pressures on teachers? Why are teachers sometimes used as scapegoats?

What are the advantages of peer review and observation processes in helping teachers improve their professional performance?

What do you think of classroom-based research? How would you go about doing it?

What Makes A Good Teacher?

Stanford research may influence national certification

Kathie Underdal never looked forward to teacher-assessment time. One day a year, an administrator would sit in the back of her 3rd grade classroom, jotting down observations. She would also suffer through multiple-choice tests that seemed unrelated to her teaching.

Last year, however, Underdal was involved in a completely different type of assessment. For the entire school year, she compiled a portfolio of examples of the methods she used to teach literacy to her pupils at Juana Briones Elementary School in Palo Alto, Calif. The portfolio included such items as students' writing samples, passages from their "literature logs," in which they commented on stories they had read, and a videotape of her teaching.

"Other forms of assessment really don't show what you can do with a group of children," Underdal says. "This allows you to pick certain areas and really show what you can do, and to learn as you go."

Underdal was one of 40 teachers—20 elementary school literacy teachers and 20 high school biology teachers—who compiled portfolios last year as part of Stanford University's Teacher Assessment Project. The closely watched project is a three-year, $2.5 million effort to develop a new generation of assessments for teachers. It is viewed as a key element in the move to professionalize teaching.

Evaluation of the portfolios, which took place in June, marked the end of the project's second phase. In its first phase, the research team designed a number of exercises that could be used at special teacher-assessment centers.

During the project's final few months, staff will analyze data from the two phases. But most of the work is now complete, and Lee Shulman, the education professor who designed and directed the project, says his team has accomplished its main objectives.

According to Shulman, today's methods of assessing teachers are "utterly inadequate." He is convinced that the portfolio and assessment-center approach offers a workable alternative that "gets at teachers as thinking, decisionmaking individuals working in a context that has real history."

The new assessments place teachers, rather than administrators, at the center of the evaluation process. "We think that putting the experienced teacher—the expert teacher—in the key role in both setting standards and implementing them is at the very heart of any conception of the professionalization of teaching," Shulman says.

The portfolio and assessment-center prototypes that Shulman and his team designed and tested could serve as models for the new National Board for Professional Teaching Standards, which is establishing a national voluntary certification system. If such a system is to gain widespread acceptance, workable and acceptable teacher assessments are essential, so the standards board is keeping a close eye on Shulman's work.

Although the standards board and the assessment project are both sponsored by the Carnegie Corporation of New York, Shulman points out that there are no formal ties between the two efforts. His prototypes are among the most detailed working models of new forms of teacher assessment developed to date, but the board will look at many sources in constructing its national certification system.

Shulman envisions national certification as a "marriage of insufficiencies." By themselves, all forms of assessment—written tests, classroom observation, portfolios, and assessment centers—have weaknesses. But if integrated into a comprehensive certification process, they could provide a fair and accurate mirror of the complexities of teaching.

What's more, Shulman believes that the new assessment process will help produce better teachers. "Our assessments are so much more closely related to teaching that if you take preparation for the assessment seriously, you are going to improve your teaching," he says.

The assessment-center phase of the Stanford project culminated with teachers of high school history and elementary school mathematics from around the country participating in a two-day field test. During the test, they were run through a series of teaching exercises and then evaluated. Some exercises were common to all teachers, such as delivering a lecture or planning a lesson with colleagues. Others focused on the subject matter: Math teachers were asked to select various items—such as poker chips, a ball of string, measuring cups, and a clock—from a box and explain how the items could be used to teach equivalent fractions; history teachers critiqued a videotape of another teacher delivering a lesson on the Spanish-American War. In all, the teachers completed about 10 exercises, each ranging from 45 minutes to three hours.

The assessment-center exercises, however, lack important elements—the school setting and students. That's where the portfolios enter in.

"We designed our portfolio to allow varieties of style," says Angelo Collins, who has taken over as the project director while Shulman is on sabbatical. "There is no one right way to teach. One of the values of the portfolios is that they allow teachers to bring some of their uniqueness."

Collins, a former biology teacher, typifies the central role teachers have played in designing and evaluating the assessments. She and four other experienced biology teachers designed the different sections of the biology portfolio. Teachers also served as evaluators when the portfolios were presented.

Nancy Knight, a 2nd grade teacher at Juana Briones Elementary School, was one of the evaluators of the literacy portfolios. Knight, who has been teaching for 25 years, says that the teachers she was evaluating were not the only ones to gain from the experience.

"It made me think about my role as a teacher, and it made me more reflective about what I do and why I do it," she says. "It was like putting a microscope on something I have to do all the time."

Furthermore, Knight says she intends to incorporate some of the things she saw in the portfolios into her own teaching. For example, she discovered some new ways to approach the often difficult task of communicating students' progress to parents.

Evaluating the portfolios and assessment-center exercises posed the biggest challenge, but Shulman says disagreement among evaluators was not as extreme as he had expected. Even in areas of practice where there is a great deal of controversy over theory, he says, "when you get down to the concrete examples, there's much less disagreement." When evaluators critiqued an example of teaching photosynthesis in a high school biology course, for instance, they reached a high level of consensus.

Shulman says the key is to set standards for good teaching that are reasonable and flexible enough to allow for differences in style. "I think there will be a lot of room for variation" in portfolios and assessment-center activities, he adds. "The beauty of this kind of assessment strategy is that, unlike multiple-choice tests, you don't have to decide on one right answer or the best answer. You can leave open the possibility of pluralism, what I would call a pluralism of excellence."

Less encouraging were reports from participants about the many hours it took to compile portfolios. "Schools are organized almost to prevent teacher reflection on their work," Shulman says. "There simply is no time and space for teachers to do the kind of careful analysis that you have in other professions. The teachers who worked with us did beautiful portfolios, but a fair amount of what they did really had to come out of their hides."

Shulman came away convinced that improved teacher assessments cannot stand alone; they must be part of a more general movement to restructure schools and teaching. "Restructured schools, as we envision them," he says, "are places where teachers have the opportunity to carefully document what they do, what their students are doing, and to work collaboratively with their peers on drawing the proper inferences from that kind of documentation. That's a very rare opportunity for teachers today."

—Daniel Gursky

Fixing the teaching, not the kids

Reversing the trend in special education in Rochester

To Rochester schools' Superintendent Peter McWalters, American public education has become the grim sorter. "If we start out with 100 students, eventually we'll sort them out into groups and categories and we'll end up with two kids in a room," observes McWalters, his sarcasm born of experience. "And then we'll ask for help with one of *them*."

Over the past two decades, Rochester has done its share to make special education a growth industry in America. Today, one sixth of the district's 2,400 teachers and an almost equal percentage of its 32,000 students are assigned to special-education classes. Those labeled learning disabled are the largest single group, with nearly 1,900 students.

As part of an ambitious, 2-year-old effort to reform its entire troubled school system, Rochester's administrators are now trying hard to cut the rolls of special-education classes, which they believe have too often been used as a convenient way to avoid facing up to the problems of regular education. "When a student isn't learning, we've always assumed there's something wrong with the kid," says Joseph Accongio, a middle-school administrator in Rochester. "Now, we're looking to see what's wrong with the way we're teaching."

Having to deal with difficult students has been a leading cause for otherwise dedicated, regular-education teachers to leave the profession. In Rochester, as the number of poor, minority students greatly increased in recent years, many teachers

who stayed came to rely on the special-education system to handle the problem for them. "We have to learn to deal with a different population," says McWalters. "Filling special-ed classes full of black children is not the way." In a school system where 8 of 10 kindergartners arrive lacking some basic skills, referrals begin early. The cultural and economic gap between teachers and students is widely seen as a factor in such decisions.

Mixing it up. Discovery, an experimental program at Frederick Douglass Middle School aimed at developing new methods of teaching, is an example of Rochester's efforts to tackle those problems. There are 255 regular-education children enrolled in Discovery, as well as 36 special-education students who spend at least one period each day in the program. A part of Discovery's mandate is to help special students return to regular classes and to keep borderline regular-education students from being referred to special classes in the first place.

One method being tried, called cooperative learning, is based on the premise that peer acceptance is a primary motivation for students in the sixth, seventh and eighth grades. For a few periods each day, Discovery's students are placed in groups of two to six and given assignments as mundane as spelling or as challenging as profiling a foreign country. The emphasis is on group achievement and accountability with students learning not just from the teacher, but from each other. This approach gives LD students a chance to contribute from their strong suits while getting help in their weak areas from other students. At last month's science fair, the fruits of cooperative learning were on abundant display. Discovery-student teams made more than 100 projects, far more than regular

science classes made in any previous year at Douglass.

One of the biggest criticisms of special education is that often it simply perpetuates low achievement among borderline students. One way Discovery tries to avoid that cycle is by grabbing students' attention with programs that take advantage of their most popular interests, such as television. Joe Accongio, for example, teaches a group of 20 students who have shown little or no interest in learning math. They have also been identified by the district as likely dropouts as soon as they reach the minimum legal age of 16. Accongio is trying to reach them by using a program called Square One Television, which he helped to develop at the Children's Television Workshop in New York. With the help of videotapes that include skits, songs and colorful graphics, Accongio hopes to make staples such as fractions, decimals and prime numbers more interesting to his students. One segment, called Mathnet, is a takeoff on the television series "Dragnet" and features characters trying to solve math problems over a five-day period. Another one is called Mathman, a numerical version of the popular Pac Man video game.

Part of Discovery's value is in removing some of the stigma associated with special education. At Douglass, which with 1,150 students is overcrowded, special-education students are grouped in Cluster I, located in classrooms at one end of the building. Many students try to hide their status by requesting lockers on different floors or blotting out the I on their bus passes.

Discovery's experiment in integrating regular and special education is likely to be extended next year at Douglass in a more intensive and formal program that will bring together about 120 students.

This report is the third in a series of articles examining the experiment launched by Rochester, N.Y., to overhaul its troubled school system.

Half of them will be "at risk" regular-education kids and one fourth of them borderline special-education students who currently attend some regular classes. Proponents argue that it combines the best of both worlds—teachers steeped in traditional subject areas such as math and social studies working with teachers who have special pedagogic training to deal with slow learners.

Rochester is making progress in reducing the ranks of its special classes. The 1,666 new referrals to special education last year were down from 1,900 four years ago. In the past two years, 284 learning-disabled students have been returned to the regular classroom. At Douglass, there is a special push to mainstream LD students before they enter high school, where the schedule becomes less flexible and the emotional stigma more firmly ingrained. Accongio says every student returned to the regular classroom is a strong role model. "These kids see special ed as a hole they're trying to climb out of," he says. "When one makes it, it shows the others it can be done."

The mainstream. Ultimately, Rochester's success in reaching slow learners through regular-education channels will depend a great deal on the commitment of its teachers. A few months ago, Discovery teacher Donna Gattelaro-Andersen was assigned Angelo Cruz, a student one step away from being added to the ranks of the learning disabled. The sixth grader was self-conscious about being bigger than most of his classmates, and he was unable or unwilling to focus on his studies. To a school psychologist, he was another kid with "attention-deficit disability."

But to Gattelaro-Andersen, Angelo was a kid "who needed to be understood before he could be taught." With help from other teachers and counselors, she found out that he was being raised without a father and that he was receiving medication for hyperactivity. She knew that Angelo was in dire need of self-esteem. But she also sensed that the "slow class" was not the place to find it.

Gattelaro-Andersen began with a time-tested method, enlisting Angelo as her classroom helper. Lunch periods spent cleaning blackboards, straightening desks and stapling papers boosted Angelo's confidence. In a special class period set aside to address students' individual strengths and weaknesses, "Mrs. G's" soft voice and patient instruction have helped him to improve his reading.

Today, Angelo is still a below-average student, but thanks to Discovery, he has remained in the regular classroom. "I don't teach English," Gattelaro-Andersen says. "I teach students." For Rochester's reformers, that may be the best weapon against learning disabilities, real or imagined.

Jerry Buckley

Now You See Them, Now You Don't: Anonymity Versus Visibility in Case Studies of Teachers

JUDITH H. SHULMAN

JUDITH H. SHULMAN *is at the Far West Laboratory for Educational Research and Development, 1855 Folsom Street, San Francisco, California 94103.*

Many teachers, in collaborative relationships with researchers, no longer want anonymity. They seek recognition for their contributions to the studies in which they engage. Yet revealing the names of the people, schools, and districts participating in research raises a new set of problems about the conduct of such inquiries. Difficulties arising from the need for anonymity and the desire for visibility in collaborative studies are the subject of this paper.

Educational Researcher, Vol. 19, No. 6, pp 11–15

Collaborative research with teachers has put a new twist on the old problem of protecting the rights of informants in qualitative research. In most discussions of the qualitative researcher's obligations to his or her informants, the emphasis is on protecting their rights to privacy, confidentiality, and anonymity. As new research paradigms in the study of teaching and teacher education call for teachers as collaborators in the research that studies their work, a new issue arises. Many teachers no longer wish to remain hidden behind a cloak of anonymity; they prefer to be credited and recognized for their contributions. This raises new problems for research on teaching. How do scholars weigh their competing responsibilities to teacher collaborators who wish well-deserved recognition against obligations to schools, districts, and other teachers who may wish to remain anonymous? When teacher/authors forego the protection of anonymity, in what ways do they become vulnerable to the disapproval or recriminations of peers or administrators?

In my own research, a school-based collaborator, Joel Colbert, and I worked with two groups of teachers to write narratives about their teaching. With the district's blessing, our goal was to publish their vignettes in casebooks and use them during district-sponsored inservice training. Each group of teachers was given the option of individual authorship or anonymity for their published work. Their decisions differed, which had contrasting implications for the researchers's rela-

tionships with the district. The purpose of this paper is to describe how the tension between anonymity and visibility for each group of teacher/authors was handled in this research. I will also discuss the manner in which such problems are either dealt with or ignored in selected books on qualitative research. I will conclude with a discussion of the implications of this analysis for the growing body of collaborative and teacher-authored studies of teaching.

Two primary theoretical perspectives are used to analyze these accounts. One is the importance of the teacher's voice to the literature on teaching and teacher education (McDonald, 1986; Shulman, 1989; Shulman & Colbert, 1987), which has traditionally been dominated by educational scholars. If research and practice are truly interdependent, then researchers must provide opportunities for teachers to be recognized for their own accomplishments. The second is the absence of ethical discussions of informants' desires to be recognized in textbooks and journal articles on qualitative research methods (Ellen, 1984; Georges & Jones, 1980; Hammersley & Atkinson, 1983; Whyte, 1984; Yin, 1985). In general, when researchers discuss ethical issues, they deal only with the recognized right of *anonymity* for informants and the responsibilities they have to their sponsors, school districts, and collaborators with whom they have worked.

Background

This research was conducted collaboratively among two groups of teacher/authors, Joel Colbert, a district staff developer, and myself, a researcher from a regional educational laboratory. During the first year of activity, we developed a casebook on the complexity of the new mentor–teacher role (in California) with 22 mentor teachers from the district (Shulman & Colbert, 1987). They were all enrolled in a master's level course on staff development for mentor teachers taught by Colbert. Each teacher contributed at least one case to the book. The casebook was later used during inservice training for experienced mentor teachers. Their cases dealt with successful and less successful interactions with new teachers, constructive and harmful relationships with school principals, and the rewards and frustrations of being a mentor teacher (see Shulman & Colbert, 1989, for a description of the analysis of the data). All persons and schools mentioned in each case were given pseudonyms to preserve the privacy of the participants involved. When we asked the teachers how to attribute authorship of their cases, they decided to list their names as a group on the title page and to leave individual cases anonymous. For these teachers, the risk of hurt feelings and compromised relationships with their colleagues and administrators was greater than their need for personal recognition for their own writings. Getting permission from the district to publish this casebook was no hassle, because there appeared to be no controversial material in the book. We were not prepared for what occurred during our next project.

The following year we planned another casebook, this time authored by beginning teachers, working on emergency credentials, who were each assigned a mentor teacher (Shulman & Colbert, 1988). The book was intended to serve as a partner to the first casebook for mentor training, and as a staff development tool for incoming new teachers. Though 17 novices volunteered for the project, 8 dropped out the first week. The nine who remained appeared motivated by the carrot of publication. The teachers, one African American and the rest Caucasian, had stories to tell about their early experiences in teaching, and they wanted to be recognized for their efforts. Unlike the previous group of teacher/authors, these teachers wanted their names associated with their own cases. Because the feeling was unanimous, we agreed to their decision.

During the introductory session with the intern/authors, we discussed a set of guidelines for writing the cases (see Shulman & Colbert, 1988, for a description of the methodology and data analysis of this project). We asked them to write candidly about their teaching circumstances and to select events that would help others understand the dilemmas of new teachers during their first few months of teaching. We said that their cases would be accompanied by interpretive comments by other new and veteran teachers and scholars, and the compiled casebook would be used for training mentor teachers and teachers new to the district. Our experiences working with the district to approve the contents of the intern-authored casebook—in contrast with its predecessor—yielded the experiences discussed in this paper.

I used three sources of information for this paper: (a) *The Intern Teacher Casebook*, (b) suggested changes by district staff on drafts of individual cases, and (c) the subsequent struggles and negotiations needed to receive approval for the book's publication. The casebook consisted of 15 cases, each with commentary from at least two other educators. The cases were classified in three categories. The first group dealt with instructional episodes that are problematic either in their conception or their implementation. The second focused on interactions with individual students who persistently act out or refuse to do work. The last category examined the neophytes' relationships with mentor teachers and other experienced teachers. Because of the delicacy of this third category, the teachers decided to leave these cases anonymous.

Permeating all the cases were descriptions of the teachers'

culture shock with the poverty and living conditions of their students. Most of the teachers came from middle-class backgrounds and had never entered an inner-city school before their teaching assignment. Their cases often depicted their initial perceptions of their students as unmotivated and unruly, who tested teachers with foul language and constant disruptions. Their teaching problems were exacerbated by circumstances such as limited materials, inappropriate textbooks, minimal planning time, and isolation from colleagues.

Colbert and I felt that these honest, often poignant, descriptions of initial teaching experiences were excellent teaching tools for preservice and inservice education. Though perhaps exaggerated by some of the urban placements, the cases depicted experiences that are common to all beginning teachers. They provided opportunities for practitioners and researchers to test theoretical principles within the context of real classrooms and teaching episodes. They also provided guidance for appropriate teaching strategies, both from mistakes that the interns described and their reflective comments about them, and from the commentary by the experienced teachers and educational scholars.

We soon discovered, however, that others thought differently. When we gave the cases to three other officials in the staff development office for review, we received abundant recommendations for changes in the text. We agreed with the suggestions to eliminate any information that might identify persons and places mentioned in the cases to protect the privacy of those involved. Yet we objected to other suggestions: censor all foul language that might be offensive to some readers; change selected phrases and delete paragraphs that might appear embarrassing to the district; and *withhold the identity of the case writers* from their narrative accounts. The next section provides selected examples of the kinds of changes that were suggested.

Recommended Changes to Text

The recommended changes below are grouped in three categories: (a) foul and other questionable language, (b) perceptions and descriptions of students, and (c) judgements about working conditions.

Foul and Other Questionable Language

All of the reviewers felt that persons in the district could get into trouble if we allowed any language that could be considered "swearing" in the text.[1] For example, we were asked to change words in phrases such as the following:

> [After a teacher described what he thought was a good presentation of a lesson, students asked questions such as:] "What's all this bullshit, Rossbach?...Yeah, where are the fuckin handouts for this shit?"
> [After a junior high school teacher asked his class to name sources of air pollution, one student said,] "I know teacher! Farts!" [Amidst the subsequent laughter and "farting" sounds, another student blurted out,] "Teacher, Malcom told me to suck his cock."

Perceptions and Descriptions of Students

All of the reviewers recommended some changes in this category. Some felt that a few teachers used questionable language and suggested that the teacher choose alternative adjectives. For example, one teacher described her teenagers as "squirrelly" with "out-to-lunch" brains. Another teacher called his life science class a "dumping ground for noncollege bound, nonacademic dropouts."

Most controversial were the ways in which some of the teachers described their initial impressions of their students. For example, all reviewers thought that the following descriptions showed extreme bias toward minorities and should be modified.

It's hard to describe the shock I experienced during my first weeks of school. Many students were loud, vulgar, poorly dressed, and many had obvious physical problems, such as extremely crooked teeth, which in almost any other environment would have been taken care of by doctors. My heart went out to these kids, but at the same time they made me very angry. Every day I tried to get control of my classes. Every day it was an effort....[After describing several failed strategies to encourage student cooperation in completing schoolwork and reducing tardiness, the teacher continued] I talked with parents whose voices were slurred. They had trouble following the conversation as if they were under the influence of drugs or alcohol.

[Another teacher said] My descent from innocence was swift and brutal. I was given a temporary roll sheet, assigned a room—actually three different rooms—and with little other preparation was thrust into the world of teaching. Suddenly I was faced with classes populated by unruly students, gang members, and other children with only rudimentary scholastic skills.

[While reflecting on a metric lesson that went awry, one teacher wrote] Not only did the students have no knowledge of the metric system, they were ignorant of measuring using the English system.

One reviewer suggested that we delete whole paragraphs. For example, this reviewer said the following entire paragraphs about two small groups of students who were not attending to their assigned task were irrelevant.

I arrived just in time to witness the finishing touches that Juan was adding to his self-inspired metric project. He had beautifully carved his gang symbol into the meter stick with an eight inch knife he had been carrying. He also asked me if, perchance, I would like to buy some "ludes" from him...

At table four, Miguel, who had just been released from jail the day before, was sharing with his lab partners the economics lesson he learned while incarcerated. The going rate for the striker part of a matchbook is five dollars. Those in the lower economic brackets can borrow the striker from a fellow inmate for the cost of a cigarette...

Judgements About Working Conditions

One of the reviewers also objected to the ways that some teachers characterized their own or others' teaching situations. As this reviewer said, "[the statements] are evaluative and imply that all inner-city secondary schools are the bottom of the barrel. Can they be edited so as not to be so biased?"

[One junior high teacher wrote] Most of the teachers must work with the texts which (1) are several years beyond the reading level of their students and (2) have content which only partially satisfies the objectives of the course outline.

[In a reaction to a high school teacher's case, an experienced teacher said] I definitely admire anyone who can survive an assignment in an inner-city school, especially in a junior high, and still want to continue teaching.

Ethical Dilemmas: How to Respond?

The above recommendations raised several ethical issues for project staff. We wanted to maintain the integrity of the cases because of their perceived educative value. Yet, as a regional educational laboratory, we had to be responsible to our sponsors and to our clients. We asked ourselves questions such as: Who were our clients, the teacher/authors or the districts whom we serve? How could we renege on a commitment to the authors? Yet what was our responsibility if publication of their accounts had negative repercussions for them personally? What was our position about changes in written perceptions? In foul language? Were there any circumstances under which we would change the text? Were there any particular constraints around publishing a federally funded document?

> **Permeating all the cases were descriptions of teachers' culture shock.**

These questions prompted hours and weeks of deliberation among many staff members of the Laboratory. We consulted lawyers about liability issues and discovered that apparently neither we nor the teachers could be held liable. We consulted our funding agent, who warned that certain political groups routinely scrutinize all published documents for "appropriate content." My collaborator and I also consulted the teacher/authors. We explained our dilemmas, explored potential repercussions for their professional lives, and shared with each individual the recommended changes to his or her own accounts. Their response was uniform. The teachers felt that the cases represented the reality of their teaching situations and they understood why their accounts might be controversial, but they preferred to stand by and be recognized for what they wrote.

Because of the delicacy of the situation, Colbert and I developed a 3-stage negotiating plan to gain approval for the book. First, we would meet face to face with two senior officials in the district staff development office to negotiate differences. Next, we would send a revised draft to an associate superintendent, who then, we hoped, would pass it on to the superintendent for final approval.

A few days before the initial negotiating meeting, I met with senior staff at the Laboratory to develop some ground rules for the negotiations. We realized that we were defining new turf in certain areas of collaborative research. Whereas the literature provided guidance on the treatment of data in qualitative research and the rights of informants, collaborators, and school districts to remain anonymous (e.g., Georges & Jones, 1980; Hammersley & Atkinson, 1983; Whyte, 1984; Yin, 1985), it was devoid of ethical discussions of informants' desires to be recognized.

We also had to consider several programmatic themes that had developed at our office. One was the importance of the teacher's voice to the literature on teaching, which is currently dominated by researchers (Nelson & Shulman, 1989; Shulman, 1989; Shulman & Colbert, 1987). We at Far West Laboratory were committed to providing opportunities for teachers and administrators to publish their writing, and we were creating a casebook series by practitioners as our medium. If we truly defended the importance of this line of work, then we believed that our teacher/collaborators should be able to decide how they wanted to be recognized. And if the teacher/authors preferred visibility to anonymity, we wanted to respect their wishes.

The following list represents the ground rules that we developed for negotiating this casebook. It is sequenced in order of importance.

1. This casebook will definitely be published. We would prefer to use the district's real name, but we would create a pseudonym if we could not come to a mutual agreement.
2. All information in the accounts that might lead to the identification of persons or schools would be edited or altered.
3. The narratives as written would be treated like data in a research report, and thus the substance could not be changed. We would, however, consider adding ''in my opinion'' to a statement that was judged to be highly controversial.
4. Any language in the text that might be considered particularly offensive would be altered. This included ''foul'' language, with the possible exception of *farts*, which most adult readers found fairly benign and rather fitting. It also included words and phrases that might be particularly offensive to minority groups.
5. A strong argument for the rights of teacher/authors to be individually recognized would be raised. However, if this were the only item of disagreement, we would compromise and list the authors' names in a group.

As it turned out, the meeting with the two district officials was easier that we had anticipated. It was clear that the officials wanted to come to some mutual agreement and were quite willing to compromise. They appreciated the ground rules that I developed for the discussion and understood the rationale behind them. As we proceeded to wade through each suggested modification, we found few disagreements. We dismissed most of the suggestions for changes in teachers' perceptions, and added ''in my opinion'' to the three most controversial statements.[2] The district officials felt that this addition prevented the assertion that the comments were generalizable to all teachers. We also censored all foul language, including, reluctantly, the substitution of *flatulence* for *farts*. By the end of the meeting, we had arrived at a mutual agreement on all issues except how to attribute recognition to the authors. District officials strongly recommended withholding individual authors' names on each case. Though we deferred that decision subject to further consultation at the Laboratory, everyone present felt that the meeting was productive and a revised draft had a good chance for acceptance.

The next phase of deliberations continued back at the Laboratory. We approved all of the modifications except the two troublesome issues: We decided to hold out for individual recognition of individual authors, and to return *farts*

to the text, because *flatulence* was simply too ridiculous. We knew that these decisions were chancy, but we felt they were worth the risk. Colbert concurred with these recommendations, and, with high hopes, he gave the revised draft to an associate superintendent. We were not prepared for what happened next.

In a few days, Colbert called in shock. He reported that, as far as the district was concerned, the project was dead. The associate superintendent refused to give the manuscript to the superintendent and recommended that the district disassociate itself from it. He said that is was much too controversial for district sponsorship. Colbert suggested that if we wanted to keep the project alive, the next step would have to come from the Laboratory.

Again the scene shifted to the Laboratory. We decided that our only hope was a letter to the superintendent by the director, followed by the manuscript itself. Once more we were surprised. Within a few days after we had mailed the manuscript, Colbert ecstatically called. He had just received a message that the superintendent approved the manuscript under two conditions: (a) the Laboratory assume full responsibility and liability for its contents and (b) the district collaborator (Colbert) approved the text. Neither of us could believe that our 6-month ordeal was settled so quickly.

The rest is local history. The book was published and disseminated to a wide audience of educators and scholars by both the Laboratory and two Educational Research and Information Clearinghouses (ERICs)—the first such collaboration between the ERIC centers on educational management and on teacher education. Feedback on its utility as an educative tool by preservice and inservice teacher educators has been uniformly enthusiastic. We were particularly pleased, however, with the district's response. The book is currently being used in seminars with new teachers. The instructor reports that the cases stimulate discussions about how to motivate students and tailor instruction to fit the needs of inner-city youngsters. To our relief, there have been no negative repercussions for the professional lives of the teacher/authors.

Implications

This paper deals with the hitherto unexplored problem of maintaining identification and recognition for teachers rather than confidentiality and privacy. The question of identifying teacher informants/collaborators can no longer be automatically answered on the side of anonymity. The ethnographer's traditions of rendering informants invisible were produced in an era when informants were seen as powerless and in need of protection. In our day, research on teaching has become one of the vehicles for the professionalization and empowerment of teachers. The anonymous teacher may no longer be an appropriate focus for all studies of teaching. Textbooks on qualitative or ethnographic research must include new sections that alert researchers to their obligation to treat teachers as professional colleagues who deserve as much recognition as the traditional scholar.

We must recognize, however, that when teachers forego the protection of anonymity, they become vulnerable to the disapproval and recrimination of their peers and administrators. Unlike qualitative researchers who leave the scene when their work is over, teachers rarely leave the scene. They must bear the burden of their written words, for they remain participants long after they complete their roles as formal observers and writers. Ironically, the school district also becomes more vulnerable under these circumstances. We are justifiably committed to providing opportunities for the expression of the teacher's voice. Yet as teachers cast aside their cloaks of anonymity, they place their institutions at some risk as well. We as a research community must learn to consider the rights of all individuals and institutions who collaborate with us.

Some colleagues have urged me to propose a set of general principles or rules of thumb for dealing with such dilemmas in the future. I do not believe that general principles are of much use in these situations. These circumstances represent a serious tangle of competing ethical obligations complicated by political realities. They are best handled on a case-by-case basis, through negotiation and deliberation among all the relevant stakeholders. Even in the domain of ethical and moral reasoning (e.g., Jonsen & Toulmin, 1988) philosophers have generally come to recognize the limitations of general principles and the critical importance of deciding ethical problems by focusing on the particularities of individual situations.

Notes

Work on this paper was supported by the Office of Educational Research and Improvement, Department of Education, under Contract No. 400-86-0009 to the Far West Laboratory for Educational Research and Development. The contents of this paper do not necessarily reflect the position or policies of the Department of Education.
[1]*From the Editors desk:* The tale of discomfort continues. The Los Angeles public schools and the Far West Laboratory were not the only institutions that experienced difficulties with these records of student language, as reported by practicing teachers, for use by other teachers and teacher educators. The editor of this manuscript did not want to censor a document that had been through review processes and found acceptable, but he also wondered at the propriety of the language for our journal, and whether any of our readers would be offended. Editorial sense, sense of propriety, and issues of censorship and research ethics all became topics of conversation after this manuscript was submitted. Concerns were voiced and discussed with colleagues and the author—concerns that never arise when we publish a cost–benefit analysis of educational programs, or a conceptual piece on situated cognition.

Ultimately, the editor decided not to ask the author to change the language. We are a research journal. These data are real. Our readers are adults. And because our experiences differ, each of us would have a different vision of what words were actually used if we did not instantiate the term *foul language.* Nevertheless, the discomfort continues. (David C. Berliner, Features Editor).

[2]Adding "in my opinion" to the three most controversial statements turned out to be a key element in negotiating the retention of these statements. The district officials felt that this addition emphasized the individual perspectives of the writers, thus preventing the inclination to generalize the same perspectives to other teachers.

References

Ellen, R. F. (1984). *Ethnographic research: A guide to general conduct.* Orlando: Jovanovich; London: Academic Press.

Georges, R. A., & Jones, M. O. (1980). *People studying people.* Berkeley: University of California Press.

Hammersley, M., & Atkinson, P. (1983). *Ethnography: Principles in practice.* London: Tavistock Publications.

Jonsen, A. R., & Toulmin, S. (1988). *The abuse of casuistry: A history of moral reasoning.* Berkeley: University of California Press.

McDonald, J. P. (1986). Raising the teacher's voice and the ironic role of theory. *Harvard Educational Review, 56*(4), 355–378.

Nelson, L., & Shulman, J. H. (1989, March). *Case writing as professional development: Practitioner perspectives.* Paper presented at the Annual Meeting of the American Educational Research Association, San Francisco, CA.

Shulman, J. H. (1989). Blue freeways: Traveling the alternate route with big city teacher trainees. *Journal of Teacher Education, 40*(5), 2–8.

Shulman, J. H., & Colbert, J. A. (1987). *The mentor teacher casebook.* San Francisco: Far West Laboratory for Educational Research and Development.

Shulman, J.H., & Colbert, J.A. (1988). *The intern teacher casebook.* San Francisco: Far West Laboratory for Educational Research and Development.

Shulman, J. H., & Colbert, J. A. (1989). Cases as catalysts for cases. *Action in Teacher Education, 11*(1), 44–52.

Whyte, W. F. (1984). *Learning from the field: A guide from experience.* Beverly Hills: Sage Publications.

Yin, R. K. (1985). *Case study research: Design and methods.* Beverly Hills: Sage Publications.

Research on Teaching and Teacher Research: The Issues That Divide

MARILYN COCHRAN-SMITH
SUSAN L. LYTLE

MARILYN COCHRAN-SMITH *is Assistant Professor of Education in the Graduate School of Education, University of Pennsylvania, Philadelphia.* SUSAN L. LYTLE *is Assistant Professor of Education in the Graduate School of Education, University of Pennsylvania, Philadelphia.*

Neither interpretive nor process–product classroom research has foregrounded the teacher's role in the generation of knowledge about teaching. What is missing from the knowledge base for teaching, therefore, are the voices of the teachers themselves, the questions teachers ask, the ways teachers use writing and intentional talk in their work lives, and the interpretive frames teachers use to understand and improve their own classroom practices. Limiting the official knowledge base for teaching to what academics have chosen to study and write about has contributed to a number of problems, including discontinuity between what is taught in universities and what is taught in classrooms, teachers' ambivalence about the claims of academic research, and a general lack of information about classroom life from a truly emic perspective. This article proposes that teacher research has the potential to provide this perspective; however, several critical issues divide teacher research from research on teaching and make it difficult for the university-based community to acknowledge its potential. The article also proposes that in order to encourage teacher research, the educational community will need to address incentives for teachers, the creation and maintenance of supportive networks, the reform of organizational patterns in schools, and the hierarchical power relationships that characterize much of schooling.

Educational Researcher, Vol. 19, No. 2, pp. 2–11

Although there has been considerable emphasis in current educational research on developing a systematic and rigorous body of knowledge about teaching, little attention has been given to the roles teachers might play in generating a knowledge base. That few teachers participate in codifying what we know about teaching, identifying research agendas, and creating new knowledge presents a problem. Those who have daily access, extensive expertise, and a clear stake in improving classroom practice have no formal way to make their knowledge of classroom teaching and learning part of the literature on teaching.

In the first part of this article we argue that efforts to construct and codify a knowledge base for teaching have relied primarily on university-based research and ignored the significant contributions that teacher knowledge can make to both the academic research community and the community of school-based teachers. As a consequence, those most directly responsible for the education of children have been disenfranchised. We propose that teacher research, which we define as systematic, intentional inquiry by teachers, makes accessible some of the expertise of teachers and provides both university and school communities with unique perspectives on teaching and learning. In the second part of this article we identify a number of critical issues that divide research on teaching from teacher research and thus make it extremely difficult for the academic community to recognize the contribution that teacher research can make. Finally, we assess the value of teacher research for the school and university communities, claiming that a broader context for research on teaching requires the systemic reform of school structures.

In this article we hope to contribute to the dialogue recently begun among practitioners and researchers, to explore audiences for teacher research in the academy and in schools, and to argue for the potential of teacher research to help in the reform of schooling. We do not pretend or presume to speak for the school-based teachers whose activities as teacher-researchers are the focus of this paper. Rather we address this topic from our own perspectives as university-based teachers, teacher educators, and researchers.

Theoretical and Research Frameworks

Research on Teaching

Two paradigms have dominated research on teaching over the last 2 decades (Shulman, 1986a). The first, which has been characterized as process-product research, accounts for the majority of studies. For more than 15 years, researchers have been exploring effective teaching by correlating particular processes, or teacher behaviors, with particular products, usually defined as student achievement as measured by standardized tests. (See, for example, Brophy & Good, 1986; Denham & Lieberman, 1980; Dunkin & Biddle, 1974.) Underlying this research is a view of teaching as a primarily linear activity wherein teacher behaviors are considered "causes," and student learning is regarded as "effects."

This approach emphasizes the actions of teachers rather than their professional judgments and attempts to capture the activity of teaching by identifying sets of discrete behaviors reproducible from one teacher and one classroom to the next. Research of this kind has been associated with the view of teacher-as-technician (Apple, 1986), wherein the teacher's primary role is to implement the research findings of others concerning instruction, curriculum, and assessment. With this view, the primary knowledge source for the improvement of practice is research on classroom phenomena that can be observed. This research has a perspective that is ''outside-in''; in other words, it has been conducted almost exclusively by university-based researchers who are outside of the day-to-day practices of schooling.

The second paradigm includes a diverse group of qualitative or interpretive studies that Shulman (1986) refers to as studies of ''classroom ecology.'' This family of inquiries draws from anthropology, sociology, and linguistics, and from the traditions of qualitative, interpretive research. (See, for example, recent syntheses by Cazden, 1986; Erickson, 1986; Evertson & Green, 1986.) Research from these perspectives presumes that teaching is a highly complex, context-specific, interactive activity in which differences across classrooms, schools, and communities are critically important. Interpretive research provides detailed, descriptive accounts of customary school and classroom events that shed light on their meanings for the participants involved. For example, many interpretive studies explore the perspectives and experiences of teachers and students through extensive interviews, and some studies are conducted cooperatively by classroom teachers and university-based researchers (Bussis, Chittenden, & Amarel, 1976; Erickson, 1989; Perl & Wilson, 1986; Yonemura, 1986). Although a small number of research reports are coauthored by university-based researchers and school-based teachers (Edelsky & Smith, 1984; Heath & Branscombe, 1985; Smith & Geoffrey, 1968), most are published singly by university researchers and are intended for academic audiences. Cooperative research provides valuable insights into the interrelationships of theory and practice, but like more traditional interpretive research, often constructs and predetermines teachers' roles in the research process, thereby framing and mediating teachers' perspectives through researchers' perspectives.

We propose that current research on teaching within both process-product and interpretive paradigms, constrains, and at times even makes invisible, teachers' roles in the generation of knowledge about teaching and learning in classrooms. The contents of the *Handbook of Research on Teaching* (Wittrock, 1986), widely viewed as the most comprehensive synthesis of research in the field, is indicative of this exclusion. Described on the dust jacket as ''the definitive guide to what we know about teachers, teaching, and the learning process,'' the 1037-page handbook contains 35 research reviews. Although a few of these include studies carried out by university researchers in cooperation with teachers, and several focus explicitly on teachers' thinking, knowledge, and the cultures of teaching (e.g., the syntheses by Clark & Peterson, 1986, and by Feiman-Nemser & Floden, 1986), none are written by school-based teachers nor, as far as we can determine, are published accounts of teachers' work

cited. Rather, in most of the studies included, teachers are the objects of researchers' investigations and then ultimately are expected to be the consumers and implementors of their findings. Missing from the handbook are the voices of the teachers themselves, the questions that teachers ask, and the interpretive frames that teachers use to understand and improve their own classroom practices.

Teacher Research

We take here as a working definition for teacher research *systematic and intentional inquiry carried out by teachers*. This definition is based in part on the work of Lawrence Stenhouse (as cited in Rudduck & Hopkins, 1985), who defines research in general as ''systematic, self-critical enquiry,'' and in part on an ongoing survey of the literature of teacher writing. This literature includes journal articles written by teachers, in-house collections of teachers' work in progress, monographs about teachers' classroom experiences, as well as published and unpublished teachers' journals and essays. With this definition we wish to emphasize that there already exists a wide array of writing initiated by teachers that is appropriately regarded as research. By *systematic* we refer primarily to ways of gathering and recording information, documenting experiences inside and outside of classrooms, and making some kind of written record. By *intentional* we signal that teacher research is an activity that is planned rather than spontaneous. And by *inquiry* we suggest that teacher research stems from or generates questions and reflects teachers' desires to make sense of their experiences—to adopt a learning stance or openness toward classroom life. We have proposed four categories as a working typology of teacher research: teachers' journals, brief and book-length essays, oral inquiry processes, and classroom studies. Teacher research in these four categories begins to make accessible some of the knowledge and interpretive frames of teachers that are missing from the literature. (See Lytle & Cochran-Smith, in press, for a detailed discussion of the working typology and an analysis of the contribution of teacher research in these categories to the university-based and school-based educational communities.)

The term *teacher research* has been used as a kind of umbrella to describe a wide range of activities, which many trace to the ''action research'' notion of the 1950s and 1960s. Characterized by Lewin (1948) as ''comparative research on the conditions and effects of various forms of social action, and research leading to social action'' (pp. 202–203), action research presented an implicit critique of the usefulness of basic research for social change. Corey (1953), one of the first to use action research in education, emphasized that its major value was increasing the individual teacher's effectiveness with subsequent classes in similar situations over time rather than extending generalizations across educational contexts. Schaefer (1967), on the other hand, asserted that schools could be organized as centers of inquiry, actively producing knowledge in the field of education. In the 1960s and early 1970s, action research by teachers was typically carried out in collaboration with consultants, partly in response to critique that action research was not scientifically valid. Many of the action research initiatives have aimed both to improve school and classroom practice and to contribute to knowledge about teaching and research itself

(Elliott, 1985; Oja & Smulyan, 1989, Tikunoff, Ward & Griffin, 1979).

One of the most influential interpretations of action research is found in the work of Lawrence Stenhouse and his colleagues, who established the Center for Applied Research in Education at the University of East Anglia in 1970. The goal of the center was to "demystify and democratize research, which was seen as failing to contribute effectively to the growth of professional understanding and to the improvement of professional practice" (Stenhouse as cited in Rudduck & Hopkins, 1985, p. 1). Stenhouse, and later his colleagues (e.g., Elliott & McDonald, 1975; Nixon, 1981; Rudduck & Hopkins; and others) encouraged teachers to become intimately involved in the research process. They believed that through their own research, teachers could strengthen their judgment and improve their classroom practices. Stenhouse's argument was radical: He claimed that research was the route to teacher emancipation, and that "researchers [should] justify themselves to practitioners, not practitioners to researchers" (Stenhouse as cited in Rudduck & Hopkins, 1985, p. 19). (For more extensive discussions of the historical roots of action research, see Kyle & Hovda, 1987; and Oja & Smulyan, 1989).

Like action research, the work of Patricia Carini and her teacher colleagues at the Prospect Center and School in Bennington, Vermont, is related to the current concept of teacher research. For almost 2 decades, the Prospect group has developed a number of processes for documenting children's learning in school contexts; for helping teachers uncover and clarify their implicit assumptions about teaching, learning, and schooling; and for solving a variety of school-based educational problems. (See, for example, Carini, 1975, 1979, 1986.) Carini's work is unique; it not only provides formats for teacher research and collaboration, but also, through the Prospect Archives of children's work and records of teacher's deliberations, serves as a living resource for the study of children's development over time. The work of the Prospect School group has influenced many teachers to document and reflect on their classroom practices. Similarly, the North Dakota Study Group on Evaluation, guided by Vito Perrone and many teachers, has long provided a forum for collaborative teacher inquiry into their own and children's work. (See, for example, North Dakota Study Group monographs on children's thinking and language, teacher support systems, in-service training, and the school's relationship to the larger community.)

While the terms *teacher research* and *action research* are relatively new, their underlying conceptions of teaching and the roles of teachers certainly are not. Early in the century Dewey (1904) criticized the nature of educational development, pointing out that it tended to proceed reactively by jumping uncritically from one new technique to the next. He argued that the only remedy for this situation was teachers who had learned to be "adequately moved by their own ideas and intelligence" (p. 16). Dewey emphasized the importance of teachers' reflecting on their practices and integrating their observations into their emerging theories of teaching and learning. He urged educators to be both consumers and producers of knowledge about teaching, both teachers and students of classroom life. Dewey's notion of teachers as students of learning prefigures the concept of teachers as reflective practitioners more recently developed

in the work of Schön and others. Unlike those who characterize teaching as the acquisition of technical skills, Schon (1983, 1987) depicts professional practice as an intellectual process of posing and exploring problems identified by teachers themselves.

Some teacher-researchers model their classroom and school-based inquiries on more traditional university-based social science research. Myers (1985) has been influential in arguing for the adaptation of basic and applied social science research paradigms to teacher research. He suggests that the norms of generalizability, tests of significance, and optimizing controls of problems apply to teacher research, but need to be defined differently by classroom teachers. Myers calls for teacher researchers to be well grounded in problem definition, research design, and quantitative data analysis, and suggests that they begin by replicating the studies of university-based researchers. In contrast to Myers (1985), Mohr and MacLean (1987) and Bissex and Bullock (1987) argue that teacher research is essentially a new genre not necessarily bound by the constraints of traditional research paradigms; they urge teachers to identify their own questions, document their observations, analyze and interpret data in light of their current theories, and share their results primarily with other teachers. Berthoff (1987) puts little emphasis on data gathering and, instead, asserts that teachers already have all the information they need and should reexamine, or in her word "RE-search" their own experiences.

Each of these sets of recommendations for teacher research contains an image of what the genre might look like—an approximation of university-based research; a more grassroots phenomenon that has its own internal standards of logic, consistency, and clarity; or a reflective or reflexive process that is for the benefit of the individual. Each of these images, although quite different, also implicitly compares teacher research to university-based research on teaching. In the section that follows we argue that several critical issues underlying these comparisons account for the exclusion of teacher research from research on teaching.

The Issues That Divide

We argue in this section that comparison of teacher research with university-based research involves a complicated set of assumptions and relationships that act as barriers to enhancing our knowledge based about teaching. Researchers in the academy equate "knowledge about teaching" with the high-status information attained through the traditional modes of inquiry. They fault teachers for not reading or not implementing the findings of such research, even though teachers often find it irrelevant and counterintuitive. Yet teacher research, which by definition has special potential to address issues that teachers themselves identify as significant, does not have a legitimate place. If simply compared with university research, it can easily be found wanting. Regarding teacher research as a mere imitation of university research is not useful and ultimately condescending. It is more useful to consider teacher research as its own genre, not entirely different from other types of systematic inquiry into teaching, yet with some quite distinctive features. But it is also important to recognize the value of teacher research for both the school-based teaching community and the university-based research community.

To compare teacher research and research on teaching, we explore two major issues in educational research: (a) institutionalization, including content and ownership as well as supportive structures and (b) standards for methodological rigor, including research questions, generalizability, theoretical frameworks, and documentation and analysis. Exploring teacher research along these lines points out some of the salient features of this genre, suggests questions raised by the comparison of university-based research and teacher research, and identifies conflicting conceptions of the nature and purposes of teacher research.

Institutionalization

Ownership and content. Although some teacher-researchers are university teachers who reflect on their own teaching at the university level (Duckworth, 1987; Freeman, 1989; Kutz, 1989; Rorschach & Whitney, 1986), most of those engaged in teacher researcher are K–12 classroom teachers or student teachers who have participated in some institute, in-service training, or graduate program based at a university where they have been exposed to particular ideas about teaching and learning. They do teacher research as dissertations, graduate coursework projects, as part of their work as cooperating teachers or student teachers, or as ongoing work in teacher collaborative projects. Some teacher-researchers work on collaborative research projects with university-based researchers or teacher educators (Buchanan & Schultz, 1989; Edelsky & Boyd, 1989; Lytle & Fecho, 1989); others form research partnerships with their teacher colleagues (Boston Women's Teachers Group, 1983; The Philadelphia Teachers Learning Cooperative, 1984) or with their own students (Cochran-Smith, Garfield, & Greenberger, 1989; Goswami & Shultz, in press).

Encouraged by the widespread activities of the National Writing Project, the Breadloaf School of English, and the work of influential researchers/practitioners such as Donald Graves (1983) and Lucy Calkins (1986), the focus of much of the K–12 teacher research of the last decade has been writing—children's development as writers (Avery, 1987), classroom environments that support students' progress (Atwell, 1987), classroom and schoolwide strategies for writing assessment (*Making Room for Growth*, 1989), teachers' own writing and classroom inquiry processes (Frutkoff, 1989), and the generation of theory through sustained reflection on classroom practice (Johnson, 1989). Other teacher researchers have focused on classroom teaching and learning more broadly by looking, for example, at the interrelationships of children's oral and written language development (Strieb, 1985), the complexities of a single class or a teacher's experience over time (Harris, 1989), the corpus of a single child's artistic or written work (Buchanan, 1988), children's growing and changing conceptions of the world and how these are expressed in their stories, play, and drama (Paley, 1981), and thematic analyses of teachers' curriculum theory and design (Wiggington, 1985). Many of these address the interactive relationships of students' language, literacy, and learning (Ashton-Warner, 1963), whereas others focus on the acquisition of discipline-based knowledge (Tierney, 1981), and a few center on more general issues of school organization, policy, and multicultural education (Palonsky, 1986).

Supportive structures. Recently, a number of organizations have begun to focus their efforts on teacher research. For example, both the National Council of Teachers of English (NCTE) and the U.S. Department of Education's Office of Educational Research and Improvement (OERI) have begun to sponsor national efforts to support and sanction teacher research through direct funding. These two funding efforts represent different approaches to supporting teacher research.

The guidelines for OERI's funds require that teachers must be the principal investigators and that proposed projects must address issues important to local school improvement; specified topics are broad, including teachers' roles and functions, instructional processes and materials, subject matter teaching, assessment, professional development, alternative patterns of school management and organization, and ways for schools to find, understand, and use research and practice-based knowledge. This represents a significant federal effort to institutionalize teacher research in planning and decision making at school and district levels. Funding efforts like OERI's seem very promising, but in order for these initiatives to make a difference, those in positions of power in school districts would need to believe in and act on the following assumptions: (a) that the questions teachers ask about theory and practice ought to be the starting points for classroom inquiry; (b) that teachers can and should play a central role in the creation of new knowledge about teaching and learning; (c) that the benefits of this new knowledge would outweigh the problems inherent in altering standard school routines and practices; and (d) that power in decision making can and ought to be distributed among teachers, specialists, and administrators across the school system.

In contrast, NCTE provides funds for individual teacher-researchers who are asked to identify a study based on concerns directly relevant to their own work. NCTE's guidelines for would-be teacher-researchers specify that funds may not be used for teacher release time, travel, or other organizational changes or staffing arrangements. Furthermore, to support their proposals, teacher-researchers are asked to include evaluations by three knowledgeable reviewers who may or may not include school-based personnel. Unlike OERI's efforts, which require school-level commitment and the creation of systemic structures that support changing roles for teachers, the NCTE program emphasizes the professional development of teachers inside their own classrooms. However, the structures of NCTE as an organization, as well as those of the Breadload School of English and the National and local sites of the National Writing Project, function as infrastructures that make it possible for teachers to present their work at conferences and publish their writing.

There are no simple ways to create systemic supports for teacher research that, on one hand, encourage teacher autonomy and initiative, but, on the other hand, recognize that teacher research occurs within the context of broad-based efforts of school improvement. Unlike the academic research community, which is organized to provide formal and informal structures to support research on teaching, the community of teacher researchers is disparate, and there are few structures that support their work. Variations in the efforts of OERI, NCTE and other organizations reflect the complexity of the problem.

Standards for Methodological Rigor

Research questions. It may appear to be self-evident that the research questions in teacher research emanate from the day-to-day experiences of teachers themselves, but this is not a trivial issue. In traditional university-based classroom research, researchers' questions reflect careful study of the theoretical and empirical literature and, sometimes, negotiation with the teachers in whose classrooms the researchers collect data. Teachers' questions, on the other hand, often emerge from discrepancies between what is intended and what occurs: Initially these questions may be the result of a concern about a student's progress, a classroom routine that is floundering, conflict or tension among students, or as a desire to try out some new approach. This questioning process is highly reflexive, immediate, and referenced to particular children and classroom contexts: What happens when my "high-risk" second graders shift from a basal reading program to a whole language curriculum? How will I know when my students are on the way to thinking like mathematicians rather than simply learning new routines? How do my digressions from lesson plans contribute to or detract from my goals for the students? How do my students' theories of teaching and learning shape and become shaped by writing conferences?

There is little disagreement that teachers who engage in self-directed inquiry about their own work in classrooms find the process intellectually satisfying, they testify to the power of their own research to help them understand and transform their teaching practices.

Although these questions are not framed in the language of educational theory, they are indeed about discrepancies between theory and practice. Although they are not always motivated by a need to generalize beyond the immediate case, they may in fact be relevant to a wide variety of contexts. The questions of teacher-researchers are, at once, more general than questions that concentrate on the effectiveness of specific techniques, materials, or instructional methods and more specific than interpretive questions that explore the meanings of customary school and classroom events. Teachers' questions are not simply elaborated versions of What can I do Monday morning? or What will work in my

classroom? Embedded in the questions of teacher-researchers are many other implicit questions about the relationships of concrete particular cases to more general and abstract theories of learning and teaching. For example, when a teacher asks, What will happen if I use journals with my first graders at the beginning of the school year before they have begun to read? she is also asking, more generally, How does children's reading development relate to their writing development? Does some explicit instruction in letter–sound relationships have to precede children's expressive uses of those relationships? Do children have knowledge of these relationships before they begin formal reading instruction? If they do, where does this knowledge come from? Will the children collaborate on the journals? What kind of a context should I provide for sharing? Who will they imagine is their audience? What is the relationship between "errors" and growth in writing? For which students will this activity be effective and useful, and for which students will it not be? Why? The unique feature of the questions that prompt teacher research is that they emanate solely neither from theory nor from practice, but from critical reflection on the intersection of the two.

Generalizability. The criterion of generalizability has been used to discount the value of research prompted by the questions of individual teachers and conducted in single classrooms. As Zumwalt (1982) effectively argues, however, there is a growing realization in the research community that the positivistic paradigm that attempts to formulate general laws is probably not the most useful for understanding educational phenomenon. Zumwalt points out that generalizations about teaching and learning are by definition context-free. She quotes Guba's (1980) assertion that "it is virtually impossible to imagine any human behavior which is not mediated by the context in which it occurs" (in Zumwalt, 1982, p. 235), to make the case that rather than laws about what works generically in classrooms, we need insight into the particulars of how and why something works and for whom, within the contexts of particular classrooms.

A similar argument is made by interpretive researchers who demonstrate that understanding one classroom helps us better to understand all classrooms. Teachers are uniquely situated to conduct such inquiries: They have opportunities to observe learners over long periods of time in a variety of academic and social situations; they often have many years of knowledge about the culture of the community, school and classroom; and they experience the ongoing events of classroom life in relation to their particular roles and responsibilities. This set of lenses sets the perspectives of teachers apart from those of others who look in classrooms. Knoblauch and Brannon (1988) make a related point in their discussion on the phenomenological basis of teacher research. "The story-telling of the teacher-inquirer in a classroom devoted to language practices has its peculiar features and makes a distinctive contribution to our knowledge of school experience.... The telling aims not at selectivity or simplification but at richness of texture and intentional complexity" (p. 24).

Holt (1964) did not use the phrase "teacher research" when he called for teachers to observe more closely their children's classroom activities and then meet to talk about their observations, but his words are very much in keeping with its spirit: "Once we understand that some of the things we teachers do may be helpful, some merely useless, and some downright harmful, we can begin to ask which is which. But only teachers can ask such questions and use their daily work with students to test their answers. All other kinds of research into ways of improving teaching lead mostly to expensive fads and nonsense" (p. 54). While Holt's critique probably responds to the experimental research of the 1950s and early 1960s, his point about the unique potentialities of teacher questions and classroom inquiry remains significant.

Theoretical frameworks. Not only is the status of teacher questions at issue, but there is also considerable disagreement about the way in which teacher research is grounded in theory. In a discussion of practical theories of teaching, Sanders and McCutcheon (1986) argue that teaching requires intentional and skillful action within real-world situations. The success of these actions depends on the ability to perceive relevant features of complex, problematic, and changeable situations and to make appropriate choices. The knowledge necessary to perform these professional tasks has been called "theories of action" (Argyris, 1982). Rather than make a distinction between professional knowledge and educational theory, as is usually done, Sanders and McCutcheon make the case that professional knowledge essentially is theoretical knowledge.

This position contrasts with North's (1987) analysis of practitioners' knowledge in composition. North calls professional knowledge "lore," and defines it as "the accumulated body of traditions, practices, and beliefs in terms of which practitioners understand how writing is done, learned and taught" (p. 22). Although North seems critical of the fact that practitioner knowledge has been devalued, conceptions like his may contribute to its devaluation by suggesting that the structure of this knowledge is experiential and driven only by pragmatic logic. We wonder how "lore," which North claims is a "very rich and powerful body of knowledge" can be, as he also points out, totally unselective, self-contradictory, and framed only in practical terms. From North's perspective, then, teachers' knowledge would hardly qualify as theory, and indeed in North's discussion of practical inquiry, his version of teacher research, there is little mention of theory.

Juxtaposing North's concept of "lore" with the recent work of Shulman (1986b, 1987), which explores the knowledge base for teaching, reveals a major discrepancy among views of teachers' knowledge and theories. By working intensively with beginning and experienced teachers, Shulman is exploring the wide variety of categories of knowledge that teachers have and use. His work suggests that the base for teaching is complex, encompassing knowledge of content, pedagogy, curriculum, learners and their characteristics, educational contexts, purposes and values and their philosophical and historical grounds (p. 8). Our own work with teachers leads us to believe that all of Shulman's categories of knowledge can be seen as leading to theoretical frameworks that teachers not only bring to the identification of their research questions but also utilize in the analysis and interpretation of their findings.

These debates demonstrate that the status and role of theory are central issues in teacher research. Just as our earlier discussion indicated that there are controversies in

the academic community about the feasibility of discovering generalizable laws, similar questions are raised about the kinds of theory appropriate to applied fields like education. In these fields, various combinations of facts, values, and assumptions may better capture the state of knowledge than conventional scientific theories (Zumwalt, 1982; House, 1980). It may be that the notion of theory as a combination of perspectives will be particularly compatible with, and productive for, the emerging genre of teacher research. Indeed, how and whether teachers theorize is an empirical question being explored in a variety of interesting ways (Clark & Peterson, 1986; Elbaz, 1983; Munby, 1987; Shavelson & Stern, 1981; Shulman, 1987). Teacher research itself may provide evidence of the unique theoretical frameworks underlying teachers' questions and decisions and grounded in their classroom practice. If we regard teachers' theories as sets of interrelated conceptual frameworks grounded in practice, then teacher researchers are both users and generators of theory. If, however, we limit the notion of theory to more traditional university-based definitions, then research by teachers may be seen as atheoretical, and its value for creation of the knowledge base on teaching may be circumscribed.

Documentation and analysis. In many respects the forms of documentation in teacher research resemble the forms used in academic research, particularly the standard forms of interpretive research. Field notes about classroom interactions, interviews with students and teachers, and classroom documents (e.g., students' writing and drawing, test scores, teachers' plans and handouts) are commonly collected by teacher researchers. In addition, teacher researchers often keep extensive journals and audiotape or videotape small and large group discussions, peer and teacher–student conferences, students' debates, role plays, and dramatic productions, as well as their own classroom presentations. Like university-based qualitative research, a strength of teacher research is that it often entails multiple data sources that can be used to confirm and/or illuminate one another.

Questions about the demands of rigorous documentation emerge from both teacher researchers and university researchers. Although many teachers collect some of these data in the course of the normal activity of teaching, as teachers readily point out, the complex and extensive demands on teachers' time and attention place obvious limitations on what teachers can manage to do. Some university researchers, who equate data collection with training in the traditions of social science research, question whether teachers' data can be sufficiently systematic and teacher researchers sufficiently well prepared as classroom observers. As we have demonstrated elsewhere, however, many teachers have sophisticated and sensitive observation skills grounded in the context of actual classrooms and schools. In analyzing the patterns and discrepancies that occur, teachers use the interpretive frameworks of practitioners to provide a truly emic view that is different from that of an outside observer, even if that observer assumes an ethnographic stance and spends considerable time in the classroom. (See Lytle & Cochran-Smith, in press, for a detailed analysis of the texts and contexts of teacher research).

Teacher Research: Contributions and Future Directions
Underlying much of the debate about methodological rigor in teacher research is a limited concept of what kinds of

research can contribute to our knowledge about teaching. This limited concept is the basis of our critique of *The Handbook of Research on Teaching* (Wittrock, 1986), whose dust jacket describes the contents as "the definitive guide to what we know about teachers, teaching, and the learning process." As we have shown, the "we" refers only to the academic community, and privileges its particular ways of knowing, writing, and publishing about teaching. In this arena the academy decides what counts as knowledge according to its own traditions. We have been arguing that teacher research constitutes another legitimate arena of formal knowledge about teaching. The status and value of teacher research, however, have yet to be determined by school-based teachers, the interpretive community for whom it is primarily intended. Just as academics have evolved a complex set of criteria and standards for judging the quality and contribution of research in the academic community, teachers over time will develop a similarly complex set of standards for evaluating the research generated in and for their community.

Value for the Teaching Community

There is little disagreement that teachers who engage in self-directed inquiry about their own work in classrooms find the process intellectually satisfying; they testify to the power of their own research to help them better understand and ultimately to transform their teaching practices. In *Reclaiming the Classroom: Teacher Research as an Agency for Change*, the most widely disseminated collection of conceptual pieces about teacher research as well as studies by teachers, Goswami and Stillman (1987) provide a compelling summary of what happens when teachers conduct research as a regular part of their roles as teachers:

1. Their teaching is transformed in important ways: they become theorists, articulating their intentions, testing their assumptions, and finding connections with practice.
2. Their perceptions of themselves as writers and teachers are transformed. They step up their use of resources; they form networks; and they become more active professionally.
3. They become rich resources who can provide the profession with information it simply doesn't have. They can observe closely, over long periods of time, with special insights and knowledge. Teachers know their classrooms and students in ways that outsiders can't.
4. They become critical, responsive readers and users of current research, less apt to accept uncritically others' theories, less vulnerable to fads, and more authoritative in their assessment of curricula, methods, and materials.
5. They can study writing and learning and report their findings without spending large sums of money (although they must have support and recognition). Their studies, while probably not definitive, taken together should help us develop and assess writing curricula in ways that are outside the scope of specialists and external evaluators.
6. They collaborate with their students to answer questions important to both, drawing on community resources in new and unexpected ways. The nature of classroom discourse changes when inquiry begins. Working with teachers to answer real questions provides students with intrinsic motivation for talking, reading, and writing and has the potential for helping them achieve mature language skills. (preface)

Similar claims about the value of teacher research for the teachers themselves have been made by a number of groups of teacher-researchers and university researchers working together (e.g., Bissex & Bullock, 1987; Mohr & MacLean, 1987; Strickland et al., 1989). When more teachers have opportunities to collaborate across classrooms, schools, and communities and when they develop their own set of evaluative standards, it is likely that they will find avenues for broader dissemination and that the value of their work will increase dramatically.

Value for the Academic Community

We are not suggesting that the audience of teacher research is or ought to be limited to teachers. Just as teachers read and use the research of university-based researchers, many academics committed to teacher education and/or the study of teaching and learning undoubtedly will find the research of teachers a rich and unique sources of knowledge. We can imagine at least four important ways in which the academic community can learn from teacher research. (See Lytle & Cochran-Smith, in press, for a more extensive analysis.) First, teachers' journals provide rich data about classroom life, which can be used by academics to construct and reconstruct theories of teaching and learning. In this capacity, teachers serve primarily as collectors of data, but their data are unlike other classroom descriptions that have been selected, filtered and composed in the language of researchers. Second, because teacher research emanates from teachers' own questions and frameworks, it reveals what teachers regard as the seminal issues about learning and the cultures of teaching. Third, as Shulman (1986a) argues, both "scientific knowledge of rules and principles" and "richly described and critically analyzed cases" need to constitute the knowledge base of teaching. Teacher research provides these rich classroom cases. Because cases are often more powerful and memorable influences on decision making than are conventional research findings in the form of rules and generalizations (Nisbett & Ross, 1980; Shulman, 1986a), teacher educators can use teachers' cases to study how practitioners learn from the documented experiences of others. Finally, through their research, teachers can (a) contribute to the critique and revision of existing theories by describing discrepant and paradigmatic cases, and (b) provide data that ground or move toward alternative theories. What teachers bring will alter, and not just add to, what is known about teaching. As the body of teacher research accumulates, it will undoubtedly prompt reexamination of many current assumptions about children, learning, and classroom processes.

Communities for Teacher Research

Participation in teacher research requires considerable effort by innovative and dedicated teachers to remain in their classrooms while carving out opportunities to inquire and reflect on their own practice. Teacher research is unlike university-based research, which occupies an unquestioned position at the center of the institution's mission. Furthermore, the academic research community is organized to provide formal and informal opportunities for response and critique. On the other hand, teacher research struggles on the margins of K–12 schools, and teacher researchers often work outside school systems. The Philadelphia Teachers'

Learning Cooperative, which has met weekly in private homes for more than a decade to reflect on classroom practices (Philadelphia Teachers' Learning Cooperative, 1984), and the Boston Women's Teachers' Group, which studies the effects of teaching on teachers throughout their professional careers (Boston Women's Teachers' Group, 1983), are good examples of self-initiated and sustained teacher inquiry groups.

Cautioning against simply adding research to teachers' work loads, Myers (1987) has argued persuasively for the institutionalization of teacher research by making inquiry an integral part of the professional lives of teachers. Recently, a few school districts have moved in this direction by establishing new positions that combine teaching and researching responsibilities, such as lead teachers, teacher-mentors, or peer supervisors. For example, the Pittsburgh public school system has created positions for researchers-in-residence who collect and manage data for the principal and faculty (P. LeMahieu, personal communication, 1988), and in the Philadelphia public schools, teacher-consultants combine classroom teaching with teacher research through a unique cross-visitation program initiated by teachers in the Philadelphia Writing Project (Fecho, 1987; Lytle & Fecho, 1989). These efforts are part of a trend to differentiate teachers' roles in schools and capitalize on teacher expertise. It is unclear at this time what the impact of innovations like these will be. It would be unfortunate, however, if they inadvertently buttressed the traditional association between gaining increased power and responsibility in the school system and abandoning the classroom.

A variety of arrangements have been proposed to enable teachers to do research. These include: reduced loads, release time, paid overtime, and summer seminars or institutes in which teachers write and reflect about their teaching practices (Mohr & MacLean, 1987); collaborative networks, study groups, or research teams; opportunities to visit the classrooms of teachers in other grade levels, subject areas, schools, and school districts; financial support for their research projects; and a number of formal and informal channels for the dissemination of teachers' work. We contend that the most important factor in determining where and how these arrangements work is whether school systems allow teachers to participate on a voluntary basis, in designing and revising these new structures. This new approach will come about if schools and school systems realize that there is a direct connection between supporting the systematic inquiries of teacher-researchers and improving the quality of teaching and learning.

However, in many school systems teachers have not been encouraged to work together on voluntary, self-initiated projects or to speak out with authority about instructional, curricular, and policy issues. When groups of teachers have the opportunity to work together as highly professionalized teacher-researchers, they become increasingly articulate about issues of equity, hierarchy, and autonomy and increasingly critical of the technocratic model that dominates much of school practice. This notion of highly professionalized teachers is consonant with Aronowitz and Giroux's (1985) concept of teachers as "transformative intellectuals" who have the potential to resist what Apple (1986) refers to as "deskilling" mandates and to change their own teaching practices. In a recent collection of case studies by

teachers of writing, editors Bissex and Bullock (1987) suggest that "by becoming researchers teachers take control over their classrooms and professional lives in ways that confound the traditional definition of teacher and offer proof that education can reform itself from within" (p. xi). In the same vein, they also argue that teacher research is a natural agent of change: "Doing classroom research changes teachers and the teaching profession from the inside out, from the bottom up, through changes in teachers themselves. And therein lies the power" (p. 27).

Although we agree with the direction of these claims, we are concerned about school reform efforts that depend primarily on the efforts of teachers without school restructuring. Because many structural features of school systems constrain bottom-up, inside-out reform, it seems unlikely that school systems traditionally organized to facilitate top-down change will readily acknowledge and build on the potential impact of teacher-initiated reforms. Furthermore, as teachers empower themselves by adopting a more public and authoritative stance on their own practice, they are more likely to create the contexts for their own students to be empowered as active learners. Ironically, and indeed unfortunately, many school systems are slow to realize the potential link between teacher research and enhanced student learning.

If teachers are to carry out the systematic and self-critical inquiry that teacher research entails, networks will need to be established and forums created by teachers so that ongoing collaboration is possible. These networks begin to function as intellectual communities for teachers who, more typically, are isolated from one another. Two examples in which we are involved are PhilWP (The Philadelphia Writing Project, a site of the National Writing Project at the University of Pennsylvania) and Project START (Student Teachers as Researching Teachers, a school–university collaborative teacher education program at the University of Pennsylvania). Both of these involve groups of experienced and beginning teachers who meet regularly to read, write, problem-solve, and ask each other a wide range of significant questions abut theory and practice. In addition to collaborating with each other, PhilWP teachers are involved in a program designed by project teachers whereby they visit, are visited by, and consult with other teachers not in the project. The cross-visitation program constitutes teacher research in two respects: teachers conduct classroom inquiries across classrooms and schools, and a smaller research group is documenting the evolution of the program as an innovative model of collegial in-service development. This arrangement allows teachers to develop a broad range of perspectives on what goes on in their own classrooms and schools (Fecho, 1987; Lytle and Fecho, 1989). In Project START experienced teachers, in-service teachers, and teacher-educators form teacher-researcher teams to study learning and teaching in single classrooms from their three different perspectives. Part of what preservice teachers learn are the intellectual frames of experienced teachers who in turn examine and develop their own interpretive strategies (Cochran-Smith, 1989a, 1989b). For PhilWP teachers, the school district provides "writing support teachers" who substitute while PhilWP teachers and their teacher partners cross-visit and confer. For Project START, most schools have set aside time in the school day for weekly teacher-researcher group meetings. In both projects, school systems have provided in-school resources to support these unusual collaborative structures.

Teacher research has the potential to play a significant role in the enhanced professionalization of teaching, but it will certainly not be the entire agenda for school reform. As we have shown, there are complex problems involved even in calling for teacher research. As Myers (1985) rightly argues, "telling teachers they should do teacher research is…an inadequate way to begin" (p. 126). To encourage teacher research, we must first address incentives for teachers, the creation and maintenance of supportive networks, the reform of rigid organizational patterns in schools, and the hierarchical power relationships that characterize most of schooling. Likewise, to resolve the problematic relationship between academic research and teacher research it will be necessary to confront controversial issues of voice, power, ownership, status, and role in the broad educational community. We are not arguing that teacher research ought to occupy a privileged position in relation to research on teaching. Rather we are suggesting that an exploration of the issues the divide research on teaching and teacher research may help raise critical questions about the nature of knowledge for teaching and hence enhance research in both communities.

References

Apple, M. (1986). *Teachers and texts: A political economy of class and gender relations in education.* New York: Routledge and Kegan Paul.

Argyris, C. (1982). *Reasoning, learning and action: Individual and organizational.* San Francisco: Jossey-Bass.

Aronowitz, S., & Giroux, H. (1985). *Education under siege.* New York: New World Foundation.

Ashton-Warner, S. (1963). *Teacher.* New York: Simon & Schuster.

Atwell, N. (1987). *In the middle: Writing, reading and learning with adolescents.* Portsmouth, NH: Boynton/Cook.

Avery, C. S. (1987). Traci: A learning-disabled child in a writing-process classroom. In G. Bissex & R. Bullock (Eds.), *Seeing for ourselves.* Portsmouth, NH: Heinemann.

Berthoff, A. (1987). The teacher as researcher. In D. Goswami and P. R. Stillman (Eds.), *Reclaiming the classroom: Teacher research as an agency for change.* Upper Montclair, NJ: Boynton.

Bissex, G., & Bullock, R. (1987). *Seeing for ourselves: Case study research by teachers of writing.* Portsmouth, NH: Heinemann.

Boston Women's Teachers' Group (Freeman, S., Jackson, J., & Boles, K.). (1983). Teaching: An imperilled "profession." In L. Shulman & G. Sykes (Eds.), *Handbook of teaching and policy.* New York: Longman.

Brophy, J. E., & Good, T. L. (1986). Teacher behaviors and student achievement. In M. C. Wittrock (Ed.), *Handbook of research on teaching* (3rd edition). New York: Macmillan.

Buchanan, J. (1988). *Looking closely at one student's work: Anwar's fourth grade year.* Paper presented at teacher-researcher conference. Lehman College, New York.

Buchanan, J., & Schultz, K. (1989). *Looking together: Communities of learners in an urban third-fourth grade classroom.* Paper presented at National Council of Teachers of English, Spring Conference, Charleston, SC.

Bussis, A. M., Chittenden, E. A., & Amarel, M. (1976). *Beyond surface curriculum.* Boulder, CO: Westview Press Inc.

Calkins, L. (1986). *The art of teaching writing.* Portsmouth, NH. Heinemann Educational Books.

Carini, P. (1975). *Observation and description: An alternative methodology for the investigation of human phenomena.* Grand Forks, ND: University of North Dakota Press.

Carini, P. (1979). *The art of seeing and the visibility of the person.* Grand Forks, ND: University of North Dakota.

Carini, P. (1986). *Prospect's documentary processes.* Bennington, VT: Manuscript.

Cazden, C. (1986). Classroom discourse. In M. C. Wittrock (Ed.), *Handbook of research on teaching* (3rd edition). New York: Macmillan.

Clark, C. C., & Peterson, P. L. (1986). Teachers' thought processes. In M. C. Wittrock (Ed.), *Handbook of research on teaching* (3rd edition). New York: Macmillan.

Cochran-Smith, M. (1989a). *Of questions, not answers: The discourse of student teachers and their school and university mentors.* Paper presented at American Educational Research Association, San Francisco.

Cochran-Smith, M. (1989b). *Rethinking student teaching: Project START.* Paper presented at American Association of College Testing Education, Anaheim, CA.

Cochran-Smith, M., Garfield, E., & Greenberger, R. (1989). *Student teachers and their teacher: Talking our way into new understandings.* Paper presented at National Council of Teachers of English Spring Conference. Charleston, SC.

Corey, S. (1953). *Action research to improve school practices.* New York: Teachers College, Columbia University.

Denham, C., & Lieberman, A. (Eds.). (1980). *Time to learn.* Washington, DC: NIE.

Dewey, J. (1904). The relation of theory to practice in education. *The third NSSE yearbook (Part 1).* Chicago, IL: University of Chicago Press.

Duckworth, E. (1987). *The having of wonderful ideas.* New York: Teachers College Press.

Dunkin, M. J., & Biddle, B. J. (1974). *The study of teaching.* New York: Holt, Rinehart and Winston.

Edelsky, C., & Boyd, C. (1989). *Collaborative research.* Keynote address presented at National Council of Teachers of English Spring Conference, Charleston, SC.

Edelsky, C., & Smith, K. (1984). Is that writing or are those marks just a figment of your curriculum? *Language Arts, 61*(1): 24–32.

Elbaz, F. (1983). *Teacher thinking: A study of practical knowledge.* New York: Nichols Publishers.

Elliott, J., & MacDonald, B. (1975). *People in classrooms.* Occasional Paper No. 2, University of East Anglia, Center for Applied Research in Education.

Elliott, J. (1985). Facilitating action research in schools: some dilemmas. In R. Burgess (Ed.), *Field Methods in the study of education.* Lewes: Falmer Press.

Erickson, F. (1986). Qualitative methods in research on teaching. In M. C. Wittrock (Ed.), *Handbook of research on teaching* (3rd edition). New York: Macmillan.

Erickson, F. (1989). Research currents: Learning and collaboration in teaching. *Language Arts, 66*(4): 430–442.

Evertson, C. M., & Green, J. L. (1986). Observation as inquiry and method. In M. C. Wittrock (Ed.), *Handbook of research on teaching* (3rd edition). New York: Macmillan.

Fecho, R. (1987). *Folding back the classroom walls: Teacher collaboration via cross visitation.* Work in Progress. Philadelphia; University of Pennsylvania, Philadelphia Writing Project.

Feiman-Nemser, S., & Floden, R. E. (1986). The cultures of teaching. In M. C. Wittrock (Ed.), *Handbook of research on teaching* (3rd edition). New York Macmillan.

Freeman, C. (1989). *The case study method in teacher education: A teacher researcher study.* Paper presented at Ethnography in Education Forum, Philadelphia, PA.

Frutkoff, J. (1989). *Journal keeping: A teacher looks inward and backward.* Paper presented at Ethnography in Education Forum, University of Pennsylvania, Philadelphia, PA.

Goswami, D., & Schultz, J. (in press). *Reclaiming the classroom: Teachers and students together.* Portsmouth, NH:Boynton/Cook.

Goswami, D., & Stillman, P. (1987). *Reclaiming the classroom: Teacher research as an agency for change.* Upper Montclair, NJ: Boynton/Cook.

Graves, D. (1983). *Writing: teachers and children at work.* Exeter, NH: Heinemann Educational Books.

Guba, E. G. (1980). *Naturalistic and conventional inquiry.* Paper presented at American Educational Research Association, Boston, MA.

Harris, M. (1989). *Looking back: 20 years of a teacher's journal.* Paper presented at Ethnography in Education Forum, University of Pennsylvania, Philadelphia, PA.

Heath, S. B., & Branscombe, A. 91985). 'Intelligent writing' in an audience community: Teacher, students, and researcher. In S. Freedman (Ed.), *The acquisition of written language: Response and revision.* Norwood, NJ: Ablex.

Holt, J. (1964). *How children fail.* New York: Dell Publishing Co.

House, E. R. (1980). *Mapping social disconsensus onto social theory.* Paper presented at American Educational Research Association, Boston.

Johnston, P. (1989). A scenic view of reading. *Language Arts, 66*(2): 160–170.

Knoblauch, C. H., & Brannon, L. (1988). Knowing our knowledge: A phenomenological basis for teacher research. In Smith, L. Z. (Ed.), *Audits of meaning: A festschrift in honor of Ann E. Berthoff.* Portsmouth, NH: Boynton/Cook.

Kutz, E. (1989). *Preservice teachers as researchers: Developing practice and creating theory.* Paper presented at Ethnography and Education Forum, University of Pennsylvania, Philadelphia, PA

Kyle, D., & Hovda, R. (1987). The potential and practice of action research, parts I and II. *Peabody Journal of Education, 64*(2) and (3).

Lewin, K. (1948). *Resolving social conflicts.* New York: Harper & Row.

Lytle, S. L., & Cochran-Smith, M. (in press). *Learning from teacher research: A Working Typology.*

Lytle, S. L., & Cochran-Smith, M. (1989, March). Teacher research: Toward clarifying the concept. *National Writing Project Quarterly.*

Lytle, S., & Fecho, R. (1989). *Meeting strangers in familiar places: Teacher collaboration by cross-visitation.* Paper presented at American Educational Research Association, San Francisco, CA.

Making room for growth: A documentary portrait of the 1987–1989 writing assessment program in the School District of Philadelphia. (1989). Conducted by Paths/PRISM in Partnership with the School District of Philadelphia.

Mohr, M., & MacLean, M. (1987). *Working together: A guide for teacher-researchers.* Urbana, IL: National Council of Teachers of English.

Munby, H. (1987). Metaphors and teachers' knowledge. *Research in the Teaching of English, 21*(4): 337–397.

Myers, M. (1985). *The teacher-researcher: How to study writing in the classroom.* Urbana, IL: National Council of Teachers of English.

Myers, M. (1987). Institutionalizing inquiry. *National Writing Project Quarterly, 9*(3).

Nisbett, R. E., & Ross, L. (1980). *Human inference: Strategies and shortcomings of social judgment.* Englewood Cliffs, NJ: Prentice Hall.

Nixon, J. (Ed.), (1981). *A teacher's guide to action research.* London: Grant McIntyre.

North, S. (1987). *The making of knowledge in composition: Portrait of an emerging field.* Upper Montclair, NJ: Boynton/Cook.

North Dakota Study Group on Evaluation. (The monograph series of the North Dakota Study Group on Evaluation). Center for Teaching and Learning, University of North Dakota.

Oja, S. & Smulyan, L. (1989). *Collaborative action research: a developmental approach.* London: Falmer Press.

Paley, V. (1981). *Wally's stories.* Cambridge, MA: Harvard University Press.

Palonsky, S. B. (1986). *900 shows a year, A look at teaching from a teacher's side of the desk.* New York: Random House.

Perl, S., & Wilson, N. (1986). *Through teachers' eyes.* Portsmouth, NH: Heinemann Educational Books.

Philadelphia Teachers Learning Cooperative. (1984). On becoming teacher experts: Buying time. *Language Arts, 6*(1), 731–735.

Rorschach, E., & Whitney, R. (1986). Relearning to teach: Peer observation as a means of professional development for teachers. *English Education, 18*(3): 159–172.

Rudduck, J. (1985). Teacher research and research-based teacher education. *Journal of Education for Teaching, 11*(3), 281–289.

Rudduck, J., & Hopkins, D. (1985). *Research as a basis for teaching, Readings from the work of Lawrence Stenhouse.* London: Heinemann Educational Books.

Sanders, D., & McCutcheon, G. (1986). The development of practical theories of teaching. *Journal of Curriculum and Supervision, 2*(1): 50–67.

Schaefer, R. J. (1967). *The school as a center of inquiry.* New York: Harper and Row.

Schon, D. A. (1983). *The reflective practitioner.* San Francisco, CA: Jossey-Bass Publishers.

Schon, D. A. (1987). *Educating the reflective practitioner.* San Francisco, CA: Jossey-Bass Publishers.

Shavelson, R. J., & Stern, P. (1981). Research on teacher's pedagogical thoughts, judgments, decisions and behaviors. *Review of Educational Research, 51,* 455–498.

Shulman, L. (1986a). Paradigms and research programs in the study of teaching: A contemporary perspective. In M. C. Wittrock (Ed.), *Handbook of research on teaching* (3rd edition). New York: Macmillan.

Shulman, L. (1986b). Those who understand: Knowledge growth in teaching. *Educational Researcher, 15*(2): 4–14.

Shulman, L. (1987). Knowledge and teaching: Foundations of the new reform. *Harvard Educational Review, 51,* 1–22.

Smith, L. H., & Geoffrey, W. (1968). *The complexities of an urban classroom: An analysis toward a general theory of teaching.* New York: Holt, Rinehart and Winston.

Strickland, D., Dillon, R. M., Funkhouser, L., Glick, M., & Rogers, C. (1989). Research currents: Classroom discourse during literature response groups. *Language Arts, 66*(2): 192–200.

Strieb, L. (1985). *A Philadelphia teacher's journal.* North Dakota Study Group Center for Teaching and Learning. Grand Forks, ND: Center for Teaching and Learning.

Tierney, R. (1981). Using expressive writing to teach biology. In A. Wotring & R. Tierney (Eds.), *Two studies of writing in high school science.* Classroom research study #5. Berkeley, CA: Bay Area Writing Project, University of California.

Tikunoff, W. J., Ward, B. A., & Griffin, G. A. (1979). *Interactive research and development on teaching study: final report.* San Francisco: Far West Regional Laboratory for Educational Research and Development.

Wiggington, E. (1985). *Sometimes a shining moment: The Foxfire experience.* Garden City, NY: Archer Press/Doubleday.

Wittrock, M. C. (1986). *Handbook of research on teaching* (3rd edition). New York: Macmillan Publishing Co.

Yonemura, M. (1986). *A teacher at work, Professional development and the early childhood educator.* New York: Teachers College Press.

Zumwalt, K. K. (1982). Research on teaching: Policy implications for teacher education. In A. Lieberman, & M. McLaughlin (Eds.), *Policy making in education,* 81st yearbook of the National Society for the Study of Education, Chicago, IL: University of Chicago Press.

'It Was A Testing Ground'

Suzanne Hershey is in the early stages of her teaching career. In an interview with Assistant Editor Mary Koepke, she recalled the trials and tribulations of her first year.

Hershey, 28, is in her second year of teaching 10th and 11th grade English at Eastern Senior High School in Washington, D.C. In college, Hershey took "Methods of Teaching English" and whizzed through a successful student-teaching experience. But course work and preservice training didn't prepare her for the everyday realities of starting her own classroom from scratch, such as not getting her textbooks until six weeks into the semester and then finding them to be inappropriate for her students anyway. And she wasn't prepared for the frustration of having to invent her own materials without direct access to a photocopying machine; she was strictly limited to a "budget" of one copy per student per week. Hershey didn't even have her own classroom. Instead, she had to carry her papers, books, and teaching tools to a different room each period. But the biggest shock of all was how fiercely she was tested by her students.

During my student teaching I was well-loved. The students thought I was wonderful, and they said it all the time. But when I started my own classroom, there was no other teacher there to provide the structure. I had to maintain discipline. And I felt hated.

On my first day in the classroom, two students in two different classes said, "I hate white people." So I just said, "Well, I hope you'll like one by the end of this year." But I was afraid that everybody else was going to take it personally. I was afraid that, as a white person in a mostly black school, all the other students might think that I was going to be against them based on that comment—that they wouldn't judge me based on my own merit.

The next encounter that I recall was when I told a student to put away her social studies book in my English class. I walked up to her desk and repeated the request, and then I flipped the book closed. And she was, all of the sudden, in my face, screaming at me. We were both turning purple. It was extremely upsetting. I was scared and as angry as I've ever been in my life. And I was also acutely conscious that while the student and I were screaming at each other, the rest of the class was going nuts. I realized that I had lost control of 25 people because I had let one person take over the whole class.

Later, I became good buddies with that student. I saw her on a bus once, and she wouldn't sit with her friends; she wanted to sit with me. The good side of our relationship began after one event in particular: the homecoming dance. I was one of only a few teachers who was trying to dance. She ran up and started shimmying with me, having fun with me. And then she went off with her friends. I guess it was because I was a teacher trying to dance to go-go music—that made me a human being to her. That was the first step toward acceptance.

Then there was my gum crusade. At the beginning, I thought it sounded terrible when students cracked and popped their gum. I still think that. However, I spent so much time that first year trying to get students to get rid of their gum that I wasn't teaching. Then students began to make it a joke. They began chewing their tongues or claiming that it was laxative gum. And they would insist on having me check their mouths. They really wanted me to inspect their uvula. Here I had all these kids with their mouths hanging open at me screaming, ''AAAAAAHH.''

It didn't really get smooth until March. Something clicked in my relationships with students about halfway though the year. The students decided that I was there to stay and that they might as well learn. And I started teaching better.

I gave up some of my old rules that weren't working. Rules such as ''no gum.'' And I got very serious about calling parents, holding detentions, taking away points for rudeness, and making students stay after school and talk to me about what was going wrong.

And I stopped letting some things bother me. For instance, I had one fidgety student who sat in the front row and drummed on his desk all the time. It drove me crazy. He also talked to himself. I remember separating other students who talked to each other, and turning to him and saying, ''I'm going to have to figure out how to separate you from yourself.''

One day I refused to interrupt the lesson to stop his fidgeting. Instead, I casually picked up his hand, held it, and went on teaching. He stared at my hand, stared at my fingernails, then his eyes gradually traveled up my arm, up to my face, and he paid attention to what I was saying.

Part of my writing curriculum was journal writing. I wanted them to write in their journals every night. Originally, I gave them a topic, such as, ''What is the biggest pressure facing girls or boys?'' Or, ''Describe a dream you've had.'' Or, ''If you had a million dollars and couldn't spend any of it on yourself, what would you spend it on?'' The rule was: If you turned it in late, you lost points. But that never worked. The majority of the students wouldn't do it and would then get overwhelmed knowing that they couldn't receive full credit.

So I decided to give a bunch of topics and gave them six weeks to complete them. Every week I reminded them and tried to help pace them. A lot of them started writing. Some students waited until the end and wrote them all on the last night, but at least they finished. Before they weren't even trying.

Finally, I got to see some writing samples. The journal entries gave them practice writing; a lot of them were reluctant writers. And it gave me a chance to get to know them better. I realized how creative some of them were, which was not coming out in class.

Also, I wrote comments—notes to them about what they were saying in their journals. They were amazed that I was taking an active interest in them.

I gritted my teeth every quarter and asked them to evaluate me. First of all, most of the comments were quite negative. They said that I was very sweet but that they didn't understand why I made them do certain things. I felt terrible and cracked down on myself and restructured things. Then, in the second quarter, the evaluations started getting better. One wrote, ''This is what I've learned.'' Another wrote, ''My teacher makes sure I understand, and she goes over things in different ways until I understand.'' I was so happy.

Now I have a stronger idea of why I'm doing what I'm doing. I have entirely reorganized all my plans, and I am very happy. From first year to second year, I have improved dramatically. And that is the best thing about the first year. It was a testing ground.

Who Decides What Schools Teach?

America desperately needs serious discussion of the condition of our schools and of the content and form of school programs, Mr. Eisner maintains. If curriculum scholars could significantly deepen this dialogue, they could make an important contribution to the culture at large.

ELLIOT W. EISNER

ELLIOT W. EISNER (Stanford University Chapter) is a professor of education and art in the School of Education, Stanford University, Stanford, Calif.

Illustration by Susan Hunsberger

IT IRKS those of us who have devoted our professional lives to the study of curriculum to find that, when efforts are made to improve the schools, we are the least likely to be consulted. Why doesn't the public appreciate our expertise? Why aren't we pursued by the national commissions that shape education policy, by state boards of education, by foundations eager to make U.S. schools "competitive" with those in other nations? Why are we left on the sidelines, commenting on the recommendations others make, rather than making recommendations ourselves?

In some ways the answers to the foregoing questions are not particularly subtle or complex, and I have no intention of making them so. In the first place, curriculum scholars — by which I mean those educationists whose specialty is the *broad aims and content* of schooling (as contrasted with subject-matter specialists in math, fine arts, science, and other such fields) — have not had much appetite for addressing the content of school programs. When they have had something to say, it has tended to be an attack on the way capitalism exploits students and teachers, or it has been addressed to those who already occupy the choir: namely, other educationists rather than the American public. Those Marxist and Neo-Marxist critics who have lambasted American schools can cite chapter and verse concerning what they think is wrong with our schools. But they have comparatively little to say about what is right with them or about how to go about making them better. They are adept at pulling weeds, but rather inept at planting flowers.

For those of a more centrist bent, the overall mission of schools — and of what should be taught in them — has been largely absent from the intellectual agenda. The symposium from which the ar-

From *Phi Delta Kappan*, March 1990, pp. 523-526. Reprinted by permission of *Phi Delta Kappan* and the author.

ticles in this special section of the *Kappan* have been adapted was put together in desperation by an astute program chair who recognized that curriculum scholars in the American Educational Research Association were addressing everything except the most central of educational questions: What should be taught in schools? The papers delivered at that symposium and now published in the *Kappan* were created because of her initiative, not that of the writers.

One might reasonably ask, Why this neglect? How is it that broad, central questions pertaining to the aims and content of schooling should be marginalized in discourse on the curriculum? One reason is that such questions are not simply broad, they are unabashedly normative in character. In an age when discourse analysis, hermeneutics, feminism, and Foucault bombard us from one direction and a view of specialized scientific inquiry that regards only value-neutral description as cognitively respectable assails us from the other, the appetite for broad, "messy," normative questions that hark back to Herbert Spencer's "What knowledge is of most worth?" seems a touch too romantic. Intellectual respectability leads us in other directions. The result is that in academic circles we find a preponderance of papers that offer interpretations of interpretations or present highly specialized studies of individual disciplines that neglect central issues entirely. Both approaches avoid the broader question of what is worth learning anyway.

Furthermore, many curriculum scholars have, in this day of research on teaching, shifted their focus from curriculum to matters of teaching and teacher education. Both are no doubt important areas of research, but they cannot replace attention to curricular matters. No matter how well something is taught, if it is not worth teaching, it's not worth teaching well.

Thus within the academy there is 1) a neglect of the broad aims and overall content of school programs, because of the growing interest in social criticism writ large and because of the difficulty of doing scientifically respectable work on issues that are scientifically intractable, and 2) a growing interest in teaching and teacher education that has shifted attention away from what should be taught. We appear to want better messengers more than better messages.

There are some exceptions to the picture I have just painted. For example, John Goodlad, a curriculum scholar par excellence, has not been quiet about what

schools should teach. In *A Place Called School*, Goodlad not only identifies the strengths and weaknesses of schooling, but also identifies and justifies what should be taught there.[1] Similarly, within the academy, Theodore Sizer has offered Americans a view of curricula and a conception of the proper mission of schools that is built on a "less is more" principle.[2] Sizer argues that the compromises that teachers make in order to survive could be ameliorated if schools attempted less but did it better.

From outside the academy, Ernest Boyer's *High School* provides an articulate conception of what is worth students' attention and what schools would be well-advised to address.[3] And there is Mortimer Adler who, in his eighties, has much to say about curriculum and the forms of teaching that really count.[4] It is interesting to note that Goodlad, Sizer, and Adler have not only written books that are widely read and say something about what should be taught in schools, but they have also created organizations to build the kinds of schools they envision.

As noteworthy as these efforts to improve schooling in America have been, they are, alas, but minor themes within the larger score that is American education; more factors are at work to stabilize schools than to change them. What confers such stability on schools? Why do they appear so intractable? What will be necessary to change them? And what role, if any, can those who have studied schooling and curriculum best play in reforming the schools? It is to these questions that I now turn.

STABILITY AND CHANGE IN SCHOOLS

When I was a student at John Marshall High School in Chicago some 40 years ago, I was enrolled in a curriculum that consisted of four years of English, two years of math, three years of social studies, two years of science, two years of foreign language (Spanish), one year of music, four years of physical education, and four years of art.

The school day was divided into nine 45-minute periods. We had about five minutes to move from one class to another. There were between 30 and 35 students in each of my classes, except in choral music and in gym, in which there were about 75. The school year lasted 40 weeks, beginning after Labor Day and ending in mid-June. Teachers usually sat at a desk situated in the front of the room, while we sat at desks that were screwed to the floor and arranged in rows. We

were graded four times each semester, largely on the basis of our performance on teacher-made tests and on homework assignments.

Aside from the fixed seating, I submit that the 4,000-student high school I attended 40 years ago is not fundamentally different, structurally and organizationally, from the high schools operating today. Furthermore, I believe that the school I attended is much like the ones that most *Kappan* readers attended, at least those who attended urban schools.

In the past decade or so, much of the literature on schooling has emphasized the influence of school structure on what students learn in school.[5] The content of a student's experience is shaped not only by the explicit curriculum, but by the kind of place any particular school is. And that is influenced by the way the school is organized, by the way teachers' roles are defined, by the way students are rewarded, and by the priorities that the school sets. From a structural perspective, American schools, particularly secondary schools, have been extremely stable.

Another source of stability derives from the content of the curriculum. In broad terms, the content areas that are emphasized in schools have been extremely stable: English, social studies, math, science, foreign language, art, music, and physical education. Today computer literacy has replaced typing, but where is anthropology or law or child development or political science or feminist studies? I am well aware that each of these subjects is taught in some schools somewhere. But these subjects are not among the mainstream subjects that have been staples in American schools for more than six decades. Why?

Part of the reason is tradition. We do what we know how to do. Furthermore, our professional associations of subject-matter specialists also stabilize the curriculum. When the American Anthropological Association developed an anthropology curriculum for American secondary schools in the 1960s, it had to disguise it as a social studies course rather than as a course in anthropology. We protect our turf.

Another stabilizing factor is our textbooks. They are designed to take no risks, and they strive to alienate no one. They are usually models of the dull, the routine, and the intellectually feckless. Typically, they are dense collections of facts that read much like the Los Angeles telephone book: a great many players, but not much plot. The recent efforts in California to create a framework for history and social science that *does* look interesting may motivate publishers to be a bit more courageous. Generally speaking, however, since textbooks define the content and shape the form in which students encounter that content, their conservative character serves to resist change.

Teachers with limited time for planning and little intellectual contact with their professional colleagues are unlikely to redefine curriculum content radically. In any case, the changes teachers make are almost always within the confines of the courses they teach, and these courses operate within the constraints of the traditional school. The 50-minute hour is as much a sacred cow in the school as it is on the psychiatrist's couch. In a conservative educational climate, such as we have today, the difficulty of substantially altering curriculum content is even greater.

Yet another stabilizing agent is standardized testing, which neither teachers nor school administrators can afford to ignore. As long as teachers are held accountable by tests other than the ones they design, testing programs are likely to foster conservative educational practices. Standardized tests are intended to measure the achievement of large groups of students for whom there are common expectations. Deviation from the content to be covered constitutes a political and professional hazard for teachers. Indeed, if the virtue of test scores is their ability to predict future grades or future test scores, a conservative function is built into the test: stability, not variability, of conditions is likely to increase the predictive validity of the tests.

But educational innovation is predicated on change — not only in the *form* of educational method used, but also in the *content* and *goals* of education. Innovation is also predicated, I believe, on the desire to cultivate productive idiosyncrasy among students. While some common educational fare is reasonable and appropriate for all students, standardized tests that make invisible the unique and productively idiosyncratic in students perform a conservative function in school programs. *A Dictionary of Cultural Literacy* is a testament to such a conservative function.[6]

Moreover, such conservatism in education is attractive, particularly when schools are receiving bad press. The past always seems to exude a rosy glow, and Americans seem to require an absence of ambiguity. Thus it is reassuring to have a cultural dictionary that identifies, once and for all, "what every American should know." This need for stability — more

than the educationally trivial but publicly visible drop in scores on the Scholastic Aptitude Test (SAT) — is what Americans should really be concerned about. Why do we need such security? Why do we require a blueprint to follow on matters that beg for interpretation, for consideration of context, for flexibility, and most of all for judgment? If American educators have something to worry about, it is the national fear of exercising judgment, coupled with our political apathy, that must rank highest.

Methods of evaluation that are operationalized through standardized tests are given even more significance in the American university than in the public schools. With a few exceptions, American universities are not notable for adopting an adventurous — or even liberal — attitude toward defining admissions criteria. Universities protect tradition. They take SAT scores more seriously than they are willing to admit, and many now consider enrollment in Advanced Placement courses as admissions criteria. What were once "options" for students have become prescriptions for university admission. Not to have such courses on your transcript is tantamount to an admission of intellectual sloth, at least for those seeking entrance to our most prestigious universities.

Such expectations exert a chilling effect on innovative course development and on students' enrollment patterns. When students have the opportunity to take really innovative courses during that blue-sky period in high school known as the eighth semester, what are academically oriented students doing? They are taking courses in high school that they will have available to them in college six months later. Is faster always better?

Such practices and norms are essentially conservative. Collectively, tradition, textbooks, and evaluation systems work to stabilize the curricular status quo. As a result, when calls for change are made, they almost always focus on the least significant aspects of schooling: more days in school, higher standards, more years of math and science, more of the same.

DESPITE THESE stabilizing factors, what effects might curriculum scholars have if we reclaimed our voice in the public conversation about the schools? What would we have to say about what should be taught in schools? What if we were given a platform from which to address the public? The results, I think, would be as follows.

It would quickly become clear that

there is a profound lack of consensus about what schools should teach among those whose line of work is curriculum. The Neo-Marxists would continue to complain. The feminists would want attention paid to gender issues in schools. Curriculum analysts would continue to analyze, to avoid commitment, and to advocate the need for more data and more deliberation. Curricular conservatives would advance (or is it retreat?) to a reemphasis on the disciplines. The developmentally oriented among us would begin with the needs of the individual child as a foundation for what should be taught in schools. Those still interested in the power of process would claim that what is taught is less important than how it is taught. Cognitive skills, they would argue, can be developed by repairing a Mazda as well as by studying *Macbeth*. The re-conceptualists would continue to remind us that it is personal experience that really counts and that other starting points for curriculum are essentially coercive or irrelevant. In short, we would have not a symphony, but a cacophony.

Would this be bad? I think not. What *is* bad is a false sense of certainty, and that has characterized too many of the recent recommendations for education reform. President Bush is going to improve American education the old-fashioned way: he's going to reward good schools with more money. Chrysler Corporation is going to improve American schools by frightening the American public with a Japanese boogieman. William Bennett's approach was to create a James Madison High School curriculum that would be good medicine for everyone.

The debate could use more voices and deeper, more penetrating analyses of what schools should teach and the kinds of places schools should be. America desperately needs serious discussion of the condition of our schools and of the content and form of school programs. If curriculum scholars, having once reclaimed their voices, could significantly deepen the dialogue by exploring the options, we would have made an extremely important contribution to the culture. Does anybody hear any voices?

1. John I. Goodlad, *A Place Called School* (New York: McGraw-Hill, 1984).

2. Theodore R. Sizer, *Horace's Compromise* (Boston: Houghton Mifflin, 1984).

3. Ernest Boyer, *High School* (New York: Harper & Row, 1983).

4. Mortimer J. Adler, *The Paideia Proposal* (New York: Macmillan, 1982).

5. Robert Dreeben, *On What Is Learned in School* (Reading, Mass.: Addison-Wesley, 1968).

6. E. D. Hirsch, Jr., *A Dictionary of Cultural Literacy* (Boston: Houghton Mifflin, 1988).

Developing and Sustaining Critical Reflection in Teacher Education

John Smyth

Smyth is Associate Professor and Chair of the Educational Studies Centre, Deakin University, Australia.

Smyth provides background information on the emergence of reflectivity as a conceptual thrust in teacher education. He also discusses some of the impediments to empowerment that teachers and teacher educators confront as they attempt to implement critical reflection in their curricula. Smyth concludes that if teachers (and teacher educators) are going to uncover the forces that inhibit and constrain them, they need to engage in four forms of action with respect to teaching. These "forms" are characterized by four sequential stages and are linked to a series of questions: (a) describing (What do I do?), (b) informing (What does this mean?), (c) confronting (How did I come to be like this?), and (d) reconstructing (How might I do things differently?).

It is interesting to speculate on the reasons for the recent upsurge of interest in what might be broadly described as a reflective approach to teacher education. While there is a good deal of contention at the moment as to precisely what this might mean, it is clear that we have been down a very similar track before, most notably with the work of Dewey (1904/1965) earlier this century. So what makes the current revival so significant? For an answer to that question we have to look carefully at the social, economic, and political times in which we live and at the way in which the emphasis on reflective approaches represents something of a calculated response to the prevailing views about the nature of schooling and knowledge. There can be little doubt that as we rush headlong into this era of neoconservative ways of thinking and acting educationally, the reflective approach represents an interesting and challenging counter discourse to the ensconced technicist views. At the same time that we are being increasingly courted and urged by technologically minded policymakers and educational reformers into believing that all our social and economic ills will somehow magically dissolve if we place our faith in their capacity to get the mix of techniques right, significant questions are being asked as to whether the applied science mentality that lies behind their thinking and their strategies has the efficacy to resolve the complex issues in the ways being suggested.

It is clear that the work of Donald Schon in his *Reflective Practitioner: How Professionals Think in Action* (1983), and his more recent work, *Educating the Reflective Practitioner* (1987), has been important in all of this. Indeed, Schon's work has come to be something of a rallying point for besieged liberal progressive educators who are under tremendous threat at the moment as a consequence of educational conservatism. Connelly and Clandinin (1988) regard as remarkable "the speed with which Schon's . . . recent works [have] penetrated the reference lists of teacher education writers" (p. 1).

Schon's work does provide something of a convenient focus by which to reinforce and keep alive the tradition of experiential knowledge, but his substantive arguments are of major importance. In the face of widespread and continuing demands for technocratic ways of operating, Schon argues that proposals for more stringent forms of accountability based on research evidence are entirely wrongheaded. For Schon the problem has much more to do with a deep-seated "crisis of confidence" (as distinct from "competence") that amounts to a manifest inability of the professions to deliver solutions on the pressing environmental, economic, and social problems of our times. His claims are rooted in the argument that those who persist in arguing that professional practice should have a demonstrated 'scientific' basis and should adhere closely to prescriptions deriving from large-scale, objective, outsider-initiated research ignore the extent to which *practitioner-derived knowledge* is, in fact, trustworthy and relevant in and of itself (see Smyth, 1987a). By choosing to focus exclusively on the products of other peoples' research, at the expense of the process by which understandings are reached, proponents of such views actually misconstrue the value of research, which lies not in its being definitive, but rather in the tentativeness of discipline-based research as something to be explored, confirmed, or rejected in the light of experience.

From *Journal of Teacher Education*, March/April 1989, pp. 2-9. Copyright © 1989 by the American Association of Colleges for Teacher Education.

Continuing to seize upon the instrumental applicability of other people's research findings about professional practice is tantamount to placing a level of certainty on research that social scientists themselves would deny. Schon argues that across a range of professional areas, the nature of professional practice seems to have shifted from "problem solving" to "problem setting" (or problem posing); that is to say, from a rational process of choosing from among possibilities that best suit agreed-upon ends, to a situation that opens up for contestation and debate the nature of those decisions, the ends to which they are to be directed, and the means by which they are achievable (Schon, 1983). Rather than relying upon discipline-based knowledge, the scene, according to Schon, is becoming increasingly characterized by the application of practitioner knowledge acquired from previous particular cases. What this amounts to is a quite dramatic shift: from a position where scientifically derived knowledge was deemed superior, to a circumstance in which artistic and intuitive knowledge may have a claim to being equally appropriate; from an *a priori* instrumental view of knowledge, to one that reflects knowledge as being tentative and problematic; and, from a view that presupposes answers to complex social questions, to one that endorses the importance of problem posing and negotiated resolution (Smyth, 1986).

What Schon (1983) does is to provide us with a way of fundamentally re-thinking how we view professional practice, and the relationship between theory and practice. His thesis rests on the claim that whereas in the past, professionals laid claim to "extraordinary knowledge in matters of great social importance" (p. 4) and in return were granted unique rights and privileges, a number of factors have occurred to change those circumstances. In addition to the media exposure of the extensive misuse and abuse of these privileges for personal gain, Schon (1983) points to a more important public loss of confidence in and questioning by society of professionals' claims to extraordinary knowledge. Schon illustrates this by way of example:

a series of announced national crises — the deteriorating cities, poverty, the pollution of the environment, the shortage of energy — seemed to have roots in the very

practices of science, technology, and public policy that were being called upon to alleviate them. . . . Government sponsored 'wars' against such crises seemed not to produce the expected results; indeed, they often seemed to exacerbate the crises. (p. 9)

Increasingly, professionals of all kinds (teachers included) are being confronted by situations in which the tasks they are required to perform no longer bear any relationship to the tasks for which they have been educated. As Schon (1983) so aptly put it, "The situations of practice are not problems to be solved but problematic situations characterized by uncertainty, disorder and indeterminacy" (pp. 15-16). Practitioners are therefore becoming increasingly engulfed in wrangles over conflicting and competing values and purposes. Teachers, for example, are

faced with pressures for increased efficiency in the context of contracting budgets, demands that they rigorously "teach the basics," exhortations to encourage creativity, build citizenship, (and to) help students examine their values. (p. 17)

Impediments to Empowerment

While it is true that this largely undefined call for a reflective approach to teacher education has occurred as a consequence of moves to empower teachers, particularly in a climate characterized by centralized authorities acting in ways to reduce teacher autonomy, many of these calls are remarkably unreflexive of their own agenda. Indeed, the way the term is picked up and used on some occasions generates major problems. Liston and Zeichner (1987) argue that reflection is becoming something of an "educational slogan . . . that lacks sufficient conceptual elaboration and programmatic strength" (p. 2). As Gore (1987) points out, what happens in circumstances like these is that people like Cruickshank (1985) are able to use it as a way of appearing to give legitimation to a focus on the pedagogical and behavioral skills of teachers (or the means of teaching), to the exclusion of the ends of valued social and moral purposes to which teaching is (or should be) directed. For example, while Cruickshank and Applegate (1981) define reflection in terms of "helping teachers to think about what happened, why it happened, and what else they could have done to reach their goals" (p.

553), it is clear that their conception of the reflective amounts to nothing short of prescribing what teachers ought to teach within tight guidelines, while coopting one another into policing the implementation of predetermined goals. Activity of this kind gives the reflective approach a bad name.

Whether we are speaking about a reflective stance for experienced teachers or those in training, it is important that the process be clearly seen as based on moves that actively recognize and endorse the decidedly historical, political, theoretical, and moral nature of teaching. When teaching is removed from an analysis of contextual determinants like those within which it is located, it takes on the aura of a technical process. The notion of reflection, therefore, that I want to deal with here is not one that is related at all to passive deliberation or contemplation — a meaning that is sometimes ascribed to reflection in everyday life. Rather, what I am arguing for is a notion of the reflective in teacher education that is both active and militant (Mackie, 1981; Shor, 1987), that reintroduces into the discourse about teaching and schooling a concern for the "ethical, personal and political" (Beyer and Apple, 1988, p. 4), and that is above all concerned with infusing action with a sense of power and politics. Beyer and Apple (1988) put this succinctly:

It involves both conscious understanding of and actions in schools on solving our daily problems. These problems will not go away by themselves, after all. But it also requires critically reflective practices that alter the material and ideological conditions that cause the problems we are facing as educators in the first place. (p. 4)

Clearly, the major impediment (but at the same time the major challenge) to the reflective approach envisaged above has been recent attempts to 'reform' schooling in the USA and other western democracies by ensuring that what goes on *inside* schools is directly responsive to the economic needs *outside* of schools. In large measure this has meant deliberately constructing the mythology that somehow schools and teachers are the cause of the economic failure, but that if certain narrowly prescribed forms of action (a return to the teaching of basic skills, better teacher appraisal schemes, tighter classroom discipline, longer school days, more sophisticated performance indicators, state-wide testing, performance budgeting, and other cost-efficient and cost-effectiveness measures) are adopted, then schools can be magically restored to their rightful role as servants of the economy (Walker and Barton, 1987). The claim of the policy-making technocrats is that it is just a matter of entrusting schools to them so that they can come up with the right mix of variables to be prescribed for teachers to follow in achieving the required strategic, economic, and social goals. It is precisely this kind of common-sense thinking that is in fact imbued with all manner of undisclosed political agendas that ought to be the object of discussion about teaching and teacher education. To paraphrase a comment by Dippo (1988), teacher education should provide practitioners with

> the tools and resources they need to recognize, analyze, and address the contradictions, and in so doing open-up the possibility that conditions in schools . . . can be different . . . [S]uch empowering educational goals [are] clearly linked to the larger political project of redefining existing social and economic relations. (p. 486)

Tom (1985) points out that while always a minority viewpoint, the reflective (or inquiry-oriented) approach to teacher education goes back a long way, but the confusion that arises is with respect to what is defined as the "arena of the problematic." As Tom puts it, while there is a view that "to make teaching problematic is to raise doubts about what, under ordinary circumstances, appears to be effective or wise practice" (p. 37), the object of that problematizing (or reflective action) is by no means agreed upon. According to him, "the objects of our doubts might be accepted principles of good pedagogy, typical ways teachers respond to classroom management issues, customary beliefs about the relationship of schooling to society, or ordinary definitions of teacher authority — both in the classroom and in the broader school context" (p. 37). Reflection can, therefore, vary from a concern with the micro aspects of the teaching-learning process and subject matter knowledge, to macro concerns about political/ethical principles underlying teaching and the relationship of schooling to the wider institutions and hierarchies of society. How we conceptualize teaching, whether as a set of neutral, value-free technical acts, or

as a set of ethical, moral, and political imperatives holds important implications for the kind of reflective stance we adopt.

For myself, I am of the view that focusing on the reductionist aspects of the teaching-learning process that have a technocratic orientation to them, in the absence of the wider ethical and political scenery, is to fail to make the crucial linkage between issues of agency and structure and to relegate teachers to being nothing more than "a cog in a self-perpetuating machine" (Tom, 1985, p. 38). Teaching, and reflection upon it, has a lot more to do with intentionality and the way in which teachers are able to be active agents (Ross and Hannay, 1986) in making the linkages between economic structures, social and cultural conditions, and the way schooling works.

Countering the dominant view that educational phenomena are natural and capable of detached analysis requires a viewpoint that embraces the essentially political, historical, and theoretical nature of teaching. Such a socially constructed view, which regards teaching as serving certain human interests, posits the entire educational system as potentially part of the arena of the problematic (Tom, 1985) and incorporates reflection that focuses primarily on the way in which schooling contributes (or does not, as the case might be), to the creation of a less oppressive, more just, humane, and dignified society.

The idea that teaching is a political process serving certain interests in demonstrable ways while actively excluding and denying others is not a notion that has general acceptance either among teachers or the wider community (White and White, 1986; Stevens, 1987; Lightfoot, 1973). To some extent this is understandable given the often technicist ways in which the teacher education enterprise trains teachers to engage in the transfer of knowledge to students, rather than to question the notions of power and ideology behind that knowledge (Freedman, 1986). Only rarely have teachers been required (or indeed permitted) to confront the knowledge/power issue. When they do, it is generally in the context of someone else's teaching, not their own. Teachers struggle hard, therefore, to see the importance or even the relevance of "accommodation" and "resistance" in their work, especially

in a system which increasingly demands that schools be responsive to the needs of the economy. Because of the way in which capitalist systems in general have been able to ascribe the causes of our economic ills to the personal inadequacies and failings of individuals (illiteracy, lack of incentive, and poor work habits among students) rather than deficiencies of the system itself, it has not been difficult to link this with the systematic failure of schools to meet the needs of industry. The argument is such a compellingly simplistic one that it is proving extremely difficult to dislodge — get students in schools to conform through more compliant forms of education, and all our economic woes will disappear. The kind of position represented by these ideas needs to be challenged and roundly critiqued through the kind of reflective process being spoken about here.

Requiring that teachers develop a sense of personal biography and professional history is one way of having them begin to overcome their inertia and unwillingness to question where particular teaching practices came from, and to that extent, no longer accepting teaching actions as natural or common sense and unquestionable. It is to attune them to the fact that perhaps silences on these matters are perhaps not accidental at all, but may be socially constructed responses to wider societal agenda. As Gadamer (1975) argues, understanding practice involves coming to grasp the way in which beliefs and values (which are themselves historical constructions) amount to powerful forces that enable us to ascribe particular meaning and significance to events. Put another way, our experiences as teachers give meaning and significance to events. Put another way, our experiences as teachers have meaning for us in terms of our own historically located consciousness; what we need to do is to work at articulating that consciousness in order to interpret meaning. Failure to understand the breaks and the discontinuities in our history makes it difficult for us to see the shifts in the nature of power relationships, with the result that we end up denying their very existence. Elsewhere I have put it in these words:

> Reflection, critical awareness, or enlightenment on its own is insufficient — it must be accompanied by action . . .

[As Freire so aptly put it] reflection without action is verbalism; action without reflection is activism . . . [What we need to do is to open up] dialogue between teachers about actual teaching experiences but in a way that enables questions to be asked about taken-for-granted, even cherished assumptions and practices, the reformulation of alternative hypotheses for action, and the actual testing of those hypotheses in classroom situations. (Smyth, 1984, p. 63)

Confronting the Cultural Dispositions of Schooling

The notion of empowerment (even if it is becoming an overused term) has to do with teachers taking charge of aspects of their lives over which they have been prevented from gaining access in the past (Fried, 1980a). The intention is to critique and uncover the tensions that exist between particular teaching practices and the larger cultural and social contexts in which they are embedded. Willis (1977) expressed it in terms of the social actors themselves reflecting upon, challenging, and refuting, rather than accepting, the structural conditions which envelop their lives. There is a sense in which people who do this embark on a process of *becoming different,* by thinking critically and creatively to pursue meanings that enable them to make increasing sense of the world in which they live. As Mishler (1986) put it, empowerment entails a shift in the balance of power as participants move *beyond* the description of the "text" of their teaching, to embrace possibilities for action: "To be empowered is not only to speak one's own voice and to tell one's own story, but to apply the understanding arrived at to action in accord with one's own interests" (p. 119).

There is no longer a preparedness to accept things the way they are, but to see instead, "patterned inequalities, institutional power, ideologies [and] . . . the internal dynamics of how a system works, and for whom the system is not functional" (Everhart, 1979, p. 420). My argument is that teachers are only able to reclaim the power they have lost over their teaching if they place themselves in critical confrontation with their problems. Empowerment through reflection, thus, has less to do with "a handing down of knowledge . . . [and is more like] a partnership, a mutual sharing of ideas, intuitions

and experiences" (Fried, 1980b, p. 30). In Greene's (1986) terms, this means "a sense of agency is required of . . . teacher[s]" in which they can "become challengers, when they can take initiatives" (p. 73) and in which schools become places where spaces are created in which worthwhile questions can be asked. For most teachers, this is in stark contrast to the 'delivery of services' mentality created by centralized bureaucratic educational authorities who insist on presenting the educational world in terms of

. . . one rank of people (service deliverers) who have been trained and hired to treat the rest. They diagnose our problems, assess our needs, and then provide us with anything from a prescription to an entire program to fix what's lacking, or leaking, in us. (Fried, 1980a, p. 4)

Simon (1987) expressed the way in which teachers become empowered through reflection:

It literally means to give ability to, to permit or enable. When we hear the word empowerment used in education, it is usually being employed in the spirit of critique. Its referent is the identification of oppressive and unjust relations within which there is an unwarranted limitation placed on human action, feeling and thought. Such limitation is seen as constraining a person from the opportunity to participate on equal terms with other members of a group or community to whom have accrued the socially defined status of "the privileged," "the competent." . . . To empower is to enable those who have been silenced to speak. (p. 374)

According to Anderson (1987), beyond an ill-defined and rhetorical call for teacher empowerment, there have been few indicators about how teachers themselves "can reflect on the structural conditions that inform their practice" (p. 14). Whether we are talking about preservice or inservice teacher education matters little at this stage. What is important is the stance taken toward knowledge about teaching: who has the right to create it, under what circumstances, and what are the implications of that knowledge on the working lives of people in classrooms. If teachers (or those in training) are denied the opportunity to articulate, critique, and culturally locate principles about their own (or one another's) teaching, then, politically speaking, such teachers are being treated no differently than disempowered workers who have historically been oppressed and denied access to power over their

work.

If consciousness raising is in fact about teachers becoming aware of their own alienation and coming to recognize the nature and sources of the forces that keep them subjugated, then as Harris (1979) says, this has to start with their sketching out the contours of actual situations and posing problems about those concrete situations. This process of distancing themselves from classroom events and processes can be difficult and perplexing for teachers (Pollard, 1987) because classrooms present such a kaleidoscope of events that it is difficult for teachers to obtain a stable image of themselves and of the interactive part they play in the creation of those events. Before we can engage teachers in untangling the complex web of ideologies (Berlak, 1987) that surround them in their teaching, they first need to focus on those manifestations of their teaching that perplex, confuse, or frustrate them; that is to say, the practicalities of the here- and-now that teachers pride themselves in being so vitally concerned about.

If teachers are going to uncover the nature of the forces that inhibit and constrain them, and work at changing those conditions, they need to engage in four forms of action with respect to their teaching (each of which has its origins, broadly speaking, in the work of Paulo Freire). They can perhaps be best characterized by a number of sequential stages that can be linked to a series of questions:

1. Describe . . . what do I do?
2. Inform . . . what does this mean?
3. Confront . . . how did I come to be like this?
4. Reconstruct . . . how might I do things differently?

Describing

Starting with the hermeneutic notion that teaching is a form of text (Gordon, 1988) to be described and then untied (Young, 1981) for the meaning it reveals provides a form of accessibility that has a lot of appeal to teachers. Because teaching is the kind of activity that can only be adequately explicated and critiqued in a post-factum manner, Elliott (1987) argues that "rational action is logically prior to rational principles" (p. 151). The latter, he says, "are the result of reflection on the former" (p. 151), and any critique of teaching must therefore be in the context of practice if it is to go beyond being partial. In essence, the claim is that to articulate adequately the principles that lie behind teaching, teachers must start with a consideration of current practice as the way of gaining entree to the "knowledge, beliefs, and principles that [they] employ in both characterizing that practice and deciding what should be done" (p. 151). Both Harris (1986) and Bonser and Grundy (1988) claim that written codification can be a powerful guiding device for practitioners engaging in reflective deliberation.

As teachers reflect about their own (or one another's) teaching, they describe concrete teaching events. The teachers I have worked with (Smyth, 1987b; Smyth, 1988) use a journal or diary (Holly, 1984; Tripp, 1987) as a way of building up an account of their teaching as a basis for analysis and discussion with colleagues. Having to write a narrative of what was occurring in confusing, perplexing, or contradictory situations helps them to organize an account of their teaching in a way that is crucial to their finding and speaking their own voices (McDonald, 1986). These descriptions don't have to be complex or in academic language; on the contrary, if there is to be any genuine ownership by teachers, it is important that such descriptions be in their own language (cf. Lortie, 1975). The rationale is that if teachers can create a text that comprises the elements of their teaching as a prelude to problematizing it, then there is a likelihood that they will have the basis upon which to speak with one another so as to see how their consciousness was formed, and how it might be changed. Creating personalized narratives is also a way of guarding against the rampant "intellectual imperialism" (Harris, 1979) so prevalent in teaching, whereby outsiders provide the packaged answers to the issues that are non-questions for teachers. In Shor's (1980) terms, when teachers keep journals they are able to "extra-ordinarily re-experience the ordinary" in a way that is clearly based on a sense of the concrete in their working lives, but in a manner that enables them to see how the elements of particular situations alienate and confuse them and impose real "limit situations" (Fay, 1977) on what

it is possible for them to do.

Informing

When teachers describe their teaching, it is not an end in itself; it is a precursor to uncovering the broader principles that are informing (consciously or otherwise) their classroom action. As Kretovics (1985) put it, it is a way of beginning to confront the "structured silences" that abound in teaching. Developing narratives is a way of uncovering what Argyris and Schon (1977) called "theories-in-use," what Hirst (1983) labelled "operational theories," or what Tripp (1987) has characterized as "local theories." By whatever term we choose to describe them, when teachers engage in the activity of unpacking descriptions of their teaching in order to make a series of "it looks as if . . ." statements, then they are really recapturing the pedagogical principles of what it is they do. For example, on the basis of descriptions of the way a teacher treats children, it could be said that such a teacher holds a view of classroom management that says "the extent to which a teacher is going to have discipline problems is related to factors like the consistency and firmness of his or her reactions to breaches of classroom rules, the types of punishment he or she metes out, and their severity" (Gordon, 1988, p. 431). In trying to work out their operational theories, teachers are in effect seeking to develop defensible practical principles "grounded in a largely tacit knowledge of complex and particular situations" (Elliott, 1987, p. 152). Such theories or thematic representations may well fall short of being generalizable, but the contradictions they contain may nevertheless be highly significant in explaining the nature of idiosyncratic work contexts. What teachers are trying to do in this process is to move their teaching out of the realm of the mystical, as it were, into a situation in which they are able to begin to see through discussion with others the nature of the forces that cause them to operate in the way they do and how they can move beyond intellectualizing the issues to concrete action for change.

Developing short-range theories or explanatory principles about practice is not without its own set of complex problems and impediments, a major one being the generally enforced sep-

aration of theory from practice. Most educational research assumes that theories about teaching are developed by people from outside of classrooms and then transfused into classrooms to be applied by teachers. Such an applied view of the nature of research is, to say the least, highly problematic in that it takes no account of the extensive experiential wisdom possessed by most teachers. Carr (1982) speaks in terms of the prevalent but quite erroneous view of educational theory as being akin to a collage of "maps, guides, itineraries and rule-books produced in some far off land and then exported to the 'world of practice' so that its inhabitants can understand where they are, what they are doing and where they are supposed to be going" (p. 26). The problem, then, is primarily a political one of who has the legitimate right to define what counts as knowledge about teaching. While teachers may have been reluctant in the past to be seen as publicly exercising that claim, others outside of classrooms have been far less reticent. As Kohl (1983) so aptly put it:

> Unless we [as teachers] assume the responsibility for theory making and testing, the theories will be made for us by . . . the academic researchers and many other groups that are simply filling the vacuum that teachers have created by bargaining away their educational power and giving up their responsibility as intellectuals. (p. 30)

Confronting

Theorizing and describing one's practice is one thing, but being able to subject those theories to a form of interrogation and questioning that establishes something about their legitimacy and their legacy is altogether another matter. Yet, if we are to be clear about what it is that we do as educators, and why we do it, then it is imperative that we move to this stage. Above all we need to regard the views we hold about teaching not as idiosyncratic preferences, but rather as the product of deeply entrenched cultural norms that we may not even be aware of. Locating or situating teaching in a broader cultural, social, and political context amounts to engaging in critical reflection about the assumptions that underlie those methods and classroom practices. Regarded this way, teaching becomes less of an isolated set of technical procedures, and more of a historical expression of shaped values about what is considered to be important about the nature of the educative act. When teachers write about their own biographies and how they feel these have shaped the construction of their values, then they are able to see more clearly how social and institutional forces beyond the classroom and school have been influential.

As a way of providing some structure, teachers can approach the confrontation of local theories of teaching through a series of guiding questions, that might include the following:

- What do my practices say about my assumptions, values, and beliefs about teaching?
- Where did these ideas come from?
- What social practices are expressed in these ideas?
- What is it that causes me to maintain my theories?
- What views of power do they embody?
- Whose interests seem to be served by my practices?
- What is it that acts to constrain my views of what is possible in teaching? (Smyth, 1987c)

In Freire's (1972) terms this amounts to a way of problematizing teaching by asking poignant questions about the "social causation" (Fay, 1977) of those actions. Untangling and reevaluating taken-for-granted (even cherished) practices require breaking into well entrenched and constructed mythologies that may not always be easily dislodged.

Reconstructing

Being able to locate oneself both personally and professionally in history in order to be clear about the forces that have come to determine one's existence, is the hallmark of a teacher who has been able to harness the reflective process and can begin to act on the world in a way that amounts to changing it. This amounts to being able to see teaching realities not as immutable givens but as being defined by others, and as essentially contestable. If teachers, and those aspiring to enter teaching, are to experience their lives in authentic terms, then they will have to expel the internalized images that researchers, administrators, and policymakers are so deft at perpetuating. By constructing portrayals of their own teaching that are embedded in the particularities of that teaching, they are able to gain

a measure of control through self-government, self-regulation, and self-responsibility that will enable them to trumpet the virtues of "what's best in teaching." Adopting this kind of perspective on reflection is to deny the artificially constructed separation of thought from action, of theory from practice, of mental from manual labor, and ultimately to jettison the false and oppressive view that people outside of classrooms know what is best about teaching. Put quite simply, the people who do the work of teaching should be the same people who reflect upon it.

When teachers are able to begin to link consciousness about the processes that inform the day-to-day aspects of their teaching with the wider political and social realities within which it occurs, then they are able to transcend self-blame for things that don't work out and to see that perhaps their causation may more properly lie in the social injustices and palpable injustices of society, which is to say that deficiencies in teaching can be caused by the manner in which dominant groups in society pursue their narrow sectional interests. Although teachers are by no means a numerically small group in society, it is becoming increasingly clear that they are being acted upon by educational systems and governments in ways that bear an uncanny resemblance to the oppressive treatment meted out to minority groups. Indeed, only when teachers take an active reflective stance (see Freedman, Jackson and Boles, 1983) are they able to challenge the dominant factory metaphor of the way schools are conceived, organized, and enacted. Being reflective, therefore, means more than merely being speculative. It means starting with reality, with seeing the injustices of reality's limits, and beginning to overcome reality by reasserting the importance of learning.

Conclusion

To adopt the more expansive and politically informed kind of reflective pose being argued for in this paper is to proceed in a mutually reinforcing direction so that both preservice and inservice teacher education are able to support one another in the effort to reclaim the classroom (Goswami and Stillman, 1987). To argue, for example, that such a reflective process is

only possible for experienced teachers who have a lifetime of teaching behind them is to deny a long and sometimes harsh history of being treated in certain ways as students that trainee teachers bring with them to programs of teacher training. These histories are most decidedly worth unpacking in some considerable detail for the more just and humane alternatives they will reveal. Adopting an exclusionist policy over matters like this is only justified in a context that construes teacher education as a narrow process of infusing skills. Besides, to operate otherwise is to ignore what we already know about the powerful socializing effect of the profession on neophyte teachers.

Reflective practitioners and nonreflective practitioners are not two fundamentally irreconcilable groups. Rather, they are at different points in working to overcome the social, cultural, and political amnesia that has gripped the entire teaching profession in recent times (McLaren, 1987). To be sure, there are problems with the reflective approach, but they are not of a kind that have to do with developing a formula and having everyone march in the same direction to the sound of the same drum. The problems are not about ensuring neat and system-wide uniform dissemination of packaged arrangements, but rather have to do with winning the hearts and minds of people committed to a common struggle (Spring, 1977). There are other problems, too, because of the in-built presumption that teachers will necessarily want to become self-aware and act in ways that promote their own interests and those of their students in preference to the forces of dogma and irrationality that blind them to the nature of reality. This, of course, may be quite an erroneous presumption and one that Elbaz (1988) is right to point to as a persisting dilemma. But none of these is adequate justification for not embarking on the process, for as Rudduck (1984) put it: "Not to examine one's practice is irresponsible; to regard teaching as an experiment and to monitor one's performance is a responsible professional act" (p. 6).

References

Anderson, G. (1987, April). *Towards a critical ethnography of educational administration*. Paper presented at the annual meeting of the American Educational Research Association, Washington DC.

Argyris, C., & Schon, D. (1974). *Theory in practice: Increasing professional effectiveness.* London: Jossey Bass.

Berlak, A. (1987, April). *Teaching for liberation and empowerment in the liberal arts: Towards the development of a pedagogy that overcomes resistance.* Paper presented at the annual meeting of the American Educational Research Association, Washington DC.

Beyer, L., & Apple, M. (1988). *Curriculum: Problems, politics and possibilities,* Albany: State University of New York.

Bonser, S., & Grundy, S. (1988). Reflective deliberation in the formulation of a school curriculum policy. *Journal of Curriculum Studies, 20* (1).

Carr, W. (1982). Treating the symptoms, neglecting the cause: Diagnosing the problems of theory and practice. *Journal of Further and Higher Education, 6* (2), 19-29.

Connelly, M., & Clandinin, J. (1988, April). *Narrative, experience and the study of curriculum.* Paper presented at the American Educational Research Association, New Orleans.

Cruickshank, D. (1985). Uses and benefits of reflective teaching. *Phi Delta Kappan, 66,* 704-706.

Cruickshank, D., & Applegate, J. (1981). Reflective teaching as a strategy for teacher growth. *Educational Leadership, 38* (7), 553-554.

Dewey, J. (1965). Theory and practice in education (National Society for Study of Education Yearbook, 1904). In M. Borromann, (Ed.), *Teacher education in America: A documentary history.* New York: Teachers College Press.

Dippo, D. (1988). Making ethnographic research count. Review of "Becoming Clerical Workers" by Linda Valli. *Curriculum Inquiry, 18* (4), 481-488.

Elbaz, F. (1988). Critical reflection on teaching: Insights from Freire. *Journal of Education for Teaching, 14* (2), 171-181.

Elliott, J. (1987). Educational theory, practical philosophy and action research. *British Journal of Educational Studies, 35,* 149-69.

Everhart, R. (1979). Ethnography and educational policy: Love and marriage or strange bedfellows. In R. Barnhardt, et al., *Anthropology and educational administration* (pp. 409-428).

Tucson, AZ: Impresora.

Fay, B. (1977). How people change themselves: The relationship between critical theory and its audience. In T. Ball (Ed.), *Political theory and praxis: New perspectives* (pp. 200-283). Minneapolis: University of Minnesota Press.

Freedman, S., Jackson, J.; & Boles, K. (The Boston Womens' Teachers' Group). (1983). Teaching: An imperilled "profession." In L. Shulman & G. Sykes (Eds.), *Handbook of Teaching and Policy* (pp. 261-299). New York: Longmans.

Freedman, P. (1986). Don't talk to me about lexical meta-analysis of criterion-referenced clustering and lap-dissolve spatial transformations: A consideration of the role of practicing teachers in educational research. *British Educational Research Journal, 12* (2), 197-206.

Freire, P. (1972). *Pedagogy of the oppressed.* Harmondsworth: Penguin.

Fried, R. (1980a). *Empowerment vs. delivery of services.* Concord, NH: New Hampshire Department of Education.

Fried, R. (1980b). *Learning in community: An empowerment approach.* Concord, NH: Office of Community Education, New Hampshire State Department of Education.

Gadamer, H. (1978). *Truth and method.* (G. Barden & J. Cumming's Ed. & Trans.). New York: Seabury Press.

Gordon, D. (1988). Education as text: The varieties of educational hiddenness. *Curriculum Inquiry, 18* (4), 425-49.

Gore, J. (1987). Reflecting on reflective teaching. *Journal of Teacher Education, 38* (2), 33-39.

Goswami, D., & Stillman, P. (Eds.). (1987). *Reclaiming the classroom: Teacher research as an agency for change.* Portsmouth, NH: Boynton Cook.

Greene, M. (1986). Reflection and passion in teaching. *Journal of Curriculum and Supervision, 2* (1), 68-81.

Harris, I. (1986). Communicating the character of "deliberation." *Journal of Curriculum Studies, 18* (2), 115-32.

Harris, K. (1979). *Education and knowledge: The structured misrepresentation of knowledge.* London: Routledge & Kegan Paul.

Hirst, P. (1983). Educational theory. In P. Hirst (Ed.), *Educational theory and its foundation disciplines.* London: Routledge & Kegan Paul.

Holly, M. (1984). *Keeping a personal-professional journal.* Geelong, Australia: Deakin University Press.

Kohl, H. (1983). Examining closely what we do. *Learning, 12* (1), 28-30.

Kretovics, J. (1985). Critical literacy: Challenging the assumptions of mainstream educational theory. *Journal of Education, 67* (2), 50-61.

Lightfoot, S. (1973). Politics and reasoning: Through the eyes of teachers and children. *Harvard Educational Review, 43* (2), 197-244.

Liston, D., & Zeichner, K. (1987). Reflective teacher education and moral deliberation. *Journal of Teacher Education, 38* (6), 2-8.

Lortie, D. (1975). *School teacher: A sociological study.* Chicago: University of Chicago Press.

Mackie, R. (1981). (Ed.). *Literacy and revolution: The pedagogy of Paulo Freire.* New York: Continuum.

McDonald, J. (1986). Raising the teacher's voice and the ironic role of theory. *Harvard Educational Review; 56* (4), 355-378.

McLaren, P. (1987). Critical pedagogy and the dream of emancipation. *Social Education, 51* (2), 146-150.

Mishler, E. (1986). Meaning in context and the empowerment of respondents. In E. Mishler, *Research interviewing: Context and narrative.* Cambridge, MA: Harvard University Press.

Pollard, A. (1987). Reflective teaching — the sociological contribution. In P. Woods & A. Pollard (Eds.), *Sociology and teaching: A new challenge for the sociology of education.* London: Croom Helm.

Ross, E., & Hannay, L. (1986). Toward a critical theory of reflective inquiry. *Journal of Teacher Education, 37* (4), 9-15.

Rudduck, J. (1984). *Teaching as an art, teacher research and research-based teacher education.* Second Annual Lawrence Stenhouse Memorial Lecture, University of East Anglia.

Schon, D. (1983). *The reflective practitioner: How professionals think in action.* New York: Basic Books.

Schon, D. (1987). *Educating the reflective practitioner.* San Francisco: Jossey-Bass.

Shor, I. (1980). *Critical teaching and everyday life.* Boston: South End Press.

Shor, I. (1987). (Ed.). *Freire for the classroom.* Portsmouth, NH: Boynton/Cook.

Simon, R. (1987). Empowerment as a pedagogy of possibility. *Language Arts, 64* (4), 370-82.

Smyth, J. (1984). Teacher-as-collaborators in clinical supervision: Cooperative learning about teaching. *Teacher Education, 24,* 60-68.

Smyth, J. (1986). *Reflection-in-action.* Geelong, Australia: Deakin University Press.

Smyth, J. (1987a). (Ed.). *Educating teachers: Changing the nature of pedagogical knowledge.* London: Falmer Press.

Smyth, J. (1987b, October). *A critical pedagogy of classroom practice.* Paper presented at the ninth Curriculum Theorizing and Classroom Practice Conference, Dayton, OH.

Smyth, J. (1987c). *Rationale for teachers' critical pedagogy: A handbook.* Geelong, Australia: Deakin University Press.

Smyth, J. (1988). Teachers theorizing their practice as a form of empowerment. *The Educational Administrator, 30,* 27-37.

Spring, J. (1977). *A Primer for libertarian education.* New York: Free Life Editions.

Stevens, P. (1987). Political education and political teachers. *Journal of Philosophy of Education, 21* (1), 75-83.

Tom, A. (1985). Inquiring into inquiry-oriented teacher education. *Journal of Teacher Education, 36* (5), 35-44.

Tripp, D. (1987). *Theorizing practice: The teacher's professional journal.* Geelong, Australia: Deakin University Press.

Walker, S., & Barton, L. (1987). (Eds.). *Changing policies, changing teachers: New directions for schooling.* Milton Keynes: O.U.P.

White, J., & White, P. (1987). Teachers as political activists. In A. Hartnett & M. Naish (Eds.), *Education and society today.* London: Falmer.

Willis, P. (1977). *Learning to Labour: How working class kids get working class jobs.* Westmead, G.B.: Gower.

Young, R. (1981). (Ed.). *Untying the text.* Boston: Routledge & Kegan Paul.

A Look to the Future

There are several trends developing in North America that are sure to affect the conditions of learning in the next decade. The conditions of work and leisure are changing rapidly. Regarding the schools, it is estimated that public school enrollment in the United States will increase to about 43.8 million students by the year 2000. Also it is anticipated that one million young people will drop out of school in each of the next 10 years, costing the nation over $240 billion in lost earning and taxes over their lifetimes. The changes in North American family structure will produce distressing consequences for America's youth. The supply of newly graduated teaching candidates is expected to meet only about 60% of the national demand for teachers over the next decade. These and other dramatic trends are going to force a restructuring of the form and content of schooling.

As we enter the 1990s, the forces for change and reform in American education are as real, if not more so, as they were in the latter years of the 1980s. It would appear that we are at a pivotal point in North American educational history, if many of the reforms recommended for teacher education in the past decade are actually carried through to implementation. Some of the proposed changes in teacher education and licensure, such as the National Teacher Certification Board, are in advanced planning and development stages. Other proposed reforms, such as the elimination of undergraduate teacher education programs, are not, in my view, likely to occur. We shall watch with interest to see whether their recommendations will be implemented or ignored by the states in the 1990s.

On other fronts, the student populations of North America reflect vital social and cultural forces at work. In the United States, a massive secondary school dropout problem has been developing steadily through the past decade. The 1990s will reveal how public school systems will address this and other unresolved problems brought about by dramatic upheavals in demographics. There is the issue, as well, of how great a shortfall in the supply of new teachers will be experienced in the 1990s. In the immediate future we will be able to see if a massive teacher shortage is beginning; if it is, how will "emergency" or "alternative" certification measures adopted by states affect achievement of the objectives of the reform agenda of the 1980s?

At any given moment in a people's history, several alternative future directions are open to them. Since 1970, North American educational systems have been subjected to one wave after another of recommendations for programmatic change. Is it any wonder that "change" is a sort of watchword for persons in teacher education on this continent? What specific directions it will take in the immediate future depend on which recommendations of the reform agenda are implemented. The direction of educational change depends on several other factors as well, not the least of which is the resolution of the issue of which agencies of government (local, state or provincial, and federal) will pay for the very high costs of reform.

The major demographic changes that have been occurring on this continent, particularly in the United States, will be critical in determining the needs of our educational systems in the coming years. Increased numbers of students in the schools from the faster-growing cultural groups will bring about shifts in perceived national educational priorities, and perhaps fundamental realignments of our educational goals. We shall see how state and provincial education agencies respond to these trends.

Basic changes in society's career patterns should also be considered. It is estimated that in the United States the average nonagricultural worker now makes a major job change about five times in his or her career. The schools will surely be affected, indirectly or directly, by such major social phenomena. Changes in the social structure due to divorce, unemployment, or job-retraining efforts will also have an impact. Educational systems are integral parts of the broader social systems that created them. If the larger social system experiences fundamental change, this is reflected in the educational system.

In the area of information science and computer technologies applicable for use in educational systems, the development of new products is so rapid that we cannot predict what technological capacities may be available to schools 20 years from now. In addition, basic computer literacy is becoming more and more widespread in the population. We are entering—indeed we are in—a period of human history when knowledgeable people can control far greater amounts of information (and have immediate access to it) than at any previous time. As new information command systems evolve, this phenomenon will become more and more meaningful to all of us.

The future of education will be determined by the current debate concerning what constitutes a just, national response to human needs in a period of technological change. The history of technological change in all human societies since the beginning of industrial development clearly demonstrates that major advances in technology and major breakthroughs in the basic sciences lead to more rapid rates of social change. Society is on the verge of discoveries that will lead to the creation of

entirely new technologies in the dawning years of the twenty-first century. All of the social, economic, and educational institutions on earth will be affected by these scientific breakthroughs. The basic issue is not whether the schools can remain aloof from the needs of industry or the economic demands of society, but how they can emphasize the noblest ideals of free persons in the face of inevitable technological and economic change. Another concern is how to let go of predetermined visions of the future that limit our possibilities as a free people. The schools, of course, will be called upon to face these issues. We need the most enlightened, insightful, and compassionate teachers ever educated by North American universities to prepare the youth of the future in a manner that will humanize the high-tech world in which they live.

All of the articles included in this unit touch on some of the issues previously mentioned. They can be related to discussions on the goals of education, the future of education, or curriculum development. They also reflect highly divergent perspectives in the philosophy of education.

Looking Ahead: Challenge Questions

What might be the shape of school curricula by the year 2000?

What changes in society are most likely to affect educational change?

Based on all of the commission reports of recent years, is it possible to identify any clear directions in which teacher education in North America is headed? How can we build a better future for teachers?

How can information about population demographics, potential discoveries in the basic sciences, and the rate and direction of technological change in Canada and the United States assist in planning for our educational future?

How can schools prepare students to live and work in an uncertain future? What knowledge bases are most important? What skills are most important?

EDUCATIONAL RENAISSANCE:
43 Trends for U.S. Schools

More business-and-school partnerships and increased parental participation are among the likely developments ahead, according to two education consultants.

Marvin J. Cetron and Margaret Evans Gayle

Marvin J. Cetron is president of Forecasting International, Ltd., 1001 North Highland Street, Arlington, Virginia 22210. He is author (with Owen Davies) of *American Renaissance: Our Life at the Turn of the 21st Century*, revised edition (St. Martin's Press, 1990, paperback), which is available from the Futurist Bookstore for $14.45 ($13.35 for Society members), including postage and handling.

Margaret Evans Gayle is president of the Triangle Management Group and vice president of the 21st Century Futures Corporation. She is also president of the Triangle Futures Group—Research Triangle Park chapter of the World Future Society. Her address is 3700 Pembrook Place, Raleigh, North Carolina 27612.

In the near future, American schools will have changed dramatically, and so will people's relationship to them. On the outside, most will still be the same brick-and-glass structures—literally the same, half of them nearing 75 years old. But on the inside, the changes will be obvious: Classrooms will be full of personal computers and other high-tech teaching aids. Teaching methods will have changed to reflect a growing understanding of the learning process. Teachers will be backed up by volunteers from the community and from local businesses. Most of all, educational standards will be more demanding, and they will be enforced. We will be asking far more of schools a few short years from now, and giving them more as well. And we will be getting more in return.

The first experiments in reconstruction have already begun. From them, we have learned more than enough to heal most of the ills that now afflict the U.S. school system. There is nothing to prevent school districts across the country from adopting these and many other reforms — nothing but the inertia of 16,000 school districts. But that inertia is rapidly disappearing in the face of political pressure from enraged parents.

The key, of course, is in the hands of parents themselves. If school systems are to recover their lost quality, if the United States is to survive as an economic leader, parents — and all stakeholders — must accept responsibility for the performance of their local school system. They must offer themselves as part-time teachers and teaching assistants. They must work with local political leaders to raise school budgets to pay teachers for performance (merit pay) and with school administrators to see that funds are used to promote effective classes in the core subjects. Above all, they must make certain that their own children understand the importance of a good education and have the support required for the difficult job of learning. In the years to come, more and more people will accept this challenge. The trend has clearly begun.

In the following pages, we list dozens of examples of key trends and likely developments in education and lifelong learning.

Trends in Education

1. Education will be the major public-agenda item as we enter the twenty-first century.

2. Education will continue to be viewed as the key to economic growth.

3. Technology, coupled with flexible home, work, and learning schedules, will provide more productive time for schooling, training, and working.

4. There is a growing mismatch between the literacy (vocabulary, reading, and writing skills) of the labor force and the competency required by the jobs available. Both ill-prepared new work-force entrants and already-employed workers, who cannot adapt to changing requirements and new technologies, contribute to this mismatch.

● The mismatch between the skills workers possess and the requirements of tomorrow's jobs will be greatest among the "best" jobs, where educational demands are greatest. Three-fourths of new work-force entrants will be qualified for only 40% of new jobs created between 1985 and 2000.

Students

5. The number of public-school enrollments in the United States will increase to 43.8 million by 2000, after having dipped below 40 million in the mid-1980s.

6. One million young people will drop out of school annually, at an estimated cost of $240 billion in lost earnings and forgone taxes over their lifetimes.

7. The number of students at risk of dropping out of school will increase as academic standards rise and social problems (such as drug abuse and teenage pregnancy) intensify.

Teachers

8. The United States will need 2 million new teachers in the public-school system between now and 1995, but historical projections indicate that only a little over a million will materialize.

9. The expected attrition of the aging teaching force, class-size policies, and school-enrollment projections will be major factors determining the numbers of new teachers required to staff U.S. schools.

10. The supply of newly graduated teaching candidates is expected to satisfy only about 60% of the "new hire" demand over the next 10 years.

11. The growing proportions of minorities in the general population and in the student population are not reflected among teachers. This discrepancy will be particularly acute in the southern states, where minority enrollment ranges from 25% to 56% and the proportion of minority teachers ranges from 4% to 35%.

12. Most states will implement alternative routes to certification by 1995 as a solution to teacher shortages, especially in the sciences.

13. We will see a return to teaching laboratories or development schools in the 1990s, as university programs and teaching professionals develop a new vision for schooling from the ground up.

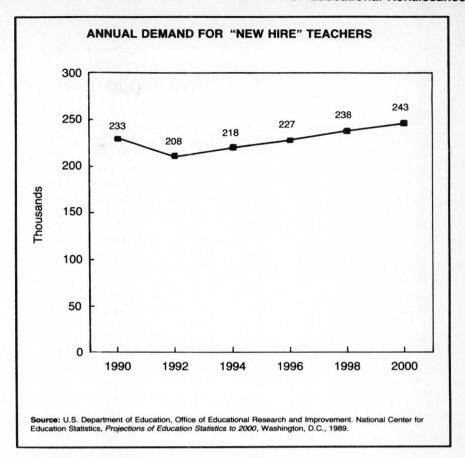

ANNUAL DEMAND FOR "NEW HIRE" TEACHERS

Source: U.S. Department of Education, Office of Educational Research and Improvement. National Center for Education Statistics, *Projections of Education Statistics to 2000*, Washington, D.C., 1989.

The supply of new teachers will fall short of demand by about 40% in the year 2000.

14. Teachers' salaries will continue to be debated in the 1990s while research regarding the relationship of financial incentives to retention of qualified teachers continues.

Curriculum and Instruction

15. Lifelong learning will generate birth-to-death curriculum and delivery systems.

16. A core curriculum for all students will emerge as parents, teachers, business leaders, and other stakeholders debate what is important for the learning enterprise: Basic skills versus arts or vocational education versus critical-thinking skills, for example, will be a major part of the debate.

17. The focus on thinking globally will make foreign language a requirement for all students entering college.

18. Foreign language and bilingual instruction will become a necessity for all students in the twenty-first century. All states will initiate or expand their programs to prepare students for a worldwide marketplace.

19. Vocational education, with emphasis on higher technical literacy, will be required for increasing numbers of students. Access to vocational education will be demanded by more parents and clients.

20. Secondary students will come to value vocational education more highly as reform efforts bring about a restructuring of schools, especially an integration of academic and technical skills.

Higher Education

21. Only 15% of the jobs of the future will require a college diploma, but more than half of all jobs will require postsecondary education and training.

22. There will continue to be an oversupply of college graduates,

The Connection to Jobs and Work

Businesses are increasingly recognizing that their futures depend on an adequately educated work force. Instead of pouring money into training employees once they're hired, more businesses will invest earlier in human resources by forming partnerships with schools.

The trends outlined below show how the world of work is changing and will force schools and businesses to strengthen their relationship.

1. Lifetime employment in the same job or company is a thing of the past. Workers will change jobs or careers five or more times; this will require lifelong training and learning.

2. The decline of employment in agricultural and manufacturing industries will continue. Exception: By 2001, manufacturing productivity will have increased 500% in those industries that have become more automated, added robotics, and remained flexible in their management and production.

3. Information processing (collecting, analyzing, synthesizing, structuring, storing, or retrieving data, text, or graphics), as a basis of knowledge, is becoming important in more and more jobs. By 2000, knowledge workers will fill 43% of available jobs.

4. Work at home will increase as office automation becomes more portable and powerful. Twenty-two percent of the labor force will work at home by the year 2000.

5. A shortage of entry-level workers, especially in the service sector, will create competition among business, the military, and institutions of higher learning for the youth labor force.

6. Eight million jobs in highly skilled occupations — executive, professional, and technical — will become available over the next decade.

7. Small businesses (fewer than 100 employees) will employ most of the labor force by the year 2000. Many of these will be small manufacturing firms.

8. Continued high levels of unemployment in some states will force over-qualified workers to take available jobs, displacing less-qualified workers who will experience longer periods of unemployment.

9. The growth in numbers of part-time workers and workers who moonlight will continue into the twenty-first century as two incomes become increasingly needed to maintain quality-of-life expectations.

— **Marvin J. Cetron and Margaret Evans Gayle**

Adapted from *Educational Renaissance* (St. Martin's Press, December 1990).

As changes occur in the world of work, businesses will have to take more responsibility for preparing their future labor force by forming partnerships with schools.

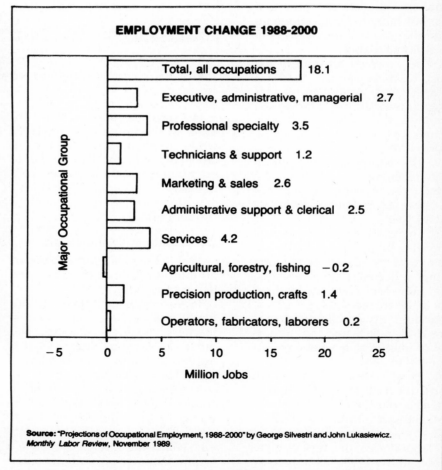

EMPLOYMENT CHANGE 1988-2000

Major Occupational Group	Million Jobs
Total, all occupations	18.1
Executive, administrative, managerial	2.7
Professional specialty	3.5
Technicians & support	1.2
Marketing & sales	2.6
Administrative support & clerical	2.5
Services	4.2
Agricultural, forestry, fishing	−0.2
Precision production, crafts	1.4
Operators, fabricators, laborers	0.2

Source: "Projections of Occupational Employment, 1988-2000" by George Silvestri and John Lukasiewicz. *Monthly Labor Review*, November 1989.

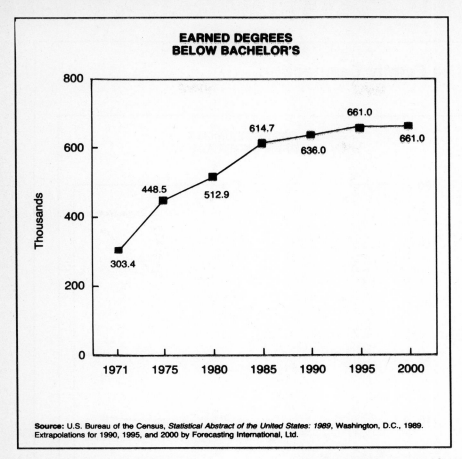

EARNED DEGREES BELOW BACHELOR'S

303.4
448.5
512.9
614.7
636.0
661.0
661.0

Thousands

1971 1975 1980 1985 1990 1995 2000

Source: U.S. Bureau of the Census, *Statistical Abstract of the United States: 1989*, Washington, D.C., 1989. Extrapolations for 1990, 1995, and 2000 by Forecasting International, Ltd.

Two-year and technical colleges offering degrees below a bachelor's will be significant factors in the technological growth of communities.

especially in liberal arts. A liberal-arts background is valued in principle, but not in pay or in competition for jobs that require specialized skills.

23. Community colleges and technical institutes will become major determinants of technological growth in communities and within regions.

24. The drop in enrollments in teacher-education programs, particularly among minority students, will reach the crisis point in the 1990s.

• Current minority enrollment in teacher education is insufficient even to replace the minority teachers who are leaving the profession.

• Fewer than half of minority teacher candidates, prepared by colleges and universities, pass the required certification tests in some 45 states.

• High failure rates on standardized tests and teacher-certification examinations are also reducing the pool of available minority teachers.

School Reform and Restructuring

25. School-reform efforts will continue to improve elements of the educational system, but without a national philosophy that stresses reform (e.g., merit pay, longer school days and years, etc.) and the commitment to fund it, American schools will remain inferior to those of other industrialized nations.

26. The emphasis on school reform and restructuring will continue throughout the 1990s, but with little improvement of national averages on standardized tests.

27. The "back-to-basics" movement will be superseded by a "forward-to-future-basics" movement, which will include the use of telecommunications technologies, together with other advanced science knowledge and technical skills, for problem solving.

28. Flexible school scheduling will result in more learning time for students.

29. Accountability at all levels will be the buzzword for the 1990s. But will the impetus be top-down or bottom-up? The trend toward school-based management suggests that local schools can carry out national standards. Accountability issues will create major conflict among federal, state, and local agencies.

30. Increased accountability and higher-paid educators will produce more-professional approaches and solutions to educating a democratic and pluralistic society.

Governance and Leadership

31. All community stakeholders (parents, students, teachers, business leaders, and others) will continue to demand more involvement in the decisions governing education, but they will have little knowledge about what should be done to restructure; much is done with little research basis.

32. Centralized control of curriculum, teacher training, and achievement standards will continue, but decentralization of school and classroom management will increase.

33. The current shortage of qualified candidates for school administration positions will continue well into the twenty-first century. Three-fourths of American school superintendents, and as many as half of all principals, will retire by 1994.

34. The principal will become the major change agent for schools. He or she will bear tremendous leadership responsibility in sharing governance with the staff of the school. This school-based-management trend will create a need to place high-quality professionals in school administration — a difficult task in light of projected shortages and the present low test scores of candidates.

35. Educational bureaucracies, local school boards, and other regulatory agencies will lose their power as the second wave of reforms takes hold during the 1990s.

36. The educational system will become more fragmented in the next decade. Implementation of

The Family Connection

Families of the twenty-first century will encounter many stresses and will increasingly turn to the community and the educational system for support. In the Ideal Community School scenario proposed by William L. Lepley, director of the Iowa Department of Education, schools will be the hub of society by the year 2010. Ideal schools will offer a range of family-aiding programs, such as health-care services, job information, childbirth and parenting classes, and pre-retirement planning.

Parents — and even members of the community without children — will form stronger ties with schools as they become increasingly recognized as crucial to the future well-being of communities. Below are just a few of the trends affecting families that will ultimately have an impact on schools and education.

1. By 2000, fewer than 4% of families will consist of breadwinner husband, homemaker wife, and two children.
2. There will be more multi-families: children living with adults who are not related.
3. Legal redefinitions of "family" will have an impact on schools.
4. By 2000, three-fourths of 3-year-olds will attend nurseries (day-care centers or nursery schools).
5. Both partners in most family units (married and unmarried) will work; this figure could rise to 75% by 2000.
6. The number of single-parent families is steadily growing in size and importance. The major reason why white children are living with only one parent is divorce; for black and

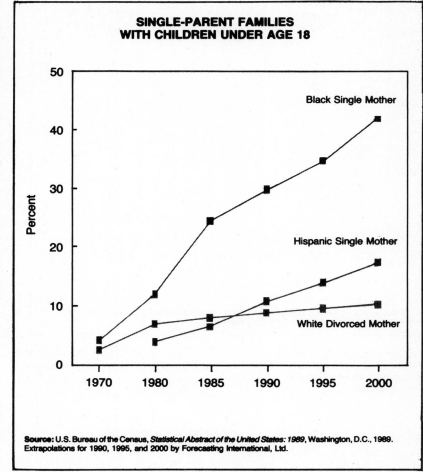

SINGLE-PARENT FAMILIES WITH CHILDREN UNDER AGE 18

Source: U.S. Bureau of the Census, *Statistical Abstract of the United States: 1989*, Washington, D.C., 1989. Extrapolations for 1990, 1995, and 2000 by Forecasting International, Ltd.

Hispanic children it is because the parent was never married. If current trends continue, by 2000:
• Eleven percent of white children will be living with a divorced mother (10% in 1988).
• Forty-two percent of black children will be living with a never-married mother (29% in 1988).
• Seventeen percent of Hispanic children will be living with a never-married mother (10% in 1988).
7. The number of people below the poverty level is not

Growing numbers of single-parent families will look to schools for more services, from pre-kindergarten day care to parenting classes and health care.

improving: Among female-headed families (no husband present) the rates are rising, especially for children.

— Marvin J. Cetron and Margaret Evans Gayle

Adapted from *Educational Renaissance* (St. Martin's Press, December 1990).

numerous schooling alternatives will erode the traditional schooling pattern.

37. New systems of school governance will be explored that go beyond centralization and decentralization to, for instance, distribution of authority among government, teaching professionals, and families.

School Finance

38. A wide spectrum of school-finance initiatives and experiments will be undertaken. These will range from extreme centralization and financial control at the state level on one end to privatization on the other, where the states will finance education through vouchers to parents (based on their choices of schools) rather than by directly financing schools. Between these extremes, there will be many traditional programs, but with an increasing number of private-sector partnerships.

39. Employers spend $210 billion annually on training. The number and effectiveness of business–education partnerships, to reduce remediation costs and to develop technical skills, will increase.

40. Regional disparities in educational resources will increase.

School Law

41. Making public education work for everyone, especially for minorities and those with low incomes, will be the challenge for the 1990s. Parents and special-interest groups will raise legal challenges to curriculum, methodology, expenditures, access, and a host of other issues.

42. Equity issues will become the major problems faced by policy makers. Legal challenges will increase as standards are raised.

43. Educational equity will be redefined not in terms of access, but in terms of expenditures.

Proper behavior for the 21st century in our global village

A challenging call for educators to change some traditional behaviors so that the needs of tomorrow's adults can be met today.

WALI GILL

Dr. Wali Gill is Assistant Professor in the College of Education at the University of Nebraska at Omaha.

"**E**ducation does not mean teaching people to know what they do not know; it means teaching them to behave as they do not behave," said English critic and author John Ruskin. As the global village approaches the 21st Century, educators will have to modify their behavior drastically in order to prepare today's students with the behaviors those students will need for tomorrow. What, then, are the issues which will manifest themselves for educational reform?

In Alvin Toffler's *The Third Wave,* predictions of an upcoming super-struggle that will form 21st century democracy are made painfully clear. (1) Second Wave people, committed to maintaining the industrial past, will be in conflict with growing millions of Third Wave people who recognize that the world's most urgent problems can no longer be resolved within the framework of the industrial order. The need for new family, educational, and corporate institutions involves the design of more appropriate systems in many nations at once.

Demographic data provide one of the most effective means for long-range planning. For example, in the last decade all NATO nations have had major declines in birthrates. (2) The current world population is 5 billion; 9 out of every 10 children born in the world are born in a developing nation; and The West is estimated to be 14 percent white now and 9 percent by the year 2010.

Two areas attracting increasing attention from educators and likely to impact on tomorrow's students are the right to literacy and moral behavior. While literacy is of general concern, the recent debate surrounding *cultural* literacy sidesteps some of the disrupting problems of sexism, racism, class exploitation, and other disheartening social issues. (3) However, the cultural literacy debate has had its own problems. Conservative scholars bent on preserving the traditions of Western civilization have avoided attending to works of literature and philosophy that are classical East Indian or Chinese. And connections have not been established between the cultural literacy of native lands and the development of character in students.

Attempting to find a place for moral education, or character development, has been under discussion in the United States since the end of the 19th century. (4) Identified by a body of activities and

> "*Education as a human right and for human rights loom on the international horizon.*

principles by which moral education can be transmitted to secular institutions, educators have become wary of trying to find common moral threads as society has become more ethnically and socially diverse. Such diversity has yet to be addressed.

The Right to Literacy

Education as a human right and education for human rights loom on the international horizon. Governments and individuals have expressed deep concern about throngs of young people who leave school without the basic knowledge and skills needed for informed life-long decisions. (5) The Committee of Ministers, the highest political body of the Council of Europe, has recommended that "throughout their school career, all young people should learn about human rights as part of their preparation for life in a pluralistic democracy." Accordingly, human rights education should permeate their whole school life—the ethos and organization of their schools as well as the content of the formal curriculum. Specifically, it should also lead to the acquisition and development of certain skills including language, judgment, social, and action skills. (6) The relationship between human rights and education must be considered by educators and policy makers who wish to weave it into an overall fabric for truly culturally literate students.

In the United States, literacy has been declining at a time when a changing society continues to demonstrate ours is a country in need of some remedial prescription. The United States lags behind the most developing nations in literacy. (7) United States students lack basic literacy and cultural literacy knowledge that corporations, businesses, writers and speakers assume their workers and audiences already know.

Interest in cultural literacy has increased. Defined as the basic information needed to thrive in the modern world, the schools are failing great numbers of children. (8) Youngsters from poor and illiterate homes remain poor and illiterate. This has

Wali Gill, "Proper Behavior for the 21st Century in Our Global Village." *Middle School Journal,* 21:20-22, National Middle School Association, September 1989.

occurred not because teachers are inept, but chiefly because they are compelled to teach a fragmented curriculum based on faulty educational theories.

Within the sphere of comparative and interdisciplinary education, numerous policies and programs have proven successful with multicultural audiences and deserve more attention. (9) Unfortunately, many of the programs designed for special learning audiences are virtually unknown within many teacher education programs and are peripheral, at best, in most national teacher efforts. (10) There are a few scholars in the United States who have urged the creation of schools to effectively educate non-white students and to consider their learning styles resulting from their non-white cultural backgrounds. (11) At the present time, however, much documentation attests to the disparities between white and non-white audiences in academic achievement, suspensions, students classified as gifted and talented and educable mentally handicapped. (12)

Pointing public school personnel in America toward a teaching process conducive to cultural sensitivities is limited by the current nature of self-centeredness, ethnocentricity and majority-culture bias in higher education. It has been suggested that the decline of higher education is directly attributable to the *Professorus Americanus* mentality. (13) That is, today's professor *is* the university, and he is self-interested, anti-intellectual, mobile and without loyalty to institutions or the values of liberal education. Further, these professors are politicans and entrepreneurs who protect their turf and shrewdly hustle research for cash while they huckster their talents to rival universities, business, foundations, and government. In the process they divert attention from themselves by blaming societal ills elsewhere. The impact on students can be devastating.

Recent investigations have addressed the decline of minority students in higher education and concomitant issues relating to minority participation in the field of teaching. (14) To illustrate: school reform movements are cyclical and the present call for excellence can be seen in previous cycles; comprehensive programs have yet to be designed to recruit, retain and graduate a more culturally and socially diverse population; and several factors have been identified that facilitate and hinder the educational development and success of minority students.

This impact of these realities is felt in public schools.

By the year 2000, when minority students are expected to make up 33 percent of the school-age population, the minority teaching force is expected to be 5 percent. (15) Though states and school districts want the best qualified teaching force available, they retain policies that exclude and deny access to education by pitting excellence against equity and do the society a serious disfavor.

> **Minority students will be 33% of school population while minority teachers will only be 5% of staff.**

Moral Aspects of Education

The effect of school on the moral behavior of children cannot be underestimated in any society. The teaching of moral values may negate to some degree family disunity, a preoccupation with hedonism and material acquisition, the impact of the media, and distrust and questionable ethical practices in public institutions, government, and industry. Schools cannot ignore moral education for it is one of their most important responsibilities, and even though human beings vary, there is common ground to stand on. (16)

Neither should the viewpoint of children be cast asunder. Children's moral outlook; how much they owe a particular viewpoint to parents, peers, and surroundings; and how much to their own inner nature, should be an ongoing concern for educators. Schools must be more active in character development. (17) In the eyes of students, teachers, and administrators, what makes someone a person of character could easily be a common overlay in schools. Character development in children can also be spurred by employing a phenomenological perspective. That is, observation must come before the explanation process of attending to and grasping, and, the belief that the individual has within himself the ability to make modifications of his character. (18)

In order to become a good teacher, one

must rise above the domain of personal circumstance of class, color, ethnicity, and religion. Teaching has been described as the practice of what it means to be human; to have a voice that names the world in relation to one's own experiences; to activate students to understand that the conditions of their own humanity are the conditions of humanity as a whole; that they do not have to accept the world as it is; and that their futures are not given. (19)

Teachers, if they consider themselves educated, have the responsibility to change society and an obligation to civilize children. (20) One of my mentors, a very talented and sage person, told me the qualifications of a good teacher were: have zeal and enthusiasm, be easy to comprehend, be a good speaker, have the opportunity to be heard before a respectful and attentive audience and have a companion to share the burden of responsibility.

Behaving with Passion

Societies will be judged by their ability to nurture their young and to prepare them to provide for themselves, the next generation and even the previous generation. Hence, education's goals must be to train all children so they can live full lives, adapt to change, and contribute to productive work and the service to others. Toffler predicts the Second Wave civilization will continue to fight against minority power; attempt to preserve the nuclear family; resist decentralization, regionalism, and diversity; and oppose effects to de-massify the schools.

> **Teachers have the responsibility to change society and an obligation to civilize children.**

By contrast, he predicts that Third Wave proponents will lobby for shared minority power, legitimate options for the nuclear family, and less standardization and more individualism in the schools. Cultural and moral training may play pivotal roles in the process. For the educational process to be effective, Second and Third Wave educators must have passion for the profession and people.

The recommendations made by educators, sociologists and psychologists have yet to be initiated with much energy. Nonetheless, there continues to be a groundswell of agreement on the importance of the following identified by the Carnegie Corporation: a. creating smaller environments for learning by dividing large schools into smaller units, especially at the middle school level; b. emphasizing

———————— " ————————

As long as there is strife and human suffering in the global village, there will be a need for educational reform.

· · · · · · · · · · · · · · · · ·

As long as there is a need for human rights, there will be a need to consider morality and literacy.

moral development; c. teaching reading and writing in the early school years; d. teaching a core curriculum aimed at producing students who are literate and understand the sciences, and who have a sense of health, ethics, and citizenship; e. eliminating the use of "tracking" by achievement level, which essentially dooms many children to failure; f. increasing teacher salaries; g. reversing the status of the "pecking order" created by top administrators, high school, junior high, middle and elementary school

teachers; h. identifying effective programs and disseminating those ideas whenever possible i. investigating effective teaching methods in which white teachers can help non-white students achieve academic excellence; j. investigating the connection between the lack of minority faculty in higher education and the shortage of minority teachers; k. involving parents and community leaders in the education of children, including in-school programs; l. and helping those who need public health care. (21)

As long as there is strife and human suffering in the global village, there will be a need for educational reform. As long as there is a need for human rights and for an informed society, there will be a need to consider morality and literacy. Until all of the world's citizens can function effectively in their native lands and be "their brother's keeper," there will be a need for educational change. After all, as Ruskin has said, "The highest reward for man's toil is not what he gets for it, but what he becomes by it."

References

1. Alvin Toffler (1980). *The Third Wave.* New York: William Morrow and Company.
2. Harold Hodginson (1988). "The Right Schools for the Right Kids," *Educational Leadership,* February, 10-14.
3. Stanley Aronowitz and Henry A. Giroux (1988). Schooling, Culture, and Literacy in the Age of Broken Dreams: A Review of Bloom and Hirsch," *Harvard Education Review,* 48, 2, May, 172-194; Allan Bloom (1987). *The Closing of the American Mind.* (New York: Simon and Schuster); E. D. Hirsch (1988). *Cultural Literacy: What Every American Needs to Know.* (New York: Random House).
4. S.M. Yulish (1980). *The Search for a Civic Religion.* (Washington, D. C.: University Press of America).
5. Norma Bernstein Tarrow, Ed. (1987). *Human Rights and Education.* (New York: Pergamon Press), ix.
6. *Ibid*, x.
7. Jonathan Kozol (1987) *Literate America.* (New York: Doubleday and Company, Inc.).
8. Hirsch, *Cultural Literacy.*
9. Tarrow, *Human Rights;* Alan C. Peters, ed. (1989) *International Comparisons* (Alexandria, VA: Association for Supervision and Curriculum Development).
10. Asa G. Hillard, III (1988). "Public Support for Successful Instructional Practices for At-Risk Students," In Council of Chief School Officers, *School Success for Students At Risk.* (Orlando, FL: Harcourt Brace Jovanovich, Inc), 195-208.
11. Janice Hale-Benson (1982). *Black Children: Their Roots, Culture, and Learning Styles.* (Provo, Utah: Brigham Young University Press).
12. *A Special Analysis of 1986 Elementary and Secondary Civil Rights Survey Data* (1988). Boston: National Coalition of Advocates for Students.
13. Charles Sykes (1988). *ProfScram: Professors and the Demise of Higher Education.* (Washington, D. C.: Regnery Gateway).
14. Faustine Jones-Wilson (1989). "Equity in Education: A Low Priority in the School Reform Movement," in Willy DeMarcell Smith and Eva Wells Chunn (Eds.) *Black Education: A Quest for Equity and Excellence* (New Brunswick: Transaction Publishers), 28-35; *Seventh Annual Status Report on Minorities in Higher Education* (1988). Washington, D. C.: American Council on Education, Office of Minority Affairs; Alexander Astin (1982). *Minorities in Higher Education.* (San Francisco: Josey-Bass).
15. Barbara J. Holmes (1989). "A Closer Look at the Shortage of Minority Teachers," *Education Week,* May 7, 29.
16. "Moral Education in the Life of the School" (1988). Association for Supervision and Curriculum Development Panel on Moral Education, *Educational Leadership,* May, 4-8.
17. Robert Coles (1986). *The Moral Life of Children.* (Boston: Houghton Mifflin).
18. R. M. Goldenson (1970). *The Encyclopedia of Human Behavior: Psychology and Mental Health,* Vol 2 (New York: Doubleday and Company, Inc., 964-965; C. R. Rogers (1951). *Client-Centered Therapy.* (New York: Houghton Mifflin; Rogers (1962) "Towards Becoming A Fully Functioning Person," In A. W. Combs (Ed.), *Association for Supervision and Curriculum Development Yearbook of 1962, Perceiving, Behaving, Becoming.* (Washington, D. C.: NEA, 21-33.
19. Alice H. Reich (1983). "Why I Teach." *The Chronicle of Higher Education,* 17, 8, October, 1.
20. James Baldwin (1988). "A Talk to Teachers," in Rick Simmons and Scott Walker (Eds.), *The Greywolf Annual Five: Multicultural Literacy, Opening the American Mind.* (St. Paul: Greywolf Press) 3-12.
21. *Turning Point: Preparing American Youth for the 21st Century* (1989), Carnegie Council on Adolescent Development Task Force (Carnegie Corporation of New York); Wali Gill, "Fostering Intellectual Growth in Minority Students," *Educational Leadership,* November, 1989 (forthcoming); Hodgkinson (1988), "Using Demographic Data For Long-Range Planning," *Phi Delta Kappan,* October, 166-170; Holmes. "A Closer Look"; Kozol, *Literate America,* 203-217; Toffler, *The Third Wave,* 436-438.

Will the Social Context Allow a Tomorrow for Tomorrow's Teachers?

Michael W. Apple

University of Wisconsin, Madison

First asking why schools and teachers should be called on to solve social and economically created structural problems in our society, Apple then raises related economic questions about how minorities and working-class students will pay for additional professional education and whether communities intent on keeping taxes low will maintain a lopsided temporary teacher workforce. He also warns of taking a scientific-technical view of teacher education.

There is a good deal to applaud in *Tomorrow's Teachers*. The report is quite insightful in a number of areas. For instance, in opposition to the very reductive proposals now surfacing in the media and elsewhere that blame the school for all of our social ills, the authors at least minimally recognize how closely tied the educational system is to social factors outside its doors. "Excellence" and responsiveness in schooling may require profound alterations in the unequal economic and political realms that dominate the larger society.

Second, the report shows its willingness to deal with complexity in its assertion (one that I believe is very well founded) that teaching is not reducible to "competencies" measured on paper-and-pencil tests. Rather, good teaching is a complex assemblage of knowledge "that," "how," and "to," none of which can be easily merged back into the others. Third, the author's recognition of the gendered specificities out of which many of the conditions of teaching were constructed is commendable. It is the case that whatever excellence our school system now has was built on the backs of the low-paid and committed labor of generations of teachers who were primarily women.[1] No other report of this type has dealt honestly with this critically important issue. I do not believe that the Holmes Group goes far enough with this recognition, but it is to the authors' credit that the question of *who* does the bulk of the teaching in the United States is at least raised. Any call for greater control over the teaching profession, any attempt to change teachers' work, is also a call to control the labor process of what is largely "women's work" and needs to be seen in the context of the frequent attempts to rationalize women's paid work in the past.[2]

Fourth, the wish to involve schools and especially teachers more directly in teacher education, to form more cooperative arrangements, is a clear sign of progress. It values the practical and political skills teachers have developed over decades of hard work. Further, and very importantly, such involvement could assist in the movement to resist the deskilling of teaching that has accelerated in the past few years.[3] The same could be said of the group's position on the necessity of more cooperative relations between faculties of education and the rest of the university.

Finally, *Tomorrow's Teachers* is clear about many of the dangers of short-term solutions to the problems confronting teaching. It rightly raises cautions about credential deregulation, a process that could have the same truly negative effects as other privatized and deregulated proposals such as voucher plans.[4] And it is self-reflective about some of the dangers of simple models of differentiated staffing. All of these points document why we should take the Holmes Group's recommendations seriously. Even though I have disagreements with a number of their specific proposals, the thoughtfulness and care that went into crafting their position is evident.

Even with the articulateness of these proposals, there are gaps and silences in the document. What I want to do here is raise a series of issues that need to be given further consideration. Obviously, these will by nature take the form of assertions that cannot be detailed in depth given space limitations. Interested readers who wish to pursue these claims will find further substantiation in the references that accompany these comments. I shall limit my attention to a few issues that may not usually surface in discussions of the document.

A number of points need to be made at the outset. The supposed crisis in teaching and in education in general is not an isolated phenomenon. It is related to a much more extensive structural crisis in the economy, in ideology, and in authority relations. As I have argued in considerably more detail elsewhere, we are witnessing an attempt to restructure nearly all of our major cultural, economic, and political institutions to bring them more closely into line with the needs of only a very limited segment of the American population.[5] Thus, we cannot fully understand why our formal institutions of education and the teachers and administrators who work so long and hard in them are being focused on so intently today unless we realize that economically powerful groups and the New Right have already been partly successful in refocusing attention away from the very real problems of inequality in the economy and in political representation and shifting most criticism to the health, welfare, legal, and especially educational systems. In technical terms, there has been a marked shift from a concern for "person rights" to those of "property rights" in our public discourse.[6]

In essence, dominant groups have been relatively successful in *exporting* the larger crisis away from themselves. When achievement is low among certain groups, when there are significant rates of negative intergenerational mobility, when workers have little enthusiasm for their jobs, and so forth, the public is asked to blame the school and the teachers. That is, rather than focusing directly on what may be the major sources of the problem—for instance, the immensely high under- and unemployment rates among working-class and especially minority youth who often see little future for themselves, an economy in which 80 percent of the benefits consistently go to the top 20 percent of the population, corporate decisions that cause millions of employees to work in low-paid, deskilled, and boring jobs (or to have no jobs at all), or an economic system that by its very nature needs to subvert traditional values, authority relations, self-discipline, and accepted conceptions of legitimate knowledge in order to create new "needs" and to stimulate the purchasing of commodities, and so forth[7]—the problem is placed on the educational system. If only teachers were better prepared, if only teaching and curricula were more tightly controlled and better managed, if only textbooks were more demanding and discipline and work skills were stressed, all of the above problems would be solved. The diagnosis and cure are actually a form of category error and would be easy to dismiss on empirical grounds if only they were not taken so seriously.

Tomorrow's Teachers, then, needs to be seen as something that follows in the footsteps of other documents such as *A Nation at Risk*. Its authors are considerably more aware of the larger structural situation in which schools and teachers exist and they are certainly not apologists for those people who wish to turn schools over to industrial and conservative needs and ideologies. The existing process of exporting the blame and bringing conservative ideologies into the heart of the educational enterprise helps, however, to construct the context in which the report of the Holmes Group will be *read* even though this may not be the authors' intention at all.

Obviously, *Tomorrow's Teachers* cannot solve all of these larger problems. No document about teachers and teaching could. But it is wise to keep the structural context in mind, since—while educators should direct their attention to what needs to be done in education—education itself must be wary of assuming that the answers to many of its very real dilemmas lie in preparing a more intellectually rigorous "profession." To do this may simply play into the hands of the attempt by dominant groups to export their crisis onto other areas. Thus, while I am in total agreement with the Holmes Group that some important things must be done in education and in teacher education, the latent

effects of limiting our attention to the internal issues need to be given a good deal of thought.

While I want to avoid being overly economistic here, let me use this larger social context as a backdrop to point to some of the economic problems that I believe will create serious difficulties in the way the report of the Holmes Group will be received. It may produce effects that its authors would not intend or approve.

There is one serious problem that needs to be given considerably more attention by those institutions and individuals that wish to take the report's recommendations seriously. Here I am speaking of the class and racial dynamics that could evolve in the elimination of an undergraduate education major. The Holmes report partly recognizes the fact that extending teacher training beyond the fourth year could present problems for some individuals. Hence, it calls for loan forgiveness for future teachers. Yet the problems go much deeper than this. Already, large numbers of students must work one and sometimes two jobs to make enough money to live on and pay college expenses during their four years of college. We are witnessing a severe downturn in minority and working-class college enrollments. Many universities have become bastions of the middle class and above. Extending professional training beyond the four years will simply have elitist effects unless large sums of money are made available not just in "forgiveable" tuition loans but in outright grants for living expenses, books, and so on. Absent this much more extensive financial commitment, the outcome of the Holmes Group recommendations will be to ultimately make it more difficult for less economically advantaged individuals to become teachers. Without such extensive financial support, movements to increase the amount of time spent in teacher education should be resisted, since their class- and race-stratifying effects could be massive.

The economic issues do not end here, however. Other elements of the report need further thought as well. The plan to have differentiated staffing patterns, for example, has major economic implications that may be hidden beneath the meritorious goals of the Holmes Group. In arguing for changes in the constitution of teaching we must realize that we live in the real world, a world of declining revenues, of anger over school budgets, of pressure to cut educational costs as much as possible. I do not like this situation, but it will not go away. These conditions—caused in large part by the fiscal crisis of the state[8]—are already creating immense pressures on local school districts to hire the least expensive teachers possible. With differentiated staffing, I would predict that many school systems will attempt to minimize costs by hiring as many Instructors as possible. These short-term, nontenured appointments would save districts a good deal of money. Pension costs would be minimal. There would be a continual large turnover of staff, even more than today. Thus, the bulk of the teaching force would be made up of those people who have less than five years seniority. The salary savings here would be enormous. The fiction of a reprofessionalized teaching force might be maintained, but there would be considerable pressure to minimize the number of Professional Teachers and to keep to a bare minimum the number of Career Professionals. The fiscal crisis is not a fiction, as anyone who works with school budgets knows. Any plan to differentiate teaching that does not include serious proposals to deal with the possible management offensive to cut costs that will undoubtedly arise from such plans is not as complete as it should be.

These economic points have important implications. The Holmes Group, as a group made up primarily of deans of major research institutions, needs to engage in intense and concerted lobbying and to put pressure on state legislatures and the federal government not only in support of its proposals, but just as importantly for considerable sums of money for students in these extended programs to live on. This can be accomplished only if organizations such as the Holmes Group join with others in questioning where financial resources are now going (i.e., into "defense," corporate tax "relief," etc.). Absent such alterations in our current "income transfer policies" (in which funding for human programs is transferred, say, to the military), the resources available to actually make a long-term difference will probably be insufficient. This may be hard for educators like ourselves to deal with, but we need to face up to how very complicated and far reaching the dilemmas we face actually are and what may actually be required to solve them.

Furthermore, guarantees need to be given by every school district that accepts models of differentiated staffing and career ladders similar to those proposed by the Holmes Group about the hiring ratios. This too will require money for financially crisis-ridden communities and will again require a significant reorientation of spending priorities at all levels, but especially at the national level. There are plans available for such changes both in spending priorities and in social goals, some of which are insightful and detailed. These take the common good, not only the needs of business, industry, and the Right, as their starting point, and integrate educational planning into proposals for more democratic planning in general.[9] These plans provide a platform on which we can stand and from which we can see the role of education in its larger context. I am afraid that without movement toward these kinds of more general changes, reports like that of the Holmes Group may play into the hands of the conservative restoration.

Let me raise one final caution. In a document produced by representatives of many of the major research institutions in education, it is not surprising that a faith in "science" as the primary road to pedagogic and curricular "progress" should be evident. I must admit, however, to having some serious reservations about the claim in *Tomorrow's Teachers* that the "promise of science of education is about to be fulfilled" (p. 52). The very metaphor of a science education is problematic. Education may not in fact "progress" in quite the same manner as even the most applied of the sciences.[10]

If by science we mean the more historical European idea of disciplined reason enlivened by a concern for value, that is one thing. If we mean a science in which the accumulation of atomistic facts that, when put together, will ultimately provide a strong empirical warrant for all we do in classrooms, that is another. Just as teaching itself is a complex assemblage of "thats," "hows," and "tos," so too is the study of pedagogy and curriculum. "Positive" science may provide a certain, actually rather limited, amount of insight into the process. Ultimately, however, decisions in and about education are not technical, but ethical and political.[11] Whatever its glory, the history of the search for a science of education has also been the history of the transformation of educational discourse from a concern with *why* X should be taught to *how* to do it. The difficult and intensely valuative questions of content (of what knowledge is of most worth) and of teaching (of how to teach fairly and in an ethically responsive, not only efficient, manner) have been pushed to the background in our attempts to determine a set of technical procedures that will "solve" all of the problems we face.

Clearly, the report *does* recognize some of this dynamic, and in the struggle for respect and necessary resources, the notion of a science of education may be important rhetorically. After all, educators deserve respect and cannot fully succeed with the all too limited human and material resources now made available to them. However, we should not confuse the use of science as what might be called a rhetoric of justification with the much more complicated process of deliberation, conflict, and compromise that constitutes the real world of educational work.

Do not misinterpret me. There *is* a need for research. Much that goes on in classrooms *can* benefit from a closer "empirical" (interpreted as broadly as possible)[12] look and the quantitative and qualitative methods developed by social and educational researchers are essential, though not totally sufficient, tools in illuminating what is actually happening in schooling. Yet, so much of the weakest kind of educational theory and practice—overly competency based instruction, systems management, reductive accountability schemes, the construction of management systems that deskill teachers, and so on—has been justified by the claim to scientificity that I think we should be very careful of the latent effects of the current resurgence of "scientific approaches" to curriculum and teaching even when it is supported in such an articulate fashion as in *Tomorrow's Teachers*. Not only must we insist on the best of science—a commodity in rarer supply in education than we would like to admit given our propensity to borrow the reconstructed logic of science, not its logic in use[13]—but we need to avoid patterning all of education on science itself. Education is simply too ethically and politically complicated, too valuative, to be totally capturable by such a language system.

Let me repeat that even with all this said, I do have sympathy with many of the positions taken in the report. However, because of the social context in which it appears and because it has chosen to highlight certain elements in its arguments over others, its reception may signal something less than what its proponents hoped for. On a national level, the report may be used to largely justify mass testing of teachers of a very inflexible kind and a further move toward "scientific" curriculum making and compentency-based teaching and teacher education. It can thereby actually depower, not empower, the very teachers the Holmes Group wishes to support.[14] At a state level, it may have the effect of reinforcing legislative intervention in the name of accountability and cost-cutting. On a local level, a number of its proposals may be used by financially troubled administrators and antagonists of teachers' unions to staff their schools with the cheapest teachers available.

These are all *possibilities*, not definites. Given the sensitivity and intelligence evident in so much of the report of

9. A LOOK TO THE FUTURE

the Holmes Group, and given the quality of the people involved in it, I trust that the next stages of their deliberations will take these issues into account. If they are not taken seriously, the Right, corporate America, and the efficiency experts who now pretend to be educators in the richest sense of that term will win. It will be the teachers and students who will suffer the loss. This will be at a cost that will be more than a little damaging not only to their futures but to all of ours as well.

Notes

1. For further discussion of the relationship between gender, class, and teaching, see Michael W. Apple, *Teachers and Texts; A Political Economy of Class and Gender Relations in Education* (New York: Routledge & Kegan Paul, 1987); and Sara Freedman, "Master Teacher/Merit Pay— Weeding Out Women from 'Women's True Profession,' " *Radical Teacher* 25 (November 1983): 24-28

2. Apple, *Teachers and Texts;* and Alice Kessler-Harris, *Out to Work* (New York: Oxford University Press, 1982).

3. See Michael W. Apple, *Education and Power* (Boston: Routledge & Kegan Paul, 1982); and Andrew Gitlin, "School Structure and Teachers' Work," in *Ideology and Practice in Schooling,* ed. Michael W. Apple and Lois Weis (Philadelphia: Temple University Press, 1983), pp. 193-212.

4. Apple, *Education and Power,* especially ch. 4.

5. Apple, *Teachers and Texts.* See also Ira Shor, *Culture Wars* (New York: Routledge & Kegan Paul, 1986).

6. See Francis Fox Piven and Richard A. Cloward, *The New Class War* (New York: Pantheon Books, 1982).

7. See, for example, Robert L. Heilbroner, *The Nature and Logic of Capitalism* (New York: Norton, 1985); Joshua Cohen and Joel Rogers, *On Democracy* (New York: Penguin Books, 1983); and Martin Carnoy, Derek Shearer, and Russell Rumberger, *A New Social Contract* (New York: Harper & Row, 1983).

8. See Manuel Castells, *The Economic Crisis and American Society* (Princeton: Princeton Universtiy Press, 1980); James O'Conner, *The Fiscal Crisis of the State* (New York: St. Martin's Press, 1973); and Apple, *Education and Power.*

9. Among the best is the masterful analysis and set of proposals in Marcus Raskin, *The Common Good* (New York: Routledge & Kegan Paul, 1987). I do not fully agree with all of Raskin's proposals for education, however.

10. Francis Schrag, "Knowing and Doing," *American Journal of Education* 89 (May 1981): 253-82.

11. This is discussed in more detail in Michael W. Apple, *Ideology and Curriculum* (Boston: Routledge & Kegan Paul, 1979). See also Dwayne Huebner, "Curricular Language and Classroom Meanings," in *Language and Meaning,* ed. James B. Macdonald and Robert R. Leeper (Washington: Association for Supervision and Curriculum Development, 1966), pp. 8-26.

12. See Eric Bredo and Walter Feinberg, eds. *Knowledge and Values in Social and Educational Research* (Philadelphia: Temple University Press, 1982).

13. Abraham Kaplan, *The Conduct of Inquiry* (San Francisco: Chandler Publishing Co., 1964).

14. See Michael W. Apple and Kenneth Teitelbaum, "Are Teachers Losing Control of Their Skills and Curriculum?," *Journal of Curriculum Studies* 18 (April-June 1986): 177-84.

Credits/ Acknowledgments

Cover design by Charles Vitelli

1. Perceptions of Education in North America
Facing overview—The Dushkin Publishing Group.

2. Reconceptualization of the Educative Effort
Facing overview—United Nations photo by O. Monsen.

3. Striving for Excellence
Facing overview—United Nations photo by Y. Nagata.

4. Morality and Values in Education
Facing overview—United Nations.

5. Discipline and Schooling
Facing overview—The Dushkin Publishing Group photo by Barbie Heid.

6. Equal Opportunity
Facing overview—United Nations photo by Milton Grant.

7. Serving Special Needs
Facing overview—United Nations photo by L. Solmssen.

8. The Profession of Teaching Today
Facing overview—United Nations photo by Marta Pinter.

9. A Look to the Future
Facing overview—Apple Computer.

ANNUAL EDITIONS ARTICLE REVIEW FORM

■ NAME: _____ DATE: _____

■ TITLE AND NUMBER OF ARTICLE: _____

■ BRIEFLY STATE THE MAIN IDEA OF THIS ARTICLE: _____

_____

_____

_____

_____

■ LIST THREE IMPORTANT FACTS THAT THE AUTHOR USES TO SUPPORT THE MAIN IDEA:

_____

_____

_____

_____

_____

_____

■ WHAT INFORMATION OR IDEAS DISCUSSED IN THIS ARTICLE ARE ALSO DISCUSSED IN YOUR TEXTBOOK OR OTHER READING YOU HAVE DONE? LIST THE TEXTBOOK CHAPTERS AND PAGE NUMBERS:

_____

_____

_____

_____

_____

_____

_____

■ LIST ANY EXAMPLES OF BIAS OR FAULTY REASONING THAT YOU FOUND IN THE ARTICLE:

_____

_____

_____

_____

■ LIST ANY NEW TERMS/CONCEPTS THAT WERE DISCUSSED IN THE ARTICLE AND WRITE A SHORT DEFINITION:

_____

_____

_____

_____

_____

We Want Your Advice

ANNUAL EDITIONS: EDUCATION 91/92

Article Rating Form

Here is an opportunity for you to have direct input into the next revision of this volume. We would like you to rate each of the 47 articles listed below, using the following scale:

1. **Excellent: should definitely be retained**
2. **Above average: should probably be retained**
3. **Below average: should probably be deleted**
4. **Poor: should definitely be deleted**

Your ratings will play a vital part in the next revision. So please mail this prepaid form to us just as soon as you complete it.
Thanks for your help!

Annual Editions revisions depend on two major opinion sources: one is our Advisory Board, listed in the front of this volume, which works with us in scanning the thousands of articles published in the public press each year; the other is you—the person actually using the book. Please help us and the users of the next edition by completing the prepaid article rating form on this page and returning it to us. Thank you.

Rating	Article	Rating	Article
	1. Now Comes the Hard Part		24. Charm School for Bullies
	2. A National Priority: The Search for Common Goals		25. Children of Poverty
	3. Rethinking Education Reform in the Age of George Bush		26. Welfare Reform: Serving America's Children
	4. The Public Schools and the Public Mood		27. Gender Issues in Teacher Education
	5. The 22nd Annual Gallup Poll of the Public's Attitudes Toward the Public Schools		28. Race and Ethnicity in the Teacher Education Curriculum
	6. A Reconceptualization of Teacher Education		29. Social Class, Race, and School Achievement: Problems and Prospects
	7. A Reconceptualization of Educational Foundations		30. The ABC's of Caring
	8. Inside the Classroom: Social Vision and Critical Pedagogy		31. *Honig v. Doe:* The Suspension and Expulsion of Handicapped Students
	9. Navigating the Four C's: Building a Bridge Over Troubled Waters		32. Teen-Age Pregnancy: The Case for National Action
	10. 'Those' Children Are Ours: Moving Toward Community		33. Home Remedy: A Mom's Prescription for Ailing Schools
	11. A Brief Historical Perspective of the Struggle for an Integrative Curriculum		34. Adolescence: Path to a Productive Life or a Diminished Future?
	12. Fixing the System From the Top Down		35. When School Is a Haven
	13. Forging a Profession		36. Is Your School Ready for AIDS?
	14. Rift Over Teacher-Certification Rules Seen Impeding Reform Movement		37. Rethinking Retention
	15. Teacher Preparation: Should It Be Changed?		38. What Makes a Good Teacher?
	16. How Do You Spell Distinguished?		39. Fixing the Teaching, Not the Kids
	17. The Moral Life of America's Schoolchildren: An Introduction		40. Now You See Them, Now You Don't: Anonymity Versus Visibility in Case Studies of Teachers
	18. The Moral Life of America's Schoolchildren		41. Research on Teaching and Teacher Research: The Issues That Divide
	19. Teaching Values in School: The Mirror and the Lamp		42. 'It Was a Testing Ground'
	20. Ethical Decision Making for Teachers		43. Who Decides What Schools Teach?
	21. Design a Classroom That Works		44. Developing and Sustaining Critical Reflection in Teacher Education
	22. Order in the Classroom		45. Educational Renaissance: 43 Trends for U.S. Schools
	23. 'I Cried in Front of Fifth Period . . .'		46. Proper Behavior for the 21st Century in Our Global Village
			47. Will the Social Context Allow a Tomorrow for Tomorrow's Teachers?

(Continued on next page)

ABOUT YOU

Name_____ Date_____
Are you a teacher? ☐ Or student? ☐
Your School Name _____
Department _____
Address _____
City _____ State _____ Zip _____
School Telephone # _____

YOUR COMMENTS ARE IMPORTANT TO US!

Please fill in the following information:

For which course did you use this book? _____
Did you use a text with this Annual Edition? ☐ yes ☐ no
The title of the text? _____
What are your general reactions to the Annual Editions concept?

Have you read any particular articles recently that you think should be included in the next edition?

Are there any articles you feel should be replaced in the next edition? Why?

Are there other areas that you feel would utilize an Annual Edition?

May we contact you for editorial input?

May we quote you from above?